Baja California

Andrea Schulte-Peevers
David Peevers
Michele Matter
Sarah Long

LONELY PLANET PUBLICATIONS
Melbourne • Oakland • London • Paris

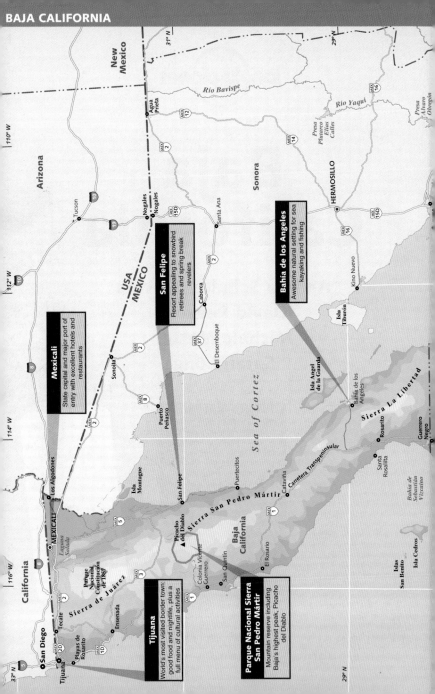

Mexicali

State capital and major port of entry with excellent hotels and restaurants

San Felipe

Resort appealing to snowbird retirees and spring break revelers

Bahía de los Angeles

Awesome natural setting for sea kayaking and fishing

Tijuana

World's most visited border town; good food and nightlife, plus a full menu of cultural activities

Parque Nacional Sierra San Pedro Mártir

Mountain reserve including Baja's highest peak, Picacho del Diablo

New Mexico

Arizona

Sonora

California

Baja California

Sea of Cortez

Sierra La Libertad

Sierra San Pedro Mártir

Sierra de Juárez

USA
MEXICO

Río Bavispe

Río Yaqui

Presa Alvaro Obregón

Presa Plutarco Elías Calles

HERMOSILLO

Agua Prieta

Nogales
Nogales

Tucson

Santa Ana

Caborca

Sonoíta

El Desemboque

Puerto Peñasco

Kino Nuevo

Isla Tiburón

Isla Angel de la Guarda

Bahía de los Angeles

Rosarito

Guerrero Negro

Santa Rosalita

Carretera Transpeninsular

Cataviña

Bahía de Sebastián Vizcaíno

Islas San Benito

Isla Cedros

Santa Rosalita

Puertecitos

San Felipe

Isla Montague

Laguna Salada

MEXICALI

Los Algodones

San Diego

Tecate

Tijuana

Playas de Rosarito

Ensenada

Colonia Vicente Guerrero

San Quintín

El Rosario

Picacho del Diablo

Parque Nacional Constitución de 1857

31° N

29° N

33° N

29° N

110° W

112° W

114° W

116° W

Río Bavispe

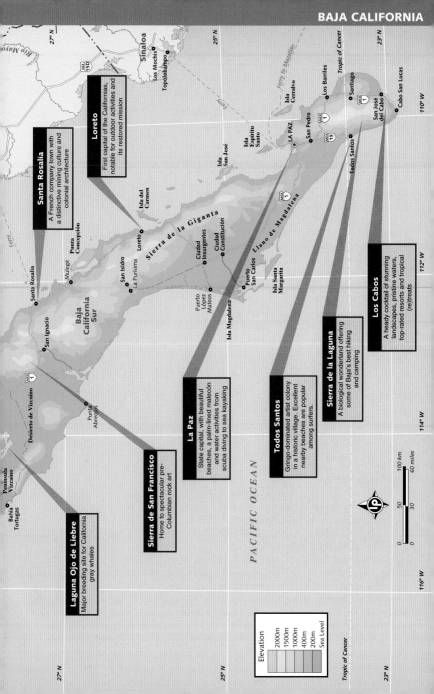

Santa Rosalia
A French company town with a distinctive mining culture and colonial architecture

Loreto
First capital of the Californias, notable for outdoor activities and its restored mission

Sierra de San Francisco
Home to spectacular pre-Columbian rock art

Laguna Ojo de Liebre
Major breeding site for California gray whales

La Paz
State capital, with beautiful beaches, a palm-lined malecón and water activities from scuba diving to sea kayaking

Todos Santos
Gringo-dominated artist colony in a historic village. Excellent nearby beaches are popular among surfers.

Sierra de la Laguna
A biological wonderland offering some of Baja's best hiking and camping

Los Cabos
A heady cocktail of stunning landscapes, pristine waters, top-rated resorts and tropical (re)treats

Sinaloa
Los Mochis
Topolobampo

Santa Rosalia
Mulegé
Punta Concepción
Isla del Carmen
Loreto
San Isidro
La Purísima

San Ignacio

Baja California Sur

Desierto de Vizcaíno

Punta Abreojos

Peninsula Vizcaíno

Bahía Tortugas

Sierra de la Giganta

Ciudad Insurgentes
Ciudad Constitución

Puerto López Mateos

Isla Magdalena

Puerto San Carlos
Isla Santa Margarita

Llano de Magdalena

Todos Santos

LA PAZ
San Pedro

Isla Espíritu Santo
Isla San José
Isla Cerralvo

Los Barriles
Santiago
San José del Cabo
Cabo San Lucas

Río Mayo

ferry to Mazatlán
ferry
ferry

Tropic of Cancer

PACIFIC OCEAN

Tropic of Cancer

Elevation
2000m
1500m
1000m
400m
200m
Sea Level

27° N
25° N
23° N

27° N
25° N
23° N

110° W
112° W
114° W
116° W

0   50   100 km
0   30   60 miles

Baja California
5th edition – March 2001
First published – March 1988

Published by
Lonely Planet Publications Pty Ltd A.B.N. 36 005 607 983
90 Maribyrnong St, Footscray, Victoria 3011, Australia

Lonely Planet Offices
Australia Locked Bag 1, Footscray, Victoria 3011
USA 150 Linden St, Oakland, CA 94607
UK 10a Spring Place, London NW5 3BH
France 1 rue du Dahomey, 75011 Paris

Photographs
All of the images in this guide are available for licensing from
Lonely Planet Images.
email: lpi@lonelyplanet.com.au

Front cover photograph
Elephant tree and cirio near Bahía de los Angeles
(Woods Wheatcroft)

ISBN 1 86450 198 7

Printed by Colorcraft Ltd, Hong Kong

Contents

2   Contents

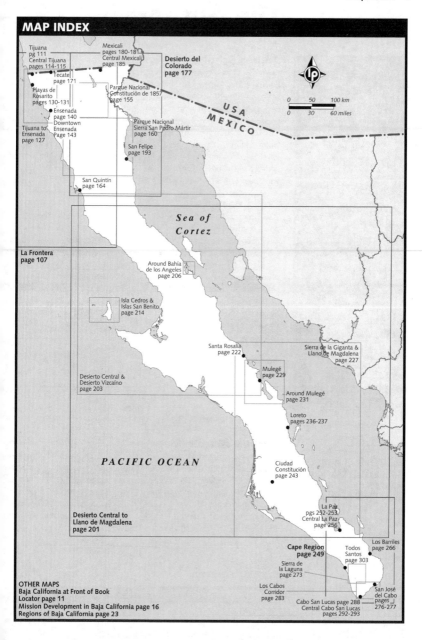

MAP INDEX

Tijuana
pg 111
Central Tijuana
pages 114-115

Tecate
page 171

Playas de
Rosarito
pages 130-131

Ensenada
page 140

Downtown
Ensenada
page 143

Tijuana to
Ensenada
page 127

Mexicali
pages 180-181
Central Mexicali
page 185

Parque Nacional
Constitución de 1857
page 155

Parque Nacional
Sierra San Pedro Mártir
page 160

San Felipe
page 193

San Quintín
page 164

Desierto del
Colorado
page 177

USA
MEXICO

0   50   100 km
0   30   60 miles

La Frontera
page 107

Sea of
Cortez

Around Bahía
de los Angeles
page 206

Isla Cedros &
Islas San Benito
page 214

Santa Rosalía
page 222

Sierra de la Giganta &
Llano de Magdalena
page 227

Mulegé
page 229

Desierto Central &
Desierto Vizcaíno
page 203

Around Mulegé
page 231

Loreto
pages 236-237

PACIFIC OCEAN

Ciudad
Constitución
page 243

Desierto Central to
Llano de Magdalena
page 201

La Paz
pgs 252-253
Central La Paz
page 256

Los Barriles
page 266

Cape Region
page 249

Todos
Santos
page 303

Sierra de
la Laguna
page 273

Los Cabos
Corridor
page 283

San José
del Cabo
pages
276-277

Cabo San Lucas page 288
Central Cabo San Lucas
pages 292-293

OTHER MAPS
Baja California at Front of Book
Locator page 11
Mission Development in Baja California page 16
Regions of Baja California page 23

The Authors

Andrea Schulte-Peevers

Andrea is a Los Angeles–based writer, editor and translator who caught the travel bug early in life, hitting all continents but Antarctica by the time she turned 18. After finishing high school in Germany, Andrea decided the world was too big to stay in one place and moved first to London, then to Los Angeles. Armed with a degree from UCLA, she managed to turn her wanderlust into a professional career as a travel writer and may still chase penguins around the South Pole one of these days. Since joining the LP team in 1995, Andrea has authored and/or updated the guides to *Los Angeles*, *Berlin*, *Germany*, *California & Nevada* and *Spain*. She is currently writing *San Diego & Tijuana*.

David Peevers

David holds advanced degrees in 'eclectic theoretics,' the science that posits if anything can happen, it will – except absolutely differently. He has driven spikes on the railroad, written musicals for children, guided on whitewater rivers and sailed schooners throughout the Caribbean. David has lugged cameras up mountains and medieval towers, been a publisher of art and written and photographed for magazines, governments and colleges worldwide. He flies high-performance aircraft to relax and was surprised – while at LP headquarters in Australia – to learn he is absolutely typical of Lonely Planet authors, whom he refers to as 'the species.' David has also contributed to Lonely Planet's *California & Nevada* and *Los Angeles* guides.

Sarah Long

Sarah left her home town of Highworth in Wiltshire, England, to complete a degree in European Studies at Essex University. Believing Spain to be far more glamorous than Essex, she spent a year living and studying in Valencia. Sarah now works as a publicist for Lonely Planet's London office. This is her first experience as an LP author.

Michele Matter

Michele spent her childhood in Berkeley, California, with breaks spent traveling across the US and to South America with family. After graduating from UC Berkeley, she spent some time traveling, then returned to the Bay Area and began working in Lonely Planet's marketing department. After nearly five years behind the desk promoting travel guides, Michele decided to jump the fence and venture out into the world of travel writing, starting with her contribution to LP's *Mexico* guide.

FROM THE AUTHORS

Andrea Schulte-Peevers & David Peevers Researching Baja California presented us with unique challenges, which is why the help provided by the following people was especially welcome.

In Los Cabos, a heartfelt thank you goes to Daniel Uribe Pedraza, who so generously showed us around the area, providing great insights and sharing his personal favorites. Warmest regards go to John and Jennifer Ireland, as well as Gary Webb Barnes, for being the perfect hosts on the East Cape and for being such generous and wonderful spirits.

In Cabo San Lucas, we would like to thank Dennis and Veronica Wolf for their friendly welcome and unstinting hospitality. Marco Hernandez deserves big kudos for introducing us to the rich playground that is the Sierra de la Laguna.

In Tijuana, we could not have done without Yves Lelevier: Heaps of thanks for coming through on all fronts. Also going beyond the call of duty were Javier Navarro Aragón and Gloria Acosta Bautista in Ensenada: Thank you for being smart, funny and generous and the perfect guides around town. Hector Reyes Orrantia in Playas de Rosarito, and Felizardo Palacios Pérez and Cesar Jauregui in Ensenada all deserve special mention for their help as well. Another round of applause goes to Conchita Endrino and Diego Espinosa for giving us a crash course in Tijuana bar hopping and for revealing some of the city's lesser known 'attractions' – we had a great time!

Finally, a heartfelt *gracias* to our fellow authors on this book, to our great editor, Suki Gear, to Tom Downs, Monica Lepe, Josh Schefers and everyone else at LP Oakland who had a hand in putting this edition into readers' hands.

Michele Matter Thanks to Andrea Schulte-Peevers and Suki Gear for their help and advice. Thanks to the staff of the tourist offices I stopped in for their willingness to answer my numerous questions. And thanks to my family, especially to my mother, Ligia, and my brother, Michael, for being great travel companions.

Sarah Long Many thanks to the teams at all the Secture offices, to Carlos Guillén and Laura Esquer in Mexicali, Manuel González Leon and Enrique Cervantes in San Felipe and Cynthia in Los Algodones. Casey Hamlin, thanks for the desert drive to Puertecitos and for answering subsequent email inquiries. Thanks to LP UK: Charlotte Hindle for getting me the gig, Katrina Browning, Ryan Ver Berkmoes for author words of wisdom, Sara Yorke for tricky map stuff and Jennifer Cox for the necklace of power. And of course, thanks and love to Norma and Gerry Long and the Inner Circle for their eternal support.

This Book

Andrea Schulte-Peevers and David Peevers were the coordinating authors of *Baja California*, fifth edition; they wrote the introductory chapters and back matter, La Frontera and most of the Cape Region. Michele Matter updated the Desierto Central to Llano de Magdalena chapter and part of the Cape Region. Sarah Long updated the Desierto del Colorado chapter.

Wayne Bernhardson wrote the third and fourth editions of this book. Scott Wayne wrote the first and second editions.

FROM THE PUBLISHER

Baja California was tweaked and tidied up in Lonely Planet's Oakland office. Suki Gear was the editor (she'd like to thank the Peevers for turning in another sparkly manuscript). Señorita Susan Derby stepped in to edit two chapters. Senior editor Tom 'Prom Clowns' Downs helped keep the book, and Suki, in line. Paul Sheridan and Suki proofread.

Cartographer Patrick 'Patito' Huerta was the man behind the maps, with Monica Lepe cheering him on. Also contributing to the maps were Patrick 'Peaches' Phelan, Dion Good, Colin Bishop, Ed Turley, Justin Colgan, Katherine 'Kitty Kat' Smith and John 'Worm Boy' Spelman.

Superstar designer Joshua Schefers laid out the book and pieced together the *muy bonito* color pages, with help from Katie the Latte Lady. Jennifer Steffey designed the fetching cover and livened up the office with her funky-fresh wardrobe.

The illustrations were the handiwork of Justin 'Jumping Bean' Marler, Hugh D'Andrade, Hayden Foell, Rini Keagy, Hannah Reineck, Jennifer Steffey, Lisa Summers, Scott Summers and Jim Swanson. Beca Lafore penned the prickly boxed-text border. Design manager (den mother) Susan Rimerman kept a sharp eye on the design process.

Last but not least, the new and improved index was created by Ken DellaPenta.

Foreword

ABOUT LONELY PLANET GUIDEBOOKS

The story begins with a classic travel adventure: Tony and Maureen Wheeler's 1972 journey across Europe and Asia to Australia. Useful information about the overland trail did not exist at that time, so Tony and Maureen published the first Lonely Planet guidebook to meet a growing need.

From a kitchen table, then from a tiny office in Melbourne (Australia), Lonely Planet has become the largest independent travel publisher in the world, an international company with offices in Melbourne, Oakland (USA), London (UK) and Paris (France).

Today Lonely Planet guidebooks cover the globe. There is an ever-growing list of books, and there's information in a variety of forms and media. Some things haven't changed. The main aim is still to help make it possible for adventurous travelers to get out there – to explore and better understand the world.

At Lonely Planet we believe travelers can make a positive contribution to the countries they visit – if they respect their host communities and spend their money wisely. Since 1986 a percentage of the income from each book has been donated to aid projects and human-rights campaigns.

Updates Lonely Planet thoroughly updates each guidebook as often as possible. This usually means there are around two years between editions, although for more unusual or more stable destinations the gap can be longer. Check the imprint page (following the color map at the beginning of the book) for publication dates.

Between editions, up-to-date information is available in two free newsletters – the paper *Planet Talk* and email *Comet* (to subscribe, contact any Lonely Planet office) – and on our website at www.lonelyplanet.com. The *Upgrades* section of the website covers a number of important and volatile destinations and is regularly updated by Lonely Planet authors. *Scoop* covers news and current affairs relevant to travelers. And, lastly, the *Thorn Tree* bulletin board and *Postcards* section of the site carry unverified, but fascinating, reports from travelers.

Correspondence The process of creating new editions begins with the letters, postcards and emails received from travelers. This correspondence often includes suggestions, criticisms and comments about the current editions. Interesting excerpts are immediately passed on via newsletters and the website, and everything goes to our authors to be verified when they're researching on the road. We're keen to get more feedback from organizations or individuals who represent communities visited by travelers.

Lonely Planet gathers information for everyone who's curious about the planet – and especially for those who explore it first-hand. Through guidebooks, phrasebooks, activity guides, maps, literature, newsletters, image library, TV series and website, we act as an information exchange for a worldwide community of travelers.

Research Authors aim to gather sufficient practical information to enable travelers to make informed choices and to make the mechanics of a journey run smoothly. They also research historical and cultural background to help enrich the travel experience and allow travelers to understand and respond appropriately to cultural and environmental issues.

Authors don't stay in every hotel because that would mean spending a couple of months in each medium-size city and, no, they don't eat at every restaurant because that would mean stretching belts beyond capacity. They do visit hotels and restaurants to check standards and prices, but feedback based on readers' direct experiences can be very helpful.

Many of our authors work undercover; others aren't so secretive. None of them accept freebies in exchange for positive write-ups. And none of our guidebooks contain any advertising.

Production Authors submit their raw manuscripts and maps to offices in Australia, the USA, the UK or France. Editors and cartographers – all experienced travelers themselves – then begin the process of assembling the pieces. When the book finally hits the shops, some things are already out of date, we start getting feedback from readers and the process begins again....

WARNING & REQUEST

Things change – prices go up, schedules change, good places go bad and bad places go bankrupt – nothing stays the same. So, if you find things better or worse, recently opened or long since closed, please tell us and help make the next edition even more accurate and useful. We genuinely value all the feedback we receive. Julie Young coordinates a well-traveled team that reads and acknowledges every letter, postcard and email and ensures that every morsel of information finds its way to the appropriate authors, editors and cartographers for verification.

Everyone who writes to us will find their name in the next edition of the appropriate guidebook. They will also receive the latest issue of *Planet Talk*, our quarterly printed newsletter, or *Comet*, our monthly email newsletter. Subscriptions to both newsletters are free. The very best contributions will be rewarded with a free guidebook.

Excerpts from your correspondence may appear in new editions of Lonely Planet guidebooks, the Lonely Planet website, *Planet Talk* or *Comet*, so please let us know if you *don't* want your letter published or your name acknowledged.

Send all correspondence to the Lonely Planet office closest to you:

Australia: Locked Bag 1, Footscray, Victoria 3011
USA: 150 Linden St, Oakland, CA 94607
UK: 10a Spring Place, London NW5 3BH
France: 1 rue du Dahomey, 75011 Paris

Or email us at: talk2us@lonelyplanet.com.au

For news, views and updates, see our website: www.lonelyplanet.com

HOW TO USE A LONELY PLANET GUIDEBOOK

The best way to use a Lonely Planet guidebook is any way you choose. At Lonely Planet, we believe the most memorable travel experiences are often those that are unexpected, and the finest discoveries are those you make yourself. Guidebooks are not intended to be used as if they provided a detailed set of infallible instructions!

Contents All Lonely Planet guidebooks follow the same format. The Facts about the Country chapters or sections give background information ranging from history to weather. Facts for the Visitor gives practical information on issues like visas and health. Getting There & Away gives a brief starting point for researching travel to and from the destination. Getting Around gives an overview of the transport options available when you arrive.

The peculiar demands of each destination determine how subsequent chapters are broken up, but some things remain constant. We always start with background, then proceed to sights, places to stay, places to eat, entertainment, getting there and away, and getting around information – in that order.

Heading Hierarchy Lonely Planet headings are used in a strict hierarchical structure that can be visualized as a set of Russian dolls. Each heading (and its following text) is encompassed by any preceding heading that is higher on the hierarchical ladder.

Although inclusion in a guidebook usually implies a recommendation, we cannot list every good place. Exclusion does not necessarily imply criticism. In fact, there are a number of reasons why we might exclude a place – sometimes it is simply inappropriate to encourage an influx of travelers.

Entry Points We do not assume guidebooks will be read from beginning to end, but that people will dip into them. The traditional entry points are the list of contents and the index. In addition, however, some books have a complete list of maps and an index map illustrating map coverage.

There may also be a color map that shows highlights. These highlights are dealt with in greater detail later in the book, along with planning questions. Each chapter covering a geographical region usually begins with a locator map and another list of highlights. Once you find something of interest in a list of highlights, turn to the index.

Maps Maps play a crucial role in Lonely Planet guidebooks and include a huge amount of information. A legend is printed on the back page. We seek to have complete consistency between maps and text, and to have every important place in the text captured on a map. Map key numbers usually start in the top left corner.

Introduction

Ever since the arrival of the first Spanish explorers in the 1530s, Baja California (or simply 'Baja,' as most people call it) has been a land of extremes. In modern times, it has become a land of extreme escapes and escapades. Once thought to be an island, Baja remains isolated – in its geography *and* mentality – from mainland Mexico, but it is now flooded by a steady stream of foreign visitors, primarily North Americans. Most flock to the population centers along the US-Mexico border and in the Los Cabos area in the southernmost part of the peninsula.

In between lie 600 miles (960km) of harsh desert badlands, largely undeveloped and traversed by rugged, mountainous terrain and hardy vegetation, some of it unique in all the world. Travel here has a near-meditative quality as the landscape's unrelenting sameness actually sharpens your senses, making you more receptive to its delicate, subtle beauty. On both the Pacific and Sea of Cortez sides, silvery sandy beaches, tranquil bays and lagoons – many of them isolated and remote – fringe the peninsula. In winter, Baja hosts some of the most magnificent visitors: the gray whales who find the peninsula's temperate waters ideal for giving birth to their calves before returning home to their frozen northern waters.

Baja's earliest visitors, the 16th-century European explorers, found the peninsula both enticing and forbidding, as its welcoming coastline belied the inhospitable desert interior. Settlement attempts repeatedly failed until the late 17th century, when Jesuit priests succeeded in establishing self-sufficient missions. They converted the local Indians to Catholicism and taught them how to work the fields and build churches, all in the interest of 'civilizing' them. In less than a century, these missions began to collapse as the Indians were decimated by European diseases and the Spanish crown expelled the Jesuits from the empire.

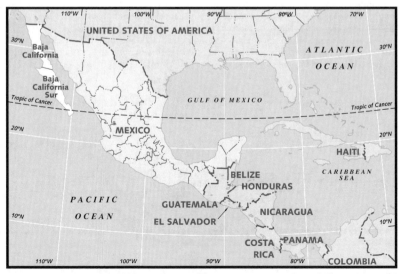

In the 19th century, ranchers and fishermen from the Mexican mainland settled parts of the peninsula. Prospectors discovered minerals and dug the first mines, prompting foreign companies to establish the first major port facilities and to acquire huge tracts of land. Encouraged by major mining discoveries, outsiders poured in to make small fortunes, but most of the peninsula remained largely undeveloped and unaffected. When the mines closed in the early 20th century, many foreigners took the money and ran.

Throughout the last century, Baja California has been a land of escape. Some of the first to seek refuge were the Magonistas, a splinter group of revolutionaries and mercenaries who briefly 'conquered' northern Baja while fleeing Mexican federal troops. Criminals from mainland Mexico also found remote Baja a good hideout, while Prohibition-era gamblers, drinkers and other 'sinners' from the USA could indulge their habits south of the border.

New hotels, restaurants, racetracks, bullrings and casinos lured a new type of escapee – the North American tourist. As tourism became a growth industry, Baja's population grew right along with it, its numbers swelled mostly by migrants from the Mexican mainland. Many of these new arrivals were escapees in their own right who fled from lack of opportunity, isolation and poverty. And not an insignificant number of them felt – and still feels – the need to escape their own country by illegally crossing the border into the US, seduced by the promise of the American Dream.

Meanwhile, millions of North Americans – and a few other international visitors – descend upon the peninsula each year in search of a quick, fairly inexpensive getaway. For many, the main attractions are shopping sprees in modern malls, markets and on the streets; sumptuous meals and exotic drinks; raucous nightclubs and bars; bullfights and dog races.

Others are drawn by Baja's natural treasures, first and foremost its splendid coastline, which gives access to numerous aquatic pursuits – fishing, scuba diving, snorkeling, windsurfing, sea kayaking, surfing and sailing among them. Landlubbers can charge down the beaches on horseback, explore rough terrain on mountain bikes, embark on multiday backpacking treks into remote mountains or view the prehistoric rock paintings left behind by Baja's earliest residents, the now extinct Cochimí Indians.

This book describes Baja's most popular attractions but also offers tips on experiencing this exceptional destination beyond stereotypical tourist activities. Detailed, practical information describes everything from marlin tacos to *mordida* (the bribe, literally, 'the bite'), and the basics are rounded out with essential environmental, cultural and historical background.

Facts about Baja California

HISTORY

At least 12,000 years ago, and perhaps much earlier, one of the most significant human migrations occurred. The accumulated ice of the great polar and continental glaciers of the Pleistocene Epoch lowered sea levels around the world, and the ancestors of American Indians crossed from Siberia to Alaska via a land bridge across the Bering Strait.

About 10,000 years ago, according to radiocarbon dating of artifacts like shell middens, stone tools and arrowheads, descendants of these migrants reached the Baja Peninsula by way of mainland California. As middens at Punta Minitas in northwestern Baja indicate, shellfish was a main food source for these peoples who also engaged in hunting, gathering and, later, rudimentary farming. A fluted point used for hunting large animals like mammoths, discovered near San Ignacio in Baja California's Desierto Central, dates from about 12,000 years ago.

Undoubtedly, the most spectacular artifacts left by Baja's early inhabitants are their petroglyphs and cave paintings – hundreds of rock art sites dot the peninsula from the US border to the tip of Cabo San Lucas. Some of these are abstract designs, while others are representations of humans and animals, reflecting the region's hunter-gatherer economy that existed until the arrival of European explorers. The tradition continued even after European contact, as some works include pack animals and Christian crosses. (For more on the subject, see the boxed text 'Rock Art of Central Baja,' in the Desierto Central to Llano de Magdalena chapter.)

Baja California Indians

Until Europeans reached the peninsula in the 16th century, upward of 48,000 mobile hunter-gatherers lived on the Baja Peninsula. Despite the early introduction of European diseases along the Gulf coast, this population remained fairly stable until the late 17th century.

The native peoples of Baja belonged to three major linguistic groups: the Yumano, the Cochimí and the Guaycura. Each group was subdivided into several tribal entities. Compared to the highly advanced native populations on mainland Mexico – the Aztecs, Maya and Incas – the Baja Indians lived in fairly primitive conditions and had not evolved beyond the early Stone Age.

The most accomplished of the trio were the Yumano in northern Baja, who counted the Diegueño or Dieguino (now commonly known as Tipai), Kamia or Kumiai (also known as Ipai), Paipai, Cucupah, Ñakipa and Kiliwa among their tribes. The Cochimí tried to eke out a living in the arid central peninsula, while the Guaycura – encompassing the Huchití and Pericú tribes – roamed the Cape Region. Written language, formal religious beliefs and agriculture were unknown among natives who also practiced polygamy, apparently because tribal warfare had led to a surplus of women.

These people lived in groups that became known as rancherías, ranging in size from a few families to upward of 200 people. They usually slept in the open, in caves or in simple dwellings made of local materials near a dependable, permanent water source such as a spring or stream. Their waking hours were primarily spent finding enough sustenance for survival. The men used a crude wooden spear or bow and arrow for hunting small animals and for fishing; the women gathered wild plant foods such as pine nuts and the fruit of the pitahaya cactus.

While groups in the north and south enjoyed a fairly dependable subsistence, by most accounts the Cochimí of central Baja, the peninsula's harshest desert, were often destitute. In times of stress they even collected pitahaya seeds from their own excrement and toasted them in what Spaniards jokingly called their 'second harvest.'

The only remaining Baja Indians live in the northernmost part of the peninsula, herding livestock and fishing. They include the Paipai (near Santa Catarina), the Kumeyaay (near Tecate in the Valle de Guadalupe) and the Cochimí (near Ojos Negros). Collecting pine nuts is an important seasonal activity, and women still produce attractive basketry and pottery.

The Era of Cortés

After the conquest of Mexico in the early 16th century, the Spanish turned their attention toward exploring the edges of their new empire. There was much fanciful speculation about a golden island beyond Mexico's western coast, and California got its name before it was explored, after a mythical island in a Spanish novel. The precise etymology and meaning of the name 'California' have never been convincingly established, though there is now wide consensus that it is a derivation of 'Calafia,' the book's heroine queen, who ruled a race of gold-rich black Amazons.

Starting in 1532, Spanish conquistador Hernán Cortés dispatched a series of expeditions in search of Calafia's riches. When the first fleet was captured by rival explorer

California: What's in a Word?

A word on terminology: In late Spanish colonial times and under Mexican rule, the general term 'California' meant Baja California (Lower California), and the present US state of California, then a backwater, became known as Alta California (Upper California). Rather than use the latter term, an anachronism except in its historical context, this book will use the more appropriate (if not precisely accurate) term 'mainland California' to refer to areas north of the Mexican border.

Modern Baja California consists of two separate states: Baja California (capital Mexicali) and Baja California Sur (capital La Paz). When necessary for clarity, this book refers to the individual states as Baja California (Norte) and Baja California Sur.

Nuño de Guzmán, Cortés sent out a second under the command of Diego Becerra. Alas, the captain met his maker during a mutiny, leaving the outlaw crew to sail on without him. They landed at Bahía de La Paz in 1534, making mutineer Fortún Jiménez the first European to set foot on the peninsula.

Local Indians, however, didn't exactly roll out the welcome mat and killed most of the hapless intruders, inspiring the survivors to beat a hasty retreat back to the mainland. The sample of black pearls they managed to bring back only fueled Cortés' visions of wealth and glory and prompted him to personally join a third expedition in 1535.

With about 400 Spanish settlers, plus black slaves and horses, Cortés went ashore at present-day Bahía Pichilingue, north of La Paz, where he founded the colony of Santa Cruz. He did find pearls, but the harsh desert proved too much of a challenge. By early 1535, disease, hostile Indians and several food and water shortages had forced the colonists to return back to the mainland.

But Cortés wouldn't give up. In 1539, he sent out a fourth expedition led by the experienced captain Francisco de Ulloa. Ulloa is credited with discovering that Baja was actually a peninsula and not an island at all. Before he could return to the mainland, his ship disappeared near Bahía Magdalena. Fortunately, one of his supply ships did make the journey back to Mexico to report on the expedition.

Upon hearing of Ulloa's demise, Cortés finally had enough: The conqueror of Mexico had been conquered by Baja California. He returned to Spain in 1541, leaving the 'golden land' to other adventurers.

In 1540, Hernando de Alarcón had also reached the mouth of the Colorado River, and in 1542 Portuguese explorer Juan Rodríguez Cabrillo explored the Pacific coast and became the first European to set foot in mainland California. After Cabrillo fell ill and died, his expedition continued north as far as Oregon, then returned to Mexico with charts and descriptions of the coast but no evidence of a sea route to the Atlantic, no cities of gold and no islands of spice. The authorities were unimpressed and showed no interest in California – upper or lower – for 60 years. It would take another 155 years before Baja would be successfully colonized.

Boats & Buccaneers

Meanwhile, the peninsula became important in other ways, in particular as a stopping point for trade ships between Mexico and the Philippines, which was also under the jurisdiction of the viceroy of New Spain. For 250 years, starting in 1565, these 'Manila galleons' traveled west from Acapulco across the Pacific to Manila, where they loaded up on Asian luxuries. Distended with goodies like silk, perfumes, spices, gold and silver, the bloated vessels then embarked on their six-to eight-month return journey to Mexico. The long voyage was arduous and, after crossing the Pacific, the crew was usually out of fresh water and starved of food. The Baja Peninsula was the first land after the crossing and made for an obvious supply stop.

Creating a settlement on the peninsula to re-equip the crew became even more crucial after bounty-hungry buccaneers caught wind of the seaborne riches and started to attack the overloaded vessels. Sir Francis Drake was among the first to stage these raids. Many other pirates, mostly from England and the Netherlands, followed suit. The Spaniards tried to hide from the marauders by seeking shelter in the bays of the Cape Region, but they were outfoxed again. In the biggest attack ever, in November 1587, Englishman Thomas Cavendish lay in wait at Cabo San Lucas, then sacked the prize galleon *Santa Ana* in a surprise attack. More than 120 years later, another Englishman, Woodes Rogers, repeated the coup with the *Encarnación*. Rogers is also remembered for rescuing stranded sailor Alexander Selkirk off an uninhabited island, providing the inspiration for Daniel Defoe's *Robinson Crusoe*.

Meanwhile, a desperate Spanish crown dispatched a skilled admiral, Sebastián Vizcaíno, to look for alternative sites to stop the riches from falling into enemy hands, but it was too little, too late. He landed on the Sea of Cortez side (also called the Gulf of California), near the same site as Cortés and Jiménez before him, and named the place La Paz. A major bay and a large desert in central Baja California are named for Vizcaíno, but permanent European settlement of the peninsula awaited the arrival of Jesuit missionaries.

The Mission Period

Having been thoroughly humiliated by repeated failures to colonize Baja, the Spanish crown now felt it was time to bring in the army – of God, that is. The first Jesuit foray into the peninsula came in 1683 when Isidro de Atondo y Antillón, governor of Sinaloa in mainland New Spain, crossed the Sea of Cortez with Jesuit priest Eusebio Kino. Together they established a settlement at La Paz, which was soon abandoned because of hostile Indians. Shortly thereafter, Padre Kino founded Misión San Bruno, just north of present-day Loreto, but attempts to catechize local Indians failed and the mission was abandoned within two years.

It would take another 12 years before a Jesuit priest named Juan María Salvatierra and six soldiers finally managed to do what had eluded countless explorers for a century and a half: they established the first *permanent* Spanish settlement in Baja California. Loreto, where they set up the first mission, Misión Nuestra Señora de Loreto, soon became the peninsula's religious and administrative capital. From here, other Jesuits swarmed out to establish missions throughout the area, founding a total of 23 over the next 70 years.

The Jesuits may have meant well in converting the Indians to Christianity and in instructing them in farming techniques and various crafts, but their altruistic intentions soon backfired. Along with God, grapes and greener pastures, the missionaries also brought an invisible evil – European microbes to which native peoples had no natural defenses. Epidemics of smallpox, plague, typhus, measles and venereal diseases decimated the Indian population. Several revolts against missionization caused further loss of life. By the end of the Jesuit period (1767) the Indian population had dwindled to only about 8000 (down from about 48,000 at contact).

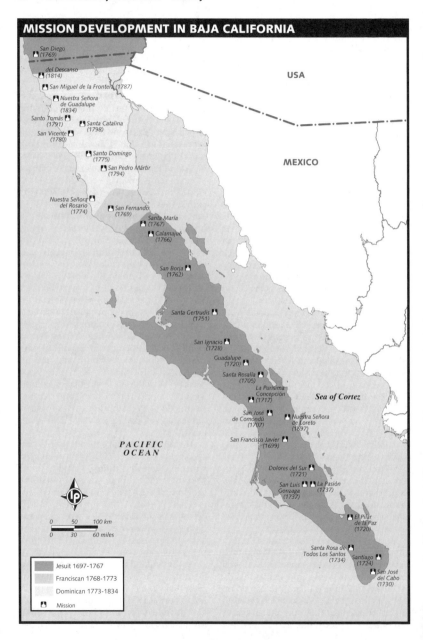

MISSION DEVELOPMENT IN BAJA CALIFORNIA

San Diego (1769)
del Descanso (1814)
San Miguel de la Frontera (1787)
Nuestra Señora de Guadalupe (1834)
Santo Tomás (1791)
Santa Catalina (1798)
San Vicente (1780)
Santo Domingo (1775)
San Pedro Mártir (1794)
Nuestra Señora del Rosario (1774)
San Fernando (1769)
Santa María (1767)
Calamajué (1766)
San Borja (1762)
Santa Gertrudis (1751)
San Ignacio (1728)
Guadalupe (1720)
Santa Rosalía (1705)
La Purísima Concepción (1712)
San José de Comondú (1707)
Nuestra Señora de Loreto (1697)
San Francisco Javier (1699)
Dolores del Sur (1721)
San Luis Gonzaga (1737)
La Pasión (1737)
El Pilar de la Paz (1720)
Santa Rosa de Todos Los Santos (1734)
Santiago (1724)
San José del Cabo (1730)

USA
MEXICO
Sea of Cortez
PACIFIC OCEAN

0   50   100 km
0   30   60 miles

Jesuit 1697-1767
Franciscan 1768-1773
Dominican 1773-1834
Mission

The declining Indian population posed a serious risk to the survival of the Jesuit missions, but ultimately it was a decision made halfway around the world that doomed their efforts. As word spread that the Jesuit Order had accumulated inordinate power and wealth, King Carlos III of Spain acted quickly to have all Jesuits arrested and expelled from their various missionary postings around the world. The Baja Jesuits had just founded their last mission in Santa María when the hammer fell and they were deported back to Spain.

In their stead came another order, the Franciscans, under the authority of Padre Junípero Serra. He closed or consolidated several of the Jesuit missions, founded only a single new one at San Fernando Velicatá, then turned his energies toward mainland California, where he established a chain of 21 missions stretching from San Diego to Sonoma.

In 1773, another order, the Dominicans, got into the mission game in Baja, setting up nine new missions north of El Rosario in today's La Frontera region. They also continued to operate the former Jesuit missions until after Mexico won independence from Spain in 1821. Three years later, Baja became a federal territory, headed by a governor. In 1832, a newly appointed governor, with support from Mexico City, put an end to the mission system by converting nearly all of them into parish churches. Only the Dominican missions in northern Baja remained intact, as they were considered the only outposts of civilization that connected barren Baja with flourishing mainland California.

The Mexican-American War

Meanwhile, on the Mexican mainland, momentous events were taking place that would bring war as far west as the Baja Peninsula and forever alter the map of Mexico. Before 1848, most of what is today the southwestern USA belonged to Mexico. North American settlers, initially welcomed by the Mexican authorities, declared Texas independent in 1836 in a surprise move. When, in 1845, the US Congress voted to annex Texas, and US president Polk demanded further Mexican territory, Mexico resisted. And so it came to the Mexican-American War (1846–48).

The main battles occurred on the Mexican mainland, but Baja was drawn into the conflict as well. American ships arrived in La Paz in 1846 and in San José del Cabo the following spring, where they brought local authorities under their control. In response, the Mexican government swiftly sent in troops under Captain Manuel Piñada. Fighting took place in Mulegé, La Paz and San José del Cabo, with Mexicans putting up such fierce resistance that the US troops had to repeatedly call for reinforcements. It wasn't until March 1848 that they finally captured the captain and his cohorts. Both sides were oblivious to the fact that war had ended one month earlier.

With the signing of the Treaty of Guadalupe Hidalgo, a destabilized Mexico was forced to sell most of New Mexico and mainland California to the US in exchange for US$15 million and the cancellation of US$3.25 million in debt. Arizona and the rest of New Mexico changed hands for another US$10 million in 1853. Mexico did, however, retain sovereignty over Baja California.

Foreign Interests & Investment

There were several other US attempts to acquire the Baja Peninsula. Though the government of Benito Juárez was willing to sell, it set too high a price but still encouraged foreign projects like Jacob Leese's Lower California Colonization & Mining Company, later known as the Lower California Company. In 1866, this company gained title to all Baja lands between 24°20'N and 31°N (roughly from La Paz to San Quintín) in a transparently fraudulent colonization attempt.

The San Francisco–based company went so far as to issue bogus paper money under the name 'The Bank of Lower California Trust and Loan Association' for the proposed city of Cortez. After an exploration in 1867, one disillusioned member warned that 'to send a party of colonists here, without previous preparation of the land at great expense, would be criminal,' but the company responded with a propaganda barrage in favor of the plan.

As an agricultural colonization project, the company failed scandalously, but its concession to collect *orchilla* (a valuable dye plant) employed about 500 gatherers in the Llano de Magdalena. This spurred the opening of a customs house and a brief boom until the development of alternative aniline dyes reduced the market. Another attempt at agricultural colonization, under the successor Chartered Company of California, also failed.

In the 1880s, the Mexican government, under autocratic President Porfirio Díaz, began encouraging US and European capital investment in Baja and other parts of Mexico. Díaz and his *científicos* (a group of largely Eurocentric, sometimes openly racist advisers), eager to raise much needed funds to grow the Mexican economy, granted major mining, railroad, manufacturing and other concessions to foreign investors. As a result, northern Baja in particular, which until then had been a complete outback without infrastructure, was transformed. The main investor was the International Company of Mexico (ICM), based in the US state of Connecticut.

The ICM made a downpayment of US$5 million toward a total price of US$16 million for the right to develop much of northern Baja as well as offshore islands and some areas on the Mexican mainland. The company constructed port facilities and flour mills at Ensenada and San Quintín. Further plans included a railroad from San Diego to San Quintín, 200 miles (320km) south of the US border and across to the state of Sonora.

In an effort to attract settlers and colonists to Baja from the USA, the ICM sent out pamphlets like the 1887 *Lower California, the Peninsula, Now Open to Colonists,* glorifying Baja's fertile land and resources, excellent climate and great agricultural potential. This was, of course, hyperbole at best and an outright lie at worst. Not too many people bought into it. After too many rainless years, the ICM cut its losses and surrendered its 'perfect title' to this 'last frontier' to a gullible English syndicate for US$7 million.

Bringing in several colonist families, the syndicate finished the mills in San Quintín and Ensenada, built part of a railroad and planted wheat. But once again the rains failed and harvests were nil. Those colonists who did not end up in San Quintín's first cemetery returned to England or moved to other parts of Baja, where British surnames like Jones and Smith are not unusual.

If agriculture proved to be a futile endeavor, mining did not. Several important mineral discoveries occurred around the peninsula, including gold and silver strikes. One of the largest projects, operated by the French syndicate Compañía del Boleo at Santa Rosalía, produced copper until the 1950s. There were also small nickel, mercury, graphite and sulphur mines, and many foreigners flocked to Baja to find their fortune underground.

Among other US investors who acquired or controlled huge tracts of land in northern Baja were Harrison Gray Otis, publisher of the *Los Angeles Times*; the Spreckels family of San Francisco, who made fortunes in the US sugar industry; and the powerful Southern Pacific Railroad.

From the beginning of the 20th century, following major agricultural development projects in the Imperial Valley just north of Mexicali, the Mexican government promoted commercial agriculture in the fields between Mexicali (which replaced Ensenada as the territorial capital) and the Colorado River delta. Water development in this region was the prime factor in Baja California's political and economic emergence.

Revolution & Its Aftermath

The Mexican Revolution of 1910 lasted a decade and temporarily interrupted growth. Warfare had very little impact on most of the peninsula, but in 1911 a ragtag army of the Liberal Party, an anarchist force under the influence of exiled Mexican intellectual Ricardo Flores Magón, swept through northern Baja's lightly defended border towns from Mexicali to Tijuana in an attempt to establish a regional power base. Militant labor organizations like the Industrial Workers of the World (IWW or 'Wobblies') from the US side of the border assisted the revolutionaries, many of

William Walker, Big Talker

Many Americans, not happy with the conditions of the Treaty of Guadalupe Hidalgo, felt that the US troops should have stayed on after the war to make Baja part of the new US state of California.

Some even decided to do something about it.

Among them was quixotic American rabble-rouser William Walker who, in 1853, got together a band of about 50 mercenaries and set sail from San Francisco with the goal of establishing a self-styled 'Republic of Lower California.' Touching land at Cabo San Lucas, he continued on to the territorial capital of La Paz where he misrepresented himself and his cohorts as commercial voyagers to gain permission to land. Walker's forces then arrested the governor, took possession of public buildings and raised the flag of the new republic. He declared himself president, installed 'cabinet officers' and, for good measure, also proclaimed annexation of the state of Sonora on the Mexican mainland.

Improvised Mexican resistance failed to dislodge Walker from La Paz, but the threat of a more organized force and the failure of his own reinforcements to arrive drove him back to Cabo San Lucas. Concerned that a Mexican warship was trailing him, Walker abandoned plans to establish a new capital at Bahía Magdalena and headed north to Ensenada. From here he led a heroically foolish attempt to conquer Sonora, ending up defeated not by Mexican troops but by the merciless Sonoran desert. Eventually, he straggled across the US border to hatch the grandiose Central American invasion schemes that led to his death in Honduras in 1860.

whom had been imprisoned or exiled in mainland California, with money and weapons.

The Magonistas, as Flores Magón's forces were also known, took Tijuana in a single morning as curious onlookers watched from across the border. However, attempts to establish a government failed because many of the Magonistas were foreign mercenaries with no interest in structured government. When the Mexican army approached Tijuana, the rebel 'government' crumbled and the Magonistas fled across the border.

After the war, Baja continued in isolation, excluded from most of the grandiose political and economic development plans under discussion in Mexico City. Ironically, it was the passage of legislation in the USA that pump-primed the Baja economy. The Eighteenth Amendment to the Constitution – better known as Prohibition – outlawed the production, transportation and sale of alcoholic beverages north of the border. Mainland Californians now flocked in droves to Tijuana, Ensenada and Mexicali for drinking, gambling and sex.

Border towns both prospered and suffered from this US invasion. Along with the money came an assortment of corrupt characters, and both Tijuana and Mexicali soon had a reputation for tawdriness and sleaze that – despite vast improvements – has proven hard to shake.

Reforms & Economic Growth

A major turning point in the history of Baja came in 1938 with the election of reformist President Lázaro Cárdenas, who instituted sweeping reforms throughout Mexico. He banned casino gambling, cracked down on crime and built the Sonora-Mexicali railroad to reduce the territory's economic dependence on the US and its isolation from mainland Mexico. He instituted various educational and agricultural reforms (such as the *ejido* system of peasant landholding cooperatives; see the boxed text) and boldly expropriated foreign oil-company operations in Mexico, forming Petróleos Mexicanos (Pemex, the Mexican Petroleum Company). After the oil expropriation, however, foreign investors avoided Mexico, which slowed the economy.

Reforms were stalled under the next president, Manuel Ávila Camacho, in part because of WWII, but continued under his successor, Miguel Alemán, who built hydroelectric stations, irrigation projects and an expanded road system. In 1952, still under Alemán, Baja's political status improved as its northern half became the Mexican state of Baja California. Voters elected a governor and state representatives, but outside of the immediate border boomtowns, most of the peninsula remained isolated for another two decades.

The Age of Tourism

After WWII, tales of fish, perpetual sunshine and beautiful bays filtered north to California, spurring the wealthy and the famous to explore the frontier south of the border. With no access road, private planes and yachts were the only means of access. In 1948, Hollywood bigwigs including Bing Crosby, John Wayne and Desi Arnaz put money toward Baja's first private resort at Las Cruces, just south of La Paz. In 1956, Rod Rodríguez (son of Abelardo L Rodríguez, the Mexican president from 1932 to 1934) built the Hotel Palmilla in Los Cabos. W Matt (Bud) Parr's Hotel Cabo San Lucas nearby and Herb Tanzi's Rancho Buena Vista on the Eastern Cape followed in 1962. Development came to Cabo San Lucas in 1967 when Rodríguez built the Hotel Hacienda (later bought and expanded by Parr), Luís Coppola put up Hotel Finisterra and Luís Bulnes the Hotel Solmar. These five families are commonly considered the founders of Los Cabos.

Despite these developments, tourism stagnated, largely because of inaccessibility. This changed in 1973 when paved México 1, the 1059-mile (1694km) Transpeninsular from Tijuana to Cabo San Lucas, opened. The population grew so quickly that less than a year later, south of the 28th parallel, Baja California Sur became Mexico's 30th state.

The highway functioned very much as a bridge to the 20th century. It allowed farmers and craftsmen to transport their goods to other parts of Baja and beyond while opening up one of the hemisphere's last frontiers to tourism. The influx of these foreigners further contributed to an improved standard of living for the local population. Southern Baja's fate as a 'destination' was sealed when the international airport near San José del Cabo opened in 1986.

1980s to the Present

Following the oil booms of the 1970s, the Mexican economy went into a tailspin in the '80s from which it did not recover until drastic measures to introduce private enterprise and free trade were taken under President Carlos Salinas de Gortari (1988–94). By the time NAFTA took effect on January 1, 1994, things seemed to have stabilized and started to move forward. Then all hell broke loose.

The same day, about 2000 indigenous-peasant rebels calling themselves the Ejército Zapatista de Liberación Nacional (EZLN, Zapatista National Liberation Army) surprised Mexico by taking over several towns in the southern Mexican state of Chiapas. Two months later, Luis Donaldo Colosio, Salinas' chosen successor as Partido Revolucionario Institucional (PRI) presidential candidate, was assassinated in Tijuana. Conspiracy theories abound about the killing – relations between Salinas and Colosio had deteriorated markedly – but by 1999, the only person who had been convicted was the one who pulled the trigger and was captured on the spot.

Baja California has also become a major gateway into the US for the drug trade. Mexican cartels, especially the Tijuana-based Arellano Félix clan, dominate the cocaine, heroin, methamphetamine and marijuana trade. Despite increased cooperation between US and Mexican authorities, officials estimate that 90% of production still makes it to market. Drug-related crime is rampant in the border towns. When Tijuana's police chief died in a hail of bullets in March 2000, he became the 70th murder victim in the city in that year alone.

All this bad news has a deleterious effect on tourism, especially from Southern California, Baja's main market. The introduction of the tourist fee of about US$16 in July 1999 for trips south of Ensenada proved unpopular as well. Many people were further scared away by recent reports of the death of an American accident victim after local officials delayed his release to a US hospital by forcing his family to post a US$7000 bond.

But despite such problems, Baja California continues its growth in economic power, population and popularity as a tourist destination. For example, in the 1990s, Los Cabos' population tripled and countless new hotels, condominium complexes and golf courses have sprouted, with no end to development in sight. Growing pains will be inevitable, but the peninsula will weather

The Ejido System

Ejidos are agricultural and residential lands held communally by a local peasant population. About 55% of Mexico's cultivated land is ejido land. Unlike in central and southern Mexico, where ejidos are divided into individual family holdings, in Baja California and other parts of northern Mexico, community members work the land collectively. Besides farm land, the ejido also consists of the fundo legal (townsite), which may include schools, wells and other infrastructure.

The origin of the ejidos goes back to colonial times, when the term referred to communal grazing lands on the outskirts of rural communities in mainland Mexico. One major land owner was the Catholic Church, which, under orders of Mexico's first president, Benito Juárez, was divested of its extensive landholdings in 1855. One side effect of this law was it cost the Indian communities the village lands they'd occupied for more than a century.

Not much changed for the landless peasants until after the Mexican Revolution of 1910. The country's 1917 Constitution was a backlash against the granting of major land concessions to foreign corporations, most notably from the US, under the pre-Revolution regime of President Porfirio Díaz. Article 27 then stipulated that only Mexican nationals could own Mexican land. This in turn set the stage for the land reform measures enacted by President Lázaro Cárdenas from 1934 to 1940.

It was Cárdenas who seized national and foreign assets and redistributed the land to peasants in the form of ejidos. The government, however, retained ownership of the land, which could not be sold and only be transferred by inheritance.

In the Mexicali area, for example, most ejidos were formed from lands once owned by the Colorado River Land Company. Like the company, some collective ejidos could take advantage of economies of scale to produce commodities like cotton, but others entered activities such as fishing, forestry, mining and livestock. In Baja, ejidos are often involved in tourism – guests in coastal campgrounds frequently rent their spaces from the local ejido and buy their gasoline from ejido-run Pemex stations.

The ejido system is now under siege from NAFTA. Nationwide, land cultivated by the ejidatarios is underutilized and among the least productive. Most ejido members lack the technological, educational or financial wherewithal to make use of the land in a more competitive manner.

An amendment to the Constitution, passed under former President Carlos Salinas de Gortari in the early 1990s, now makes it possible for ejidos to sell the lands they've been cultivating for decades. This, however, may be both a blessing and a curse. The right to sell the land will almost certainly be financially rewarding to some ejidatarios, but in the long run it may also spell an end to the very system itself, once again ending landholding rights of the agrarian workers.

this crisis as well and probably emerge triumphantly. Young in comparison with the rest of Mexico and even the US, it is still a kind of frontier state, imbued with the energy, creativity and pioneer spirit that goes along with this.

GEOGRAPHY

Baja California is a desolate but scenic peninsula of mountains, deserts, headlands and beaches flanked by the Pacific Ocean to the west and the Sea of Cortez (also known as the Gulf of California) to the east. Its irregular, snakelike outline stretches for about 800 miles (1300km) from the mainland California state border to Los Cabos, though its width ranges only from 30 to 145 miles (50 to 230km). On its northeastern edge, it also shares short borders with the US state of Arizona and the Mexican state of Sonora, both across the Río Colorado delta. With a total land mass of about 55,000 sq miles (143,000 sq km), it is about the size of the US state of Illinois or of England and Wales combined. Its coastline extends over 3000 miles (4800km).

A string of mountain ranges, which are a continuation of the sierras of mainland California, form the backbone of the entire peninsula. Out of a total of 23, the four most important are the granitic Sierra de Juárez near the US border, home to the Parque Nacional Constitución de 1857; the Sierra San Pedro Mártir, crowned by the 10,154-foot (3046m) Picacho del Diablo (Devil's Peak), Baja's highest mountain; the Sierra de la Giganta, which stretches from just beyond Loreto to nearly La Paz; and the volcanic Sierra de la Laguna, with peaks up to 7000 feet (2100m) high, which divide the southern Cape in half.

Similar to mainland California's Sierra Nevada, Baja's ranges, on their western slope, feature low foothills gradually giving way to pine forests and granitic mountain peaks. On the eastern side, the mountains rise up rather abruptly and the landscape is more arid and rugged.

Dotting Baja's Gulf waters are numerous islands that are undersea extensions of peninsular mountain ranges. The largest island, Isla Angel de la Guarda, is 42 miles (68km) long and 10 miles (16km) wide.

The Tropic of Cancer runs almost precisely through the towns of Todos Santos and Santiago, about midway between La Paz and Cabo San Lucas.

GEOLOGY

One of the world's youngest peninsulas, Baja California had an arduous birthing process that took nearly 20 million years, finally splitting off from the Mexican mainland about five million years ago. The break-up was the result of a geologic phenomenon called plate tectonics during which large sections of the earth's crust shift gradually over millions of years. Most of what today is California (both mainland and Baja) lies on the Pacific Plate, with the rest of North America on the North American Plate. The boundary between these two plates is the legendary San Andreas Fault, a gigantic fracture that stretches from just north of San Francisco all through California and into northern Baja to the Río Colorado delta, from where it continues as the Sea of Cortez Rift Zone. Over the course of millions of years, the Pacific Plate has shifted along this chasm in a northwesterly direction, gradually allowing the Pacific Ocean to invade the elongated structural trough that is now the Sea of Cortez. It continues to move to this day at a rate of about one-quarter inch a year.

Baja's unique topography is partly the result of uplift, during which the peninsula tilted westward, to form the main mountain ranges of the Sierra Juárez, Sierra San Pedro Martir, Sierra la Giganta and others. Another determining factor was volcanic activity, evidence of which still exists in the volcanoes and lava flows near San Ignacio and elsewhere on the peninsula.

CLIMATE

Baja California is famous for its sunny skies and warm temperatures, but the peninsula actually has a surprising range of climates. As a general rule, temperatures are higher in the south, along the Sea of Cortez coast and at lower elevations. They are lower in

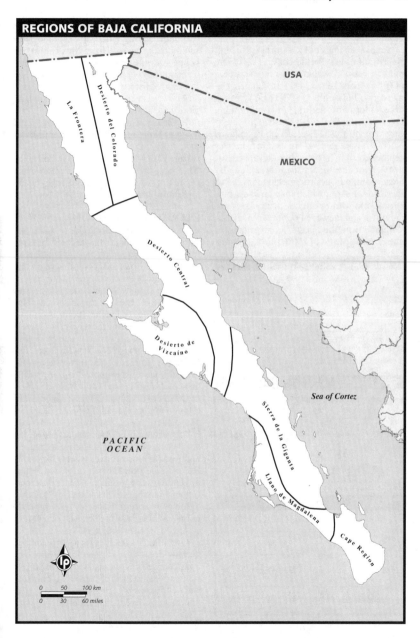

northern Baja, on the Pacific side and in the mountains.

Thanks to the cool California Current, Baja California's Pacific coast is relatively mild year round, with average temperatures of 60° to 75°F (16° to 24°C). In summer, the mercury often climbs to 85°F (30°C), but sea breezes provide natural air-conditioning. Fog often cloaks the beaches from May to July, though it usually clears up by midday. Northern Baja gets 90% of its rain from December to March. At higher elevations, especially in the Sierra de Juárez and the Sierra San Pedro Mártir, precipitation takes the form of snow, which may last well into spring. On winter nights, frosts are not unknown and may even occur at sea level.

Inland from the Pacific, summer temperatures soar upward of 110°F (43°C), humidity is almost nil and rain is rare, especially east of the sierras in the Río Colorado delta; summers in the area from Mexicali to San Felipe are murderously hot. The Desierto Central between El Rosario and San Ignacio is blistering as well, although, as in desert areas everywhere, day and night temperatures fluctuate greatly.

In the tropical Cape Region from La Paz to Cabo San Lucas, the hottest months, May to October, are also the wettest. Tropical storms called *chubascos* occasionally pelt the area, which is also visited by hurricanes once in a while. Winter is generally warm and sunny and the nicest time to visit.

ECOLOGY & ENVIRONMENT

From the international border to Cabo San Lucas, Baja California's fragile desert and maritime environments are facing a variety of challenges. Urban population growth has caused various problems. In Tijuana, for instance, the inability to build adequate housing and sewage facilities has meant serious pollution of the Río Tijuana; about 13 million gallons (58.5 million liters) of raw sewage enter the river daily and flow into the Pacific Ocean off San Diego. The New River, entering California from Mexicali, carries about 100 toxic substances and more than one billion liters of sewage and industrial waste daily.

Other environmental issues include deforestation and erosion in the Sierra de Juárez of northern Baja, potentially deleterious effects of increased salt production on the gray-whale nursery at Laguna San Ignacio and toxic mining residues at sites like Santa Rosalía. The proliferation of off-road races throughout the peninsula has done inestimable damage to its flora and fauna – hardly any place in Baja seems off-limits to noisily polluting and carelessly driven motorcycles, ATVs and 4WD vehicles.

Overfishing is another major problem, especially because of commercial fishing. The Mexican government allows Japanese fishing boats to fish for tuna with long lines within 15 miles off the shores of Baja, with billfish considered incidental catches. This poses not just a serious threat to the fish

CABO SAN LUCAS

Elevation – 7m/22ft

SAN FELIPE

Elevation – 450m/1476ft

TIJUANA

Elevation – 53m/173ft

population but ultimately also to the sport-fishing industry, which plays an important part in the tourism sector. Locals are becoming gradually educated, and most sport-fishing operators promote catch and release.

FLORA

Most people think of Baja as a desert largely devoid of vegetation. Fact is, the desert is indeed alive with more than 3000 native and introduced plants, some of which grow nowhere else on earth.

In botanical terms, much of semi-arid northern Baja is very much a continuation of Southern California. At sea level and in the lower elevations, plants like agave, buckeye, buckwheat, and bladderpod dominate. Away from the coast, these give way to chaparral vegetation including manzanita, California lilac, laurel sumac, chamise and other plants. Above the chaparral belt, the upper slopes of the Sierra de Juárez and San Pedro Mártir support a lush forest studded with pines, like the Jeffrey pine and the piñon pine, as well as spruce, cedar, fir, aspen and oak.

East of the sierras, the Sonoran Desert botanical region comprises several distinct subregions. From the US border as far as Bahía de los Angeles, there are small-leaved shrubs like ocotillo and the closely related *palo adán,* which bloom only at rare times of heavy rainfall, cactuslike *nopal* (prickly pear), cholla and saguaro cacti.

South of Bahía de los Angeles almost to La Paz, a narrow coastal strip on the Sea of Cortez features imposing cacti like the *cardón,* which reaches a height of 65 feet (20m), and many species of *biznaga* (barrel cactus). All of these cacti, especially the nopal, produce edible fruit or seeds.

The giant cardón cactus is one of the species endemic to Baja California. Others with this distinction are the *datilillo,* a yucca variety related to the Joshua tree in Southern California, and the curious *cirio* tree. Often likened in appearance to an inverted carrot, this bizarre, slow-growing species stands up to 60 feet (18m) tall. It's also called 'boojum,' in reference to the tall, twisted creature in Lewis Carroll's poem *The Hunting of the Snark.*

Farther south, on the Pacific slope, the Desierto de Vizcaíno and the Llano de Magdalena support different species of agave, plus cacti like the cardón and the galloping cactus. Also found here is the *pitahaya agria,* whose slightly acid fruit was consumed by native peoples who also used the stems as fish poison.

The Sierra de la Giganta, running from Loreto nearly to La Paz, is home to many common trees and shrubs like acacia and mesquite, a handful of native palms and many cacti, including nopal, the organ pipe cactus and the *pitahaya dulce,* which yields a sweet fruit that was the Cochimí equivalent of candy.

South of the Sierra de la Giganta, most of the Cape Region is an arid tropical zone of acacia and other leguminous trees and shrubs, sumac and fan palm. Pines and oaks, however, appear side by side with palms and cacti at higher elevations in the well-watered Sierra de la Laguna; the piñon pine produces edible seeds.

In addition to these major zones, more localized plant associations exist that are botanically significant and constitute critical wildlife habitat, especially for birds. These areas include coastal dunes, coastal salt marshes, freshwater marshes, mangrove swamps and vernal pools. The dense, salt-tolerant mangroves, present along segments of both the Pacific and Gulf coasts of Baja

Biznaga (barrel cactus)

Endangered Species

The Convention on International Trade in Endangered Species of Wild Fauna and Flora (CITES) is a diplomatic agreement regulating trade in plants and animals that are either in immediate danger of extinction or declining so rapidly that they soon may be in danger of extinction. Regulations are complex, but in general prohibit or severely restrict any exploitation – commercial or noncommercial – of such species.

Most species protected by CITES are assigned either to Appendix I (endangered: under immediate threat of extinction without remedial action) or Appendix II (threatened: perhaps regionally endangered). Appendix III covers the species that require close monitoring to determine their vulnerability.

Travelers should not hunt, purchase or collect the species of plants and animals listed below. Even buying products made from them requires explicit authorization from authorities in Mexico City. Otherwise, such products may be confiscated by US Customs. The list below is partial, and you should consult with US Customs before attempting to import any such products.

Appendix I
Flora

Otay mesa mint
  (*Pogogyne nudiuscula*)
salt marsh bird's beak
  (*Cordylanthus maritimus*)

Fauna

Baja pronghorn antelope
  (*Antilocapra americana peninsularis*)
caguama
  (green sea turtle; *Chelonia mydas agasizii*)
California least tern
  (*Sterna antillarum*)
Cedros mule deer
  (*Odocoileus hemionus cedrosensis*)
cochito
  (Gulf harbor porpoise; *Phocoena sinus*)*
Guadalupe fur seal
  (*Arctocephalus townsendii*)
hawksbill sea turtle
  (*Eretmochelys imbricata*)
leatherback sea turtle
  (*Dermochelys coriacea*)
light-footed clapper rail
  (*Rallus longirostris levipes*)
loggerhead sea turtle
  (*Caretta caretta*)
olive ridley sea turtle
  (*Lepidochelys coriacea*)
totuava
  (seatrout or weakfish; *Cynoscion macdonaldii*)

Appendix II
Flora

cacti**
cirio
  (boojum; *Idria columnaris*)

Fauna

bighorn sheep
  (*Ovis canadensis*)
California gray whale
  (*Eschrichtius robustus glaucus*)
coral
  (*Coelenterata*)***
southern sea otter
  (*Enhydra lutris nereis*)

*All whales and porpoises not in Appendix I are in Appendix II, but not all species are listed here.
**All cacti not in Appendix I are in Appendix II, but these are too numerous to list here.
***Corals of all orders are in Appendix II but are too numerous to list here.

Sea otter

California Sur, also provide spawning habitat for fish and shellfish.

FAUNA

For more details on Baja's flora and fauna, see the Books section in the Facts for the Visitor chapter.

Birds

Baja California's bird habitats are strongly correlated with its plant communities but vary with climate, elevation and latitude. The major geographical divisions of the northern Pacific coast – the mountainous Sierra San Pedro Mártir, the Desierto del Colorado, the Desierto de Vizcaíno and the Cape – each have characteristic groups of bird species, though the desert species are widespread outside those areas.

Large colonies of nesting seabirds populate the many islands in the Sea of Cortez. Among the most noteworthy species are black storm-petrels and least storm-petrels, brown pelicans, cormorants, frigate birds, boobies, Craveri's murrelets, Heerman's gulls, yellow-footed gulls, elegant terns and brown noddys.

Seabirds prosper from the Midriff Islands south to Los Cabos because nutrients upwelling from deep submarine canyons feed abundant fish and plankton near the surface.

A particularly common bird species on the peninsula itself is the turkey vulture, or buzzard. Those poor birds definitely got short-changed in the beauty department, with their blood-red, featherless heads held up by a graveyard-black hunched body. They're often seen soaring overhead, perched on a cactus or pecking away at some unfortunate carcass.

Land Mammals

Baja is home to a variety of unique mammals, including the black jackrabbit of Isla Espíritu Santo and the fish-eating bat of the Sea of Cortez. More characteristic, however, are animals like the mule deer, peninsular pronghorn antelope and endangered desert bighorn sheep. The Cedros mule deer is an endangered subspecies on its namesake Pacific island. Smaller and more common land mammals include the coyote, rabbit, fox, squirrel, chipmunk and gopher.

Marine Mammals

From January to April, visitors flock to the lagoons of central Baja to view the migration and mating of the California gray whale, but other species of whales and dolphins also frequent the waters of the Pacific and the Gulf. Among them are the finback whale and the humpback whale.

For information on whale-watching, see Organized Tours in the Activities chapter and the Guerrero Negro, Laguna San Ignacio and Bahía Magdalena entries in the Desierto Central to Llano de Magdalena chapter.

Other marine mammals include the endangered Gulf of California harbor porpoise, the recovering but still threatened southern sea otter, the threatened Guadalupe fur seal and the more common sea lion, northern elephant seal and harbor seal. Sea lions and elephant seals can be seen at several offshore Pacific islands, most notably Isla Cedros and the Islas San Benito, about midway down the peninsula. There are also smaller, easily accessible colonies at Bahía Los Frailes and Cabo San Lucas.

Fish & Marine Life

The waters of the Pacific support a cool temperate flora and fauna resembling that off the coast of mainland California, with kelp (like *Macrocystis*) and mollusks, sea urchins and barnacles. Shallow areas, like Laguna San Ignacio and Bahía Magdalena, support more tropical life forms.

Because of the range of temperatures in the Sea of Cortez, its flora and fauna are relatively limited in numbers of species, especially in the northern half. Total biomass is fairly large because of algal blooms – the frequently used term 'Vermillion Sea' derives from this phenomenon. Mangrove swamps in some shallow lagoons, especially toward the south of the peninsula, are incubators for oysters. Crustaceans such as spiny lobsters and rock crabs were already popular fare in aboriginal Baja. The venomous yellow-bellied sea snake frequents the inshore waters of southern Baja.

The Sad Tale of the Turtle

The great whales get all the press. Few travelers know as much about the sea turtles that, historically, have been as important to the peoples of the tropics as whales have been to the peoples of the Arctic. Called 'the world's most valuable reptile' by the late geographer James Parsons, the Pacific green turtle *(Chelonia mydas)* is endangered throughout the world, and its conservation should be a major priority in Baja California and the rest of Mexico.

The green turtle *(caguama negra,* or *tortuga prieta* in Baja) is a grazing reptile that feeds on marine grasses in tropical and subtropical seas, though wandering individuals have been found as far north as England and as far south as Argentina and Chile. Individuals can weigh up to 800lb (360kg), though most weigh 300lb (135kg) or less. Males rarely leave the sea, but females migrate long distances to haul out on the sandy beaches of isolated tropical islands, where they lay their eggs.

For millennia, the green turtle has provided protein to people in the tropics with its meat and eggs, but the exploration of the globe by Europeans marked the beginning of the species' decline. Northern European sailors netted the abundant turtles of the Caribbean, for example, and kept them aboard ships as sources of fresh meat on their trips around the Horn – feeding them bananas and bathing them in saltwater to keep them alive. By the 18th century, fresh turtle meat and turtle soup were luxuries in London, but a hundred years later they reached the British capital in cans.

Outside the protein-scarce tropics, turtle has always been a delicacy, and commercial pressures resulted in overhunting in such important areas as the Caribbean coasts of Nicaragua and Costa Rica. The result was a transfer of protein from the poor countries of the tropics to the rich countries of the midlatitudes.

Baja California's turtles shared this unfortunate history. At Bahía Tortugas on Península Vizcaíno, one 19th-century ship netted almost 200 turtles in a single pass. Many were canned or

---

Most of today's important marine life, especially that of interest to tourists, is pelagic (native to open seas). More than 800 species of fish inhabit the Sea of Cortez. The totuava, known commonly as sea trout or weakfish, is an endangered species in the Sea of Cortez.

Black coral is on the endangered species list, and exports to the US require a permit from Mexico City. Coral is mined with dredge hooks, and substantial reef areas are destroyed in the process of obtaining relatively small amounts of coral.

Reptiles

Desert environments support many reptiles, including snakes, lizards and turtles. Baja has an abundant and varied snake population, including king, gopher and whiptail and of course rattlesnakes, which are a serious concern throughout the peninsula. Isla Santa Catalina, southeast of Loreto, is home to the endemic rattleless rattlesnake, so called because it has only a single rattle segment, which by itself is incapable of making any sound.

Sea turtles, all of which are endangered species, inhabit the coastal areas, mostly on the Sea of Cortez side. The Pacific green turtle, colloquially known as the *caguama negra* or *tortuga prieta,* is the most important, but other species include the leatherback, the black, the olive ridley, the loggerhead and

The Sad Tale of the Turtle

shipped north to San Francisco or San Diego for sale or further processing. As recently as the 1960s, the Ruffo family's Empacadora Baja California in Ensenada was canning as much as 100 tons of turtle soup in a single season.

In the 1970s, increasing concern over the green's declining numbers resulted in its placement (and that of all other sea turtles) on Appendix I of the Convention on International Trade in Endangered Species of Wild Fauna and Flora (CITES). Mexico officially outlawed sea-turtle hunting in 1990. Despite passage of the 'Ley de Veda Permanente' in 1991, which makes it illegal to kill turtles or damage their habitat, the turtle populations continue to decline. Pollution, hunting, egg collecting, ATV use on nesting-site beaches, boat traffic and other factors contribute to the turtles' demise. Note that it is illegal to import any turtle products – such as turtle-leather boots, tortoise-shell jewelry or hair accessories, and sea-turtle oil-based cosmetics – into the US.

Several Baja-based nonprofit agencies focus their energies on turtle preservation, including Baja Tortugas (☎ 1-135-00-86) and Asupmatoma, which operates a turtle nursery at Rancho Punta San Cristobal, about 15 minutes north of Cabo San Lucas. In the 1999-2000 season, more than 15,000 hatchlings were released into the Pacific Ocean. At Bahía de los Angeles, Semarnap (the Mexican ministry of the environment) has a modest turtle conservation project, where it's possible to see leatherbacks, hawksbills and greens. For details, see the Bahía de los Angeles entry in the Desierto Central to Llano de Magdalena chapter.

Baja visitors are unlikely to come across nesting sites, which are usually in remote spots. Nevertheless, greens and other turtle species are not unusual in Baja waters; there are nesting sites on the Eastern Cape north of Cabo Pulmo. In Baja California (Norte), the green has been spotted at Gulf island sites like Angel de la Guarda, Rasa, Salsipuedes, San Luis and San Lorenzo, as well as at Bahía de los Angeles, Bahía San Luis Gonzaga, Puertecitos, San Felipe and even the mouth of the Río Colorado. On the Pacific coast, turtles have been seen at Isla Cedros, Bahía San Quintín and Ensenada.

The warmer waters of Baja California Sur are better turtle habitat, and turtles appear in many of the same areas frequented by calving gray whales: Laguna Ojo de Liebre (Scammon's Lagoon), Laguna San Ignacio and Bahía Magdalena.

the hawksbill. Mexicans most commonly apply the word *caguama* to the green, but the term can mean any species of turtle. For more on sea turtles, see the boxed text.

National Parks

Mexico has established four major *parques nacionales* (national parks) on the Baja Peninsula, officially restricting many forms of human exploitation, although enforcement is lax, and tree-cutting, hunting and grazing have carried on illegally.

Constitución de 1857 On the plateau and eastern slope of the Sierra de Juárez, this 19-sq-mile (49-sq-km) park, barely an hour's drive from Ensenada, is a good place for camping and rock climbing. Shallow, sprawling Laguna Hanson, surrounded by shady pine forests, is a major stopover for migratory birds on the Pacific flyway. For details, see the La Frontera chapter.

Sierra San Pedro Mártir Reaching altitudes above 10,000 feet (3000m) in the Sierra San Pedro Mártir, this roughly 236-sq-mile (614-sq-km) park contains Baja's highest point, the Picacho del Diablo (Devil's Peak), which measures 10,154 feet (3046m). Thanks to the park's remoteness and difficult access, it does not receive many visitors and has little infrastructure. Its varied terrain and vegetation, however, make it a good destination for backcountry camping and backpacking, especially in the spring. The park is also home to Mexico's national observatories. On its eastern escarpment, it plunges steeply down to the dry lake bed of Laguna Diablo. The La Frontera chapter provides details.

Bahía de Loreto The National Marine Park at Bahía de Loreto is Baja's newest park (established in 1996) and protects the fish, sealife and water around Loreto. Covering 799 sq miles (2077 sq km), it extends 20 miles (32km) out to sea, covering an area 12 miles (19km) north and 35 miles (56km) south of Baja's historical capital. The park includes the islands of Isla Coronado, Isla del Carmen, Isla Danzante, Isla Montserrat and Isla Santa Catalina. See Loreto in the Desierto Central to Llano de Magdalena chapter for more information.

Cabo Pulmo The 27-sq-mile (70-sq-km) National Marine Park at Cabo Pulmo was Mexico's first underwater national park when founded in 1995. It protects the only coral reef on the west coast of North America and its surrounding waters off the thinly populated Eastern Cape. See Cabo Pulmo in the Cape Region chapter for details.

Biosphere Reserves

Biosphere reserves are a result of a 1970s initiative by Unesco, the United Nations Educational, Scientific & Cultural Organization, which recognized that it was impractical for developing countries to take productive areas out of economic use. Biosphere reserves encourage local people to take part in planning and developing sustainable economic activities outside the reserves' strictly protected *zonas núcleo* (core areas).

Alto Golfo y Delta del Río Colorado

Straddling the states of Baja California and Sonora at the northern end of the Sea of Cortez, this sprawling 3609-sq-mile (9383-sq-km) reserve unites desert scrub, coastal dunes, estuaries and marine environments in a single unit. Parts of this biosphere region are covered in the Desierto del Colorado chapter.

Islas del Golfo Created in 1978, this 579-sq-mile (1505-sq-km) reserve includes all the islands in the Sea of Cortez, comprising parts of the states of Baja California, Baja California Sur and Sonora; the reserve overlaps the borders of the new marine national parks at Loreto and Cabo Pulmo (see National Parks, earlier).

Three international conservation groups are working to protect its desert scrub and thorn forest: Conservation International de México in the Midriff region, the Mexican branch of the Worldwide Fund for Nature (WWF-México) in the Midriff and The Nature Conservancy at Isla Espíritu Santo and in the new Loreto marine national park. For details about the area protected by this biosphere, see the Desierto Central chapter.

El Vizcaíno The Vizcaíno Biosphere Reserve stretches across the central peninsula just south of the border between the states of Baja California and Baja California Sur. This 9833-sq-mile (25,566-sq-km) reserve is Latin America's largest single protected area, though some of the terms of protection are ambiguous. It contains the important gray-whale calving sites of Laguna Ojo de Liebre and Laguna San Ignacio, a population of the endangered peninsular pronghorn antelope and pre-Columbian rock art sites, together designated a Unesco World Heritage Site. See Around Guerrero Negro in the Desierto Central to Llano de Magdalena chapter for more information.

Sierra de la Laguna In the high mountains of the Cape Region, this 434-sq-mile (1128-sq-km) reserve, established in 1994, protects a truly unique mixture of coniferous, deciduous and palm forests. Also see Sierra de la Laguna in the Cape Region chapter.

GOVERNMENT & POLITICS

Mexico is a federal republic of 31 states and one federal district. The peninsula of Baja

California consists of two separate states, Baja California (capital Mexicali) and Baja California Sur (capital La Paz). In this book, the state of Baja California is usually called Baja California (Norte) to distinguish it from the term used for the entire peninsula. Each state is subdivided into *municipios,* roughly equivalent to US counties, each of which is administered by a *cabecera* (county seat). Each municipio in turn consists of several smaller communities called *delegaciones.*

Baja California (Norte) encompasses the municipios of Tijuana, Playas de Rosarito, Tecate, Mexicali and Ensenada; Baja California Sur has the municipios of Mulegé, Loreto, La Paz and Los Cabos. The size of municipios can be very disproportionate – Tijuana, for instance, containing the bulk of Baja California's population, is only 576 sq miles (1498 sq km, about 2.2% of the state's area), while that of Ensenada is 18,900 sq miles (49,140 sq km, more than 73% of the state's area).

As elsewhere in Mexico, the official Partido Revolucionario Institucional (PRI) dominated politics in Baja California for most of the 20th century. But it was in Baja California (Norte) where the first cracks in the PRI's political landscape began to appear – cracks that resulted in a full-fledged chasm in the 2000 national elections.

In 1989, the state made history when it became the first in the nation to elect a non-PRI governor, Ernesto Ruffo Appel of the center-conservative Partido de Acción Nacional (PAN). In 1995, PAN held onto the governorship with the election of Hector Terán Terán. When Terán died suddenly of a heart attack in October 1998, he was succeeded by Alejandro Gonzalez Alcocer, who will govern until 2001. Many other elected officials also belong to PAN, including the mayors of Tijuana, Mexicali and Playas de Rosarito.

In the 2000 election, PAN was able to transpose its popularity in northern Baja to the national stage as, for the first time in 71 years, Mexico elected a non-PRI president, Vicente Fox. The election result was widely considered as paving the way toward a more democratic Mexico.

Fox, a brash, tough-talking rancher and former businessman, hails from the mainland

Vicente Fox, Mexico's saucy new president

Mexican state of Guanajuato, of which he was elected governor in 1995. He began his career working for Coca-Cola, where he rose from salesman to regional president in charge of Mexico. As governor, his main accomplishment was to bring about the lowest level of unemployment in any Mexican state. He is considered a pragmatist who supports free enterprise. In the same elections, PAN also won pluralities in both chambers of the Mexican Congress; 10 of the 12 largest Mexican cities are governed by PAN mayors as well.

Baja California Sur is governed by Leonel Cota Magaña of PRI.

ECONOMY

Agriculture and fishing remain major industries, but tourism and related service industries have become the motor that drives the economy. Over the past two decades, every major town and city has seen a construction boom in hotels and related infrastructure. Fonatur, Mexico's federal tourism development agency, has promoted major resort complexes at Loreto and Los Cabos (San José del Cabo and Cabo San Lucas) with foreign and Mexican capital, attempting to transform these places into luxury resorts like Cancún in the Yucatán.

Baja's popularity as a tourist destination is undeniable. More than 28 million tourists a year visit northern Baja alone, where they spend about US$1.2 billion, accounting for about 14% of all tourist dollars spent in Mexico. Tijuana is the world's busiest border city, with more than 60 million northbound person crossings annually (averaging about 165,000 a day, including the 35,000 commuters to San Diego, California). Both Mexicali and Tijuana have built cultural centers to attract more visitors, and each year more drivers explore the Transpeninsular and its side roads or jet into resorts at Loreto, La Paz and Los Cabos.

Borderlands Economy

As more North Americans head south for holidays or retirement in Baja, increasing numbers of unauthorized Mexican and other Latin American workers cross north into the USA. A 1986 immigration law made it illegal for US businesses to hire undocumented foreigners, but this has neither deterred employers nor slowed the tide of illegal immigrants. Most of the illegal immigrants are in search of better wages. The minimum wage in Mexico is around US$3.50 a day for unskilled laborers, and most trained workers earn less than US$10 a day. Even some Mexican professionals are poorly paid: A full-time university professor may earn less than a minimum-wage laborer north of the border.

But not all Mexicans crossing the border to the US are illegal immigrants. Many residents of Tijuana, Mexicali and other settlements have special 'border-crosser' status that allows them to enter the USA for shopping trips and to visit relatives. In addition, there are about 35,000 workers who reside in Tijuana and commute to work in San Diego legally.

One alternative to this massive illegal exodus to 'the other side' is the promotion of long-term foreign investment to create jobs in Mexico. Much of foreign investment takes the form of *maquiladoras*, factories (usually foreign-owned) that are allowed to import raw materials, parts and equipment duty-free for processing or assembly by inexpensive Mexican labor. More than 40% of all maquiladoras in Mexico are in Baja California (Norte). In September 1999, the state had 1136 such factories, which employed some 33.6% of the population (roughly one million), about 55% of them women.

Maquiladora workers seem generally satisfied because their wages are nearly double the average wage in Mexico (despite higher living costs along the border) and their jobs sometimes provide additional training and other benefits. Maquiladora wages still average only about US$1 per hour. Mexico is pleased with reduced unemployment and increased foreign exchange, but the maquiladoras' contribution to the country's economy and industrial base is minimal because their scope is so limited, and they provide little prospect of long-term investment.

NAFTA & the Peso Collapse

Mexico's federal government eagerly anticipated the ratification of the North American Free Trade Agreement, which took effect on January 1, 1994. Known to Mexicans as the TLC (Tratado de Libre Comercio), NAFTA is gradually (over a 15-year period) eliminating restrictions on trade and investment between the US, Mexico and Canada. The hope was that it would bring Mexico increased employment and growing exports, as well as cheaper imports. Opponents charge that the gap between rich and poor is being widened as new imports – such as maize grown cheaply by US agribusiness – damage uncompetitive sectors of the Mexican economy.

The Mexican economy's collapse at the end of disgraced President Salinas' term in 1994 led to a precipitous devaluation of the Mexican peso and a bailout in the form of massive loans from the US government. More than 1.5 million people lost their jobs, prices and crime soared, production and standards of living fell, borrowers went broke. Inflation in 1995 was more than 50%. More Mexicans looked to (usually illegal) migration to the USA as the only way out of poverty.

Recovery

Government-led austerity measures and its successful raising of new capital on private markets, coupled with big help with exports from NAFTA and the cheap peso, began to pull Mexico out of the slump surprisingly quickly. Foreign investment revived, and

Cholla (Bahía de los Angeles)

Saguaro (Cataviña)

Flowering Cardón (Cape Region)

Cactus farm (Ejido Uruapán)

Ocotillo fence (San Felipe)

Day of the Dead figurines (Ensenada)

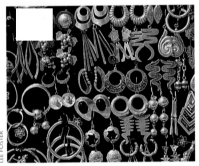

Silver jewelry, sold all over Baja

Tiles inside Riviera del Pacífico (Ensenada)

Virgin of Guadalupe shrine (Tijuana)

Mexico repaid most of its emergency debt ahead of schedule. By 1998, production was rising about 6% a year and inflation was down to around 15%. And by late 1999, Mexico's economic outlook was still brightening. Inflation for the year looked likely to better the government's target of 13%, and the crucial US market was growing steadily. Real incomes – allowing for inflation – were starting to rise again, and consumption and production were expected to grow in 2000. Baja California (Norte) now has one of the highest per capita incomes of all the Mexican states.

POPULATION & PEOPLE

Baja's population consists largely of *mestizos,* individuals of mixed Indian and European heritage, mostly immigrants or descendants of immigrants from mainland Mexico. Official results of the 1995 intercensus estimate Baja's total population as 2.5 million – 2,112,140 in the state of Baja California (Norte) and 427,193 in the state of Baja California Sur. Current figures are estimated to be considerably higher, as both states have experienced a tremendous influx of people since the mid-1990s. More accurate official figures will not become available until the completion of the 2000 census, which was still underway at the time of writing.

In Baja California Sur, 60% of the population was born in the state; in northern Baja, the figure was 53%, reflecting massive immigration from mainland Mexico. Around 2% of the population is foreign, mostly US citizens residing in Tijuana and the Cape Region. The centers of population growth are the border cities and the Cape Region, whose burgeoning tourism infrastructure generates a growing need for service-industry personnel and construction workers. Almost three-quarters of the population of Baja California (Norte) are under 35 years old.

Most *bajacalifornianos* (inhabitants of Baja California) live in cities in the extreme northern and southern parts of the peninsula. Tijuana (two million) accounts for the bulk of Baja's total population; Mexicali (950,000) is the second-largest city. Ensenada (350,000) is third, and La Paz (182,500) is the fourth-largest city and the largest in Baja California Sur. (All these figures are estimates.)

Many informed analysts suspect that, at least in the past, the PRI-controlled federal government has intentionally understated official population figures – especially in Baja California (Norte) – in order to limit the disbursement of population-based federal assistance to the state, which is governed by the opposition party, PAN. There is also suspicion that the federal government wishes to downplay the phenomenal growth of border cities because of the sensitivity of the immigration issue across the line.

Indigenous Peoples & Early Settlers

Permanent European settlements, which began in the 17th century as Jesuit missions or small military camps, exposed the indigenous population to deadly epidemics that reduced their numbers from upward of 48,000 at contact to barely 3000 by 1820. Baja's 1500 or so remaining Indians, often known by the generic term Cochimí after the now extinct peoples of the Desierto Central, live mainly in the Sierra San Pedro Mártir, the Sierra de Juárez and the lowlands near the Río Hardy. They belong to tribal groups like the Diegueño (Tipai), Paipai, Kiliwa, Cucupah and Kamia, but few follow the traditional subsistence economy of hunting and gathering. Nearly all speak Spanish, but indigenous languages are still common among the Tipai, Paipai and Cucupah.

The past decade has seen the influx of large numbers of Indians from central Mexico to the city of Tijuana in particular, often as a staging point for crossing the US border. Several thousand Mixtecs from rural Oaxaca have settled in the San Quintín area, driven by poverty in the south and attracted by farming jobs in Baja, despite relatively low wages. For this reason, mainland indigenous languages are more common than in the past; bilingual schools have even been established in Tijuana, San Quintín and elsewhere.

In the 19th century, Baja's first fishing villages, *ranchos* (rural settlements) and secular towns appeared, along with mining operations that attracted fortune-seekers from around the world. Many established bajacalifornianos are descendants of settlers whose roots were in mainland Mexico or in other parts of the world – some trace their ancestry to the USA, southern and northern Europe or even China. Thanks to these enclaves, unexpected surnames like Smith, Jones and even Crosthwaite and McLish are not unusual on the peninsula.

EDUCATION

Systematic formal education began with the arrival of the Jesuit missionaries in 1697. The first secular school opened in Santo Tomás in 1867, soon followed by others in Real del Castillo, San Vicente, Tecate and El Rosario. In the early 20th century, educational facilities improved rapidly, and by the time Baja California became a state, there were more than 230 primary schools, nine secondary schools and a university.

These days school attendance, obligatory throughout Mexico from age six to 14, is increasing but still low, especially in some rural areas. Even in Tijuana, the average child attends school for only 6.6 years (as opposed to 4.7 in other parts of Mexico). In 1990, about 40% of Tijuana students dropped out of secondary school. Despite such bleak statistics, the two Baja states also have several universities. The state-run Universidad Autónoma de Baja California now has major campuses in Tijuana, Mexicali and Ensenada, as does the private Centro de Enseñanza Técnica y Superior. El Colegio de la Frontera Norte and the Universidad Iberoamericana have campuses in Tijuana, while the Universidad Autónoma de Baja California Sur has a La Paz campus.

Several of these institutions have exchange programs and research affiliations with institutions north of the border, including San Diego State University, the University of California at San Diego and the Scripps Institute of Oceanography in La Jolla. Many wealthy Tijuana families also opt to send their children to schools in San Diego.

ARTS

Though underappreciated by most visitors, Baja California's arts scene has many figures and performers worthy of attention.

Dance

Since the mid-20th century, both traditional and experimental dance have prospered on the peninsula, mostly in association with the universities and the Casa de la Cultura de Baja California, the state-sponsored arts agency. Since 1983, Mexicali's Paralelo 32 dance group, associated with the Universidad Autónoma, has traveled widely throughout the state and the country to promote their craft.

Music

In Mexico, live music may start up at any time on streets, plazas or even buses. The musicians play for a living and range from marimba (wooden xylophone) teams and mariachi bands (trumpeters, violinists, guitarists and a singer, all dressed in smart cowboy-like costumes) to ragged lone buskers with out-of-tune guitars and sandpaper voices. Mariachi music – perhaps the most 'typical' Mexican music of all – originated in the Guadalajara area but is played nationwide.

On a more organized level, Mexico has a thriving popular music business. Its out-

Traditional mariachis

pourings can be heard live at fiestas, nightspots and concerts or bought from music shops or cheap bootleg-tape vendors. (Ask tape vendors to play cassettes before you buy them, as there are many defective or blank copies floating about.)

Regional Styles When traveling throughout the Baja Peninsula, the most common sounds blaring from boomboxes and car stereos are representative of *la música norteña*. Its roots are in *corridos*, folk ballads dealing with Latino/Anglo strife in the borderlands in the 19th century, and themes from the Mexican Revolution. Today's songs, some of which are officially banned by the Mexican government, focus more on the trials and tribulations of small-time smugglers or drug-runners trying to survive amid big-time corruption and crime. The accordion is the most characteristic instrument, although backing for the singer is also guitar-based, with bass and drums. Los Tigres del Norte from Mexicali, the superstars of this genre, added saxophone and absorbed popular cumbia rhythms from Colombia. Other major norteña bands are Los Tucanes de Tijuana, Los Martinez and Los Huaracanes del Norte.

Banda is a 1990s development of norteña, substituting large brass sections for guitars and accordion and playing a combination of Latin and more traditional Mexican rhythms. In Baja California, Banda Machos, Banda Cuisillos and Banda Aguacaliente are big names.

Ranchera is Mexico's urban 'country music.' Developed in the expanding towns and cities of the 20th century, it's mostly melo-dramatic, sentimental stuff with a nostalgia for rural roots – vocalist-and-combo music, maybe with a mariachi backing. Eugenia León, Juan Gabriel and Alejandro Fernández are among the leading ranchera artists.

Rock Baja California has a particularly vibrant rock music scene, most evident in Tijuana. Among the popular bands are Staura (a sort of Sonic Youth clone), Solución Mortal (hard-core punk), Tijuana No (Clash-inspired salsa-punk; the group has also toured

mainland California), Paradoxa (thrash), Mercado Negro (UK-style punk), Beam (California punk), Crime of the Century (a Kiss clone with members from both sides of the border) and Giovanna (pop). Ensenada's Yeo is a heavy-metal act. Sammy Hagar, once bass player for Eddie Van Halen, owns the Cabo Wabo cantina in Cabo San Lucas and occasionally performs with his band.

Popular bands from other parts of Mexico include the Def Leppard–type rockers Jaguares and talented and versatile Mexico City bands such as café Tacuba and Maldita Vecindad. The latter two took *rock en español* to new heights and new audiences (well beyond Mexico) in the '90s, mixing a huge range of influences – rock & roll, ska, punk, bolero and mariachi.

Classical Baja's larger cities, most notably Tijuana and La Paz, support classical music at venues like Tijuana's Centro Cultural. Ensembles also tour smaller towns and cities. One of the most renowned groupings is Tijuana's Orquesta de Baja California, with musicians from Russia, the US and Mexico. It is led by conductor Eduardo García Barrios, a Mexican who studied at Moscow's Tchaikovsky Conservatory prior to the breakup of the Soviet Union. Barrios also instigated the formation of Mexico's first orchestra-led music academy, which has since evolved into the Conservatorio Estatal de Música (State Music Conservatory).

Literature

Not much literature is specifically Baja Californian as opposed to Mexican in general, but two short-story collections are worth seeking out. The stories of Daniel Reveles' *Enchiladas, Rice and Beans* are set in Tecate, while Federico Campbell's *Tijuana* deals with life in Baja's border boomtown. The latter includes a useful introduction by translator Debra A Castillo.

Film

Early Hollywood directors gave such insulting treatment to the Mexican borderlands through depictions of casinos and prostitution that Baja California's first cinematic production in 1927, *Raza de Bronce* (Race of Bronze), was a nationalistic response to what director Guillermo Calles perceived as racist stereotyping. In the 1970s, Tecate built a cinema village to attract US directors of westerns, but local talent did not flourish until the video format became an inexpensive alternative.

With support from the Universidad Autónoma de Baja California, bajacalifornianos have produced documentaries on such topics as the Jesuit colonization of the peninsula and the Chinese community of Mexicali, as well as short fictional pieces like Gabriel Trujillo's quasibiography of the French poet Rimbaud. Since the mid-1980s, the city of Tijuana has occasionally sponsored a film and video festival to reward the efforts of emerging talent.

Independent US director Jonathan Sarno's oddball romance *Ramona* (1992), which won several awards and is available on video, was set partly in Tijuana. A few years later, Hollywood went south again, and 20th Century Fox custom-built a studio just south of Playas de Rosarito for the filming of James Cameron's epic, *Titanic*. Originally intended as a one-time facility, it has been turned into the permanent Fox Baja Studios and was used for other major movies, including *Tomorrow Never Dies* and *Deep Blue Sea*. See the La Frontera chapter for details.

Theater

Tijuana, Mexicali and La Paz, all of which have outstanding stage facilities, are Baja California's dramatic centers. Like film, dance and painting, peninsular theater grew with the universities and the Casa de la Cultura. Numerous theater companies have offered aspiring actors the opportunity to develop their talents. Groups like the well-established Thalía Company of Mexicali and the more experimental Los Desarraigados of Tijuana have performed in Mexico City, the USA and overseas.

Visual Arts

Few visitors appreciate what a fertile environment Baja California has provided for the visual arts. Throughout the peninsula, from Tijuana to Los Cabos, evidence of cultural links with mainland Mexican movements like the muralist tradition are apparent, but sculpture and painting flourished even before the creation of the Instituto de Ciencias y Artes del Estado (ICAE, now part of the Instituto de Bellas Artes) and the Universidad Autónoma in the 1950s. Both institutions supported local artists and others who had relocated from mainland Mexico.

After the Universidad Autónoma abandoned the arts community, individual artists combined to form groups like the Círculo de Escultores y Pintores (Circle of Sculptors and Painters) and the Profesionales de Artes Visuales (Visual Arts Professionals). Since 1977, the Bienal de Artes Plásticas de Baja California has been an important competition for artists from the region.

One informal movement in the local scene is *cholismo,* the equivalent of European or North American punk, often expressed in street murals featuring traditional Mexican figures like the Virgin of Guadalupe in unconventional contexts. Artists from both sides of the border are active in groups like the Taller de Arte Fronterizo (Border Art Workshop) and in the women-only Las Comadres. Both have direct ties to the Centro Cultural de la Raza in San Diego and the Centro Cultural in Tijuana and often stage performance-art shows and events with borderlands themes. Rubén Martínez describes Tijuana's thriving independent arts community in great detail in the essay 'Tijuana Burning,' in his collection *The Other Side.*

Baja California Sur also has a lively arts community, revolving around the village of Todos Santos, which partly but by no means exclusively derives from North Americans who have relocated to the area. Their work, however, lacks the urgency of borderland artists' work, and more closely resembles styles and themes of artists from Taos and Santa Fe in the US state of New Mexico.

SOCIETY & CONDUCT

Despite strong currents of machismo and nationalism, Mexicans are in general friendly, humorous, and helpful to visitors –

the more so if you address them in Spanish, however rudimentary.

Time

The fabled Mexican attitude toward time – *'mañana, mañana…'* – has probably become legendary simply from comparison with the USA. But it's true, especially outside the big cities, that the urgency Europeans and North Americans are used to does not exist. A running joke goes that if someone promises to meet you at 8 pm, it means any time *after* 8 pm, but definitely not before. Most Mexicans value *simpatía* (congeniality) over promptness. If something is really worth doing, it gets done. If not, it can wait. Of course, all of this is a generalization. There are many bajacalifornianos who are perfectly punctual, especially when dealing with foreigners and in business situations.

Nationalism

Most Mexicans are fiercely proud of their own country, even as they despair of it ever being governed well. Their independent-mindedness has roots in Mexico's war of independence from Spain and subsequent struggles against US and French invaders. Any threat of foreign economic domination – as many Mexicans fear will result from NAFTA – is deeply resented.

The classic Mexican attitude toward the US is a combination of the envy and resentment that a poor neighbor feels for a rich one. The word *gringo*, incidentally, isn't exactly a compliment, but it's not necessarily an insult either. Much depends on context, and it can be purely descriptive or even friendly. Another common term, which seems largely descriptive, is *güero* (blond), often applied to virtually any fair-skinned person, whether Mexican or foreign.

Machismo

A common trait throughout Latin America, machismo is an exaggerated masculinity designed to impress other men more than women. Its manifestations range from aggressive driving and the carrying of weapons to heavy drinking.

Many Mexican women, in turn, exaggerate their femininity and defer to male authority in public, but such stereotyping is not universal and is under pressure from modern influences, especially as the women's movement has been making some strides since it began in the 1970s.

Foreign women, often seen as sexually available by Mexican men, may attract unwelcome attention. Most women find such attention more of a nuisance than a danger, but some may feel more comfortable traveling with a male companion.

RELIGION

Mexicans are a religious people, and physical manifestations of their faith are evident everywhere. Baja California lacks the monumental religious architecture of mainland Mexico, but many of the original Jesuit, Franciscan and Dominican missions still survive, at least in ruin; some of these, such as Misión Santa Gertrudis in central Baja, are important pilgrimage sites despite their remoteness. Roadside shrines bear witness not just to victims of traffic accidents but also to revered religious figures like the Virgin of Guadalupe. Some of these shrines are intriguing examples of folk art and are well worth a stop on the highway.

Catholicism

Like other Mexicans, the majority of bajacalifornianos are Roman Catholic. Jesuit missionaries pioneered colonization of the peninsula and, in their domain, exercised more authority than the formal institutions of colonial government until their expulsion from the Spanish empire in 1767. Almost everyone from all social strata and racial groups belonged to the Church because, in addition to salvation, it offered education and other social services.

The Jesuits' expulsion marked the beginning of stormy church-state relations in Mexico. In the 19th and 20th centuries (up to 1940), Mexico passed numerous measures restricting the Church's power and influence. The bottom line was money and property, both of which the Church was amassing faster than the generals and political bosses. The 1917 Mexican constitution prevented the church from owning property or running schools or newspapers and banned clergy from voting, from wearing clerical garb and from speaking out on government policies and decisions. In practice, most of these provisions ceased to be enforced in the second half of the 20th century, and in the early 1990s President Salinas had them removed from the constitution. In 1992, Mexico finally established diplomatic relations with the Vatican.

Despite tensions with the state, the Church remains influential, especially as a symbol and an institution of social cohesion. Its most binding symbol is *Nuestra Señora de Guadalupe,* the dark-skinned Virgin of Guadalupe, a manifestation of the Virgin Mary who appeared to an indigenous Mexican in 1531 on a hill near Mexico City. The Guadalupe Virgin became a crucial link between Catholic and indigenous spirituality, and as Mexico grew into a mestizo society, she became the most potent symbol of Mexican Catholicism. Today, she is the country's patron, her blue-cloaked image is ubiquitous, and her name is invoked in religious ceremonies, political speeches and literature.

Protestantism

While Roman Catholicism is Mexico's dominant religion, evangelical Protestantism is growing here as elsewhere in Latin America. Protestantism in Mexico dates from the Revolution of 1910, when many Mexicans found it an effective outlet for protesting the influence of the traditional Church, but even the smallest communities now often have evangelical churches competing with the Catholics. In the larger cities

Border Spanish

Spanish-speakers on both sides of the US-Mexico border have unselfconsciously adopted many English words. Perhaps the best marker of the cultural border, as opposed to the political border, might be the geographical point where bathrooms taps start to be marked 'C' and 'F' for caliente and frío rather than 'H' and 'C' for 'hot' and 'cold.'

The following list shows a few common border terms with their English and standard Spanish equivalents. For purposes of differentiation, some of the border-Spanish (or 'Spanglish') spellings are phoneticized, but this can be misleading because the words themselves are rarely written down. Spanglish is essentially an oral language, though occasionally English words are adopted as written and given a Spanish tone.

English	Spanglish	Standard Spanish
brake	el breque	el freno
clutch	el clutch	el embrague
junk	el yonke	las chacharas
lunch	el lonche	el almuerzo
pickup truck	la pickup	la camioneta
rug/carpet	la carpeta*	la alfombra
six pack	el six pack	n/a
truck	la troca	el camión
vacuum cleaner	la vaquium	la aspiradora
yard (distance)	la yarda	vara
yard (lawn)	la yarda	el jardín

*In standard Spanish, *carpeta* means 'notebook.'

such as Tijuana, these churches frequently occupy storefronts.

LANGUAGE

Spanish is Mexico's official language, but English is fairly widely spoken along the border (where there are many hybrid 'Spanglish' usages) and at tourist-oriented businesses throughout the Baja Peninsula. Indigenous languages are frequently spoken among the Tipai, Paipai and Cucupah of northern Baja and among the mostly Mixtec immigrants in the San Quintín area and even in Tijuana.

See the Spanish for Travelers and Menu Guide chapters for a quick plunge into the primary language on the peninsula.

Facts for the Visitor

HIGHLIGHTS

Some of Baja California's finest experiences are not the ones tourist offices usually promote. For more highlights, see the color map of Baja at the front of this book. For regional highlights, see the boxed text at the top of each geographical chapter. For prime spots for particular activities – diving, hiking, surfing and so on – see the respective entries in the Activities chapter.

Towns

Many of Baja's towns are fascinating places, but for different reasons. Tijuana is a bustling border town with a cosmopolitan vibe, great restaurants, nightlife and shopping. Tecate more closely resembles a mainland Mexican town than does any other settlement in the entire state of Baja California (Norte).

Santa Rosalía has unusual residential architecture and a church designed by Gustave Eiffel (think Paris). Loreto is an ideal base for all types of outdoor activities, while La Paz is distinguished by great sunsets, nearby beaches and neocolonial architecture.

San Jose del Cabo preserves its charming, small-town center and has great shopping. Todos Santos is an artist's colony popular with North Americans.

Missions

Baja is studded with 30 mission sites in various states of repair. In most cases, little survives but a few foundations and ruined walls. There are a few exceptions: The most preserved of the Baja missions is San Francisco Javier near Loreto, which is also distinguished by a wonderful setting. Misión San Ignacio in San Ignacio, with walls made from lava block, is often considered the peninsula's most beautiful church. Misión San Borja, near Rosarito and Bahía de los Angeles, is embedded in a scenic oasis.

Beaches

With 3000 miles (4800km) of coastline, finding a fabulous beach in Baja is not difficult, but here are some of the best: In San Felipe, a long white sandy beach beckons. El Requesón, south of Mulegé, once made it on the list of *Condé Nast Traveler*'s top-ten beaches in Mexico.

Punta San Francisquito, in the bay of the same name, is one of the most beautiful, isolated beaches on the peninsula. The 50 miles (80km) of beaches south of Mulegé are popular, especially for camping.

In Bahía Pichilingue north of La Paz, Playa Balandra and Playa Tecolote are wonderful places for lounging. On the East Cape, Cabo Pulmo and Bahía Los Frailes offer seclusion, good snorkeling, calm waters and soft sands, as do the coves and beaches of the Los Cabos Corridor.

Pre-Columbian Rock Art

Declared a UNESCO World Heritage Site, the dissected (cut by irregular valleys and hills) volcanic plateau of the Sierra de San Francisco contains the most extraordinary of the many rock art sites on the peninsula. The muleback descent into the sierra's canyons from the village of San Francisco de la Sierra, north of San Ignacio, is an unforgettable experience. Another good site is Cañón La Trinidad southwest of Mulegé. There are also cave paintings near Cataviña.

Whale-Watching

Laguna Ojo de Liebre (Scammon's Lagoon) has the greatest number of whales among Baja's whale-watching sites, but Laguna San Ignacio is probably the best spot for contact with so-called friendly whales. In southern Baja, Bahía Magdalena, especially Puerto San Carlos and Puerto Adolfo López Mateos, is the best spot.

SUGGESTED ITINERARIES

The ideal way to see – and experience – the Baja Peninsula is to travel its entire 800-mile (1300km) length from border to cape. If you don't have the time, money or inclination to do this, consider any of the following route suggestions:

Northern Baja Loop Tijuana-Playas de Rosarito-Ensenada-Valle de Guadalupe-Tecate-Tijuana (this tour could also start in Tecate). All roads are paved. The tour can be done by bus.

Grand Northern Baja Loop Tijuana-Playas de Rosarito-Ensenada-San Felipe-Mexicali-Tecate-Tijuana (this tour could also start in Tecate or Mexicali). All roads are paved. The tour can be done by bus. Consider a side trip to Laguna Hanson and Parque Nacional Constitución de 1857 from Ojos Negros (off-road).

Baja's Border Towns Tijuana-Tecate-Mexicali (or vice versa). All roads are paved. The tour can be done by bus.

Dual Coast Loop Mexicali-San Felipe-Puertecitos-Bahía San Luis Gonzaga-Cataviña (cave paintings)-El Rosario-San Quintín-Ensenada-Tijuana-Mexicali (this tour could also start in Tijuana or Tecate). Roads are mostly paved, but there's rough road on the unpaved stretch from San Felipe to México 1.

National Parks Loop From Tijuana, Tecate or Mexicali to El Cóndor (on México 2)-Laguna Hanson and Parque Nacional de Constitución de 1857-Ojos Negros (on México 3) to Km 138-Mike's Sky Rancho-Observatory Road-Parque Nacional Sierra de San Pedro Mártir-Meling Ranch-San Telmo-Tijuana or other starting point. The trip is mostly off-road but partly on.

Central Coastal Towns Loreto-Mulegé-Santa Rosalía or in reverse. Consider the extension to San Ignacio and cave paintings of Sierra de San Francisco. All roads are paved. The tour can be done by bus.

Cape Loop La Paz-Todos Santos-Cabo San Lucas-Los Cabos Corridor-San José del Cabo-East Cape-La Paz (this tour could also start in San José del Cabo). Traveling the route clockwise is another alternative, or take a side trip into Sierra de la Laguna (off-road). All roads are paved. The tour can be done by bus.

PLANNING
When to Go

Baja is a year-round destination, but the best time to visit depends on where you're going and what you want to do.

The northwestern Pacific coast is busiest from May to October when the weather is reliably dry and warm. Winter here brings cooler temperatures and occasional rain but also smaller crowds and lower prices. During spring break, US university students jam all the resort areas down to San Felipe and even trickle down to Cabo San Lucas.

On the Sea of Cortez coast and in the Cape Region, tourist season peaks from November through March. The nicest time to visit here may be spring, when temperatures are moderate and tourists few. Summer is *chubasco* (tropical storm) season and can be hot, humid and unpleasant, unless fishing is your bailiwick: The biggest catches are usually brought in between July and September.

Visitors with special interests should tailor their itineraries accordingly. Whale-watching season generally runs from January to the end of March, while bird-watchers may find the colonies in the Bahía de los Angeles area most active in May. Desert bighorn sheep are easiest to spot in summer in the eastern escarpment of the Sierra de Juárez and Sierra San Pedro Mártir. In general, it's best to skirt the desert areas between May and October.

Hiking in the mountains is best in summer, when temperatures are mild; in winter be prepared for snow and icy conditions. Spring flower season peaks in April and May in the northern ranges and September and October in the Cape Region sierras.

Maps

The *Baja California Road Map,* published by the Automobile Club of Southern California, an affiliate of AAA, is the best general map of the peninsula. It is available for free to club members and sold to everyone else for US$3.95 at AAA offices and in bookstores. It is occasionally found in Baja bookstores and tourist-oriented enterprises as well.

International Travel Maps & Books (ITMB; ☎ 604-879-3621, fax 604-879-4521, itmb@itmb.com) has the most recent (2000) map of Baja California (US$8.95). Though a bit cluttered for field use, the map has a scale of 1:1,000,000 and is excellent for planning trips and getting background information. It's available in stores or by mail from ITMB, 530 West Broadway, Vancouver, BC Canada V5Z 1E9. Its Web site is at www.itmb.com.

The *Baja Almanac* (1997), by Baja Almanac Publishers, contains topographical maps at a scale of 1:100,000 and is a good resource for off-road travel. Its two volumes cover Baja California (Norte) and Baja California Sur and cost US$12.50 each.

Essential for hikers and backpackers is the series of topo maps published by INEGI (Instituto Nacional de Estadística, Geografía e Informática) at a scale of 1:50,000 (1cm:500m) and available for US$3 each. There are INEGI offices in Tijuana and La Paz.

All of these maps may be ordered from the US-based companies Map Centre (☎ 619-291-3830, 888-849-6277, fax 619-291-3840) at 3191 Sports Arena Blvd, Suite F, San Diego, CA 92110, and Maplink (☎ 805-692-6777, fax 805-692-6787, custserv@maplink.com), 30 S La Patera Lane, No 5, Santa Barbara, CA 93117. The latter publishes an extensive mail-order catalog for view online at www.maplink.com. Both stores take orders in person, by phone, fax or email.

In the UK, a good place for Baja-related maps and books is Stanfords (☎ 020-7240-3611) at 12-14 Long Acre, London, WC2E 9LP. It also offers mail-order service. Visit its Web site at www.stanfords.co.uk.

City, town and regional maps of varying quality are often available free from local tourist offices in Baja, and you can often find commercially published ones at bookstores or newsstands. Unfortunately, most are outdated and poorly produced.

What to Bring

Casual is king just about anywhere on the peninsula and is appropriate in most situations. Men will only need ties and jackets in the fanciest restaurants. Women might prefer conservative clothing outside the resort towns, especially when traveling alone. In general, when packing, choose clothes that enable you to dress in layers. The climate varies throughout the peninsula and even hot days can be followed by chilly nights. See Climate in the Facts about Baja California chapter for the kind of temperatures and rainfall you can expect.

General toiletries (shampoo, soap, shaving cream, toothpaste, etc) are readily available, but outside the tourist hubs, items like contact lens solution, tampons and contraceptives may be hard to find.

Other useful items include sunglasses, a hat and sunscreen; a lighter, pocketknife and some cord; a small sewing kit; a money belt or pouch; a Latin American Spanish dictionary and/or phrasebook; a medical kit (see the boxed text later in this chapter); and diving, snorkeling or fishing equipment, if you plan on engaging in those activities. Also carry a flashlight (torch) in case you get stranded at night or there's an electrical power outage.

RESPONSIBLE TOURISM

A responsible tourist is, perhaps, one who treats the visited place as if it were home. Would you like having your photo taken without being asked? Would you wander into your church during a service and start taking flash photos? If the drains in your home were blocked, would you put toilet paper down them to clog them further?

As for Baja's environment, everyone has an obligation to help stop it from deteriorating. For instance, don't buy turtle, iguana or black coral products, and do patronize ecotourism projects that aim to preserve or restore the environments they visit.

As the saying goes, take only photos, leave only footprints – but don't leave footprints on the coral. Help prevent overfishing by not exceeding daily catch quotas. Respect size limits when clamming. When hiking and camping on the beach or in the mountains, take out everything you bring in and make an effort to carry out trash left by others. Don't bury trash, which disturbs the ground cover and furthers erosion. Don't dig up plants, destroy tide pool organisms or pick up artifacts.

TOURIST OFFICES
Local Tourist Offices

Most of the major tourist towns on the peninsula have tourist offices, especially in Baja California (Norte). They can be helpful with maps and brochures, and usually some staff members speak English.

Offices of the Secretaría de Turismo del Estado (Secture) in Tijuana, Tecate, Mexicali, Playas de Rosarito, San Felipe, Ensenada, San Quintín and La Paz are affiliated with the state governments of either Baja California (Norte) or Baja California Sur. The staff at all these offices are helpful in providing information about those cities and perhaps other places in Baja.

Local offices of the Cámara Nacional de Comercio (Canaco, National Chamber of Commerce) and the Comité de Turismo y Convenciones (Cotuco, Committee on Tourism & Conventions) can be found in Tijuana, Rosarito, Ensenada, Tecate and Mexicali. The Ensenada Cotuco office is among the best-organized sources of information in Baja. There are also municipal tourist offices in San José del Cabo and Loreto.

Free English-language newspapers are available at tourist offices, hotels and restaurants throughout the peninsula. The most widely available is the *Baja Sun,* which comes in two editions: Baja Norte and Los Cabos. It is primarily geared toward long-time residents, property owners and frequent travelers from North America but may contain some useful information and background articles. There are several other publications, especially in the Los Cabos area. See the boxed text 'What's Up in Cabo' in the Cape Region chapter for details.

Tourist Offices Abroad

Currently, the Mexican Government Tourist Offices are undergoing complete reorganization and restructuring into a private organization funded by hoteliers, airlines and other tourism-related businesses. The new organization will be known as the Mexican Tourism Board. It is unclear whether all 13 offices around the world will remain in operation, also in view of the change in government in the 2000 national elections. Though contact information listed below was correct as of the time of writing, closures and address changes are possible.

Canada
Montréal: (☎ 514-871-1052, fax 514-871-3825, turimex@cam.org) 1 Place Ville Marie, Suite 1931, Montréal, Québec H3B 2B5
Toronto: (☎ 416-925-2753, fax 416-925-6061, mexto3@inforamp.net) 2 Bloor St W, Suite 1502, Toronto, Ontario M4W 3E2
Vancouver: (☎ 604-669-2845, fax 604-669-3498, mgto@bc.simpatico.ca) 999 W Hastings St, Suite 1610, Vancouver, BC V6C 2W2

France
(☎ 01 42 86 96 12, fax 01 42 86 05 80, otmex@world.fr) 4 rue Notre Dame des Victoires, 75002 Paris

Germany
(☎ 069 25 35 09, fax 069 25 35 55, mexiconline@compuserve.com) Wiesenhüttenplatz 26, 60329 Frankfurt/Main

Italy
(☎ 06-487-21-82, fax 06-487-36-30, mex.touroffice@arora.stm.it) Via Barberini 3, 00187 Rome

Spain
(☎ 01-561-35-20, fax 01-411-07-59, mexico@lander.es) Velázquez 126, Madrid 28006

UK
(☎ 020-7488-9392, fax 020-7265-0704, info@mexicotravel.co.uk) 41 Trinity Square, London, EC3N 4DJ

USA
California: (☎ 213-351-2075, fax 213-351-2074, 104045.3647@compuserve.com) 2401 W 6th St, 5th Floor, Los Angeles, CA 90057
Florida: (☎ 305-718-4091, fax 305-718-4098, mgtomia@gate.net) 1200 NW 78th Ave, Suite 203, Miami, FL 33126
Illinois: (☎ 312-606-9252, fax 312-606-9012, mgtochi@compuserve.com) 300 N Michigan, 4th Floor, Chicago, IL 60601
New York: (☎ 212-821-0314, fax 212-821-0367, milmgto@interport.net) 21 E 63rd St, 3rd Floor, New York, NY 10021
Texas: (☎ 713-772-2581, fax 713-772-6058, mgtotx@ix.netcom.com) 1010 Fomdren St, Houston, TX 77096

In the US, general tourist information for Mexico can also be accessed by calling ☎ 800-4463-9426 (800-44-MEXICO). Note that responses to email requests take a lot longer than those to telephone calls.

VISAS & DOCUMENTS

Every visitor beyond the immediate border area should carry a valid passport and a stamped Mexican government tourist card at all times; see Travel Permits, later, for details. Consular visas may be required for travel by citizens of some countries. Drivers must have a valid driver's license, current vehicle registration and, if planning to travel to mainland Mexico, a temporary import permit for each vehicle (including motorcycles and boats), obtainable at the border (for details, see Vehicle Permits in the Getting Around chapter). These requirements are in flux, so verify information with the Mexican consulate or embassy in your country before going.

Passport

Though it's not recommended, US tourists can enter Baja without a passport if they have official photo identification, such as a driver's license, plus some proof of their citizenship, such as a birth certificate certified by the issuing agency or their original certificate of naturalization (not a copy). Citizens of other countries who are permanent residents in the US have to take their passport and Permanent Resident Alien Card ('Green Card').

Canadian tourists may enter Mexico with official photo identification plus proof of citizenship, such as a birth certificate or notarized affidavit of it. Naturalized Canadian citizens, however, require a valid passport.

Citizens from all other countries must have a valid passport and, in some cases, a tourist visa (see Visas, next).

Visas

Citizens of the USA, Canada, EU countries, Australia, New Zealand, Norway, Switzerland, Iceland, Israel, Japan, Argentina and Chile are among those who do not require visas to enter Mexico as tourists. But they must obtain a stamped Mexican government tourist card for visits in excess of 72 hours and/or travel south of Ensenada or San Felipe (see Travel Permits, later). Countries whose nationals *do* have to obtain visas – as well as a tourist card – include most African, Asian and eastern European nations. Some nationals will also need to produce a round-trip ticket to enter Mexico. Check well ahead of travel with your local Mexican embassy or consulate.

Non-US citizens passing through the USA on the way to or from Mexico, or visiting Mexico from the USA, should check their US visa requirements.

US and Canadian citizens visiting Mexico on business must complete form FM-N, authorizing the conduct of business for 30 days. It is available from Mexican consulates or at the border. You will need a valid passport or original birth certificate plus a letter from your company stating the purpose of your trip and the source of your income.

If your stay exceeds 30 days, you will need to apply for an FM-3 card. In addition to your passport and company letter, you will need two photographs and must pay US$70. This permit is good for multiple entries for one year.

Travel Permits

The Mexican tourist card – officially the Forma Migratoria para Turista (FMT) – is a small document that is stamped by Mexican immigration when you enter Mexico and which you must keep until you leave. It is available free of charge at border crossings, international airports and ports, and often from airlines, travel agencies, Mexican consulates and Mexican Government Tourism Offices. At the US-Mexico border, you won't usually be given one automatically but must pick it up at the Instituto Nacional de Migración (INM, National Immigration Institute).

In Baja, you do not need a stamped tourist card if you're entering by land and are staying north of Ensenada or San Felipe for visits of less than 72 hours. In practice, enforcement is so limited that most people don't bother getting their card stamped even if spending more than 72 hours in the border zone.

However, everyone, regardless of age, must get a stamped tourist card for travel beyond Ensenada or San Felipe. It's likely that you will be asked to show this document at road checkpoints and may be sent back north if your papers are not in order. The Servicios Migratorios in Ensenada may also stamp tourist cards, although it's best to get the process over with right at the border. A tourist card is also necessary for travel to mainland Mexico.

One section of the card – to be filled in by the immigration officer – deals with the length of your stay in Mexico. You may be asked a couple of questions about how long you want to stay and what you'll be doing, but normally you will be given the maximum 180 days if you ask for it. It's always advisable to put down more days than you think you'll need, in case you are delayed or change your plans. The card is good for multiple entries.

Tourist Fee Since July 1, 1999, foreign tourists (of any age) and business travelers visiting Mexico have been charged a fee, which, at the time of writing, was 170 pesos (about US$18). If you enter Mexico by air, the fee is included in the price of your plane ticket.

Tourists are exempt if entering Baja by land for a visit of less than 72 hours and staying north of Ensenada on the Pacific side or San Felipe on the Sea of Cortez side. Everyone else must pay the fee at a branch of any of 27 Mexican banks listed on the back of your tourist card. If possible, pay the fee right at the bank branch at the border (usually Banco Ejército).

Hours of operation at the Tijuana-San Ysidro crossing are 8 am to 10 pm weekdays, to 6 pm Saturday, and noon to 4 pm Sunday; the bank at the Otay Mesa crossing is open 10 am to 6 pm daily. In Tecate, bank hours are 8 am to 4 pm daily, and in Mexicali it's open around the clock. When paying at the bank, you need to present your tourist card or business visitor card, which will be stamped to prove that you have paid.

Tourists only have to pay the fee once in any 180-day period and are entitled to multiple entries. If you are going to return within the stipulated period, retain your stamped tourist/business visitor's card when you leave Mexico.

Tourist Card Extensions & Lost Cards If the number of days given on your tourist card is less than the 180-day maximum, its validity may be extended one or more times, at no cost, up to the maximum.

To get a card extended, you must apply to the Servicios Migratorios, which has offices in many towns and cities. The procedure is free and usually accomplished in a few minutes. You'll need your passport, tourist card, photocopies of the important pages of these documents, and – at some offices – evidence of 'sufficient funds.' A major credit card is usually OK for the latter, or an amount in traveler's checks that could vary from US$100 to US$1000, depending on which office you are dealing with.

Most offices will not extend a card until a few days before it is due to expire – don't bother trying earlier.

If you lose your card or need more information, contact the Secture's emergency hotline in Mexico City (☎ 5-250-0123, toll-free in Mexico ☎ 01-800-903-92-00).

Consent Forms for Minors

Every year numerous parents try to run away from the USA or Canada to Mexico with their children to escape legal entanglements with the other parent. To prevent this, minors (people under 18) entering Mexico without one or both of their parents are officially required to show a notarized consent form, signed by the absent parent or parents, giving permission for the young traveler to enter Mexico. A form for this purpose is available from Mexican consulates. In the case of divorced parents, a custody document may be acceptable instead. If one or both parents are dead, or the traveler has only one legal parent, a notarized statement to that effect may be required.

These rules are aimed primarily at visitors from the USA and Canada but apparently apply to all nationalities. Enforcement, however, is fairly lax.

Travel Insurance

A travel insurance policy to cover theft, loss (including plane tickets), delay or cancellation of flights, and medical problems is a good idea. As a rule, buy insurance as early as possible. If you get it the week before departure, for example, you may find that you're not covered for delays to your flight caused by strikes.

Mexican medical treatment is generally inexpensive for common diseases and minor treatment, but most doctors and hospitals in Baja require payment at the time of service. If you suffer from a serious medical problem, you may want to fly out for treatment, and travel insurance can cover the costs.

Without insurance, even minor health concerns can easily bust your entire travel budget – and worse. In late 1999, according to a well-publicized news report, one patient requiring sophisticated medical treatment only available in the US died in a Baja hospital after the hospital refused to release him until his entire medical bill had been paid.

In order to process reimbursement through your insurance, be sure to get receipts and keep all documentation. Some policies require you to make a collect call to a center in your home country before seeing a physician, where an immediate assessment of your problem is made.

US health insurance policies may stay in effect (at least for a limited time) if you travel abroad, but it's worth checking exactly what you'll be covered for in Mexico. For people whose medical insurance or national health systems don't extend to Mexico – which includes most non-Americans – a travel policy is advisable.

Some policies offer lower and higher medical-expense options; the higher ones are chiefly for countries such as the USA, which have extremely high medical costs. There is a wide variety of policies available, so check the small print.

Some policies specifically exclude 'dangerous activities,' which can include scuba diving, motorcycling and even trekking.

Check that the policy covers ambulances or an emergency flight home. If it doesn't, consider taking out medical evacuation insurance. It can cost as little as US$50 for a 30-day trip as opposed to thousands of dollars for an actual evacuation. Reputable companies include American Care (☎ 800-941-2582, 619-486-8844) and Critical Air Medicine (☎ 800-247-8326, 619-571-0482), both San Diego based; and AirEvac (☎ 800-421-6111) in Phoenix. All companies accept collect calls in emergencies.

Plane-ticket loss is also covered by most travel insurance policies. Make sure you have a separate record of all your ticket details – or better still, a photocopy of it. Also make a copy of your policy in case the original is lost.

Driver's License & Permits

To drive in Baja, you need a valid US or Canadian driver's license or an International Driving Permit. If you are from a country other than the US or Canada, bring your International Driving Permit as well as your national license. Also bring car registration papers.

To rent a vehicle in Mexico, you will need a driver's license and a major credit card. A vehicle permit is only required for travel in mainland Mexico. For more information on either subject, see the Getting Around chapter.

Student & Youth Cards

The ISIC student card, the GO25 card for travelers 12 to 25, and the ITIC card for teachers can all help you obtain reduced-price airfare to or from Mexico at student and youth-oriented travel agencies. Once in Baja, however, these cards won't make much of a difference. Student discounts are almost unknown, though some museums may offer small discounts on already low admission fees.

Pet Permits

Under Mexican law, travelers entering the country may bring a dog, cat or up to four canaries (!) with them, provided they can present the following certificates at the border: a pet health certificate signed by a registered veterinarian and issued not more than 72 hours before the animal enters Mexico and a pet vaccination certificate showing inoculation against rabies, hepatitis, pip and leptospirosis. Certification of these papers by a Mexican consulate is *not* required. At the border you will be issued a pet permit (fee-based).

Before taking a pet to Mexico, confirm re-importation requirements for the USA. Unless you have no alternative, it's probably better to leave your pet at home.

Copies

Before you leave home, you should photocopy all important documents (passport data page and visa page, credit cards, travel insurance policy, air/bus/train tickets, driver's license, etc). Leave one copy with someone at home and keep another with you, separate from the originals.

It's also a good idea to store details of your vital travel documents in Lonely Planet's free online Travel Vault in case you lose the photocopies or can't be bothered with them. Your password-protected Travel Vault is accessible online anywhere in the world – create it at www.ekno.lonelyplanet.com.

EMBASSIES & CONSULATES

Mexico has extensive diplomatic representation around the world, though more in the USA than anywhere else. The listings below are consulates rather than embassies (embassies deal with diplomatic matters rather than tourist inquiries), though in some cases they are both at the same site.

Mexican Consulates Abroad

Mexican diplomatic offices abroad include the following:

Australia
(☎ 02-9326-1311, fax 02-9327-1110, comexsyd@bigpond.com.au) 135-153 New South Head Rd, Level 1, Edgecliff, Sydney NSW 2027

Canada
Montréal: (☎ 514-288-2502, fax 514-288-8287, comexmt@mmic.net) 2055 rue Peel, Bureau 1000, Montréal, Québec H3A 1V4

Toronto: (☎ 416-368-2875, fax 416-368-8342, consulad@interlog.com) 199 Bay St W, Suite 4440, Toronto, Ontario M5L 1E

Vancouver: (☎ 604-684-3547, fax 604-684-2485, mexico@direct.ca) 1130 W Pender St, Vancouver, BC V6E 4A4

France
(☎ 01 42 86 56 20, fax 01 49 26 02 78, consulmex.paris@wanadoo.fr) 4 rue Notre Dame des Victoires, 75002 Paris

Germany
Berlin: (☎ 030 327 6504/5/6, fax 030 327 71 121, rfaemb@edina.com) Kurfürstendamm 72, 10709 Berlin

Frankfurt/Main: (☎ 069 299 8750, fax 069 299 87 575, consulmex_@compuserve.com) Taunusanlage 21, 60325 Frankfurt/Main

UK
(☎ 020-7235-6393) 8 Halkin St, London SW1X 7DW

Mexican Consulates in the USA

Arizona
Douglas: (☎ 520-364-3107, fax 520-364-1379) 541 10th St, Douglas, AZ 85607

Nogales: (☎ 520-287-2521, 800-285-1626, fax 520-287-3175) 480 N Grand Ave, Nogales, AZ 85621

Phoenix: (☎ 602-242-7398, fax 602-242-2957) 1990 W Camelback Rd, Suite 110, Phoenix, AZ 85015

Tucson: (☎ 520-882-5595, fax 520-882-8959) 553 S Stone Ave, Tucson, AZ 85701

California
Calexico: (☎ 760-357-3863, fax 760-357-6284) 331 W 2nd St, Calexico, CA 92231

Fresno: (☎ 209-233-9770, fax 209-233-5638) 830 Van Ness Ave, Fresno, CA 93721

Los Angeles: (☎ 213-351-6800, fax 213-351-6844) 2401 W 6th St, Los Angeles, CA 90057

Sacramento: (☎ 916-441-3287, fax 916-363-0625) 1010 8th St, Sacramento, CA 95827

San Diego: (☎ 619-231-8414, fax 619-231-4802) 1549 India St, San Diego, CA 92101

San Francisco: (☎ 415-392-5554, fax 415-392-3233) 870 Market St, Suite 528, San Francisco, CA 94102

San Jose: (☎ 408-298-5581, fax 408-294-4506) 380 N 1st St, Suite 102, San Jose, CA 95112

Colorado
(☎ 303-331-1867, fax 303-830-2655) 48 Steele St, Denver, CO 80206

Florida
(☎ 305-716-4977, fax 305-593-2758) 1200 NW 78th Ave, Suite 200, Miami, FL 33126

Georgia
(☎ 404-266-2233, fax 404-266-2309) 2600 Apple Valley Rd, Atlanta, GA 30319

Illinois
(☎ 312-855-0066, fax 312-855-9257) 300 N Michigan Ave, 2nd Floor, Chicago, IL 60601

Louisiana
(☎ 504-522-3596, fax 504-525-2332) World Trade Center, 2 Canal St, Suite 840, New Orleans, LA 70115

Massachusetts
(☎ 617-426-4942, fax 617-695-1957) 20 Park Plaza, Suite 506, Boston, MA 02116

Michigan
(☎ 313-567-7713, fax 313-567-7543) 600 Renaissance St, Suite 1510, Detroit, MI 48243

Missouri
(☎ 314-436-3065, fax 314-436-2695) 1015 Locust St, Suite 922, St Louis, MO 63101

New Mexico
(☎ 505-247-2147, fax 505-842-9490) 401 5th St NW, Albuquerque, NM 87102

New York
(☎ 212-217-6400, fax 212-217-6493) 27 E 39th St, New York, NY 10016

Oregon
(☎ 503-274-1442, fax 503-274-1540) 1234 SW Morrison, Portland, OR 97205

Pennsylvania
(☎ 215-922-3834, fax 215-923-7281) Bourse Bldg, 111 S Independence Mall E, Suite 310, Philadelphia, PA 19106

Puerto Rico
(☎ 787-764-0258, fax 787-250-0042) Av Muñoz Rivera 654, Suite 1837, San Juan, Puerto Rico 00918

Texas
Austin: (☎ 512-478-2300, fax 512-478-8008) 200 E 6th St, Suite 200, Austin, TX 78701
Brownsville: (☎ 210-542-2051, fax 210-542-7267) 724 E Elizabeth St, Brownsville, TX 78520
Corpus Christi: (☎ 512-882-3375, fax 512-882-9234) 8800 N Shoreline Blvd, Suite 410, Corpus Christi, TX 78401
Dallas: (☎ 214-630-7341, fax 214-630-3511) 8855 Stemmons Freeway, Dallas, TX 75247
El Paso: (☎ 915-533-3644, fax 915-532-7163) 910 E San Antonio St, El Paso, TX 79901
Houston: (☎ 713-339-4701, fax 713-789-4060) 10440 W Office St, Houston, TX 77042
Laredo: (☎ 956-723-6369, fax 956-723-1741) 1612 Farragut St, Laredo, TX 78040
Midland: (☎ 915-687-2335, fax 915-687-3952) 511 W Ohio, Suite 121, Midland, TX 79701
San Antonio: (☎ 210-227-1085, fax 210-227-1817) 127 Navarro St, San Antonio, TX 78205

Utah
(☎ 801-521-8502, fax 801-521-0534) 458 East 200 S, Suite 110, Salt Lake City, UT 84111

Washington, DC
(☎ 202-736-1000, fax 202-797-8458, consulwas@ aol.com) 2827 16th St NW, Washington, DC 20009

Washington State
(☎ 206-448-8419, fax 206-448-4771) 2132 3rd Ave, Seattle, WA 98121

Foreign Consulates in Baja

Most of the foreign consulates in Baja are in Tijuana. Besides the countries listed below, Austria, China, Finland, Gambia, Honduras, Italy, Korea, Norway, Spain and Switzerland also have representations in this city.

Canada
(☎ 6-684-04-61, fax 6-684-03-01) German Gedovius 10411, Zona Río, Tijuana
(The Canadian consulate will also assist citizens of Australia and Belize.)
(☎ 1-142-43-33, fax 1-142-42-62) No 9 Plaza José Green, Blvd Mijares, San José del Cabo

France
(☎ 6-685-71-72, fax 6-684-20-94) Avenida Revolución 1651, 3rd Floor, Tijuana
(☎ 1-122-16-20) Zaragosa 30, La Paz

Germany
(☎ 6-680-18-30, 6-680-25-12) Cantera 400-304, Edificio Ole, Playas de Tijuana

UK
(☎ 6-681-73-23, fax 6-681-84-02) Blvd Salinas 1500, Colonia Aviación, La Mesa, Tijuana

USA

(☎ 6-681-74-00, fax 6-681-8016, 619-692-2154 answering service in San Diego) Tapachula 96, Colonia Hipódromo, Tijuana

(☎/fax 1-143-35-66) Boulevard Marina y Pedregral No 1, Local No 3, Cabo San Lucas (in the Plaza Naútica, behind the Bital bank)

Your Own Embassy

As a tourist, it's important to realize what your own embassy – the embassy of the country of which you are a citizen – can and can't do. Generally speaking, it won't be much help in emergencies if the trouble you're in is remotely your own fault. Remember that you are bound by the laws of the country you're visiting. Your embassy will not be sympathetic if you end up in jail after committing a crime locally, even if such actions are legal in your own country.

In genuine emergencies, you might get some assistance, but only if other channels have been exhausted. For example, if you need to get home urgently, a free ticket home is exceedingly unlikely – the embassy would expect you to have insurance. If all your money and documents are stolen, it might assist you in getting a new passport, but a loan for onward travel is out of the question.

CUSTOMS

The value of goods visitors may bring into Mexico duty free is limited to US$50 if arriving by land and US$300 if arriving by sea or air.

Travel-related items for personal use may also be brought in duty free. These include clothing and toiletries; medicine for personal use, with prescription in the case of psychotropic drugs (medicines that can alter perception or behavior); one still, video or movie camera; up to 12 rolls/reels of film or videocassettes; one portable computer; and, if you're 18 or older, 3 liters of wine, beer or liquor and 400 cigarettes.

These limits are not always applied very strictly. Amounts exceeding the duty-free limit are subject to a 32.8% tax. If you are entering by land, it is fairly unlikely that you will be stopped and your vehicle searched by Mexican customs inspectors.

If you are bringing a lot of expensive electronic items into the country – such as cameras, computers, radios and TVs – you may want to register them with US Customs before crossing the border unless you have the original receipts for the items. Firearms and ammunition are prohibited unless you have a permit issued by a Mexican consulate or embassy.

US residents returning to the USA from Baja or elsewhere in Mexico may bring in duty-free items with a total retail value of up to US$400, for personal use only and not for resale. The exemption may only be used once in any 30-day period.

Limits on the importation of liquor are stricter. Adult US residents (21 years or older) crossing into the US from Mexico by car or on foot may bring only 1 liter (33.8 fluid oz) of hard liquor (spirits), wine or beer into mainland California every 30 days. They may also bring in 100 cigars (though not of Cuban origin) and 200 cigarettes duty free.

There is a complex list of regulations for agricultural products, but in general, plants, seeds, soil, pork, poultry, live birds and straw are prohibited. Most fruits and vegetables are permitted, except avocados, sugar cane, potatoes, sweet potatoes and yams. Other prohibited items include fireworks, switchblade knives and products made from endangered species. For details, check under *Know Before You Go* at the Web site www.customs.gov/travel/travel.htm.

MONEY
Currency

Mexico's currency is the peso, which is divided into 100 centavos. Coins come in denominations of five, 10, 20 and 50 centavos and one, two, five, 10, 20 and 50 pesos, and there are notes of 10, 20, 50, 100, 200 and 500 pesos.

Both Mexican pesos and US dollars are commonly used in Baja, but US dollars may not be accepted in some small towns and villages. The $ sign refers to pesos in Mexico. The designations 'N$' and 'NP' (both for *nuevos pesos*) and 'MN' *(moneda nacional)* all refer to pesos. Prices quoted in US dollars will normally be written as 'US$5,' '$5 Dlls' or '5 USD.'

Because the peso's exchange value is unpredictable, prices in this book are given in US-dollar equivalents.

Exchange Rates

The peso has been relatively stable since the currency crisis of 1994–95, when it lost 60% of its value in three months. Exchange rates were as follows at press time:

country	unit		nuevos pesos
Australia	A$1	=	N$5.2
Belize	BZ$1	=	N$4.7
Canada	C$1	=	N$6.3
European Union	€1	=	N$8.3
France	FF1	=	N$1.3
Germany	DM1	=	N$4.3
Guatemala	Q1	=	N$1.2
Japan	100Y	=	N$8.8
New Zealand	NZ$1	=	N$3.9
UK	UK£1	=	N$13.8
USA	US$1	=	N$9.4

Exchanging Money

Money can be exchanged at banks, hotels and *casas de cambio* (exchange houses). Exchange rates vary a little from one bank or casa de cambio to another. Different rates are also often posted for *efectivo* (cash) and *documento* (traveler's checks). Cambios are usually quicker and less bureaucratic than banks. They also have longer hours and may be open evenings or weekends.

Banks rarely charge commissions, but cambios do. Hotels, especially at the top end of the scale, offer poor rates and often charge commissions as well.

Traveler's Checks & Cash Traveler's checks are generally accepted in tourist areas, and most banks will cash them, but the bureaucracy involved can be tiresome. Some banks will not cash more than US$200 worth of checks at a time. Major-brand checks, denominated in US dollars, are best. American Express is most widely accepted and has an efficient replacement policy; call its 24-hour hotline in Mexico City collect at ☎ 5-326-27-00 in case of theft or loss. Thomas Cook is lesser known but still accepted in most places.

Carrying cash is more risky, but you will need it when paying bus and taxi drivers, making small purchases at convenience stores, eating at casual restaurants, leaving tips and so on. It is definitely the preferred method of payment in smaller, remote parts of the peninsula.

ATMs Automated Teller Machines (ATMs) are the easiest way of obtaining cash pesos from a credit card or a bank account back home. They are common in Baja's larger cities and tourist areas, less so on the long stretch of the Transpeninsular between San Quintín and Ciudad Constitución.

Many ATMs are accessible around the clock and are affiliated with several networks, the most prevalent being Cirrus and Plus. Despite the handling fee that may be charged to your account, ATMs offer a better exchange rate.

On the downside, ATMs don't always function properly, especially outside the tourist areas. In those locales, it's best to use them during banking hours in case the machine accidentally 'swallows' your card or doesn't spit out the correct amount of money. Another good reason to use ATMs during bank hours is to guard against robbery; preferably choose one that is inside a bank building rather than those open to the street or enclosed only by glass.

Credit Cards Major credit cards are accepted by virtually all airlines, car rental companies and travel agents in Baja and by many hotels, restaurants and shops in the border zone and in the Cape Region. Outside of these major tourist hubs, however, few businesses will honor your cards, and it's never a good idea to rely on this method of payment.

MasterCard and Visa are the most widely accepted, American Express to a lesser extent. Some businesses charge a *recargo* (surcharge) for using a credit card. Note that Pemex stations will *not* take credit cards – gasoline purchases are cash only (although there are reportedly a few exceptions).

You can also use your credit card to withdraw cash from many ATMs, although you should check with your credit card company about fees.

International Transfers If you need money wired to you in Mexico, an easy and quick method is the Western Union 'Dinero en Minutos' (Money in Minutes) service, identified outside its locales by black-and-yellow signs. You'll find the service by the *telégrafos* (telegraph) offices in many cities, and by some other shops.

The sender pays the money at their nearest Western Union branch, along with a fee, and gives the details on who is to receive it and where. When you pick it up, take photo identification. Western Union has offices worldwide; information is available at ☎ 5-721-30-80 or 5-546-73-61 in Mexico, ☎ 800-325-6000 in the USA, or at www.westernunion.com.

Security
Be cautious – but not paranoid – about carrying money and other valuables. Ideally, when you're out and about, carry only what you'll need that day and leave the rest in the hotel's *caja fuerte* (safe). If there isn't a safe, you have to decide whether it's better to carry your funds with you or hide them in your room. A money belt worn under your clothes is a good place to carry excess currency when you're on the move or otherwise unable to stash it in a safe. Avoid carrying your wallet in a back pocket of your pants. Other prime pickpocket targets are handbags, the outside pockets of day packs and fanny packs (bum bags). Also see Dangers & Annoyances, later in this chapter, for more tips on safeguarding your belongings.

Costs
The cost of travel in Baja depends a great deal on the degree of comfort you require. Food and accommodations cost more in Baja than in the rest of Mexico, and in many places only slightly less than in the US. Prices are highest near the border and in tourist centers like La Paz and Los Cabos.

Unless you're camping or traveling with an RV, lodging will probably take the biggest chunk out of your travel budget. It's hard to find a decent double for less than US$25 per night. Prices are lower in RV parks or campgrounds, and beach camping is free. Most luxury resort hotels are in Los Cabos, where doubles start around US$180 per night.

You can save money by buying food from supermarkets, bakeries and fruit and vegetable stands or by eating at roadside taquerías or casual restaurants. Filling meals here can cost less than US$3, but prices at better restaurants equal or even exceed those in the US.

Gasoline is not cheap in Mexico, so using the bus and public transportation can be a money-saver. However, it will also limit your mobility and prevent you from accessing the most fascinating and remote parts of the peninsula.

Tipping & Bargaining
In restaurants, it is customary to tip 10% to 15% of the bill. Service staff are poorly paid, so if you can afford to eat out, you should be able to afford a tip. If you stay a few days in one place, leave a small tip for the cleaning person if you're satisfied with their work. A porter in a mid-range hotel would be happy with US$1 for carrying two bags. Taxi drivers don't generally expect tips unless they provide some special service, but gas station attendants do (three or four pesos will do).

Although you can attempt to bargain down the price of some hotel rooms, especially in budget and mid-range places and in the off season, the rates are normally fairly firm. In street and souvenir markets, bargaining is the rule. You should also haggle with drivers of unmetered taxis.

Taxes

In Baja, the *Impuesto de Valor Agregado* (Value-Added Tax), abbreviated IVA ('EE-bah'), is levied at 10%. By law the tax must be included in virtually any price quoted and should not be added afterward.

In addition to the IVA, some hotels – in Los Cabos, for example – also charge a 2% lodging tax to offset promotional costs. Before taking a room, ask whether the price includes IVA and/or the lodging tax. Most accommodations prices listed in this book do *not* include IVA, although other prices (bus fares, meals, admissions, etc) do. Many upscale resorts also levy a compulsory 15% service charge in lieu of tipping.

POST & COMMUNICATIONS

The Servicio Postal Mexicano (the formal name for Mexico's national postal service) sells postage stamps and sends and receives mail at every *oficina de correos* (post office) in Baja.

Unfortunately, it is not distinguished by efficiency: Letters from Tijuana, for instance, arrive in San Diego only after passing through Mexico City. Most northern Baja businesses with dealings north of the border maintain post office boxes in San Ysidro or Calexico.

Sending Mail

Most post offices are open 9 am to 4 or 5 pm weekdays and also Saturday morning.

Service is not always dependable, and packages in particular sometimes go missing. Mark all mail conspicuously with the phrase *'Vía Aérea.'* Registered *(certificado* or *registrado)* service helps ensure delivery and costs just US$0.80 extra for international mail. An airmail letter from Mexico to the USA or Canada can take four to 14 days to arrive (but don't be surprised if it takes longer). Mail to Europe may take between one and three weeks, to Australasia a month or more.

An airmail letter or postcard weighing up to 20g costs US$0.45 to the US or Canada, US$0.55 to Europe and US$0.60 to Australasia. Items weighing between 20g and 50g cost US$0.75, US$0.85 and US$1, respectively.

Receiving Mail

You can receive letters and packages care of a post office if they're addressed as follows (for example):

Jane SMITH (last name in capitals)
Lista de Correos
Tijuana
Baja California 00000 (post code)
MEXICO

When the letter reaches the post office, the name of the addressee is placed on an alphabetical list, which is updated daily. If you can, check the list yourself – it's often pinned on the wall – because the letter may be listed under your first name instead of your last. To claim your mail, present your passport or other identification. There's no charge; the snag is that many post offices hold 'Lista' mail for only 10 days before returning it to the sender.

If you think you're going to pick up mail more than 10 days after it has arrived, address the envelope as follows (for example):

Jane SMITH (last name in capitals)
Poste Restante
Correo Central
Tijuana
Baja California 00000 (post code)
MEXICO

Poste Restante may hold mail for up to a month, but no list of what has been received is posted. Again, you will not be charged for collection.

Inbound mail usually takes as long to arrive as outbound mail does, and international packages coming into Mexico may go missing, just like outbound ones.

Telephone

Local calls are cheap, but international calls can be very expensive – although they needn't be if you call from the right place at the right time. Public pay phones are common in towns and cities: You'll usually find some at airports, bus stations, and around the main square of any sizable town. Most work OK. But plenty of areas, especially in central Baja and parts of the Cape Region, still do not have phone service.

Pay phones are operated by a number of different companies: The most common, and most reliable on costs, are those marked with the name of the country's biggest phone company, Telmex. Telmex pay phones work on *tarjetas telefónicas* or *tarjetas Ladatel* (phone cards), which come in denominations of 30, 50 or 100 pesos (about US$3, US$5 and US$10). These cards are sold at many kiosks and shops – look for the blue-and-yellow sign reading *'De Venta Aquí Ladatel.'*

Cabinas (sometimes also called *casetas de teléfono)* are call stations, usually found in a shop or restaurant, where you take the call in a booth after an on-the-spot operator connects it for you. It can be more expensive than Telmex pay phones but not always so. You don't need a phone card to use them, and they eliminate street noise. Many offer off-peak discounts – for instance 50% off domestic long-distance calls and 33% off international calls at night and for much of the weekend.

Prefixes, Codes & Costs When making a direct call, you need to know what *prefijo* (prefix) and *claves* (country or area codes) to include before the number. In 1999–2000 all Mexican area codes and numbers were changed. In each case, the last one or two digits of the area code were lopped off and transferred to the start of the local number. For example, the area code of Cabo San Lucas used to be 114 and all numbers had five digits. Now the Cabo area code is 1 and all numbers have seven digits. The changes only make a difference in dialing local calls.

Calling within the same town, you don't need to add a prefix or area code to a number. Your call will cost about US$0.05/minute on a Telmex pay phone. To call another town in Mexico, add 01 + area code before the number, which will cost about US$0.40/minute. To call another country, add 00 + country code + area code. Calls will cost about US$1.25/minute to USA or Canada, US$2.50/minute to Europe or Australasia.

In other words, if you're in Tijuana (area code 6) and want to call the Tijuana number ☎ 688-11-11, just dial this seven-digit number.

If you're dialing the same number from within Mexico but outside Tijuana, you must dial ☎ 01-6-688-11-11. This is true even if you are in a town that has the same area code (eg, Rosarito or Ensenada). To call a number in the US, dial ☎ 00+1 (US country code)+area code+local number. For other international country codes, see the boxed text.

When dialing Mexican toll-free numbers – ☎ 800 followed by seven digits – always use the 01 prefix. You can call these numbers from Telmex pay phones without inserting a telephone card. Most US toll-free numbers are ☎ 800 or 888 followed by seven digits. Many US and Canadian toll-free numbers work in either of the two countries; some can also be reached from Mexico (dial ☎ 001 before the 800), but you will probably have to pay for the call. In northern Baja, some businesses have 800 numbers that work from the US, though connections are pretty unreliable.

If you need to speak to a domestic operator, call ☎ 020; for an international operator, call ☎ 090. For Mexican directory information, call ☎ 040.

To call a number in Mexico from another country, dial your international access code, then the Mexico country code (☎ 52), then the area code and number.

North American Calling Cards If you have an AT&T, MCI or Sprint card, or a Canadian calling card, you can use it for calls from Mexico to the USA or Canada by dialing the appropriate access number.

International Country Codes

Australia	☎ 61
Canada	☎ 1
France	☎ 33
Germany	☎ 49
Italy	☎ 39
New Zealand	☎ 64
Spain	☎ 34
UK	☎ 44
USA	☎ 1

These calls can be quite expensive, so check rates before going to Mexico.

AT&T	☎ 001-800-462-4240
MCI	☎ 001-800-674-7000
Sprint	☎ 001-800-877-8000
AT&T Canada	☎ 001-800-123-0201
Bell Canada	☎ 001-800-010-1990

International Calling Cards There's a wide range of international calling cards. Lonely Planet's eKno Communication Card provides budget international calls, a range of messaging services, free email and travel information. You can join online at www .ekno.lonelyplanet.com or by phone from Mexico by dialing the eKno access number (☎ 001-800-514-0287).

Collect Calls A *llamada por cobrar* (collect call) can cost the receiving party much more than if *they* call *you,* so you may prefer to find a phone where you can receive an incoming call, then pay for a quick call to the other party to ask them to call you back.

If you do need to make a collect call, you can do so from pay phones without a card. Call an operator on ☎ 020 for domestic calls, or ☎ 090 for international calls. Alternatively, use *País Directo* (a Home Country Direct service). This service, by which you make an international collect call via an operator in the country you're calling, is available for several countries. You can get information on Home Direct services from your phone company before you leave for Mexico, and you can make the calls from pay phones without any card. For Home Direct calls to the USA through AT&T, MCI or Sprint, and to Canada via AT&T Canada or Bell Canada, dial the numbers given earlier under North American Calling Cards. Mexican international operators may be able to give you access numbers for other countries.

Mexican international operators can usually speak English. Some telephone casetas and hotels will make collect calls for you, but they usually charge for the service.

Scams In Baja's tourist areas, you may notice a variety of other pay phones adver-

tising that they accept credit cards or that you can make easy collect calls to the USA on them. Stay away from these phones!

Charges for these operator-assisted calls are exorbitant: Rates of US$28 for the first minute, followed by US$10 for each additional minute are not uncommon. The operator may quote you cheaper rates, but you won't know your final tally until it's posted on your next month's credit card bill – by then, it'll be impossible to prove that you were given a different rate.

Fax
Public fax service is offered in many Mexican towns by the public *telégrafos* (telegraph) office or offices of the company Telecomm. Also look for *'Fax Público'* signs on shops, businesses and telephone casetas, and in bus stations and airports. Typically, you pay around US$1.50 to US$2 a page to the US or Canada, and US$2.50 to Europe or Australasia.

Email & Internet Access
Many Mexican cities and towns have Internet cafes or public Internet services where you can surf the net and, usually, check and send email. Typical charges are US$3 to US$5 per hour. You'll find many such services mentioned under Information in city sections in this book.

For those traveling with their own computers, CompuServe (www.compuserve.com) has nodes (access numbers) in eight Mexican cities and one node (☎ 01-800-720-00-00) that you can access from anywhere in the country. America Online (www.aol.com) has 10 AOL Globalnet nodes around Mexico, although none in Baja. There's a US$6 hourly surcharge.

Some Mexican hotel rooms have direct-dial phones and phone sockets that enable you to unplug the phone and insert a phone jack that runs directly to your computer. In others, you're confronted with switchboard phone systems and/or room phones with a cord running directly into the wall, both of which make it impossible to go online from your room. In such cases, you may try to borrow the reception's fax line for a couple of minutes.

It's also possible to plug in your computer at some telephone casetas.

When traveling with a computer, remember your PC-card modem may or may not work outside your home country – the safest option is to buy a reputable 'global' modem before you leave home, or buy a local PC-card modem if you're spending an extended time in any one country.

Telephone sockets can differ from country to country, so ensure that you have at least a US RJ-11 telephone adapter that works with your modem. You can almost always find an adapter that will convert from RJ-11 to the local variety. For more information on traveling with a portable computer, go to www.teleadapt.com.

INTERNET RESOURCES

The World Wide Web is a rich resource for travelers. You can research your trip, hunt down bargain airfares, book hotels, check on weather conditions and chat with locals and other travelers about the best places to visit (or avoid!).

There's no better place to start your Web explorations than the Lonely Planet Web site (www.lonelyplanet.com). Here you'll find succinct summaries on traveling to most places on earth, postcards from other travelers and the Thorn Tree bulletin board, where you can ask questions before you go or dispense advice when you get back. You can also find travel news and updates for many of LP's most popular guides. The subWWWay section links you to the most useful travel resources elsewhere on the Web.

Here are some Baja-specific sites to start with:

Baja Bound Run by a Mexican insurance company and packed with valuable information about current tourist and vehicle fees, your rights if in an accident, maps and mileage charts. www.bajabound.com

Baja Information Pages Well-organized, comprehensive Web site with travelers' experiences and information about many subjects (pets to tides, ATMs to weather); mostly focused on Baja Sur. The downside: it's not updated very often

(except for travelers' reports). http://math.ucr.edu/~ftm/bajaInfoPage.html

Baja Life Online Online version of glossy quarterly magazine with solidly reported and written articles; the only place to read about Alice Cooper's surf-fishing experiences near Cabo San Lucas. www.bajalife.com

Baja Links The most comprehensive and extensive compilation of links to Baja-related Web sites, with several subcategorizations from airlines to whales; updated frequently. www.bajalinks.com

Baja Nomads Free online travel club and magazine with interesting articles, a bulletin board, book and insurance discounts and good links. www.bajanomads.com

Baja Online Written by Rosarito resident Paula McDonald, this site features chatty insider information about northern Baja. www.sandiego-online.com/baja/

Baja Travel Resource Guide Excellent travel resource guide with details on destinations from Tijuana to Los Cabos; includes specialized themed information (missions, diving and snorkeling, golf, transportation, etc); there's a chat room and great links page; it's kept pretty current. www.escapist.com/baja

Baja Web Destination-specific information from Tijuana to Los Cabos, plus general information about ferries, immigration, activities from diving to windsurfing; lots of links; also in German. www.baja-web.com

Embassy of Mexico in the US www.embassyofmexico.org/english/main2.htm

San Diego Tribune Recent Mexico-related articles with particular focus on Baja. www.uniontrib.com/news/mexico/index.html

Walt Peterson's Baja Page Background information about Baja activities such as backpacking, nature watching and boating by the author of Lonely Planet's *Diving & Snorkeling in Baja California*. http://home.earthlink.net/~wepeterson/bajaindex.html

BOOKS

None of Baja's bookstores *(librerías)* specialize in English-language material, but some stock a few books, usually mainstream novels, in English. Baja's many trailer parks are full of North Americans who may be willing to swap reading material. Some hotels also have book exchanges.

Most books are published in different editions by different publishers in different countries. As a result, a book might be a hardcover rarity in one country but readily available in paperback in another. Fortunately, bookstores and libraries can search by title or author, so check with your local bookstore or library on the availability of the books recommended in this section.

California-based Howard Karno Books (☎ 760-749-2304, 800-345-2766, fax 760-749-4390, info@karnobooks.com) specializes in out-of-print books; contact them directly or check their catalog online at www.karnobooks .com. Dawson's Book Store (☎ 323-469-2186), 535 Larchmont St, Los Angeles, CA 90004, also has a wide selection of Baja books, both in and out of print, including their self-published 50-volume Baja travel series, although at US$2000 for the set, it's quite an investment.

Lonely Planet

For those planning on traveling beyond Baja to mainland Mexico, Lonely Planet's comprehensive country guide *Mexico* is an excellent investment.

A handy companion for anyone traveling in Mexico is the *Latin American Spanish phrasebook*, which contains practical, up-to-date words and expressions in Latin American Spanish.

Read This First: Central & South America offers more tips on preparing for a trip to Mexico.

World Food Mexico is an intimate, full-color guide to exploring Mexico and its cuisine. This book covers every food or drink situation the traveler could encounter and plots the evolution of Mexican cuisine. Its very useful language section includes a definitive culinary dictionary and useful phrases to help you on your eating adventure.

Diving & Snorkeling Baja California by Walt Peterson is an invaluable resource for divers and is well respected by Baja-based dive shops.

Guidebooks & Special Interest

The People's Guide to Mexico by Carl Franz (motto: 'Wherever you go…there you are')

has for a quarter of a century been an invaluable, amusing resource for anyone on an extended trip. It doesn't attempt hotel, transportation, or sightseeing specifics but does provide a great all-around introduction to Mexico.

Best Stories of Baja by Larry Stanton tries to capture the flavor of Mexican life and culture, as well as its politics and characters, though much of the book seems to revolve around duck hunting. A sequel, *Arriba! Baja,* was published in 1999.

Baja4You by Roberta Giesea offers background information on Baja – with a focus on the border area – in an easy-to-read question and answer format sprinkled with anecdotes.

Almost an Island: Travels in Baja California by Bruce Berger recounts tales from the author's three decades of traveling on the peninsula.

The National Parks of Northern Mexico by Richard Fisher includes good coverage of those parks on the peninsula.

Cooking with Baja Magic by Ann Hazard is dedicated exclusively to the cuisine of the peninsula. It contains 170 recipes, most of them fairly easy to prepare.

For general coverage of outdoor activities, easily the best choice is Walt Peterson's *The Baja Adventure Book.* Covering fishing, boating, kayaking, rock climbing, backpacking, windsurfing and many other sporty endeavors, it also contains useful maps. However, its oversized format is unwieldy for backpackers, and hardly any information on cities is included.

Jack Williams' *Baja Boaters Guide* covers practically every possible mooring along the Pacific coast (Vol I) and the Sea of Cortez (Vol II).

One of the best sources for Baja-specific camping information is Fred and Gloria Jones' *Baja Camping: The Complete Guide.* Another option is *Exploring Baja by RV,* also by Walt Peterson, in collaboration with his son Michael.

Neil Kelly and Gene Kira's *The Baja Catch* covers both inshore and deep-water fishing and is considered a 'bible' by many angling aficionados. It also contains good general information, especially on remote camping. A *No-Nonsense Guide to Fly Fishing in Southern Baja* by Gary Graham was written by a guy who's fly-fished Baja for more than 20 years and contains extensive maps and directions, charts and illustrations.

Andromeda Romano-Lax's *Sea Kayaking in Baja* describes a handful of kayaking routes, mostly on the Sea of Cortez, but some experienced kayakers have found its usefulness limited.

Flora & Fauna

Sanford Wilbur's *Birds of Baja California* is a comprehensive listing of species found throughout Baja, but its lack of illustrations makes it unsuitable for field use. Field-oriented birders might prefer RT Peterson and EL Chalif's *Field Guide to Mexican Birds*, which covers the mainland, the peninsula and offshore islands.

The *Audubon Society Field Guide to North American Birds, Western Region* by Miklos Udvardy focuses on birds of the USA and Canada but overlaps considerably with Baja and the Mexican mainland. The *Baja California Plant Field Guide* by Norman C Roberts describes more than 400 plants on the peninsula.

The *Seasonal Guide to the Natural Year: A Month by Month Guide to Natural Events – Baja California* by Judy Wade provides detailed information on the best times and locations for wildlife viewing (whales, birds, etc) and other natural phenomena like wildflower-blooming seasons.

The following are good sources of information on whales: Richard Ellis' *Book of Whales*, Steven Leatherwood and Randall Reaves' *Sierra Club Handbook of Whales and Dolphins* and Stanley Minasian's *The World's Whales*.

Daniel Gotshall's *Marine Animals of Baja California: A Guide to the Common Fish & Invertebrates* has lavish color photographs of Baja's sea life. The *Handbook of Turtles* by Archie Carr and J Whitfield Gibbons includes a section on Baja turtles.

Roadside Geology & Biology of Baja California by John, Edwin and Jason Minch is geared toward amateurs and discusses

Baja's geologic and biological make-up, including a section on birds.

Travel

John Steinbeck's classic combination of travelogue and natural history essay *The Log from the Sea of Cortez* was one of the earliest studies of marine life in the Sea of Cortez. Steinbeck's biologist companion, Ed Ricketts, was the model for Doc in the novelist's famous *Cannery Row*.

Ray Cannon's *The Sea of Cortez* is a coffee-table book, with first-rate photos, published by a lifelong Baja enthusiast. Literary naturalist Joseph Wood Krutch wrote *The Forgotten Peninsula: A Naturalist in Baja California* about his travels in pre-Transpeninsular Baja.

Cartwheels in the Sand: Baja California, Four Women and a Motor Home by Ann Hazard is an amusing and insightful account of an eventful journey down México 1 by four women traveling in a 1978 RV.

God and Mr Gomez by Jack Smith is a hilarious classic that follows the adventures of 'Mr and Mrs Smith' in their effort at building their dream house in Baja.

Into a Desert Place is Graham Mackintosh's narrative of his two-year, 3000-mile (5000km) walk around the Baja coast, which has been called 'one of the most grueling and challenging solo bipedal treks ever taken.'

Jonathan Waterman's *Kayaking the Vermilion Sea: Eight Hundred Miles Down the Baja* is an account of a two-month kayak trip by the author and his wife from the Río Colorado delta to the tip of the peninsula. *Wind, Water, Sun: A Solo Kayak Journey Along Baja California's Desert Coastline* by Ed Darack is similar, though more matter of fact. It contains numerous photos and maps.

History

Michael C Meyer and William L Sherman's *The Course of Mexican History* is one of the best general accounts of Mexican history and society.

A good source for peninsula prehistory is Campbell Grant's *Rock Art of Baja California,* which gives a basic overview of

Baja's cave paintings. Harry Crosby's *Cave Paintings of Baja California* is a more detailed effort by a dedicated enthusiast and contains excellent color and B&W photographs, plus several fairly general maps.

A modern and comprehensive history of early colonial times is Harry Crosby's *Antigua California: Mission and Colony on the Peninsular Frontier, 1697–1768.* For the perspective of an early Jesuit father, obtain Johann Jakob Baegert's *Observations in Lower California,* which was originally published in Germany in 1771, only four years after the Jesuits' expulsion from the peninsula. A new entry is *The Lost Treasures of Baja California* by James Francez et al, which deals with the history of the missions.

On the subject of piracy and the Manila galleons, see Peter Gerhard's succinct and readable *Pirates of the Pacific, 1575–1742.*

James Blaisdell's *The Desert Revolution* tells of Ricardo Flores Magón's quixotic attempt to influence the Mexican Revolution from the Baja periphery.

Norris Hundley's *The Great Thirst: Californians and Water, 1770s–1990s* details the controversy between the US and Mexico over the Colorado River delta.

Ted Conover's *Coyotes* is a compellingly readable account of undocumented immigrants by a writer who befriended Mexican workers while picking fruit with them in the orchards of Arizona and Florida, lived among them in their own country and accompanied them across the desert border despite concerns about his (and their) personal safety at the hands of the police and other unsavory characters. He concludes that 'the majority (of laborers) would make good neighbors; I'd welcome them as mine.'

Similar themes appear in Luis Alberto Urrea's grim but fascinating *Across the Wire: Life and Hard Times on the Mexican Border,* which focuses on the problems of immigrants and shantytowns in a Tijuana that very few tourists ever see. Urrea's recent *By the Lake of the Sleeping Children: The Secret Life of the Mexican Border,* a combined effort with photographer John Lueders-Booth, deals with garbage pickers – the ultimate recyclers – in Tijuana.

Rubén Martínez's collected essays on Mexican and Mexican-American culture in *The Other Side* include a lengthy piece on Tijuana. Oscar Martínez's *Troublesome Border* deals with current borderland issues like population growth, economic development, ecology and international migration.

Alan Weisman's *La Frontera: The United States Border with Mexico* explores all aspects of border life and culture, from the shiny skyscrapers of San Diego and Tijuana to poverty-stricken shantytowns and the seedy zona of Nuevo Laredo.

NEWSPAPERS & MAGAZINES

Baja California has a rich journalistic heritage and a thriving local press in addition to national newspapers. Of the nine main dailies in Baja, those with the highest circulations are Mexicali's *La Voz de la Frontera* and Tijuana's *El Mexicano.* Tijuana's *El Heraldo de Baja California,* the state's first daily, dates from 1941.

Other notable dailies include *ABC* in Mexicali and Ensenada; Tijuana's *El Día, Diario de Baja California* and *Ultimas Noticias*; Mexicali's *El Centinela*; and *Novedades de Baja California* in Mexicali, Tijuana and Ensenada.

Though published locally, *Diario 29* is a regional edition of *El Nacional,* a Mexico City paper that generally supports the Partido Revolucionario Institucional (PRI). In addition to the daily press, there are numerous magazines of varying content, including cultural supplements to the daily papers.

The Tijuana-based *Zeta* is a crusading weekly alternative to the generally conservative daily press. Its editor, J Jesús Blancornelas, received an International Press Freedom Award from the New York–based Committee to Protect Journalists for his exposés and candid criticisms of political and police corruption, drug lords, and the connections among them. Extensive readers' letters give a good sampling of the state's most articulate public opinion; *Zeta* also publishes a Mexicali edition.

In Baja California Sur, the main dailies are the La Paz–based *Diario Peninsular* and *El Sudcaliforniano. La Güicha,* a new satirical magazine whose main targets are political figures in the state capital of La Paz, also publishes arts and music reviews.

RADIO & TV

Four television stations operate in Baja California (Norte), two in Mexicali and one each in Tijuana and Ensenada, but cable and satellite services are widely available throughout the peninsula. The Mexican multinational TV network Televisa maintains a large studio and production facilities in Tijuana.

Of the 41 radio stations in Baja California (Norte), 26 are on the AM band and 15 on the FM band. All are commercial except for four FM stations, mostly associated with the Universidad Autónoma de Baja California, that emphasize cultural programming.

Travelers in northern Baja can often hear English-language broadcasts from the US, but mountainous topography often disrupts reception. At night, it's possible to hear them much farther down the peninsula.

VIDEO SYSTEMS

Like the rest of North America, Baja uses the National Television System Committee (NTSC) color TV standard, which is not compatible with other standards – such as Phase Alternative Line (PAL) or Système Electronique Couleur avec Memoire (SECAM) used in Africa, Europe, Asia and Australia – unless converted.

PHOTOGRAPHY & VIDEO
Film & Equipment

In tourist areas, print film is widely available at supermarkets, drugstores and tourist shops, but for slide film you usually have to go to a specialized photographic store. Outside the cities, slide film may be next to impossible to find and even print film may not be widely available. Stock up before heading into the boondocks or, better yet, bring your favorite film with you from home. Mexican Customs allows the duty-free import of up to 12 rolls of film, but enforcement is so lax it's almost nonexistent. Prices are generally slightly higher than what you'd pay in North America. Avoid buying film from sun-exposed shop windows.

In general, buy film for its planned usage. For general-purpose shooting – for either prints or slides – 100 ASA film is just about the most useful and versatile, as it gives you good color and enough speed to capture most situations on film. If you plan to shoot brightly lit night scenes, or in dark areas, without a tripod, switch to 400 ASA.

The best and most widely available films are made by Fuji and Kodak. Fuji Velvia and Kodak Elite are easy to process and provide good slide images. Stay away from Kodachrome: It's difficult to process quickly and generates lots of headaches if not handled properly. For print film, you can't beat Kodak Gold, though Fuji is comparable and Agfa is coming along.

Film can be damaged by excessive heat, so avoid leaving your camera and film in the car or placing them on the dash while you're driving.

Be sure to carry a spare battery for your camera to avoid disappointment if it dies in the middle of nowhere. If you're buying a new camera for your trip, do so several weeks before you leave and practice using it.

Technical Tips

Proverbially sunny Baja offers plenty of light for photography. When sunlight is strong, and the sun high in the sky, photographs tend to have harsh shadows. It's best to shoot during early morning and late afternoon, when the sun is low in the sky and the light is softer.

A polarizing filter is a most useful piece of gear as it deepens the blue of the sky and water, can eliminate many reflections and makes clouds appear quite dramatic. It's best used to photograph scenes in nature. Using one at high altitudes where the sky is already deep blue, however, can result in pictures with a nearly black and unrealistic sky. The effect of a polarizer is strongest when you point your camera 90 degrees away from the sun. By spinning the filter around, you'll see a pretty fair approximation of what the effect will be on film.

In places where light levels are low, using fast film or your camera's fill-flash function may be helpful. Just remember: A normal camera flash is only effective from 10 to 15 feet (3 to 5m), so don't waste it trying to light up an entire bull ring. A monopod or lightweight tripod is an invaluable piece of gear for 'steadying up' your camera for slow exposures or when using a telephoto lens. These will also allow you to take those great night shots of neon, theater marquees and those 'streaking taillights' shots of cars rushing by. Lacking the above gear, jam your camera against anything at hand – a church pew, a tree, a street sign – to steady up. And remember: 'Blurry is a worry. Steady is ready.'

Photographing People

Mexicans, especially in tourist areas, are normally very gracious about being photographed. No one seems to mind being photographed in the context of an overall scene, but if you want a close-up shot, you should ask first. Simply saying, *'Con su permisión?'* ('With your permission?') while pointing at the camera will usually result in broad smiles and generous posing. If you shoot several shots, they will often go back to what they were doing, which often results in pictures that are far more natural.

Families with small children are normally complimented that you've chosen them to shoot, and these photos can be very effective. People in the pueblos may be more camera-shy and harder to enlist in your cover shot for *National Geographic*. Warming them up often requires great tact and – sometimes – a few pesos. It's not a good idea to photograph soldiers.

Airport Security

All flight passengers have to pass their luggage through x-ray machines. In general, airport x-ray technology isn't supposed to jeopardize lower-speed film (under 1600 ASA). Recently, however, new high-powered machines designed to inspect *checked* luggage have been installed at major airports around the world. These machines conduct high-energy scans that may destroy unprocessed film.

Be sure to carry film and loaded cameras in your hand-luggage and ask airport security people to inspect them manually. Pack all your film into a clear plastic bag that you can quickly whip out of your luggage. It helps greatly to have a couple of rolls of 1600 ASA film right on top as this clearly shows security people that x-rays will damage your film. This not only saves time at the inspection points but also helps minimize confrontations with security staff. In this age of terrorism, their job is tough, but they can also add to your pre-flight hell, big time.

TIME

The northern state of Baja California is on Pacific Standard Time (PST), while Baja California Sur is on Mountain Standard Time (MST), which is one hour ahead of PST. PST is eight hours behind Greenwich Mean Time (GMT), while MST is seven hours behind GMT.

In summer, PST is moved ahead one hour for Pacific Daylight Time (PDT) and thus becomes the same as MST. Northern Baja is always on the same time as mainland California.

ELECTRICITY

Electrical current in Mexico is the same as in the USA and Canada: 110V, 60Hz. Though most plugs and sockets are the same as in the US, Mexico actually has three different types of electrical socket: older ones with two equally sized flat slots, newer ones with two flat slots of differing sizes, and a few with a round hole for a grounding (earth) pin. If your plug doesn't fit the Mexican socket, get an adapter or change the plug. Mexican electronics stores have a variety of adapters and extensions that should solve the problem.

WEIGHTS & MEASURES

In Mexico the metric system is official, but the colloquial use of US measurements, especially miles and gallons, is widespread in Baja. Because so many people drive to Baja in cars manufactured north of the border whose odometers read in miles, this book uses both miles and kilometers to indicate distance. Landmarks along the Trans-peninsular and other main roads may be indicated by the appropriate roadside kilometer marker (placed by the Mexican highway department).

Temperatures, weights and liquid measures are also given in both US measures and their metric equivalents. See the conversion table at the back of this book.

LAUNDRY
USA-style laundromats are becoming more common, at least in larger cities and tourist destinations. Travelers can either do the wash themselves (US$2 to US$3 per load) or leave it for the staff for a nominal additional charge.

TOILETS
Public toilets are virtually nonexistent; you should take advantage of facilities in places like hotels, restaurants, bars and bus stations. Toilet paper may not always be available, so carry some with you. If there's a basket beside the toilet, put paper, tampons, etc in it – it's there because the drains can't cope otherwise.

HEALTH
Travel health depends on your predeparture preparations, your day-to-day health care while traveling and how you handle any medical problem or emergency that does develop. While the list of potential dangers may seem frightening, with basic precautions, adequate information and a little luck, few travelers suffer anything worse than upset stomachs.

Predeparture Planning
Make sure you're healthy before you start traveling. If you are going on a long trip, make sure your teeth are OK. If you wear glasses, take a spare pair and your prescription.

If you require a particular medication, take an adequate supply, as it may not be available locally. Take part of the packaging showing the generic name rather than the brand

---

Everyday Health

Normal body temperature is up to 98.6°F (37°C); more than 4°F (2°C) higher indicates a high fever. The normal adult pulse rate is 60 to 100 per minute (children 80 to 100, babies 100 to 140). As a general rule, pulse increases about 20 beats per minute for each 2°F (1°C) rise in fever.

Respiration (breathing) rate is also an indicator of illness. Count the number of breaths per minute: Between 12 and 20 is normal for adults and older children (up to 30 for younger children, 40 for babies). People with a high fever or serious respiratory illness breathe more quickly than normal. More than 40 shallow breaths a minute may indicate pneumonia.

---

name, which will make getting replacements easier. To avoid problems, take a legible prescription or letter from your doctor to show you legally use the medication.

Most importantly, ensure that you have adequate health insurance. See Travel Insurance under Visas & Documents earlier in this chapter for details.

Immunizations Travelers to Mexico, including Baja, are not required to get any vaccinations, but it's a good idea to at least be up to date on your diptheria and tetanus vaccines. If your plans include onward travel to rural areas on mainland Mexico, polio and typhoid shots are recommended.

Plan ahead for vaccinations: Some of them require more than one injection, while some should not be given together. It's recommended that you seek medical advice at least six weeks before travel. Record all vaccinations on an International Health Certificate, available from your doctor or government health department.

Diphtheria, Tetanus and Measles Diphtheria can be a fatal throat infection, and tetanus can be a fatal wound infection. Everyone should have these vaccinations. After an initial course of three injections, boosters are necessary every 10 years. You should be up to date with your measles immunity too.

Medical Kit Check List

The following is a list of items you should consider including in your medical kit – consult your pharmacist for brands available in your country.

❏ **Aspirin or acetaminophen** – for pain or fever

❏ **Antifungal cream or powder** – for fungal skin infections and thrush

❏ **Antihistamine** (such as Benadryl) – for allergies (eg, hay fever), to ease the itch from insect bites or stings and to prevent motion sickness

❏ **Antibiotics** – consider including these if you're traveling well off the beaten track; see your doctor, as they must be prescribed, and carry the prescription with you

❏ **Antiseptic** (such as Betadine) – saturated swabs or ointment, and an antibiotic powder or similar 'dry' spray, for cuts and grazes

❏ **Bandages, Band-Aids** (plasters) and other wound dressings

❏ **Calamine lotion, sting relief spray or aloe vera** – to ease irritation from sunburn and insect bites or stings

❏ **Cold and flu tablets, throat lozenges and nasal decongestant**

❏ **Insect repellent, sunscreen, lip balm and eye drops**

❏ **Kaolin preparation (Pepto-Bismol), Imodium or Lomotil** – for stomach upsets

❏ **Prochlorperazine or metaclopramide** – for nausea and vomiting

❏ **Rehydration mixture** – to prevent dehydration, which may occur, for example, during bouts of diarrhea; particularly important when traveling with children

❏ **Scissors, tweezers and a thermometer** – note that mercury thermometers are prohibited by airlines

❏ **Syringes and needles** – in case you need injections; ask your doctor for a note explaining why you have them

❏ **Water purification tablets or iodine**

Hepatitis A This is the most common travel-acquired illness after diarrhea and can put you out of action for weeks. Havrix 1440 is a vaccination that provides long-term immunity (possibly more than 10 years) after an initial injection and a booster at six to 12 months. Gamma globulin is not a vaccination but is a ready-made antibody collected from blood donations. It should be given close to departure because, depending on the dose, it only protects for two to six months.

Hepatitis B This disease is spread by blood or by sexual activity. Travelers who should consider a Hepatitis B vaccination include those who might be exposed to blood (for example health-care workers), have sexual contact with the local population, stay longer than six months, or be exposed through medical treatment (for instance by inadequately screened blood transfusions). It involves three injections, the quickest course being three weeks with a booster at 12 months. The US Centers for Disease Control & Prevention recommend Hepatitis B vaccine for all infants and for children 11 or 12 years old who did not receive it as infants.

Rabies Vaccination should be considered if you are spending a month or longer in the country, especially if you will be cycling, handling animals, caving or traveling to remote areas; it should also be considered for children (who may not report a bite). Pre-travel rabies vaccination involves three injections over 21 to 28 days. If someone who has been vaccinated is bitten or scratched by an animal, they will require two booster injections of vaccine; those not vaccinated require more.

Travel Health Guides If you plan to travel in remote areas for a long period of time, you might consider taking a more detailed health guide, such as one of the following:

Healthy Travel Central & South America by Dr Isabelle Young (Lonely Planet Publications, 2000) is a user-friendly guide to minimizing health risks and dealing with problems while on the road.

Staying Healthy in Asia, Africa & Latin America by Dirk Schroeder (Moon Publications, 1994) is probably the best all-around guide to carry; it's compact, detailed and well organized.

Travelers' Health by Dr Richard Dawood (Oxford University Press and Random House, 1994) is comprehensive, easy to read, authoritative and highly recommended, though rather large to lug around.

Travel with Children by Maureen Wheeler (Lonely Planet Publications, 1995) includes advice on travel health for younger children.

There are also a number of excellent travel health Web sites. Links to the World Health Organization and the US Centers for Disease Control & Prevention can be found on the Lonely Planet home page (www .lonelyplanet.com).

Basic Rules

Many Baja travelers worry about potential health problems from food and water, which can include dysentery, giardiasis, hepatitis A and, in extremely rare instances, typhoid and polio. The common maladies – upset stomach and diarrhea – can be minimized or even avoided by taking a few precautions.

Food It is generally safe to eat cooked food, as long as you don't punish your stomach by consuming large portions immediately upon arrival.

Take it easy – you may even want to have your first meal in one of the many restaurants that cater mainly to foreign visitors. This is not to say you should avoid local restaurants, taco stands and street-corner fish and fruit carts – they're part of the Baja experience, after all. Just introduce yourself to them gradually. Some travelers recommend taking a preventive dose of Kaolin preparation (such as Pepto-Bismol) for the first two or three days of your stay to stave off stomach problems.

Avoid uncooked or unpasteurized dairy products like raw milk and homemade cheeses. Dairy products from supermarkets are usually *pasteurizado,* but in restaurants you can't be sure.

Vegetables and fruit should be washed with purified water or peeled when possible. In tourist-oriented hotels and restaurants, salads are usually safe. If thoroughly cooked, meat, chicken and most types of seafood are safe.

If a place looks clean and well run and the vendor also looks clean and healthy, the food is probably safe. In general, places that are packed with travelers or locals are fine, but empty restaurants are questionable. The food in busy restaurants is cooked and eaten quickly, with little standing around, and it is probably not reheated.

Water Everyone has heard the infamous warning about Mexico: Don't drink the water. It's often true – the water can be potable, but bacterial differences can still make you sick. Generally, it is best to avoid tap water for drinking, brushing your teeth, washing fruit and vegetables or making ice cubes. *Agua purificada* (purified water) and *hielo* (ice from purified water) are available throughout Baja from supermarkets and liquor stores. Restaurants are supposed to make ice with purified water, and hotels will generally make you aware of the quality of the water; finding a bottle of water in the room is a good indication that the *agua* from the tap is not the purest.

Licuados con leche (milkshakes) from juice stands are usually safe because the government requires the use of pasteurized milk and purified water. Tea or coffee should also be OK, since the water should have been boiled.

Off the main roads, some sort of water purification system is advisable, unless you carry enough bottled water with you.

The simplest way to purify water is to boil it thoroughly, but for longer trips consider purchasing a water filter. There are two main kinds of filters. Total filters remove all parasites, bacteria and viruses and make water safe to drink. While expensive, they can be more cost-effective than buying bottled water. Simple filters (which can even be a nylon mesh bag) remove dirt and larger foreign bodies from the water, so that chemical solutions work much more effectively; if water is dirty, chemical solutions may not work at all. When you're buying a filter, it's very important to read the specifications, so you know exactly what it removes from the water and what it doesn't.

Simple filtering does not remove all dangerous organisms, so if you cannot boil water, it should be treated chemically. Chlorine tablets kill many pathogens, but not some parasites such as giardia and amoebic cysts. Iodine is more effective in purifying water and is available in tablet form. Follow the directions carefully, and remember that too much iodine can be harmful.

Medical Problems & Treatment

If you come down with a serious illness, find a competent doctor, and don't be afraid to get second opinions. You may want to telephone your doctor at home as well. Self-diagnosis and treatment can be risky, so seek qualified help if possible. Treatment dosages indicated in this section are for emergency use only. Correct diagnosis is vital.

Antibiotics should ideally be administered only under medical supervision. Take only the recommended dose at the prescribed intervals, and use the whole course, even if symptoms cease earlier. Stop immediately if there are any serious reactions, and don't use the antibiotic at all if you are unsure that you have the correct one. If you are allergic to commonly prescribed antibiotics such as penicillin, carry this information when traveling.

Almost every locale in Baja has either a hospital or medical clinic and Cruz Roja (Red Cross) emergency facilities, all of which are indicated by road signs showing a red cross. Hospitals are dependable for non-life-threatening ailments (like diarrhea or dysentery) and minor surgery (such as stitches, sprains). Medical bills are comparatively low, but both hospitals and doctors require payment at the time of service; doctors usually insist on cash payment. Only a few facilities accept credit cards.

Clinics, especially those in small towns, are often understaffed and ill-equipped to deal with serious medical problems needing immediate, sophisticated attention. In these cases, it may be advisable to fly elsewhere for treatment, which is why you might consider taking out medical evacuation coverage in addition to travel health insurance (see Travel Insurance, earlier in this chapter).

Environmental Hazards

Heat Exhaustion Dehydration or salt deficiency can cause heat exhaustion. Take time to acclimatize to high temperatures, and make sure you drink enough liquids. Salt deficiency is characterized by fatigue, lethargy, headaches, giddiness and muscle cramps. Salt tablets or adding salt to your food may help. Vomiting or diarrhea can also deplete your liquid and salt levels.

Anhydrotic heat exhaustion, caused by an inability to sweat, is rare. Unlike other forms of heat exhaustion, it is likely to strike people who have been in a hot climate for some time rather than newcomers.

Heat Stroke Long, continuous periods of exposure to high temperatures can leave you vulnerable to this serious, sometimes fatal, condition, which occurs when the body's heat-regulating mechanism breaks down and body temperature rises to dangerous levels. On arriving in a hot climate, avoid strenuous activity and excessive alcohol intake, and do drink other liquids well before you desperately need them.

Symptoms include feeling unwell, lack of perspiration and a high body temperature of 102° to 105°F (39° to 41°C). When sweating ceases, the skin becomes flushed and red. Severe, throbbing headaches and lack of coordination also occur, and victims may become confused or aggressive. Eventually they become delirious or go into convulsions. Hospitalization is essential, but meanwhile get victims out of the sun, remove their clothing, cover them with a wet sheet or towel and fan them continually. Give fluids if they are conscious.

Hypothermia Too much cold can be just as dangerous as too much heat. If you are hiking at high altitudes or simply taking a long bus trip over mountains, particularly at night, be prepared. Hypothermia occurs when the body loses heat faster than producing it, causing the body's core temperature to drop. It is surprisingly easy to progress from very cold to dangerously cold due to a combination of wind, wet clothing, fatigue and hunger, even if the air temperature is above freezing. It is best to dress in layers; silk, wool and some of the new artificial fibers are all good insulating materials. A hat is important, as a lot of heat is lost

GREG ELMS

Mole poblano, served for special occasions

DAVID PEEVERS

Traditional pastries (Tecate)

WOODS WHEATCROFT

Bottled goodies (Ensenada)

GREG ELMS

Limes, Mexico's citrus of choice

GREG ELMS

Fresh produce, market style

WOODS WHEATCROFT

Calling all gringos (Loreto)

Choose your poison.

Curbside soup (Cabo San Lucas)

Fresh abalone (San Quintín)

Chilies and beans for sale (Tijuana)

through the head. A strong, waterproof outer layer (and a 'space' blanket for emergencies) is essential. Carry basic supplies, including food containing simple sugars to generate heat quickly and fluid to drink.

Symptoms of hypothermia are exhaustion, numb skin (particularly toes and fingers), shivering, slurred speech, lethargy, stumbling, dizzy spells, muscle cramps, violent bursts of energy, or irrational or violent behavior. Irrationality may take the form of sufferers claiming they are warm and trying to take off their clothes.

To treat mild hypothermia, first get victims out of the wind and/or rain, remove their clothing if it's wet and replace it with dry, warm clothing. Give them hot liquids – not alcohol – and some high-calorie, easily digestible food. Do not rub victims: Instead, allow them to slowly warm themselves. This should be enough to treat the early stages of hypothermia. Early recognition and treatment of mild hypothermia is the only way to prevent severe hypothermia, which is a critical condition.

Prickly Heat This is an itchy rash caused by excessive perspiration trapped under the skin. It usually strikes people who have just arrived in a hot climate. Keeping cool, bathing often, drying the skin, using a mild talcum or prickly heat powder or resorting to air-conditioning may help.

Sunburn In Baja's desert climate, you can get sunburned quickly, even through cloudy skies. Use a sunscreen, a hat and a barrier cream for your nose and lips. Calamine lotion and commercial after-sun preparations are good for mild sunburn. Protect your eyes with good-quality sunglasses, particularly if you will be near water, sand or snow. Remember: The sunshine on the beach and in the water is deceptive and will burn you quickly. Wear a T-shirt while snorkeling or swimming.

Motion Sickness
Eating lightly before and during a trip reduces the chances of motion sickness. If you are prone to motion sickness, try to find a place that minimizes disturbance: near the wing on aircraft, close to midship on boats or near the center on buses. Fresh air usually helps; reading and cigarette smoke don't. Commercial anti-motion-sickness preparations, which can cause drowsiness, have to be taken before the trip commences; when you're feeling sick, it's too late. Ginger (available in capsule form) and peppermint (including mint-flavored candy) are natural preventatives. Acupressure wrist bands have also proven effective for many people.

Jet Lag
This condition is experienced when a person travels by air across more than three time zones. It occurs because many of the functions of the human body (such as temperature, pulse rate and emptying of the bladder and bowels) are regulated by internal 24-hour cycles. When we travel long distances rapidly, our bodies take time to adjust to the 'new time' of our destination, and we may experience fatigue, disorientation, insomnia, anxiety, impaired concentration and loss of appetite. These effects will usually be gone within three days of arrival, but to minimize the impact of jet lag, do the following:

- Rest for a couple of days prior to departure.
- Try to select flight schedules that minimize sleep deprivation; arriving late in the day means you can go to sleep soon after you arrive. For very long flights, try to organize a stopover.
- Avoid excessive eating (which bloats the stomach) and alcohol (which causes dehydration) during the flight. Instead, drink plenty of noncarbonated, nonalcoholic drinks such as fruit juice or water.
- Avoid smoking.
- Make yourself comfortable by wearing loose-fitting clothes and perhaps bringing an eye mask and ear plugs to help you sleep.
- Try to sleep at the appropriate time for the time zone to which you're traveling.

Infectious Diseases
Diarrhea Almost every Baja traveler fears diarrhea, popularly known as Montezuma's Revenge or *turista*. Simple things such as a change of water, food or climate can all cause a mild bout of diarrhea, but a few rushed

toilet trips with no other symptoms are not indicative of a major problem. Introduce yourself gradually to exotic and/or highly spiced foods.

Dehydration is the main danger with any diarrhea, particularly in children or the elderly, because it can occur quite quickly. Under all circumstances, fluid replacement (at least equal to the volume lost) is the most important thing to remember. Weak black tea *(té negro)*, chamomile tea *(agua de manzanilla)*, mineral water *(agua mineral)* or soft drinks allowed to go flat and diluted 50% with clean water are all good. About 24 to 48 hours should do the trick, but if symptoms persist, see a doctor.

With severe diarrhea, using a rehydrating solution is preferable to replace lost minerals and salts. Commercially available oral rehydration salts (ORS) are very useful; add them to boiled or bottled water. In an emergency, you can make up a solution of 6 teaspoons of sugar and a half teaspoon of salt to a liter of boiled or bottled water. You need to drink at least the same volume of fluid that you are losing in bowel movements and in vomit. Urine is the best guide to the adequacy of replacement – if you have small amounts of concentrated urine, you need to drink more. Keep drinking small amounts often. Stick to a bland diet as you recover.

Gut-paralyzing drugs such as loperamide or diphenoxylate can be used to bring relief from symptoms, although they do not actually cure the problem. Only use these drugs if you do not have access to toilets, for example, if you *must* travel. Note that these drugs are not recommended for children under 12.

Antibiotics may be required in certain situations: diarrhea with blood or mucus (dysentery), any diarrhea with fever, profuse watery diarrhea, persistent diarrhea that does not improve after 48 hours and severe diarrhea. These suggest a more serious cause of diarrhea, and in these situations gut-paralyzing drugs should be avoided. In these situations, a stool test may be necessary to diagnose what bug is causing your diarrhea, so you should seek medical help urgently. When this is not pos-

sible, the recommended drugs for bacterial diarrhea (the most likely cause of severe diarrhea in travelers) are norfloxacin 400mg twice daily for three days or ciprofloxacin 500mg twice daily for five days. These are not recommended for children or pregnant women. The drug of choice for children is co-trimoxazole, with dosage dependent on weight. A five-day course is given. Ampicillin or amoxycillin may be given in pregnancy, but medical care is necessary.

Two other causes of persistent diarrhea in travelers are giardiasis and amoebic dysentery. Giardiasis is caused by a common parasite, *Giardia lamblia.* Symptoms include stomach cramps, nausea, a bloated stomach, watery, foul-smelling diarrhea and frequent gas. Giardiasis can appear several weeks after you were exposed to the parasite. The symptoms may disappear for a few days and then return, which can go on for several weeks.

Amoebic dysentery, caused by the protozoan *Entamoeba histolytica,* is characterized by a gradual onset of low-grade diarrhea, often with blood and mucus. Cramping abdominal pain and vomiting are less likely than in other types of diarrhea, and fever may not be present. It will persist until treated and can recur and cause other health problems.

You should seek medical advice if you think you have giardiasis or amoebic dysentery, but when this is not possible, tinidazole or metronidazole are the recommended drugs. Treatment is a 2g single dose of tinidazole (Fasigyn) or 250mg of metronidazole (Flagyl) three times daily for five to 10 days.

Fungal Infections Hot-weather fungal infections are most likely to occur on the scalp, between the toes or fingers (athlete's foot), in the groin (jock itch or crotch rot) and on the body (ringworm). You get ringworm (a fungal infection, not literally a worm) from infected animals or by walking on damp surfaces, like shower floors.

To prevent fungal infections, wear loose, comfortable clothes, avoid artificial fibers, wash frequently and dry carefully. If infected, wash the area daily with a disinfectant or medicated soap and water, rinse and dry well and apply an antifungal cream or powder like tolnifate (Tinaderm). Try to expose the infected area to air or sunlight as much as possible. Wash towels and underwear in hot water and change them often.

Hepatitis Hepatitis is a general term for inflammation of the liver. It is a common disease worldwide. Several different viruses cause hepatitis, and they differ in the way that they are transmitted. Symptoms are similar in all forms of the illness and include fever, chills, headache, fatigue, feelings of weakness and aches and pains, followed by loss of appetite, nausea, vomiting, abdominal pain, dark urine, light-colored feces, jaundiced (yellow) skin and yellowing of the whites of the eyes. People who have had hepatitis should avoid alcohol for some time after the illness, as the liver needs time to recover.

Hepatitis A is transmitted by contaminated food and drinking water. You should seek medical advice, but there is not much you can do except rest, drink lots of fluids, eat lightly and avoid fatty foods. Hepatitis E is transmitted in the same way as hepatitis A; it can be particularly serious in pregnant women.

There are almost 300 million chronic carriers of hepatitis B in the world. It is spread through contact with infected blood, blood products or body fluids (for example, through sexual contact, unsterilized needles and blood transfusions, or contact with blood via small breaks in the skin). Other risk situations include having a shave, tattoo or body piercing with contaminated equipment. Symptoms of hepatitis B may be more severe than those of type A, and the disease can lead to long-term problems such as chronic liver damage, liver cancer or a long-term carrier state. Hepatitis C and D are spread in the same way as hepatitis B and can also lead to long-term complications.

There are vaccines against hepatitis A and B, but there are currently no vaccines against the other types of hepatitis. Following the basic rules about food and water (hepatitis A and E) and avoiding risk situa-

tions (hepatitis B, C and D) are important preventative measures.

Intestinal Worms These parasites are most common in rural, tropical areas. The different worms infect people in different ways. Some, like tapeworms, may be ingested from food such as undercooked meat; some, like hookworms, enter through your skin. Infestations may not show up for some time, and although they are generally not serious, some can cause severe health problems later if left untreated. Consider having a stool test when you return home to check for these and determine the appropriate treatment.

HIV & AIDS Infection with the human immunodeficiency virus (HIV) may lead to acquired immune deficiency syndrome (AIDS), which is a fatal disease. Any exposure to blood, blood products or body fluids may put the individual at risk. The disease is often transmitted through sexual contact or dirty needles – vaccinations, acupuncture, tattooing and body piercing can be potentially as dangerous as intravenous drug use. HIV/AIDS can also be spread through infected blood transfusions; some developing countries cannot afford to screen blood used for transfusions. If you do need an injection, ask to see the syringe unwrapped in front of you, or take a needle and syringe pack with you.

Fear of HIV infection should never preclude treatment for serious medical conditions.

Sexually Transmitted Diseases HIV/AIDS and hepatitis B can be transmitted through sexual contact – see those sections, earlier, for more details. Other STDs include gonorrhea, herpes and syphilis; sores, blisters or rashes around the genitals and discharges and pain when urinating are common symptoms. In some STDs, such as wart virus or chlamydia, symptoms may be less marked or not observed at all, especially in women.

Chlamydia infection can cause infertility in men and women before any symptoms are noticed. Syphilis symptoms eventually disappear completely, but the disease continues and can cause severe problems in later years. Although abstinence from sexual contact is the only 100% effective prevention, using condoms is also effective. Gonorrhea and syphilis are treated with antibiotics. The various sexually transmitted diseases each require specific antibiotics.

Cuts, Bites & Stings

See Less Common Diseases, later in this section, for details on rabies, which is passed on through animal bites.

Wash all cuts well and treat them with an antiseptic such as povidone-iodine. When possible, avoid bandages and Band-Aids (plasters), which can keep wounds wet. Coral cuts are notoriously slow to heal, and if they are not adequately cleaned, small pieces of coral can become embedded in the wound. Various fish and other sea creatures can sting or bite dangerously or may be dangerous to eat – seek local advice.

Bee and wasp stings are usually painful rather than dangerous. However, people who are allergic to them may experience severe breathing difficulties and require urgent medical care. Calamine lotion or a sting relief spray will give relief, and ice packs will reduce the pain and swelling.

Bedbugs & Lice Bedbugs live in various places, but particularly in dirty mattresses and bedding. They may be evidenced by spots of blood on bedclothes or on the wall. Bedbugs leave itchy bites in neat rows. Calamine lotion or a sting relief spray may help.

All lice cause itching and discomfort. They make themselves at home in your hair (head lice), clothing (body lice) or pubic hair (crabs). You catch lice through direct contact with infected people or by sharing combs, clothing and the like. Powder or shampoo treatment will kill the lice, and infected clothing should then be washed in very hot, soapy water and left in the sun to dry.

Ticks *Garrapatas* may be present in dense vegetation, where hikers often get them on their legs or in their boots. Pulling them off increases the likelihood of infection, but an insect repellent may keep them away. Smearing chemicals on the tick is not recommended; instead, press down around the tick's head with tweezers, grab the head and gently pull upward. Avoid pulling the rear of the body, as this may increase the risk of infection and disease.

Snakes Rattlesnakes *(cascabeles)* are common in the desert. To minimize the odds of being bitten, always wear boots, socks and long trousers when walking through undergrowth where snakes may be present. Keep your hands out of holes and crevices, and be cautious when collecting firewood.

Though painful, snake bites do not cause instantaneous death, and antivenins are usually available. Immediately wrap the bitten limb tightly, as you would for a sprained ankle, and then attach a splint to immobilize it. Keep the victim still and seek medical help. If possible, bring the dead snake for identification. (Don't attempt to catch the snake if there is a possibility of being bitten again.) Tourniquets and sucking out the poison are now comprehensively discredited.

Scorpions Stings from scorpions are notoriously painful, although almost never fatal for adults. Shoes, bedspreads and clothing are all likely places for them to hang out. If bitten, place ice packs on the affected area and/or take an aspirin to relieve the swelling and pain. Small children should seek medical treatment.

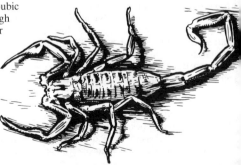

Women's Health

Gynecological Problems Antibiotic use, synthetic underwear, sweating and contraceptive pills can lead to fungal vaginal infections, especially when you're traveling in hot climates. Fungal infections are characterized by a rash, itch and discharge and can be treated with a vinegar or lemon-juice douche or with yogurt. Nystatin, miconazole or clotrimazole suppositories or vaginal cream are the usual treatments. Maintaining good personal hygiene and wearing loose-fitting clothes and cotton underwear may help prevent these infections.

Sexually transmitted diseases are a major cause of vaginal problems. Symptoms include a smelly discharge, painful intercourse and sometimes a burning sensation when urinating. Medical attention should be sought, and male sexual partners must also be treated. Also see Sexually Transmitted Diseases, earlier. Besides abstinence, the best thing is to use condoms.

Pregnancy Most miscarriages occur during the first three months of pregnancy. Miscarriage is not uncommon and can occasionally lead to severe bleeding. The last three months should also be spent within reasonable distance of good medical care. A baby born as early as 24 weeks stands a chance of survival, but only in a good modern hospital. Pregnant women should avoid all unnecessary medication, although vaccinations and malarial prophylactics should still be taken when needed. Additional care should be taken to prevent illness, and particular attention should be paid to diet and nutrition. Alcohol and nicotine, for example, should be avoided.

Less Common Diseases

Lyme Disease This tick-transmitted infection may be acquired throughout North America, Europe and Asia. The illness usually begins with a spreading rash at the site of the tick bite, accompanied by fever, headache, extreme fatigue, aching joints and muscles, and mild neck stiffness. If untreated, these symptoms usually resolve over several weeks, but disorders of the nervous system, heart and joints may develop over subsequent weeks or months. Treatment works best early in the illness. Medical help should be sought.

Rabies This fatal viral infection is found in many countries. Many animals can be infected (such as dogs, cats and bats), and it is their saliva that is infectious. Any bite, scratch or even lick from a warm-blooded furry animal should be cleaned immediately and thoroughly. Scrub with soap and running water, and then apply alcohol or iodine solution. If there is any possibility that the animal is infected, medical help should be sought promptly to receive a course of injections to prevent the onset of symptoms and death. For those in a high-risk category (eg, if you will be exploring caves or working with animals), a rabies vaccination is available – see Immunizations, earlier.

Tetanus This disease is caused by a germ that lives in soil and in the feces of horses and other animals. It enters the body via breaks in the skin. The first symptom may be discomfort in swallowing or stiffening of the jaw and neck; this is followed by painful convulsions of the jaw and whole body. The disease can be fatal, but it can be prevented by vaccination.

WOMEN TRAVELERS

In a land of machismo, women have to make some concessions to local custom – but don't let that put you off. In general, Mexicans are great believers in the difference (rather than the equality) between the sexes. Foreign women without male companions will inevitably be confronted with catcalls and attempts to chat them up. Many men may only want to talk to you, but it can get tiresome. A good way to discourage unwanted attention is to avoid eye contact (sunglasses help here) and, if possible, ignore the attention altogether. Otherwise, use a cool but polite initial response and a consistent, firm 'No.' It is possible to turn uninvited attention into a worthwhile conversation by making clear that you *are* willing to talk, but no more.

Don't put yourself in peril by doing things Mexican women would not do, such as challenging a man's masculinity, drinking alone in a cantina, hitchhiking without a male companion or going alone to isolated places.

Although informal 'dress codes' are more permissive than in the recent past, avoid clothing that Mexican men may interpret as provocative. Except in beach resorts, it's advisable to wear shorts only at swimming pools. Some women have found it useful to swim in shorts and a T-shirt, as many Mexican women do.

Women must recognize the extra threat of rape, which is more of a problem in tourist than in rural areas. You're more vulnerable if you've been drinking or using drugs than if you're sober. At night, if you're going out with friends, take care not to become separated from the group. Don't hitchhike, especially when alone, and don't pick up hitchhikers when you're driving alone. Driving at night is not a good idea either.

GAY & LESBIAN TRAVELERS

Though it might appear to be one of the world's more heterosexual countries, Mexico is more broad-minded than visitors might expect. Gays and lesbians tend to keep a low profile but in general rarely attract open discrimination or violence. In Baja California, Tijuana is the city with the liveliest scene, although smaller ones exist in Ensenada and Mexicali – though, perhaps surprisingly, not in Los Cabos.

A great source of information on the Internet is *Frontera Gay* (www.fronteragay .com), which focuses on the border-town scene. Although mostly in Spanish, the site also has an extensive English-language section. It's also available in magazine form in the border towns as well as in San Diego. The 'mother' of all Mexican gay Web sites, though, is *The Gay Mexico Network* (www .gaymexico.net), sort of the central clearinghouse for information on all things gay throughout Mexico. *Sergay* is a Spanish-language magazine, focused on Mexico City but with bar and disco listings for the whole country. You can find it on the Internet at www.sergay.com.mx.

Gay Mexico: The Men of Mexico by Eduardo David and *Ferrari's Guide to Gay Mexico* by Richard Black are two of the most established and useful gay guides to the country. *Men's Travel in Your Pocket, Women's Travel in Your Pocket* and *Gay Travel A to Z* (for men and women) are not specifically focused on Mexico but are popular nonetheless. One of the oldest publications (now in its 29th edition) is the *Spartacus International Gay Guide* by Bruno Gmunder. All titles should be available at gay- and lesbian-oriented bookstores and may also be ordered on the Internet.

DISABLED TRAVELERS

Mexico doesn't yet make many concessions to the disabled, though some hotels and restaurants (mostly toward the top end of the market) and public buildings are starting to provide wheelchair access. Mobility is easiest in the major tourist resorts, where dropped curbs are more common than elsewhere. Public transportation is mainly hopeless.

Mobility International USA (☎ 541-343-1284), PO Box 10767, Eugene, OR 97440, USA, runs exchange programs (including in Mexico) and publishes *A World of Options: A Guide to International Educational Exchange, Community Service & Travel for People with Disabilities*. Its Web site is at www.miusa.org. In Europe, Mobility International (☎ 02-201-5608, mobint@arcadis .be) is at Boulevard Baudouin 18, Brussels 1000, Belgium.

Twin Peaks Press (☎ 360-694-2462), PO Box 129, Vancouver, WA 98666-0129, USA, publishes and sells many books for disabled travelers. Its Web site is at www.pacifier .com/~twinpeak.

An excellent general Web site for disabled travelers is www.access-able.com.

SENIOR TRAVELERS

Discounted seniors' rates for sights, hotels, restaurants and other establishments are nonexistent in Baja.

Senior's advocacy groups may be able to help in planning your travels. These include the American Association of Retired Persons

(AARP; ☎ 800-424-3410), 601 E St NW, Washington, DC 20049, USA. Catering to Americans 50 years and older, it is also a good resource for travel bargains. Membership for one/three years is US$8/20. Its Web site is at www.aarp.org.

Membership in the National Council of Senior Citizens (☎ 301-578-8800), 8403 Colesville Rd, Suite 1200, Silver Spring, MD 20910, USA, gives access to discount information and travel-related advice. Check its Web page at www.aoa.dhhs.gov/AOA/dir/149.html.

Grand Circle Travel (☎ 800-597-3644), 347 Congress St, Boston, MA 02210, USA, offers escorted tours and travel information in a variety of formats. It's Web site is at www.gct.com.

TRAVEL WITH CHILDREN

Successful travel with young children requires planning and effort. Most children are excited and stimulated by the colors, sights and sounds of Mexico, but younger children especially don't like traveling all the time – they're happier if they can settle into places and make friends. Try to give them time to do some of the activities they are used to back home. Include the kids in the trip planning; if they've helped to work out where you are going, they will be much more interested when they get there.

Lonely Planet's *Travel with Children,* by Maureen Wheeler, has lots of practical advice on the subject, as well as firsthand stories from many Lonely Planet authors and others who have done it.

Mexicans as a rule like children. Any child whose hair is less than jet black will get called *güera* (blond) if she's a girl, *güero* if he's a boy. Children are welcome at all kinds of hotels and in virtually every cafe and restaurant.

Children are likely to be more affected than adults by heat or disrupted sleeping patterns. They need time to acclimatize and extra care to avoid sunburn. Replacing fluids if a child gets diarrhea is essential (see the Health section, earlier in this chapter).

Diapers (nappies) are widely available, but you may not easily find creams, lotions, baby foods or familiar medicines outside of larger cities and tourist towns. Bring what you need.

Many hotels and motels allow children to share a room with their parents for free or for a modest fee. Larger hotels often have a baby-sitting service, and others may be able to help you make arrangements.

On flights to and within Mexico, children under two generally travel for 10% of the adult fare, and those between two and 12 normally pay 67%. Children pay full fare on Mexican long-distance buses unless they're small enough to sit on your lap.

DANGERS & ANNOYANCES

Official information can make Mexico sound more alarming than it really is, but you might still find advice dispensed by your country's foreign affairs department to be of value. In the USA, contact ☎ 202-647-5225 or http://travel.state.gov; in Canada ☎ 800-267-6788, 613-944-6788 or www.dfait-maeci.gc.ca; in the UK ☎ 020-7238-4503, www.fco.gov.uk; in Australia ☎ 02-6261-3305, www.dfat.gov.au. If you're already in Mexico, you can contact your embassy.

Safety & Theft

Crime is unfortunately on the rise throughout Mexico, in large part because of low apprehension and conviction rates. In Baja California, Tijuana is the only city where violent crimes occur frequently, though cases involving tourists are rare. Crime rates are lower in coastal resorts, which tend to have a large and visible police presence.

More at risk than your physical safety are your possessions, particularly those you carry around with you. In order to minimize risk, leave valuables in hotel safes *(caja fuertes)* and carry only the cash or credit cards you'll be needing that day. Expensive jewelry and irreplaceable items are best left at home. Avoid accessing ATMs outside of a bank's business hours, and make sure no one can see you punching in your PIN code.

Car break-ins are fairly common, especially in Tijuana. Don't leave anything valuable-looking in your car, and park it in a guarded garage or lot rather than on the street (even if you have a car alarm). Car theft in itself is a serious problem, especially if your vehicle is conspicuous.

Recreational Hazards

Many of Baja's Pacific beaches have dangerous offshore rip currents, so ask before entering the water and be sure someone on shore knows your whereabouts. Only hire sports and aquatic equipment from reputable sources, such as those listed in this book. Safety standards are generally lower than in countries like the US or Australia, and the operator may not carry any accident liability insurance. Several tourists have been injured and even killed in jet-ski and diving accidents and have been subjected to dangerous landings when parasailing.

LEGAL MATTERS

Mexico's judicial system is based on Roman or Napoleonic law, presuming an accused person guilty until proven innocent. There is no jury trial. In all but the most minor car accidents, everyone involved is considered guilty and liable until proven otherwise. Without car insurance, you will be detained until fault has been established. For more on the subject, see the boxed text 'In Case of a Car Accident' in the Getting Around chapter.

Drivers found with drugs or weapons on board are likely to have their vehicle confiscated and be detained in jail for months while their cases are investigated. The minimum jail sentence for possession of anything more than a token amount of any narcotic, including marijuana and amphetamines, is 10 years; it may take up to one year before a verdict is reached. As in most other countries, the purchase of controlled medication requires a doctor's prescription (also see the boxed text 'The Drug Business').

Bringing in a firearm or ammunition (even unintentionally) is punishable by up to five years in prison, unless a permit was obtained in advance from a Mexican embassy or consulate.

Drinking on Mexican streets is illegal, as is fighting and disturbing the public order.

If arrested, you have the right to notify your embassy or consulate. Consular officials can tell you your rights and provide lists of local lawyers. They can also monitor your case, make sure you are treated humanely and notify your relatives or friends – but they can't get you out of jail. More Americans are in jail in Mexico than any other country outside of the USA – about 450 at any one time.

If you encounter minor legal hassles with public officials or local businesspeople in Baja California (Norte), you can contact La Procuraduría de Protección al Turista (Attorney General for Tourist Protection), now

The 'Drug' Business

Pharmacies, especially those in Baja's border towns, do box office with US travelers because many prescription drugs (such as antibiotics and Viagra) are available over the counter here at much lower prices. When returning to the US, you are supposed to declare all prescription medications purchased and may be asked to show a prescription from a US or Mexican doctor if the medication requires a prescription in the US.

Under US Customs regulations, you cannot bring back drugs that have not been approved by the Federal Drug Administration, even if they're legal in Mexico and have been prescribed by a local physician. Under a new ruling, US residents are allowed to legally bring back up to 50 dosage units of medications on the Drug Enforcement Agency's (DEA) controlled substances list, provided they have a prescription issued by a DEA-approved physician. Medications on this list include Valium and Librium, cough medicine with codeine, anabolic steroids and some barbiturates. For a full list, click on Traveler Information – Medications/Drugs on the US Customs Web site (www.customs.gov/travel/travel.htm). Penalties for abuse are stiff.

If you purchase a controlled medication in Mexico, the pharmacy will need to keep the prescription, so be sure to make a copy in case you need to show it to the customs inspector when re-entering the US. If you're buying noncontrolled medications, the pharmacy will let you keep the prescription.

under the auspices of the state-run tourist office, Secture. The numbers to contact are as follows:

Ensenada	☎ 6-172-30-22
Mexicali	☎ 6-566-11-16
Playas de Rosarito	☎ 6-612-02-00
Tecate	☎ 6-654-10-95
Tijuana	☎ 6-688-05-05
San Felipe	☎ 6-577-11-55
San Quintín	☎ 6-163-38-33

Each office has English-speaking aides and can help with complaints and reporting crimes or lost articles. The 24-hour national hotline maintained by Secture (☎ 5-250-01-23, 01-800-903-92-00) also provides advice on tourist protection laws and where to obtain help. The hotline is valid in both Baja California (Norte) and Baja California Sur.

If Mexican police wrongfully accuse you of an infraction (as they have often been known to do in the hope of obtaining a bribe), you can ask for the officer's identification or to speak to a superior or be shown documentation about the law you have supposedly broken. You can also note the officer's name, badge number, vehicle number and department (federal, state or municipal). Then make your complaint to Secture.

BUSINESS HOURS

Shops are generally open Monday to Saturday from 9 or 10 am to 7 pm. Siesta, or break time, is between 2 and 4 pm, although it is not usually observed by shops in big-city malls or tourist resorts. These places also tend to open on Sunday. In rural areas, though, some shops are closed Saturday afternoon and all day Sunday.

Offices have similar weekday hours. Those with tourist-related business might open a few hours on Saturday.

PUBLIC HOLIDAYS & SPECIAL EVENTS

Bajacalifornianos (residents of Baja) observe all major national and Catholic holidays, but special festivities and fairs like Carnaval and saints' days usually take place only in major towns and cities. See the regional entries for information on local holidays. Banks, post offices and government offices are closed during most of the holidays, celebrations and events listed below and may be closed on local holidays as well.

Travelers expecting to stay at hotels in Tijuana, Tecate, San Felipe, Ensenada, Mulegé, La Paz, San José del Cabo or Cabo San Lucas during religious holidays, special fairs or US holidays, such as Memorial Day, July 4, Labor Day and Thanksgiving, should make reservations.

January

Año Nuevo (New Year's Day) – January 1

Día de los Reyes Magos (Three Kings' Day; Epiphany) – January 6. Mexican children traditionally receive gifts this day, rather than at Christmas.

February

Día de la Candelaría (Candlemas) – February 2. Processions, bullfights and dancing in many towns commemorate the presentation of Jesus in the temple 40 days after his birth.

Día de la Constitución (Constitution Day) – February 5

Día de la Bandera (Flag Day) – February 24

Carnaval (Carnival) – late February to early March. Celebrated in Ensenada, San Felipe and La Paz, usually the week before Lent, with parades, music, food and fireworks.

March

Día del Señor San José (St Joseph's Day) – March 19. Bajacalifornianos celebrate the festival of St Joseph, San José del Cabo's patron saint, with street dances, horse races, food fairs and fireworks.

Día de Nacimiento de Benito Juárez (Anniversary of Benito Juárez's Birth) – March 21

Semana Santa (Holy Week) – March/April. Starting on Palm Sunday, a week before Easter, it is celebrated in every church in Baja; business closures are usually from Good Friday to Easter Sunday.

May

Día del Obrero (Labor Day) – May 1

Cinco de Mayo – May 5. Marks the anniversary of victory over the French at Puebla (1862).

Día de la Madre (Mother's Day) – May 10

June

Día de la Armada (Navy Day) – June 1

September

Día de Nuestra Señora de Loreto (Our Lady of Loreto) – September 8. Festival of the founding of Loreto.

Día de la Independencia – September 15 to 16. Commemorates Mexican independence from Spain (1821). The biggest celebrations take place in Tijuana and La Paz, with fireworks, horse races, folk dances and mariachi bands.

October

Día de la Raza (Columbus Day) – October 12. Celebrates the country's Spanish heritage.

November

Día de Todos los Santos (All Saints' Day) – November 1

Día de los Muertos (Day of the Dead) – November 2. Mexico's most characteristic fiesta; the souls of the dead are believed to return to earth this day. Families build altars in their homes and visit graveyards to commune with their dead on the night of November 1 as well as the next day. Festivities are especially colorful in Tijuana and La Paz. Breads and candies resembling human skeletons are sold, and papier-mâché skeletons and skulls appear everywhere.

Día de la Revolución (Anniversary of the Mexican Revolution of 1910) – November 20

December

Día de Nuestra Señora de Guadalupe (Festival of Our Lady of Guadalupe) – December 12. Tecate hosts one of the most interesting celebrations of this day. Groups come from all over Baja to display their costumes and dancing, while Mexicali holds colorful nightly processions from the first of the month.

Posadas – December 16 to 24. Candlelit parades of children and adults, reenacting the journey of Mary and Joseph to Bethlehem, held for nine nights, more in small towns than big cities.

Día de los Muertos artwork

Navidad (Christmas Day) – December 25. Marks the end of a week of posadas. Children also celebrate by breaking a *piñata* (papier-mâché animal) full of candy.

LANGUAGE COURSES

Baja's most popular language schools are in Ensenada and La Paz. In Ensenada, the Colegio de Idiomas de Baja California (☎ 6-174-56-88, in the US ☎ 619-758-9711, 877-444-2252, college@bajacal.com) offers Spanish immersion programs at its new campus at Barcelona y Belgrado 191, in the hills about 1 mile (1.6km) from the coast. Besides standard language courses at levels from beginner to advanced, the Colegio also offers one-on-one tuition as well as specialized instruction for business professionals. It can also arrange community college or university credit in the USA.

One-week programs (30 hours) cost US$240; weekends (13 hours) cost US$140; classes are taught in groups of five or less. The day rate (6 hours) is US$60. One-on-one tuition is available for US$80/day (6½ hours). Its Web site is at www.bajacal.com.

Also in Ensenada, the International Spanish Institute (☎ 6-178-21-01, fax 6-178-14-55, ☎ 888-308-9048 in the US, intlspan@telnor.net) offers intensive instruction on its campus at Blvd JA Rodríguez 377, about 1½ miles (2.4km) inland. Class size is also limited to five students. Each day starts with four hours of language study, followed by two hours of discussions, singing, game playing or local tours. An optional conversation session at a restaurant or cafe takes place in the evening. The cost here is US$125 a week (30 hours) or US$80 for a weekend (eight hours); there's also a one-time US$125 registration fee. Its Web site is at www.sdro.com/spanishinstitute.

Both schools can help arrange hotel accommodations, though they recommend (and will arrange) a stay with a Mexican family for maximum immersion (US$25 a day, including three meals). Weeklong classes start on Monday.

In Baja California Sur, language instruction is concentrated in La Paz. Centro de Idiomas, Cultura y Communicación (☎ 1-125-

75-54, fax 1-125-73-88, info@cicclapaz.com) is at Calle Madero 2460 y Legaspi and offers a wide range of courses. Spanish for Travelers is a one- or two-week program with two hours of instruction daily Monday to Saturday (US$86). For dedicated students, Intensive Spanish is 23 hours per week, with four levels of instruction; class size is limited to six. The recommended length of study is four weeks (US$1050, including registration fee), though shorter periods are possible. One-on-one instruction costs 20% more. Homestays are US$12 per day, including two meals. Its Web site is at www.cicclapazcom.

New on the scene in La Paz is SeHabla…La Paz (☎/fax 1-122-77-63, sehablalapaz@baja .net.mx) at Calle Madero 540 between Republica and Guerrero. This school specializes in courses for healthcare professionals but also offers general language instruction. The cost is US$15 per hour for an individual session, US$12.50 each for groups of two or US$10 for groups of four. Rates drop about 20% after 20 hours. Homestays cost US$105 for the seven-day minimum, including private room and three meals. The US contact is Salomon Smith Barney, 5255 E Williams Circle, Suite 5000, Tucson, AZ 85711. The Web site is at www.sehablalapaz.com.

WORK

Except for those directly involved in tourist specialties, like natural history tours or diving, paid work is not an attractive option in Baja. Wages are low by US or European standards, and permits are hard to obtain. English tutoring may be feasible in Tijuana or Mexicali, but competition is stiff because of the proximity to the border.

However, volunteer opportunities are offered by several organizations in Baja. Baja Outreach (☎ 619-428-4011 in the US) provides education and recreational centers, as well as nutritional programs, to disadvantaged children in Tijuana. Volunteers spend one summer to two years working in positions that include teaching, public relations, office work and fundraising. Fluent Spanish may be required, and room and board are provided.

One World Workforce (☎ 800-451-9564) accepts volunteers for eight-day trips to the Sea Turtle Station in Bahía de los Angeles. The cost is US$750, including transportation, food and lodging. Duties include cleaning and filling turtle tanks, collecting research data and food (for the turtles), weighing the turtles and other chores. Its Web site is at www.1ww.org.

A similar pay program is offered by the Earthwatch Institute whose two-week trips to the same Sea Turtle Station cost US$1695. It has offices in the US (☎ 800-776-0188 ext 250), in the UK (☎ 01865-318-831) and Australia (☎ 03-9682-6828). For details, see its Web site at www.earthwatch.org.

Baja Animal Sanctuary in Playas de Rosarito is the first and only no-kill animal shelter in northern Baja. It is dedicated to the caring and feeding of abandoned and abused animals, mostly dogs and cats, with the goal of putting them up for adoption. Volunteer opportunities exist on an informal basis. For details, contact founder Sunny Benedict in Rosarito at ☎ 6-631-32-49 or basdogs@telnor.net. Its Web site is at www.bajadogs.org.

ACCOMMODATIONS

Baja's accommodations cover the full spectrum, from primitive campsites to luxurious resorts.

Camping

Most organized campgrounds are actually trailer parks, set up for RVs (camper vans) and trailers (caravans), but many accept tent campers at lower rates. Some are very basic, others quite luxurious. Expect to pay about US$3 to US$5 to pitch a tent, and US$8 to US$15 for two people to use the full facilities of a good campground. Some restaurants or guesthouses in small beach spots will let you pitch a tent on their land for a few (US) dollars per person.

If you're planning to camp extensively, get a copy of Fred and Gloria Jones' *Baja Camping: The Complete Guide* or *Exploring Baja by RV* by Walt Peterson for suggestions on camping topics such as what to bring, how and where to camp, and cooking. AAA's Baja California guidebook is another good source.

All Mexican beaches are public property. You can camp for free on most of them, but they can be risky places for your belongings.

Hostels

There are no Hostelling International–affiliated hostels in Baja, but hostel-style accommodations are offered in Playas de Rosarito, El Sauzal near Ensenada and in Puerto San Isidro.

B&Bs

Bed and breakfast inns are not a traditional Mexican form of accommodations, which explains why most are run by North American expatriates. B&Bs are usually small, luxurious, favorably located and characterized by a personal atmosphere. Prices vary widely and may range from US$40 to US$120 a night.

Hotels & Motels

By US or European standards, many hotels and motels are in the budget range, with double-room rates starting around US$30, but a handful are cheaper and still tolerable. Don't judge a hotel by its facade: Go inside, ask to see a room, sniff around and test the mattress.

In the tourist areas – especially in the northern coastal areas and Los Cabos – seasonal price fluctuations are quite common, as are differences between weekend and midweek rates. Room rates often vary by type and location of room. While price differences between single and double occupancy are small or nonexistent, it does matter whether you're staying in a room with one or two double beds. The location of the room may also affect the price; larger hotels spread over different buildings may charge more for rooms in recently renovated structures. Those with a view naturally cost more than those without.

Note that rates are particularly fickle and may change spontaneously if business is slow or under new management. Prices quoted throughout this book should be regarded as guidelines only. Where available, we have listed email addresses in addition to phone and fax numbers. In our experience, though, inquiries made over the Internet do not always get a response.

FOOD

Mexican cuisine is enormously varied, full of regional differences and subtle surprises, and Baja is one of the best places to sample it. Baja's population is almost entirely made up of people who've migrated here from other parts of the country, bringing their regional cooking with them. In addition to Mexican fare, you'll find all sorts of international food too. For inexpensive fresh fruit, vegetables, tortillas, cheese and bread, pop into the local market.

Mexicans generally eat three meals a day: *desayuno* (breakfast), *almuerzo* (lunch) and *cena* (dinner). When eating in a restaurant, note that waiters will not bring the check until you ask for it – for them to do otherwise would be extremely rude. Note that *el menú* can mean either the menu or the special fixed-price meal of the day. If you want the menu, ask for *la carta*.

All meals usually include one or more of the following staples:

tortillas – thin, round patties of pressed corn or wheat-flour dough cooked on griddles. *Harina* (flour) tortillas are common in northern Mexico and Baja, but *maíz* (corn) tortillas are more traditional. Both can be served under, on or wrapped around just about any type of food.

frijoles (beans) – served boiled, fried, refried, in soups, on tortillas or with eggs as part of almost every meal.

chiles – these come in numerous varieties. Some, such as the *habanero* and *serrano*, are spicy hot, while others, such as the *poblano*, vary in spiciness according to when they were picked. If your tolerance is limited, ask whether the chile is *picante* (spicy hot) or *muy picante* (very spicy hot). If you exceed your tolerance and start to choke, start eating or drinking sugar, beer, milk, bread or anything else that might extinguish the fire. Note, however, that water usually exacerbates the pain.

For a full list of menu items with translations, see the Menu Guide at the back of this book.

Meals

Breakfast can either be continental or US-style. A light, continental-style breakfast consists of coffee or tea and *pan dulce* (sweet rolls). Many restaurants offer combination breakfasts for about US$1.50 to US$3.50, typically featuring *jugo de fruta* (fruit juice), *café* (coffee) or *pan tostado* (toast) with *mantequilla* (butter) and *mermelada* (jam), and *huevos* (eggs) served in a variety of styles (see the Menu Guide).

When ordering eggs, never ask *'¿Tiene huevos?'* ('Do you have eggs?'), because *huevos* is slang for 'testicles' in this context. Instead, ask *'¿Hay huevos?'* ('Are there eggs?').

In resorts and tourist areas, American-style breakfasts are common; these may include eggs, hash browns, hot cakes, sausages and bacon. Granola, *ensalada de frutas* (fruit salad) and various kinds of cereals are often available too.

La comida, the main meal of the day, is usually served between 1 and 3 or 4 pm. Most restaurants offer not only à la carte fare but also special fixed-price menus called *comida corrida* or *menú del día.* These menus constitute the best food bargains, because you get several courses (often with some choice) for much less than such a meal would cost à la carte. Prices may range from US$2 at a lonchería (casual eateries, often counters in markets) for a simple meal of soup, a meat dish, rice and coffee to US$10 or more for elaborate meals beginning with oyster stew and finishing with profiteroles. Often a soft drink is included as well.

La cena, the evening meal, is usually lighter than the comida and served about 7:30 pm. Fixed-price meals are rarely offered, so you can save money by eating your main meal at lunchtime.

Fish & Seafood

Available year round, *pescado* (fish) and *mariscos* (seafood) are the best of Baja cuisine, although choices usually depend on what's in season and/or what's been caught that day. Fish is often eaten as a *filete* (filet), *frito* (fried whole fish) or *al mojo de ajo* (fried in butter and garlic). One of the great delights is the fish taco *(taco de pescado),* a piece of deep-fried fish that you can dress up with a range of condiments including salsa, raw or browned onions, white or red cabbage, limes and mayonnaise.

Ceviche, the popular Mexican cocktail, is raw seafood (fish, shrimp, scallops, etc) marinated in lime and mixed with onions, chilies, garlic and tomatoes. There are other seafood *cocteles* (cocktails) as well. Unfortunately, seafood is also a major source of intestinal problems, so check for cleanliness and freshness, especially with uncooked fare.

Meat

Meat dishes usually feature beef or pork. *Chorizo* is a spicy sausage, often served scrambled with eggs for breakfast. *Machaca* is dried and cured beef that's been shredded and reconstituted in a sauce. It's delicious in burritos *(burrito de machaca)* or with eggs *(huevos con machaca).*

Carnitas is a specialty dish from the state of Michoacán that involves slow-roasting an entire pig; it is served by weight and eaten with a variety of side dishes and condiments. *Carne asada* is grilled meat, usually beef, often sliced thinly and used as a stuffing for tacos, burritos and other *antojitos* (traditional Mexican snacks or small meals).

Soups & Desserts

Sopa (soup) does not figure big on Baja's menus. Popular varieties include *(menudo),* a hominy-based soup with some unusual animal parts (eg, stomach, intestines) and its lighter version *(pozole),* often made with chicken and vegetables. Menudo in particular is considered an excellent remedy against hangovers.

Most desserts *(postres)* are an afterthought, and the selection is usually limited to flan, ice cream *(helado)* or rice pudding *(arroz con leche).*

DRINKS

As befits a region with a warm climate, a huge variety of *bebidas* (drinks) are imbibed in Baja. Don't drink any water, ice or drinks made with water unless you know the water has been purified or boiled (see the Health section, earlier in this chapter). You can buy bottles of inexpensive purified or mineral water everywhere.

Nonalcoholic Drinks

Tea & Coffee *Té* and *café* are available throughout Baja. If you simply ask for tea, you'll likely be given *té de manzanilla* (chamomile), so specify if you want *té negro* (black tea). Regular coffee is mostly instant Nescafé but is sometimes ground; it will almost always be served heavily sweetened unless you request otherwise. Unless requested, coffee or tea rarely arrives before a meal. In tourist centers like Playas de Rosarito, Ensenada and Los Cabos, cappuccino, lattes and other espresso drinks are also widely available.

The following are some common variants offered:

café con crema – coffee with cream; cream is usually served separately.

café con leche – about half hot milk and half coffee.

café negro or *café americano* – black coffee with nothing added except sugar.

café sin azúcar – coffee without sugar; ordering this keeps the waiter from adding heaps of sugar but doesn't mean that coffee won't taste sweet (sugar is often added to coffee beans during processing).

Juices Fresh fruit and vegetable *jugos* (juices), *licuados* (shakes) and *aguas frescas* (flavored waters) are all popular. At reputable chains like La Michoacana, these are made with purified water.

A basic licuado is a blend of fruit or juice, water and sugar. Other items can be added or substituted, such as raw egg, milk, ice and flavorings like vanilla or nutmeg. Delicious licuado combinations are practically limitless.

Aguas frescas are made by mixing fruit juice or syrup (made from mashed grains or seeds) with sugar and water; look for them in big glass jars on the counters of juice stands. Try the delicious *agua fresca de arroz* (rice water), which has a sweet, nutty taste; it is sometimes called *horchata*. *Cebada,* made with barley, is also tasty and refreshing.

Soft Drinks Almost every *refresco* (soft drink) available in the USA is also available in Baja, although not always as the 'diet' (light) version. Among the better Mexican brands are apple-flavored Sidral and Manzanita. Other flavors, like *fresa* (strawberry), *limón* (lime) and *cereza* (cherry), tend to be very sweet.

Alcoholic Drinks

Mescal, Tequila & Other Spirits Mescal, often spelled mezcal, can be made from the sap of several species of the maguey plant, a spray of long, thick spikes sticking out of the ground. Tequila is a type of mescal made only from the maguey grown in Jalisco and a few other states. The production method for both is similar, except that for mescal, the chopped-up *piña* (core) of the plant is baked, whereas for tequila it's steamed. The final product is a clear liquid (sometimes artificially tinted) that is at its most potent as tequila. The longer the aging process, the smoother the drink and the higher the price. A repugnant *gusano* (worm) is added to some bottles of mescal.

The most popular mixed drink on the peninsula is the *margarita,* made with tequila, a sweet liqueur (like Triple Sec, Grand Marnier or Controy), blended with ice or served on the rocks, usually in a salt-rimmed glass.

Baja is a shopper's paradise for inexpensive spirits and liqueurs made in Mexico: Bacardi rum, brandy (the Pedro Domecq brand comes from Baja), Controy (an orange liqueur), Kahlua (coffee liqueur) and Oso Negro vodka.

Beer & Wine Late-19th-century German immigrants first established breweries in Mexico, and their techniques and technology have been a major factor in Mexican beer's popularity throughout North America. The landmark Tecate brewery now belongs to Cervecería Cuauhtémoc, Mexico's second largest brewery conglomerate, and also produces other brands, such as Carta Blanca. Tecate is still one of the most popular beers in Baja, but other favorites include Corona, Carta Blanca, Dos Equis and Sol Especial.

Wasting Away: The Glorious & Sad Fate of Tequila

In the glory days of westerns, Clint or the Duke would lick the salt off a knuckle, throw back a grimy shot glass, bite the lime wedge and hiss loudly through clenched teeth. This was a manly ritual. This was tequila, hombre. The little bite of death. And generations of ill-prepared students have joined in this ritual only to find themselves 'hugging the bowl' and awaking to thoughts and sensations akin to those felt in the brain of a wolverine on angel dust.

Tequila, then as now, is not for the meek. But what began as the home brew of Mexican peasants ('Okay, Juan. We need to get drunk so let's boil that blue agave over there and see what happens. Maybe toss a worm in it too, just for effect') has steadily escalated in alcoholic lore to the point where its legendary qualities are threatening its existence.

Now found in every chic bar from Moscow to Melbourne, tequila has become the choice of connoisseurs whose tastes formerly ran to the dry martini or the ancient brandy. Whipping up a 'killer margarita' has made the reputation of many a trendy publican and resulted in a global gulping frenzy. Not bad for a spiky desert plant related to the lily family, you say? Sorry, but actually es muy malo for the Weber blue agave of Jalisco, the only plant authorized by the Mexican government for tequila production.

Global demand resulted in sales of US$296 million in 1998. But it takes this humble plant eight to 12 years to mature before its heart – in true Aztec fashion – is ripped out, mashed and distilled. And as the World Trade Organization has designated tequila – like champagne – the unique status of a geographically distinct liquor, Jalisco is running out of…juice.

This has resulted in waves of agave smugglers, harvesting inferior plants and pawning them off as the real deal. And the price for Jimmy Buffett's favorite vegetable has gone through the roof: A ton of agave sold a year ago for US$40 now costs well over US$600. This means you'll be 'paying at the pump' as well, with a bottle of Herradura's Seleccion Suprema going for around US$500.

You can still get mescal – tequila's bastard cousin – at a fair price, though you can't serve it at the yacht club. Plata tequila – the silver variety – is the most affordable legit stuff, but if you want to get toasty with a paramour, better shell out for a Reposada, aged in wood. And if you're asking for the hand of Don Jaime's lovely daughter, you'd best sell off your AT&T stocks and pony up with an Anejo of 100% agave, if you know what's good for you, hombre.

La Cervecería de Tijuana, which opened in that city in early 2000, is Baja's first micro-brewery.

In restaurants and bars unaccustomed to tourists' tastes, beer may be served at room temperature. If you want cold beer, order *'una cerveza helada, por favor.'*

Wine is less popular than beer and tequila, but Baja has several significant wineries, all in and around Ensenada, including LA Cetto, Vinícolas Domecq and Bodegas de Santo Tomás, plus several smaller ones.

ENTERTAINMENT

Historically, Baja California has had a reputation for border-town bawdiness, but this notoriety is largely outdated despite the continued existence of Tijuana's Zona Norte and the tawdrier parts of Mexicali's La Chinesca.

Both Tijuana and Mexicali are increasingly cosmopolitan cities with a variety of nightlife, ranging from spectator sports like baseball and dog racing to glitzy nightclubs and pop music concerts to symphony orchestras and serious drama. In tourist resorts like San Felipe and Cabo San Lucas, bars and nightclubs stay open nearly all night for live music and dancing. Sports bars with satellite TV connections, even in very remote places, attract tourists to Monday-night American football and other athletic events.

The cinema was once a dominant form of entertainment throughout Mexico, but the video revolution has subverted the big screen almost everywhere in Baja; only in Tijuana, Playas de Rosarito, Mexicali, Ensenada and La Paz will moviegoers still find first-run features.

SPECTATOR SPORTS
Baseball
Soccer may be bigger than *béisbol* in Mexico, but not so in Baja. You'll often see small boys, using broken table legs for bats and balls coming apart at the stitches, play into the twilight on empty sandlots, and nearly every sizable town has a groomed sandlot field or even a stadium. While Mexican professionals have not matched the success of their Caribbean counterparts in the US major leagues, the Liga Mexicana del Pacífico offers outstanding competition, good facilities and a chance to see young players, including the occasional American, on the way up.

Bullfights
The bullfighting season runs from late April to late September. Tijuana has the two most prominent arenas: the Plaza de Toros Monumental and the El Toreo de Tijuana. There's also a bullring in Mexicali. For more on bullfights, see the boxed text 'Death in the Afternoon' in the Tijuana section of the La Frontera chapter.

Rodeos
Mexican *charreadas,* which frequently take place during fiestas and other special occasions, are particularly popular in northern Mexico but occur throughout the peninsula. Unlike North American rodeo riders, however, *charros* (Mexican cowboys) rely on style and skill rather than speed and strength; rodeos are competitive events, but there are no cash prizes. Admission fees go to offset the costs of staging the events.

Female riders, known as *escaramuzas,* play an important but different role in the rodeo. While athletic, this role is ambiguous, derived from aristocratic traditions of equestrianism but also, at least symbolically, from female couriers in the Revolution of 1910. In style, escaramuzas ride sidesaddle – a dubious symbol of feminism. Readers particularly interested in the subject should read Kathleen Mullen Sands' *Charrería Mexicana: An Equestrian Folk Tradition.*

Soccer
Mexico has twice hosted the World Cup soccer finals, but on neither occasion did the home side advance beyond the quarterfinals. Mexican players lag behind those in other Latin American countries – the best tend to go to Europe for better competition and higher salaries. Although there's a decent professional league and several impressive stadiums, attendance is low, in part because TV coverage is so extensive.

SHOPPING
Baja's tourist centers are full of souvenirs from throughout Mexico, but relatively few crafts come from Baja itself. Several jewelry stores carry traditional silver jewelry and cutlery from Taxco. Carved doors and other woodwork from Guadalajara can be bought or ordered in Playas de Rosarito. A variety of other crafts are also available: woven baskets, colorful *rebozos* (shawls), brightly painted ceramic animals, hand-painted tiles, intricately decorated leather boots and wrought-iron staircases.

Many crafts sold in Baja qualify as junk or kitsch, like wrought-iron cages with stuffed birds, black velvet paintings, oversized embroidered sombreros, bull horns and onyx chess sets. The exceptions to this general rule are Paipai, Kumiai and Cucupah Indian basketry, pottery and jewelry, which are available in those communities as well as in major tourist cities like Ensenada.

The importation to the US of any product made from any of the endangered species listed under Appendices I or II of the Convention on International Trade in Endangered Species of Wild Fauna and Flora (CITES) is strictly prohibited. (See the boxed text 'Endangered Species' in the Facts about Baja California chapter for more information.) This includes black-coral jewelry, a specialty from the Cape Region, as well as cacti, sea-turtle and marine-mammal products. These products can be confiscated and those in possession of them can be prosecuted under civil and criminal laws.

Baja's best bargains are medical services, such as dentistry and optometry, and prescription pharmaceuticals (see the boxed text 'The Drug Business,' earlier). Border towns like Tijuana and Mexicali also do a thriving business in car body repair, painting and upholstery, at prices from one-third to one-half of their cost north of the border. Mufflers, brakes and similar repairs are equally inexpensive.

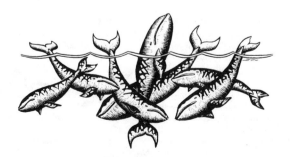

Activities

Much of Baja's appeal springs from its outdoor activities, especially when winter weather makes pastimes like camping, hiking and water sports difficult or impossible in most of the US and Canada.

Mexicans are less enamored of camping and hiking than beachgoing and water sports, but visitors will find some mountain areas suitable for the former activities. Tents-only campgrounds are rare, though tent camping is possible at most trailer parks and beaches. In some areas, horses are available for rent.

A good general guidebook to outdoor activities in Baja is Walt Peterson's *The Baja Adventure Book*. For sport-specific books, see the Books section in the Facts for the Visitor chapter.

DIVING & SNORKELING

Both the Pacific Ocean and the Sea of Cortez are water wonderlands for divers and snorkelers. Rock and coral reefs, shipwrecks and kelp beds all invite exploration and attract a great variety of ocean dwellers and tropical fish.

Dive sites on the Pacific side, in general, are better suited for advanced divers and, thanks to chilly water temperatures, wetsuits are advisable year round. Both Islas Todos Santos and Islas Coronado are popular playgrounds for Southern Californians. Species you're likely to encounter include rockfish, the luminescent garibaldi and bat rays.

The central and southern Sea of Cortez beckons with calmer and warmer waters and an even greater diversity of species: You may well feel as if you're diving in a giant tropical aquarium. There are sites for snorkelers as well as divers of all skill and experience levels. Hubs for underwater explorations are (north to south): Bahiá Los Angeles; the Midriff Islands; Isla Santa Inéz and Bahía Concepción; La Paz with Isla Espiritú Santo, Isla Partida, Los Islotes, El Bajo Seamount (famous for schooling hammerhead sharks, mantas and whale sharks); the East Cape's Cabo Pulmo (the only coral

reef on the North American west coast); and Los Cabos' Land's End sandfalls, Playa Santa María and Playa Chileño.

Dive shops at or near all of these areas lead tours and rent equipment, though you may prefer to bring your own. For more on the subject, read Lonely Planet's well-respected *Diving & Snorkeling Baja California* by Walt Peterson.

San Diego–based Baja Expeditions (☎ 858-581-3311, 800-843-6967, fax 858-581-6542, travel@bajaex.com) and Horizon Charters (☎ 619-277-7823, fax 619-560-6811, dives@aol.com) both organize multi-day diving excursions, as does Baja Adventures (☎ 541-386-7610, 800-533-8452, fax 541-386-4899, bajasales@windriders.com), based at Los Barriles on the East Cape.

FISHING

Sportfishing, for good reason, is one of the most popular activities off the Pacific coast and in the Sea of Cortez. The waters of Baja are among the most fecund anywhere, and few places offer a greater variety of fish. The southern peninsula enjoys a legendary reputation for big game fish like marlin and dorado. The most detailed and respected source on Baja fishing is *The Baja Catch* by Neil Kelly and Gene Kira.

Also see the individual entries for Ensenada, San Quintín, San Felipe, Bahía San Luis Gonzaga, Bahía de los Angeles, Mulegé, Loreto, La Paz, the East Cape, San José del Cabo and Cabo San Lucas.

When to Fish

You can catch fish in Baja waters year round, but what's biting, how many, where and when

Marlin

depends on such variables as water temperature, currents, bait supply and fish migrations. In general, the biggest catches occur from April to July and between October and December. Keep in mind that summer and late fall is also prime tropical storm and hurricane season. Also see the fish calendars that appear throughout the book, indicating at what time certain species are most prevalent in a particular area.

Where to Fish

The waters around Ensenada and San Quintín Bay are rich in yellowtail, halibut, sea bass, bonito and albacore tuna. On the Sea of Cortez side, grouper, sierra and corvina are common off San Felipe. Mulegé and Bahía Concepción have many of the same species as well as yellowtail, dorado and even the occasional marlin. Loreto is famous for roosterfish.

The most abundant fishing grounds are in the Cape Region. Both Los Cabos and the East Cape are rich in migratory species such as dorado, tuna and wahoo, but Cabo San Lucas especially is the epicenter for year-round billfish such as marlin, sailfish and swordfish. The East Cape also swarms with roosterfish.

Charters

Fishing charters are available at all of Baja's fishing hubs, and you'll find reputable local companies listed throughout this book. Always ask what's included in the rates. Fishing licenses, tackle, crew and ice are standard, but sometimes charters may also include bait, cleaning and freezing, meals, drinks and tax. Your live bait – usually available dockside for a few dollars – should be checked for absolute freshness. Tips for the crew are at your discretion, but US$20 (per angler) for a successful eight hours is considered adequate. Bring along a hat, sunscreen, polarized sunglasses and Dramamine (or equivalent) if you suffer from sea sickness.

Prices depend on boat type and size. The most common is the flybridge cruiser, usually 26 to 42 feet (8.6 to 14m) in length. It usually has two fighting chairs in the stern to reel in the big fish. Prices range from US$260 to US$650.

The cheapest boats are pangas, the vessel of choice of Mexican commercial fishermen, as they put you right up close with the sea. About 18 to 24 feet (6 to 8m) long, these sturdy skiffs are made from heavy-duty fiberglass and wood and powered by an outboard motor. They get cruising speeds of up to 25mph (40km/h) and are capable of beach landings. Superpangas are larger, more comfortable and often feature toilets and a canvas top for shade. Rates start around US$30 per hour for three people, with a six-hour minimum.

Angler's Glossary

The following list should help English-speaking fishing enthusiasts avoid confusion when talking with Mexican guides and anglers. Note that in Mexico, some terms may be understood differently than they are in other Spanish-speaking countries. *Jurel*, for instance, commonly means 'mackerel' elsewhere.

barracuda	picuda
black marlin	marlín negro
blue marlin	marlín azul
crevalle	toro
dolphin fish (mahi mahi)	dorado
grouper	garropa
halibut	lenguado
mackerel	macarela
needlefish	agulón
octopus	pulpo
pompano	palometa
roosterfish	pez gallo
sailfish	pez vela
sea bass	cabrilla
shark	tiburón
sierra	sawfish
skipjack	barrilete
snapper	pargo
squid	calamar
striped marlin	marlín rayado
swordfish	pez espada
triggerfish	cochi
yellowfin tuna	atún de aleta
yellowtail	jurel

On the northwest Pacific coast, operators based at San Diego or Ensenada go out on larger powerboats (40 to 60 feet/13 to 20m) that can accommodate up to 30 anglers.

Licenses & Bag Limits

Anyone 16 years or older aboard a private vessel carrying fishing gear must have a Mexican fishing license, whether they're fishing or not. Licenses are usually included in any charters but can also be obtained in the USA from the Mexican Fisheries Department (☎ 619-233-6956, fax 619-233-0344), 2550 5th Ave, Suite 101, San Diego, CA 92103. In Mexico, licenses are issued by the Oficina de Pesca in the respective towns. The cost of the license is US$18 per week, US$29 per month and US$38 per year. Day licenses for US$9 are sometimes issued by the local oficinas.

The daily bag limit is 10 fish per person with no more than five of any one species. Billfish like marlin, sailfish and swordfish are restricted to one per day per boat; tarpon, roosterfish and halibut to two. We strongly recommend catch and release of the billfish, as these majestic lords of the deep are being disastrously overfished, both by sportsmen and Japanese commercial fleets (also see the boxed text 'Catch & Release' in the Cape Region chapter). Protected species like totuava and sea turtles, as well as mollusks and crustaceans, may not be taken at all.

US Customs allows fish caught in Mexico to enter the US as long as it conforms with Mexican bag limits, the species is somehow identifiable (an ice chest filled with fillets is a no-no; the head, tail or part of the skin should be left on) and you can produce a Mexican fishing license. Contact the California Department of Fish & Game (☎ 619-467-4201) at 4949 Viewridge Ave, San Diego, CA 92123, for information about declaration forms, permits and limits. For requirements of other US states or Canadian provinces, check with the respective authorities.

SEA KAYAKING

Baja California is a top-rated destination for sea kayaking, which is often the only way to access some of the most pristine and beautiful coves and inlets along the coast and the offshore islands.

The Sea of Cortez offers calmer waters than the Pacific and is a great place to learn or hone your kayaking skills. The most interesting areas are the Gulf islands of the Midriff from Bahía de los Angeles south to La Paz. These feature abundant wildlife and countless anchorages for well-equipped campers. Sheltered Bahía Concepción, south of Mulegé, is another major hot spot for recreational kayakers and especially suited for novices. Kayaking is also possible along the East Cape and in Los Cabos.

Rougher seas on the Pacific side attract more advanced and adventurous kayakers, although most beginners should also be able to cope with the waters in sheltered Punta Banda south of Ensenada.

Hazards to sea kayakers include the large swells of the open Pacific and high winds on the Gulf, both of which can swamp unsuspecting novices. But even experts respect these natural phenomena and inquire about local conditions. Note also that Mexican government regulations prohibit sea kayaking when whales are present in the Pacific coastal lagoons of Baja California Sur.

Many aficionados bring their own equipment, but kayaks are also for rent at hotels, resorts and sports outfitters, many of whom also offer guided tours. The following operators in the USA offer a variety of extended trips: Sea Trek (☎ 415-488-1100, fax 488-1707, paddle@seatrekkayak.com) in San Francisco; Baja Expeditions (☎ 858-581-3311, 800-843-6967, fax 858-581-6542, travel@bajaex .com) and Southwest Sea Kayaks (☎ 619-222-3616, fax 619-222-3671, kayaked@aol .com) in San Diego; Kayak Port Townsend (☎ 360-385-6240, 800-853-2252, fax 360-385-6062, info@kayakpt.com) in Port Townsend, Washington; and Sea Kayak Adventures (☎ 208-765-3116, fax 765-5254, skadvent@ iea.com) in Coeur D'Alene, Idaho.

SURFING

Virtually the entire Pacific coast of Baja and areas along the East Cape as far north as Punta Arenas contain a multitude of surf sites. Wetsuits are de rigeur year round, except in Los Cabos, where you can usually get away with wearing shorties.

The most popular (and crowded) sites are in easily accessible areas, such as those along the northern Pacific coast along the Tijuana-Ensenada Corridor, and on the Los Cabos Corridor, such as Zipper's Beach. Dedicated surfers favor isolated spots with difficult access, such as the Islas de Todos Santos near Ensenada and Isla Natividad near Guerrero Negro.

The most popular spots are south of points *(puntas)* offering right-point breaks (where swells peak up into steep waves as they encounter a shelflike point), especially during winter swells. Beaches north of Punta Santa Rosalillita, southwest of the Bahía de los Angeles junction with the Transpeninsular, are renowned among surfers for exceptional breaks. Punta Rosarito, about 18 miles (30km) south of here, known among surfers as 'The Wall,' may be the most consistent break on the entire peninsula.

To reach the best spots, surfers need sturdy vehicles, should carry extra parts and gasoline, plenty of water and all supplies, and should be especially conscientious about carrying out their trash. Those who speak Spanish will find that local fishermen are good sources of information – they know where to find the *olas* (waves).

México Surf Spot's Map (sic) has considerable information on Baja California and is sold in many surf shops and sometimes in beach supply stores.

For organized tours, contact Baja Surf Adventures (☎ 760-744-5642, 800-428-7873, fax 760-744-5921, info@bajasurfadventures.com). For details, including equipment rental, see individual geographical entries in this book.

WINDSURFING

Baja's windsurfing capital is Los Barriles, a fast-growing settlement on the East Cape, but Bahía de la Ventana, southeast of La Paz via a good paved highway, has more consistent wind and is rapidly gaining popularity. The season runs from mid-November to early March. In these areas, equipment is easy to come by, but elsewhere, windsurfers will have to bring their own.

On the Pacific side, popular spots include Punta Baja, Punta Abreojos and Punta San Carlos, named 'best wave sailing spot in the world' by *Windsurfing* magazine. Another insider spot is Bahía de Los Angeles. The season here runs from February to October, peaking in the summer.

Vela Windsurf Resorts and Baja Adventures both organize windsurfing trips. See Los Barriles and Buena Vista in the Cape Region chapter for details.

WHALE-WATCHING

In winter, the coastal lagoons of Baja California Sur become a nursery for the California gray whale, and thousands of visitors, both Mexicans and foreigners, gather to observe mothers and their calves cavorting in the lagoons' shallow waters. It's possible to arrange informal full- or half-day whale-watching trips on local fishing boats at Guerrero Negro, at Ojo de Liebre and San Ignacio lagoons and at Bahía Magdalena. These are much cheaper than organized trips arranged in the USA but are also less extensive and informative.

If you decide to go on a multi-day tour, there are several companies from which to choose, most of them based in San Diego: Baja Expeditions (☎ 858-581-3311, 800-843-6967, fax 858-581-6542, travel@bajaex.com); Baja Discovery (☎ 619-262-0700, 800-829-2252, bajadis@aol.com); Searcher Natural History Tours (☎ 619-226-2403, fax 619-226-1332);

and the San Diego Natural History Museum (☎ 619-232-3821 ext 203, fax 619-235-9446). Natural Habitat Adventures (☎ 303-449-3711, 800-543-8917) is based in Boulder, Colorado.

BICYCLING & MOUNTAIN BIKING

Bicycling is increasingly popular as both bicycles and roads improve – bicycling the length of Baja may now be more common than driving it was before completion of the Transpeninsular. However, the distance between settlements and lack of water in some areas can be serious drawbacks without logistical support; cyclists should be adept mechanics and carry spare parts. Narrow shoulders on most highways can be hazardous, although most drivers are courteous and keep their distance. According to one of our readers, the same is not true of bus drivers. But he also reported that most of the hotels where he stayed let him take the bike into his room.

Even better than biking along the highway is getting off-road into the backcountry to experience desert and sierra close up and personal. Tracks may take you along ridges, past remote ranches and through cactus forests. 'Slime tubes' (self-sealing

puncture tubes) are essential on these thorn-paved trails. You'll also need fairly wide tires to deal with frequent sand.

The Baja border areas, particularly the cities of Tecate, Playas de Rosarito and Ensenada, host a variety of bicycling events annually; for details, see the respective city entries. For additional information about bicycling in Baja, see the Getting Around chapter.

Rental bikes are readily available in resort areas like Loreto, La Paz and Los Cabos. Outfitters of organized multi-day trips include two Northern California companies: Backroads Bicycle Touring (☎ 510-527-1555, 800-462-2848, fax 510-527-1444, backtalk@backroads.com) and Pedaling South (☎ 707-942-4550, 800-398-6200, 707-942-8017, tourbaja@aol.com).

HIKING

Hiking and backpacking are less common in Baja than they are north of the border, but there are many areas suitable for these activities – for example, Parque Nacional Constitución de 1857 (including canyons on the eastern escarpment of the Sierra de Juárez), Parque Nacional Sierra San Pedro Mártir, the Sierra de San Francisco of the Desierto Central, the Sierra de la Giganta west of Loreto and the Sierra de la Laguna in the Los Cabos area. (For more information, see those entries in the geographical chapters.) Services anywhere are basically nil.

The two national parks have the best trail infrastructure, often following the routes walked by Indians hundreds of years ago, although trails are not always well maintained. In the central and southern areas, trails are less worn and it's fairly easy to get lost. Even locals rarely venture on multi-day trips, and many recommend taking a guide unless you're a very experienced navigator.

Part of the problem is reliable maps are nonexistent. The Instituto Nacional de Estadística, Geografía e Informática (INEGI) publishes large-scale topographical maps covering the entire country, but these are rather outdated. Both Map Centre and Maplink are good sources for maps; see the Maps entry in the Facts for the Visitor chapter.

We recommend that you always carry a compass (or GPS) to help you stay oriented. It's best not to hike alone. At the very least, let someone know precisely the route you're planning on taking. Bring plenty of water and food supplies with you. Wear light to medium boots for day hikes, sturdy ones for extended trips; make sure they're broken in and have a good heel. Dress in layers, as temperatures may fluctuate from hot to chilly within a single day. Other useful items to take, especially on longer trips, include a flashlight, a small first-aid kit, a knife, waterproof matches and/or a lighter, sunscreen, a hat and a whistle in case you're injured and need rescuing. Be aware of hazards like rattlesnakes, flash floods and unanticipated heat (even in winter), which can lead to dehydration.

If you prefer not to go it alone, check out the hiking calendar of Baja Discovery (in the USA ☎ 619-262-0700, 800-829-2252, bajadis@aol.com).

GOLF

Developers, mostly from the USA, have turned Los Cabos into a new mecca for the golfing set. New courses are sprouting at a frightening pace, irrevocably turning the pristine coastline between Cabo San Lucas and San José del Cabo into a 'Palm Springs by the Sea.' For a complete run-down of golf options, see the Los Cabos Corridor section in the Cape Region chapter.

Getting There & Away

Most of the travel to Baja California, whether by air, land or sea, is from the USA – in fact, it is largely from California. Canadians constitute the second-largest visitor contingent, many of them seeking to escape harsh winters. Since there are no direct flights from overseas into Baja airports, travelers from Europe, Australia or elsewhere must change planes in the US or Mexico City.

AIR
Airports & Airlines
Most visitors to Baja California arrive at the international airport in Los Cabos, although there are also direct flights from US and Mexican cities to Tijuana, Mexicali, Guerrero Negro, Loreto and La Paz. Destinations on the Baja Peninsula are served by Mexican airlines like Aero California, Mexicana, AeroMéxico and its subsidiary Aerolitoral and by US carriers such as Alaska

Airlines, America West, American Airlines, Northwestern Airlines and Continental Airlines. For flight information, contact any of these airlines by phone or via the Internet.

Aero California (☎ 800-237-6225)

Aerolitoral (☎ 800-237-6639)
www.aerolitoral.com.mx

AeroMéxico (☎ 800-237-6639)
www.aeromexico.com

Alaska Airlines (☎ 800-426-0333)
www.alaskaair.com

America West Airlines (☎ 800-235-9292)
www.americawest.com

American Airlines (☎ 800-433-7300)
www.americanair.com

Continental Airlines (☎ 800-231-0856)
www.flycontinental.com

Delta Air Lines (☎ 800-221-1212)
www.delta-air.com

Horizon Air (☎ 800-547-9308)
www.horizonair.com

Mexicana (☎ 800-531-7921)
www.mexicana.com.mx

Northwest Airlines (☎ 800-225-2525)
www.nwa.com

The US is the only country with direct international flights to Baja California. Most flights originate on the West Coast, from Los Angeles in particular, although there are also some from Phoenix, Tucson, Dallas-Fort Worth, Chicago and Denver. All Mexican airlines also operate flights to and from the Mexican mainland.

For details about travel to and from a particular destination, see the Getting There & Away section in the relevant chapter.

Buying Tickets
An air ticket alone can gouge a great slice out of anyone's budget, but stiff competition has resulted in widespread discounting – good news for travelers! The only people likely to be paying full fare these days are travelers flying in 1st or business class. For long-term travel, plenty of discount tickets are avail-

able that are valid for 12 months, allowing multiple stopovers with open dates. For short-term travel, cheaper fares are available by traveling midweek, staying away at least one Saturday night or taking advantage of short-lived promotional offers.

Phone travel agents for bargains rather than contacting the airlines directly. Occasionally, airlines have promotional fares and special offers, but generally they only sell fares at the official listed price. One exception is reserving on the Internet. Many airlines offer excellent fares to Web surfers, selling seats by auction or by giving discounts to reflect the reduced cost of electronic selling.

The days when some travel agents routinely fleeced travelers by running off with their money are, happily, almost over. Paying by credit card generally offers protection, as most card issuers provide refunds if you can prove you didn't get what you paid for. Similar protection can be obtained by buying a ticket from a bonded agent, such as one covered by the Air Transport Operators License (ATOL) scheme in the UK. Agents who only accept cash should hand over the tickets straight away and not tell you to 'come back tomorrow.' After you've made a reservation or paid your deposit, call the airline and confirm that the reservation was made. It's generally not advisable to send money (even checks) through the mail unless the agent is very well established – some travelers have reported being ripped off by fly-by-night mail-order ticket agents.

You may decide to pay more than the rock-bottom fare by opting for the safety of a better-known travel agent. Firms such as STA Travel and Council Travel with offices worldwide, Travel CUTS with offices in Canada and the UK, usit CAMPUS (formerly Campus Travel) in the UK and Flight Centre in Australia are not going to disappear overnight, and they do offer good prices to most destinations. These companies also sell discounted tickets for students and people under 26.

Departure Tax

A departure tax equivalent to about US$18 is levied on international flights from

Travelers with Special Needs

Most international airlines can cater to people with special needs – travelers with disabilities, people with young children and even children traveling alone.

Travelers with special dietary preferences (vegetarian, kosher, etc) can request appropriate meals with advance notice. If you are traveling in a wheelchair, most international airports can provide an escort from the check-in desk to the plane when needed, and ramps, lifts, toilets and phones are generally available.

Airlines usually allow babies up to two years of age to fly for 10% of the adult fare, although a few may allow them free of charge. Reputable international airlines usually provide diapers (nappies), tissues, talcum and all the other paraphernalia needed to keep babies clean, dry and half-happy. For children between the ages of two and 12, the fare on international flights is usually 50% of the regular fare or 67% of a discounted fare.

Mexico. If you buy your ticket in Mexico, the tax is included in your ticket cost. If you buy it outside Mexico, ask if it has been included. If it is, make sure that that the letters 'XD' appear somewhere on your ticket; otherwise, you must pay the tax again when checking in.

The USA

Discount travel agents in the USA are known as consolidators (although you won't see a sign on the door saying 'Consolidator'). San Francisco is the country's ticket consolidator capital, but good deals can also be found in Los Angeles, New York and other big cities. Consolidators are listed in the Yellow Pages or in the major daily newspapers. The *New York Times,* the *Los Angeles Times,* the *Chicago Tribune* and the *San Francisco Examiner* all produce weekly travel sections in which you will find a number of travel agency ads.

Council Travel, the USA's largest student travel organization, has around 60 offices in the country; its head office (☎ 800-226-8624) is at 205 E 42nd St, New York, NY 10017. Call for the office nearest you or visit its Web site at www.ciee.org. STA Travel (☎ 800-777-0112) has offices in Boston, Chicago, Miami, New York, Philadelphia, San Francisco and other major cities. Call the toll-free number for office locations or visit its Web site at www.statravel.com.

Fares fluctuate widely because of seasonal variations and advance purchase requirements. Midweek departures are generally cheaper than those leaving on a Friday or Saturday. Many airlines offer bargain packages – including air, hotel and sometimes meals, for short-term visitors – especially to resorts in the Los Cabos area. Check airline Web sites or call the numbers listed under Airports & Airlines earlier in this chapter. Also check the travel sections of major US newspapers for current promotions.

Canada

There are no direct flights from Canada to Baja California, but Alaska Airlines has direct flights to Los Cabos from Seattle. Canadian discount travel agents are also known as consolidators; their airfares tend to be about 10% higher than those sold in the USA. The *Globe & Mail,* the *Toronto Star,* the *Montreal Gazette* and the *Vancouver Sun* carry travel agents' ads and are good places to look for cheap fares.

Travel CUTS (☎ 800-667-2887) is Canada's national student travel agency and has offices in all major cities. Check out its Web site at www.travelcuts.com.

Australia & New Zealand

The cheapest and most direct route across the Pacific is to fly to a US West Coast city (preferably Los Angeles) and make the short hop south to Baja from there. The main carriers are Qantas, Air New Zealand and United. Prices are higher if you wish to stop over in Hawaii or plan to stay abroad for more than two months.

Several travel offices specialize in discount air tickets. Some travel agents, particularly smaller ones, advertise cheap airfares in the travel sections of weekend newspapers, such as the *Age* in Melbourne and the *Sydney Morning Herald.*

Two well-known agents for cheap fares are STA Travel and Flight Centre. The main office for STA Travel (☎ 03-9349-2411, 131-776 in Australia) is at 224 Faraday St, Carlton, VIC 3053. It has offices in all major cities and on many university campuses, as well as a Web site at www.statravel.com.au. Flight Centre (☎ 131-600) has a central office at 82 Elizabeth St, Sydney, and dozens of offices throughout Australia. Its Web address is www.flightcentre.com.au.

In New Zealand, the *New Zealand Herald* has a travel section in which travel agents advertise fares. Flight Centre (☎ 09-309-6171) has a large central office in Auckland at National Bank Towers (corner of Queen and Darby Sts) and many branches throughout the country. STA Travel's main office (☎ 09-309-0458) is at 10 High St, Auckland. It has other branches in Auckland, as well as in Hamilton, Palmerston North, Wellington, Christchurch and Dunedin.

The UK

There are no direct flights from the UK to Baja California – you must first fly to North America or Mexico City and from there fly to Baja. Usually, it's cheapest to fly to Los Angeles and then head south, rather than fly to Mexico City and travel north.

Airline ticket discounters are known as 'bucket shops' in the UK. Discount air travel is big business in London. Travel agent ads appear in the travel pages of the Saturday edition of the *Independent* and the *Sunday Times.* Also look for the free magazines, such as *TNT,* widely available in London outside the main railway and underground stations.

For students or travelers under 26, popular travel agencies include STA Travel (☎ 020-7361-6161), which has an office at 86 Old Brompton Rd, London SW7 3LQ, and other offices in London and Manchester. Visit its Web site at www.statravel.co.uk. Usit CAMPUS (☎ 020-7730-3402), 52 Grosvenor Gardens, London SW1W 0AG, has branches throughout the UK. The Web address is www.usitcampus.com. Both

Air Travel Glossary

Cancellation Penalties If you have to cancel or change a discounted ticket, there are often heavy penalties involved; insurance can sometimes be taken out against these penalties. Some airlines impose penalties on regular tickets as well, particularly against 'no-show' passengers.

Courier Fares Businesses often need to send urgent documents or freight securely and quickly. Courier companies hire people to accompany the package through customs and, in return, offer a discount ticket, which is sometimes a phenomenal bargain. However, you may have to surrender all your baggage allowance and take only carry-on luggage.

Full Fares Airlines traditionally offer 1st class (coded F), business class (coded J) and economy class (coded Y) tickets. These days there are so many promotional and discounted fares available that few passengers pay full economy fare.

Lost Tickets If you lose your airline ticket, an airline will usually treat it like a traveler's check and, after inquiries, issue you with another one. Legally, however, an airline is entitled to treat it like cash and if you lose it then it's gone forever. Take good care of your tickets.

Onward Tickets An entry requirement for many countries is that you have a ticket out of the country. If you're unsure of your next move, the easiest solution is to buy the cheapest onward ticket to a neighbouring country or a ticket from a reliable airline that can later be refunded if you do not use it.

Open-Jaw Tickets These are return tickets where you fly out to one place but return from another. If available, this can save you backtracking to your arrival point.

Overbooking Since every flight has some passengers who fail to show up, airlines often book more passengers than they have seats. Usually excess passengers make up for the no-shows, but occasionally somebody gets 'bumped' onto the next available flight. Guess who it is most likely to be? The passengers who check in late.

Promotional Fares These are officially discounted fares, available from travel agencies or direct from the airline.

Reconfirmation If you don't reconfirm your flight at least 72 hours prior to departure, the airline may delete your name from the passenger list. Call to find out if your airline requires reconfirmation.

Restrictions Discounted tickets often have various restrictions on them – such as needing to be paid for in advance and incurring a penalty to be altered. Others are restrictions on the minimum and maximum period you must be away.

Round-the-World Tickets RTW tickets give you a limited period (usually a year) in which to circumnavigate the globe. You can go anywhere the carrying airlines go, as long as you don't backtrack. The number of stopovers or total number of separate flights is decided before you set off and they usually cost a bit more than a basic return flight.

Transferred Tickets Airline tickets cannot be transferred from one person to another. Travelers sometimes try to sell the return half of their ticket, but officials can ask you to prove that you are the person named on the ticket. On an international flight, tickets are compared with passports.

Travel Periods Ticket prices vary with the time of year. There is a low (off-peak) season and a high (peak) season, and often a low-shoulder season and a high-shoulder season as well. Usually the fare depends on your outward flight – if you depart in the high season and return in the low season, you pay the high-season fare.

agencies sell tickets to all travelers but cater especially to young people and students.

Other recommended travel agencies include the following:

Bridge the World (☎ 020-7734-7447) 4 Regent Place, London W1R 5FB

Flightbookers (☎ 020-7757-2000) 177-178 Tottenham Court Rd, London W1P 9LF

Trailfinders (☎ 020-7938-3939) 194 Kensington High St, London W8 7RG

Continental Europe

Although London is the travel discount capital of Europe, some continental cities also offer good deals. All the major airlines usually have some sort of promotional fare, and price does not vary much between cities. Travel agents may also have special deals on offer, so shop around.

Across Europe, many travel agencies have ties with STA Travel, where cheap tickets can be purchased and STA-issued tickets can be altered (usually for a US$25 fee). Outlets in major cities include the following:

France

Voyages Wasteels (☎ 08 03 88 70 04, fax 01 43 25 46 25) 11 rue Dupuytren, 756006 Paris

Germany

STA Travel (☎ 030 311 0950, fax 030 313 0948) Goethestrasse 73, 10625 Berlin

Greece

ISYTS (☎ 01-322-1267, fax 01-323-3767) 11 Nikis St, Upper Floor, Syntagma Square, Athens

Italy

Passaggi (☎ 06-474-0923, fax 06-482-7436) Stazione Termini FS, Gelleria Di Tesla, Rome

France has a network of student travel agencies that can supply discount tickets to travelers of all ages. OTU Voyages (☎ 01 44 41 38 50) has a central Paris office at 39 Ave Georges Bernanos (5e) and 42 offices around the country. Its Web site is at www.otu.fr. Acceuil des Jeunes en France (☎ 01 42 77 87 80), 119 rue Saint Martin (4e), is another popular discount travel agency.

General travel agencies in Paris that offer some of the best services and deals include Nouvelles Frontières (☎ 08 03 33 33 33), 5 Ave de l'Opéra (1er), with a Web site at www.nouvelles-frontieres.com; and Voyageurs du Monde (☎ 01 42 86 16 00), 55 rue Sainte Anne (2e).

Belgium, Switzerland, the Netherlands and Greece are also good places for buying discount air tickets. In Belgium, Acotra Student Travel Agency (☎ 02-512-86-07), at rue de la Madeline, Brussels, and WATS Reizen (☎ 03-226-16-26), at de Keyserlei 44, Antwerp, are both well-known agencies. In Switzerland, SSR Voyages (☎ 01-297-11-11) specializes in student, youth and budget fares. Its Zurich branch is at Leonhardstrasse 10, and there are others in most major Swiss cities. Its Web site is at www.ssr.ch.

In the Netherlands, NBBS Reizen is the official student travel agency. You can find it in Amsterdam (☎ 020-624-09-89) at Rokin 66, and there are several other agencies around the city. Another recommended travel agent in Amsterdam is Malibu Travel (☎ 020-626-32-30), at Prinsengracht 230.

In Athens, check the many travel agencies in the back streets between Syntagma and Omonia Squares. For student and non-concessionary fares, try Magic Bus (☎ 01-323-7471, fax 01-322-0219).

Mainland Mexico

Internal Mexican flights are generally a bit cheaper than comparable flights in the USA. Direct daily flights depart from several mainland Mexican cities to Tijuana, Mexicali, Loreto, La Paz and Los Cabos. Consult AeroMéxico, Aero California or Mexicana. For specific route details, see the Getting Around sections in the respective city chapters.

LAND
Border Crossings

From west to east, there are six official border crossings from the US state of California to Baja. At any crossing, Mexican Customs & Immigration will issue and stamp tourist cards and process car permits free of charge.

Andrade–Los Algodones Open 8 am to 10 pm daily, this bustling crossing is about 7 miles (11km) west of Yuma, Arizona, via US Interstate 8 and California State Hwy 186.

Calexico–Mexicali Open 24 hours a day, this congested crossing is about 8 miles (13km) south of El Centro via California State Hwy 111.

Calexico East–Mexicali Open 6 am to 10 pm daily, this crossing has relieved some of the pressure from the downtown crossing.

Mesa de Otay–Tijuana Open 6 am to 10 pm daily, this crossing offers a far less congested port of entry than the San Ysidro crossing; it is east of downtown Tijuana near the airport.

San Ysidro–Tijuana Open 24 hours a day, this border crossing, 15 miles (24km) south of downtown San Diego, is one of the world's busiest.

Tecate Open 6 am to midnight daily, the Tecate border crossing is about 30 miles (50km) southeast of San Diego via California State Hwys 94 and 188.

Bus & Trolley

For details about bus and trolley travel from US cities to Tijuana, see Getting There & Away in the Tijuana section of the La Frontera chapter. Information about how to get to Mexicali and beyond is under Mexicali in the Desierto del Colorado chapter. Both entries also provide details about travel from either city to other destinations in Baja California.

Buses run regularly from major centers throughout Mexico to Mexicali and Tijuana, from where you can continue to other Baja destinations. See the Getting There & Away section in either city chapter for details.

Train

Amtrak runs about 10 passenger trains daily from Los Angeles' Union Station at 800 N Alameda St to its San Diego terminal at 1050 Kettner Blvd near Broadway. One-way/roundtrip fares are US$25/33. From the San Diego terminal, trolleys go directly to the border at San Ysidro. For current fare and schedule information, phone Amtrak (☎ 800-872-7245) or check its Web site at www.amtrak.com.

Car & Motorcycle

Countless visitors drive their own vehicles into Baja California from the USA. Those traveling no farther south than San Felipe or Ensenada and staying less than 72 hours do not need a tourist card or vehicle permit. If you're headed farther south, you will need a stamped tourist card. If you're taking your car to mainland Mexico, either by ferry from Baja or overland from Mexicali, you will need a car permit and a tourist card for everyone aboard.

Liability insurance, purchased from a Mexican company, is essential for driving in Mexico; Mexican law does not recognize policies from companies based in other countries, though some US policies will pay claims in Mexico. While insurance is not obligatory, it can prevent serious legal problems for anyone involved in an accident. According to Mexican law, the principals in an accident are guilty until proven innocent. Understandably, it is common for the victims of a nonlethal accident to leave the scene before the police arrive.

For more on the subject, see the Legal Matters section in the Facts for the Visitor chapter and the boxed text 'In Case of a Car Accident' in the Getting Around chapter. The latter also contains information about how to obtain insurance. For more details on Motorcycles, see the Getting Around chapter.

SEA
The USA

Cruise ships and private yachts are the only ways to travel by sea from the US to Baja.

Cruise Ships Carnival Cruises (☎ 888-2276-4825 in the USA) and Royal Caribbean (☎ 800-327-6700 in the USA) both offer three-night (Friday to Monday) and four-night cruises (Monday to Friday) to Ensenada with year-round departures from the port in San Pedro in Los Angeles County. Prices start at US$299/339, respectively, but vary widely between seasons and also depend on cabin location and amenities. Meals, entertainment, port charges and taxes are included.

Carnival Cruises also operates seven-day cruises from San Pedro to Cabo San Lucas every Sunday aboard the *Elation*. Prices are

Shuffleboard anyone?

highest in summer and winter, with the lowest rates available during fall's *chubasco*, or tropical-rain season. A mid-September cruise in a standard room with queen-size bed runs $812. Add $100 more for a 'picture window' in your cabin and $20 additional for each deck the higher you go.

Private Yachts If you know something about boats and sailing, try looking for a crew position on one of the many boats that sail south from Southern California. Marinas at Dana Point, Newport Beach, Belmont Shores and Marina del Rey are all good places to ask, but one correspondent has offered these detailed suggestions for southbound travelers on the Pacific coast:

From October through February, sailboats converge on San Diego to rest, make repairs and purchase provisions. Crews also frequently change, and it is a perfect place for crew to be added. Crews with experience are in demand, and just about any type of deal they want with regard to costs is possible. There is a place for the novice. A person who is willing to ask questions and learn can also do quite well. Many of the skippers are engaged in their first open-ocean experience and may not be

all that relaxed. I would encourage potential crews to have frank discussions about costs, equipment, safety, nudity and expectations. The last is very important for females (crew) and male skippers.

Shelter Island in San Diego is where almost all skippers meet and are available. Throughout the boating communities, we are linked via radio for news and information. The radio networks are referred to as UHF nets or simply local nets. The key is that you do not need to have a radio to participate. Yachties are more than happy to broadcast that potential crew is available. Shyness has no place.

Make inquiries and/or send three-by-five cards for posting on the bulletin board to Downwind Marine (☎ 619-224-2733, fax 619-224-7683), 2804 Cañon St, San Diego, CA 92106, where 'Dennis' operates the local VHF (very high frequency) net. For vessels in Baja, Downwind is a complete nautical chandler specifically geared toward cruising. It is also a supplier of spare parts, and drivers buying parts will often take passengers as far as La Paz to share gas. Downwind also publishes a free cruising guide, available in person from its San Diego offices.

Any vessel traveling south along the Baja coast beyond Ensenada or staying more than three days in Ensenada must file a crew list with a Mexican consulate before entering Mexican waters. All registration papers and other relevant documentation must also be on board.

Semarnap (☎ 619-233-6956), Mexico's ministry of the environment, natural resources and fisheries, maintains an office at 2550 5th Ave, Suite 101, San Diego, CA 92103, and can provide necessary forms and information. It's open 8 am to 2 pm weekdays only.

Mainland Mexico

An alternative to car travel between mainland Mexico and Baja is the ferry service across the Sea of Cortez. Boats sail between Santa Rosalía and Guaymas twice weekly and between La Paz and Topolobampo (near Los Mochis), and La Paz and Mazatlán daily.

Grupo Sematur de California, a Mexico-based conglomerate, has improved ferry services over the last few years, but fares have risen considerably, especially for vehicles. See La Paz in the Cape Region chapter and the Santa Rosalía entry in the Desierto Central to Llano de Magdalena chapter for schedule and fare information.

Note that if you bring a vehicle from Baja into mainland Mexico on a ferry, you will need a permit; see the Vehicle Permits entry in the Getting Around chapter for more information.

ORGANIZED TOURS

Green Tortoise (☎ 415-956-7500, 800-867-8647, tortoise@greentortoise.com), based out of San Francisco, operates its Baja Beach Daze tour from November to April. Sort of a hostel on wheels, Green Tortoise appeals to the young and adventurous who put camaraderie over comfort. Tours may be joined in San Francisco, Los Angeles or San Diego and run either nine or 14 days. The tours cover the length of the peninsula as far as La Paz, and stops include Ensenada, Bahía Concepción, San Ignacio and Mulegé, as well as lots of secluded beaches. The cost is US$329 (plus US$71 for food) for the nine-day trip and US$399 (plus US$91 for food) for the 14-day trip. Its Web site is at www.greentortoise.com.

Adventure Bus (☎ 909-797-7366, 888-737-5263, info@adventureplanet.com) offers its similar nine-day Baja Sun Safari from Los Angeles (with pickups in Orange County and San Diego) for US$329 plus US$75 for food. Departures are year round – twice monthly in winter and monthly otherwise.

Baja Discovery (☎ 619-262-0700, 800-829-2252, bajadis@aol.com), operating out of San Diego, offers several tours around Baja, including its popular four- to eight-day walking excursions. Other tours focus on special themes, such as whale-watching, missions, wildlife of the Sea of Cortez, or cave painting. Most last a week and cost from US$1495 to US$1795. Its Web site is at www.bajadiscovery.com/tours.

Baja California Tours (☎ 858-454-7166, 800-336-5454, fax 858-454-2703) in La Jolla, California, specializes in short-term guided tours to northern Baja, including Tijuana, Playas de Rosarito, Puerto Nuevo and Ensenada. A three-day/two-night package to Ensenada, for instance, starts at US$99 per person, including accommodations and transportation. It also offers themed specialty tours, often set around special events like wine festivals or bicycle races. Its Web site is at www.bajacaliforniatours.com.

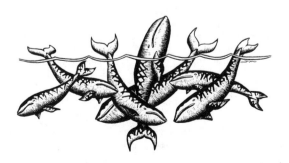

Getting Around

AIR

Three major domestic carriers and several smaller ones connect the airports at Tijuana, Mexicali, Loreto, La Paz and Los Cabos with mainland Mexico. In addition, Ensenada, Guerrero Negro and Isla Cedros have very limited commercial aviation. For details on what airlines serve which destinations, see Getting There & Away in the respective city sections.

For contact information for Aero California, AeroMéxico and Mexicana, which have direct flights within Baja California, to the mainland and to the USA, see the Getting There & Away chapter. Airfares are notoriously volatile, but in general, advance bookings – even for one-way flights – can yield significant savings. Promotional fares are common on competitive routes, such as Tijuana-Guadalajara, but available seats may be limited. In addition to IVA (the consumer tax, which is 10%), air tickets are subject to an airport tax of about US$12.50. Taxes are normally added to your quoted fare and paid when you buy the ticket.

Nearly every town and village in Baja California has an airstrip suitable for small private aircraft. Arnold Senterfitt's self-published *Airports of Baja California & Mainland Mexico* (US$49) provides details about every airstrip and airport on the peninsula. Though out of print, it is still available from Baja Bush Pilots (in the USA ☎ 480-730-3250, fax 480-730-3250, jack@bajabush.com), 1255 W Baseline, Suite 138, Mesa, AZ 85202, USA. This group's Web site, at www.bajabush.com, also contains information about landing fees, fuel prices, airport conditions, insurance, border crossings and other aspects of plane travel.

Another useful resource is Galen L Hanselman's *Air Baja! A Pilot's Guide to the Forgotten Peninsula* (US$49.95).

BUS

Air-conditioned buses operate daily between towns all along the Baja Peninsula. Most have on-board sanitary facilities (bring your own toilet paper), and amenities like videos, drinks and snacks are common on long-distance carriers. Some companies, like Norte de Sonora, offer *elite* services, which are more comfortable, faster and only slightly more expensive. ABC's similar Servicio Plus only operates in northern Baja.

Travel from top to bottom of the peninsula takes about 27 hours (with a change in La Paz), as buses stop in almost every town to drop off and pick up passengers. Tickets may not be reserved, but seats are assigned at the time of purchase. To guarantee one for long-distance trips, buy tickets a day or two before departure. There is no guarantee of a seat at intermediate stops, but it is rare *not* to get one, except around holidays. For long journeys, work out which side the sun will be on and sit on the other side; also try to avoid the back of the bus, which is where the toilets are and the ride is bumpier. Food at interim stops can be expensive and may not always be appealing, so you may want to bring some along.

Regional buses (some air-conditioned) also run frequently between La Paz and Cabo San Lucas (via San José del Cabo or Todos Santos), Tijuana and Ensenada, Tijuana and Playas de Rosarito, Tijuana and Mexicali (via Tecate), and Ensenada and San Felipe.

For fares and details, see the Getting There & Away entries in the respective city sections.

CAR

Car travel is usually more convenient than bus travel and often the only way to reach isolated towns, villages, mountains and beaches, but it is more expensive. To drive in Baja California, you need a valid US or Canadian driver's license or an International Driving Permit. See the Visas & Documents entry in the Facts for the Visitor chapter for more information.

Vehicle Permits

Ostensibly in an effort to curb the illegal sale of US vehicles in Mexico, Mexican Customs now requires anybody planning to take their car into mainland Mexico to obtain a *permiso de importación temporal de vehículos* (temporary vehicle import permit).

You do *not* need this permit if you'll be traveling in Baja California only, are staying within the 25 to 30km border zone in mainland Mexico or are traveling in Sonora (in which case you need a special Sonora Only permit). A caveat: While this information is correct at the time of writing, regulations have been known to change periodically, and we recommend checking with a Mexican consulate before leaving.

Permits may be obtained at the *aduana* (customs) office at any border crossing, in Ensenada or at the Pichilingue (La Paz) ferry terminal. Note that permits are not available at Santa Rosalía, the other Baja ferry port. If at all possible, we recommend obtaining your permit right at the border. The Tijuana-San Ysidro office is on the right-hand side of the border-post just beyond the crossing, but the less congested Mesa de Otay office is more expeditious.

The person importing the vehicle will need a passport (or proof of US or Canadian citizenship) and originals plus two photocopies of each of the following documents, which must all be in his/her own name:

• certificate of title for the vehicle
• current registration card
• driver's license (see Visas & Documents in the Facts for the Visitor chapter)

You will also need a major credit card or cash to pay a very large bond (see below). If the vehicle is not fully paid for, bring a notarized letter from the lender authorizing its use in Mexico for a specified period. If the vehicle is leased or rented, bring the original contract (plus a copy), which must be in the name of the person importing the car, and a notarized letter from the rental firm authorizing the driver to take it into Mexico. To find out which companies allow their cars to be taken south of the border, see Rental, later in this chapter.

One person cannot bring in two vehicles. If you have a motorcycle attached to your car, another adult traveling with you will need to obtain a permit for the motorcycle. If the motorcycle is registered in your name,

Paved in 1973, the Transpeninsular (México 1) stretches from Tijuana to Baja's southern tip.

you'll need a notarized affidavit authorizing the other person to take it into Mexico.

At Mexican Customs, you will be asked to fill out three forms: the 'temporary import permit' form, the 'vehicle return promise agreement' and the 'tourist card' (see Travel Permits in Facts for the Visitor). You will then be directed to a branch of the Banco del Ejército (also called Banjército; it's the army bank), which is usually nearby, where your credit card will be charged a fee (US$16.50 at the time of writing). Eventually someone at customs will put a sticker on your windshield and give you a permit (with another sticker) and your tourist card, stamped *'con automóvil.'* Make sure you get back the originals of all documents.

If you don't have an international credit card, you will have to deposit a *fianza* cash bond with the Banco del Ejército or an authorized Mexican *afianzadora* (bonding company). The amount depends on the age and make of your vehicle. For example, a 1998 compact (Honda, Volkswagen, etc) would require a bond of US$6000; a 1994 BMW comes in at US$12,000. There may be taxes and processing fees to pay too. This bond, plus interest, will be totally refunded when you leave Mexico.

When you do leave the country, you must have your permit canceled by the Mexican authorities. Drivers leaving a credit card deposit may exit at any border crossing, but those leaving a bond must exit by the same border crossing that they entered, in order to redeem the bond. Go to the Banjército office at the border, or one within the 20 to 30km border zone, and turn in the three forms mentioned earlier. If you leave Mexico without having the permit canceled, authorities will assume you've left your car in the country and start charging fines to your credit card.

Only the owner can take the vehicle out of Mexico. If it breaks down or is wrecked, you must obtain permission to leave it in the country from the Registro Federal de Vehículos in Mexico City or a *hacienda* (treasury department) office in another city. If you have to leave the country in an emergency, the vehicle can be stored temporarily at an airport or seaport, or with an aduana or hacienda office.

Insurance

Mexican law recognizes only Mexican *seguro* (car insurance), so a US or Canadian policy won't help. Driving in Mexico without Mexican insurance would be extremely foolish (see the boxed text 'In Case of a Car Accident'). At the very minimum, you should get liability insurance, although we recommend obtaining full coverage (collision, liability, fire, theft, glass, medical and legal).

Insurance offices are at every Baja border crossing, some of them open 24 hours a day. Some insurance companies also issue policies via fax and the Internet. Rates are government controlled and thus fairly standard on both sides of the border, but policies may also be arranged through representatives in the USA. Most major US insurance companies and automobile clubs (which usually require membership) can arrange coverage.

Prices depend on the age and make of your vehicle and the length of the insurance policy. For example, full coverage for a car valued between US$5000 and US$10,000 costs about US$12 a day; those valued between US$15,000 to US$20,000 are US$16. In general, the longer your stay, the cheaper the per-day rate. If you're planning on spending a lot of time in Baja (two weeks or more), you should consider an annual policy, which works out much cheaper (about US$150 for cars under US$10,000 or US$200 for cars under US$20,000).

Below is a list of some US-based companies offering Mexican insurance policies:

Applied Risk Insurance Services (☎ 619-296-4706, 800-654-7504, fax 619-296-4715) 3900 Harney St, Suite 250, San Diego, CA 92110. Offers home, business and legal services protection in addition to car insurance; open weekdays from 8 am to 5 pm.

Baja Bound (☎ 619-437-0404, 888-552-2252, fax 888-265-7834, administrator@bajabound.com) 2222 Coronado Ave, Suite H, San Diego, CA 92154. Offers car, boat and aircraft insurance in person, by fax or via the Internet. Office hours are 8:30 am to 4:30 pm weekdays. Its information-packed Web site is at www.bajabound.com.

Borderline Insurance (☎ 619-428-0095, 800-332-2118) 2004 Dairy Mart Rd, Suite 103, San Ysidro, CA 92073. Provides car insurance and tourist information on weekdays from 9 am to 5 pm.

Instant Mexico Insurance Services (☎ 619-428-4714, 800-345-4701, fax 619-690-6533) 223 Via de San Ysidro, San Ysidro, CA 92173. Open 24 hours a day for car insurance, tourist information, currency exchange, maps, tourist cards, and fishing and boat permits. It also issues policies over the phone.

International Gateway Insurance Brokers (☎ 619-422-3028, 800-423-2646) 3450 Bonita Rd, Suite 103, Chula Vista, CA 92013. Issues coverage for cars, aircraft, homes, RVs and motorcycles. Hours are 8:30 am to 5 pm weekdays and 9 am to noon on Saturday.

Lewis & Lewis Insurance Agency (☎ 310-657-7112, 800-966-6830, fax 310-652-5849) 8929 Wilshire Blvd, Suite 220, Beverly Hills, CA 90211. Handles only annual policies.

Mex-Insur (☎ 619-428-1121) US Interstate 5 at the Via de San Ysidro exit, San Ysidro, CA 92173, and (☎ 619-425-2390) US Interstate 805 at F St & Bonito Rd, Chula Vista, CA 91910. Arranges car, RV, airplane and boat insurance and also provides information.

Oscar Padilla Mexican Insurance (☎ 619-550-1122, 800-258-8600, fax 619-550-1130) 4330 La Jolla Village Dr, Suite 110, San Diego, CA 92122. This is California's oldest and largest Mexican insurer, with a full line of insurance plans. There are two offices at the border in San Ysidro and one in Calexico.

Sanborn's Insurance (☎ 956-686-3601, 800-222-0158, fax 956-686-0732, info@sanbornsinsurance.com) 2009 S 10th St, McAllen, TX 78503. Sanborn's has been in business since 1948 and sells insurance via phone, fax, Internet or in person. Its Web site is at www.sanbornsinsurance.com.

Fuel

All *gasolina* (gasoline) and diesel fuel in Mexico is sold by the government-owned, Pemex (Petróleos Mexicanos) at gas stations all along the Transpeninsular; in some towns, private individuals also sell fuel out of drums, usually at a considerable markup. Almost all gas stations accept only cash, although there are apparently some newer ones that also take credit cards.

All gasoline is *sin plomo* (unleaded) and comes in both Magna Sin, equivalent to US regular unleaded, and Premium, equivalent

Gas Pump Scams

A few gas stations are now self-service, most notably the 24-hour one north of El Rosario, but most stations along the Transpeninsular still have pump attendants (who expect tips). While most stations are trustworthy, there are a variety of scams out there to guard against.

Check that the pump registers '0 pesos' to start with, and be quick to check afterward that you have been given the amount you requested – the attendants often reset the pump before you get a chance to look at the total, then charge you whatever amount they feel like. Your best protection is to get out of the car, open the gas tank yourself, and then watch the entire operation from start to finish.

When buying fuel, it's better to ask for a peso amount than to say *lleno* (full) – lleno usually finishes with fuel gushing down the side of your car. When paying, try to give the attendant the exact amount you are charged or risk getting shortchanged. If you protest, the person will simply claim that you gave them a smaller note than you actually did.

to US super unleaded. Diesel fuel is also widely available; regular diesel has a higher sulfur content than US diesel, but a newer 'Diesel Sin' has less sulfur than before. If diesel drivers change their oil and filter about every 3500km, they should have no problems.

In central Baja (south of El Rosario to Loreto), it's a good idea to top up your tank at every gas station you pass. Occasionally, massive caravans of 20 or more RVs can deplete supplies, particularly at isolated stations like the one at Cataviña in the Desierto Central. Carrying at least a 5-gallon (23-liter) spare can will also keep you out of trouble, especially if you're planning on doing any off-road traveling.

Service

The Mexican tourism ministry, Secture, maintains a network of *Ángeles Verdes* (Green Angels) – bilingual mechanics in green uniforms and green trucks who patrol

In Case of a Car Accident

Two points cannot be stressed often enough:

• Do *not* drive in Baja California without Mexican insurance.

• Do *not* drive while drunk or under the influence of drugs.

Adhering to this advice will make your life a lot less complicated if you are involved in an accident – regardless of whether you are at fault or not.

If you're in an accident, you and the other parties should wait at the scene until the police arrive. In case of minor damage, it's not very likely that you'll be arrested and detained – unless, of course, you are intoxicated or without insurance. In an ideal scenario, the parties will be asked to arrive at a settlement of the damages, and you and your vehicle will be released on the spot. Contact your insurance company before signing any agreement.

If a settlement cannot be reached, the damage is significant and/or there are injuries, you will most likely be detained, and your vehicle impounded, while responsibility is assessed. You will be asked to make a statement. While you have the right to refuse to make a statement, this is not a good idea. You should, however, ask for a lawyer to be present, as well as an interpreter if your Spanish isn't great. Under Mexican law, you have the right to both. If you don't know a lawyer, call your consulate for a referral.

Determining responsibility can take weeks or even months. Except in the case of fatalities, it may be possible to be released on bail, as long as you can ensure that you will pay restitution to the victims – plus fines, towing costs and other expenses – should you be found guilty. This is where your insurance comes in especially handy, as it serves as a payment guarantee. And, of course, you lose the right to bail if you were driving while intoxicated.

For more on the Mexican justice system, see Legal Matters in the Facts for the Visitor chapter.

major stretches of highway daily during daylight hours looking for motorists in trouble. They make minor repairs, replace small parts, provide fuel and oil, and arrange towing and other assistance by radio if necessary. Service is free; parts, gasoline and oil are provided at cost. Patrols are said to be most prevalent in the northernmost and southernmost stretches of the highway, but we've never actually seen them.

If you are near a telephone when your car has problems, you can call the patrols on their 24-hour hotline in Mexico City (☎ 5-250-82-21) or through the national 24-hour tourist assistance numbers in Mexico City (☎ 5-250-01-23, 01-800-903-92-00).

Most serious mechanical problems can be fixed efficiently and inexpensively by mechanics in Baja's towns and cities if the parts are available. On the other hand, don't expect miracles if your problems are linked to state-of-the-art computerized systems or other features foreign to Mexican mechanics. Volkswagens (without fuel-injection engines) are the most common cars and thus the easiest to have repaired in Baja.

Because Baja's notoriously bad roads take a heavy toll on tires, *llanteras* (tire repair shops) are ubiquitous, even in many out-of-the-way spots. However, they cannot work miracles on a tire that's been shredded by sharp rocks or other hazards, so avoid driving too fast. Ordinary llanteras, especially those in remote areas, may have only a limited selection of spares. Other than major cities like Tijuana, Ensenada, Mexicali and La Paz, the best places to buy tires along the Transpeninsular are Guerrero Negro, Santa Rosalía and Ciudad Constitución.

Road Conditions

In towns and cities, beware of *alto* (stop) signs, potholes and *topes* (speed bumps). Wide one-way streets in Tijuana, for example, are infamous for stop signs placed on one street corner or the other, but not on both. Consequently, drivers in the far-left lane may not see a stop sign on the right corner until they are already in the intersection. Sometimes stop signs are not posted on corners but painted in bold letters on the street just before the intersection, and drivers looking at the corner can miss the painted letters. Driving slowly and carefully should eliminate the danger of overlooking stop signs.

Speed-bump signs, speed bumps and potholes can also be easy to miss until it's too late, but highway driving has its own set of problems and challenges (see the boxed text 'A Few Words of Advice'). The toll portion (México 1D) of the Transpeninsular between Tijuana and Ensenada is the best-maintained highway in Baja – four lanes wide, smooth and fast, with spectacular coastal views. Baja's other highways offer equally spectacular scenery – multicolored desert landscapes, dark, craggy volcanoes, verdant valleys and vineyards – but the landscape can distract your attention from sharp curves and narrow lanes.

Off-Highway Driving

Thousands of miles of rough dirt roads and tracks crisscross Baja's backcountry. Many unpaved roads are graded and passable even for ordinary passenger vehicles, but others require a 4WD vehicle with high clearance. Sharp stones and other hazards can shred even heavy-duty tires, forcing wise drivers to travel at much slower speeds than on paved roads. In such circumstances, Mexican drivers regularly deflate their tires, to as little as 20 or 22lbs per square inch, in order to avoid punctures and smooth out the rough surfaces. This obviously reduces fuel efficiency, but gas is cheaper than a set of new tires.

Make sure your vehicle is in excellent condition; some areas are so isolated that getting stuck can be dangerous. Heat, drought, rain,

---

A Few Words of Advice

Traveling the Transpeninsular requires a lot of heightened awareness behind the wheel and one all-important purchase: Mexican car insurance. An uninsured accident anywhere in Mexico can easily land you in jail with all the attendant horrors. Don't forget this, as the roads present many tricky turns – so to speak.

First off, most of the highway is only the width of a country road, which provides little margin for error. Potholes can be real axle busters, and animals – including burros and cows – can pop up around any corner. Large debris is also a frequent menace, and many drivers will often signal this problem ahead of you by waving their hands downwards, which means you should slow down.

When you approach a large, slow-moving truck from behind, the driver will frequently throw on the left-turn signal, indicating that it's safe for you to pass. Just remember that you're relying on someone else's judgment; when you accelerate to pass the driver, make sure the person is not actually signaling to turn left!

Night on the roads of Baja is like the witching hour – sinister and with amplified mayhem. Either don't drive at all or do so like a nun with a load of school children.

As you're driving along the Transpeninsular, you'll pass numerous black-and-white signs bearing safety instructions and admonishments. In case your Spanish isn't up to it, here's a quick translation of some of the more common ones:

Cuida Su Vida, Maneje Con Precaución	Protect Your Life, Drive with Caution
No Rebase con Raya Continua	Don't Drive with Your Lights On
Por Su Seguridad Disminuye La Velocidad	Decrease Speed for Your Safety
Precaución Zona de Ganado	Careful: Cattle Zone
Si Toma No Maneje	Don't Drink and Drive
Utilice Cinturón de Seguridad	Use Your Seatbelt

Lastly, when you're back north of the border, change that air filter, as the dust of village and field will have given your new SUV a choking case of automotive emphysema.

flash floods and snakes are among the hazards that may bedevil an unprepared driver. Essentials for excursions off paved highways include water, extra fuel, a first-aid kit, flashlight (torch), tools, flares, matches and a disposable lighter, and sleeping bags.

One way to avoid trouble is by checking conditions with the locals before setting out. Roads often deteriorate quickly, especially after rains, and what was an easy, if bumpy, ride last week, may have become impassable. If you've already headed out and find conditions questionable, turn back. Some travelers may prefer to form an informal convoy with other vehicles.

For more information, consult the *Baja California Guidebook* by the Automobile Club of Southern California, which also publishes a detailed map of Baja that shows almost every off-road route described in the book (also see Maps in the Facts for the Visitor chapter).

Police & Military Checkpoints

Road travelers should expect occasional roadblocks set up by armed police or military personnel to check vehicles for drugs, weapons or illegal migrants. Many checkpoints will have a red flag marker and are operated by uniformed officials; however, others are unmarked and manned by police/military officers in civilian clothing.

Intimidating as this may seem, these stops usually just involve answering a few questions before you'll be waived through. Occasionally, however, officials will insist on searching your car, trailer or RV. These inspections can be anything from cursory to complete. Sometimes, the searches seem to be motivated by curiosity: Many of these men are young soldiers from rural parts of Mexico and are unaccustomed to seeing equipment, clothes and other gear from the US or other parts of the world.

Your best strategy is to be cooperative and courteous. Some travelers say that establishing a rapport helps in speeding up the process; offering a cold Coca-Cola apparently goes a long way in some cases. But there have also been many authenticated cases of Mexican police planting drugs on unsuspecting tourists, then demanding exorbitant bribes to let them go. If you are driving alone and they ask to see the trunk of your car, lock the front doors (as inconspicuously as possible, to avoid angering them).

At the time of writing, travelers reported checkpoints just north of La Paz, halfway between Loreto and Mulegé, just north of San Ignacio, in Guerrero Negro and in Maneadero, but these are subject to change any time.

La Mordida

Officially, no policeman is authorized to accept money, and all traffic fines should be paid at the police station or by mail. Historically, however, Mexico has been notorious for *la mordida* (literally 'the bite,' or bribe). The most frequent opportunity for the mordida is a traffic violation, such as speeding, driving the wrong way on a one-way street or running a stop sign. Realists do not expect the mordida to disappear from Mexican life any time soon, but petty harassment of tourists for minor matters seems to be declining.

If you get pulled over, you can either try to pay the bribe and get on with your day, or you can argue the validity of the citation. Some people simply pretend not to understand, let alone speak, any Spanish in the hopes that the officers become exasperated enough to just let them go. Insisting on going to the police station to pay the fine can also be a deterrent, especially if you've been pulled over for no good reason. If you end up going to the station, be sure to get a receipt.

If, however, you are willing to pay the bribe, don't offer money to police officers directly; it's illegal. One strategy is to tell officers that, if they forgive you, you will be extremely grateful (*'Si me perdona, se lo podría agradecer'*). Sometimes officers will signal their willingness to take a bribe, but this too is usually done in a roundabout way, for instance, by saying: 'Are you a friend of President Jackson?' (Jackson is featured on the US$20 bill.)

Rental

Auto rental in Mexico is expensive by US or European standards, but it can be worthwhile if you want to visit several places in a short time and have three or four people to share the cost. It can also be useful for getting off the beaten track, where public transport is scarce or nonexistent.

Cars can be rented in most of Baja's cities and resorts, at airports and sometimes at bus and train stations. Most big hotels can also arrange a car. Sometimes it's necessary to book a few days ahead.

Renters must have a valid driver's license (US and Canadian licenses are accepted; everyone else should bring an international driver's license as well as their national license), passport and major credit card. You are usually required to be at least 23 (sometimes 25) years old. Sometimes age 21 is acceptable, but you may have to pay more.

In addition to the basic daily or weekly rental rate, you must pay for insurance, tax and fuel. Ask exactly what the insurance covers – sometimes it covers only minimal liability insurance of, say, US$200, which would put you in big trouble in case of an accident (see the boxed text earlier in this chapter). In such situations, you should purchase additional liability or comprehensive insurance.

Most agencies offer a choice between a per-kilometer deal or unlimited kilometers. The latter is usually preferable if you intend to do some hard driving. Local firms are sometimes cheaper than the big international ones. You can usually find a Volkswagen Beetle – often the cheapest car available – for around US$40 a day with unlimited kilometers and including insurance and tax, and you can often get a weekly rate equivalent to six single days. The extra charge for drop-off in another city, when available, is usually about US$0.30 per kilometer.

You can book cars in Mexico through the large international agencies, which may get you lower rates. Here's contact information for some major firms operating in Mexico (☎ US, ☎ Mexico):

Avis (☎ 800-331-1084, ☎ 800-288-88-88)
www.avis.com
Budget (☎ 800-472-3325, ☎ 800-700-17-00)
www.drivebudget.com
Dollar (☎ 800-800-4000, N/A)
www.dollar.com
Europcar (N/A, ☎ 800-003-95-00)
www.europcar.com
Hertz (☎ 800-654-3001, ☎ 800-709-50-00)
www.hertz.com
Thrifty (☎ 800-847-4389, ☎ 800-021-22-77)
www.thrifty.com

No agency in Baja allows its cars to be taken to the US, but some US-based agencies do permit their rental cars to be taken into Mexico provided you buy supplemental Mexican car insurance.

Avis and Dollar allow their vehicles to be driven anywhere on the peninsula if cars are rented from certain locations, including the airports in San Diego and Los Angeles. The supplemental insurance is US$18 and US$25 per day, respectively.

Budget allows you to take a car 200 miles down the peninsula and charges US$20 a day for insurance. Cars may be rented from any Budget office. Hertz may allow it, but only if the car is rented from an office in Orange County or San Diego. Permission to take the car into Mexico is granted at the time of pick-up, not at the time of reservation.

MOTORCYCLE

Traveling Baja California's paved roads and highways by motorcycle is fast, thrilling and economical, but recommended only for experienced drivers. The challenges of traveling by car in Baja become dangers on a motorcycle. A good helmet and protective clothing are essential because the graveled, potholed roads can easily cause a spill.

Exercise extreme caution on corners, especially those that are marked *¡Peligro!* (Danger!) – gasoline often sloshes out of Pemex trucks on curves and makes the roads slippery. Livestock on the road can also pose a serious hazard.

Carry extra water and food if traveling alone, because if you have mechanical problems on an isolated stretch of road, you should avoid leaving your bike unattended. Many street bikes are not suitable for off-road riding. Parts are scarce, although street mechanics are geniuses at repair and improvisation.

Note that one person cannot take two vehicles into Mexico (including a car with a motorcycle in tow). See the Car section, earlier, for permit information and additional tips on driving in Baja.

BICYCLE

Bicycling is an increasingly popular way to tour Baja. If you are bringing your bicycle to Baja California, check for wear and tear before you arrive and fill your repair kit with every imaginable spare part. As with cars and motorcycles, you won't necessarily be able to buy that crucial gismo for your machine when it breaks down somewhere in the back of beyond.

In northern Baja, annual summer races and recreational rides on the paved routes between Tecate and Ensenada, and Playas de Rosarito and Ensenada, attract more and more people, mostly mainland Californians.

Many others ride the entire length of the peninsula, occasionally solo, but such a trip requires a tent, sleeping bag, flashlight (torch), tools, spare tubes and tires, food, several water jugs, a first-aid kit and other supplies. Cyclists should be in top physical shape, have excellent equipment and be prepared to handle their own repairs, even in the middle of nowhere. Small towns and villages often have bicycle mechanics, but they may lack replacement parts for complex repairs.

Racing bicycles are suitable for paved roads like the Transpeninsular, but potholes are numerous and highway shoulders are very steep and narrow; even though most Mexican drivers are courteous to cyclists,

there are likely to be anxious moments when an 18-wheeler blows by at 70mph (112km/h). On the graveled or dirt roads that crisscross much of the peninsula, a mountain bike *(todo terreno)* is a much better choice, but even then thorns are a major hazard to bicycle tires.

Bicycles can travel by air. You can take them apart and put them in a bike bag or box, but it's much easier to simply wheel your bike to the check-in desk, where it should be treated as a piece of baggage. You may have to remove the pedals and turn the handlebars sideways so that it takes up less space in the aircraft's hold. Check all this with the airline well in advance, preferably before you pay for your ticket.

One of our readers also reports that it's possible to take bicycles aboard long-distance buses, although this seems to depend on where you're boarding the bus. A small fee may be charged.

All the major cities in Baja California have sporting-good and department stores that sell bicycles. Places to rent them are rare, except at some tourist resorts (noted throughout the book).

HITCHHIKING

Hitchhiking is never entirely safe in any country, and we don't recommend it. Travelers who decide to hitchhike should understand that they are taking a small but serious risk. You're not likely to be able to identify the local rapist/murderer before you get into his vehicle. Hitchhiking is definitely not advisable for single women, but anyone can fall into a difficult or unpleasant situation.

If you choose to hitchhike, keep in mind that temperatures in the desert can plunge at night, and being stranded can be dangerous. Expect long waits, and carry sun protection in addition to warm, windproof clothing. A water bottle and snack food are imperative. Displaying your destination on a readable sign is a good idea.

LOCAL TRANSPORTATION
Bus

Generally known as *camiones,* local buses are the cheapest way to get around cities and to nearby villages. In Baja California, they exist in Tijuana, Ensenada, San Quintín, Mexicali, La Paz and Los Cabos. They run everywhere, frequently, and are cheap (about US$0.50). Most buses are surprisingly modern, clean and uncrowded.

Taxi

Every large town and city in Baja California has taxi service. Most taxis are private, with government-regulated fares, though haggling over fares is still the rule. In Tijuana, Loreto, San José del Cabo and Cabo San Lucas, you will also find bright-yellow, government-run minivans called Aeroterrestre taxis, which provide transportation to and from major airports; fares are government-controlled and not subject to bargaining.

Route taxis are an efficient and inexpensive way to get around town. They are station wagons that operate along designated routes, just like city buses, only slightly more expensive and much faster. The cars are painted in particular colors corresponding to their routes; the destination is also painted on the body of the vehicle and/or on the windshield. You can board them at their designated route terminus or after flagging them down. The driver will stop wherever you want to get off.

La Frontera

La Frontera is that part of Baja California (Norte) corresponding roughly to the Dominican mission frontier. It's also the area most heavily frequented by visitors from

Highlights

- Soaking up Baja history at the Museo de las Californias in Tijuana
- Browsing for crafts, furniture and art in Tijuana's Bazar de México or in Playas de Rosarito
- Catching the perfect wave south of Playas de Rosarito
- Camping under the stars in Parque Nacional Constitución de 1857 or Sierra San Pedro Mártir
- Feasting on lobster without breaking the bank in Puerto Nuevo
- Sailing into port in San Quintín with a fat catch of the day

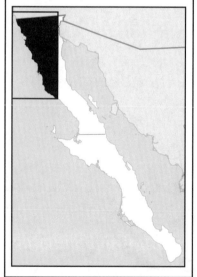

north of the border. For mainland Californians who view its cities and beaches as centers of hedonism, La Frontera is undeniably a playground. But this superficial image hides a more complex and interesting reality.

The Mexican federal government's *fideicomiso*, a 30-year bank trust, eased restrictions on property ownership and promoted the construction of resort complexes and time-share condominiums along the coast. Some US citizens also find Baja's low rents attractive – substantial numbers of them rent Tijuana apartments at a fraction of the cost of comparable housing in San Diego and commute to jobs just across the border.

The border region is one of Mexico's fastest-growing, most innovative and most prosperous areas, and not only because of US influence. Tijuana and Mexicali are major cities and important manufacturing centers in their own right, while Mexicali's Río Colorado hinterland is, like mainland California's Imperial Valley, an important agricultural producer. Unlike most US cities, whose centers are virtually empty after dark, the border towns enjoy a lively street life in which the tawdry attractions of the *zonas de tolerancia* (literally 'zones of tolerance,' the Mexican equivalent of a red-light district) play only a minimal role.

Commerce is booming as well, due in part to foreign investors (mostly US and Japanese) who underwrite construction of new factories, commercial centers, shopping centers and housing complexes. Baja's duty-free status permits the sale of many imported goods at prices lower than those in the USA and attracts US, European, South Korean and Japanese manufacturers.

More than 40% of all *maquiladoras* (industrial assembly plants) in Mexico are in Baja California (Norte). In September 1999, the state had 1136 such factories – nearly all of them in the border region – employing roughly one million people (some 33.6% of the region's population). At these plants, raw materials or components for items like TV

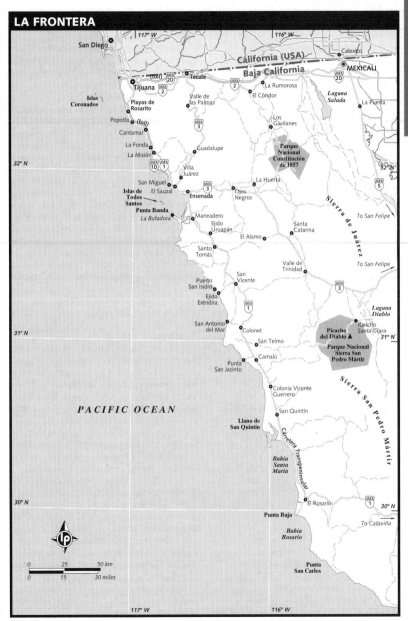

LA FRONTERA

117° W
116° W

San Diego

California (USA)
Baja California

Calexico

MEXICALI

Tijuana

(toll)

MEX 2D

Tecate

MEX 2

La Rumorosa

El Cóndor

MEX 2D

Islas Coronados

Playas de Rosarito

Valle de las Palmas

Los Gavilanes

Laguna Salada

La Puerta

Popotla (toll)

Cantamar

MEX 3

La Fonda

La Misión

Guadalupe

Parque Nacional Constitución de 1857

MEX 5

32° N

MEX 1D

MEX 1

Villa Juárez

32° N

San Miguel

El Sauzal

Ensenada

MEX 3

La Huerta

Islas de Todos Santos

Ojos Negros

Punta Banda

La Bufadora

Maneadero

Ejido Uruapán

Santa Catarina

Sierra de Juárez

To San Felipe

El Alamo

Santo Tomás

Valle de Trinidad

To San Felipe

Puerto San Isidro

San Vicente

MEX 3

Ejido Eréndira

MEX 1

Laguna Diablo

San Antonio del Mar

Colonet

Picacho del Diablo ▲

Rancho Santa Clara

31° N

San Telmo

Parque Nacional Sierra San Pedro Mártir

31° N

Camalú

PACIFIC OCEAN

Punta San Jacinto

Colonia Vicente Guerrero

Sierra San Pedro Mártir

San Quintín

Llano de San Quintín

Carretera Transpeninsular

30° N

Bahía Santa María

El Rosario

MEX 1

30° N

Punta Baja

To Cataviña

Bahía Rosario

0   25   50 km
0   15   30 miles

Punta San Carlos

117° W
116° W

sets and refrigerators can be imported duty free and then exported back to the USA with duty payable only on the value added to the original materials. Mexico's low labor costs – a fraction of those in the USA – are a major incentive to foreign investors.

This chapter follows the coast south from Tijuana to El Rosario with side trips to the wine regions of Valle de Guadalupe and Baja's two national parks, the Parque Nacional de Constitución de 1857 and the Parque Nacional Sierra de San Pedro Mártir. It then hooks back north to the border town of Tecate, en route to Mexicali, which is covered in the next chapter.

TIJUANA

For all its modern stresses, burgeoning population and seeming inability to deal effectively with drug and infrastructure problems, Tijuana (population two million) is a fun city where you can take an easy, quick dip into Mexican culture. It still suffers from an exaggerated, largely outdated reputation as a tawdry booze-and-sex border town, a gaudy place whose curio stores overflow with kitschy souvenirs like wrought-iron birdcages and ceramic burros. That Tijuana still exists, but the developing cityscape of modern office buildings, housing developments and maquiladoras marks Baja California's largest border city as a place of increasing sophistication.

These days, Tijuana is thriving and suffering simultaneously. Newcomers from more impoverished areas of Mexico stream in for job opportunities, mostly in maquiladoras (though many, of course, opt to try their luck in the US, illegally crossing the border as undocumented immigrants). Since 1994, more than 300,000 new jobs have been created in Tijuana; the city's growth rate of 6% is more than three times the national average.

But more people also generate more problems. The city is bursting at its seams and providing even basic infrastructures like housing, drinking water and education is becoming increasingly difficult. In some colonias (districts and neighborhoods), residents inhabit hillside dwellings of scrap wood and cardboard, where retaining walls of worn tires keep the soil from washing away during winter storms.

Nevertheless, for many residents – new and old – Tijuana is a city of hope. Thanks in part to its proximity to southern mainland California's large retail markets and the heavy influx of US tourists (up to 30 million a year), it is one of Mexico's most prosperous cities. San Diego traffic reports now include an obligatory mention of rush-hour delays at the border.

Tijuana has also become a major educational center, thanks to the growth of institutions like the Universidad Autónoma de Baja California and the Universidad Iberoamericana del Noroeste. The city's cultural importance also extends to the arts, an influence deriving in part from official institutions like the Centro Cultural Tijuana, as well as from independent individuals and groups. Meanwhile, the city's inability to provide basic infrastructure – demand for Río Colorado water is expected to exceed supply by 2003 if a new aqueduct is not built – threatens to stop its economic and physical growth.

History

In colonial times, the area of Tijuana fell under the jurisdiction of Misión San Diego, Alta California, but with the secularization of the missions in 1832, the Kumiai neophytes of Punta Tía Juana became peons. Then, at the end of the Mexican-American War (1848), the newly relocated international border turned this modest rancho (rural settlement) into a port of entry overnight, but it remained a backwater even after the government opened a formal customs depot in 1874.

In 1889, the rancho was subdivided and Pueblo Zaragoza (Tijuana's official name until 1929) was created, but the population grew very slowly, to only 242 in 1900 and less than 1000 at the end of WWI. The fledgling city, however, drew upscale tourists from north of the border to facilities like the US-owned Tijuana Hot Springs Hotel and soon became a center for gambling, greyhound racing, boxing matches and cockfights. Bars and bordellos further 'diversified' the local economy.

In 1911, the forces of anarchist leader Ricardo Flores Magón's Partido Liberal (Liberal Party) tried to use Baja as a territorial foothold during the Mexican Revolution. After holding the town for six weeks, however, the indecisive rebels fled federal reinforcements. The intellectual Flores Magón, who remained in exile in Los Angeles where he edited a weekly newspaper, was later tried for espionage in the USA. Convicted on flimsy evidence, he died years later in prison in Leavenworth, Kansas.

After 1915, despite restrictive US wartime measures, Tijuana's tourist industry recovered, then positively flourished during Prohibition, when thirsty Americans flocked to Tijuana for alcohol, gambling and sex. During these years, the municipal administration paved streets, improved the water system, built schools and attracted industries like breweries, distilleries and even an aircraft factory (headed by the former Mexican President Abelardo Rodríguez, for whom Tijuana's international airport was named).

After Prohibition, President Lázaro Cárdenas outlawed casinos and prostitution: Tijuana's main casino became a high school, the Instituto Tecnológico Industrial Agua Caliente. But the Great Depression of the 1930s probably had a greater impact than executive intervention. As bankrupt US-owned businesses reverted to Mexican control and northern Baja became a customs-free zone, jobless Mexican returnees from the US remained in Tijuana rather than going back to their hometowns, doubling the city's population (to about 16,500) by 1940. The presently notorious borderside Colonia Libertad dates from this period.

During WWII, with the US Army absorbing nearly all able-bodied American men, the US and Mexican governments established the *bracero* (guest worker) program, allowing Mexican workers north of the border to alleviate serious labor shortages. This program, lasting until 1964, led to major growth in border-area commerce, and by 1960 Tijuana's population had grown tenfold to more than 180,000.

In each succeeding decade, the city's population has more or less doubled. Uncontrolled growth has brought serious social and environmental problems, as the municipal administration finds itself unable to keep up with demand for adequate housing, potable water and public health services for many parts of the city. Contamination of the Río Tijuana, which enters the USA west of the San Ysidro border crossing, is one of several major binational environmental issues.

Tijuana has never completely overcome its image as a paradise for sinners. During

The Porous Border

In recent years, the exploding job market in the border towns has brought hundreds of thousands of migrants from Mexico City and poorer states like Jalisco, Michoacán, Sinaloa and Sonora to the country's northern edge. Most find work in a maquiladora or elsewhere and settle down. But many use the region as a jumping-off point to the US.

In 1994, the Clinton administration initiated Operation Gatekeeper, a costly effort to curb illegal immigration. Stepped-up measures included a metal fence, a huge contingent of border patrol agents and sophisticated equipment such as floodlights, infrared scopes and movement-detecting ground sensors.

While these measures have certainly made life harder for potential border crossers, they have done little to seal off the flow of illegal immigrants. It is estimated that for every undocumented worker arrested, at least two manage to get through to the US. In San Diego alone, almost half a million people are caught each year.

Illegal immigration is big business. Many would-be illegal immigrants (called *pollos* or chickens) engage the services of a *coyote* or *pollero*. These smugglers charge as much as US$2000 for merely crossing the border, more for transportation to Los Angeles or elsewhere in California. Most coyotes operate as individuals, but others are part of highly organized gangs with members on both sides of the border.

and immediately after WWII, the city experienced probably its seamiest era as the infamous Avenida Revolución attracted US servicemen from nearby San Diego. In recent years, it has cleaned up its act considerably, though the Zona Norte at the northern end of Avenida Revolución retains some of the style (and substance) of the postwar era.

Most of 'La Revo,' though, now appeals to a younger crowd of US university students and their cohorts, who take advantage of Mexico's permissive drinking laws (the legal drinking age is 18 as opposed to 21 in the US) to party until dawn. At the same time, families feel more comfortable in the city's streets and stores than they did in former times.

Fans of Carlos Santana should note that as a child in the late 1950s, the musician got his start playing with local bands along this strip. Also of note, actress Rita Hayworth, born Margarita Cansino (albeit in New York), was discovered here in the early 1930s. A Hollywood bigwig saw her performing with her father in the local nightclubs as the 'Dancing Cansinos.'

Orientation

Tijuana parallels the US border for about 12 miles (19km). Downtown Tijuana is about a 10- to 15-minute walk southwest of the San Ysidro border crossing and features a regular grid pattern of north-south *avenidas* (avenues) and east-west *calles* (streets). Most streets have numbers that are more frequently used than their names. Avenida Revolución, five blocks to the east, is the city's main tourist-oriented artery; the parallel Avenida Constitución features shops and other businesses catering more to locals.

East of downtown, the Zona Río, Tijuana's new commercial center, flanks the Río Tijuana. Paseo de los Héroes, Via Poniente and Blvd Sánchez Taboada, the principal streets in this part of town, all parallel the river. Northeast of here, on a broad hilltop, is the new sector of Mesa de Otay, home to another border crossing, the airport, maquiladoras, residential neighborhoods and shopping areas.

Traffic along Paseo de los Héroes is regulated by several *glorietas* (traffic circles), each anchored by huge monuments. Going west to east, they are the Monument de la Raza, nicknamed 'Scissors' for its spiky shape; the monument to Aztec emperor Cuauhtémoc; the monument to Abraham Lincoln; and the monument to General Ignacio Zaragoza, a war hero during the French invasion of 1862.

Other important glorietas are located north of here along Avenida Independencia; one is dedicated to Mexican independence martyr Padre Miguel Hidalgo, while another features Diana, the goddess of hunting in Roman mythology.

West of downtown lie both spiffy suburbs and hillside shantytowns that are known as *asentamientos irregulars* (literally, irregular settlements). Formally, all Tijuana boroughs or neighborhoods are known as *colonias* (or sometimes as *fraccionamientos)*, and addresses are much easier to locate if one knows the name of the colonia.

A new numbering system for street addresses has created some confusion. Because most businesses still rely on the old system, this section generally uses the new system but also locates sites by their cross streets when any ambiguity exists. Another source of confusion is that some streets have more than one name, such as Paseo de Tijuana, also known as Avenida del Centenario.

Maps The maps in this book should suffice in most cases, but the tourist offices also hand out an adequate free map. If you're planning an extensive stay or want to look up specific streets, you will need to buy a more detailed map. These are available in bookstores and also at the Sanborn's department store on Avenida Revolución and Calle 8a (Hidalgo).

Choices include the Guías Urbanas *Tijuana* map, published by Mexicali's Ediciones Corona; the Guía Roji *Ciudad de Tijuana* map; and the commercial Guía T *Plano de la Ciudad de Tijuana*. Guía T also publishes a street atlas. All of these have shortcomings, but they're good enough for anyone but a cartographic perfectionist.

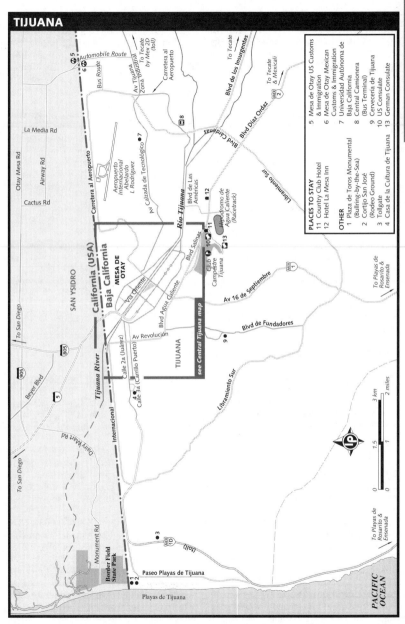

TIJUANA

see Central Tijuana map

PLACES TO STAY
11 Country Club Hotel
12 Hotel La Mesa Inn

OTHER
1 Plaza de Toros Monumental (Bullring-by-the-Sea)
2 Cortijo San José (Rodeo Ground)
3 Tollgate
4 Casa de la Cultura de Tijuana
5 Mesa de Otay US Customs & Immigration
6 Mesa de Otay Mexican Customs & Immigration
7 Universidad Autónoma de Baja California
8 Central Camionera (Bus Terminal)
9 Cervecería de Tijuana
10 US Consulate
13 German Consulate

Information

Tourist Offices Tijuana has several tourist offices at the border, downtown and in the Zona Río. If you need information prior to arrival, call ☎ 888-775-2417, which is the number for Cotuco (but also known as Fondo Mixto de Tijuana, or the Tijuana Tourism Board).

The Information Center at the border is operated by Cotuco (Comité de Turismo y Convenciones or Committee on Tourism & Conventions; ☎ 6-683-14-05) and is next to the yellow cabs (look for the totem pole). It's open 9 am to 7 pm Monday to Saturday and 10 am to 2 pm Sunday. The Cotuco head office (☎ 6-684-05-37, fax 6-684-77-82, info@ seetijuana.com), open to the public weekdays from 9 am to 6 pm, is at Paseo de los Héroes 9365, Suite 201, in the Zona Río. It also operates a kiosk, open sporadically, on Avenida Revolución between Calle 3a (Carrillo Puerto) and Calle 4a (Díaz Mirón).

Secture (Secretaría de Turismo del Estado; ☎ 6-688-05-55) has an office on Avenida Revolución at Calle 1a. It's open 8 am to 5 pm (from 10 am on weekends) and has friendly, English-speaking staff. The Tourist Assistance Office (☎ 6-688-05-05), which helps if you have a legal problem, is also here.

Money Everyone accepts (even prefers) US dollars. Numerous *casas de cambio* will change money and traveler's checks at almost any hour. Banks, though slower and more bureaucratic, offer slightly better rates; most also have ATMs. Beware of cambios on the US side, some of which advertise 'no commission' on exchanges of pesos for US dollars but charge up to 8% for converting US dollar cash or traveler's checks into pesos. Change money on the Mexican side instead.

There's also a cambio at the Central Camionera, Tijuana's long-distance bus station; the ATM at the Terminal Turística Tijuana at Avenida Revolución 1025 dispenses dollars.

Post & Communications Tijuana's main post office is at the corner of Avenida Negrete and Calle 11a (Calles). Hours are 8 am to 7 pm weekdays and 9 am to 3 pm weekends, though some services stop earlier.

Tijuana has many Ladatel public telephones and long-distance offices both downtown and in the outskirts. The Central Camionera has several booths with an operator in attendance and a public fax machine as well.

There's an Internet cafe right off Avenida Revolución at Calle 8a (Hidalgo) and another in a mini-mall at Blvd Sánchez Taboada 4002 (look for Sam's Club). Expect to pay about US$5 per hour.

Internet Resources The following are a few Web sites – all in English – with more or less accurate and up-to-date information about Tijuana:

Tijuana Tourism Trust Official tourism site with comprehensive information about hotels, restaurants, sightseeing, events and services. www.seetijuana.com

Baja Life On-line Commercial site with nightlife, restaurant and hotel listings, as well as information about car insurance and other business services. www.bajalife.com/tijuana

Tijuana.com Commercial site that's fairly up to date if not too comprehensive. www.tijuana.com.

Travel Agencies One of Tijuana's most respected travel agencies is Viajes Honold's (☎ 6-688-11-11, fax 6-688-38-00), Avenida Revolución 828 at Calle 2a (Juárez). Many others are downtown and in the Zona Río.

Bookstores Sanborn's (☎ 6-688-14-62), at Avenida Revolución and Calle 8a (Hidalgo), is a venerable Mexican department store chain that also has a good book department and the city's best selection of international magazines.

Librería El Día (☎ 6-684-09-08), Blvd Sánchez Taboada 10050 in the Zona Río, has books on Mexican history and culture, though none in English.

Cultural Centers An imposing neoclassical brick building (in the former Escuela Alvaro Obregón from 1929) houses the Casa de la Cultura de Tijuana (☎ 6-687-26-04) on pleasant grounds at Calle Lisboa 5 about 1 mile (1.6km) west of Avenida Revolución.

It presents lectures, art exhibitions and film festivals; its small Café Literarío is open 1 to 8 pm weekdays. Take any blue-and-white taxi (marked 'Colonia Altamira') westbound from Calle 3a (Carrillo Puerto) or walk up Calle 4a (Díaz Mirón); instead of the busy street, go up the hillside staircase for fine city views.

Tijuana's most important cultural center is the Centro Cultural Tijuana (Cecut); see the separate entry later this chapter. The delightful El Lugar de Nopal (see Cafes under Entertainment, later) is a good place for checking out the local cultural scene.

Medical & Emergency Services Tijuana's Hospital General (☎ 6-684-09-22) is north of the river on Avenida Padre Kino. For an ambulance, call the Cruz Roja (Red Cross; ☎ 066). Many clinics also cater to US visitors.

The central police station (☎ 060) is at Avenida Constitución 1616; the fire station (☎ 068) is next door.

Dangers & Annoyances Ain't no lie: The air quality in Tijuana on any given day will knock a buzzard off a shit wagon. The Mexican genius in the arts, astronomy and cuisine is only equaled by their unerring ability to disable any catalytic converter ever devised by humankind. Sleep well away from main traffic thoroughfares, and be aware that your migraine isn't solely due to last night's margarita.

'Coyotes' and *polleros* (smugglers) and their clients *(pollos)* (undocumented border-crossers) congregate along the Río Tijuana west of the San Ysidro border crossing. After dark, avoid this area and also Colonia Libertad, east of the crossing.

The Zona Norte, Tijuana's seedy red-light district west of Avenida Revolución and north of Calle 1a (Artículo 123), is not recommended for foreigners lacking street savvy, at least after dark. City officials prefer not to dwell on its continued existence, but the area is still of sufficient economic importance such that authorities cannot, or will not, eradicate it. Neon-lit Calle Coahuila is

especially notorious for its street prostitution and hardcore clubs.

Theft and pickpocketing are not uncommon in Tijuana. If you are the victim of a crime, you can call the state government's tourist protection number at ☎ 6-688-05-55.

La Revo

Virtually every visitor to Tijuana has to experience at least a brief stroll up raucous Avenida Revolución, also known as 'La Revo,' between Calle 1a (Artículo 123) and Calle 8a (Hidalgo). It's a mishmash of nightclubs, bellowing hawkers outside seedy strip bars, brash taxi drivers, tacky souvenir stores, street photographers with zebra-striped burros, discount liquor stores and restaurants. If you're walking north to south but find the sensory assault from high-tech sound systems too overwhelming to return the same way, try the more conventional shopping street of Avenida Constitución, paralleling La Revo one block west.

Oddly baroque in style, **Frontón Palacio Jai Alai** was begun in 1926 but not completed until 1947. This striking Tijuana landmark fronts almost the entire block of Avenida Revolución between Calle 7a (Galeana) and Calle 8a (Hidalgo). For decades it hosted the fast-moving ball game of *jai alai* – kind of a hybrid between squash and tennis, originating from Basque (in northern Spain). But alas, the game's obscurity and lack of attendance forced the owner to close down the operation. The building's future is pending, but it may be turned into a general events arena.

The **Bazar de México** (☎ 6-638-47-37) at Calle 7a (Galeana) is an interesting showcase of arts and crafts from around Mexico. This is, hands-down, the best place for buying crafts in Tijuana. You can watch many of the artisans at work, like Alberto, the Zapotec Indian who weaves intricate rugs, or the guitar maker from Michoacán. Other products include wood masks from the state of Guerrero, crêpe flowers from Jalisco and silver from Taxco. Everything's for sale, of course, but vendors will not hustle you. Bargaining is OK, but quality is high and prices are not as inflated as in other stores.

LA FRONTERA

CENTRAL TIJUANA

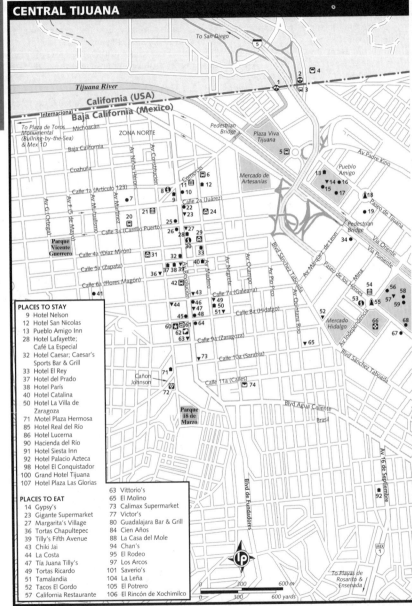

To San Diego

Tijuana River

California (USA)
Baja California (Mexico)

Internacional
Michoacán

To Plaza de Toros
Monumental
(Bullring-by-the-Sea)
& Mex 1D

Baja California

ZONA NORTE

Coahuila

Pedestrian
Bridge

Plaza Viva
Tijuana

Mercado de
Artesanías

Av Padre Kino

Pueblo
Amigo

Paseo de Tijuana

Calle 1a (Artículo 123)

Calle 2a (Juárez)

Parque
Vicente
Guerrero

Calle 3a (Carrillo Puerto)

Calle 4a (Díaz Mirón)

Calle 5a (Zapata)

Calle 6a (Flores Magón)

Calle 7a (Galeana)

Calle 8a (Hidalgo)

Mercado
Hidalgo

Calle 9a (Zaragoza)

Calle 10a (Sarabia)

Cañón
Johnson

Calle 11a (Calles)

Blvd Agua Caliente

Brasil

Parque
18 de
Marzo

Blvd de Fundadores

Pedestrian
Bridge

Vía Oriente
Vía Poniente

Paseo de los Héroes

Blvd Sánchez Taboada

To Playas de
Rosarito &
Ensenada

Av 16 de Septiembre

MEX
1

0   300   600 m
0   300   600 yards

PLACES TO STAY

9   Hotel Nelson
12 Hotel San Nicolas
13 Pueblo Amigo Inn
28 Hotel Lafayette;
     Café La Especial
32 Hotel Caesar; Caesar's
     Sports Bar & Grill
33 Hotel El Rey
37 Hotel del Prado
38 Hotel París
40 Hotel Catalina
50 Hotel La Villa de
     Zaragoza
71 Motel Plaza Hermosa
85 Hotel Real del Río
86 Hotel Lucerna
90 Hacienda del Río
91 Hotel Siesta Inn
92 Hotel Palacio Azteca
98 Hotel El Conquistador
100 Grand Hotel Tijuana
107 Hotel Plaza Las Glorias

PLACES TO EAT

14 Gypsy's
23 Gigante Supermarket
27 Margarita's Village
36 Tortas Chapultepec
39 Tilly's Fifth Avenue
43 Chiki Jai
44 La Costa
47 Tía Juana Tilly's
49 Tortas Ricardo
51 Tamalandia
52 Tacos El Gordo
57 California Restaurante

63   Vittorio's
65   El Molino
73   Calimax Supermarket
77   Victor's
80   Guadalajara Bar & Grill
84   Cien Años
88   La Casa del Mole
94   Chan's
95   El Rodeo
97   Los Arcos
101 Saverio's
104 La Leña
105 El Potrero
106 El Rincón de Xochimilco

CENTRAL TIJUANA

ENTERTAINMENT
10 Hard Rock Café
15 Cafe del Mundo
16 Señor Frog's
17 Zoo'll
25 El Torito Pub
26 Iguanas-Ranas
41 El Lugar de Nopal
45 Las Pulgas
59 Multicinemas Río
69 Cinepolis Rio
82 ZKA
83 Baby Rock
103 Cinema Las Torres Plus

OTHER
1 Mexican Customs & Immigration
2 US Customs & Immigration
3 Intercalifornias Buses
4 San Diego Trolley Station
5 Border Bus Terminal
6 Downtown Bus Terminal
7 Mercado Municipal
8 Secture Tourist Office
11 Museo de Cera
18 Monument to Diana (the Huntress)
19 Palacio Municipal
20 Buses to Playas de Tijuana
21 Galeria de Arte de la Ciudad
22 Viajes Honold's
24 Route Taxis to Central Camionera
29 Route Taxis to Playas de Rosarito
30 Cotuco Tourist Office
31 Route Taxis along Blvd Agua Caliente
34 Aerolíneas Internacionales
35 Monument to Padre Miguel Hidalgo

42 Terminal Turístico
46 Bazar de México
48 Frontón Palacio Jai Alai
53 Cotuco Head Office
54 Centro Cultural Tijuana (Cecut);
   Museo de las Californias;
   Cine Planetario
55 Monumento de la Raza
56 Aero California
58 AeroMéxico
60 Police Station; Fire Station
61 Internet Cafe
62 French Consulate
64 Sanborn's Department Store,
   Bar & Restaurant
66 Plaza Fiesta Mall: Mi Barra; Monte
   Picacho; Ah Jijo; Bar Sótano Suizo;
   La Sonrisa Bakery; Lo Ma' Bonita
67 Plaza de Zapato
68 Dorian's
70 Hospital General
72 Vinícola LA Cetto
74 Post Office
75 Monument to Cuauhtémoc
76 Budget Rent A Car
78 Librería El Día
79 Mexicana
81 Monument to Abraham Lincoln
87 Monument to General
   Ignacio Zaragoza
89 Canadian Consulate
93 El Toreo de Tijuana
96 Internet Cafe
99 National Car Rental
102 UK Consulate

MESA DE OTAY

To Abelardo L Rodriguez
International Airport &
Mesa de Otay Border Crossing

Paseo de Tijuana

Calle 16

Via Ferrocarril

Pedestrian Bridge

Plaza Río

ZONA RÍO

Via Oriente

Via Poniente

Av Cuauhtémoc

Paseo de los Heroes

Av Defensores de Baja California

Av Padre Kino

Pedestrian Bridge

Universidad Autónoma

Av Calzada de Tecnologico

Av Rivera

Av Siqueiros

José Maria Velasco

Av Rodriguez

Pedestrian Bridge

Av La Paz

Río Tijuana

To Central Camionera
(Long-Distance Bus Terminal)

Privado
Valencia
Rivera

Blvd Salinas

Av Sonora

Av Escuadron

Blvd Agua Caliente

Club Campestre
Tijuana

To Hipódromo de
Agua Caliente,
US Consulate, Tecate
& Mexicali

MEX 2

Centro Cultural Tijuana (Cecut)

This modern cultural center (☎ 6-684-11-11), at Paseo de los Héroes and Avenida Independencia, goes a long way toward undermining Tijuana's reputation as a cultural wasteland and is a facility that would be the pride of any comparably sized city in the world. It's the city's premier showcase for high-brow events – concerts, theater, readings, conferences, dance recitals, etc. Ticket prices vary but tend to be lower than north of the border; student discounts are usually available.

The distinctive complex is fronted by a humongous cream-colored sphere – sort of a giant golf ball – locally known as La Bola (the ball) and was designed by noted architects Pedro Ramirez Vasquez and Manuel Rosen Morrison. It also houses a fascinating new museum, an Omnimax theater, several art galleries, conference rooms and a well-stocked bookstore.

The state-of-the-art **Museo de las Californias** chronicles the history of Baja California from prehistoric times to the present. It's an excellent introduction to the peninsula for any visitor and should not be missed. The exhibit kicks off with replica cave paintings, then covers important historical milestones, including the earliest Spanish expeditions under Hernán Cortés, the mission period, the Treaty of Hidalgo, the Chinese immigration, the irrigation of the Colorado River delta and the advent of the railroad. Displays in glass cases mix with scale replicas of ships, missions, other objects and fairly realistic dioramas. All explanatory paneling is in English and Spanish, and touch-screen terminals provide additional information. It's all presented along gentle ramps in an airy space without encumbering walls. The museum is open 10 am to 7 pm daily except Monday; admission is US$2.

Housed within Cecut's 'golf ball,' **Cine Planetario** is a popular Omnimax-style theater showing a changing roster of films – usually in Spanish – on a 180-degree screen. Admission is US$4.50; half-price for students.

The **Jardín Caracol** is a charming garden whose layout is intended to resemble a snail (hence the name) and often hosts free events and exhibits, many of them children-oriented. In summer, the Voladores de Papántla (Totonac Indian performers) can be seen here.

Museo de Cera

Leave any expectations at the door and you might actually enjoy a visit to Tijuana's wax museum (☎ 6-688-24-78), strategically placed right along the walking route to downtown from the border at the corner of Madero and Calle 1a (Comercio). On view are about 90 waxen figures from Mexican history, world politics and entertainment, plus the obligatory House of Horrors. Speaking of horror, things start off rather gory with an Aztec warrior triumphantly posing with the heart of his poor victim. Controversial displays include Iran's Ayatollah Khomeini and Cuba's Fidel Castro, complemented by crowd pleasers like former Tijuana resident Rita Hayworth, an uncanny Frida Kahlo and a really bad Elvis.

The museum is open 10 am to 7 pm daily; admission is US$1.25.

Galería de Arte de la Ciudad

This municipal art gallery (☎ 6-685-01-04), at the corner of Avenida Constitución and Calle 2a (Juárez), presents exhibits and events involving the arts community from both sides of the border. It is housed on the ground floor of the former Palacio Municipal (City Hall), home to the city government from 1921 until its move to a new, modern building on Paseo de Tijuana in the Zona Río in 1986. At the gallery's entrance are two modest but interesting murals; the tranquil courtyard also contains a library and a worthwhile bookstore.

The gallery is only a block from La Revo and is open 9 am to 7 pm weekdays. Admission is free.

Vinícola LA Cetto

LA Cetto (☎ 6-685-30-31), at Cañón Johnson 8151, a diagonal in Colonia Hidalgo just southwest of Avenida Constitución, is Mexico's largest winery and has opened its Tijuana branch to tours and tastings. Still operated by descendants of Italian immigrants who arrived in Baja in 1926, it produces some 50 million liters annually, about 30% of which is exported. With vineyards in the fertile Valle de Guadalupe between Tecate and Ensenada, LA Cetto produces a range of tasty red and white varietals, as well as sparkling wines (about US$6 each), decent brandy (also US$6) and quality tequila (US$12).

Tours for individual visitors are offered on demand between 10 am and 5 pm weekdays and to 4 pm on Saturday for US$2, which includes a sampling of two wines. Prices at the winery store are about 25% cheaper than around town.

Cervecería de Tijuana
If you're a beer-drinker, make a pilgrimage to this microbrewery, which opened in early 2000 at Blvd Fundadores 2951, about 1½ miles (3.2km) south of downtown. Owner José González Ibarra's vision was to make a potent brew in the tradition of pilsner beer, which originated in Pilsen in the Czech Republic. He imported not only all the technology from that country but also a young Czech brewmaster whose efforts have clearly paid off. Sold under the brand name Tijuana, this is a superior and full-bodied beer that easily measures up to some of Europe's finest. It is best enjoyed in the atmospheric, timbered brewery pub.

Mercado Hidalgo
This is where locals come to buy spices, dried chilies, exotic produce, fresh tortillas and seasonal specialties made from Aztec grains. The partially covered stalls open on to a central square, usually filled with delivery trucks, which takes up several blocks bounded by Avenida Independencia and Blvd Sánchez Taboada.

On Calle 9a between Avenida Pío Pico and Avenida Sánchez Taboada, tiny La Tortilleria las 4 Milpas is a good place to see tortillas being made in the traditional way.

Playas de Tijuana
Popular with locals, Tijuana's beaches tend to get crowded, especially during summer bull-

fights (the Plaza de Toros Monumental is located here). A blue-and-white bus marked 'Playas' runs along Calle 3a (Carrillo Puerto) from downtown and goes westward to the beaches.

Organized Tours
New narrated English-language bus tours cover downtown, the Zona Río, the Agua Caliente racetrack, the LA Cetto winery (including a tasting) and the Museo de las Californias. They leave once daily from the Secture tourist office on Avenida Revolución at Calle 1a. Tours last 3½ hours and cost US$16.

Special Events
From late March to early April, Tijuana hosts an international dance festival with performances by regional, national and international troupes at the Centro Cultural.

The Feria de Tijuana is the city's annual fair with rides, food, big-name Mexican entertainment and cockfights. It takes place from mid-August to mid-September at the Agua Caliente racetrack.

Food-related festivals include the Annual Mexican Food Fair, held around September 10 at the Pueblo Amigo mall, and the 'World's Biggest Caesar Salad Festival' on Avenida Revolución in late October.

Places to Stay
Tijuana has a wealth of accommodations in all categories, from the really seedy to the truly luxurious. Note that tourist authorities try to steer visitors away from less expensive but sometimes very acceptable alternatives.

Budget Most of Tijuana's cheapest accommodations are in the Zona Norte, but because many places here do double duty as bordellos or safe houses for pollos, we cannot recommend any.

The closest acceptable place is *Hotel San Nicolas* (☎ 6-688-04-18, *Avenida Madero 768),* which exhibits a surprising artsy vibe, with Frida Kahlo posters for decoration. Rooms are small but clean and cost US$23/29 singles/doubles.

Probably the cheapest place downtown is *Hotel del Prado* (☎ 6-688-23-29, Calle 5a [Zapata] 8163), which is no-frills but clean and comfortable with friendly management. Rates are US$14 for singles/doubles with shared facilities or US$17 with private bath. Just a little more expensive, but at least as good, is *Hotel Catalina* (☎ 6-685-97-48), on the same street at Madero, which charges US$16/21 for rooms with shower and toilet; those with TV are US$26. Extra persons are charged US$5 each. Owners of this family hotel stress security, and rooms appear clean and tidy. You can even order room service from the cafeteria below.

The older *Hotel El Rey* (☎ 6-685-14-84, Calle 4a [Díaz Mirón] 8235) has sagging mattresses in rather dingy rooms that are overpriced at US$28.

Offering the best value in the budget category is *Hotel Lafayette* (☎ 6-685-39-40, Avenida Revolución 325). Well-maintained and spick and span, it charges US$20 to US$26 for rooms with TV, phone and bath. It's a safe place, as the staff has zero tolerance for riff-raff.

For visitors with vehicles, perhaps a better bargain is *Motel Plaza Hermosa* (☎ 6-685-33-53, Avenida Constitución 1821) at Calle 10a (Sarabia). Rooms cost US$24/30 weekdays, US$30/35 weekends, with secure parking.

Friendly if a tad tawdry, *Hotel París* (☎ /fax 6-685-30-23, Calle 5a [Zapata] 8181) has rooms with telephone, color TV and air-con from US$30 to US$47. In *Hotel Caesar* (☎ 6-685-16-06, fax 6-685-34-92, Avenida Revolución 1079), at Calle 5a (Zapata), historic bullfighting posters line the hallways. Its original restaurant supposedly created the Caesar salad (see Places to Eat, later). Rooms cost US$32/42.

Mid-Range One of the best downtown hotels is *Hotel La Villa de Zaragoza* (☎ 6-685-18-32, fax 6-685-18-37, Avenida Madero 1120), which has large, quiet rooms, all with TV, telephone, heater and air-con for US$43/53. Nonsmokers and the disabled can be accommodated.

Hotel Nelson (☎ 6-685-43-03, fax 6-685-43-04, Avenida Revolución 721) has long

been a travelers' favorite for its central location and 92 clean, basic and carpeted rooms, plus its bar and inexpensive coffee shop. Rooms with telephone, satellite TV and squeaky-clean bathrooms cost US$42.

The inviting *Hotel Palacio Azteca* (☎ /fax 6-681-81-00, palacio@telnor.net, Blvd Cuauhtémoc Sur 123), near the toll-free road to Playas de Rosarito and Ensenada, is a good value for US$52/63.

Tropical gardens and friendly faces behind the reception desk make the 120-room *Hotel La Mesa Inn* (☎ 6-681-65-22, fax 6-681-28-71, 800-303-2684 in the US, Blvd Díaz Ordaz 50) one of the nicest properties in town. Modern and immaculate rooms have satellite TV, telephone, air-con and bottled water. There's plenty of free parking, a lovely swimming pool and a small restaurant. Rates are a very reasonable US$55 to US$70.

Also nice is the *Country Club Hotel* (☎ 6-681-77-33, fax 6-681-76-92, 800-303-2684 in the US, bajainn@telnor.net, Tapachula 1) next to the Agua Caliente racetrack. Spacious suites and rooms overlook the golf course and the city. All have air-con, cable TV, telephone, private bath and bottled water; some are nonsmoking. Amenities include a swimming pool and a coffee shop/restaurant. Rates are US$63 to US$75.

Also try the colonial-style *Hotel El Conquistador* (☎ 6-681-79-55, fax 6-686-13-40, Blvd Agua Caliente 10750) nearby. All 105 rooms have air-con, cable TV and telephone; rates start at US$50.

Another good choice is the *Hacienda del Río* (☎ 6-684-86-44, fax 6-684-86-20, 800-303-2684 in the US, Blvd Sánchez Taboada 10606) in the Zona Río, which charges US$64 to US$77. Amenities include a restaurant, heated pool and gym. Rooms for nonsmokers are available.

Top End Modern and efficient *Hotel Real del Río* (☎ 6-634-31-00, fax 6-634-30-53, José María Velasco 1409) in the Zona Río charges US$75/82. *Hotel Siesta Inn* (☎ 6-634-69-01, fax 6-634-69-12, Paseo de los Héroes 18818) is similar and charges US$88.

The 200-room, high-rise **Hotel Plaza Las Glorias** (☎ 6-622-66-00, fax 6-622-66-02, plgtij@icanet.com.mx, Blvd Agua Caliente 11553) caters primarily to business clients, with rooms – all with color TV, air-con and telephone – starting at US$90.

Much in the same vein is **Hotel Lucerna** (☎ 6-633-39-00, fax 6-634-24-00, 800-582-3762 in the US, lucernat@telnor.net, Paseo de los Héroes 10902), with rooms starting at US$110. It has a restaurant, a business center, data ports and a heated pool.

Occupying a shiny 23-story tower, the **Grand Hotel Tijuana** (☎ 6-681-70-00, fax 6-681-70-16, 800-343-7825 in the US, ghotel2@telnor.net, Blvd Agua Caliente 4500) is certainly the city's most prominent hotel. Amenities include cable TV and minibars; there's also a heated pool, Jacuzzi and tennis court, as well as two restaurants and a cocktail bar. Rates range from US$70 to US$130.

A relative newcomer, **Pueblo Amigo Inn** (☎ 6-683-50-30, fax 6-683-50-32, 800-386-6985 in the US, htlpuebl@telnor.net, Via Oriente 9211) in the Pueblo Amigo mall is a welcoming facility offering state-of-the-art rooms with the usual conveniences. Rates start at US$150.

Places to Eat

Tijuana's cuisine scene is one of the city's big surprises. You'll find everything from traditional antojitos to Chinese, Italian, Spanish and French cuisine – and at a high level of quality. Other than on Avenida Revolución, places cluster in the Zona Río and along Blvd Agua Caliente.

Huge supermarkets abound on Blvd Agua Caliente and Paseo de los Héroes, with Gigante, Comercial and Calimax being the major chains. On Avenida Revolución, look for a Calimax branch at Calle 10a, and a brand-new Gigante in the small mall between Calle 2a and Calle 3a. Both are open 24 hours and sell fresh produce, meats, dairy, beverages and general goods.

For delicious bakery items, go to **El Molino** (☎ 6-684-90-40), at Avenida Quintana Roo and Calle 10a (Sarabia). In business since 1928, it makes everything from ordinary bolillos (typical Mexican bread) to

fanciful wedding cakes. **La Sonrisa** in the Plaza Fiesta mall specializes in pastries and whole-grain breads and also makes sandwiches to go. Next door, the brightly pigmented **Lo Ma' Bonita** is a good place for aguas and licuados.

La Revo & Downtown People coming to Avenida Revolución for booze, music and raucous partying have plenty of places to pick from. Many places also serve fairly decent Mexican food, albeit calibrated to gringo tastes. Better ones include **Margarita's Village** (☎ 6-685-38-62), at Calle 3a (Carrillo Puerto); the cheerfully decorated **Tía Juana Tilly's** (☎ 6-685-60-24), next to the Frontón Palacio Jai Alai (see La Revo, earlier); and the related **Tilly's Fifth Avenue** (☎ 6-685-90-15), near Calle 5a (Zapata).

Wedged in between are several restaurants that have stood the test of time. **Chiki Jai** (☎ 6-685-49-55, Avenida Revolución 1388) has been packed with patrons since 1947, thanks to its consistently good Spanish/Basque food. They make a mean paella for US$9. Lunch is busiest, and it closes at 9 pm.

Whether the Caesar salad really was invented in 1929 at what is now called **Caesar's Sports Bar & Grill** in the Hotel Caesar, we may never know for sure, but it's definitely fun watching your waiter go through the ritual of preparing one tableside (US$5).

Hidden away in a small basement shopping arcade on La Revo, between Calle 3a and Calle 4a next to the Hotel Lafayette, is another old-timer, the **Café La Especial** (☎ 6-685-66-54). It serves solid Mexican food at reasonable prices and is an oasis of silence compared to other downtown places.

Sanborn's (☎ 6-688-14-62), at Calle 8a (Hidalgo), belongs to a Mexican department store chain also known for its cafeterias. Prices here are low, but we found the food unexciting and rather bland. Its adjacent bar is good for a quiet drink – normally an oxymoron on La Revo.

Locals and turistas give top marks to **La Costa** (☎ 6-685-84-94, Calle 7a [Galeana] 8131), a classy and warmly lit seafood restaurant. Main courses start at US$10 and come with soup, appetizer, salad, rice and coffee. For generous portions of good pizza and pasta from US$5 to US$10, try *Vittorio's* (☎ 6-685-17-29), at Calle 9a (Zaragoza). Its lunch special is just US$4.

Step one block east or west off Avenida Revolución and you'll find plenty more culinary candidates worth your attention. One of Tijuana's best values is the diner-style *Tortas Ricardo* (☎ 6-681-86-55), a bright and cheerful place on Avenida Madero at Calle 7a (Galeana). Breakfasts are excellent, and the tortas are among the best in town. It's a nonsmoking place. *Tortas Chapultepec* (☎ 6-685-14-12), at Avenida Constitución and Calle 6a, is just as good.

Tamalandia (☎ 6-685-75-62, Calle 8a [Hidalgo] 8374) is a cheery little place selling homemade tamales stuffed with beef, chicken or cheese, plus the dessert-like dulce (all US$0.75 each). It's mostly take-out food, although there are a couple of tables.

Zona Río For the cheapest restaurants in the Zona Río, and perhaps the city, visit the Mercado Hidalgo, bordering Avenida Independencia and Blvd Sánchez Taboada; one recommendation is *Rincón del Oso*. Also here is the 24-hour *Tacos El Gordo*, which enjoys cult status among night owls. The quality of the tacos, which are perhaps a tad *too* authentic for most gringos, is debatable, but lines are often three-deep in the wee morning hours.

If you are feeling tropical, head to *La Casa del Mole* (☎ 6-634-69-20, Paseo de los Héroes 1501) for Tijuana's best mole-based dishes served in a glass-roofed jungle setting. You can eat and drink well here for under US$10.

The same cannot be said about *Cien Años* (☎ 6-634-30-39, Avenida José María Velasco 1407), one of Tijuana's temples of alta cocina (haute cuisine). The chefs have dug deep into a box of ancient Mexican recipes, some going back to the Aztecs and Mayans, and have come up with some rather unusual – but by all accounts, delicious – concoctions (how does 'spinal-cord soup' sound?). It's a formal place, so dress well.

Go casual at *Guadalajara Bar & Grill* (☎ 6-634-30-65, Avenida Diego Rivera 19), a dependable standby with an energetic vibe and good Mexican favorites; try the succulent fajitas. This is also a good place just for a drink.

Caesar's restaurant may have invented it, but many feel that the honor of 'best' Caesar salad goes to *Victor's* (☎ 6-634-33-09, Blvd Sánchez Taboada 9848). The restaurant is divided into a cafeteria and a more formal steakhouse, where prices are higher and live piano jazz may accompany your meal.

You'll eat well and plentifully at *California Restaurante* in the Plaza Río mall. It's a cafeteria-style restaurant popular for its lavish buffets (breakfast or dinner cost US$8.50; lunch is US$10).

Gypsy's (☎ 6-683-60-06) in the Pueblo Amigo mall is a lively tapas bar with decor inspired by Spanish artists Miró, Gaudí and Dalí. Its menu of more substantial main courses includes paella valenciana for US$7.

Chan's (☎ 6-634-27-66, Blvd Sánchez Taboada 10880) is a quite respectable Chinese restaurant, although flavors are adjusted to Mexican tastes.

Blvd Agua Caliente Although Blvd Agua Caliente, and its eastern spin-off, Blvd Salinas, is a bit distant for pedestrians, it has many eateries worth trying.

Youthful family restaurant *El Rincón de Xochimilco* (☎ 6-686-24-91, Privada Valencia Rivera 157), in a residential area just north of Blvd Agua Caliente, serves a range of delicious antojitos, including flautas, sopes, huaraches and gorditas prepared Mexico City–style (the owners are from there). A huge plate of food, including rice and beans, costs about US$3.

El Rodeo (☎ 6-686-56-40, Blvd Salinas 10332) is a fine beef restaurant with eccentric decor – antique gas pumps, Coke machines and a shrine to assassinated PRI presidential candidate Luis Donaldo Colosio.

Serving some of the city's best wood-fired Sonoran beef is *La Leña* (☎ 6-686-47-52, Blvd Agua Caliente 11191), just east of the Grand Hotel Tijuana; its carne asada is particularly good. Lunches and dinners cost from US$10 to US$25.

Los Arcos (☎ 6-686-47-57), at the corner of Blvd Salinas and Avenida Escuadrón, is the Tijuana branch of a popular Mexican seafood chain.

At the junction with Blvd Salinas, *El Potrero* (☎ 6-686-38-26) deserves a look not so much for its fairly straightforward food as for its oddball architecture – it's literally in the shape of a classic Mexican sombrero.

The Italian *Saverio's* (☎ 6-684-36-04, *Carlos Robirosa 250*), near the Grand Hotel, is an outstanding Italian restaurant serving pizza, pasta and seafood from throughout the Boot with prices to match; it is closed Monday.

Entertainment

Nightclubs & Bars Rowdy Avenida Revolución vibrates with venues for earsplitting live and recorded music. Classic haunts include the *Hard Rock Café* (☎ 6-685-02-06) at No 520; *Iguanas-Ranas* at Calle 3a (Carrillo Puerto); and *El Torito Pub* (☎ 6-685-16-36) at No 643. *Las Pulgas* (☎ 6-688-13-68) at No 1501 has live banda music.

Most self-respecting Tijuana hipsters wouldn't be caught dead on La Revo. The Zona Río is where it's at for locals, and there, the Flintstone-esque *Baby Rock* (☎ 6-634-24-04, *Avenida Diego Rivera 1482*) is particularly popular. This cavernous disco-bar gets the crowds going with its energetic vibe and alternative rock in English and Spanish, although it's also considered a major 'meat market' (there's usually a US$10 cover charge).

Across the street, upscale *ZKA* (☎ 6-634-71-40, *Paseo de los Héroes 10501*) is a modern disco-bar with '80s and '90s music. The cover here is usually US$10. Dress well at either place.

What La Revo is to gringos, the Plaza Fiesta mall is to locals. The dozen or so bars and restaurants are good places to knock back a few tequilas and hear the local rock talent thrash it out. The party is loudest at *Mi Barra*, *Monte Picacho* and *Ah Jijo*. *Bar Sótano Suizo* (☎ 6-684-88-34) is another popular place.

Pueblo Amigo has *Señor Frog's* (☎ 6-682-49-62, *Via Oriente 60*), where international dance music rings through the air nightly. After the Sunday corrida, bullfighting aficionados pack this place to toast the brave matadors – and vanquished bulls.

In the same complex is the industrial-style *Zoo'll* (☎ 6-683-62-55, 6-686-62-56, *Via Oriente 9211-9*), which plays house and techno (cover is about US$10).

Cafes The low-key *Cafe del Mundo* (☎ 6-683-56-84) is a mostly student-age hangout in the Pueblo Amigo mall. The clientele passes time chatting, playing cards or table games or listening to live music. Gourmet coffees, snacks and even decent wines are served.

Art, poetry, handmade music and other cultural fare are on the menu at *El Lugar de Nopal* (☎ 6-685-12-64, *Callejón 5 de Mayo*), a delightful Tijuana surprise. This sophisticated cafe-bar-cum-restaurant-cum-cultural center is a fervent supporter of local artists and an enchanting place at that, especially in the garden patio. It's tucked away in a residential area and is a bit hard to find but worth the effort.

Cinemas Most of Tijuana's cinemas are multiplexes showing first-run Hollywood blockbusters, often in English with Spanish subtitles, with the occasional Mexican or Latin American production thrown into the mix. Tickets cost about US$4.

Plaza Río has two large theaters, the *Multicinemas Río* (☎ 6-684-04-01) and *Cinepolis Río* (☎ 6-684-10-32). *Cinema Las Torres Plus* (☎ 6-686-55-70, *Blvd Agua Caliente 4558*) is near the racetrack.

Spectator Sports

Bullfights Tijuana bullfights (see the boxed text) take place on Sunday at 4 pm every two or three weeks from the last weekend in April to late September/early October.

Of the town's two bullrings, the larger, more spectacular venue is the Plaza de Toros Monumental, the renowned bullring-by-the-sea in Playas de Tijuana, only a short distance from the border fence. The other is El Toreo de Tijuana, on Blvd Agua Caliente between central Tijuana and the Agua Caliente racetrack. Spring bullfights take place at El Toreo, which has room for 12,000 spectators. In July or August, corridas move to the ring in Playas, which holds up to 25,000 people.

Tickets are available at the bullrings daily from noon to 6 pm and from 10 am on the day of the corrida. There's also a ticket desk in the Grand Hotel (see Places to Stay,

earlier). In San Diego, go to Five Star Tours (☎ 619-232-5049, 800-553-8687, fax 619-232-7035) in the Amtrak station at Broadway and Kettner Blvd. Prices range from US$8 for general admission to US$45 for prime seats in the shade.

Greyhound Races Ever since the Hipódromo de Agua Caliente's owner, Tijuana

Death in the Afternoon

It's said that Mexicans arrive on time for only two events – funerals and bullfights. To many others, *corridas de toros* (bullfights) hardly seem to be sport or, for that matter, entertainment, but Mexicans see it as both and more: It's as much a ritualistic dance as a fight.

The corrida begins promptly at 4, 4:30 or 5 pm on a Sunday. To the sound of music, usually a Spanish paso doble, the matador, in his *traje de luces* (suit of lights), and the *toreros* (his assistants) give the traditional *paseillo* (salute) to the fight authorities and the crowd. Then the first of the day's bulls (there are usually six in an afternoon) is released from its pen for the first of the ritual's three *suertes* (acts) or *tercios* (thirds).

The cape-waving toreros tire the bull by luring him around the ring. After a few minutes two picadores, on heavily padded horses, enter and jab *picas* (long lances) into the bull's shoulders. This is usually the most gruesome part of the whole process, as it instantly weakens the bull from the sudden pain and blood loss.

After the picadores leave the ring, the suerte de banderillas begins, as two toreros take turns sticking three pairs of elongated darts into the bull's shoulders without getting impaled on his horns. After that, the suerte de muleta is the climax, in which the matador has exactly 16 minutes to kill the bull.

Starting with fancy cape work to tire the animal, the matador then exchanges his large cape for the smaller muleta and takes sword in hand, baiting the bull to charge before delivering the fatal *estocada* (lunge) with his sword. The matador must deliver the estocada into the neck from a position directly in front of the animal.

If the matador succeeds, and he usually does, the bull eventually collapses and dies. If the applause from the crowd warrants it, he will be awarded an *oreja* (ear) or two and sometimes the tail. The dead bull is dragged from the ring to be butchered for sale.

A 'good' bullfight depends not only on the skill and courage of the matador but also on the spirit of the bulls. Animals lacking heart for the fight bring shame on the ranch that bred them. Very occasionally, a bull that has fought outstandingly is *indultado* (spared) – an occasion for great celebration – and will then retire to stud.

Tijuana's two bullfighting arenas are the most famous in Baja California, but there's also one in Mexicali. The veteran Eloy Cavazos, from Monterrey, is often acclaimed as Mexico's best matador. Alfredo Lomeli and Eulalio 'El Zotoluco' López are younger stars. Bullfights featuring star matadors from Spain, such as Enrique Ponce, El Julí, José Tomás and El Cordobés, have added spice.

multimillionaire Jorge Hank Rhon, refused to give in during a sustained labor dispute several years ago, the ponies no longer circle this landmark racetrack, and the place has literally gone to the dogs. In fact, it would be more accurate to call it a *galgodromo*, because greyhound races with pari-mutuel wagering take place at 7:45 pm daily and at 2 pm weekends. Just beyond the Club Campestre Tijuana on Blvd Agua Caliente, the track (☎ 6-681-78-11 ext 637) is open all year; admission is free and parking is cheap.

Rodeos *Charreadas* usually take place Sunday afternoons from May to September at one of four venues in the Tijuana area – ask Secture or Canaco (see Information, earlier) for the latest details. One popular rodeo ground is the Cortijo San José in Playas de Tijuana, just south of Plaza de Toros Monumental.

Shopping
Avenida Revolución is the main tourist-oriented shopping street. Local handicrafts are plentiful, especially jewelry, wrought-iron furniture, baskets, silver, blown glass, pottery and leather goods. Bargaining is the rule in smaller stores.

Tequila, Kahlua and other liquors are popular buys, but you can save a couple of dollars by buying in supermarkets rather than liquor stores. Also here are a few designer outlet stores like Nautica, Quicksilver and Guess. At Calle 7a is the excellent Bazar de México (see La Revo, earlier).

Avenida Constitución, one block west, has shoe stores, flower shops, hardware stores and other places primarily catering to locals.

Markets are fun places to shop. The Mercado Municipal (municipal market) on Avenida Niños Héroes between Calle 1a (Artículo 123) and Calle 2a (Juárez), and the sprawling Mercado de Artesanías (Artisans' Market) at Calle 1a (Comercio) and Avenida Ocampo near the border, are both good for browsing. The Mercado Hidalgo is where the locals shop (see its entry, earlier in the chapter).

In the Zona Río, the sprawling Plaza Río is a pleasant, modern outdoor mall an-

chored by the Comercial superstore and Dorian's department store. Other shops here sell shoes, music, lingerie, computers, clothes and more. Also here are travel agencies and two large movie theaters. Plaza de Zapato across the street has a couple dozen shoe stores.

Tiles are another popular purchase. Stores with huge assortments congregate along Blvd Salinas near the Grand Hotel's Twin Towers.

Many US visitors take advantage of Tijuana's low-priced car body and upholstery repair shops with prices typically less than half of those north of the border. Most shops have English-speaking staff and do good work, but clarify your expectations beforehand and get a written estimate before committing yourself to repairs. Shops cluster on Ocampo and Pío Pico between Calle 3 and Calle 8.

Other visitors frequent Tijuana's equally low-priced dentists for fillings, crowns, bridges and dentures. Pharmacies also do box office with US travelers, but read the boxed text 'The Drug Business' in the Facts for the Visitor chapter before stocking up.

Getting There & Away
Air Mexico's fourth-busiest airport, Aeropuerto Internacional Abelardo L Rodríguez (☎ 6-683-24-18) is in Mesa de Otay east of downtown. It has become a popular departure and arrival point, and fares may be cheaper than in the US.

AeroMéxico (☎ 6-684-84-44, 6-683-27-00 at the airport, ☎ 800-237-6639 in the US), along with its commuter subsidiary Aerolitoral, has an office in Plaza Río. Aerolitoral flies to Tucson (Arizona) and La Paz via the mainland Mexican city of Hermosillo (Sonora). AeroMéxico has one daily direct flight each to La Paz and to Mazatlán and up to 10 flights to Mexico City; it also serves numerous other destinations throughout Mexico.

Mexicana (☎ 6-634-65-66, 6-682-41-83 at the airport, ☎ 800-531-7921 in the US) has an office at Avenida Diego Rivera 1511 in the Zona Río and offers direct flights to Guadalajara, Zacatecas and Mexico City.

Aero California (☎ 6-684-28-76, 6-682-87-54 at the airport, ☎ 800-237-6225 in the US) has an office in the Plaza Río at the corner of Paseo de los Héroes and Avenida Independencia and flies daily to La Paz and Los Cabos. It also serves many mainland destinations from Mexico City northward.

Aerolíneas Internacionales (☎ 6-684-07-27, 6-682-94-32 at the airport), with an office at Avenida Vía Poniente 4246, at the corner of Leona Vicario in the Zona Río, flies to Hermosillo, Culiacán, Guadalajara, Aguascalientes, Cuernavaca and Mexico City.

Bus Just about every town in Mexico is served from Tijuana, but there is a bewildering number of stations and companies. For more on bus travel in Baja California and beyond, see the Getting Around chapter.

Central Camionera de la Linea The Border Bus Terminal (☎ 6-683-56-81) is on the southern edge of Plaza Viva Tijuana and is used by ABC (☎ 6-686-90-10), Estrellas del Pacifico (☎ 6-683-50-22) and Turi-Mex (☎ 6-682-94-34). Services include the following:

Ensenada – US$8, 1½ hours; every 30 minutes with ABC, with easy connections south to San Quintín hourly with Estrellas del Pacifico (same fares)

Mexicali – US$9.50, three hours; every 90 minutes with ABC

San Felipe – US$20, 5½ hours; twice daily with ABC

Mazatlán – US$87, 25 hours; up to nine times daily with Estrellas del Pacifico

Guadalajara – US$100, 42 hours; up to nine times daily with Estrellas del Pacifico

Antigua Central Camionera The Downtown Terminal (☎ 6-688-07-52) is at Avenida Madero and Calle 1a (Comercio), a short taxi ride or 10-minute walk from the border. It offers services by ABC (local buses only), Greyhound (☎ 6-688-19-79, 800-231-2222 in the US; www.greyhound.com) and Elite/Norte de Sonora (☎ 6-688-19-79). ABC also offers Servicio Plus to some destinations, which is slightly faster and uses more-comfortable buses. Fares are about 15% higher than those quoted here:

Playas de Rosarito – US$1, 30 minutes; about every 20 minutes from 6 am to 8 pm with ABC (Subur Baja buses)

Tecate – US$3, one hour; every 20 minutes from 5:30 am to 8 pm with ABC (Subur Baja)

Crossing the Border

One of the world's busiest border crossings, the San Ysidro-Tijuana port of entry is open 24 hours a day. If you are crossing the border on foot, take the pedestrian bridge and go through the turnstile into Mexico. To reach Avenida Revolución, walk through the Plaza Viva Tijuana shopping mall to the pedestrian bridge over the river, cross the street and proceed along Calle Comercio. The entire walk takes about 10 to 15 minutes.

For drivers, there are usually no delays coming into Mexico, but returning can be a nightmare, especially at the end of holiday weekends. Lanes 9 to 12 are reserved for carpools of at least three passengers, but only on weekdays from 5 am to 10 pm. Be sure to arrange vehicle insurance either before crossing the border or at the border (Mesa de Otay is much quicker than San Ysidro). See Insurance in the Getting Around chapter for details.

If Tijuana is your only destination, it may be better to leave your car on the northern side of the border and either walk or take a shuttle across. Parking lots include Border Station Parking at 4570 Camino de la Plaza (turn right at the last exit off the I-5 before the border), which charges US$7 per day. Also here is a small tourist information kiosk with maps and other information.

This parking lot also doubles as the northern terminus of the Mexicoach shuttle (☎ 6-685-14-70, 619-428-9517 in the US) to the Terminal Turístico Tijuana on Avenida Revolución. Buses depart at 15- to 30-minute intervals from 9 am to 9 pm daily. One-way fares are US$1.

The alternative crossing at Mesa de Otay, east of downtown near the airport, is open 6 am to 10 pm daily. Remember that it takes time to drive to Otay and return to US I-5 after crossing the border.

Ensenada – US$5.50, 1½ hours; at least hourly from 5 am to 6 pm with ABC

Mexico City – US$140, 42 hours; every two hours with Elite

Central Camionera La Mesa Tijuana's main station for long-distance buses (☎ 6-621-76-40) is about 3 miles (5km) southeast of the city center at Blvd Lázaro Cárdenas and Río Alamar. Companies include ABC (☎ 6-621-29-82), Elite (☎ 6-621-26-02), Norte de Sonora (☎ 6-621-29-55) and Greyhound (no number).

To reach the Camionera from downtown, take any 'Buena Vista,' 'Centro' or 'Central Camionera' bus (US$0.50) from Calle 2a (Juárez) east of Avenida Constitución; these buses also stop at the border bus lot.

For the same price, the quicker and more convenient gold-and-white *taxis de ruta* (route taxis; marked 'Mesa de Otay') stop on Avenida Madero between Calle 2a (Juárez) and Calle 3a (Carrillo Puerto). A taxi costs about US$14.

Tecate – US$3.25, 1½ hours; at least hourly from 5:30 am to 10 pm with ABC

Ensenada – US$8, 1½ hours; at least hourly from 5 am to 10 pm with ABC

Mexicali – US$11, 2½ to three hours; hourly from 6:30 am to 9:30 pm with ABC

San Quintín – US$17, five to six hours; four times daily with ABC

San Felipe – US$20, six hours; twice daily with ABC

El Rosario – US$21, eight hours; four times daily with ABC

Santa Rosalía – US$48, 11 to 13 hours; four times daily with ABC

Mulegé – US$53, 18 hours; four times daily with ABC

Loreto – US$59, 20 hours; four times daily with ABC

La Paz – US$76, 22 to 24 hours; four times daily with ABC

Mazatlán – US$102, 26 hours; hourly with Elite

Mexico City – US$140, 42 hours; every two hours with Elite

Mexico City – US$120, 45 hours; several times daily with Norte de Sonora

Terminal Turístico From Friday to Sunday, Mexicoach operates its Rosarito Beach Express with departures at 11 am and 1, 3 and 5 pm (US$6 roundtrip) from this termi-nal on Avenida Revolución between Calle 6a (Flores Magón) and Calle 7a (Galeana). Buses stop outside the Rosarito Beach Hotel.

To/From the USA Several companies offer services between Los Angeles, San Diego, San Ysidro and Tijuana.

From Los Angeles, Greyhound (☎ 800-231-2222 in the US) runs buses at least hourly from its downtown terminal (☎ 213-629-8401) at 1716 E 7th St (US$15.50, 3½ to 5¼ hours). Buses stop first at Tijuana's Downtown Terminal, then continue on to the Central Camionera (same fare), adding about 20 minutes to the journey. Its Web site is at www.greyhound.com.

Intercalifornias (☎ 6-683-62-81), on the eastern side of the road just south of the San Ysidro border crossing, also travels to Los Angeles for US$22.

From San Diego, Greyhound buses depart almost hourly from the terminal (☎ 619-239-3266) at 120 W Broadway (US$5.50, 1¼ hours from Tijuana, 50 minutes to Tijuana).

A cheaper alternative is bus No 932, operated by ATC/Vancom (☎ 619-427-6438), which goes from various stops along Broadway in downtown San Diego (eg, 4th and Broadway) to San Ysidro on the US side of the border (US$1.75, 90 minutes).

Train Amtrak (☎ 800-872-7245 in the US) runs daily trains between Los Angeles and San Diego. For schedule and fare information, see the Train entry in the Getting There & Away chapter.

Trolley The San Diego Trolley (☎ 619-233-3004, 800-266-6883) travels from San Diego's Amtrak station at Broadway and Kettner Blvd to the US side of the San Ysidro border (with several other stops along the way) in about 45 minutes (maximum fare is US$2.25). Trolleys depart every 15 minutes or so from about 5 am to midnight.

From San Diego International Airport (Lindbergh Field), bus No 992 goes directly to the trolley stop at Plaza America in San Diego, across from the Amtrak station, at 15-minute intervals (US$2.25). If you're making the bus-trolley connection, be sure to request a free transfer.

Getting Around

To/From the Airport Cabs to the airport from downtown or the border cost between US$10 and US$20, depending on your bargaining skills. The blue-and-white taxis behind the huge fleet of yellow cabs just south of the border are usually the cheaper option.

You can save a bundle by using public transportation. From the border, take any bus marked 'Aeropuerto' from the bus stop on the southeastern edge of Plaza Viva Tijuana, for about US$0.50.

From downtown or the Zona Río, catch the airport bus or a blue-and-white route taxi on Calle 4a (Díaz Mirón) between Avenida Constitución and Paseo de los Héroes.

Bus From the border, you can take any bus marked 'Centro' to go downtown. The bus stop is on the southeast side of Plaza Viva Tijuana; a man with a notebook is usually there to direct people toward the right bus to any destination in town. The standard fare is about US$0.50.

Car Rental cars may be cheaper in San Diego, and several of the large companies permit their cars to be taken across the border if you buy supplemental insurance. For details, see the Car section in the Getting Around chapter. Companies include the following:

Avis (☎ 6-683-06-03, 6-683-23-10) Blvd Cuauhté-moc 406, Colonia Aeropuerto

Alamo (☎ 6-686-40-40, 6-683-80-84 at the airport) Blvd Sánchez Taboada 10285, Zona Río

Budget (☎ 6-634-33-04, 6-683-29-05 at the airport) Av Paseo de los Héroes 77, Zona Río

Dollar (☎ 6-681-84-84) Blvd Sánchez Taboada 10285, Zona Río

Europcar (☎ 6-686-21-03) Blvd Agua Caliente 5000

Hertz (☎ 6-686-12-12, 6-683-20-80 at the airport) Blvd Agua Caliente 3402

National (☎ 6-686-21-03) Blvd Agua Caliente 10598

Taxi Tijuana taxis lack meters, and cabbies sometimes overcharge gringos, especially for the five-minute trip from the border to central Tijuana. The fare should not be more than US$5 per car. Do not agree to a per-person charge; try out your bargaining skills here and elsewhere in town. In general, expect to pay from US$3 to US$6 for most city taxi rides. A ride to the Central Camionera from the border costs about US$14.

Route taxis are an efficient and inexpensive way to get around town. They are station wagons that operate along designated routes, just like city buses and only slightly more expensive. You can board them at their designated route terminus or by flagging them down. Fares depend on the distance traveled but are usually five or six pesos (about US$0.60) within town. The driver will stop wherever you want to get off.

From Avenida Madero and Calle 3a (Carrillo Puerto), brown-and-white route taxis (marked 'Mesa de Otay') go to the Zona Río, the Central Camionera and the airport along Paseo de los Héroes. Red-and-black cabs travel along Blvd Agua Caliente to the El Toreo bullring, the country club and the Agua Caliente racetrack. You can pick them up at Calle 4a and Avenida Niños Héroes in downtown. Yellow-and-blue route taxis to Rosarito depart from Avenida Madero and Calle 4a (Díaz Mirón).

TIJUANA TO ROSARITO

When you're traveling south from Tijuana via the toll road, the urban sprawl quickly gives way to open coastal road and unrestricted ocean views. The first toll booth for México 1D is at Km 9. About 8 miles (13km) south of here is the village of San Antonio del Mar with the hilltop ***KOA Trailer Park/Campground*** (☎ 6-631-33-05). Mostly catering to long-term residents, it keeps a few spaces for passing RVs (water and electric) and there's also space for tent camping. Sites cost US$19 per night for two people, US$1 for each additional person.

Another 2 miles (3.2km) south, at Km 25, is the Moorish-architecture-inspired ***Oasis***

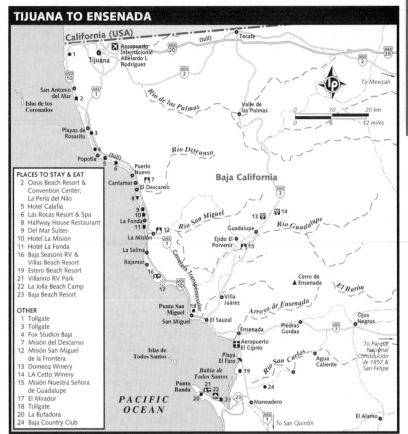

TIJUANA TO ENSENADA

PLACES TO STAY & EAT
2 Oasis Beach Resort &
   Convention Center;
   La Perla del Nilo
5 Hotel Calafia
6 Las Rocas Resort & Spa
8 Halfway House Restaurant
9 Del Mar Suites
10 Hotel La Misión
11 Hotel La Fonda
16 Baja Seasons RV &
   Villas Beach Resort
19 Estero Beach Resort
21 Villarino RV Park
22 La Jolla Beach Camp
23 Baja Beach Resort

OTHER
1 Tollgate
2 Tollgate
4 Fox Studios Baja
7 Misión del Descanso
12 Misión San Miguel
   de la Frontera
13 Domecq Winery
14 LA Cetto Winery
15 Misión Nuestra Señora
   de Guadalupe
17 El Mirador
18 Tollgate
20 La Bufadora
24 Baja Country Club

Beach Resort & Convention Center *(☎ 6-631-32-50, fax 6-631-32-52, 800-818-3133 in the US),* a luxurious beachfront hotel/RV park resort. It has 55 paved sites with small patios, brick barbecues and full hookups, including cable TV.

Facilities include a tennis court, two pools and Jacuzzis, a market, mini-golf as well as a clubhouse with bathrooms, sauna, TV, laundry and weight room. RV rates are US$49/59 midweek/weekend during peak periods for two people, US$10 more for each extra person. Its 100 spacious suites

sleep up to four people with rates starting at US$109/119 (for two), US$15 more for each extra person.

The resort's gourmet restaurant, ***La Perla del Nilo***, serves top-quality international fare at top pesos.

PLAYAS DE ROSARITO

In 1827, José Manuel Machado obtained a grant of 11 leagues of land south of Rancho Tijuana that, now divided into several ranchos, also includes the city of Rosarito (population 100,000), officially founded in

1885. The valley of Rosarito marks the original boundary between Alta and Baja California, which after the Mexican-American War was moved north to Tijuana.

In 1916, the Compañía Explotadora de Baja California purchased 14,000 acres (5600 hectares) of the Machado concession; in 1927 this became Moreno & Compañía, which began the Hotel Rosarito. Completed by Manuel Barbachano, it became the landmark Rosarito Beach Hotel.

Until several years ago, Rosarito was a modest fishing village with its single posh resort hotel (known mainly to Hollywood stars and hangers-on), long sandy beaches (frequented only by a handful of surfers) and a few taco stands. Since the 1990s, its 'discovery' has fostered a busy commercial strip lined by resort-style hotels, interesting crafts stores and fine restaurants. Its beaches, fishing, organized bicycle rides, races and horseback riding are the main attractions.

Rosarito's population nearly doubled in the 1990s and, with a growth rate of more than 14%, it continues to be the fastest-growing community in Baja California. In recognition of the town's increased size and importance, the state government granted Rosarito *municipio* status in 1995. Both the municipio and the town are now known formally as Playas de Rosarito.

Hollywood also did its part to anchor Rosarito even more prominently on the map and in people's minds. In 1996, Twentieth Century Fox opened its Fox Studios Baja just a few miles south of town. Originally built just for the filming of the *Titanic*, it is now a permanent facility, bringing a touch of glamour to this part of northern Baja.

Rosarito is a party town and a popular getaway for Southern Californians. From April to October, it's often flooded with revelers on weekends and especially during US college spring break. Prices – and noise levels – skyrocket during those times, so avoid visiting unless you're a party animal yourself.

Orientation

Rosarito's main artery, Blvd Benito Juárez, is a segment of the Transpeninsular and is lined by hotels, restaurants, shops and most other businesses. On most weekends, it becomes a two-way traffic jam, as hordes of visitors stream in. On either side of this road is a maze of narrow streets, most of

México 1 or México 1D?

Free road or toll road? That's the question you'll have to ask yourself when driving south from Tijuana to Ensenada.

México 1D, the divided toll road, is faster, more easily accessed and offers spectacular coastal views over its entire length. From the border at San Ysidro, simply follow the (slyly manipulative) 'Ensenada Scenic Road' signs along Calle Internacional. Paralleling the border fence, the road turns south in Playas de Tijuana, just before plunging into the ocean, and passes through the first of three tollgates.

Tolls for the entire 68-mile (110km) stretch, which takes about 1½ hours, are about US$6.60 for an ordinary passenger vehicle or motorcycle and twice that for any larger vehicle. One-third of the toll is charged at each of three gates – Playas de Tijuana, Playas de Rosarito and San Miguel – though there are several other exits along the route. Watch out for livestock jumping the fences to graze on the irrigated median strip.

Two-lane, toll-free México 1 (the Transpeninsular) passes through equally spectacular scenery, but heavier traffic makes it slower. From the Tijuana border crossing, follow the signs to central Tijuana and continue straight (west) along Calle 3a (Carrillo Puerto), turning left (south) at Avenida Revolución. Follow Avenida Revolución to the end, where it veers left (east) and becomes Blvd Agua Caliente. Turn right just before the twin towers of the Grand Hotel Tijuana and head south.

México 1 hits the coast just north of Playas de Rosarito. From here, the free road and the toll road run parallel for several miles. Just past La Fonda, the Transpeninsular turns inland and zigzags through the countryside for 21 miles (34km) before returning to the coast and crossing the toll road again near San Miguel.

them still unpaved. A few of the cheaper hotels can be found in the area west of the boulevard.

Rosarito's 'downtown' is toward the southern end around the Rosarito Beach Hotel. This is where most of the tourist-oriented places are located, while northern Rosarito has a more local flair.

Most places do have street addresses, but the numbering system is maddeningly erratic. Adding to the confusion, outside of downtown, most east-west streets crossing Blvd Juárez do not have signs. Most people use landmarks such as the Rosarito Beach Hotel as points of reference. Whenever possible, this section uses cross streets to help you locate a particular place, but you may still find that you'll need to refer to the map a little more often than usual.

Information

Secture (☎/fax 6-612-02-00), the local representative of the state-run tourist agency, occupies an office in the Plaza Villa Floresta, a mini-mall at Blvd Juárez 2000, on the far northern end of town. It has a few brochures and leaflets, along with recent issues of the *Baja Sun*. English-speaking staff will deal with tourist hassles and try to answer questions. It's open 9 am to 7 pm weekdays, 10 am to 4 pm weekends.

A bit more central is the Rosarito Beach Convention & Visitors Bureau (Cotuco; ☎ 6-612-03-96, 6-612-30-78, 800-962-2252 in the US) in the Oceana Plaza mall on Blvd Juárez at Encino. This office is usually open weekdays 9 am to 6 pm and Saturday to 3 pm.

The immigration office is Rosarito's Servicios Migratorios (☎ 6-613-02-34), on Calle Acacias directly behind the police station.

Nearly all merchants accept US dollars. Banks include Bital on Blvd Juárez between Cedro and Abeto, Banamex at Blvd Juárez and Ciprés, and Banca Serfin on Blvd Juárez between Roble and Acacias. American Express, which cashes its own traveler's checks for free, is represented by Viajes Carousel (see below).

Rosarito's post office is on Acacias east of the police station; the postal code is 22710. Several pharmacies and other stores along Blvd Juárez have private phone facilities.

For Internet access, go to El Tunel.com (☎ 6-613-12-97), at Blvd Juárez 208, just north of Lucio Blanco, where one hour of surfing costs US$3.

Viajes Carousel (☎ 6-613-08-32), on Blvd Juárez at Roble in the Oceana Plaza mall, is a full-service travel agency and also the local representative of American Express.

Take your dirty clothes to Lavamática on Blvd Juárez at Calle Tijuana in northern Rosarito, or to the eastern side of Blvd Juárez between Acacias and Roble.

Hospital Santa Lucía (☎ 6-612-04-40) is at Avenida Mar del Norte 557 behind the police station (☎ 6-612-11-10/1) at Blvd Juárez and Acacias. For the Cruz Roja, call ☎ 6-612-04-14 or ☎ 132.

Museo Wa Cuatay

The name of Rosarito's small historical and anthropological museum, near the Rosarito Beach Hotel, translates as 'Place of the Waters,' the Indian name for the area. It is lovingly maintained by Pedro Aries, who's also been a bartender at the hotel for the past four decades, and offers a good introduction to the area from pre-Columbian times to the present. Subjects include the missions, the creation of the ejidos and the beginnings of tourism. Indigenous artifacts, good historical photographs and the occasional traveling show from mainland Mexico round off the exhibit. It's open 10 am to 4 pm Thursday to Sunday; admission is free.

Parque Municipal Abelardo L Rodríguez

The amphitheater at Rosarito's beachfront plaza contains the impressive 1987 mural *Tierra y Libertad* (Land and Liberty) by Juan Zuñiga Padilla, proof that Mexico's celebrated muralist tradition is still alive and well. Traditional motifs include the eagle and plumed serpent and Emiliano Zapata and his followers.

Horseback Riding

Horses can be hired at several locations on the western side of the Transpeninsular in

PLAYAS DE ROSARITO

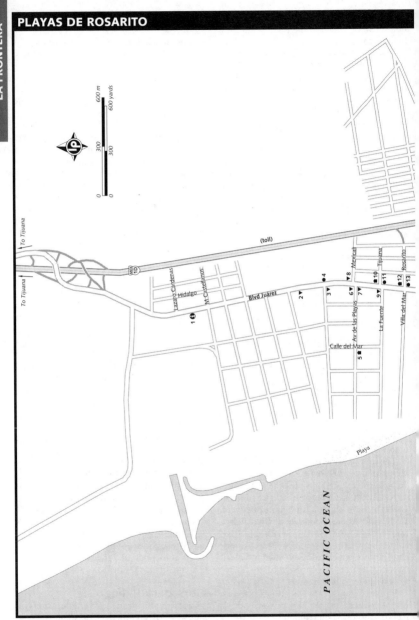

LA FRONTERA

PLAYAS DE ROSARITO

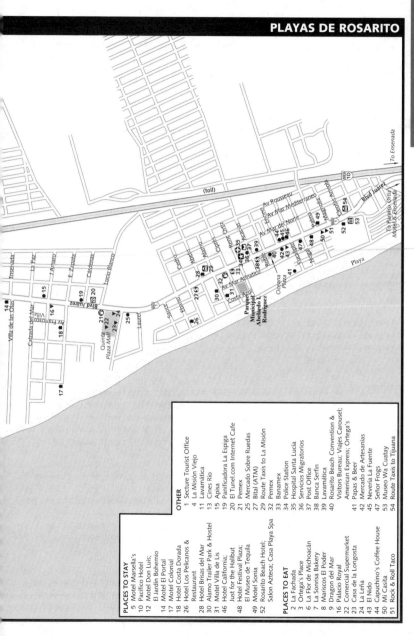

To Ensenada

(toll)

Av Rousseau

Av Mar Mediterraneo

Av Mar del Norte

Blvd Juárez

To Paraiso Ortiz
Motel & Ensenada

Playa

Parque
Municipal
Abelardo L
Rodríguez

Av Mar Atlántico

Oceana
Plaza

Costa Azul

Av Mar Atlántico

Blvd Juárez

Quinta
Plaza Mall

Av Francisco Villa

Villa de las Olas

Calzada del Mar

Ensenada
La Paz
E Zapata
Cárdenas
A Amaro
Iuco Blanco

Sauca
Ródano
Cedros
Rene Ortiz
Abril
Cipres
Alamo
Nardo
Eucalipto
Palma
Mar Báltico
Cedros Arroba

PLACES TO STAY
5   Motel Marsella's
10 Pacifico Hotel
12 Motel Don Luis;
    El Jardín Bohemio
14 Motel El Portal
17 Motel Colonial
18 Hotel Costa Dorada
26 Hotel Los Pelicanos &
    Restaurant
28 Hotel Brisas del Mar
30 Alamo Trailer Park & Hostel
31 Motel Villa de Lis
46 Hotel California;
    Just for the Halibut
48 Hotel Festival Plaza;
    El Museo de Tequila
49 Motel Sonia
52 Rosarito Beach Hotel;
    Salon Azteca; Casa Playa Spa

PLACES TO EAT
2   La Fachada
3   Ortega's Place
6   La Flor de Michoacán
7   La Sonrisa Bakery
8   Mariscos El Poder
9   Dragon del Mar
16 Palacio Royal
22 Comercial Supermarket
23 Casa de la Longosta
24 La Leña
43 El Nido
44 Capuchino's Coffee House
50 Mi Casita
51 Rock & Roll Taco

OTHER
1   Secture Tourist Office
4   La Misión Viejo
11 Lavamática
13 Cines Rio
15 Apisa
19 Panificadora La Espiga
20 El Tunel.com Internet Cafe
21 Pemex
25 Mercado Sobre Ruedas
27 Route Taxis to La Misión
29 Pemex
32 Bital (ATM)
33 Banamex
34 Police Station
35 Hospital Santa Lucia
36 Servicios Migratorios
37 Post Office
38 Banca Serfin
39 Lavamática
40 Rosarito Beach Convention &
    Visitors Bureau; Viajes Carousel;
    American Express; Ortega's
41 Papas & Beer
42 Mercado de Artesanias
45 Nevería La Fuente
47 Señor Frogs
53 Museo Wa Cuatay
54 Route Taxis to Tijuana

Rosarito and on the beach by the Rosarito Beach Hotel. The average rate is US$5 per hour. Bargain, if necessary.

Places to Stay

Because it's a resort town and so close to the border, Rosarito lacks consistent budget accommodations. Rates vary both seasonally and between weekdays (Monday to Thursday) and weekends (Friday to Sunday). Given this fickle market, prices given in the following sections are only intended to give you an idea of what to expect.

Budget A camping option is the German-owned *Alamo Trailer Park & Hostel* (☎ 6-613-11-79, alamo15@telnor.net, Calle Alamo 15). It's basic and cramped but convivial – and it's only half a block from the beach. Bunks in the single coed 'dorm' cost US$15 in summer and US$8 to US$10 in winter. Trailers rent for US$140 to US$275 per month, and you can also put up your own tent for about US$10.

For the truly cash-strapped, *Motel Sonia* (☎ 6-612-12-60), a time-worn hotel on Blvd Juárez at Palma, may be the best bet; rooms here cost US$25 to US$30 singles/doubles year round. A step up is the nearby *Hotel California* (☎ 6-612-25-50, 800-399-22-55 in the US, Blvd Juárez 32), where comfortable rooms with cable TV cost about US$40 to US$50. Both are right in the heart of downtown Rosarito near the Festival Plaza and the Rosarito Beach Hotel.

A number of affordable lodging options can be found just a block or two from the beach. Quiet and clean, the sky-blue *Motel Villa de Lis* (☎ 6-612-23-20, fax 6-613-16-51) on Alamo at Costa Azul, is a popular choice among budget travelers. Rooms have cable TV and cost US$32 midweek, US$42 on weekends. Rooms with ocean view are US$10 more. Rates drop US$10 in winter.

Another good choice is the 24-room *Motel Marsella's* (☎ 6-612-04-68, Calle del Mar 75), where clean, carpeted and spacious rooms with wood paneling, large beds and cable TV range from US$20 to US$40.

In the same general neighborhood, *Motel Colonial* (☎ 6-612-15-75), on Calle 1a at

Calle de Mayo 71, is an aging building whose rooms are still a good value. Most are suites with separate living and dining areas, kitchenette, double bed and enough space for cots and sleeping bags. Prices start around US$25.

In the northern end of town, *Motel Don Luis* (☎ 6-612-11-66, Blvd Juárez 272), near Calle Rosarito, has rooms with TV and aircon from US$30. A pool, Jacuzzi and sauna are also on the premises. Adequate if nondescript is the *Hotel Costa Dorada* (☎ 6-613-06-51, Avenida Francisco Villa 32), where rooms cost US$35/50.

Probably the best choice in this part of town is the brightly painted *Motel El Portal* (☎ 6-612-00-50), on Blvd Juárez at Vía de las Olas, where rooms cost US$31 to US$49, but rates can plunge to as low as US$16 during lulls in visitor activity.

Mid-Range The *Pacífico Hotel* (☎ 6-612-25-16, fax 6-612-22-56, Blvd Juárez 286), between Calles Mexicali and Tijuana, has 47 comfortable rooms with cable TV, phone, heater and air-con. Weekday rates are a steal at US$45 but climb to US$95 to US$110 on weekends. Continental breakfast is included.

About half a mile (1km) south of the Rosarito Beach Hotel, the friendly *Paraíso Ortiz Motel* (☎ 6-612-10-20) has cottage-style rooms for US$30 during the week, but rates rise to US$35 on weekends and US$45 in summer. It's a fair bit quieter than accommodations in Rosarito proper.

One of Rosarito's better values is the oceanside *Hotel Los Pelicanos* (☎ 6-612-04-45, Calle de Cedro 115). Basic rooms cost US$38 to US$48, plus US$7.50 for each additional person. Rooms with oceanview balconies cost US$60. There's also a good restaurant with a deck overlooking the beach.

Top End Between the ocean and Blvd Juárez, the *Rosarito Beach Hotel* (☎ 6-612-11-11, fax 6-612-11-76, in the US ☎ 619-498-8230, 800-343-8582) opened in the late 1920s during Prohibition and quickly became a popular watering hole and gambling haven for Hollywood stars like Orson Welles and Mickey Rooney. Larry Hagman of *Dallas* fame, Vincent Price and several Mexican presidents have also been guests. Facilities include two pools, a gym and two restaurants. The Casa Playa Spa offers a full menu of treatments, massages, facials and body wraps.

The best rooms are suites in the new building closest to the beach. Summer rates range from US$89 to US$129 midweek and US$109 to US$179 on weekends for rooms that include a welcome margarita and dinner. Special packages and rates are usually available.

The high-rise *Hotel Festival Plaza* (☎ 6-612-29-50, 800-453-8606 in the US), on Blvd Juárez just north of the Rosarito Beach Hotel, looks like a colorful children's playground – for adult 'children,' that is. This place is party central and any illusions of a quiet night's sleep quickly disappear when you discover that all rooms face the outdoor plaza where live concerts take place! Some 10 clubs and restaurants, a tequila 'museum' and even a small Ferris wheel are part of the complex. Standard doubles in summer cost about US$80 midweek and US$100 weekends. More expensive penthouses, suites and villas are also available.

A bit more away from the action, *Hotel Brisas del Mar* (☎ /fax 6-612-25-47, 888-871-3605 in the US, Blvd Juárez 22), between Alamo and Abeto, has 71 carpeted, contemporary rooms with air-con, heater and cable TV. There's secured parking, a heated pool and volleyball courts. Rates range from US$45 to US$95 midweek and from US$65 to US$95 on weekends.

Places to Eat

To stock up on produce, cookies, drinks, cheese and the like, head to the giant Comercial supermarket in the Quinta Plaza shopping center. The best bakery is *Panificadora La Espiga*, with several branches around town, including one at Blvd Juárez and Calle Cárdenas. For delicious whole-grain pastries and breads, head to *La Sonrisa* (Blvd Juárez 285), next to the Dragon del Mar restaurant.

Central Rosarito Next to Hotel Festival Plaza, *Mi Casita* (☎ 6-163-02-77) is the oldest

taco place in town and, many say, still the best. At US$0.75 per taco and US$1.50 for burritos, you'll fill up without going broke. In the mood for fish tacos? Head across the street to *Just for the Halibut*, where you'll be given large chunks of deep-fried fish (or shrimp) to dress up with a wide range of condiments. Tacos cost US$1 each.

Also nearby is *Rock & Roll Taco*, a full bar/restaurant that was allegedly a favorite hangout of Leonardo di Caprio and Kate Winslet during the filming of *Titanic*. It's built on the site of a former mortuary, which may explain the numerous skeletons in the splashy decor. This is more a place for drinking and partying than eating, but it does serve decent tacos and other antojitos.

For more substantial fare, one of the best places in downtown Rosarito is *El Nido* (☎ 6-612-14-30, Blvd Juárez 67), which enjoys a good reputation for its prime cuts of meat as well as solidly prepared seafood dishes. *Salon Azteca* (☎ 6-612-01-44), inside the Rosarito Beach Hotel, is an all-gringo enclave but does good weekend buffets (breakfast US$7.95, lunch US$10.95, dinner US$8.95).

Northern Rosarito The venerable *La Flor de Michoacán* (☎ 6-612-18-58, Blvd Juárez 291) specializes in authentic carnitas, served with rice, beans, guacamole, salsa and tortillas. Individual portions cost US$6, while pork tacos cost US$0.80; it's closed Wednesday. Across the street is *Mariscos El Poder*, a simple stand that makes delicious fish tacos and other inexpensive seafood fare.

Upscale *La Fachada* (☎ 6-612-17-85, Blvd Juárez 317) gets rave reviews from almost everyone for grilled specialties like steak and lobster. *Ortega's Place* (☎ 6-612-17-57, Blvd Juárez 200) serves tasty lobster dinners; its weekly Sunday champagne brunch is also a big attraction for US$8. Another Ortega's (☎ 6-612-27-91) is in the Plaza Oceana, Blvd Juárez at Roble.

El Jardín Bohemio (☎ 6-612-11-66, Blvd Juárez 272), part of Motel Don Luis toward the northern end of town, serves Caribbean food, with an emphasis on Cuban fare, and often has live music.

Good Chinese restaurants are the ***Palacio Royal*** (☎ 6-612-14-12), at the Centro Comercial Ejido Mazatlán between J Amaro and E Zapata, and the banquet-style ***Dragon del Mar*** (☎ 6-612-06-04, Blvd Juárez 283). Both have the usual wallet-friendly lunch specials.

La Leña (☎ 6-612-08-26), in the Quinta Plaza shopping center, specializes in beef. At the same location is ***Casa de la Langosta*** (☎ 6-612-09-24), a seafood restaurant that makes some of the best Puerto Nuevo–style lobster in town for about US$15.

Near the beach, between Ebano and Cedro, ***Los Pelicanos Restaurant & Bar*** (☎ 6-612-17-37) serves juicy steaks and solid Mexican fare. It's not cheap, but its upstairs oceanview deck is a great place to watch the sunset.

Entertainment
On weekends, throngs of college students, soldiers and young Mexican-Americans descend on Rosarito from Southern California for a dose of serious partying. Many of the most raucous haunts are in or near the Hotel Festival Plaza complex. The Rosarito Beach Hotel presents performances by mariachis, singers and gaudy cowboys doing rope tricks on weekends.

El Museo de Tequila (☎ 6-612-29-50) competes with Pancho's in Cabo San Lucas for having the world's biggest tequila collection. There's often live mariachi music. Also here is Rock & Roll Taco (see Places to Eat, earlier), an imaginatively decorated bar that extends outdoors to a wooden deck and a small swimming pool.

Next to the hotel, another party palace – ***Señor Frogs*** – offers much the same mix of music, drinking and dancing.

Behind the hotel, by the beach, is ***Papas & Beer*** (☎ 6-612-04-44), one of a chain of dedicated watering holes. A small cover is usually charged, and a hefty bouncer keeps rowdies, minors (under 18) and other undesirables from entering this outdoor bar and its sandlot volleyball court.

Cines Río (☎ 6-612-11-05), on Blvd Juárez kitty-corner from Motel El Portal de Rosarito at the northern end of town, is a two-screen cinema showing recent movies,

usually Hollywood fare (often dubbed in Spanish).

A more subdued hangout is ***Capuchino's Coffee House*** (☎ 6-612-29-79, Blvd Juárez 890-3), between Encino and Eucalipto, which makes good espresso drinks and pastries. Next door, ***Nevería La Fuente*** offers an excellent selection of fruit-flavored juices and ices.

From June to October, *charreadas* (Mexican rodeos) often take place on Saturday afternoon. Check with the tourist offices for details.

Shopping
Rosarito has a reputation for being the best place in northern Baja for quality rustic furniture, which can be handmade to order for a fraction of what it would cost north of the border. Several businesses are on Blvd Juárez in Rosarito proper, but you'll find the biggest concentration – and lower prices – on the Transpeninsular a few miles south of town.

In downtown, the 150 stalls of the Mercado de Artesanías at Blvd Juárez 306, offer a huge selection of curios, crafts and souvenirs. This is where you should haggle for serapes, wind chimes, hats, T-shirts, pottery and glass items. It's open 9 am to 6 pm daily.

For better quality and more unique items, you might want to browse the 18,000 square feet of Apisa (☎ 6-612-01-25), at Blvd Juárez 2400 in northern Rosarito. It has an astonishing assortment of colonial-style furniture, sculptures and crafts, though none of it is cheap. Prices are lower at La Misión Viejo (☎ 6-612-15-76), Blvd Juárez 139, the oldest of Rosarito's fine crafts stores a bit farther north near Calle de Mexicali.

On Sunday, from early morning to late afternoon, the Mercado Sobre Ruedas, a produce-cum-flea market, takes place near the Ejido Mazatlán mall in northern Rosarito.

Getting There & Around
Bus From Friday to Sunday, Mexicoach operates its Rosarito Beach Express from the Terminal Turístico in downtown Tijuana, on Avenida Revolución between Calle 6a (Flores Magón) and Calle 7a (Galeana). Buses to Rosarito depart at 11 am and 1, 3 and 5 pm

and return at noon, 2, 4 and 8 pm. The fare is US$3 each way.

ABC buses between Tijuana and Ensenada stop at the tollgate at the southern end of Rosarito but do not enter the town itself. Southbound travelers may find it more convenient to take a route taxi (see below) to La Misión and flag down the bus there. ABC's commuter line, Subur Baja, comes through about every 20 minutes from 6 am to 8 pm (US$1) and goes to Tijuana's downtown terminal near the border.

Route Taxi Yellow route taxis leaving from a stand near the Rosarito Beach Hotel connect Rosarito with Tijuana (US$1). White taxis with yellow/green stripes, running to points as far south as La Misión, leave from the southern side of Hotel Brisas del Mar at Alamo and Blvd Juárez. Because all cabs travel along Blvd Juárez, Rosarito's main commercial drag, they are also a good way to travel from one end of town to the other; simply flag one down.

ROSARITO TO ENSENADA
Popotla

Until 1996, Popotla, about 3 miles (5km) south of Rosarito, at Km 33 on the Transpeninsular, was a rustic fishing village. Then Fox Studios Baja moved in. Planned as a temporary facility built for the filming of *Titanic* (1997), the site has evolved into a permanent studio. Its giant water tank has been used for scenes from several other movies, including *Tomorrow Never Dies* (1997) and *Deep Blue Sea* (1999). In 2000, parts of *Pearl Harbor*, starring Ben Affleck, were filmed here.

No studio tours are available, but visitors may explore the **Titanic Museum**, open weekends from 10 am to 6 pm for US$6. You'll see a 25-minute video about the making of the *Titanic* before you admire sets and props from the movie like the boiler room and the 1st-class smoking lounge. The replica ship itself, alas, has been turned into scrap metal.

To Baja insiders, Popotla was a favorite destination long before Hollywood arrived. The main attraction was – and still is – the super-fresh fish and seafood served here at prices much lower than in Rosarito, Ensenada or Puerto Nuevo. Most places are informal, family-run affairs that don't serve alcohol (bring your own), take only cash and are open for lunch only.

Places to Stay At Km 34 on the Transpeninsular, *Popotla Trailer Park* (☎ 6-612-15-02) caters to long-term campers. About 30 spaces are available to short-termers for US$20 a night; tent sites are US$17. The park has an oceanview restaurant, a clubhouse, showers, toilets and easy beach access.

At Km 35.5 on the Transpeninsular, *Hotel Calafia* (☎ 6-612-15-80, fax 6-612-02-96, 877-700-2093 in the US, calafia1@telnor.net) is a curious open-air museum showcasing important moments in Baja history. The ground's Plaza de las Misiones presents replicas of the facades of several of the peninsula's missions. As a tribute to recent events, there's even a small exhibit about the making of the *Titanic* inside the main building. The hotel itself has an attractive oceanfront setting with summer rates of US$55/79 midweek/weekend for rooms with ocean or garden views or US$70/85 for oceanfront rooms with balcony. Prices include dinner for two. On weekends, the restaurant does a famous brunch for US$7.95; the best tables are right above the waves.

The nicest hotel along the Tijuana-Ensenada corridor is the Mediterranean-style *Las Rocas Resort & Spa* (☎/fax 6-612-21-40, in the US ☎ 619-234-9810, 888-527-7622, lasrocas@telnor.net) at Km 38.5 on the Transpeninsular. Its 34 luxury suites and 40 standard rooms all have private, oceanview balconies, satellite TV and telephones. Suites are appointed with stylish furniture and have microwaves, coffeemakers and fireplaces. Guests relax by the free-form 'infinity' pool or luxuriate at the first-rate hotel spa; the long menu of treatments ranges from a regular facial to the more exotic basalt-rock massage. Also popular are the baths in private tubs in sun-flooded rooms with views of the waves. Two restaurants, both with attentive service, serve delicious seafood and Mexican dishes.

Summer rates start at US$89 for the standard rooms, surging to US$169 for the deluxe suites. From October to April, midweek rates are US$65/119 singles/doubles. Spa packages are available.

Puerto Nuevo

If tectonic uplift were not raising this section of the coastline from the sea, the village of Puerto Nuevo, at Km 44 on the Transpeninsular, might sink beneath the weight of its 35 or so seafood restaurants. They all specialize in lobster, usually cooked in one of two manners: *ranchera* (simmered in salsa) or *frito* (buttered and grilled) and served with flour tortillas, beans, rice, butter, salsa, chips and limes. All have similar prices, about US$15 for a full lobster dinner and US$10 for a grilled fish dinner.

It was the Ortega family who opened the first lobster restaurant in Puerto Nuevo, and their restaurant *Ortega's Patio* is one of the nicest places in town, especially if you get to sit on the outdoor terrace. They have several other branches here and two more in Playas

Lobster, Puerto Nuevo's specialty

de Rosarito. The ordinary-looking *Miramar* also serves good food.

For the best deals, go to the smaller places on the southern edge of the village, which get less foot traffic and often outdo each other with amazing specials. On our last visit, four half lobsters with all the fixings went for just US$12.

Within steps from Puerto Nuevo, on the Transpeninsular, are two luxury resorts with a full range of facilities like pools, tennis courts, Jacuzzis and restaurants. The *Grand Baja Resort (☎ 6-614-14-93, in the US ☎ 858-496-1216, 800-275-3280)* at Km 44.5 offers junior suites for two from US$55 off season (October to March) and US$69 the rest of the year. Studios with kitchenette are slightly more expensive. One- and two-bedroom apartments (sleeping four people) start at US$99 and US$120, respectively.

Next up, at Km 45, the sprawling *New Port Beach Hotel (☎ 6-614-11-88, fax 6-614-41-74, 800-582-1018 in the US)* has rooms from US$70 to US$189.

Cantamar

At about Km 47 on the Transpeninsular is this blip of a village, with a few small grocery stores, a bakery, tire store, taco stands, a Pemex and an interchange to the toll road. The spectacular Cantamar Dunes immediately south of here are regularly subjected to assaults by ATVs and other off-road vehicles. Admission is US$5 and there's primitive camping as well.

The *Halfway House (☎ 6-625-47-23)* is a popular restaurant serving Mexican combinations for less than US$5 and steak and seafood dinners for around US$15. Well known among mainland Californians who surf the reef breaks at nearby Punta Mesquite, the restaurant is about 3 miles (5km) south of Puerto Nuevo on the Transpeninsular. The garden on the northern side of the house is a great viewpoint for afternoon photographs.

Misión del Descanso

The Dominican Misión del Descanso was one of the last missions founded in California. When Misión San Miguel, about 5 miles (8km) south, lost its irrigation-friendly lands to floods, Fray Tomás de Ahumada moved part of its operations north to this site around 1817. The two missions operated simultaneously for some time, but Descanso was also known as San Miguel Nuevo. As of the historian Peveril Meigs' visit in 1927, adobe ruins still existed; an apparent guardhouse overlooked the mission from a 150-foot (45m) slope on the southern side of the valley.

A large marker commemorates the original mission, but there are no ruins. Instead, another church built in the early 20th century occupies the site. An abandoned adobe house on a knoll to the east was part of the 1827 Machado grant that assumed control of the mission lands.

The original boundary between the Dominican and Franciscan mission provinces, and thus between Baja and Alta California prior to the Treaty of Guadalupe Hidalgo, was just north of here but was later moved to Tijuana.

To get to the site, turn east onto a sandy road about 1½ miles (2.4km) south of Cantamar on the Transpeninsular (look for the sign of Vivero La Central nursery), which passes beneath the toll road and reaches the church after about half a mile (1km).

La Fonda

La Fonda is a tiny beach community presiding over a broad, sandy beach between Km 58 and Km 60 on the Transpeninsular. At Km 58.5, *Del Mar Suites* (☎ 6-155-03-92, 949-369-5686 in the US) offers spacious oceanview studios with private patios, full kitchens and couches for just US$40 to US$50. Its owner also rents tents for beach camping for US$20 and bikes for US$8/20 for three hours/day. Excellent surfing is nearby.

Next door, *Hotel La Misión* (☎ 6-155-03-33, fax 6-155-03-34, 562-420-8500 in the US) has regular doubles with king-size beds, fireplaces and ocean views for US$42/55 midweek/weekend. Suites with Jacuzzi and refrigerator are larger and cost US$79/80, plus tax. Rates drop in winter.

Its restaurant/bar has cheap dinner specials and margaritas, plus live music on weekends.

The nearby *Hotel La Fonda* (☎ 6-155-03-07) has themed rooms for US$75 and is often filled with gringos. The restaurant serves Mexican fare and seafood; some tables are on a deck above the sand. Despite its popularity, security here seems a bit suspect. The night watchman saw nothing odd in the arrival of a rickety station wagon at 3:30 am and the subsequent hot-wiring and high-speed departure of a Lonely Planet author's 4WD pickup.

If you're traveling on the toll road, take the Alisitos exit (from the south) or La Misión (from the north) to get to any of these places.

La Misión

The village of La Misión, on the Transpeninsular's inland turn, is most notable as the site of the Dominican **Misión San Miguel de la Frontera**, also known as San Miguel Encino and San Miguel Arcángel. Founded in 1787 at a site unknown today, the mission moved up the valley of the Río San Miguel when the spring it depended on dried up. This valley dissects a broad fault surface known locally as a mesa, which is surrounded by higher lava flows.

Fishing from balsa rafts, local Indians relied mostly on seafood for their subsistence, but the mission also grew wheat, maize, barley and beans and grazed more than 1600 cattle and 2100 sheep at its peak. The highest Indian population, about 400, occurred in 1824 – a fairly large number at this late date.

The few remaining ruins are behind the Escuela Primaria La Misión (the elementary school) at Km 65.5, about 1 mile (1.6km) south of the bridge over the Río San Miguel. They include the foundations and some adobe walls of the church and adjacent buildings.

Bajamar

Continuing on México 1D will take you to this rambling resort and residential complex at Km 77.5, built around an 18-hole golf course and a newer nine-holer. Both are open to the public; greens fees are US$65 for 18 holes midweek and US$80 on weekends. After 4 pm, rates drop to US$33/40. Club rentals are US$30.

The resort's *Hotel Hacienda Las Glorias* (☎ *6-615-01-51/2, 888-311-6076 in the USA for information/reservations*) has summer rates of US$110/135 midweek/weekends for standard rooms and US$152/176 for suites. Golf packages are available.

Free camping is possible on an attractive beach at Km 71 on México 1D.

At Km 72, *Baja Seasons RV & Villas Beach Resort* (☎ *6-628-61-28, fax 6-648-71-06, in the US* ☎ *619-422-2777, 800-754-4190*) has 154 landscaped spaces with full

---

Surf's Up

The entire coast south of Rosarito to Ensenada is legendary with the surf crowd, including Cantamar, La Fonda and San Miguel (see their respective sections).

A good place to get information is the Inner Reef Surf Shop, at Km 34.5 on the Trans-peninsular, whose owner Roger has been surfing these shores for nearly four decades. He also rents surfboards for US$2/hour (three-hour minimum) or US$20/day. Boogie boards rent for US$1.50/hour, US$10/day.

Many surfers camp out at *Surfpoint Camping* (at 'Uncle Benny's Point'), a small campground at Km 38, just past the Las Rocas Resort & Spa. Full hookups for RVs up to 25 feet (7.5m) cost US$15; tent sites cost US$5. There are hot showers, and a restaurant is nearby.

---

hookups on a nice stretch of beach. Facilities include a restaurant, a swimming pool, tennis courts and a laundry. There's also a small grocery and a clubhouse with big-screen TV.

Peak rates are US$67 for oceanfront sites and US$56 for inland sites. Tent spaces cost US$10 per person, US$5 for children. To get here, use the La Salina exit off México 1D.

El Mirador

El Mirador, a roadside viewpoint at Km 84 on México 1D, is spectacularly situated above the ocean. There are a few picnic tables and a children's playground, but no food or beverage service was in sight during our visit.

San Miguel

San Miguel is a small beach community about 7 miles (11km) north of Ensenada, just south of the third tollgate, which consists mostly of US retirees in mobile homes. Its main claim to fame, however, is a famous right point break with waves that draw in hordes of surfers, especially in the cooler months.

Ramona Beach Motel & Trailer Park (☎ *6-174-60-45*) at Km 104 has 50 sites with full hookups for US$12, less for tents. Rooms rent for US$25/35 singles/doubles.

Down by the beach, *San Miguel Village RV Park* (☎ *6-174-62-25*) offers 100 sites with full hookups, tent camping, hot showers and rustic toilets for about US$8 per night. A small *seafood restaurant* is at the entrance to the RV park.

El Sauzal

The seafood cannery at sedate El Sauzal, about 2 miles (3km) north of Ensenada, gives off a powerful fishy odor. However, there are several *trailer parks* and *camp-grounds* here that charge only US$4 to US$10 a night (though it's difficult to find one that doesn't cater mostly to long-term RVers.)

You can also try camping for free on any unclaimed stretch of beach. For hotels, see Places to Stay under Ensenada.

ENSENADA

About 75 miles south of the border on Bahía de Todos Santos, Ensenada (population 350,000) is the most sophisticated and well rounded of the northern coastal towns. It's a fairly wealthy city with great civic pride. Several museums are dedicated to its history, and generously designed public areas – rather than hotels – line the waterfront. These include Plaza Cívica, known colloquially as 'Plaza de Las Tres Cabezas' (Three Heads Plaza) for its massive busts of historical icons Benito Juárez, Miguel Hidalgo and Venustiano Carranza. The circular Plaza Ventana al Mar is anchored by a gigantic Mexican flag. Lining the harbor is a tranquil *malecón* (waterfront promenade), which culminates at the historic Riviera del Pacífico, perhaps the most beautiful building in northern Baja.

Ensenada enjoys great popularity among tourists; about four million of them descend upon the town each year, including 350,000 arriving by cruise ship from Southern California. Most visitors are drawn to Avenida López Mateos, a clean, nicely landscaped and pedestrian-oriented artery lined with interesting shops, cafes and restaurants with sidewalk seating, and many hotels.

If tourism forms one leg of the economy, ocean-based industries such as fishing, processing and shipping constitute the other: Baja's largest seaport is on Bahía de Todos Santos, where more than 900,000 tons of cargo are transshipped annually. While downtown has no beaches, a full menu of water-sports activities awaits a few miles south at Punta Banda, also the site of La Bufadora (the blowhole). Ensenada is also the capital of Baja's wine production and the gateway to the vineyards and wineries in nearby Valle de Guadalupe.

History

Located on the harbor of Bahía de Todos Santos, Ensenada has sheltered explorers, freighters and fishing boats for more than four centuries. Juan Rodríguez Cabrillo, searching for the Strait of Anián (the mythical Northwest Passage) with his caravels *San Salvador* and *Victoria,* entered the bay to replenish his water supply in September 1542, encountering a small group of Indian hunter-gatherers.

In 1602, Sebastián Vizcaíno named Ensenada de Todos los Santos after All Saints' Day, November 1. During colonial times, the harbor was an occasional refuge for Spanish galleons returning to Acapulco from Manila; the last one sailed through in 1815.

Far northern Baja was the last part of the peninsula to be missionized. The nearest missions were San Miguel de la Frontera (founded 1787) some 30 miles (48km) north, Nuestra Señora de Guadalupe (founded 1834) about 25 miles (40km) northeast, and Santo Tomás de Aquino (founded 1791) around 30 miles (48km) south.

Ensenada's first permanent settlement was established in 1804, when the Viceroy of New Spain granted the surrounding area to José Manuel Ruiz, whose Rancho Ensenada became a prosperous cattle ranch. It was purchased in 1824 by Francisco Gastelum, whose family consolidated farming and ranching interests in the area.

In 1869, discovery of gold at Real del Castillo, 22 miles (35km) inland, transformed the sleepy backwater. Bahía de Todos Santos was the closest harbor, the ranchos the closest food suppliers, and Ensenada boomed with an influx of miners, merchants and hangers-on. In 1882, the city became the capital of Baja territory (until 1915).

In the 1880s, the US-owned International Company of Mexico failed to attract agricultural colonists to the region and sold out to a British enterprise, the Mexican Land & Colonization Company. Closure of the mines and the failure of agricultural colonization ended the boom.

Ensenada briefly revived in the spring of 1911, when a splinter group of anarchist Magonistas occupied the mining hamlet of El Alamo, 40 miles (64km) southeast, but soon thereafter lost its political primacy when the territorial capital was shifted to Mexicali.

LA FRONTERA

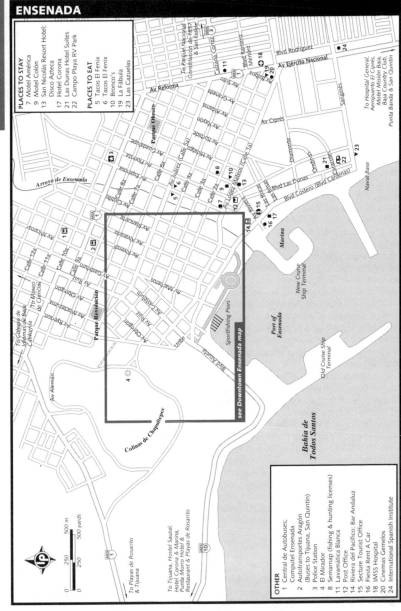

ENSENADA

PLACES TO STAY
7 Motel América
9 Motel Colón
13 San Nicolás Resort Hotel;
    Disco Azteca
17 Hotel Corona
21 Las Dunas Hotel Suites
22 Campo Playa RV Park

PLACES TO EAT
5 Tacos El Fénix
6 Tacos El Fénix
10 Bronco's
19 La Fábula
23 Las Cazuelas

OTHER
1 Central de Autobuses;
   Computel Ensenada
2 Autotransportes Aragón
   (Buses to Tijuana, San Quintín)
3 Police Station
4 El Mirador
8 Semarnap (fishing & hunting licenses)
11 Lavamática Blanca
12 Post Office
14 Riviera del Pacífico; Bar Andaluz
15 Secture Tourist Office
16 Fiesta Rent A Car
18 IMSS Hospital
20 Cinemas Gemelos
24 International Spanish Institute

After the Revolution, Ensenada, like Tijuana, began to cater to the 'sin' industries of drinking, gambling and sex during US Prohibition. The Playa Ensenada Hotel & Casino opened in the early 1930s but closed when Mexico's federal government outlawed casino gambling only a few years later. Renamed the Riviera del Pacífico, the Spanish-style hotel functioned as a resort for about another decade. Today, it's a cultural center that also offers facilities for wedding receptions and similar social occasions.

As more visitors came to Ensenada, entrepreneurs built more hotels and restaurants and the town became a tourist resort and weekend retreat for more than four million visitors annually.

Orientation

Ensenada, 68 miles (110km) south of Tijuana and 119 miles (192km) north of San Quintín, is a major fishing and commercial port on sheltered Bahía de Todos Santos. Most hotels and restaurants line Avenida López Mateos (also known as Calle 1a), which is one block inland from the waterfront Blvd Costero, also known as Blvd Lázaro Cárdenas.

Five blocks inland, Avenida Benito Juárez has shops and businesses catering to the local population. On the western end of downtown is Ensenada's 'party district,' centered on Avenida Ruiz. Legendary Hussong's Cantina (see Entertainment, later) is here as well. Farther west, the hills of Colinas de Chapultepec are an exclusive residential zone.

Just north of town, México 3 heads east and then north through the wine-growing country of the Valle de Guadalupe to the border at Tecate. From the southern end of Ensenada, México 3's southern continuation leads to Ojos Negros, Laguna Hanson in Parque Nacional Constitución de 1857 and San Felipe.

Heading southbound, the Transpeninsular (México 1) leads to the military checkpoint at Maneadero, beyond which foreigners must have a tourist card (see Visas & Documents in the Facts for the Visitor chapter).

Information

Tourist Offices Ensenada's Cotuco office (☎ 6-178-24-11, fax 6-178-36-75) is at Blvd Costero 540, across from the Pemex station. The staff are friendly, obliging and well informed, and lots of free maps and brochures are available. Hours are 9 am to 7 pm weekdays, 10 am to 6 pm Saturday and 11 am to 3 pm Sunday.

Secture (☎ 6-172-30-22, 6-172-30-81) is at Blvd Costero 1477 at Las Rocas near the Riviera del Pacífico. It's open 8 am to 5 pm weekdays, 10 am to 3 pm weekends. The Tourist Assistance Office, which can help with legal problems, is here as well.

Immigration Servicios Migratorios (☎ 6-674-01-64), Blvd Azueta 101, issues tourist cards required for travel south of Maneadero. It's open 9 am to 5 pm daily.

Money Most businesses accept dollars, but if you're traveling farther south you will need pesos.

Ensenada has plenty of banks that have ATMs and also change money. Banco Santander, Banco Serfin and Bancomer are all on Avenida Ruiz. Banamex is on Avenida Ryerson at Calle 3a. Cambio Yesan, Avenida Ruiz 201, keeps longer hours, but rates may not be as favorable. American Express (see Travel Agencies, later) cashes its own checks free of commission.

Post & Communications Ensenada's main post office, at López Mateos and Riviera, is open 8 am to 6 pm weekdays, 9 am to 1 pm Saturday. The postal code is 22800.

Telnor public telephones are widespread in Ensenada, but the Computel Ensenada office at the bus terminal (Avenida Riveroll 1075) conveniently allows payment by Visa or MasterCard. Avoid the extortionate non-Telnor street phones when calling outside of Mexico.

Cafe Internet 2000, upstairs at López Mateos 582, has about 50 fast computers and charges US$2.25 per hour. The Lost Civilizations, at Avenida Ruiz 168 across from Hussong's, is smaller and slightly more expensive. Both are open daily from 9 am to 11 pm.

Internet Resources Writer Connie Ellig runs a thorough Web-based English-language newspaper about Ensenada and surroundings at www.gazette.ensenada.net.mx.

Travel Agencies Reputable Viajes Damiana (☎ 6-174-01-70), on Calle 2a 300-4, is a full-service travel agency that is also the local American Express representative.

Bookstores The Bookseller (☎ 6-178-89-64), at Calle 4a 240, has used English-language magazines and books. It's closed Sunday and Monday. Librería Ramirez, at Avenida Ruiz 408, has a good selection of current US magazines.

Laundry Lavamática Blanca, located in the mall at the corner of Avenida Reforma and Calzada Cortez, offers self-service washers and dryers.

Medical & Emergency Services Ensenada's Hospital General (☎ 6-176-78-00) is at Km 111 on the Transpeninsular south of the city. The IMSS Hospital (emergency ☎ 6-172-45-00) is on Avenida Reforma at Blvd Ramirez Méndez, east of downtown. For an ambulance, call the Cruz Roja at ☎ 066. The police (☎ 060) have a station on Calle 9a at Espinosa, north of downtown.

El Mirador
Atop the Colinas de Chapultepec, El Mirador offers panoramic views of the city and Bahía de Todos Santos. Climb or drive up Avenida Alemán from the western end of Calle 2a in central Ensenada to the highest point in town.

Bodegas de Santo Tomás
Founded in 1888 near the vineyards of the Valle de Santo Tomás south of Ensenada, Santo Tomás (☎ 6-178-33-33, 6-178-25-09), Avenida Miramar 666, is one of Baja's premier vintners. After purchasing the winery in 1937, former Mexican president

Abelardo Rodríguez moved its facilities to Ensenada to expedite shipping. Today, it's owned and operated by the Mexico-based multinational Corporación Elías Pando y Cosio.

Varieties include pinot noir, chardonnay and cabernet; up to 120,000 cases are shipped annually throughout Mexico and to Western Europe, but not to the US.

The winery offers daily 30-minute tours at 10 and 11 am, noon, 1 and 3 pm for US$2, including tasting of four wines. For US$5, you can sample up to 15 wines and also get a souvenir glass.

Riviera del Pacífico
An extravagant waterfront complex with Spanish-Moorish architectural touches, the Riviera del Pacífico opened in 1930 as the Playa Ensenada Hotel & Casino. The second casino in northern Baja (after the Agua Caliente in Tijuana), this lavish facility was once the haunt of Hollywood figures including ex-Olympic swimmer Johnny Weissmuller ('Tarzan'), Myrna Loy, Lana Turner, Ali Khan and Dolores del Río. Briefly managed by US boxer Jack Dempsey, the facility closed in 1938 when President Lázaro Cárdenas outlawed casino gambling.

Rescued from the wrecking ball in the early 1990s, the building was reborn as the **Centro Social, Cívico y Cultural de Ensenada** and now hosts cultural events, weddings, conventions and meetings.

Open to the public, the Riviera del Pacífico – framed by splendid gardens – is well worth exploring. The lobby (which is entered from the Jardín Bugambillias courtyard on the parking lot side behind the building) contains an impressive **relief map** of the mission sites throughout Baja and Alta California. Most rooms feature carved and painted ceilings, elaborate tile work, giant wrought-iron chandeliers and creaky parquet floors. The Dining Room and the circular Casino Room are especially impressive, as is the elegant Bar Andaluz (see Entertainment, later) with its arched wooden bar.

DOWNTOWN ENSENADA

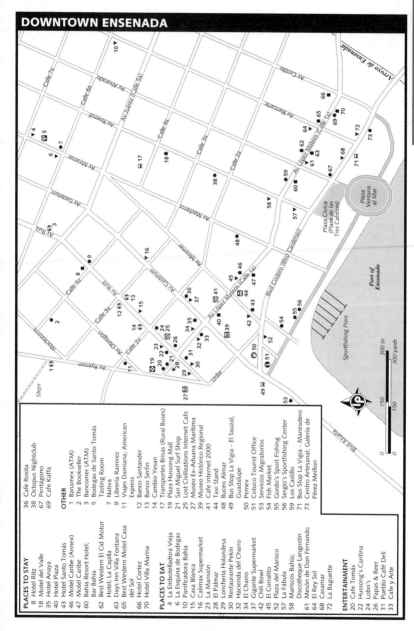

PLACES TO STAY
8 Hotel Ritz
18 Motel del Valle
35 Hotel Anaya
40 Hotel Plaza
43 Hotel Santo Tomás
46 Motel Caribe (Annex)
47 Motel Caribe
60 Bahía Resort Hotel;
     Bar Bahía
62 Best Western El Cid Motor
     Hotel; La Capilla
63 Days Inn Villa Fontana
65 Best Western Motel Casa
     del Sol
66 Hotel Cortez
70 Hotel Villa Marina

PLACES TO EAT
4 La Embotelladora Vieja
6 La Esquina de Bodegas
10 Panificadora Bahía
15 Casa Blanca
16 Calimax Supermarket
23 La Mansión
28 El Palmar
29 Lonchería Holandesa
30 Restaurante Pekín
32 Hacienda del Charro
34 El Charro
37 Gigante Supermarket
42 Chili Bowl
45 El Corralito
52 Plaza del Marisco
57 La Fábula
58 Mariscos Bahía;
     Discotheque Langostín
61 Mesón de Don Fernando
64 El Rey Sol
68 Casamar
72 La Baguette

ENTERTAINMENT
20 Cafe Tomás
22 Hussong's Cantina
24 Lobo's
26 Papas & Beer
31 Pueblo Café Deli
33 Cafe y Arte

36 Cafe Rosita
38 Octopus Nightclub
67 Pentágono
69 Cafe Kaffa

OTHER
1 Banamex (ATM)
2 The Bookseller
3 Bancomer (ATM)
5 Bodegas de Santo Tomás
     Tasting Room
7 Nativa
9 Librería Ramírez
11 Viajes Damiana; American
     Express
12 Banco Santander
13 Banco Serfín
14 Cambio Yesan
17 Transportes Brisas (Rural Buses)
19 Plaza Hussong Mall
21 San Miguel Surf Shop
25 Lost Civilizations Internet Cafe
27 Museo Ex-Aduana Marítima
39 Museo Histórico Regional
41 Cafe Internet 2000
44 Taxi Stand
48 Buceo Almar
49 Bus Stop La Vigía - El Sauzal,
     Guadalupe
50 Pemex
51 Cotuco Tourist Office
53 Servicios Migratorios
54 Fish Market
55 Gordo's Sport Fishing
56 Sergio's Sportfishing Center
59 Los Castillo
71 Bus Stop La Vigía - Maneadero
73 Centro Artesanal; Galería de
     Pérez Meillon

The complex also contains the **Museo de Historia**, which traces northern Baja history from the indigenous Indians to the mission period. A new wing features changing themed exhibits and an art gallery. The museum is open daily 9 am to 2 pm and 3 to 5 pm (Monday from 10 am); admission is US$1. On the building's basement level is the **Galería de la Cuidad**, with monthly exhibits featuring Baja California artists. It's open 9 am to 6 pm weekdays; admission is free.

Museo Histórico Regional

This modest exhibit about the 'People and Cultures of Meso-America' is housed in an 1886 military barracks that served as the city's jail until as recently as 1986.

Perhaps more intriguing than the exhibit is the cell block where several of the tiny, windowless concrete cubicles sport some rather accomplished murals by the former inmates. Staying in one of these 'private' cells was actually a privilege that had to be paid for; the alternative was the crammed and explosive general holding cell. (Apparently, this practice is still common in some Mexican prisons.)

The museum (☎ 6-178-25-31), on Avenida Gastelum near López Mateos, is open 10 am to 5 pm daily except Monday; a donation is requested.

Museo Ex-Aduana Marítima

Built in 1887 by the US-owned International Company of Mexico, the former Marine Customs House is Ensenada's oldest public building. It houses rotating exhibitions with a cultural or historical angle. The museum is at Avenida Ryerson 99 at Uribe and is open 10 am to 5 pm but closed Monday; donations are encouraged.

Museo de Ciencias

More school-oriented than general interest, Ensenada's science museum contains exhibits on both the natural and physical sciences, stressing marine ecology along with endangered species and habitats. At Avenida Obregón 1463 between Calles 14a and 15a north of downtown, the museum is open from 9 am to 5 pm Tuesday to Friday and noon to 5 pm Saturday. A donation is requested.

Markets

Ensenada's largest outdoor market, the **Mercado Los Globos** is heaven on earth for collectors of bric-a-brac. Sprawled over an area of eight square blocks on Calle 9a east of Avenida Reforma, vendors sell everything from old radios and typewriters to fruit and vegetables. It's open Wednesday to Sunday, but more stalls are open on weekends.

By the sportfishing piers is the colorful **Fish Market**, where you can admire – and purchase – the day's catch daily between 6:30 am and 7 pm. The taquerías in the market area do not have a good reputation.

Diving

Buceo Almar (☎ 6-178-30-13), Avenida Macheros 149, is the local dive shop (sales only). For equipment rentals and excursions, see La Bufadora in the Around Ensenada section, later.

Fishing

Among the popular species in the area are albacore, barracuda, bonito, halibut, white sea bass and yellowtail, depending on the season. Most people join an organized fishing trip for about US$40 per person. Groups traveling together can also charter an entire boat. Rates depend on the vessel, but figure on about US$600 for a 12-passenger cruiser or around US$200 for a four-person panga (less during the week).

The two main operators are Gordo's Sport Fishing (☎ 6-178-35-15, fax 6-178-04-81) and Sergio's Sportfishing Center (☎/fax 6-178-21-85, sergios@telnor.net), both with offices right next to the sportfishing piers near the Fish Market. Organized trips leave year round at 7 am and return at 2:30 pm.

Everyone on board (whether fishing or not) must have a Mexican fishing license. These are available from Semarnap (☎ 6-176-38-37), which has offices on Calle 2a at Avenida Guadalupe.

Whale-Watching

Between December and March, California gray whales pass through Bahía de Todos Santos on their way to southern Baja calving sites at Laguna Ojo de Liebre (Scammon's Lagoon), Laguna San Ignacio and Bahía Magdalena. Besides observing whales swimming, breaching and diving, you'll be able to see pelicans, gulls, cormorants and other seabirds skimming the ocean's surface. Sea lions and harbor seals dot the buoys and guano-covered rocks in the harbor and around the islands.

Both Gordo's and Sergio's (see Fishing, above) operate four-hour whale-watching trips for about US$20. The Museo de Ciencias also organizes tours that are accompanied by a – usually – bilingual guide and also cost about US$20.

Golf

Two golf courses are within easy reach from Ensenada. About 10 miles (16km) to the south is the 18-hole Baja Country Club (☎ 6-177-55-23), at the end of a canyon and open daily 7 am to 7 pm. Greens fees are US$35/45 weekday/weekend, including the golf cart; equipment may be rented for US$12. Golf packages through the Hotel Las Dunas (see Places to Stay, later) cost US$49 per person, including lodging and unlimited golf.

The Gray Eminences of Baja

Along with the mysterious spawning runs of salmon up the great rivers and streams of the Pacific Northwest, the migration of the great gray whales from Siberian and Alaskan waters to the lagoons of Baja is one of the world's most amazing animal accomplishments. Sliding majestically along the shore – at the stately clip of 3 to 4mph (5 to 7kph) – the whales will have swum between 10,000 and 14,000 miles (6250 to 8750km) before reaching the sanctuary of Baja's warm and protected shallow waters. There, in calving grounds such as Scammon's Lagoon southeast of Guerrero Negro and Laguna San Ignacio southeast of San Ignacio, 1500lb calves will draw their first breath and begin learning the lessons of the sea from their ever-watchful mothers.

Mature grays can range from 45 to 50 feet (15 to 18m) in length and weigh from 30 to 40 tons (27 to 36 tonnes). Of the three gray populations that once flourished, the North Atlantic branch was wiped out and the western North Pacific is faltering. This fate nearly befell the grays of Baja when their slaughter began in the calving grounds in the 1850s. Almost one century later, they were given total protection and their numbers have risen steadily to more than 20,000 – quite close to their original population.

Peak months to spot mothers and calves in the lagoons are February to early April. During the later days of their stay in Baja, the calves will have grown strong enough to slip the parental guidance of their leviathan moms. This can result in a curious calf swimming directly up to a rolling panga or zodiac to have its snout scratched and petted – an awesome close encounter. After two to three months of sheltered waters and a near doubling in their birth weight, the calves will follow their mothers back to the open sea and the long three-month glide home to their rich feeding grounds in the frozen north. And the following year, they will return.

The other golf course, on the ocean and generally considered nicer, is at Bajamar, about 22 miles (35km) north of town. For details, see the Bajamar entry, earlier.

Special Events

More than 70 sporting, tourist and cultural events take place in Ensenada each year; the ones listed below are only a sample. Dates are subject to change, so contact one of the tourist offices or event organizers for specifics.

Carnaval (Carnival or Mardi Gras) February. Ensenada's biggest truly Mexican celebration.

Spring Bicycle Ride Rosarito-Ensenada early April. For details, contact Bicycling West (☎ 619-583-3001 in the US).

Newport Beach Regatta late April. Yacht race from Newport Beach in California to Ensenada.

Fiesta de los Viñedos en Flor early May. Celebrates the beginning of the vintners' season; for details, contact Viajes Damiana at ☎ 6-174-01-70.

Fiesta La Misión late May. Two days of dancing, food and music at Misión San Miguel de la Frontera.

SCORE Baja 500 early June. Off-highway race; for details, call ☎ 818-853-8068 in the US.

Baja Open mid-July. Beach volleyball tournament at El Faro beach; for details, call Ensenada Sports Promotions (☎ 6-177-66-00).

Fiesta de la Vendimia (Wine Harvest) early August. Kicks off harvest season with cultural events in Guadalupe Valley and Ensenada.

International Seafood Fair mid-September. Seafood cooking competition judged by chefs from San Diego; for details, call ☎ 6-174-04-48.

Mexican Independence Day mid-September. Weeklong celebration of independence from Spain in 1810.

Annual Juan Hussong International Chili Cook-Off late September. Takes place at Hotel Quintas Papagayo, north of town.

Bicycle Ride Rosarito-Ensenada late September.

Mexican Surf Fiesta early October. Top competitors vie for the perfect wave at Playa San Miguel.

Fiesta de Real del Castillo mid-October. Anniversary of gold strike in the mountains east of Ensenada, with period costumes; takes place in the village, with music, dance and prizes.

SCORE Baja 1000 mid-November. Classic off-highway race from Ensenada to Cabo San Lucas.

Christmas Posadas nine nights starting December 16. Candle-lit processions that end at a nativity scene, usually built by locals.

Places to Stay

Although Ensenada has many hotels, demand can exceed supply at times. On weekends and in summer, reservations are advisable. Unless there's a special event, weekday accommodations are not a problem, but as in Playas de Rosarito, rates vary both seasonally and between weekdays and weekends, making it difficult to categorize hotels by price.

Budget At the southern end of downtown, at Blvd Las Dunas and Sanginés, **Campo Playa RV Park** (☎ 6-176-29-18) has 90 small, grassy campsites with shade trees for pitching a tent or parking a camper or motor home. Fees are US$18 for camping and US$20 for hookups, both including access to hot showers.

There's free **camping** on Playa Hermosa starting about 1 mile (1.6km) south of town. At Km 12.5 on the Transpeninsular is the **Joker Hotel & RV Park** (☎ 6-176-72-01, fax 6-177-44-60, 800-256-5372 in the US), which charges US$17 but has just 12 sites. Rooms at the hotel, built to look like a castle, cost US$43.

One of the few hostels in northern Baja, **Hostel Sauzal** (☎ 6-174-63-81, 344 Avenida L) is a friendly alcohol-free place in the suburb of El Sauzal, about 6 miles (10km) north of Ensenada. Bunks in four-person oceanview dorms cost US$10, including breakfast. To get there, take the local bus called 'El Vigia' from the corner of Costero and Gastelum (near the Cotuco tourist office); it costs US$0.50.

Central Ensenada's best bargain is **Motel Caribe** (☎ 6-178-34-81, Avenida López Mateos 628), whose clean rooms cost US$25 without TV or US$30 with TV. Larger ones are US$5 to US$15 more. In the annex across the street, considerably less comfortable rooms cost just US$15.

Another good choice is **Motel América** (☎ 6-176-13-33, López Mateos 1309), which has clean, simple singles/doubles with kitchenette for US$22/33. **Motel Colón** (☎ 6-176-19-10, fax 6-176-47-82), at López Mateos and Guadalupe, is similar and charges the same.

A step up is the **Hotel Ritz** (☎ 6-174-05-01, fax 6-178-32-62, Calle 4a 381), a remodeled downtown hostelry that's managed to retain some character; rates are US\$25/35 for carpeted rooms with cable TV and telephone.

Those who can afford a little more may like the modern, well-kept *Motel del Valle* (☎ *6-178-22-24, Avenida Riveroll 367)*. Its 21 carpeted rooms with cable TV cost US\$38 to US\$47, but rates may rise after the completion of a new annex.

A bit south of town, *Motel Misión Baja* (☎ *6-176-65-51, fax 6-177-66-80, Avenida Topacio 287)* offers good-value rooms with satellite TV, kitchen and telephone for around US\$40.

If all these places are full, consider *Hotel Anaya* (☎ *6-178-27-21, Avenida Gastelum 127)*, whose charm-free rooms cost US\$20/25. Its one redeeming feature is the restaurant-bar with cheap breakfasts and lunches.

Nearby *Hotel Plaza* (☎ *6-178-27-15, Avenida López Mateos 542)* is an architectural gem that's sadly been allowed to decay into a dump. Rates of US\$25/30 for rooms with bath and TV attract not just the budget-minded but also the 'ladies of the night' and their customers.

Mid-Range Many places in this category flank Avenida López Mateos, the main tourist drag. Ask for a room away from the street if you're not part of the party crowd.

Those looking for character and comfort should encamp at the venerable *Hotel Cortez* (☎ *6-178-23-07, fax 6-178-39-04, 800-303-2684 in the US, Avenida López Mateos 1089)*. Rooms spread out over three structures and come with air-con, heater and color TV. Free coffee, newspaper, bottled water and room service are available as well. Rates range from US\$55 for standard rooms to US\$70 for small suites. This is a popular place; it's often booked solid on summer weekends, so make reservations.

Another favorite is *Bahía Resort Hotel* (☎ *6-178-21-03, fax 6-178-14-55, 888-308-9048 in the US, htlbahia@telnor.net)*, Avenida López Mateos at Alvarado, whose 64 clean, carpeted rooms with balcony, heater and small refrigerator range from US\$36 to US\$65. The bar here serves up tasty margaritas.

Renovated and upgraded, *Days Inn Villa Fontana* (☎ *6-178-34-34, 800-422-5204 in the US, Avenida López Mateos 1050)* has a bar, coffee shop, swimming pool, Jacuzzi and parking. Comfortable rooms with full carpeting, air-con, cable TV and balcony cost from US\$50 to US\$60.

The *Best Western El Cid Motor Hotel* (☎ *6-178-24-01, fax 6-178-36-71, 800-352-4305 in the US, info@hotelelcid.com, Avenida López Mateos 993)* has rooms from US\$50 to US\$70 during the week and US\$75 to US\$100 on weekends. The hotel has a swimming pool, a great restaurant and secure parking.

Ensenada's only high-rise, the *Hotel Villa Marina* (☎/fax 6-178-33-51)*, located between Castillo and Blancarte, offers a swimming pool and restaurant as well as harbor views from many of its rooms. Rooms start at US\$60 on weekdays but climb to US\$100 on weekends.

Special touches at the *Best Western Motel Casa del Sol* (☎ *6-178-15-70, fax 6-178-20-25, 800-528-1234 in the US, Avenida López Mateos 1001)* include a welcome cocktail and free HBO cable TV. Rates range from US\$40 to US\$55.

Close to the tourist office, *Hotel Santo Tomás* (☎ *6-178-15-03, fax 6-178-15-04, 800-303-2684 in the US, Blvd Costero 609)* has some rooms set aside for nonsmokers. There's plenty of free parking, coffee and newspapers, and a small range of business services. Rates range from US\$55 to US\$70. Golf packages with the Bajamar course are available as well.

South of the downtown area, the pleasant *Las Dunas Hotel Suites* (☎ *6-176-27 71, fax 6-177-24-08, Calle Caracoles 169)* offers family suites with bedroom, living room with sofabed, dining area and full kitchens from US\$66. There's also a pool, Jacuzzi and barbecue area. Golf packages with the Baja Country Club cost US\$49 per person.

Top End The 140-room *San Nicolás Resort Hotel* (☎ *6-176-19-01, fax 6-176-49-30, Avenida López Mateos 1534)* is popular with groups and has a coffee shop, bar, nightclub and restaurant. There's an outdoor and new indoor pool. Rooms with all the modern conveniences, including coffee-maker, start at US$75.

Facing the harbor near the Riviera del Pacífico, the tile-roof **Hotel Corona** *(☎ 6-176-09-01, fax 6-176-09-04, h.corona@microsol .com.mx, Blvd Costero 1442)* has 93 rooms, all with balcony, color TV, heater and air-con, from US$70 to US$120.

Punta Morro Hotel Suites *(☎ 6-178-35-07, fax 6-174-44-90, 800-526-6676 in the US)* is a stylish, quiet and relaxing oceanside resort at Km 106, about 1½ miles (2.4km) north of Ensenada. Beautifully appointed suites have kitchens and terraces with views of the waves. The restaurant is among the best in the area (see Places to Eat). Rates are US$86/130/175 for suites with one/two/three bedrooms, dropping by about 20% from Sunday to Thursday.

Currently the fanciest lodging Ensenada has to offer, the **Hotel Coral & Marina** *(☎ 6-175-00-00, fax 6-175-00-05, in the US ☎ 619-523-0064, 800-862-8020)* is at Km 103 on the Transpeninsular, a short drive north of town. The luxurious facility has spacious ocean-view suites, three pools, Jacuzzis, tennis courts and other lush stuff. Rates start at US$135 for the standard double suite.

Places to Eat

As a popular tourist spot, Ensenada has eateries ranging from corner taco stands and basic restaurants offering antojitos to places featuring varied seafood, Chinese and sophisticated French cuisine.

Large supermarkets in the downtown area include a branch of Gigante on Gastelum between López Mateos and Calle 2a and a Calimax one block north on the same street.

La Baguette, on Blvd Costero near Blancarte, makes delicious fruit tarts, cheesecakes, croissants and other European-style pastries. One of Ensenada's largest and most popular bakeries is **Panificadora Bahía** at Calle 6a and Blancarte. More than three dozen types of pan dulce, as well as bolillos, are baked here daily.

Seafood For the city's best fish tacos, you should head to **Tacos El Fenix**, at the corner of Juárez and Espinosa. A local institution and always thronged by regulars, it's clean, fresh and friendly. Each taco costs US$0.60; shrimp tacos are US$0.90.

Seafood lovers should also try **Mariscos Bahía** *(Avenida Riveroll 109)*, where portions are generous, prices reasonable and service friendly. The sautéed garlic shrimp for US$10 is a great value, and there's a nice sidewalk terrace from which to observe the action.

Plaza del Marisco, on Blvd Costero near the Fish Market, is a cluster of seafood taco stands with more reliable quality than those adjacent to the market itself.

Lively **El Palmar** *(☎ 6-178-87-88, Avenida López Mateos 328)*, canopied by a giant palapa, is another casual place to enjoy the day's catch. There's live banda music from Thursday to Sunday.

Casamar *(☎ 6-174-04-17, Blvd Costero 987)* is a costlier choice specializing in items like lobster salad, Filet Manila (a broiled fish filet smothered in mango sauce), a variety of shrimp dishes, fried frog legs and octopus.

For a special treat, book a table at the cliffside **Punta Morro Restaurant** *(☎ 6-178-35-07)*, at Km 106 on the Transpeninsular, about 1 mile (1.6km) north of Ensenada. You'll be seated above crashing waves that will compete for your attention with the impeccably prepared and tasty seafood and meat dishes (about US$20). This classy establishment is also part of a resort complex (see Places to Stay, earlier).

Mexican Though it serves standard antojitos, **Las Cazuelas** *(☎ 6-176-10-44, Blvd Sanginés 6)* has a chef whose repertory is more creative than most. Choices may include stuffed squid, quail in orange sauce and abalone with lobster sauce, all at fairly reasonable prices. It's also famous for its breakfast omelets.

At **Bronco's** *(☎ 6-176-49-00, Avenida López Mateos 1525)*, vaquero culture is alive in the decor as well as in the hearty and humongous fare coming from the steamy kitchen. Its mesquite-grilled steaks are top quality, and it's open for breakfast, lunch and dinner.

Casa Blanca (☎ 6-174-03-16, *Avenida Ruiz 254*) is a simple coffee shop with decent set lunches for about US$3. A better choice is **Lonchería Holandesa**, on Ruiz south of López Mateos, in business since 1962. The comida corrida is also US$3, but the burrito de machaca for US$4, including salad, is a favorite. Both places close at 9 pm.

Tourist-oriented **Mesón de Don Fernando** (☎ 6-174-01-55, *Avenida López Mateos 627*) has adequate, if slightly pricey, fare. The best deal is the weekday breakfast buffet for US$5. Otherwise, the best reason to come is for the excellent margaritas, best enjoyed on the sidewalk terrace.

For marinated Mexican-style chicken, grilled or roasted over an open flame, try **Hacienda del Charro** (☎ 6-178-40-45, *Avenida López Mateos 454*). Freshly made tortillas, salsa and other condiments accompany all orders, many of which cost around US$5. The related **El Charro** across the street is more casual but has the same food.

The 24-hour **El Corralito** (☎ 6-178-23-70, *Avenida López Mateos 627*) serves OK antojitos but really shines on weekends when the nighttime crowd arrives for refueling sessions between bar visits. Also popular for this purpose is **Chili Bowl** (☎ 6-178-84-74), on Miramar near López Mateos, serving its namesake as well as breakfast around the clock.

International The Santo Tomás winery complex on Avenida Miramar between and Calle 6a and 7a features two outstanding dining establishments. **La Esquina de Bodegas** (☎ 6-178-75-57) is worth a look for its decor alone. Metamorphosed from a former brandy distillery, it integrates the ancient drums, vats and pipes into a hip industrial environment. En route to the dining area, you'll pass a wine boutique and an art gallery. The menu is Mediterranean with Mexican inflections and starts at US$7.50 for pasta to about US$40 for a seven-course gourmet meal.

The more formal **La Embotelladora Vieja** (☎ 6-174-08-07) is an ambience-laden wine cellar decorated with wooden casks and other wine-making implements where the culinary focus is Spanish-Mexican. The weekday set lunch (three courses and a glass of wine) is an excellent value at US$10. Dinners run about US$20 to US$30. It's closed Tuesday.

One of Baja's finest dining experiences, venerable **El Rey Sol** (☎ 6-178-23-51, *Avenida López Mateos 1000*) is an elegant but relaxed French-Mexican restaurant. Full dinners start at US$35, but if you pick carefully, you can get away with less. Drinks are excellent and reasonably priced, and the service attentive but unobtrusive. Leave room for the killer pastries.

Easier on the wallet is **La Mansión** (☎ 6-178-32-71, *Avenida Ruiz 149*), popular for its breakfasts, including eggs benedict. At dinnertime, the juicy chateaubriand is a favorite (US$22).

Pizza places include the chain restaurant **La Fábula** on Avenida Riveroll, just north of Blvd Costero; there's another branch at Avenida Balboa 169, near the movie theater.

Families flock to **Restaurante Pekín** (☎ 6-178-11-58, *Avenida Ruiz 98*), an established Chinese favorite where you can fill up for as little as US$3.

Entertainment

Bars Potent, tasty and inexpensive beer, margaritas and other liquors are prime attractions for gringos, especially those under the mainland California drinking age of 21. On weekends, most bars and cantinas along Avenida Ruiz, which might more accurately be called 'Avenida Ruido' (Avenue Noise), are packed from midday to early morning.

Spit-and-sawdust **Hussong's Cantina** (☎ 6-178-32-10, *Avenida Ruiz 113*) is probably the best-known watering hole in the Californias – though its namesake beer now comes from Mazatlán. After arriving from Germany in the late 19th century, the Hussong family used their knowledge of traditional German brewing to establish one of Ensenada's first cantinas in 1892. Initially a stagecoach stop frequented by miners and ranchers, it later hosted Hollywood glam queen Marilyn Monroe, rough rider Steve McQueen and a host of other celebs. These days it's the 'mecca of margaritas and mariachis' for a motley crowd of college students, tattooed bikers, honeymooning cruise-ship couples and retirees. It's open from 10 am to 1 am, but tables – and even spots at the bar – are often at a premium after mid-afternoon.

Nearby **Papas & Beer** (☎ 6-174-01-45, *Avenida Ruiz 102*) caters mostly to rowdy college students, and a small army of bouncers keeps things under control. Roaring music drowns out conversations, but the margaritas are sweet and fruity; hours are 10 am to 3 am.

For a complete change in ambience, visit the cultured **Bar Andaluz** (☎ 6-177-17-30) inside the Riviera del Pacífico, where having a drink is an exercise in nostalgia. You can almost visualize Lana Turner sipping a martini at the polished walnut bar.

In Search of the Best Margarita

Hordes of gringos descend on Ensenada in search of the perfect margarita, and many become derailed as a result – the victims of their successful 'research.' Solely as a service to you, dear readers, we undertook this most grueling sort of legwork, put our bodies – and brains – on the line, and narrowed down the choices. Here's our top three 'Margie' list, as far as we can recall...

Margaritas at Hussong's Cantina look small and innocent but pack a mean and sneaky punch. They're also a good value at US$2.50. At Mesón de Don Fernando, you'll need both hands to hoist the 'birdbath' glasses – ask for 'on the rocks' and expect to fork over about US$5. Another convincing contender is Bar Bahía, inside the Bahía Hotel, whose heady concoctions keep the karaoke crowd howling like demented coyotes in heat. So pick your poison and, if memory serves us, let us know about your favorite 'cactus cocktail.'

Please note: Lonely Planet accepts no responsibility for the behavior of those who wake up with racy tattoos or lost articles of intimate apparel.

Nightclubs Above the Mariscos Bahía restaurant, **Discotheque Langostín** (☎ 6-174-03-18, *Avenida Riveroll 109*) is where low-key locals take to the dance floor to disco, banda and rock, depending on the day. Friday is Ladies Night, with free drinks until 10 pm. Cover is about US$3. Up the street, the trendy **Octopus** caters more to a younger (18 to 25) crowd and charges a slightly higher cover. Both places have live music on weekends.

Lobo's, at Avenida Ruiz and Calle 2a, is a good place to swing your hips to a tropical Latin beat. Locals and tourists come here and there's usually no cover. **Pentágono** (☎ 6-178-18-69, *Avenida Alvarado 12*) also specializes in salsa music.

Another popular haunt for the mid-20s-and-up crowd is **Disco Azteca** (☎ 6-176-19-01 ext 257, *Avenida López Mateos 1534*), inside the Hotel San Nicolás, which also puts on Latin and tropical tunes nightly with live bands on weekends.

The smallish **La Capilla** (☎ 6-178-24-01, *Avenida López Mateos 993*), inside the El Cid Motor Hotel, is also popular.

Cafes For a serious java jolt, head to **Cafe Kaffa**, on López Mateos between Castillo and Blancarte, or **Cafe Tomás**, in the Plaza Hussong mall farther west. Nearby, **Pueblo Café Deli** (☎ 6-178-80-55, *Avenida Ruiz 96*) serves pasta, salads and sandwiches (under US$10) in addition to delicious coffee drinks.

Cafe y Arte (*Avenida López Mateos 496*) is an artsy place where most of the decoration is also for sale. Catering more to Ensenada's local population is the down-to-earth **Cafe Rosita**, on Gastelum near Calle 2a.

Cinemas The **Cinemas Gemelos** (☎ 6-176-36-16), at López Mateos and Balboa, shows recent Hollywood fare (often dubbed into Spanish).

Shopping

Many items sold in Tijuana stores are available here at slightly lower prices (see Shopping in the Tijuana section, earlier), but the selection is smaller. Liquors and beers from all over Mexico are also available at discount prices. Wine prices are fairly reasonable due to the nearby wineries in the Guadalupe and Santo Tomás Valleys. Wine bought at the Santo Tomás tasting room is about 15% cheaper than in the stores.

Stores along Avenida López Mateos are tourist-oriented but fairly classy. Most sell crafts from throughout Mexico, including woven blankets, leather goods, wood carvings, wrought-iron candlesticks and margarita glasses. Los Castillo, with several branches along López Mateos, is a reputable store selling silver jewelry.

Galería de Pérez Meillon (☎ 6-174-03-94), in the Centro Artesanal, Blvd Costero 1094, Local 39, sells first-rate indigenous pottery and other crafts from Baja California's Paipai, Kumiai and Cucupah peoples, as well as the famous Mata Ortiz pottery from mainland Mexico. Nativa on Avenida Miramar next to the Bodega Santo Tomás has a smaller and less exclusive selection; it's closed Monday and Tuesday.

For quality surfing gear, try San Miguel Surf Shop in the Plaza Hussong mall on Avenida Ryerson.

Getting There & Away
Air Aerolinea Aerocedros (☎ 6-177-35-34) is a private company operating flights to Isla de Cedros on Tuesday and Friday for about US$100 each way from the military Aeropuerto El Ciprés south of town. Contact Elvia or Rosa Irene for details.

Bus Ensenada's Central de Autobuses is at Avenida Riveroll 1075 at the corner of Calle 11a, 10 blocks north of Avenida López Mateos.

ABC (☎ 6-178-66-80) is the main peninsular carrier, with numerous buses from Ensenada to Playas de Rosarito and Tijuana as well as points south:

Tecate – US$7.50, two hours; three times daily

Playas de Rosarito/Tijuana – US$8, 1½ hours; every 30 minutes

San Felipe – US$16, 3½ hours; daily at 8 am and 6 pm

Mexicali – US$18, four hours; twice daily

Loreto – US$50, 16 hours; at 10 am, 2, 8 and 11 pm

La Paz – US$67, 24 hours; at 10 am, 2, 8 and 11 pm

Note that Tijuana-bound buses drop Rosarito passengers at the tollgate rather than in Rosarito proper.

Between 6 am and 7 pm, Autotransportes Aragón (☎ 6-177-09-09), Avenida Riveroll 861 at Calle 8a just south of the main bus terminal, goes hourly to Tijuana (US$8) and every other hour to San Quintín (US$10).

Estrellas de Oro (☎ 6-178-67-70) operates from the same counter at the bus terminal, with buses to mainland Mexican destinations like Mazatlán (US$94) and Guadalajara (US$110).

Getting Around
Local bus services are provided by La Vigia's blue-and-white minibuses and by Transportes Brisas (☎ 6-178-38-88), whose buses are yellow. Both travel within Ensenada and as far as outlying farming communities like El Sauzal or Guadalupe to the north or Maneadero to the south. There are several stops along Blvd Costero, Avenida Reforma and Blvd Azueta. The destination usually appears on the windshield. Transportes Brisas also has a terminal at Calle 4a 771. The fare is about US$0.50.

Renting a car is much cheaper in Tijuana or in San Diego, even with additional daily charges for Mexican insurance, than it is in Ensenada. The only local agency, Fiesta Rent A Car (☎ 6-176-33-44), Avenida Club Rotarío, Local 11, near the Hotel Corona, usually has competitive rates for the area.

Taxis are available 24 hours a day at several corner stands along Avenida López Mateos – one major stand is at the corner of Avenida Miramar.

AROUND ENSENADA
The following sites appear on the Tijuana to Ensenada map, earlier in the chapter.

Resorts
So sprawling that it issues its own map, ***Estero Beach Resort*** (☎ 6-176-62-35, fax 6-176-69-25, estero@telnor.net) is a luxurious gringo enclave immediately south of Playa El Faro (see below). Besides a luxury hotel and RV park, it includes tennis courts, a

convention center and a restaurant. Road signs are in English only.

Also part of the complex is the **Museo de la Naturaleza y de las Culturas Precolombinas**, displaying quality replicas of ceramics and statuary from various Mexican cultures, including Olmec, Maya, Aztec and Teotihuacán. It also contains a well-arranged seashell collection that unfortunately lacks any explanation of their biological or ecological context.

RV sites cost US$25/20 with/without full hookups for two people; extra persons are US$5. Rates drop US$5 from October to March. Hot showers and clean toilets are available, and horses can be hired nearby. Hotel doubles range from US$55 to US$90 (October to March) and rise to US$75 to US$110 the rest of the year. San Diego's Southwest Sea Kayaks offers introductory weekend sea kayak classes here for US$140, including kayak rental. For contact information, see the Activities chapter.

About 10 miles (16km) south of Ensenada, the **Baja Beach Resort** (☎ 6-154-02-20, 888-265-9421 in the US) is a large hotel/resort complex with 100 hotel rooms, four tennis courts, two swimming pools, watersports equipment rental, a charter fishing boat, bars, a restaurant and coffee shop. Rooms cost US$55/75 midweek/weekend.

Islas de Todos Santos

Professional surfers frequent these two islands, about 12 miles (19km) west of Ensenada, especially when winter storms bring towering surf to the smaller Isla Norte. In early 1997, the islands hosted the Torneo Mundial de Surfing, the world surfing championships. A Japanese-sponsored mari-culture project on the larger Isla Sur is cultivating abalone for the Asian market. While there's no scheduled transportation to the islands, it's possible to hire a launch. To do so, ask around the Ensenada sportfishing piers.

Playa El Faro

Playa El Faro, accessible from Km 14.8 on the Transpeninsular (look for the signs for the Estero Beach Resort), has the small *El Faro Beach Motel & Trailer Park* (☎ 6-177-46-25, *fax 6-177-46-20*). The motel has eight clean, simple rooms with bath and shower for US$40, but proximity to the beach is its only attraction. Camping is possible on a sandy lot next to the beach, with electricity, water, showers and toilets for US$12; sites without hookups cost US$8.

Nearby are the **Corona Beach Trailer Park**, where sites with water and electrical hookups cost US$10, and the more elaborate **Rancho Mona Lisa Trailer Park**, with full hookups for US$14 to US$18. Look for the signs. Neither have phones.

La Bufadora

La Bufadora is a tidal blowhole that spews water and foam through a V-shaped notch in the headlands of the Punta Banda peninsula. Hope to arrive on a day when the sea is rolling heavy and you'll see a spectacle. Other times, the blowhole just puffs. Nevertheless, it remains the area's most popular weekend destination for tourists and locals alike.

La Bufadora has undergone recent improvements: The endless souvenir stands are tidier than before, there's regular trash collection and the public toilets (US$0.50) at the otherwise empty exhibition center (now the site of a small cactus garden) are clean enough.

BCN-23, the paved road to La Bufadora and Punta Banda, leaves the Transpeninsular at Maneadero and passes several campgrounds and roadside stands that sell chile peppers and olives. Beyond the Baja Beach Resort are a few isolated campsites and, past a gaggle of taco stands and dozens of souvenir stalls at the end of the road, La Bufadora itself roars – or sighs tiredly.

Diving Probably the best reason to visit the area, Dale's La Bufadora Dive Center (☎ 6-174-29-92) offers underwater excursions to view sea anemones, sea urchins, sponge colonies, nudibranchs and dozens of fish species.

The Canadian operator has three boats and charges from US$20 to US$35 per person, depending on the number of people in the boat. Full sets of dive and snorkeling gear cost US$35/20, respectively. Tanks are US$7. Dale also rents kayaks for US$20/30 singles/doubles for a half-day and US$30/40 for a full day. Oceanside camping is possible too.

Places to Stay Camping at the clifftop **Rancho La Bufadora** (☎ 6-178-71-72), with a view, outhouse access and use of a few fire rings costs US$5 per night for two people. There's electricity, but it's best to bring in your own water. Local ejidos rent slightly cheaper sites above La Bufadora.

Punta Banda has two other main campgrounds. **La Jolla Beach Camp** (☎ 6-154-20-05) has about 400 spaces without hookups for US$8 for two; extra persons cost US$2, and so does electricity. Hot showers are available.

Next door, and markedly shadier, **Villarino RV Park** (☎ 6-154-20-45, fax 6-154-20-44) charges US$10/15 for sites without/with hookups; many spaces are occupied by permanent mobile-home residents. Both have clean bathrooms with hot showers and small grocery stores selling canned goods, milk and purified water. All are on the road to La Bufadora.

Places to Eat Many stalls at La Bufadora serve fish tacos, shrimp cocktails and *churros* (deep-fried dough dipped in sugar and cinnamon). There are also seafood restaurants with lower prices and better ocean views than those in Ensenada.

Los Panchos has served tourists and locals for three decades; the octopus in ranchero sauce is a popular dish, but the 'Siete Mares' (Seven Seas) soup – loaded with shrimp, octopus, fish, crab claws and other fresh seafood – is superb. It's open 9 am to sunset everyday but Thursday.

Near the entrance to Rancho La Bufadora is **Los Gordos**, where photographs, memorabilia and graffiti exude an Old Baja ambience. Specialties include a Mexican combo, deep-fried calamari, lobster and shrimp in garlic butter. The bar is a favorite watering hole for US expatriates.

Celia's has a Sunday breakfast buffet for just US$3.50, while **El Dorado**, with its

palapa-covered patio, is the place for a romantic seafood dinner.

Getting There & Away Cab rides to La Bufadora from downtown Ensenada cost about US$8. Transportes Brisas (☎ 6-178-38-88), at Calle 4a 771 in Ensenada, offers regular bus service as far as Maneadero; from the turnoff to La Bufadora, you can probably hitch a ride. Several Ensenada travel agencies offer package tours by van or bus on weekends.

Maneadero

The farm settlement of Maneadero, on the Transpeninsular about 10 miles (16km) south of Ensenada and just beyond the turnoff to Punta Banda, contains little of note. A military guns-and-drugs checkpoint south of town checks for tourist cards; if yours is not in order, you'll have to return to Ensenada. Some travelers without proper ID have used *la mordida* (a bribe) to get past the police in the past, but the military is a different matter.

Guadalupe

The village of Guadalupe is at Km 78 on México 3 (the highway from Ensenada to Tecate), about 20 miles (32km) northeast of Ensenada, in the heart of Baja's wine country. Buses from Ensenada to Tecate will drop passengers at the paved lateral to the village on México 3.

Settled by Russian immigrants in the early 20th century, the village contains ruins of the Dominican **Misión Nuestra Señora de Guadalupe**, the last mission built in the Californias, founded in 1834 and destroyed by Indians only six years later. Set in a fertile zone for grain farming and grazing, it was a powerful and important mission during its brief existence. There are Indian pictographs on a huge granite boulder known as Ojá Cuñúrr, where the canyon of the Río Guadalupe narrows, but almost nothing remains of the mission.

The Russians, pacifist refugees from the area of present-day Turkey, first arrived in Los Angeles but found the lands not to their liking and chose to head south across the border in 1905. They first lived in Indian dwellings known by their Kumiai name of *wa,* but soon built adobe houses that the Kumiai later emulated; the present museum is a Russian adobe. Across from the site of the former Dominican mission are the arches of the former Russian school, demolished some years ago. The nearby Russian cemetery still contains headstones with Cyrillic inscriptions.

Museo Comunitario de Guadalupe Only a handful of families of demonstrably Russian descent remain in the area. The private Museo Comunitario keeps alive their heritage with photographs and artifacts like samovars, a Russian bible and traditional clothing. In addition to the interior exhibits, antique farming machinery and a Kumiai tribal dwelling (wa) decorate the museum grounds.

Part of the house is still inhabited by the family of Franziska San Marín, herself married to a descendant of the early Russian settlers (ask to see the authentic sauna in the back of the house). In the attached 'restaurant,' her young daughter serves Russian dishes on weekends. To reach the museum (coming from Ensenada), turn left off México 3 onto the paved lateral at the town's Pemex station; bear to the right at the fork and follow the dirt road to the museum. Hours are 10 am to 6 pm, and it's closed Monday; a donation is requested.

Museo Historico Opposite the Museo Comunario is this INAH-maintained facility that tells the story of the local mission and also has an exhibit about the Russian settlers. It's open 10 am to 5 pm, closed Monday; a donation is requested.

Wineries The surrounding valley is now one of Mexico's major wine-growing regions, but grapes arrive at the huge Domecq Winery (at the edge of town) from vineyards throughout the peninsula. Domecq offers tours of its facility, followed by a tasting, for US$1 from 10 am to 4 pm weekdays and to 1:30 pm on Saturday.

Nearby Vinícola LA Cetto is open for tours and tastings 9 am to 5 pm daily (free).

Its products are available at the winery and at most liquor stores throughout the peninsula. In August, the Fiesta de La Vendimia (wine harvest festival) takes place at several of the valley's wineries.

PARQUE NACIONAL CONSTITUCIÓN DE 1857

In the Sierra de Juárez southeast of Ensenada and north of the highway to San Felipe, a striking plateau of ponderosa pines comprises most of Parque Nacional Constitución de 1857, a 12,350-acre (5000-hectare) park whose shallow and marshy but pleasant and solitary **Laguna Hanson** abounds with migratory birds – ducks, coots, grebes and many others – in fall. Hunting is prohibited, so bird-watchers will find the park an exceptional destination at this time of the year. Check the dying pines for woodpeckers. Anglers may hook catfish, bluegills and large-mouth bass.

The low granite outcrops north and west of Laguna Hanson offer stupendous views but require difficult ascents through dense brush and over and beneath massive rockfalls – watch for ticks and rattlesnakes. The easiest view route is to take the abandoned road northwest from near the ruined cabins and pit toilets to the first dry watercourse, and then follow it toward the peaks. Expect dead ends that are too steep to climb, but follow tunnels through the rockfalls before emerging on a saddle below the two main peaks. This short climb, which should take only about an hour, is nevertheless very tiring.

Technical climbers will find challenging routes up the open granite despite the limited relief – most pitches do not exceed 200 to 300 feet (60 to 90m). The terrain resembles mainland California's Joshua Tree National Park.

On the eastern side of the park at the base of the Sierra de Juárez are several beautiful desert palm canyons, the most accessible of which is Cañón Guadalupe – but unfortunately only from the eastern side. For more information, see the Around Mexicali entry in the Desierto del Colorado chapter.

PARQUE NACIONAL CONSTITUCIÓN DE 1857

Near Laguna Hanson, you'll find a visitor center/ranger station where you can pick up information about hiking, climbing, flora and fauna. There's a US$5 admission to the park per vehicle.

Places to Stay & Eat

Primitive but well-maintained *campsites* with pit toilets, barbecue pits and picnic tables are on the western shore of the lake at an approximate elevation of 4000 feet (1200m). There are also several rustic *cabins* that rent for US$35 per person. Reservations can be made by contacting the park administration in Mexicali (☎ 6-566-78-87, fax 6-566-78-67, sanpedro@sys.net.mx), at 1711 Fco L Montejano Ave, 21280, Mexicali, Baja California, México.

Because livestock is plentiful, the water is only suitable for dousing your campfire, so bring your own. Fuel wood is scarce in the shoreline campgrounds but more abundant in the surrounding hills; dry and not-so-dry cow patties are an easily acquired addition in a pinch. Camp robbers such as gray squirrels, and even coyotes, will abscond with any food left in the open, but the coyotes' howling at least seems to quiet the cattle. Expect hordes of mosquitoes in late spring.

Southeast of Ensenada at Km 39 on México 3 toward San Felipe, a paved lateral reaches the village of Ojos Negros, whose decent *Restaurant Oasis* has an English-speaking owner who's happy to provide tourist information.

Getting There & Away

As there is no public transportation to the park, visitors must drive. From Ojos Negros, a 27-mile (43km) dirt road, passable for almost any passenger car despite its frequent washboard surface, climbs eastward onto the plateau and into the park. Another access road lies about 10 miles (16km) east of Ojos Negros at Km 55.

Approaching from the north, the best route into the park is from the El Cóndor turnoff, west of La Rumorosa at about Km 83 on México 2 (the Tijuana-Tecate-Mexicali highway). Drivers with low-clearance vehicles will undoubtedly prefer the Ojos Negros road, although the road from Km 55 should be passable for most, especially after the first 4.4 miles (7km); the total distance is about 20 miles (32km).

EL ALAMO & VALLE DE TRINIDAD

From Ojos Negros, México 3 continues south to a marked junction with a dirt road leading west to the once-bustling mining town of El Alamo. After the discovery of gold here in 1888, El Alamo boomed with thousands of gold-seekers, but the ore gave out quickly and it's now almost deserted.

From the junction, the highway leads south into the verdant Valle de Trinidad – a prosperous agricultural development and, in the late 19th century, a mining zone – before crossing the San Matías pass toward San Felipe. Just south of the junction with El Alamo, but 5 miles (8km) east of the highway, is the site of the former Misión Santa Catarina de los Paipais, one of two Dominican missions in the peninsula's northern interior, now known officially as Santa Catarina.

Founded in 1798, with a population of more than 600 at its peak in 1824, Santa Catarina was the Dominicans' largest mission but also one of the most precarious. Its altitude (about 3500 feet, or 1050m) and cool climate meant it was not agriculturally self-sufficient, and neophytes continued to collect wild foods, like piñon nuts, in the surrounding countryside. Indian hostility was widespread, and an uprising in 1840 destroyed the mission. Parts of the adobe walls are the only remaining ruins, on a hill above the present village cemetery. An easily identifiable circular mound marks the remains of the mission watchtower.

The village is a sprawling hodgepodge of wrecked cars and a few adobe houses, trailers and abandoned greenhouses (remnants of a federal government scheme to raise jojoba. Competing Catholic and Pentecostal churches, both emphasizing the term *indígena* in their formal titles, compete for the souls of the remaining Paipai, who still speak their native language, as well as Spanish, and continue to collect piñon nuts in the fall.

EJIDO URUAPÁN

About 10 miles (16km) south of Maneadero, near Km 41, Ejido Uruapán is known for sea urchins, strawberries and quail – which draw hunters from north of the border in the winter months. The sea-urchin processing plant, established with Japanese aid, exports countless *erizos* across the Pacific Ocean. The Japanese have also built greenhouses for cultivating strawberries, mostly for export to California.

The well-shaded and well-maintained *campground* right at the turnoff from the Transpeninsular has brick barbecue pits and is a fine site for primitive camping or picnicking. A sign mentions a fee of US$5, but often no one is there to collect it. From inside the village, more signs direct you to a hot spring about 2km via a dirt road. This is primarily where the townspeople come to bathe and do their laundry, but it's open to visitors as well.

SANTO TOMÁS

The Dominican mission village of Santo Tomás (population 350) at Km 51, some 6½ miles (10.5km) south of Ejido Uruapán, takes its name from the surrounding Valle de Santo Tomás, one of Baja's key wine-producing areas. Founded in 1791 as the last link in the chain connecting Alta and Baja California, Misión Santo Tomás de Aquino soon moved upstream from its original site

DAVID PEEVERS

to escape infestations of gnats and mosquitoes, which made it both uncomfortable and unhealthy. Winter rains bring forth hordes of harmless toads who stage Darwinian sprint trials across the Transpeninsular in reckless defiance of the thundering 18-wheelers passing north and south.

The wine industry is a legacy of the Dominicans, who planted thousands of vines and other crops, most notably olives. At the mission's peak, in 1824, neophytes may have exceeded 400. Abandoned in 1849, it was the last Dominican mission to maintain a priest. A few crumbling ruins of the original mission remain on an alluvial fan where the river canyon narrows west of the Transpeninsular. But only a few faint foundations denote the upstream site, just south of El Palomar's campground/RV park behind the new church.

Places to Stay & Eat

For modern visitors, Santo Tomás' key institution is venerable El Palomar, a cluster of businesses including a Pemex, a general store, a restaurant, a motel, an RV park/campground and a picnic area.

El Palomar's *campground* sits among a grove of olive trees and bamboo; the olives are harvested, bottled and sold in the general store. In summer, the park's two tennis courts, volleyball court, children's playground, swimming pool and 100 barbecue pits attract up to 2000 visitors daily, sometimes including rowdy and unpleasant groups of middle-aged off-roaders from Southern California. Also part of the complex is another pool with waterslides about 1½ miles (2km) north of here and connected by shuttle. El Palomar has 30 spaces with full RV hookups, at US$12.50 for two people; tents are US$10.

On the slope behind the restaurant, *Motel El Palomar* (☎ 6-153-80-02) offers clean, simple singles/doubles with hot water and heating for US$35 to US$45. Portions at the restaurant are huge, but prices are fairly high. The specialty is lobster tacos, accompanied by small but potent margaritas, but other specials include breaded shrimp, rib steak, abalone chowder, beef tacos and cheese enchiladas. The 'big margaritas' live up to the billing.

EJIDO ERÉNDIRA & PUERTO SAN ISIDRO

The paved lateral off the Transpeninsular at about Km 78 leads to the beachside Ejido Eréndira, a small farming community, reached after about 10½ miles (17km). Here you can stock up on bread, milk, gasoline and other basic supplies for a beach trip to Puerto San Isidro, an appealing fishing cove another mile or so north along the coast via a rather rough dirt road. In Eréndira itself is *Motel Eréndira* (☎ 6-165-11-55), which charges US$25 to US$35 for simple rooms with bath.

Puerto San Isidro is home to *Castro's Fishing Place* (☎ 6-176-28-97, fax 6-177-25-85), where Fernando Castro Ríos rents rustic ocean-facing *cabañas* (cabins) for US$25 per night; camping is free. Toilets are outside, but refrigerator, sink, stove and six bunks are inside. Jorge Arballo leads all-day (7 am to 2 pm) fishing trips in superpangas for US$30 per person. For more information, call or write to Apdo Postal 974, Ensenada, Baja California 22800, México.

About another mile or so past Castro's Fishing Place is *Coyote Cal's* (no phone), the area's only hostel. Run by a young team of energetic surfers, this is a great and remote place to hang for a few days. The Crow's Nest – for an intimate twosome on the top floor – offers spectacular 360-degree views. Dorms sleep four to 10 people and face the ocean. Amenities include a well-equipped communal kitchen, guest laundry, swimming pool and ping-pong tables. A prime sandy beach is about a quarter-mile north and there's good surfing everywhere. Bunks cost US$15; the Crow's Nest rents for US$35 (for two). Prices include breakfast, and free beans and rice at dinner time. Many backpackers hitch a ride in from the Transpeninsular, where buses from Tijuana or other points north make drop-offs.

South of Puerto San Isidro via a rough dirt road, optimistically named *Malibu Beach Sur* (no phone), is a poorly maintained RV park offering camping, fishing and surfing. Sites for up to four people are US$10. En route, you'll pass a depressing barbed wire camp for migrant field workers.

SAN VICENTE

The agricultural community of San Vicente (population 3500) bustles on its namesake arroyo at Km 90, about 7 miles (11km) south of the Ejido Eréndira junction. **Misión San Vicente Ferrer** (1780), one of the few Dominican missions that never moved from its original site, was founded here. In some ways, it was the most important of them all, both for its centrality (convenient to the other Pacific coast missions) and its strategic location (protected from Indian attacks from the east). Though the largest and most heavily fortified Dominican mission, it never enjoyed the protection of more than 31 soldiers, but it controlled more than 300 Indian neophytes at its peak in 1787.

These neophytes cultivated maize, wheat and beans and tended the mission's livestock, which numbered up to 750 cattle and 1150 sheep, plus horses, burros and goats. After Yuman Indians destroyed most of the mission, it closed in 1833, but for another 16 years the Mexican army maintained its garrison here.

Substantial foundations and some walls of the fort and mission are in a state of arrested decay in a gated park northwest of the town. You're free to walk around the site and study the panels describing (in English and Spanish) what the various buildings looked like.

San Vicente has a post office and Telnor long-distance service at the bus terminal. Buses running between Tijuana and points south stop here.

To get there, follow the well-signed, graded dirt road west across from the *llantera* (tire repair shop), at about Km 88 just north of town. Look for the northbound sign that says 'Santo Tomás 37, Ensenada 80.' The ruins are about 1 mile (1.6km) away from the road.

San Vicente boasts a small **Museo Comunitario** on the northern side of the plaza. It contains the usual information on the missions as well as agricultural development. Note the vintage machinery outside the building. Hours are 9 am to 3 pm weekdays; admission is free.

At Km 90 on the eastern side of the Transpeninsular, *La Estrella del Sur* (☎ 6-165-66-76) has good, reasonably priced meals and four rooms with private baths and hot showers for US$25 double and US$35 triple. Bicycle riders should ask for special rates. For a better value, go next door to the new *Mini-Hotel Valentina*, which has six nicely decorated, clean rooms with TV and fan for US$17 (one bed) to US$27 (two beds). Both places also have restaurants.

At the southern edge of town, *Motel El Camino* (☎ 6-165-66-11) has monastic, unheated but fairly clean rooms. Those with shared facilities are US$10 to US$12; others with private bath are US$15 to US$20. There's also a nice-looking restaurant.

COLONET

Colonet, a major farming community 23 miles (37km) south of San Vicente, is a good place to replenish supplies and fill your gas tank or backpack if you're heading to the beach at San Antonio del Mar or inland to Rancho Meling and Parque Nacional Sierra San Pedro Mártir. No accommodations are in the town itself, but *Hotel Sonora*, north of town just past Km 122, has basic singles/doubles for US$15. The beach at San Antonio del Mar, 4 miles (6.5km) northwest, has good camping and clamming.

SAN TELMO

The village of San Telmo is 4 miles (6.5km) east of the Transpeninsular on the graded dirt road to Rancho Meling, Parque Nacional Sierra San Pedro Mártir, Picacho del Diablo and the observatory. It is subdivided into San Telmo de Abajo (lower San Telmo) and San Telmo de Arriba (upper San Telmo).

San Telmo's most notable cultural feature is the very faint remains of a Dominican chapel, built between 1798 and 1800; this was part of an *asistencia* (way station) under the jurisdiction of the mission at Santo Domingo near present-day Colonia Vicente Guerrero to the south. Look for its foundations behind a small, much newer chapel at the entrance to San Telmo de Arriba.

Rancho Meling (☎ 6-177-58-97, meling@ ensenada.net.mx), also known as Rancho San José, some 27 miles (43km) east of San Telmo, is a beloved Baja institution. The 10,000-acre (4000-hectare) cattle ranch was established by Norwegian immigrant Salve Meling in the early 1900s and run by his daughter, Aida, as a guest house until she passed away in 1998.

Her children renovated the cozy ranch house and reopened in July 2000 with 12 rustic, spacious and clean rooms (more are still under renovation). All have private baths with hot showers and a fireplace or pot-bellied stove; rates include three hearty meals served family-style. Horseback riding and pack trips into Parque Nacional Sierra San Pedro Mártir are available as well. Rates are US$75/145 for one/ two people, US$44 each for children six to 12. Reservations are a must. For more details, check out the Rancho Meling Web site at http://meling-ranch.ensenada.net.mx.

PARQUE NACIONAL SIERRA SAN PEDRO MÁRTIR

Baja California's most notable national park comprises 236 sq miles (614 sq km) of coniferous forests and granitic peaks reaching above 10,000 feet (3000m), plus deep canyons leading down into their steep eastern scarp. Major native tree types include several species of pines, plus incense cedar, Douglas fir and quaking aspen, while the most conspicuous fauna includes raccoon, fox, coyote and mule deer. The rare desert bighorn sheep inhabits some remote canyon areas.

Unlike Parque Nacional Constitución de 1857, this park has no major bodies of water. Westward-flowing streams like the Río San Rafael, Arroyo Los Pinos and Arroyo San Antonio support the endemic San Pedro Mártir rainbow trout, but wildfowl no longer breed here, as they did a century ago, because of a history of grazing and timber cutting.

Among the typical breeding land birds are the mountain quail, pinyon jay, mountain chickadee, pygmy nuthatch, western bluebird, Cassin's finch, pine siskin, red crossbill and dark-eyed junco.

The ranger station at the park entrance has maps and information. Admission is US$7 per vehicle. Details may also be ob-

tained from the park administration (☎ 6-566-78-87, fax 6-566-78-67, sanpedro@sys.net.mx), at 1711 Fco L Montejano Ave, 21280, Mexicali, Baja California, México.

Maps
The best map of the area is Centra Publications' *Parque Nacional San Pedro Mártir*, with an area map at a scale of 1:100,000 and details at a scale of 1:31,680.

Determined hikers and climbers should also obtain the latest edition of Walt Peterson's *The Baja Adventure Book*, which includes decent maps and describes several routes up Picacho del Diablo. The Mexican government topographic maps *San Rafael H11B45* and *Santa Cruz H11B55* may be useful too. All are available from Map Centre and Maplink (see Maps in the Facts for the Visitor chapter).

Climate
The Sierra San Pedro Mártir has a temperate climate similar to the mountains of southern mainland California; most precipitation falls in winter, when the snow depth at higher altitudes can be 3 feet (1m) or more, but snow is possible any time from October to May. In summer, the area gets a lot of rainfall in the form of thunderstorms. The average annual temperature is around 59°F (16°C), with highs around 68°F (22°C),

but winter temperatures can drop well below freezing. At higher elevations, even in summer, changeable weather is a potential hazard. The best time to visit is in spring when days are getting longer, temperatures are still moderate, the wildflowers are in bloom and there's plenty of water following the snow melt.

Things to See & Do

The Sierra San Pedro Mártir is an under-appreciated area for hiking, camping and backpacking, in part because access is awkward and it's a little far for weekend trips from mainland California. Still, most visitors are from the US, usually small groups of college students or families. Anyone seeking the solitude that only total wilderness can offer will be rewarded, especially since off-road vehicles are not allowed in the park.

Within the park are many suitable car-camping areas and hiking trails, though trail maintenance is minimal and hikers should carry a compass (or GPS) along with the usual cold- and wet-weather supplies, canteens and water purification tablets. Below about 6000 feet (1800m) or even a bit higher, beware of rattlesnakes. A detailed topographic map (see Maps, earlier) will be essential.

The **Observatorio Astronómico Nacional**, Mexico's national observatory, features an 84-inch diameter telescope but may only be visited by prior arrangement. Contact the government agency Semarnap in Mexicali (☎ 6-566-78-87, fax 6-566-78-67) or send an email to sanpedro@sys.net.mx. However, even if you don't get inside, you're likely to enjoy the stupendous views from up here, which extend all across the forest and over to the Pacific, the Sea of Cortez and the Mexican mainland.

To get to the observatory, follow the park access road to the end, then walk the final 1½ miles (2km). It's odd that while the access

PARQUE NACIONAL SIERRA SAN PEDRO MÁRTIR

1 Mike's Sky Rancho
2 Rancho Santa Clara
3 Observatorio Astronómico Nacional
4 Campo Noche
5 Rancho Meling
6 Park Entrance; Ranger's Station
7 Rancho Santa Cruz
8 Ruins of Misión Santo Domingo
9 Ruins of Misión San Pedro Mártir

To Mexicali
To Ensenada
Cerro El Chinero
Valle San Matías
El Michoacano
Crucero La Trinidad
Sea of Cortez

0   10   20 km
0   6   12 miles

Valle de Trinidad
To Ensenada
San Vicente
Ejido Los Pocitos
Ejido San Matías
Cerro del Borrego

Carretera Transpeninsular
Río San Rafael
Colonet
Cerro San Matías
Laguna Diablo
Cañón del Diablo

San Telmo
Picacho del Diablo
Cerro Juan
San Felipe
Bahía San Felipe

Ejido Sinaloa
Río San Telmo
Parque Nacional Sierra San Pedro Mártir
Cerro Kino
Aeropuerto Internacional San Felipe

Punta San Jacinto
Camalú
Río Santo Domingo

PACIFIC OCEAN
Colonia Vicente Guerrero
To San Quintín
El Salto
Arroyo Huatamote
To Puertecitos

road is graded dirt, the walkway to the observatory is paved!

The 10,154-foot (3046m) summit of **Picacho del Diablo**, also known as Cerro Providencia, draws climbers from throughout the Californias, but only a handful actually reach the summit because finding the route is so difficult.

Getting There & Away

There is no public transportation to Sierra San Pedro Mártir, and all access roads are dirt and in various conditions. Check road conditions locally before heading out.

To/From San Telmo From San Telmo de Abajo, south of Km 140 on the Trans-peninsular, a graded dirt road climbs eastward through San Telmo de Arriba past Rancho Meling to the park entrance, about 50 miles (80km) from the highway. Abounding with quail, rabbits, chipmunks and roadrunners, the road is passable for most passenger vehicles – and usually even small RVs – despite two major fords of the Río San Telmo. Spring runoff may cause problems for cars with low clearance, and drivers should probably avoid the road immediately after snowfall, when the warm sun can melt the snow very quickly. The one-way trip from Ensenada can take as long as six to seven hours.

To/From San Felipe The summit of Picacho del Diablo – and the network of trails at its foot – can also be accessed from the eastern edge of the park via a difficult climb along Cañón del Diablo. Access is through Rancho Santa Clara.

To get to the mouth of the canyon from San Felipe, take the sandy road northwest to Laguna Diablo, a dry salt lake, and Rancho Santa Clara. The road is reportedly safe and the surface mostly hard and dry, but ask for up-to-date information in San Felipe before attempting it.

Another route to Rancho Santa Clara is a good graded road that leaves México 3, just east of the Ensenada-San Felipe highway, just east of Km 164; rather than going down the middle of Laguna Diablo, the road keeps to high

ground along its eastern shoreline. A roadside tire marks the turnoff to Rancho Santa Clara, which also is marked by a tire.

From Rancho Santa Clara, pick up the dirt road that leads west for about 5½ miles (9km) to Cañón Diablito. This is where you must park the car. The mouth of Cañón del Diablo is another 2 miles (3km) west.

Once in the canyon, you'll come upon a striking waterfall after about half a mile (800m). This is also the biggest obstacle on the trail, but cables should be there to help you across. At about the 8-mile (13km) point, you reach Campo Noche, a good campsite before starting the ascent the next day.

AROUND PARQUE NACIONAL SIERRA SAN PEDRO MÁRTIR

Mike's Sky Rancho

Thirty-seven miles (60km) west along México 3 from the junction with Highway 5, at Km 138, is the turnoff to a 22-mile (35km) road to Mike's Sky Rancho (mobile ☎ 6-181-55-14), in a small valley framed by the pine-covered foothills of the Sierra San Pedro Mártir. The graded dirt road makes it accessible to most passenger vehicles, but those seeking quiet and solitude should know that it's a popular destination with the off-road crowd. Motorcycles by the pool are a common sight, and the lounge is decorated with racing posters. At a few points, the road is steep and tricky for ordinary passenger cars.

The rancho offers worn but tidy motel-style rooms with kerosene stove and private bath, plain but hearty meals and a large swimming pool. Rooms cost around US$22 per person, breakfast and lunch US$6 each, dinner US$12 and full board US$45. Call Mike's Sky Rancho at the number above or write to PO Box 5376, San Ysidro, CA 92073.

Misión San Pedro Mátir

Founded in 1794 in the mountains east of San Quintín, Misión San Pedro Mártir de Verona was the most isolated Dominican mission. The initial site at Casilepe proved inadequate, according to founder Fray Cayetano Pallás, when the crops froze. The new mission site at Ajantequedo, at an altitude of 5500 feet (1650m), was marginal but adequate for a neophyte population that never exceeded about 100.

Established as a possible link to *rancherías* (groups of Indians) on the Sea of Cortez and on the Río Colorado delta, the mission lasted only until 1824 because of its insecure location and the area's relatively small number of Indians. After the mission's demise, San Pedro's neophytes relocated to Misión Santo Domingo. Only a few brittle foundations still exist and may be reached on foot either from Rancho Santa Cruz or from La Grulla, north of the mission in Parque Nacional Sierra San Pedro Mártir.

Camalú

Back on the Transpeninsular, at about Km 157, this little town has a Pemex, a few stores and cafes and other infrastructure. About 4 miles (7km) before town, at Km 150, is the turnoff to **Punta San Jacinto**, reached after a (usually) easy 6-mile (11km) dirt road. This is a great surf beach where Baja Surf Adventures (see the Activities chapter) runs surf resorts. Primitive oceanfront campsites cost US$5. Nearby is the wreck of a stranded freighter.

COLONIA VICENTE GUERRERO

This booming agricultural center straddles the Transpeninsular, the town's main street. It now has a single traffic light, a bank and a casa de cambio. Otherwise, there's little of interest to visitors except its shady plaza, Parque General Vicente Guerrero, a small community museum and nearby Misión Santo Domingo. However, the long sandy beaches west of town are well worth a visit; in the summer months, surf fishing is excellent.

The bus terminal is in the center of town on the Pacific side of the highway.

Misión Santo Domingo

Founded in 1775 by Manuel García and Miguel Hidalgo at the mouth of the canyon of the Río Santo Domingo, Misión Santo Domingo de la Frontera was the second of nine Dominican missions in Baja California; it soon moved to a verdant upstream confluence about 5 miles (8km) east of the present-day Transpeninsular. At first the

mission was chaotic and undisciplined, with many Indians deserting, but by 1796 more than 350 neophytes tended livestock and harvested grain here. Unfortunately, by 1839, measles and smallpox had wiped out most of them, and the mission was abandoned.

To reach the ruins, the best-preserved of any Dominican frontier mission, go east on the dirt road on the northern side of the Río Santo Domingo, at the northern entrance to town. Note the massive landmark **Peñón Colorado**, the reddish bluff that rises out of the sediments at the entrance to the canyon.

Though many walls are standing, the ruins are truly ruins; historian Peveril Meigs remarked in 1939 that the mission church then served as a pigpen. Parts of the system of irrigation canals from mission times are still in use, though, and the ruins are now fenced off from animals.

Every year in the first week of August at the site of the ruins, the Fiesta de Santo Domingo features horseracing, rodeos, dancing and food stalls. A short distance west is a pleasant private park with a swimming pool and cafe – a good spot for a picnic, accessible for a very modest admission.

Places to Stay & Eat

Colonia Vicente Guerrero has only two motels, but at the southwestern end of town are two RV parks/campgrounds. The turnoff for both campgrounds is near Km 173 on the western side of the highway, but their signs are visible only for southbound travelers. If you're traveling north, look for the Fagro Shipping building, which leads to Don Pepe's; the turnoff to Don Diego's is about 1/16 mile (100m) before here.

Mesón de Don Pepe RV Park & Restaurant (☎ 6-166-22-16, fax 6-166-22-68), which suffers from the noise of trucks on the highway, charges US$10 per night for RV sites with full hookups for two people, plus US$2 for each extra person; sites without hookups cost US$8. Tent sites on a pleasant grassy area cost US$6.50. Hot showers are available, and the restaurant serves reasonably priced seafood and typical Mexican meals.

Spacious sites with full hookups for US$11 can be had at *Posada Don Diego*

RV Park (☎ 6-166-21-81); tent sites cost US$8.50. Only a few of its sites are in the shade, but it has hot showers, a laundry room, a restaurant and a bar. The restaurant has a good reputation. This campground is a little closer to the beach, but the often-muddy road beyond the RV park can be difficult for ordinary passenger vehicles. Hiking to the beach, which offers great clamming (respect size limits), takes 30 to 45 minutes.

Motel Sánchez (☎ 6-166-29-63), in the town center by the traffic light, has large, fairly clean rooms for US$17/22/28 singles/doubles/triples. On the northern end of town is *Motel Ortiz* (☎ 6-166-26-55), which has rooms with double bed and hot water for US$15; rooms with two beds cost US$20.

El Vaquero is a steakhouse at the northern end of town, easily spotted for its 'Wild West' decor. There are also numerous taco stands and a few small stores selling fruit, vegetables, bread and other staples.

SAN QUINTÍN

San Quintín (population 60,000) is the focus of an increasingly important agricultural region on the Llano de San Quintín (San Quintín Plain), but attractive Pacific beaches at the foot of a group of cinder cones also make it an ideal area for camping, clamming, beach-combing and fishing.

Offshore Isla San Martín is part of the volcanic cordon that protects the plain from the ocean's erosive power. Plans to develop San Quintín into a major tourist resort are, so far at least, still confined to the drawing board.

History

Several briny coastal lagoons near San Quintín provided salt for the nearby Dominican missions in colonial times; 19th-century Russian settlements north of San Francisco Bay in the US also acquired their salt here. The Russians and Americans hunted sea otters nearly to extinction, bringing Northwest Indians and their canoes along for the venture.

In the late 19th century, San Quintín was the focus of settlement schemes by the English-based Mexican Land & Coloniza-tion Company, which bought the concession of the International Company of Mexico – a US-based corporation that had obtained land rights to most of northern Baja for a massive colonization effort during the Porfiriato. The International Company attracted few settlers, but the Land & Colonization Company introduced English colonists and established a steam-powered flour mill, a customs house, a pier, schoolhouses, fertilizer plants and, after a few years, a cemetery.

The company also laid about 19 miles (31km) of track, hoping to link up with the Southern Pacific Railroad in San Diego, but insufficient rainfall prevented the sustained cultivation of the wheat they had hoped to market north of the border. Today, only the remains of the Molino Viejo (Old Mill), the Muelle Viejo (Old Pier) and the cemetery testify to the English presence.

High-tech irrigation has at least temporarily overcome some of the problems encountered by early colonists, but fields west of the Transpeninsular are suffering because growers have extracted so much fresh water that brackish seawater has contaminated the aquifers on which they rely. Cultivation has largely moved east of the highway, but some observers believe that this strategy may only provide a short reprieve for an unsustainable system. As of now, the San Quintín area is the world's largest producer of tomatoes, plus many other crops.

Recent years have seen an influx of Mixtec Indians from impoverished rural Oaxaca. Many previously worked for mainland growers and labor contractors who have expanded operations into the San Quintín area. During peak picking season, up to 60,000 farm workers work the fields. Many are here on a permanent basis, but many others move on at the end of the harvest. Some unscrupulous contractors pay these Indians, poorly educated and with large families, US$4 or less per day, low even by Mexican standards. Child-labor violations and inadequate housing are commonplace. We saw some workers, and their families, housed in primitive camps with barbed-wire fencing.

In addition to low wages, long hours and miserable housing, farm laborers suffer

LA FRONTERA

SAN QUINTÍN

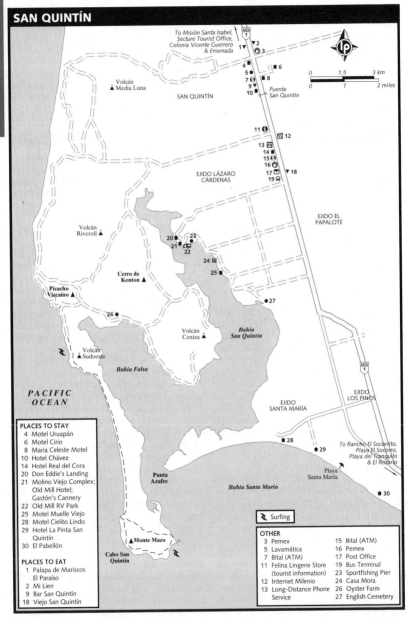

To Misión Santa Isabel,
Secture Tourist Office,
Colonia Vicente Guerrero
& Ensenada

Volcán
Media Luna

SAN QUINTÍN

Puente
San Quintín

0   1.5   3 km
0   1   2 miles

EJIDO LÁZARO
CÁRDENAS

EJIDO EL
PAPALOTE

Volcán
Riveroll

Cerro de
Kenton

Picacho
Vizcaíno

Bahía
San Quintín

Volcán
Ceniza

Volcán
Sudoeste

Bahía Falsa

PACIFIC
OCEAN

EJIDO
LOS PINOS

EJIDO
SANTA MARÍA

To Rancho El Socorrito,
Playa El Socorro,
Playa del Tranquilo
& El Rosario

Playa
Santa María

Punta
Azufre

Bahía Santa María

Monte Mazo

Cabo San
Quintín

Surfing

PLACES TO STAY
4 Motel Uruapán
6 Motel Cirio
8 Maria Celeste Motel
10 Hotel Chávez
14 Hotel Real del Cora
20 Don Eddie's Landing
21 Molino Viejo Complex;
    Old Mill Hotel;
    Gastón's Cannery
22 Old Mill RV Park
25 Motel Muelle Viejo
28 Motel Cielito Lindo
29 Hotel La Pinta San
    Quintín
30 El Pabellón

PLACES TO EAT
1 Palapa de Mariscos
   El Paraíso
2 Mi Lien
9 Bar San Quintín
18 Viejo San Quintín

OTHER
3 Pemex
5 Lavamática
7 Bital (ATM)
11 Felina Lingerie Store
    (tourist information)
12 Internet Milenio
13 Long-Distance Phone
    Service
15 Bital (ATM)
16 Pemex
17 Post Office
19 Bus Terminal
23 Sportfishing Pier
24 Casa Mora
26 Oyster Farm
27 English Cemetery

serious health problems because local agriculture relies heavily on chemical fertilizers and pesticides, with almost no protective equipment or instruction for those who apply them. Angus Wright's *The Death of Ramón González* deals with the theme of pesticide poisoning in a different part of Mexico.

Groups from north of the border occasionally offer health clinics in the area, but their efforts are largely ineffectual because itinerant workers following the harvest do not receive regular medical attention for their ailments.

Orientation

San Quintín sits on a sheltered harbor 116 miles (187km) south of Ensenada on the Transpeninsular. The name San Quintín commonly refers to an area that includes not only San Quintín proper but also ejidos and colonias to the south – Lázaro Cárdenas, El Papalote, Los Pinos and Santa María. San Quintín and Lázaro Cárdenas stretch out along the Transpeninsular for about 3 miles (5km), while the Ejido El Papalote is about 4 miles (6.5km) south of Lázaro Cárdenas. Santa María, another farming area, surrounds Hotel La Pinta San Quintín and Motel Cielito Lindo.

Because none of the streets are named, except for the highway, and there are no street addresses whatsoever, it can be difficult to find anything in the San Quintín area. Refer to the map, but trust your own eyes as well. Because San Quintín is so spread out, it's much better to drive than to rely on public transportation – off the highway, transportation is basically nonexistent.

Information

The local branch of the state-run Secture tourist office (☎/fax 6-166-27-88) is in a sparkling new building at Km 178 between Colonia Vicente Guerrero and San Quintín. The friendly, English-speaking staff can help with information about the area from San Vicente all the way south to the Parallelo 28, which marks the boundary between Baja California (Norte) and Baja California Sur. The office is usually open 8 am to 5 pm weekdays and 10 am to 3 pm weekends. In the

town of San Quintín, printed information may also be picked up at the lingerie store Felina.

Opposite the plaza in Lázaro Cárdenas, half a block off the highway, Bital bank has an ATM and cashes traveler's checks. There's another branch in San Quintín, just past Puente San Quintín on the west side of the road.

The post office (postal code 22930) is in Lázaro Cárdenas, and you'll find pharmacies, Pemex stations and grocery stores along the Transpeninsular in both Lázaro Cárdenas and San Quintín.

A long-distance phone service is adjacent to the Hotel Real del Cora at Km 193, and several Internet cafes, including Internet Milenio (☎ 6-165-21-38) at Km 193.5, are open daily (US$3 per hour).

A Lavamática in San Quintín is on the western side of the highway.

Warning: The San Quintín area has seen an increasing number of vehicle break-ins and the occasional robbery; especially vulnerable are those camping in remote areas. It's not cause for paranoia, but do take precautions. In an emergency, Secture's tourist assistance service can be reached at ☎ 163-38-33 or ☎ 078.

Things to See & Do

San Quintín has a few modest cultural landmarks from the period of the early English settlement. The old wheat mill, the **Molino Viejo**, established in the early 20th century, was turned into a cannery by the Mexican government in 1940 and remained in operation until the 1970s. The mill was originally set up here because the local tides came through the narrow channel with such force that they could easily power the millwheel – both ebbing and flowing. You can still see the phenomenon of these surging waters by simply walking to the shore.

The mill's last manager started a modest hotel on the premises, which has evolved into a comprehensive tourist site today. The former cannery is now a restaurant that's the center of local nightlife (such as it is), and also featured are a couple of good hotels and an attractive waterfront area for hanging out.

Midway between the Molino Viejo and the old pier, the wood-framed **Casa Mora** is the only remaining residence from the English period. An Ensenada businessman moved it from a site near the Molino Viejo a few years back, saving it from demolition for the time being, but it seems to be up for sale again.

Pilings alone now remain of the **Muelle Viejo** (old pier), but it's a good place to watch wildlife, especially birds. The motel restaurant here has good bay views. From November to February, tens of thousands of black Brant geese descend upon Bahía San Quintín. In those months, the area also attracts hunters from around the world. Hunting is only allowed from Friday to Sunday and must be done with a guide; hunting licenses and gun permits are required.

At the **English Cemetery**, south of the Muelle Viejo, the single identifiably English headstone is a recent construction memorializing Francis Barthemelon Henslowe of Wermigley, Norfolk and Santa María, who died July 24, 1896.

The oyster farm on Bahía Falsa is another popular destination, although it's rather remote and the drive here is rough.

Activities in the region center around the **beaches** and the ocean; the best easily accessible beaches are near Hotel La Pinta San Quintín in the Santa María area. North of town, at Km 183, in the Ejido Leandro Valle, is a turnoff to Playa San Ramón, which – year round, during low tide – offers the best **clamming** in the area. Yields are limited to 12 clams per person, and no clams under 4 inches (10cm) may be taken.

Breaks at the southern end of Cabo San Quintín, southwest of town, are good for **surfing**, but getting there can be a problem without a 4WD vehicle or a boat. Always inquire locally about road conditions before heading out.

Fishing licenses are necessary for both clamming and fishing; the tourist office and sportfishing guides are both authorized to issue licenses to anyone over 16 years of age.

Daily rates for **fishing**, including guide and panga, start at around US$160 per boat for up to three people. Larger superpangas

and cruisers are more expensive. The day starts early, around 6 or 6:30 am, and ends before 2 pm because the winds make the water too choppy later in the day. Surf fishing is also a favorite here.

Tiburón's Pangas (☎/fax 6-165-27-68, 6-170-08-21), Pedro's Pangas (☎ 6-171-18-24, 888-568-2252 in the US) and Old Mill Sportfishing (☎ 619-585-0244, 888-828-2628 in the US) are all based at the Molino Viejo complex. They enjoy excellent reputations, but locals also recommend El Capitan Sportfishing (☎ 6-162-17-16, 6-171-30-87), whose captain Kelly Catian goes out on a custom-built superpanga.

The following list indicating which fish are most common each month in the San Quintín area was provided by Kelly:

Albacore	June to October
Bluefin tuna	July to October
Cabrilla, Corvina	year round
Dorado	July to October
Halibut	January to June
Marlin	July to October
Rock Cod	January and February
White Sea Bass	March to June, November and December
Yellowfin tuna	June
Yellowtail	April to June

Places to Stay

The cheapest lodgings are right on the Transpeninsular, but heavy truck and car traffic makes them the noisiest as well. If you're planning to stay at any place off the main highway, try to arrive in daylight because the maze of dirt roads west of the Transpeninsular is poorly signed and difficult to negotiate in the dark. The exception is the paved road to Hotel La Pinta San Quintín and Motel Cielito Lindo.

Camping Free beach camping is theoretically possible but can be dangerous (theft is common). Try the area near Hotel La Pinta San Quintín, but stay well above the water line. Formal campsites with pleasant palapas – tents, vans and pickups only – and access to hot showers are available at Motel

Cielito Lindo for US$5. There are also full hookups for RVs, also for US$5. Motel Muelle Viejo has eight modest but shady campsites with hot showers and toilets for US$5 per night.

The **Old Mill RV Park** in the Molino Viejo complex charges US$15 per site with hookups, or US$10 for tents; it's hooked into the local grid for reliable electricity, but it's still windy, barren and close to breeding mosquitoes in summer.

About 10 miles (16km) south of San Quintín and half a mile (1km) west of the Transpeninsular, *El Pabellón* has basic facilities for tents and RVs – with access to showers and toilets – for US$5 per night on a lovely sandy beach. A grocery store is a 20-minute walk away, and clamming and surf fishing are superb.

Another 6 miles (9km) or so farther south, *Rancho El Socorrito* has primitive beachfront camping, also for US$5; Playa El Socorro has free camping about another half-mile (800m) south. There are also reports of a new trailer park being built at Playa del Tranquilo, about 3 miles (5km) farther south. Keep us updated.

Hotels & Motels The best budget option is the newly upgraded *Motel Uruapán* (☎ 6-165-20-58), at Km 190, whose 50 nice and clean rooms have shower and toilet, TV and fan and cost US$14/17.

A surprising island of charm in gritty San Quintín is the *Hotel Real del Cora* (☎ 6-166-85-76), at Km 193, which has 25 rooms with telephone and TV, tall ceilings and sparkling baths for US$32/35. Rooms at the well-kept *Hotel Chávez* (☎ 6-165-20-05, fax 6-165-38-05), at Km 194 just before the Puente San Quintín bridge, are nice and go for US$26/32.

For newer rooms and great comfort, try the *María Celeste Motel* (☎ 6-165-39-99), where amenities include bottled water, spic-and-span bathrooms, full carpeting, TV and phone. Rooms cost US$30/33. *Motel Cirio* (☎ 6-165-30-15), one block away east off the highway (the turnoff is just north of the Maria Celeste Motel) charges US$20 per room; its rooms are small but quieter

than those in motels along the main road. It also has a communal kitchen and a barbecue area.

Signs on the Transpeninsular also point to the American-run *Old Mill Hotel* (☎ 6-165-33-76, 877-800-4081 in the US, oldmill@telnor.net), on the site of the former wheat mill 3 miles (5km) west of the highway. Some of the old machinery still remains. The motel has a range of attractive rooms, starting at about US$28/30 and climbing to US$90 for comfortable two-bedroom suites sleeping four people.

Just north of the Molino Viejo, *Don Eddie's Landing* (☎ 6-162-27-22, 6-162-31-43, 909-315-1236 in the US) is a new motel and sportfishing center that has 17 clean and spacious rooms with tile floor, TV and oceanview patio for US$45 to US$55. A restaurant-bar serves seafood and Mexican fare. Fishing pangas for three people go out for US$160.

About 2½ miles (4km) south of here is the friendly *Motel Muelle Viejo* (☎ 6-613-42-06), also known as Motel San Carlos. Simple but nice rooms, each with bathroom, hot shower and bay view, range from US$20 to US$35. It's about 2 miles (3.2km) west of the Transpeninsular in the Ejido El Papalote; look for the wooden sign.

Farther south in Ejido Santa María, *Hotel La Pinta San Quintín* (☎ 6-165-28-78, 800-336-5454 in the US) falls short of the standards of its sister hotels elsewhere on the peninsula, but its beachfront location is suitable for clamming, surf fishing and other beach activities. Each room has two double beds and a shower/bath, plus balconies facing a wide sandy beach. Rates are about US$45/73 midweek/weekend.

Motel Cielito Lindo (no local phone, ☎ 619-593-2252 in the US, cielitolindo@bajasi.com), south of town near Hotel La Pinta San Quintín, occupies attractive grounds near the beach. Rooms all have two queen-size beds and a shower/bath for US$45; it also has a bar, a restaurant (try the cracked-crab dinner) and a full sportfishing fleet. To get there, turn west near the new packing plant. The road is paved except for the final mile or so.

Places to Eat

The San Quintín area is famous for its clams, which are sold by nearly every roadside stand and restaurant. For reliable quality, go to the casual *Palapa de Mariscos El Paraiso* (☎ 6-165-29-06) near Km 192, which has a great menu of cocteles, fish tacos, ceviche tostadas, abalone (in season) and, of course, clams. Across the street is *Mi Lien*, the area's lone Chinese restaurant.

Bar San Quintín, alongside Motel Chávez in San Quintín proper, has good breakfasts, filet mignon for about US$8 and burgers from US$3. North of the Pemex station, *Misión Santa Isabel* (☎ 6-165-23-09) is a favorite locals' hangout and always full. Portions are huge and cheap with breakfast costing about US$4 and lunch and dinner averaging US$6.

Also recommended is *Viejo San Quintín*, an expatriate hangout that makes good Mexican combinations in addition to American-style burgers and sandwiches.

The area's most expensive restaurant is *Gastón's Cannery*, at the Molino Viejo. You're paying for the atmosphere of an adapted cannery as much as for the food, but decent live entertainment in the bar is a plus. The *Muelle Viejo* in the namesake motel farther south specializes in mid-priced seafood and meat dishes and also has good bay views.

Getting There & Away

The long-distance bus terminal (☎ 6-165-30-50) is in Lázaro Cárdenas on the western side of the Transpeninsular. ABC is the main carrier, with scheduled service to points north and south.

El Rosario – US$3.50, one hour; three times daily

Ensenada – US$10, 3½ hours; hourly from 6 am to 7 pm

Tijuana – US$17.50, 5½ hours; seven times daily (two direct, others change in Ensenada)

Guerrero Negro – US$19, six hours; three times daily

San Ignacio – US$23, 7½ hours; three times daily

Mexicali – US$24, eight hours; three times daily

Santa Rosalía – US$33, 8½ hours; three times daily

Mulegé – US$36, 10 hours; three times daily

Loreto – US$47, 12 hours; three times daily

La Paz – US$59, 18 to 20 hours; four times daily

Getting Around

Transportes Ejidales vans shuttle between Camalú and Ejido El Papalote to the south, roughly every 15 minutes daily. You can flag them down anywhere en route. Their primary clientele is farm workers; fares range from US$0.85 to US$1.50.

EL ROSARIO

About one hour (36 miles or 57km) south of San Quintín, El Rosario (population 3500) is regarded by seasoned Baja travelers as the terminus of the 'civilized' part of Baja and the gateway to the untamed stretches of the central peninsula.

Historically, the town forms the southern border of the Dominican mission frontier. Known in pre-Spanish times as the Cochimí Indian ranchería of Viñadaco, it was officially founded in 1774 as Misión Nuestra Señora del Rosario Viñadaco. An abundant water supply permitted cultivation of wheat, corn and fruit, including almonds and peaches; missionaries also directed the harvesting of lobster, abalone and clams. After relocating once when the major spring dried up, the mission closed in 1832 because epidemics had so ravaged the Cochimí population that no laborers remained for the mission fields.

After the mission closed, El Rosario was the seat of military government for northern Baja but remained thinly populated until the late 1840s, when retired soldier Carlos Espinosa received a grant of 4000 acres (1600 hectares) from Governor José Castro. The Espinosa family is still prominent in the area.

Orientation & Information

El Rosario, about 36 miles (58km) south of San Quintín, consists of two parts: the larger Rosario de Arriba, along the Transpeninsular north of the Arroyo de Rosario, and Rosario de Abajo, 1½ miles (2.5km) downstream. The few tourist services are in Rosario de Arriba. The postal code is 22960. On the north end of town is a rare self-serve Pemex that's open 24 hours.

Misión Nuestra Señora del Rosario

Only limited remains of the mission's two sites are still standing. The initial mission site is at the end of a short dirt road above the highway, about 150 yards (137m) west of Motel Sinai, but only the outlines of the foundations are still visible. At Rosario de Abajo, across the Río del Rosario, several standing walls make up the ruins of the later mission.

Places to Stay & Eat

Next to the Pemex station at the northern end of town, *Motel Rosario* (☎ 6-165-88-50) is a low building with a satellite dish in front. Rooms are clean but very basic and plain and cost US$17/21 singles/doubles. At Km 56.5 at the eastern end of town, the newer *Motel Sinai* (☎ 6-165-88-18) has a range of rooms for US$18 to US$30, plus an RV park that charges US$16 for full-size RVs. Electricity and water are available, and campers may use the shower in the motel office, but only a rustic (read: challenging) pit toilet is available. The laundromat next door is now part of the motel and can wash clothes for guests or campers.

With the completion of the Transpeninsular in late 1973, *Casa Espinosa*, between the two motels, became a favorite stop for a variety of travelers. In the early days of Baja road races, celebrities Steve McQueen, James Garner and Parnelli Jones sampled Doña Anita Espinosa's lobster burritos here. The restaurant has modernized and expanded into souvenirs and accommodations, offering very clean and pleasant rooms with two beds for US$25.

Yiyo's, at the eastern end of town beyond Motel Sinai, serves Mexican food and has palatable breakfasts. *El Grullense*, at the bus terminal, serves basic cheap antojitos. There are also several good taco stands.

Getting There & Away

Buses stop at El Rosario's terminal on a schedule similar to that of San Quintín's terminal (see earlier this chapter). Southbound buses depart about an hour later than those leaving San Quintín; northbound buses depart about an hour earlier.

AROUND EL ROSARIO

At the end of a good but sometimes rough road that leads west 10½ miles (17km) from

El Rosario, the fish camp of **Punta Baja** also attracts surfers and sea kayakers to a good right-point break in the winter, but no tourist services are available.

From the hill overlooking the camp, arriving tourists and local goatherds can see the five volcanoes of the San Quintín area to the north, as well as the camp's satellite dish and school basketball courts.

Some 46 miles (74km) south of El Rosario by a series of decent graded and not-so-decent dirt roads, **Punta San Carlos** is one of the best windsurfing spots on the Pacific side of the peninsula.

TECATE

The sleepy but fast-growing border town of Tecate (population 75,000) more closely resembles a mainland Mexican *pueblo* (town) than does any other locality in northern Baja California. Town life revolves around the *zócalo* (central plaza), known as Parque Hidalgo, which is canopied by mature trees and is a favorite gathering spot for locals and visitors. On weekends, mariachi bands play here, and fiestas take place throughout the year.

Tecate is in a bowl-shaped valley surrounded by mountains. The most famous of them is Mt Cuchumá (3885 feet or 1165m), which is sacred to the Kumeyaay tribe, whose surviving elders and shaman still hold occasional ceremonies atop the summit. It offers numerous opportunities for nature lovers and recreationists and is especially nice in spring when the wildflowers are in bloom. There's also abundant birdlife. At the foot of the mountain is Rancho La Puerta, one of the oldest and most exclusive health spas in North America (see separate entry later in this section).

History

Tecate's origins derive from an 1831 land grant to a Peruvian named Juan Bandini (who became the mayor of San Diego immediately before the US takeover of Alta California), but the establishment of early businesses and the development of agriculture in the 1880s really put the town on the map. The surrounding countryside yielded both grains and fruit crops such as grapes and olives.

In 1911, Ricardo Flores Magón's Liberal Party army occupied Tecate before marching west to Tijuana, but the Mexican federal government regained control after six weeks. After 1919, the railroad linked Tecate with Tijuana and Arizona. Completion of México 2, the last link on the Tijuana-Mexico City highway, was a further boost to the economy.

Tecate's onetime whiskey factory, a major employer, folded with the repeal of US Prohibition. Businessman Alberto Aldrete's malt factory, founded in 1928, expanded into a major brewery by 1944 but soon went bankrupt. Acquired by a Mexican conglomerate after several years' management by the Banco de Mexico, it is still an important employer, producing up to 1200 cans per minute of two of Mexico's best-known beers, Tecate and Carta Blanca.

Maquiladoras, however, are the major employers; the largest is Schlage Locks, employing about 3000 people. Since its opening in 1986, the Universidad Autónoma de Baja California's extension center has enhanced the town's cultural environment.

Orientation

Tecate is about 34 miles (55km) east of Tijuana and 90 miles (145km) west of Mexicali. México 2 – the east-west route linking Tijuana and Mexicali – divides into Avenida Benito Juárez to the north and Avenida Hidalgo two blocks south as it enters town.

Avenida Juárez runs past Parque Hidalgo, the main square, and the bus terminal, while Avenida Hidalgo runs past the brewery. Lázaro Cárdenas runs north from Avenida Hidalgo to the border crossing. Ortiz Rubio runs south one block east of Cárdenas to become México 3 to Ensenada.

Information

The Customs & Immigration posts on both sides of the border are open 6 am to midnight daily. Saturday is the busiest day; Sunday, surprisingly, is relatively quiet.

Secture has a small information office (☎ 6-654-10-95) on the southern side of Parque Hidalgo, but English-speaking staff are not always available. Office hours are 8 am to 5 pm weekdays, 10 am to 3 pm weekends. Right by the border, Canaco (☎ 6-654-58-92) has a kiosk, which usually opens 8 am to 5 pm weekdays and has adequate town maps. Car insurance is also available here.

The travel agency Viajes Segovia (☎ 6-654-27-55, fax 6-654-27-56) is at Ortiz Rubio 260-2, south of Parque Hidalgo.

Most businesses readily accept US dollars, but Tecate also has several banks on Avenida Juárez and around Parque Hidalgo. These include Banamex, Bancomer and Banco Internacional (Bital). Multi-Servicio Cox operates an exchange service on Avenida Juárez between Aldrete and Santana; it's open 9 am to 7 pm and closed Sunday.

Tecate's post office is at the corner of Ortiz Rubio and Callejón Madero, three blocks north of Parque Hidalgo. The postal code is 21400. Tecate has plenty of public telephones, but the best place to make a long-distance call is the bus terminal, which has several phone booths and a fax machine.

For medical service, the Cruz Roja (☎ 132) is at the western end of Avenida Juárez. Tecate has numerous medical clinics, dentists and pharmacies that serve visitors from north of the border. The police station (☎ 6-654-11-77, emergency ☎ 134) is on México 2, east of downtown.

Things to See & Do

Tecate's street life centers on **Parque Hidalgo**, the main plaza, which features a band gazebo surrounded by well-tended gardens and a statue of independence hero Miguel Hidalgo. Unlike in most Mexican cities, Tecate's main church, the **Iglesia Nuestra Señora de Guadalupe**, is not on the plaza but one block south, at the corner of Cárdenas and Avenida Hidalgo.

The **Instituto de Cultura de Baja California** (☎ 6-654-14-83) is on the southern side of Parque Hidalgo. It offers art exhibits, films (usually in video format) and other cultural events. The **Universidad Autónoma's Centro de Extensión**, just south of the bridge over the Río Tecate, hosts occasional traveling exhibitions of bajacaliforniano art.

LA FRONTERA

TECATE

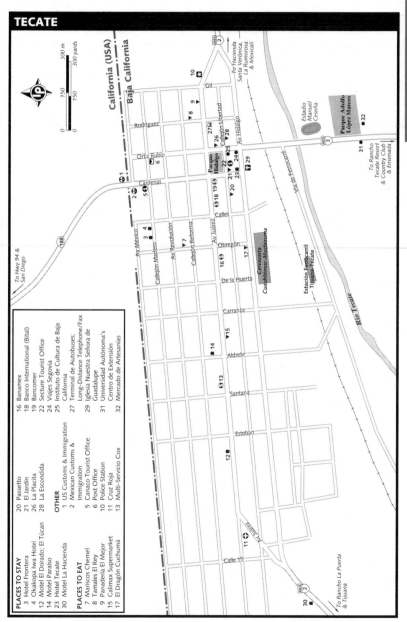

0   150   300 m
0   150   300 yards

California (USA)
Baja California

To Hwy 94 &
San Diego

To Hacienda
Santa Verónica,
La Rumorosa
& Mexicali

Estadio
Manuel
Ceseña

Parque Adolfo
López Mateos

To Rancho
Tecate Resort
& Country Club
& Ensenada

Gil
Rodríguez
Ortiz Rubio
Cárdenas
Av México
Callejón Madero
Av Revolución
Callejón Reforma
Av Juárez
Calles
Obregón
De la Huerta
Carranza
Aldrete
Santana
Esteban
Calle 15
Av Juárez

Libertad
Callejón
Av Hidalgo

Parque
Hidalgo

Cervecería
Cuauhtémoc-Moctezuma

Estación Ferrocarril
Tijuana-Tecate

Vía del Ferrocarril

Río Tecate

To Rancho La Puerta
& Tijuana

PLACES TO STAY
3 Hotel Frontera
4 Okakopa Iwa Hotel
12 Motel El Dorado; El Tucan
14 Motel Paraíso
23 Hotel Tecate
30 Motel La Hacienda

PLACES TO EAT
7 Mariscos Chemel
8 Tamales El Rey
9 Panadería El Mejor
15 Calimax Supermarket
17 El Dragón Cuchumá

20 Passetto
21 El Jardín
26 La Placita
28 La Escondida

OTHER
1 US Customs & Immigration
2 Mexican Customs &
   Immigration
5 Canaco Tourist Office
6 Post Office
10 Police Station
11 Cruz Roja
13 Multi-Servicio Cox

16 Banamex
18 Banco International (Bital)
19 Bancomer
22 Secture Tourist Office
24 Viajes Segovia
25 Instituto de Cultura de Baja
   California
27 Terminal de Autobuses;
   Long-Distance Telephone/Fax
29 Iglesia Nuestra Señora de
   Guadalupe
31 Universidad Autónoma's
   Centro de Extensión
32 Mercado de Artesanías

Rails Across the Border

The Tijuana & Tecate Railway was originally part of the San Diego & Arizona Railway and an extensive cross-border route system, built by Southern Pacific and completed in 1919. The line actually began in Lakeside, a northeastern suburb of San Diego, linked up just south of Chula Vista with a spur from Coronado and entered Mexico at Tijuana. It reentered the US at Tecate before descending the rugged eastern scarp of the Jacumba Mountains, including the difficult Carrizo Gorge, via a series of switchbacks and tunnels. At El Centro, it joined another route, the Inter-California line, recrossed the border at Mexicali and re-entered the US just beyond Los Algodones.

The San Diego & Arizona Railway continued to operate (carrying freight in its later years) until 1970, when Southern Pacific sold the Tijuana & Tecate segment to the Mexican government. In 1976, Hurricane Kathleen demolished several trestles on the route, ending operations between San Diego and El Centro. In 1997, during the privatization of the Mexican railroad, the segment was bought by the Texas-based Railtex company, which hauls freight along here and through San Diego County under the name San Diego & Imperial Valley Railroad.

Currently, no passenger service is available, except on the occasional trips aboard historic trains offered by the San Diego Railroad Museum between Tijuana and Tecate and, more frequently, from Campo (Arizona) to Tecate.

Tecate's other main landmark, the **Cervecería Cuauhtémoc-Moctezuma** (☎ 6-654-11-11), on Avenida Hidalgo between De la Huerta and Obregón, offers brewery tours at 10 am daily by reservation only, preferably for at least 10 people. It's best to call no less than two weeks in advance for reservations, but it's worth trying to hook up with another tour or to persuade the publicity people to offer one on the spot. The brewery, Tecate's largest building, produces some of Mexico's best-known beers, including Carta Blanca and the town's namesake, Tecate; after the tour, you can sample the products in the Jardín Cerveza (beer garden).

Behind the brewery, the newly revived **Estación Ferrocarril Tijuana-Tecate** (railway station, 1915) served the San Diego & Arizona Railway that ran along and across the border for more than 60 years (see the boxed text 'Rails Across the Border').

On selected dates throughout the year, the San Diego Railroad Museum (☎ 619-595-3030, 888-228-9246, fax 619-595-3034) runs excursions to Tecate aboard historic trains. Occasional day trips from Tijuana include a three-hour stay in Tecate; fares are US$50/100 for coach/1st class. More frequent outings embark from the museum's headquarters in Campo, across the border in eastern San Diego County. These half-day trips cost US$40/100 with trains chugging downhill from 2500 feet, passing three tunnels on the way.

Special Events

While less extroverted than Tijuana and Ensenada, Tecate holds several festivals that draw in locals from throughout the region. Those listed below are in addition to regular Mexican holidays (see the Facts for the Visitor chapter). Double-check with the tourist offices, as event dates may change.

Nacional de Bicicleta de Montaña late June. National Mountain-Biking Championships; for details, call ☎ 6-654-22-46.

Feria Tecate en Marcha mid-July, sometimes in September. Celebrated with parades and rodeos. Takes place in Parque Adolfo López Mateos. For details, call ☎ 6-654-13-19.

Romería de Verano early August. Popular local summer festival in Parque Hidalgo, including food stalls, artisanal goods and regional music and dance.

Fundación de Tecate early October. Two-week celebration of city's anniversary.

Día de Nuestra Señora de Guadalupe December 12. Tecate's Festival of Our Lady of Guadalupe is one of the peninsula's most interesting celebrations of this holiday, with groups from all over Baja visiting Tecate to display their costumes and dancing.

Posadas de Tecate throughout December. Annual Pre-Christmas parades.

Places to Stay

Low-key Tecate has a fair amount of accommodations in the budget and mid-range price brackets.

Camping About 13 miles (21km) east of Tecate is the pleasant *Tecate KOA Kampground* (☎ 6-655-30-14, fax 6-655-30-15, *rojai@telnor.net*), part of Rancho Ojai, a working ranch. Charges are US$15 for tent spaces, US$25 for RVs with full hookups and US$40 to US$50 for self-contained cabins. A heated pool, mini-golf and nature trail are among the many assets. It's by the side of México 2, the free road to Tijuana (look for the Rancho Ojai sign).

Motels & Hotels The best true budget option is the hospitable *Motel Paraíso* (☎ 6-654-17-16, Calle Aldrete 83). Rooms are ragged around the edges, but rates are OK for US$17/24 singles/doubles. Also good in this price range is the super-friendly *Hotel Frontera* (☎ 6-654-13-42, Callejón Madero 131), which offers basic but tidy rooms for US$17 with shared bath, US$28 with private bath.

Next door is Tecate's prettiest hotel, the *Okakopa Iwa Hotel* (☎ 6-654-11-44, *okakopa@todito.com, Callejón Madero 141*), one block west of the border post. Rooms exhibit style and personality through their decor and come with air-con, color TV and telephone. Parking is secure as well. Rates are US$42/52.

The best value in town is offered by *Motel La Hacienda* (☎ 6-654-12-50, 6-654-09-53, Avenida Juárez 861), on Tecate's outskirts. A flower-festooned courtyard gives way to clean, carpeted, air-conditioned doubles with TV for US$32/36. Amenities include secure parking, a swimming pool and a guest fax.

Also west of the center, the 41-room *Motel El Dorado* (☎ 6-654-11-02, fax 6-654-13-33, Avenida Juárez 1100) has comfortable rooms with air-con, cable TV, telephone and carpeting for US$59 to US$83.

If every place is full, you could also try *Hotel Tecate* (☎ 6-654-11-16), on Cárdenas half a block south of Parque Hidalgo, whose spartan, unheated rooms cost US$19, or US$26 with color TV. The hot showers are dependable and the toilets are clean. The entrance is upstairs from within the courtyard, accessed from either Parque Hidalgo or Cárdenas.

Places to Eat

Despite its modest size, Tecate has a number of good eateries. Self-caterers may find the assortment at the Calimax supermarket on Juárez between Aldrete and Carranza useful. Locals swear that *Panadería El Mejor* (☎ 6-654-00-40, Avenida Juárez 331), near the bus terminal, bakes the best bread and pastries in Baja – and they may well be right. It's open 24 hours a day (with free coffee).

La Placita, an outdoor kitchen on the eastern side of Parque Hidalgo, serves some of Tecate's juiciest tacos. The southern side of Avenida Juárez between the bus terminal and Parque Hidalgo has wall-to-wall taquerías of good to excellent quality. The prize, though, is *Mariscos Chemel* (☎ 6-654-41-12, Obregón 250), where locals swarm for succulent, inexpensive fish and shrimp tacos. *Tamales El Rey* (☎ 6-654-61-26), on Rodríguez just north of Juárez, makes good tamales with various fillings, including chicken and pork.

La Escondida (☎ 6-654-21-64) definitely lives up to its name, 'the hidden one' – see if you can locate the entrance at Callejón Libertad 174 between Ortiz Rubio and Rodríguez. If you do, you'll be treated to some great Mexican standards at next-to-nothing prices. The three-course comida corrida is less than US$3. It's open 7 am to 6 pm, weekends to 5 pm.

For a change from Mexican fare, try *Passetto* (☎ 6-654-13-61, Callejón Libertad 200), which makes moderately priced Italian dishes. *El Dragón Cuchumá* (☎ 6-654-05-40), on Hidalgo at Obregón, is a Chinese restaurant named after a nearby mountain.

El Jardín, on the south side of Parque Hidalgo, is Tecate's only outdoor restaurant and serves beer in Oktoberfest-size mugs (1 liter).

The mediocre restaurant at Hotel Tecate, *El Túcan*, does a passable weekend buffet for US$9.

Shopping

Shopping in Tecate is not as good as in Tijuana or the beach towns. Selection is small and prices are about the same or higher. Hand-painted clay tiles and Tecate beer are the town's specialties.

A small Mercado de Artesanías (☎ 6-654-17-50) is just south of Parque Adolfo López Mateos. A few more shops are on Cárdenas just south of the border crossing.

Getting There & Away

Tecate's Terminal de Autobuses is at Avenida Juárez and Rodríguez, one block east of Parque Hidalgo. ABC's Subur Baja buses go to Tijuana's Central Camionera at least hourly (US$3, 1½ hours) and more frequently to the downtown terminal (US$3, one hour).

ABC also goes to Mexicali (US$8.50/10 for 2nd/1st class) hourly from 6:30 am to 10 pm. Five buses leave daily for Ensenada (US$5.25/8.50) and one each to Santa Rosalía (US$56, at 2:30 pm) and to La Paz (US$82, at 7 pm).

If you're driving from San Diego, take Hwy 94 to the Tecate turnoff. Coming from Arizona, take the I-8 and switch to Hwy 94 just east of Jacumba. From Tijuana, you can choose between the free México 2 or the toll road México 2D, which starts just east of Mesa de Otay. The latter is easier to find and faster once you're actually on it. The downside is the exorbitant fee of US$5.50 per vehicle for what amounts to a 20-mile (32km) drive on the actual toll road. From Mexicali, simply follow México 2 all the way west to Tecate; parts of it are a divided four-lane highway.

AROUND TECATE
Rancho Tecate Resort & Country Club

On México 3, about 6 miles (10km) south of Tecate in the Tanama Valley, Rancho Tecate Resort & Country Club (☎ 6-654-00-11, fax 6-654-02-41) features a hotel, tennis courts, a restaurant, two artificial lakes, a swimming pool and Jacuzzi. There's also a 'golf course,' but because only three of the nine holes are operating, you have to play three rounds.

The greens fee is US$10 per person, and the course is open to the public. Rooms range from US$55 to US$100.

Rancho La Puerta

If restoring body, mind and soul is your foremost concern, a stay at the exquisite health spa and resort of Rancho La Puerta (☎ 6-654-11-55, fax 6-654-11-08, in the US ☎ 760-744-4222, 800-443-7565, fax 760-744-5007, reservations@rancholapuerta.com) may be what you need. Founded in 1940 by self-improvement gurus Deborah and Edmund Szekely, the lushly landscaped resort snuggles up against the foot of Mt Cuchumá, also known as 'Holy Mountain.'

The one-week stay (Saturday to Saturday) at this nonsmoking facility is anchored in a low-fat diet and lots of exercise. Days start with a sunrise hike before breakfast, then continue with as many classes as you like; choose from about 50 different ones, including African dance, cardio boxing, Pilates, t'ai chi and postural alignment. In addition, there are tennis courts, pools, Jacuzzis and saunas. Meals are served three times daily.

Accommodations range from *rancheras* (studio bedrooms) to larger villas, all decorated with folk art, handcrafted furniture and tiles, and vibrant weavings. Guest capacity is limited to 160, and vacancies fill up as much as a year in advance. Cancellations do happen, though, so it's worth calling or checking the Web site at www.rancholapuerta.com.

Rates start at US$1727 per person, double occupancy, and include accommodations, meals and classes, as well as transportation to and from San Diego International Airport (Lindbergh Field). The rancho is on México 2, about 3 miles (5km) west of Tecate.

Hacienda Santa Verónica

Climbing to a high plateau, México 2 passes through a zone of small farms and ranches. Hacienda Santa Verónica (☎ 6-681-74-28, fax 6-681-74-29), about 15 miles (24km) southeast of Tecate, is reached via a lateral off the main highway. The Spanish Colonial–style resort is on a 5000-acre former bull breeding ranch and offers roomy cabins with fireplace and patio, a large swimming

pool, six tennis courts, volleyball and basketball courts. Horseback riding is available
too. Visitors seeking peace and quiet should
know that the ranch also has an off-road
racing track.

Rooms cost US$53 per night for a
double. RV spaces with full hookups cost
US$28 and tent camping is US$10 per
person, including access to restrooms,
showers, laundry, and sports and fossil-fuel
facilities.

La Rumorosa

East of Tecate, for about 40 miles (64km),
México 2 passes through an imposing
panorama of immense granite boulders to
La Rumorosa. Here it descends the precipitous Cantú Grade, with extraordinary views
of the shimmering Desierto del Colorado.
At Km 83, the village of El Cóndor gives
access to a northern route into the Parque
Nacional de Constitución de 1857. For
details, see the park's entry, earlier.

Desierto del Colorado

The Desierto del Colorado stretches out east of the Sierra de Juárez and the Sierra San Pedro Mártir and encompasses the bustling border town of Mexicali, the lowlands of the Río Colorado delta and the region south to the Gulf port of San Felipe. It's a popular destination for Canadians and Americans from the cold northern states and for party-ing college students on spring break. From June to October, the area turns into a roaring furnace, when temperatures often exceed 110°F (45°C).

Initially slow to be settled by Europeans, the agricultural Valle de Mexicali area grew rapidly in the 20th century as irrigation allowed farmers to take advantage of rich soils and a long, productive growing season.

San Felipe's beaches and sportfishing draw more visitors than any other regional attraction, but the eastern canyons of the sierras attract increasing numbers of campers and hikers. South of San Felipe, the village of Puertecitos is the starting point for a rugged but rewarding alternative southbound connection to the Transpeninsular for drivers, motorcyclists and even bicyclists. Plans to improve this route have yet to materialize.

Highlights

- Enjoying seafood and worldwide cuisine at Mexicali's excellent restaurants
- Visiting Mexicali's Sol del Niño science museum, fun for children of all ages
- Camping at Cañón Guadalupe amid hot springs, natural pools and waterfalls
- Kicking back on San Felipe's white-sand beach
- Exploring the Valle de los Gigantes, home to giant cardón cacti

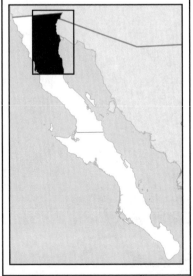

MEXICALI

Bustling Mexicali, capital of the state of Baja California, is a prosperous agricultural and industrial center that relies on Río Colorado irrigation water to grow vegetables, wheat and cotton in the delta's silt-laden soil.

Of all Mexico's northern border cities, Mexicali (population 950,000) most impressively dwarfs its US counterpart, with a population at least 10 times that of neighboring Calexico and the Imperial Valley. Making an enormous economic contribution to the US border cities, at least three times as many Mexicans cross the line into mainland California than do foreigners southbound into Baja – it's a popular saying that when Mexicali gets a cold, Calexico gets pneumonia. Many visitors pass through Mexicali on their way south to San Felipe or east to Sonora and mainland Mexico, but only a handful stop for more than gasoline, cheap liquor, brief shopping sprees or visits to tawdry bars.

However, Mexicali, like Tijuana, is shedding its stereotypical border-town image. In the southern part of the city, the Centro Cívico-Comercial (Civic & Commercial Center) includes local, state and federal

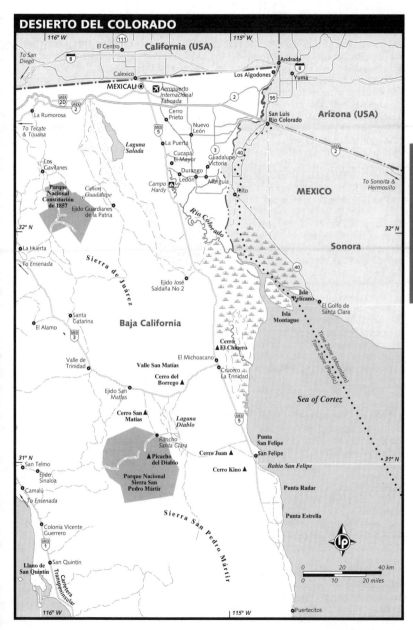

DESIERTO DEL COLORADO

116° W
115° W

To San Diego
El Centro
California (USA)
Andrade
Yuma

Calexico
Los Algodones

MEXICALI
Aeropuerto Internacional Taboada
San Luis Río Colorado
Arizona (USA)

La Rumorosa
Cerro Prieto
Nuevo León
La Puerta

To Tecate & Tijuana
Laguna Salada
Cucapá El Mayor
Guadalupe Victoria
MEXICO

Los Gavilanes
Durango León
Murguía

Parque Nacional Constitución de 1857
Cañon Guadalupe
Campo Hardy
Riíto
To Sonoita & Hermosillo

Ejido Guardianes de la Patria
Río Colorado

32° N
32° N

La Huerta
Sonora

To Ensenada
Sierra de Juárez

Ejido José Saldaña No 2

Isla Pelícano
El Golfo de Santa Clara

Santa Catarina
Baja California
Isla Montague

El Alamo

Valle de Trinidad
El Michoacano
Sea of Cortez

Valle San Matías
Crucero La Trinidad

Cerro El Chinero
Ejido San Matías
Cerro del Borrego

Cerro San Matías
Laguna Diablo

Rancho Santa Clara
Punta San Felipe
San Felipe

31° N
Cerro Juan
Bahía San Felipe
31° N

San Telmo
Picacho del Diablo
Cerro Kino

Ejido Sinaloa
Parque Nacional Sierra San Pedro Mártir
Punta Radar

Camalú
To Ensenada
Punta Estrella

Colonia Vicente Guerrero
Sierra San Pedro Mártir

San Quintín
Llano de San Quintín
Carretera Transpeninsular

0   20   40 km
0   10   20 miles

116° W
115° W
Puertecitos

Time Zone (Mountain)
Time Zone (Pacific)

government offices, a medical school, a bullring, cinemas, a bus terminal, hospitals and restaurants. Mexicali, unlike San Felipe or Cabo San Lucas, is reluctant to pander to tourists and is thus all the more interesting; its historic core along the border makes for a rewarding excursion that reveals as much about mainland California as it does about Baja.

The city enjoys excellent cultural and educational facilities, thanks largely to institutions of higher education like the Universidad Autónoma de Baja California, the Universidad Pedagógica Nacional, the Instituto Tecnológico Regional and the Centro de Enseñanza Técnica y Superior.

History

In pre-Columbian times, relatively dense populations of sedentary Yuman farmers inhabited the Río Colorado delta, an area that the early Spaniards failed to colonize because of its remoteness, hostile climate and determined peoples who resented missionary intrusions. Conditions changed in the early 20th century, when entrepreneurs from north of the border realized the agricultural potential of the deep river-borne sediments, if only they could be irrigated.

Events north of the border both contributed to and detracted from Mexicali's development. Since the mid-19th century, ambitious speculators and their engineers had sought to convey water from the Colorado to the Imperial Valley in California, but the sprawling Algodones Dunes were an insurmountable obstacle with the available technology. Charles Rockwood's California Development Company circumvented this problem by diverting water from the Colorado's main channel into its westward-flowing Alamo channel, south of the border, and hence to the Imperial Valley. In return for permission to cross Mexican territory, Rockwood promised Mexico half the diverted water.

With completion of the Alamo Canal in 1902, the site known as Laguna del Alamo began to prosper and the following year was formally founded as the city of Mexicali. In succeeding years, however, floodwaters silted up the canal's Hanlon Headgate and several bypasses near Andrade in mainland California, so the company excavated a newer, more direct channel between the river and the canal. It did not, however, build a headgate that could accommodate the major floods of 1905.

These floods poured water into the dry channel of the Río Nuevo for months, obliterating parts of the fledgling settlement of Mexicali as it swept north into mainland California's Salton Sink – which soon became the Salton Sea. Not until early 1907 did massive efforts by the Southern Pacific Railroad, which acquired the California Development Company shortly after the 1905 fiasco, succeed in returning the Colorado to its main channel.

After this reprieve, Mexicali rebounded only to falter and then benefit from the Revolution of 1910, when it was briefly occupied by anarchist Magonistas. The Mexican government grew alarmed at the Magonistas' internationalist membership and at agricultural developments north of the border – especially since Mexico had lost so much territory by the 1848 Treaty of Guadalupe Hidalgo. In 1915, these concerns led Colonel Estéban Cantú, a military political appointee, to relocate the territorial capital from Ensenada to Mexicali, though he governed more or less independently of the revolutionaries and the established government. In 1952, Mexicali became capital of the new state of Baja California.

In Mexicali's early decades, nearly all the land was under control of the Colorado River Land Company, a US company that engaged in large-scale cotton cultivation with imported Chinese laborers, who were later replaced by Mexicans from the mainland states. In the 1920s, US Prohibition fostered drinking, gambling and prostitution south of the border.

In 1937, after the famous 'Asalto a las Tierras' (Assault on the Lands) by laborers in the Mexicali valley, the government of President Lázaro Cárdenas forced the Colorado River Land Company to sell most of its land to Mexican farmers and *ejidos* (peasant cooperatives). Around the same time, the

Colorado River Compact among the US states in the great river's watershed led to the construction of the All-American Canal, north of the border, which bypassed Mexico and reduced the amount of water available to Mexican growers.

The company's imprint on the cityscape is still apparent – its historic headquarters is now an office building, while the open spaces along the railway line, now giving way to shopping malls, are reminders of the numerous cotton mills that employed many city residents.

In 1947, the Ferrocarril Sonora-Baja California linked Mexicali to mainland Mexico via the rail junction of Benjamín Hill (Sonora); highways and airline and communication links followed in short order.

Orientation

On the eastern bank of the intermittent Río Nuevo, most of Mexicali's main streets run east-west, paralleling the border. From Mexican Customs & Immigration, Avenida Francisco Madero heads east past Parque Niños Héroes de Chapultepec, running through Mexicali's central business district of modest restaurants, stores, bars and budget hotels. The other streets that run parallel to Avenida Madero are also key shopping areas; better hotels and restaurants begin to appear a few blocks east of the border crossing. The largely residential area west of the Río Nuevo is known as Pueblo Nuevo.

Unfortunately, much of Mexicali is no longer pedestrian-friendly – mostly because local, state and federal authorities have consciously shifted government services to the new Centro Cívico-Comercial and discouraged commercial development near the border zone. From the border, the broad diagonal Calzada López Mateos heads southeast through Mexicali's relatively new industrial and commercial section, where cotton and flour mills once lined the rail route.

For pedestrians, the new decentralization isn't so bad when the weather is cool, but the lack of trees or any other shade is almost lethal in summer heat. Drivers are mostly

courteous, but the busy boulevards have their own momentum – even Olympic sprinters may find crossing them difficult.

The *zona hotelera,* an area of posh lodgings and restaurants just beyond the Centro Cívico-Comercial, is about 2¼ miles (3.5km) southeast of the border post. Calzada López Mateos continues south another 3 miles (5km) before dividing into México 5 (to San Felipe) and México 2 (to Sonora).

Information

Border Crossings Calexico-Mexicali's border crossing in downtown is open 24 hours, but drivers should avoid the northbound afternoon rush hour. To relieve congestion, US and Mexican authorities have opened a new border complex, Calexico East, in the industrial-park area east of downtown, at the junction of Avenida República Argentina and Blvd Abelardo L Rodríguez. This one is open 6 am to 10 pm daily.

If you're traveling east to mainland Mexico or south beyond Ensenada or San Felipe, obtain a tourist card. If you're driving to mainland Mexico, you need a vehicle permit and a tourist card; both are available from Mexican Customs & Immigration at either crossing. For details about the tourist card, see Travel Permits in the Facts for the Visitor chapter. For vehicle permits, see the Getting Around chapter.

US Customs & Immigration officials at Calexico sometimes x-ray the luggage of pedestrians crossing the border, so it's wise to remove photographic film from bags and backpacks.

Tourist Offices The Secretaría de Turismo del Estado (Secture; ☎ 6-566-11-16, fax 6-558-10-00, secture@hotmail.com) is on Calzada Benito Juárez, just past the Benito Juárez monument. It's open 8 am to 5 pm weekdays, 10 am to 3 pm Saturday. An English-speaker is always on duty, and Secture's city map is very useful.

The Comité de Turismo y Convenciones (Cotuco or Committee on Tourism & Conventions; ☎ 6-557-23-76, 6-557-25-61) is at the corner of Calzada López Mateos and Camelias, about 1¾ miles (3km) southeast

MEXICALI

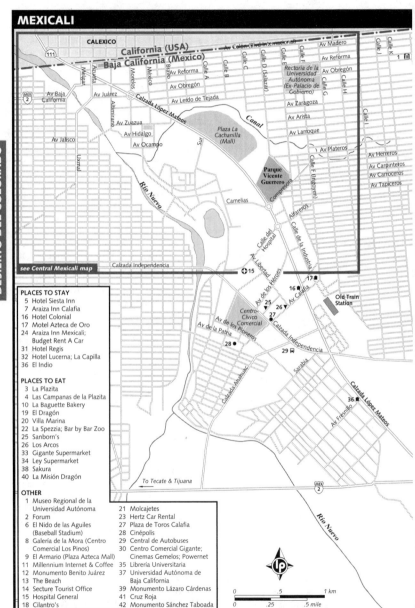

see Central Mexicali map

PLACES TO STAY
5 Hotel Siesta Inn
7 Araiza Inn Calafia
16 Hotel Colonial
17 Motel Azteca de Oro
24 Araiza Inn Mexicali;
   Budget Rent A Car
31 Hotel Regis
32 Hotel Lucerna; La Capilla
36 El Indio

PLACES TO EAT
3 La Plazita
4 Las Campanas de la Plazita
10 La Baguette Bakery
19 El Dragón
20 Villa Marina
22 La Spezzia; Bar by Bar Zoo
25 Sanborn's
26 Los Arcos
33 Gigante Supermarket
34 Ley Supermarket
38 Sakura
40 La Misión Dragón

OTHER
1 Museo Regional de la
   Universidad Autónoma
2 Forum
6 El Nido de las Aguiles
   (Baseball Stadium)
8 Galería de la Mora (Centro
   Comercial Los Pinos)
9 El Armario (Plaza Azteca Mall)
11 Millennium Internet & Coffee
12 Monumento Benito Juárez
13 The Beach
14 Secture Tourist Office
15 Hospital General
18 Cilantro's
21 Molcajetes
23 Hertz Car Rental
27 Plaza de Toros Calafia
28 Cinépolis
29 Central de Autobuses
30 Centro Comercial Gigante;
   Cinemas Gemelos; Powernet
35 Librería Universitaria
37 Universidad Autónoma de
   Baja California
39 Monumento Lázaro Cárdenas
41 Cruz Roja
42 Monumento Sánchez Taboada

To Tecate & Tijuana

0   .5   1 km
0   .25   .5 mile

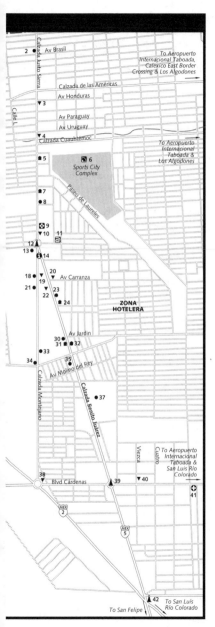

of the downtown border crossing. The staff usually includes an English-speaker. Hours are 8 am to 7 pm weekdays.

Across the border, Calexico's Chamber of Commerce (☎ 760-357-1166), 1100 Imperial Ave (Hwy 111), is also a good source of information; it's open 8:30 am to 5 pm weekdays.

Money *Cambios* (currency exchange offices) are especially abundant in the immediate border area; they do not charge commission on exchanges. Downtown banks with ATMs include Bancomer at Azueta and Avenida Madero, Banco Internacional (Bital) at the corner of Avenida Madero and Morelos, and Banamex across the street to the south. Many other banks in both Mexicali and Calexico have 24-hour ATMs.

Travelers passing through Calexico can change money (cambios here usually offer slightly better rates than their Mexicali competitors) and buy car insurance along Imperial Ave (Hwy 111), which leads straight to the border.

Post & Communications Mexicali's central post office is on Avenida Madero at the corner of Morelos. Downtown Mexicali's postal code is 21000.

Phone booths are common in pharmacies and similar businesses, but public telephones are numerous.

To surf the Web or check email, go to Powernet (☎ 6-566-25-50) at Calzada Benito Juárez 1400. They charge US$1.70 for 30 minutes and US$2.70 for 60 minutes of access and are open 9 am to 11 pm Monday to Saturday and noon to 9 pm Sunday. Closer to the border, but more expensive, is Café Internet Mexicali (☎ 6-554-12-49) at Avenida Reforma and Calle D (Salazar). A cheaper option is Millennium Internet & Coffee (☎ 6-568-38-40) at Calzada Justo Sierra 1700.

Travel Agencies Mexicali has many downtown travel agencies, among them Aero Olímpico Tours (☎ 6-552-50-25), Avenida Madero 621, and Viajes Ana Sol (☎ 6-553-47-87), Avenida Madero 1324-A near the rectory of the university. The American Express representative is KL International (☎ 6-554-12-00), Calzada Justo Sierra at Avenida Zaragoza.

Bookstores Librería Universitaria, across from the Universidad Autónoma on Calzada Benito Juárez just south of Calzada Independencia, has a good selection of books (mostly in Spanish) on Mexican history, archaeology, anthropology and literature. Closer to the border, on Avenida Madero between Altamirano and Morelos, Librería Alethia has a smaller but still respectable selection of books on similar subjects. Another store with a small selection of high-quality books is Librería INAH (☎ 6-557-11-04), Avenida Reforma 1310, Local 3.

Cultural Centers The Instituto de Cultura de Baja California (☎ 6-553-58-74) presents film series at the Teatro del Estado's Café Literario on Calzada López Mateos.

The main campus of the Universidad Autónoma de Baja California, located on Calzada Benito Juárez just south of Calzada Independencia, has a theater that hosts numerous cultural events, including live drama and lectures.

Medical & Emergency Services For emergencies, the Cruz Roja (Red Cross; ☎ 066, 6-561-81-01) is at Blvd Cárdenas 1492. The Hospital General (☎ 6-556-11-23) is at the corner of Calle del Hospital and Calzada Independencia near the Centro Cívico-Comercial.

Near the border are many clinics, laboratories, pharmacies and hospitals catering to US visitors, such as the Hospital México-Americano (☎ 6-552-27-49), Avenida Reforma 1000 at the corner of Calle B. Dentists trained at the Mexicali campus of the Universidad Autónoma offer quality work at a fraction of the cost north of the border.

La Chinesca

Mexicali's Chinatown, mostly centered along Avenida Juárez and Altamirano south of Calzada López Mateos, has its origin in the labor shortages experienced in the early 20th century when the Colorado River Land Company began agricultural operations in the Valle de Mexicali. From its beginnings, La Chinesca was a center of commerce and social interaction for the immigrant community, peaking around the 1920s. Today, the neighborhood is no longer what it once was, but it still contains many Chinese restaurants, other businesses and typically Sino-Mexican architecture.

Near the corner of La Chinesca's Altamirano and Avenida Zuazua, a concentration of rehearsal halls for banda groups has developed. The groups proclaim their presence by displaying their names and telephone numbers on bass drums on the sidewalk. In late afternoon, after band members finish their day jobs, it's possible to hear them practice – or hire them for a gig. For more about Mexicali's Chinese residents, see the boxed text.

Centro Cívico-Comercial

The highlights of Mexicali's modern civic center, located along Calzada Independencia, are the state government's Poder Ejecutivo (Governor's Office), Cámara de Diputados (Legislature) and Poder Judicial (Supreme Court). The plaque on the monument between them describes Mexicali as 'La Ciudad Cuyo Cielo Capturó Al Sol' (The City Whose Sky Captured the Sun).

Museums & Galleries

Local artists display their paintings, sculptures and photographs (for sale at reasonable prices) at **Galería de la Ciudad** (☎ 6-553-50-44), Avenida Obregón 1209 just east of Calle D (Salazar). This private gallery is open 9 am to 7 pm weekdays, to 1 pm Saturday.

Permanent displays at the **Museo Regional de la Universidad Autónoma** – also known as El Museo Hombre, Naturaleza y Cultura (Museum of Man, Nature & Culture) – cover subjects like geology, paleontology, human evolution, colonial history and photography. There are also traveling exhibitions with themes such as indigenous textiles from mainland Mexico. The modest eight-room museum (☎ 6-554-19-77) is located at the corner of Avenida Reforma and Calle L and

The Story of La Chinesca

Near Mexicali's main border crossing, a pagoda gracing the Plaza de la Amistad (Friendship Plaza) is the first visitors see of La Chinesca, one of Mexico's largest Chinatowns.

Chinese immigrants came to the Valle de Mexicali largely because the onset of WWI left companies like the Colorado River Land Company and other landowners in short supply of cheap labor. Trying to meet the increasing worldwide demand for American agricultural products, these companies looked to immigrants to prepare the land for cultivation. The Colorado River Land Company leased areas of land of up to 1000 acres (400 hectares) to individuals who then assumed complete responsibility for management and production. Many lessees were wealthy Chinese from California who imported contract labor from China. Eventually, some of the imported workforce formed cooperatives to work the land, pooling resources and sharing profits.

After the war ended in 1918, Mexicans from mainland Mexico flocked to the valley, attracted by the fervor of development. As the area started to experience a surplus of labor, resentment against the hard-working and entrepreneurial Chinese grew quickly, culminating in 1937 when President Lázaro Cárdenas ordered the confiscation of large landholdings, forcing thousands of Chinese off the land and into Mexicali city or back to China.

Meanwhile, in the mid-'20s, Mexicali's economy was booming, thanks in large part to US Prohibition. Americans flooded into Mexicali for boozing binges, gambling and sex: Most of the action was centered in and around La Chinesca. A huge fire in 1923 revealed a series of tunnels leading to underground bars, brothels and opium dens. At least one tunnel burrowed under the international border to surface in Calexico, undoubtedly for the transportation of contraband to the dry US.

Today's Chinese population in Mexicali is around 2000, the largest Chinese population in Mexico originating from Canton. The Asociación China de Mexicali, set up in 1918 to unify the Chinese laborers, is still going strong, providing representation, support and advice to the community. It also organizes cultural events, the big one being Chinese New Year. Preservation of the Chinese culture is most apparent in the Chinese language school, which runs Cantonese language classes for children on weekends.

Unfortunately, La Chinesca itself is pretty run-down, but it retains a buzz that leaves the newer parts of town feeling a bit soulless. Since the early 1990s, Nanjing, China, has been Mexicali's sister city, but so far the exchange is a passive one; cultural visits have yet to be organized.

is open 9 am to 6 pm weekdays, 10 am to 4 pm weekends. Admission is US$0.80.

The focus of **Sol del Niño** (☎/fax 6-553-83-83) is science, technology and the environment. Visitors are encouraged to experiment and play with what they experience here; the interactive exhibits include working TV and radio stations and are especially fun for kids. Located next to Parque Vicente Guerrero, the museum is open 8:30 am to 5 pm Monday to Friday, 10 am to 7 pm weekends. Admission is US$3.30.

Historic Buildings

The **Catedral de la Virgen de Guadalupe**, at the corner of Avenida Reforma and Morelos,

is Mexicali's major religious landmark. One block north, on Avenida Madero between Altamirano and Morelos, the former Escuela Cuauhtémoc is a neoclassical building that now serves as the city's **Casa de la Cultura** (☎ 6-552-96-30), which hosts rotating art exhibitions.

Now housing the rectory of the Universidad Autónoma, the grounds of the former **Palacio de Gobierno** (Government Palace, built between 1919 and 1922) interrupt Avenida Obregón just east of Calle E. Just north of this imposing building, at the intersection of Avenida Reforma and Calle F (Irigoyen), the former headquarters of the **Colorado River Land Company** (1924) is now used for offices, but its attractive patio fountain and restored balcony murals merit a visit.

At the corner of Avenida Zaragoza and Calle E, two blocks southwest of the rectory, the former **Cervecería Mexicali** (Mexicali Brewery) sits vacant but in a good state of preservation despite fire damage in 1986. Opened in 1923 under a German master brewer, it satisfied local demand for half a century and even managed to export some of its production.

City Monuments

Mexicali's monuments, which appear on its *glorietas* (traffic circles), are dedicated to past presidents, peasants, the fishermen of San Felipe and various other luminaries. Some notable figures honored in stone and steel are Benito Juárez, where Calzada Justo Sierra meets Calzada Benito Juárez; Lázaro Cárdenas, at the intersection of Blvd Cárdenas and Calzada Benito Juárez; Vicente Guerrero, on Calzada López Mateos; and Rodolfo Sánchez Taboada, also on Calzada López Mateos.

Special Events

Mexicali hosts a multitude of annual festivals and events, ranging from dog shows and golf tournaments to off-highway races; most are less gringo-oriented than those in other parts of the peninsula. The list below is a sample of the more important events.

Aniversario de Mexicali March 14. Celebration of the city's founding in 1903

Triatlón Campo Mosqueda May 18. Mexicali's triathlon

Festejos de Independencia September 16. Celebrates Mexico's Independence Day

Feria del Libro (Annual Book Fair) late September

Fiesta del Sol (Festival of the Sun) late September to mid-October. Commemorating the city's founding, this event includes pop music concerts, art exhibits, theatrical performances and parades.

Paseo Ciclista Mexicali-San Felipe (Mexicali-San Felipe Bicycle Race) late October

Feria de Muestra Gastronómica (Gastronomic Fair) early November. Cooking competition among Mexicali chefs

Places to Stay

Accommodations are less expensive here than in Tijuana, but adequate budget places are hard to find. If you don't fancy sleeping in a hotel whose reception has iron bars on the windows, you're going to have to pay for it.

Ordinary accommodations are better and no more expensive in Calexico, just across the border; most motels on 4th St charge US$30 to US$40.

Budget In and around La Chinesca are several places including *Hotel Nuevo Pacífico* (☎ 6-552-94-30, Avenida Juárez 95), near the corner of Altamirano, offering cheap but noisy doubles in dubious surroundings from about US$13. Central Mexicali's best bargain may be the family-oriented *Hotel México* (☎ 6-554-06-69, Avenida Lerdo de Tejada 476), between Altamirano and Morelos. Rooms are clean but small and cost US$21/30 for singles/doubles.

Close to the Central de Autobuses, *El Indio* (☎/fax 6-557-22-77, Avenida Fresnillo 101), off Blvd Lopez Mateos, offers good and clean standard rooms set in a flowered courtyard for US$32/42.

Mid-Range The slightly isolated *Motel Azteca de Oro* (☎/fax 6-557-14-33, Calle de la Industria 600), across from the train station, equips all rooms with telephone, TV and air-con for US$38/48.

Hotel Casa Grande (☎ 6-553-57-71, Avenida Cristóbal Colón 612) faces the border fence in downtown Mexicali. It offers rooms with air-con and TV for US$33/46 and also has a swimming pool. Conveniently close to the border crossing, the landmark art-deco-style *Hotel del Norte* (☎ 6-552-81-01, Melgar 205) has 52 rooms, some with color TV and air-con, for US$39/50. Its downstairs restaurant serves moderately priced Mexican dishes, lunch and dinner specials and huge margaritas.

Friendly *Hotel Regis* (☎ 6-566-34-35, fax 6-566-88-01, Calzada Benito Juárez 2150) is close to good restaurants and nightspots in the zona hotelera. Rooms cost US$38/51.

The 173-room *Araiza Inn Calafia* (☎ 6-568-33-11, fax 6-568-20-10, Calzada Justo

DESIERTO DEL COLORADO

CENTRAL MEXICALI

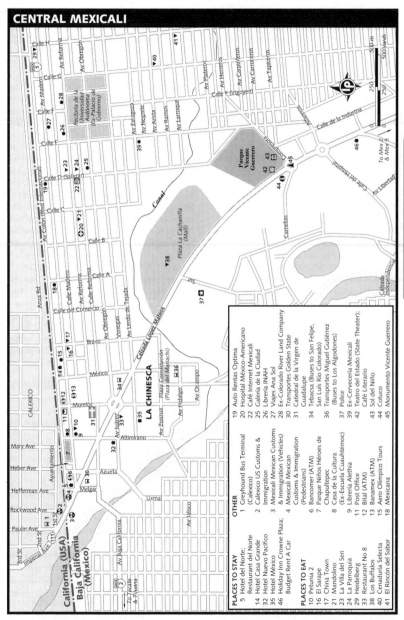

PLACES TO STAY
5 Hotel del Norte;
   Restaurant del Norte
14 Hotel Casa Grande
32 Hotel Nuevo Pacifico
35 Hotel México
46 Holiday Inn Crowne Plaza;
   Budget Rent A Car

PLACES TO EAT
10 Petunia 2
16 El Sarape
17 China Town
21 Mandolino
23 La Villa del Seri
24 La Parroquia
29 Heidelberg
33 Restaurant No 8
38 Los Buffalos
40 Cenaduría Selecta
41 El Rincón del Sabor

OTHER
1 Greyhound Bus Terminal
   (Calexico)
2 Calexico US Customs &
   Immigration
3 Mexicali Mexican Customs
   & Immigration (Vehicles)
4 Mexicali Mexican
   Customs & Immigration
   (Pedestrians)
6 Bancomer (ATM)
7 Parque Niños Héroes de
   Chapultepec
8 Casa de la Cultura
   (Ex-Escuela Cuauhtémoc)
9 Librería Alethia
11 Post Office
12 Bital (ATM)
13 Banamex (ATM)
15 Aero Olímpico Tours
18 Mexicana
19 Auto Rentas Optima
20 Hospital México-Americano
22 Café Internet Mexicali
25 Galería de la Ciudad
26 Librería INAH
27 Viajes Ana Sol
28 Ex-Colorado River Land Company
30 Transportes Golden State
31 Catedral de la Virgen de
   Guadalupe
34 Tebasca (Buses to San Felipe,
   San Luis Río Colorado)
36 Transportes Miguel Gutiérrez
   (Buses to Los Algodones)
37 Police
39 Ex-Cervecería Mexicali
42 Teatro del Estado (State Theater);
   Café Literario
43 Sol del Niño
44 Cotuco
45 Monumento Vicente Guerrero

Sierra 1495) is located about 1½ miles (2.5km) southeast of central Mexicali. Rates start around US$83 for simple but comfortable and air-conditioned rooms with cable TV; secure parking is available.

Hotel Siesta Inn (☎ *6-568-20-01, fax 6-568-23-05, 800-426-5093 in the US, Calzada Justo Sierra 899)* has carpeted rooms starting around US$66 and better rooms for only a little more. There's a coffee shop next to the lobby.

Top End Many, though not all, of Mexicali's upscale hotels are in the zona hotelera, a designated hotel area off Calzada Benito Juárez about 2¼ miles (3.5km) southeast of the border crossing and north of Calzada Independencia.

Rooms at the *Araiza Inn Mexicali* (☎ *6-564-11-00, fax 6-564-11-13, Calzada Benito Juárez 2220)* start around US$99/103, IVA (value-added tax) included. The Web site is at www.araizainn.com.mx. The inn's erstwhile sister, the *Holiday Inn Crowne Plaza* (☎ *6-557-36-00, fax 6-557-00-35, 800-227-6963 in the US)*, is at the junction of Calzada López Mateos and Avenida de los Héroes. Rooms cost US$123, including buffet breakfast.

Highly regarded *Hotel Colonial* (☎ *6-556-13-12, fax 6-556-11-41, 800-437-2438 in the US, colonial@mv.net.mx, Calzada López Mateos 1048)* charges US$104.

Hotel Lucerna (☎ *6-564-70-00, fax 6-566-47-06, Calzada Benito Juárez 2151)* is known among Mexicali's yuppies and business community for its nightclub. In an idyllic setting of fountains and colonial-style courtyards, its 192 rooms have color TV and air-con; those overlooking the pool usually have balconies. Rates are US$125/135.

Places to Eat

Mexicali has a variety of quality restaurants throughout the city. However, the city lacks small general stores and fresh produce markets, so you'll have to head to one of the big chain supermarkets. Gigante, in the Centro Commercial Gigante, just off Calzada Benito Juárez, sells everything, as does Ley, at the corner of Calzada Montejano and

Calle Independencia and in the Plaza La Cachanilla. *La Baguette* bakery, on Calzada Benito Juárez opposite the monument, sells excellent empanadas and muffins. It's open daily from 7 am to 9 pm.

Mexican Family-run *Cenaduría Selecta* (☎ *6-552-40-47, Avenida Arista 1510)*, at Calle G, is a Mexicali institution that specializes in antojitos like beef tacos and burritos, but they're not cheap. It's open 8 am to 11 pm and gets very busy on Sunday afternoons. *El Rincón del Sabor* (☎ *6-554-08-88, Avenida Larroque 1500)*, at Calle H, is another good choice for Mexican food.

Part of the Hotel del Norte (see Places to Stay), *Restaurant del Norte* is a US-style coffee shop offering large and inexpensive but rather ordinary specials for breakfast, lunch and dinner. A good and cheap breakfast place is *Petunia 2*, a friendly nonsmoking oasis on Avenida Madero between Altamirano and Morelos.

La Plazita (☎ *6-565-60-94, Calzada Justo Sierra 377)* offers Mexican and international dishes in a pleasant atmosphere at moderate prices (especially with discount coupons). *Las Campanas de la Plazita* (☎ *6-565-60-94)*, down the street on Calzada Justo Sierra and under the same management, is comparable.

El Sarape (☎ *6-554-22-87, Nicolás Bravo 140)*, between Avenidas Madero and Reforma, is a popular, even raucous, spot with live mariachi music nightly; it has a great tequila selection.

La Villa del Seri (☎ *6-553-55-03)*, at the corner of Avenida Reforma and Calle D (Salazar), specializes in Sonoran beef but also has excellent seafood and antojitos. Prices are on the high side, but portions are large. Animal lovers may be disturbed by the stuffed dear adorning the piano.

Across the street is *La Parroquia* (☎ *6-554-23-13, Avenida Reforma 1200)*, which doubles as a sports bar. *Los Buffalos* (☎ *6-566-31-16)*, in the Plaza La Cachanilla mall on Calzada López Mateos, also specializes in beef and seafood.

The Mexican institution *Sanborn's* (☎ *6-557-04-11)* maintains a branch at the corner of Calzada Independencia and Avenida de los Héroes.

Chinese Mexicali's 150-plus Chinese restaurants offer the opportunity to dine well and relatively cheaply. At the corner of Avenida Juárez and Morelos, *Restaurant No 8* is open 24 hours. Another downtown choice is *China Town* (☎ 6-554-02-120, *Avenida Madero 701*), at the corner of Bravo.

The pricier but highly regarded *El Dragón* (☎ 6-566-20-20, *Calzada Benito Juárez 1830*) occupies a huge pagoda. It's open 11 am to 11 pm. The same proprietors operate *La Misión Dragón* (☎ 6-566-43-20, *Blvd Cárdenas 555*), which is set among lovely gardens complete with pagoda and miniature lake, a quarter-mile (0.5km) east of Calzada Benito Juárez. This enormous restaurant also has take-away service.

German Mexicali's only German restaurant, *Heidelberg* (☎ 6-554-20-22), at the corner of Avenida Madero and Calle H, serves hearty Middle European–style food, in addition to Mexican specialties, in a very Germanic setting.

Italian Like every other Italian restaurant in Mexico, *Mandolino* (☎ 6-552-95-44, *Avenida Reforma 1070*), located between Calle B and Calle C, features the obligatory *Godfather* photograph of Marlon Brando, but its food is excellent and the atmosphere very relaxed. *La Spezzia* (☎ 6-567-95-55, *Calzada Benito Juárez 1198*) has just been remodeled, featuring Dalíesque murals.

Japanese Intimately lit by lanterns hung over an indoor pool, *Sakura* (☎ 6-566-48-48, *Blvd Cárdenas 200*), at the corner of Calzada López Mateos, serves sushi and other Japanese dishes. Karaoke nights run from Wednesday to Saturday; closed Sunday.

Seafood Perhaps Mexicali's most popular seafood restaurant is *Los Arcos* (☎ 6-556-09-03, *Avenida Calafia 454*), near the Plaza de Toros in the Centro Cívico-Comercial. Another possibility is the beautifully re-designed *Villa Marina* (☎ 6-568-29-67, *Avenida Venustiano Carranza 1199*), at the corner of Calzada Benito Juárez in the zona hotelera. The choice of shrimp dishes is quite overwhelming.

Entertainment
Nightclubs There are lots of lively restaurant/bars around the zona hotelera. *Cilantro's* (☎ 6-557-03-95, *Calzada Montejano 1100*), just behind the Secture tourist office, and *Molcajetes* (☎ 6-556-07-00) next door, are both fun for a night out. They get going after about 10 pm.

Especially popular with university students, *La Capilla* (☎ 6-566-11-00, *Calzada Benito Juárez 2151*) is a music and dance club at Hotel Lucerna. Its hours are 8 pm to 2 am. Other nightspots include *The Beach* (☎ 6-556-10-88 *Calzada Montejano 1058*) and *Bar by Bar Zoo* (☎ 6-567-95-55), above La Spezzia restaurant. *Forum* (☎ 6-552-40-91) is at the corner of Avenida Reforma and Calzada Justo Sierra.

Theater A variety of theatrical and musical performers, such as Cuba's La Tropicana dance troupe, appear throughout the year at the state theater, Teatro del Estado, an ultra-modern building seating 1100 and equipped with the 'latest acoustical technology.' Its Instituto de Cultura de Baja California also presents retrospective film series in the Café Literario. The theater (☎ 6-554-64-18) is on the eastern side of Calzada López Mateos, just north of Avenida Tapiceros, opposite the Cotuco tourist office.

Cinemas Mexicali has several movie complexes showing first-run films: *Cinemas Gemelos Cachanilla* (☎ 6-555-67-27) is on Calzada López Mateos in the Plaza La Cachanilla; *Cinépolis* (☎ 6-557-19-85) is located at Avenida de los Héroes and Avenida de la Patria in the Centro Cívico-Comercial; and *Cinemas Gemelos* (☎ 6-566-07-48) is in the Centro Comercial Gigante at Calzada Benito Juárez.

Spectator Sports
Baseball Mexicali's professional baseball team, Las Aguilas (The Eagles), plays in the

Liga Mexicana del Pacífico, which begins its official season in October shortly after the World Series in the US. The regular season ends in early January, when a series of play-offs determines the league's representative to the Caribbean Series, which rotates among Mexico, Puerto Rico, the Dominican Republic and Venezuela.

Mexicali's stadium, nicknamed 'El Nido de las Aguilas' (Eagles' Nest), is on Calzada Cuauhtémoc (also known as Avenida Cuauhtémoc) about 3 miles (5km) east of the border post. Games begin at 7:30 pm on weeknights, at 6 pm on Saturday and at noon on Sunday. Tickets range from US$2 to US$8 (call ☎ 6-567-51-29).

Bullfights *Corridas de toros* take place once a month from October to May in the Plaza de Toros Calafia (☎ 6-557-38-64), at the corner of Avenida Calafia and Calzada Independencia next to the Centro Cívico-Comercial. Tickets (US$6 to US$19) are available at the gate.

Shopping

Curio stores selling cheap leather goods and kitschy souvenirs are concentrated on Melgar and Avenida Reforma, a short walk from the border. For a more sophisticated selection, try El Armario (☎ 6-568-19-06), Calzada Justo Sierra 1700, Suite 1-A, in the Plaza Azteca mall, or Galería de la Mora (☎ 6-568-12-55), Calzada Justo Sierra 1515, Locales 2 & 3, in the Centro Comercial Los Pinos. Shopping sprees can be had at Plaza La Cachanilla, the huge pink shopping mall at Calzada López Mateos.

Mexican beer and hard liquor are cheaper than in the USA, but duty-free quantities permissible by customs are limited to one liter.

Pharmaceuticals and medical services, including dentistry and optometry, are much cheaper on the Mexican side of the border. Many clinics and hospitals are located on the streets that parallel the US border, including Avenida Reforma and Avenida Obregón. (Be sure to read the boxed text 'The Drug Business' in the La Frontera chapter before buying drugs.)

Getting There & Away

Air Aeropuerto Internacional General Rodolfo Sánchez Taboada (☎ 6-553-51-58, 6-553-40-23) is about 12 miles (20km) east of town via Carreterra Aeropuerto Algodones. Mexicana (☎ 6-553-54-01, 6-552-93-91 at the airport), Avenida Madero 833 just west of Calle A, flies all over Mexico and daily to Guadalajara (some of these flights continue on to Mexico City) and Hermosillo.

Bus Major intercity bus companies have offices at the Central de Autobuses (☎ 6-557-24-20, 6-557-24-50), on Calzada Independencia near Calzada López Mateos.

The following are the main companies:

Autotransportes de Baja California (ABC; ☎ 6-552-65-48) Operates exclusively on the peninsula as far south as La Paz, via Tijuana. Web site: http://abc.com.mx.

Autotransportes Estrellas del Pacífico (☎ 6-557-18-30) Around the corner from the main terminal at Calzada Anahuac 553. Buses go to Guadalajara and intermediate points every two hours daily from 11 am and to Tijuana every two hours daily from 5 am.

Transportes del Pacífico (☎ 6-557-24-61) Goes to mainland destinations along the Sea of Cortez before turning inland at Tepic and continuing to Mexico City.

Transportes Norte de Sonora/Elite (☎ 6-556-01-10) Competes with Transportes del Pacífico and also serves northern Mexican destinations such as Ciudad Juárez, Chihuahua, Monterrey and San Luis Potosí. Elite offers slightly more expensive 1st-class services. There are about 14 departures daily to Guadalajara and another nine to Mexico City.

ABC fares to destinations within Baja California are as follows:

destination	fare
Tijuana	US$13
Ensenada	US$19
San Quintín	US$24
Guerrero Negro	US$51
Vizcaíno	US$55
San Ignacio	US$59
Santa Rosalía	US$63
Mulegé	US$66

Loreto	US$73
Ciudad Constitución	US$81
La Paz	US$91

ABC offers an hourly service to San Luís Río Colorado (US$5.50, 1 hour) on the Sonora/Arizona border and four buses daily to Sonora's Gulf resort of Puerto Peñasco (US$19, five hours). Tebacsa (☎ 6-554-04-54), on Calzada López Mateos between Morelos and Calle México, runs buses to San Luís Río Colorado every 90 minutes (US$1.60).

Transportes Miguel Gutiérrez (☎ 6-554-68-26, 6-557-76-50) runs hourly buses to Los Algodones (only 8 miles/13km from Yuma, Arizona). These leave from Avenida Hidalgo between Aldana and Morelos at the southern end of Plaza Constitución (Plaza del Mariachi).

The following are typical times and fares to other mainland Mexican destinations:

destination	duration	fare
Hermosillo	10 hours	US$35
Ciudad Obregón	14 hours	US$48
Los Mochis	17 hours	US$62
Ciudad Juárez	18 hours	US$56
Chihuahua	19 hours	US$78
Culiacán	21 hours	US$73
Mazatlán	24 hours	US$81
Monterrey	29 hours	US$117
Guadalajara	33 hours	US$101
San Luis Potosí	37 hours	US$112
Mexico City	41 hours	US$123

Across the border in Calexico, Greyhound (☎ 760-357-1895, 800-231-2222) is at 121 1st St, directly opposite the pedestrian border-crossing entrance. It has four buses daily to Los Angeles at 9 am and 1:45, 2 and 6 pm (six to seven hours, US$28/49.50 one way/ roundtrip). From the Los Angeles terminal (☎ 213-629-8405), there are five buses daily to Calexico, leaving at 7:40 and 10:00 am and 2:15, 6 and 8 pm.

There are frequent daily buses between Calexico and El Centro, Indio, El Cajon, San Diego, Riverside, San Bernardino, Phoenix, Yuma and a few other cities. Schedules and fares change monthly, so call Greyhound for the latest information or check their Web site at www.greyhound.com.

From a stop at Calzada López Mateos 234 at the corner of Melgar near the border, Transportes Golden State (☎ 6-553-61-59) has services to the mainland California destinations of Indio and Mecca (US$18) and El Monte and Los Angeles (US$30). Buses for LA leave at 6 and 8 am, 2:30, 7:30 and 10:30 pm daily. It also maintains offices on the Calexico side and picks up passengers at Church's Fried Chicken, 344 Imperial Ave (Hwy 111).

Getting Around

Most city bus routes start from Avenida Reforma just west of Calzada López Mateos, two blocks from the border crossing. The ':Justo Sierra' bus goes to the museum and the Secture tourist office. Any 'Centro Cívico' bus goes to the Cotuco tourist office and the bullring. The 'Central Camionera' bus goes to the Centro Cívico-Comercial and the bus terminal. Local bus fares are about US$0.50.

International car rental agencies include Budget at Araiza Inn Mexicali, Calzada Juárez 2220 (☎ 6-566-48-40), and at the Holiday Inn Crowne Plaza, Calzada López Mateos and Avenida de los Héroes (☎ 6-557-08-88). Hertz (☎ 6-568-19-73) is at Calzada Benito Juárez 1223. A local independent agency is Auto Rentas Optima (☎ 6-552-36-17), at Avenida Madero 1183.

A taxi ride from the border to the central bus station or zona hotelera costs about US$5 to US$6. Try bargaining, but agree on the fare before accepting the ride. A reliable alternative is to arrange a cab in advance with Ecotaxi (☎ 6-562-65-65), which has slightly cheaper fares. Taxis are the only method of transport to the airport (US$15).

AROUND MEXICALI

South of Mexicali, México 5 proceeds through a prosperous farming region en route to the Gulf resort of San Felipe, 120 miles (193km) south.

Some 17 miles (27km) south of Mexicali and 2 miles (3km) east of the highway, rising clouds of steam mark the **Cerro Prieto** geothermal electrical plant, whose 620-megawatt

DESIERTO DEL COLORADO

capacity makes it the largest of its kind in North America. It is not open to the public.

Cerro El Chinero (Chinese Hill), just east of México 5 and north of the junction with México 3, on the way to San Felipe, memorializes a group of Chinese immigrants who died of thirst in the area.

Cucapá El Mayor

At Km 56, 35 miles south of Mexicali, this Indian village has the Museo Comunitario, with exhibits on subsistence life and indigenous artifacts; outside are examples of traditional Cucupah nomadic dwellings. A small store within sells a selection of crafts, including attractive bead necklaces. Both museum and store are open 10 am to 5 pm daily.

Laguna Salada

Another 23 miles (37km) south, around Km 93, is the edge of the vast, desolate Laguna Salada – 500 sq miles (1300 sq km) of salt flats when dry (as is usual). Although these flats were part of the Gulf of California four centuries ago, today they constitute one of Baja's most arid regions. Unusually heavy rains in the mid-1980s, however, swelled the nearby Colorado and Bravo Rivers, turning the landscape into an ephemeral marsh. Southeast of the lake is the Río Colorado delta, a 60-mile (97km) expanse of alluvium (soil deposited by floodwaters).

Cañón Guadalupe

Southwest of Mexicali, and descending the eastern scarp of Parque Nacional Constitución de 1857 (see the La Frontera chapter), palm-studded Cañón Guadalupe is a delightful hot-springs area superb for hiking, swimming and car camping. Because it's in the rain shadow of the coast range, Cañón Guadalupe is dry and pleasant except in summer when it's brutally hot. The best time to visit is from November to late May. In addition to the cold canyon pools and small waterfalls, there are rock art sites in the vicinity.

On México 2 about 22 miles (35km) west of Mexicali, a smooth graded road (passable for passenger vehicles in dry weather) leads 27 miles (43km) south to a junction that leads another 8 miles (13km) west to Cañón

Guadalupe. For northbound travelers from San Felipe, the canyon is also accessible by a difficult sandy road (4WD recommended, though not essential) leading northwest from the southern end of Laguna Salada, at the turnoff from México 5 to Ejido José Saldaña No 2. This road is slow, tiresome, sometimes difficult to follow and not really worth doing unless there's no alternative.

The **Guadalupe Canyon Hot Springs & Campground** (☎ 949-673-2670 in the US, CanyonmanRob@earthlink.net) has comfortable camping facilities starting at US$15 per site from June to mid-November but rising to US$70 for two nights the rest of the year, including use of hot tubs with water temperatures up to 110°F (43°C). There's a restaurant (which may run out of food) and a swimming pool. The campground gets crowded on weekends. (Note the two-night minimum stay on weekends and three-night minimum stay during holiday periods.) Visa and MasterCard are accepted for reservations but not in the canyon itself.

LOS ALGODONES

Settled by ranchers from Sonora in the mid-19th century, the border town of Los Algodones (population 9,500) next to Andrade, California, was a stagecoach stop on the route from Yuma (Arizona) to San Diego when the Río Colorado was navigable. Named for the surrounding cotton fields, Los Algodones is about 40 miles (64km) east of Mexicali but only about 8 miles (13km) west of Yuma across the Río Colorado.

Nearly deserted in the brutally hot summer, Los Algodones bustles in winter, when more than a million foreigners cross the border. Many of these are retirees from Yuma who find prescription drugs, eyeglasses and dental work much cheaper here than in the US. So many 'snowbirds' frequent the town that Mexican professionals organize bus charters from Yuma for their benefit.

The border is open 8 am to 10 pm daily, but Mexican authorities will process car permits from 8 am to 3 pm only. There's a tourist information office (☎ 6-517-76-35) at Avenida B 261. There are many cambios, but dollars are accepted widely here.

'Snowbirds' head south for the winter.

Besides its pharmacies, dentists and opticians, Los Algodones is virtually a wall-to-wall assemblage of kitschy souvenirs, but resolute shoppers may find attractive textiles from mainland Mexico here.

Hanlon Headgate
Just north of the border, the Hanlon Headgate was part of the Alamo Canal, built by the California Development Company to carry Colorado River water through Mexican territory en route to mainland California's Imperial Valley. In the wet winter of 1905, the headgate burst and water flowed west through Mexico and then north, creating mainland California's Salton Sea and obliterating whatever benefits Mexican farmers had gained from water development. It was two years before the Southern Pacific Railroad, which acquired the California Development Company, halted the flow to the north.

Places to Stay & Eat
The misnamed *Motel Olímpico (no phone)*, really a hotel in the middle of the block opposite the Delegación Municipal, charges US$22/38 for singles/doubles. Its entrance is not particularly inviting, but it's the only hotel in town.

In Andrade on the US side of the border, the Quechan Indians of Fort Yuma Reservation operate the spacious but basic *Sleepy Hollow RV Park* (☎ 760-572-5101); rates are US$15 without or US$25 with hookups.

Los Algodones' most popular eateries are *Carlota's Bakery*, mobbed by snowbirds at breakfast, and the adjacent courtyard restaurant *El Paraíso* in the Real Plaza del Sol. *Restaurant Tucán*, just off the main street, has more elaborate meals at reasonable prices, with live music at lunchtime. Opposite, *El Gourmet* is a quieter choice with a stylish bar area.

Getting There & Away
There is no public transportation across the border at Los Algodones. Hourly bus service from Los Algodones to Mexicali exists, but not from Andrade to Yuma. California State Route 186 is now paved to US Interstate 8, which leads east to Yuma.

SAN FELIPE
Beautifully located between the desert and the Sea of Cortez, San Felipe (population 23,000) is perfect kick-back territory. The white-sand beach is the town's main pulling card for visitors and is clean and safe. Paddleboats can be rented on the beach.

San Felipe has somewhat of a split personality. Normally tranquil to the extreme, the town's noise levels rise and accommodations are hard to find during national holidays and US spring break, when visitors stream in. However, the action doesn't last long and can be easily avoided with a bit of preplanning. If you can't avoid the busy times, then the margaritas at sundown, fresh shrimp tacos and generous nature of the locals will make the frenzy more than bearable. Try to visit between November and April, before temperatures soar as high as 120°F (49°C).

History
In 1721, Jesuit missionary Juan de Ugarte landed at the port of San Felipe de Jesús, which appears in Fernando Consag's map of 1746. In 1797, Fray Felipe Neri, a Dominican priest from Misión San Pedro Mártir, established a small supply depot and settlement here in the hope of replenishing his struggling mission, located in an isolated, mile-high valley about 45 miles (72km) to the west. Both the depot and the mission failed in the early 19th century, in part because of water shortages. Mission ruins can still be

seen, but access is difficult; see the Misión San Pedro Mártir entry in the La Frontera chapter for more information.

Bahía San Felipe remained almost undeveloped until 1876, when speculator Guillermo Andrade decided to exploit a Mexican government grant of approximately 117 sq miles (304 sq km). Andrade, who had obtained the concession almost two decades earlier, built a road to the gold mines at Real del Castillo, 120 miles (193km) to the northwest, but his attempt to attract business from the mines was largely unsuccessful because well-established Ensenada was much closer to them.

After establishing control over Mexicali in 1915, Colonel Estéban Cantú opened a rough road south to San Felipe and even planned a railroad, but it was shrimpers from Guaymas, Loreto and Santa Rosalía who really turned San Felipe into a town. In 1925, San Felipe's population was only about 100, but by 1948, when the improved highway made travel from Mexicali much easier, it had reached nearly 1000.

Today, half a dozen fishing cooperatives operate out of San Felipe, exporting shrimp and various fish species to the USA, Canada and elsewhere. The San Felipe fleet has 41 boats, several of which can remain at sea for as long as 40 days.

Sportfishing and warm winters have attracted hundreds of North American retirees, while large hotels and sprawling trailer parks have sprung up to accommodate growing numbers of visitors. Many houses, subdivisions and condominiums are under construction.

Orientation

San Felipe hugs the shoreline of its namesake bay, a curving inlet of the northern Gulf of California, 120 miles (193km) south of Mexicali. North-south avenidas bear the names of seas around the world, while east-west calles bear the names of Mexican ports. Avenida Mar de Cortez is the main north-south drag, while Calzada Chetumal leads west to a junction with México 5, the highway north to Mexicali. Downtown along the beach is San Felipe's attractive *malecón* (waterfront promenade).

Northwest of San Felipe is the eastern approach to Parque Nacional Sierra San Pedro Mártir and the famous peak of Picacho del Diablo, via a turnoff from México 3. For more details, see the park's entry in the La Frontera chapter.

Information

One source of information is the English-language monthly *San Felipe Newsletter,* available free around town. Although its main audience is US residents, the newsletter contains some useful travel information. The mailing address is PO Box 5259, Heber, CA 92249, USA.

Tourist Offices Secture (☎ 6-577-11-55) is at the corner of Avenida Mar de Cortez and Manzanillo, across from El Capitán Motel. It's open 8 am to 5 pm weekdays, 10 am to 3 pm weekends; the staff is extremely helpful and someone usually speaks English.

Money Nearly all merchants accept dollars as readily as pesos. San Felipe has two banks, both with an ATM. Bancomer, on Avenida Mar de Cortez just north of Calzada Chetumal, is open 8:30 am to 4 pm weekdays and 10 am to 2 pm Saturday. Banco Bilbao Vizcaya, on Avenida Mar de Cortez Sur, is open 9 am to 5:30 pm weekdays. Curios Mitla, at Calzada Chetumal and Avenida Mar de Cortez, operates a cambio.

Post & Communications San Felipe's post office is on Avenida Mar Blanco between Calzada Chetumal and Ensenada. It's open 8 am to 3 pm weekdays and 9 am to 1 pm Saturday. The postal code is 21850. A quick way of sending post is to use the Yet Mail service at Avenida Mar del Cortez. Daily collections take the post over the border to San Diego and mail it from there.

Increasing numbers of public telephones are available on the street, in addition to private phone booths, but they can be expensive.

The Net (☎ 6-577-16-00), on Avenida Mar de Cortez Sur just north of Hotel El Cortez, offers Internet and email services. Fees are an exorbitant US$16 per hour. It's open 9 am to

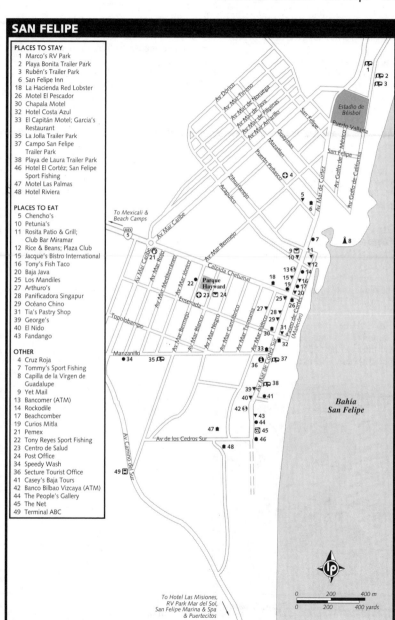

SAN FELIPE

PLACES TO STAY
1 Marco's RV Park
2 Playa Bonita Trailer Park
3 Rubén's Trailer Park
6 San Felipe Inn
18 La Hacienda Red Lobster
26 Motel El Pescador
30 Chapala Motel
32 Hotel Costa Azul
33 El Capitán Motel; García's Restaurant
35 La Jolla Trailer Park
37 Campo San Felipe Trailer Park
38 Playa de Laura Trailer Park
46 Hotel El Cortéz; San Felipe Sport Fishing
47 Motel Las Palmas
48 Hotel Riviera

PLACES TO EAT
5 Chencho's
10 Petunia's
11 Rosita Patio & Grill; Club Bar Miramar
12 Rice & Beans; Plaza Club
15 Jacque's Bistro International
16 Tony's Fish Taco
20 Baja Java
25 Los Mandiles
27 Arthuro's
28 Panificadora Singapur
29 Océano Chino
31 Tia's Pastry Shop
39 George's
40 El Nido
43 Fandango

OTHER
4 Cruz Roja
7 Tommy's Sport Fishing
8 Capilla de la Virgen de Guadalupe
9 Yet Mail
13 Bancomer (ATM)
14 Rockodile
17 Beachcomber
19 Curios Mitla
21 Pemex
22 Tony Reyes Sport Fishing
23 Centro de Salud
24 Post Office
34 Speedy Wash
36 Secture Tourist Office
41 Casey's Baja Tours
42 Banco Bilbao Vizcaya (ATM)
44 The People's Gallery
45 The Net
49 Terminal ABC

DESIERTO DEL COLORADO

4 pm Monday to Saturday from October to July and 8 am to 1 pm from July to September.

Laundry Speedy Wash, at the corner of Avenida Camino del Sur and Manzanillo, is open 8 am to 4:30 pm Monday to Saturday. Some staff speak English, and a drop-off service is available.

Medical & Emergency Services San Felipe's Centro de Salud (☎ 6-577-15-21) is on Avenida Mar Bermejo between Calzada Chetumal and Ensenada. For 24-hour emergency service, contact the Cruz Roja (☎ 066, 6-577-15-44), at the corner of Avenida Mar Bermejo and Puerto Peñasco.

Capilla de la Virgen de Guadalupe
The local shrine of the Virgen de Guadalupe, Mexico's great national symbol, is a small monument atop a hill north of the malecón. The climb to the top offers panoramic views of town and bay.

Clamming
Clamming is popular, particularly when very low tides reveal wide expanses of firm, wet sand. The best beaches for clamming are south

Virgen de Guadalupe, Mexico's sweetheart

of town beyond Playa El Faro and north of town beyond Campo Los Amigos. Small, tasty butter clams can be found around rocks, while the larger, meatier white clams are just beneath the wet sand. Check with locals about minimum acceptable sizes and per-person limits – clammers caught with undersized specimens are subject to hefty fines.

Fishing
This sport draws many visitors to San Felipe, and Bahía San Felipe has become a parking lot of *pangas* (skiffs), shrimpers, trawlers and tuna clippers. Fishing licenses are obligatory for any type of fishing, including surf fishing (also see the Activities chapter).

Tommy's Sport Fishing, at the north end of the malecón, just past Rosita Patio & Grill, rents out local 25-foot (7.5m) pangas. A whole day's fishing, including license equipment and bait, costs US$40 per person. The boats fit up to five people. Travelers with their own boats will find several launching ramps, including a convenient one at Hotel El Cortez, where San Felipe Sport Fishing (☎ 6-577-22-93) is located. Tony Reyes Sport Fishing (☎ 6-577-11-20) is at Avenida Mar Bermejo 130.

Enchanted Island Excursions (☎ 6-550-42-02 cell phone), runs all day excursions on the 36-foot *Viento Loco* for US$240 (plus tax) for a maximum of eight people. Passengers must buy the appropriate licences.

The following list indicates when the various species are most common in the vicinity of San Felipe:

Albacore	July to August
Barracuda	May to October
Bonefish	June to August
Cabrilla	year round
Corvina	July to November
Halibut	January to April
Marlin	June to September
Rockfish	year round
Sea Bass	May
Yellowtail	March to November

Special Events
On holidays like Thanksgiving, Christmas and New Year's, San Felipe's population prac-

tically doubles. The main street becomes a surge of motorcycles, dune buggies and other ATVs and noise levels rise significantly. Do as the locals do: If you can't beat 'em, join 'em.

San Felipe also hosts many special events, though the hot summer months are usually quiet. For racecar events, see Spectator Sports, later.

Carnaval San Felipe early March. This celebration starts off the party year with a parade of floats and general merriment.

US Spring Break mid-March. University students from north of the border flock here to party.

Día de la Marina Nacional (National Navy Day) June 1.

La Fiesta Maristaco August. A festival celebrating the fishing industry; San Felipe's chefs gather to make enormous amounts of ceviche, a seafood cocktail made with 150 kilos of vegetables and 250 kilos of fish.

Feria del Camarón (Shrimp Festival) November. This celebration has become a tourist and gastronomic success despite the decreasing shrimp population in the Gulf.

Bienvenida a los Pájaros de la Nieve December. Perhaps the antithesis of spring break, this event acknowledges the annual arrival of snowbird retirees from the frozen north.

Organized Tours

Casey's Baja Tours (☎/fax 6-577-14-13, casey@ canela.sanfelipe.com.mx) runs excursions to Puertecitos (US$55), Valle de los Gigantes, home to the giant cardón cactus (12 miles/ 20km away; US$25), a petrified forest (5 miles/8km away; US$35) and waterfalls (40 miles/65km away; US$50). Prices do not include tax. Casey's office is on Mar y Sol, just off Avenida Mar de Cortez Sur.

Places to Stay

Accommodations in San Felipe, as in other coastal resorts, can be hard to categorize because rates vary so much both seasonally and between weekdays and weekends. A budget hotel during the week may well be a mid-range place on the weekend or during spring break.

Budget Campgrounds and RV parks are abundant in San Felipe itself and also dot the beaches to the north and south. The quality of sites varies considerably; prices range from US$7 to US$28 per night. Most places have drinkable water, electricity and hot showers.

Pete's Camp (☎ 909-676-4224 in the US, rafael@petescamp.com) is 6 miles (10km) north of San Felipe at Km 177 of México 5. It has basic campsites (only a few with shade) for US$8 per night for one car. Showers, toilets and cold beer are available. Rustic *Playa Blanca* at Km 183 has 70 spaces, some with full hookups; toilets and showers are available.

San Felipe's cushiest trailer park, *El Dorado Ranch* (☎ 6-550-01-57, fax 6-550-07-04, 303-790-1749 in the US, ranchres@ telnor.net) is 7 miles (12km) north of town. It has 200 RV sites (100 on the beach) with full hookups for US$28 per night. Its extensive amenities include swimming pool, Jacuzzi, tennis courts, restaurant, bar, laundry and grocery store.

At the northern end of town, *Marco's RV Park* (☎ 6-577-18-75, Avenida Golfo de California 868) has small but well-equipped campsites and RV sites (full hookups) for US$7. Across the street, *Playa Bonita Trailer Park* (☎/fax 6-577-12-15, 626-967-4250 in the US, playabonita@aol.com) has 35 sites with hookups, as well as toilets, showers and a restaurant. The cost is US$25 per site for two people – plus US$10 per additional person; prices rise slightly on holidays. New condominiums are also for rent at US$129 for six people.

Rubén's Trailer Park (☎/fax 6-577-20-21, Avenida Golfo de California 703), just south of Playa Bonita Trailer Park, has 54 shaded sites with full hookups. There's a boat launch, restaurant, toilets, showers and a patio. Rates are US$15 per night for two people, US$2 for each additional person.

La Jolla Trailer Park (☎/fax 6-577-12-22), near the center of town at the corner of Avenida Mar Bermejo and Manzanillo, offers 50 fully equipped sites, toilets, showers and laundry facilities. Sites cost US$15 per night for two people, US$2.50 for each additional person.

Playa de Laura Trailer Park (☎ 6-577-11-28), between Avenida Mar de Cortez and the beach, has 40 sites, half with full hookups and the rest with water and electricity only. Hot showers and rental boats are also available. Sites cost US$21 and up per night for two people, US$3 for each additional person.

Also in town and on the beach is the *Campo San Felipe Trailer Park*. It has 39 fully equipped sites with showers and toilets for US$15 to US$25 for two people (rates depend on beach proximity), plus US$2 for each additional person. Reservations are not accepted.

RV Park Mar del Sol (☎ /fax 6-577-10-88, 800-336-5454 in the US, Avenida Misión de Loreto 149) is in the southern end of town next to Hotel Las Misiones. It has 84 RV sites with full hookups for US$20 (US$5 for each additional person) and 30 tent sites for US$12 per night for two people (US$3 for each additional person). Amenities include access to hotel facilities (October to June), showers, toilets, a small grocery store, laundry room and swimming pool.

Friendly *Chapala Motel* (☎ 6-577-12-40, Avenida Mar de Cortez 142) offers clean, decent singles/doubles for US$33/38; most rooms have air-con and others have a kitchenette. One-star *Motel El Pescador* (☎ 6-577-26-48), at the corner of Calzada Chetumal and Avenida Mar de Cortez, has 24 rooms with air-con for US$35/40. Newly remodeled *La Hacienda Red Lobster* (☎ /fax 6-557-15-71, Calzada Chetumal 125) has a very good adjoining restaurant. Rates are US$25 Sunday to Thursday, US$30 on Friday and Saturday.

Mid-Range The two-star, 40-room *El Capitán Motel* (☎ /fax 6-577-13-03, Avenida Mar de Cortez 298) is just across from the state tourist office. All rooms have air-con and satellite TV, and there's a restaurant and swimming pool. Sunday to Thursday, rooms cost US$37; Friday and Saturday US$50.

San Felipe Inn (☎ 6-577-16-08, Avenida Mar de Cortez 472) is just north of Puerto Peñasco. Rooms cost US$40 Sunday to Thursday, US$50 Friday and Saturday.

The three-star *Motel Las Palmas* (☎ 6-577-13-33, fax 6-577-13-82, palma@wotw.com, Avenida Mar Báltico 1101) has 45 clean, air-conditioned rooms for about US$41/51 Sunday to Thursday and US$45/62 Friday and Saturday. It has a lovely pool area with plenty of lounge chairs, a poolside bar and a view of the Gulf of California.

Overlooking the town from Avenida de los Cedros Sur near Avenida Mar Báltico, the *Hotel Riviera* (☎ 6-577-11-85) has air-conditioned rooms with private bath and shower. Its two bars and small swimming pool are shelters from the summer heat. Rooms cost US$55.

Hotel El Cortez (☎ 6-577-10-55, 800-800-9632 in the US, cortezho@telnor.net) is a 90-room beachfront place on Avenida Mar de Cortez Sur near the center of town. Singles/doubles with sea views, air-con, TV and private bath with shower begin at US$62/76; a few smaller rooms have beachfront patios. Amenities include a restaurant/bar (with satellite TV), a swimming pool and a boat ramp.

Dwarfing others in its category in size (140 rooms) and amenities (pool, satellite TV, bar, restaurant, coffee shop, phones and the like), the extravagantly landscaped *Hotel Costa Azul* (☎ 6-577-15-48, fax 6-577-15-49), at Avenida Mar de Cortez and Ensenada, charges US$65/79. This is the main place for 'spring breakers,' so it can get noisy.

Top End Two miles (3km) south of San Felipe, the 190-room *Hotel Las Misiones* (☎ 6-577-17-08, fax 6-577-712-80, 619-454-7166 in the US, Avenida Misión de Loreto 148) has extensive facilities including a trailer park, two tennis courts, restaurants, bars, cafeterias and swim-up bars in two of its three swimming pools. Rooms cost about US$78; all have air-con, color TV, telephone and shower bath. There's a 20% AAA discount. It's Web site is at www.hotellasmisiones.com.

San Felipe Marina Resort & Spa (☎ 6-577-14-35, fax 6-577-15-66, 800-291-5397 in the US, snmarina@telnor.net) is a luxurious facility with RV park at Km 4.5 on the road to the airport. Rates normally start around US$105 for a double, but substantial weekday and off-season discounts are possible.

Places to Eat
As a popular tourist destination, San Felipe has a good selection of restaurants serving the usual antojitos as well as outstanding seafood specialties. For excellent, inexpensive tacos, try the numerous stands along the malecón, most of which specialize in fish and shrimp. *Tony's Fish Taco* is a good choice.

For freshly squeezed juice, paletas, aguas, ice cream, milkshakes and similar treats, try *La Michoacana*, with several locations on and around Avenida Mar de Cortez. *Panificadora Singapur*, on Avenida Mar de Cortez just south of Calzada Chetumal, offers a selection of sugary Mexican pastries, and American-owned *Tia's Pastry Shop*, on Avenida Mar del Cortez, sells fattening homemade cakes and muffins.

George's (☎ 6-577-10-57, *Avenida Mar de Cortez Sur 336*) is a US-style coffee shop and breakfast favorite among local expatriates. Hours are 6:30 am to 9:30 pm. *Chencho's* (☎ 6-577-10-58, *Puerto Peñasco 233*) is also a breakfast choice. *Petunia's* (*Avenida Mar de Cortez 241*) serves cheap Mexican dishes.

Next to The People's Gallery (see Shopping, later) on Avenida Mar de Cortez Sur, *Fandango* (☎ 6-577-11-22) is an overlooked bargain for Mexican specialties like *chilaquiles* (scrambled eggs with chiles and bits of tortillas). On the street side at the northern end of the malecón, *Rosita Patio & Grill* (☎ 6-577-17-70) has a large and varied menu, emphasizing seafood at moderate prices. Around the corner on the malecón, *Rice & Beans* (☎ 6-577-17-70), run by the same owners, has similar fare.

Open 7 am to 9 pm, *Los Mandiles* (☎ 6-577-11-68), at the corner of Calzada Chetumal and Avenida Mar de Cortez, serves seafood and steak. *Arthuro's* (*Avenida Mar Báltico 148*), just south of Calzada Chetumal, serves Mexican and American dishes. *Océano Chino* (*Avenida Mar de Cortez 146*) is San Felipe's only Chinese restaurant.

Baja Java (☎ 6-577-24-65), upstairs at the corner of Calzada Chetumal and Avenida Mar de Cortez, is a great spot for lunch and one of the only places in town where you can get a cappuccino. *Garcia's Restaurant*, based in El Capitán Motel, gets very busy and serves delicious *burritos verdes.*

Jacque's Bistro International (☎ 6-577-19-16), on Avenida Mar de Cortez just north of Calzada Chetumal, serves excellent, mainly French, dishes. It's a bit more expensive but worth it for the wine list and life-size stuffed crocodile gracing the entrance.

El Nido (☎ 6-577-10-28, *Avenida Mar de Cortez Sur 348*) is perfect for a romantic meal. It serves various seafood dishes and steaks cooked over mesquite charcoal; the chicken tacos are excellent. Main courses crest at US$15. Hours are 2 to 9 pm (closed Wednesday).

Entertainment
There are several clubs on and around the malecón. The *Rockodile* is a bar/disco on Avenida Mar de Cortez attracting the party crowd on weekends. Just south of here, at the corner of Calzada Chetumal, the *Beachcomber* (☎ 6-577-21-22) is a combination bar/grill. *Club Bar Miramar* (☎ 6-577-11-92, *Avenida Mar de Cortez 315*) also has an entrance on the malecón and is similar in concept. Another is the *Plaza Club* on Avenida Mar de Cortez just north of Acapulco.

Spectator Sports
A preferred destination for fossil-fuel fanatics, San Felipe boasts Mexico's only racing stadium, which serves as both the start and finish of some off-highway races, though most start and finish at the arches on the approach to town. The stadium is about 5 miles (8km) south of town; the main annual events are the SCORE San Felipe 250 in mid-March, San Felipe Grand Prix in early April, mid-June's Corp San Felipe 200 and Carrera Mexicali – San Felipe, which takes place at the beginning of December.

Shopping
San Felipe's big source for souvenirs from around Mexico is Curios Mitla, at the corner of Avenida Mar de Cortez and Calzada Chetumal, but the entire length of Mar de

Cortez is lined with stores. For arts and crafts by local and expatriate artists, as well as crafts classes, visit The People's Gallery at Avenida Mar de Cortez Sur 5 just north of Hotel El Cortez. It opens seven days a week but sometimes closes in the heat of summer.

Getting There & Away
Aeropuerto Internacional San Felipe is 8 miles (13km) south of town via a spur off México 5, but there are presently no commercial flights.

Terminal ABC (☎ 6-577-15-16) is on Avenida Mar Caribe, just south of Avenida de los Cedros Sur. Buses to Mexicali (US$12, 2½ hours) leave at 6 and 7:30 am, noon and 4 and 8 pm. Buses leave for Ensenada (US$16, four hours) at 8 am and 6 pm daily. The Tijuana service (US$25, 5½ hours) leaves at 6, 7:30 and 8 am, noon and 4 pm daily. Buses to Puertecitos, south of San Felipe (US$4, two hours) leave at 10:30 am and 7 pm daily. Buses leave Puertecitos for San Felipe at 7 am and 5 pm.

There is no public transportation available, but Francisco Padilla taxi (☎ 6-577-12-93) is a very reliable operator.

PUERTECITOS
As paved México 5 gradually extends southward, access to the once-isolated string of communities stretching to Puertecitos and beyond is becoming easier. The road to Puertecitos is very good despite numerous *vados* (fords) and potholes, which require slowing down; the last 14 miles (22.5km) are still slow going.

On the way to Puertecitos, it's well worth visiting the **Valle de los Gigantes** (Valley of the Giants), home to huge cardón cacti (some supposedly 100 years old), about 12 miles (20km) from San Felipe. You'll feel like you've just stepped into the movie set of a spaghetti western.

Puertecitos itself (population 130), 52 miles (84km) south of San Felipe, is popular with North American retirees who festoon their driveways with street signs pilfered from their hometowns.

There is a Pemex station (rarely open), one public telephone, two small shops and

decent sportfishing in the area. Camino Compadre takes you to several warm, spring-fed pools near the point just south of town. They make for good bathing, but be careful, the water can reach boiling point at certain times of the day.

Fishing
The following list indicates when the various fish species are most common around Puertecitos:

Cabrilla	October to May
Corvina	January to August
Grouper	year round
Marlin	June to September
Rockfish	June and September
Roosterfish	August
Sierra	May to October
White Sea Bass	November to March
Yellowtail	May to October

Places to Stay & Eat
Playa Escondida Trailer Park charges about US$10 per site. Remodeled *Puertecitos Motel & Restaurant* has four double rooms for US$40, plus four RV sites (US$8) with cold water. Puertecitos only has electricity for four hours a day, from 6 to 10 pm. Make reservations by calling the shop Las Palmas (☎ 6-650-20-14); ask for Doña Clara. The restaurant is closed on Thursday.

SOUTH OF PUERTECITOS
Within a few years, the road south of Puertecitos is likely to be paved to its intersection with the Transpeninsular south of Cataviña. For the time being, however, ask about conditions, because much of the road is very rough and subject to washouts as far as Bahía San Luis Gonzaga, about 50 miles (80km) south. While vehicles with high clearance and short wheelbase are desirable, they are not absolutely essential, and 4WD is not necessary. Allow at least five hours to Bahía San Luis Gonzaga, and drive slowly to avoid punctures of tires or oil pan.

Trailers and large RVs, with luck and skill, can go as far as La Costilla, approximately

5 miles (8km) south of Puertecitos. **Punta Bufeo** is 91 miles (147km) from San Felipe. The mountains meet the water here, making this small resort mostly steep and rocky. There are cabins for rent, a restaurant, dirt landing strip and boat anchorage.

Beyond Punta Bufeo, the road becomes easier but still requires caution as far as Rancho Grande. For more details on the highway, see the Bahía San Luis Gonzaga entry in the Desierto Central to Llano de Magdalena chapter.

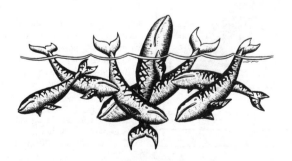

Desierto Central to Llano de Magdalena

The area between Baja's Desierto Central (Central Desert), roughly starting at El Rosario, to Llano de Magdalena (Magdalena Plain), northwest of La Paz, is one of the least frequented parts of the peninsula. In pre-Columbian times, Cochimí Indians foraged its vast deserts and fished its extensive coastlines. The area is still more rural than other parts of the peninsula, with few resort-style hotels or restaurants with English-language menus. Many of its small farming towns, fishing villages and century-old *ranchos* (rural settlements) are accessible only by dirt and gravel roads.

Most visitors come to central Baja to fish its hidden coves or explore its isolated beaches – ideal for camping, clamming and lounging in the sun. Verdant valleys of grapes and tomatoes, extinct volcanoes and massive granite boulders on high plateaus are all accessible to well-outfitted travelers, and Baja's historical heritage is more palpable here than it is farther north. Well-preserved or restored mission churches and modest plazas in San Ignacio, Loreto and elsewhere reveal close links to mainland Mexican life and culture. In Santa Rosalía, French colonial clapboard buildings and a prefabricated Eiffel church recall a 19th-century copper boom that drew miners from around the world.

Highlights

- Fishing in Bahía San Luis Gonzaga or Bahía de Los Angeles
- Whale-watching at Laguna Ojo de Liebre, Laguna San Ignacio or Bahía Magdalena
- Viewing pre-Columbian rock art in the Sierra de San Francisco
- Camping along the beaches south of Mulegé
- Surfing at San Juanico
- Diving and kayaking in Loreto

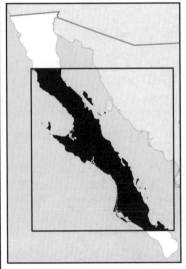

Desierto Central & Desierto de Vizcaíno

The sinuous 76-mile (122km) stretch of the Transpeninsular between El Rosario and Cataviña traverses a surrealistic landscape of huge boulders among stands of the *cardón* cactus (resembling the saguaro of the southwestern USA) and the twisted, drooping *cirio* (nicknamed 'boojum' for its supposed resemblance to an imaginary creature in Lewis Carroll's *The Hunting of the Snark*). The cirio grows only here and in parts of the mainland Mexican state of Sonora.

Beyond Guerrero Negro, the Desierto de Vizcaíno is a harsh, desolate expanse, but the oasis of San Ignacio reflects the semitropical

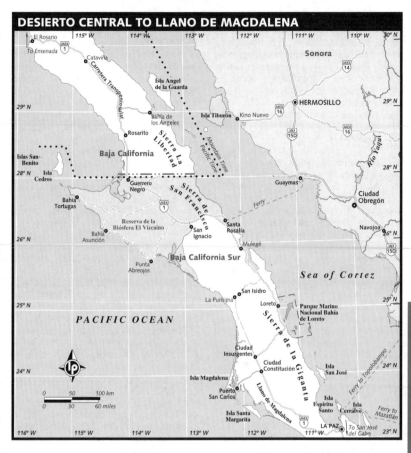

DESIERTO CENTRAL TO LLANO DE MAGDALENA

environment of the Gulf coast between Mulegé and Cabo San Lucas.

MISIÓN SAN FERNANDO

About 35 miles (56km) southeast of El Rosario, near the site of the Franciscan mission of San Fernando Velicatá, the roadside settlement of Rancho El Progreso offers simple food and cold drinks. From Km 121 on the Transpeninsular, just west of the rancho, a dirt spur leads west about 3 miles (5km) to the mission ruins. Despite a couple of sandy spots, the road is passable for anything but a low rider.

The famed Franciscan Padre Junípero Serra founded the mission in 1769, but the Dominicans assumed control four years later when Serra decided to concentrate his efforts in Alta California. A few years later, epidemics nearly obliterated the native population, and the mission closed in 1818.

Some of the mission church's adobe walls are still standing, but of greater interest are the **petroglyphs** on a conspicuous granite outcrop a few hundred yards down the arroyo. Dating from about AD 1000 to 1500, these include both abstract (curvilinear and geometric) and representational (human and animal) designs. Some of the latter appear to be shaman figures. These resemble sites in mainland California's Imperial, Inyo, Mono and San Bernardino Counties more closely than they do Cochimí designs to the south. Unfortunately, vandals have damaged some paintings and others have weathered poorly, but together with the mission ruins they make the trip worthwhile.

EL MÁRMOL

At Km 149, an excellent graded lateral off the Transpeninsular leads to a major onyx quarry presently worked by nearby Ejido Revolución. Once trucked to the Pacific and shipped north to San Diego's Southwest Onyx and Marble Company, the decorative stone now takes the modern highway north to Tijuana, where it's turned into tabletops and similar items. Some still reaches the USA, as it did in the late 19th century.

Well worth seeing are the ruins of the **onyx schoolhouse**, which sheltered the children of the quarry workers when North Americans still ran the operation. The school closed around 1967, but its huge buttresses and unpolished, yard-thick walls are an imposing sight to this day.

At Km 149 of the Transpeninsular just beyond the El Mármol turnoff, **Rancho Sonora** has basic tourist facilities, including RV parking (US$3) and a restaurant.

CATAVIÑA

Set in a landscape of massive granite boulders, the isolated oasis of Cataviña, roughly midway between El Rosario and Bahía de Los Angeles, is a good place to fill the tank. There's no Pemex station, but you can buy gas next to the RV park; the next Pemex station on the Transpeninsular is at Villa Jesús María, 123 miles (198km) south.

For great *free camping*, follow any of the sandy tracks off into the desert north of the arroyo, which runs to the north of Cataviña and west of the Transpeninsular among the boulders and towering cardones. Firewood is plentiful (keep it small), but bring food and water. A bonus is a series of Cochimí cave paintings east of the highway, just beyond the arroyo. (There's a dirt road that leads

from the highway at the arroyo. Once you drive in a short distance, there is a sign leading to the paintings.)

Those who prefer to stay in Cataviña proper can use the barren **Parque Natural RV Park**, for about US$5 per site. It lacks both showers and electricity. Economical rooms are available at **Cabañas Linda** for US$21 on the eastern side of the highway; fatigued visitors with a bigger budget can stay at **Hotel La Pinta** (☎ 1-151-46-04), perhaps the best kept of any of the La Pinta chain. With rooms at US$63 single/double, it features an attractive cactus garden, a swimming pool and a children's playground.

On the eastern side of the highway is reasonably priced **Café La Enramada**, successful enough to have built a pleasant new *palapa* (palm-leaf shelter) with cardón walls and glass windows to keep out the wind. The cafe offers quality antojitos, seafood specialties and traditional Mexican chocolate (ask for 'chocolate Ibarra' or you may get instant Quik). It's a much better value than the more elaborate restaurant at Hotel La Pinta and has a small grocery store.

Rancho Santa Inés, a fourth-generation ranch, at the end of a paved road half a mile (1km) south of Cataviña, permits camping and has toilets and hot showers (US$4 per site). It also has very clean dormitory accommodations for US$10 per person. A restaurant provides good meals, and the proprietors can arrange excursions to the isolated ruins of **Misión Santa María**, which Walt Peterson's *The Baja Adventure Book* called 'Mission Impossible.' The ruins are 17 miles (27km) east of the highway by a road difficult even for 4WD vehicles – the trip takes about three days out and back.

BAHÍA SAN LUIS GONZAGA

About 32 miles (52km) south of Cataviña, near Laguna Chapala and across from the **Lonchería Los Cirios** (a basic restaurant between Km 234 and Km 235), a graded but rough road, passable even for large RVs, cuts northeast to Bahía San Luis Gonzaga, Puertecitos and the popular Gulf resort of San Felipe. Bahía San Luis Gonzaga is a quiet, beautiful area now experiencing in-

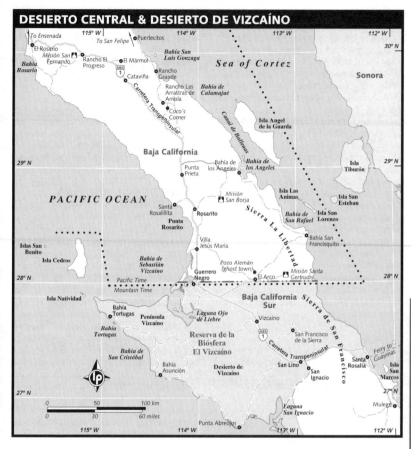

creased but not overwhelming tourist development, primarily attracting fishing enthusiasts. It is one of the most beautiful bays in Baja. Except for a few large vacation homes, accommodations are fairly basic, though good food is available.

The road to Bahía San Luis Gonzaga is one of the worst in Baja, so before starting out, ask about current conditions at the *llantera* (tire repair shop) next to Lonchería Los Cirios and deflate your tires – the road's sharp rocks can shred even heavy-duty tires that are fully inflated. Driving at speeds higher than 15mph (24kph) is not advisable.

About 13 miles (21km) east of the junction is **Coco's Corner**, a wild assemblage of ready-made objets d'art, including beer-can ornaments, a cactus garden, ocotillo 'street trees,' hubcaps, fan belts and other odds and ends. Radiator water, motor oil and automatic transmission fluid are all available here, as are cold drinks and modest meals. Camping is encouraged (free, with pit toilets).

From Coco's Corner, another dirt road leads east to little-visited Bahía de Calamajué; a branch off this road leads to the site of the short-lived Misión Calamajué and ruins of a gold mill on the Arroyo de Calamajué.

The same road continues south toward Bahía de Los Angeles but is only suitable for high-clearance vehicles with short wheelbases.

The main road continues about 4 miles (6km) north to **Rancho Las Arrastras de Arriola**, which has water, a mechanic, a llantera and cold drinks. The sandy parallel tracks sometimes offer better driving than the main roadway on the 20-mile (32km) stretch to Rancho Grande on Bahía San Luis Gonzaga itself. The entire stretch from the Transpeninsular to Rancho Grande, where Magna Sin gasoline is available for US$4 per gallon, takes about three hours.

Beyond Bahía San Luis Gonzaga, storms have damaged sections of the roadway to Puertecitos and San Felipe. For more details on this route, which is now very difficult for vehicles with low clearance and impossible for those without a short wheelbase (in other words, no RVs), see the South of Puertecitos entry in the Desierto del Colorado chapter. While 4WD is not necessary, the road is often steep, narrow, washboarded and difficult for any vehicle larger than a camper van.

Fishing

Anglers usually bring their own boats to Bahía San Luis Gonzaga, though boats and guides may be locally available. The following list indicates at what times the various fish species are most common:

Bass	April to June
Cabrilla	July
Corvina	March to September
Grouper	April to October
Sierra	July to September
White Sea Bass	November to March
Yellowtail	May to October

Places to Stay & Eat

RV Park Villas Mar de Cortez rents beach-front RV campsites for US$5 per car plus US$5 per palapa; facilities are limited to pit toilets, and gringo morons sometimes use the nearby airstrip for nighttime drag races. Drinkable water and cold showers are both available at Rancho Grande's Minimarket San Luis across the highway.

Just to the north, *Alfonsina's* also has its own airstrip, much improved and expanded motel-style accommodations (US$40 for rooms with two double beds and private bath) and a fine seafood restaurant. There's also a single beachfront palapa for car campers for US$5 per night, but how long it will last is questionable.

Two and a half miles (4km) north is the turnoff for *Papá Fernández*, a popular fish camp with basic accommodations (around US$10 per site) and an excellent restaurant. Service is a little slow, but the shrimp omelet and the fresh tortillas are worth the wait.

BAHÍA DE LOS ANGELES & AROUND

In colonial times, Bahía de Los Angeles (population 520) was a supply port for the interior mission of San Borja. About 107 miles (172km) southeast of Cataviña via a paved spur off the Transpeninsular, it is now a popular fishing village on the shore of its sparkling namesake bay, an inlet of the Sea of Cortez. The surface of the 42-mile (68km) spur, which meets the Transpeninsular at a junction 65 miles (105km) south of Cataviña, is paved but full of potholes; drive carefully.

People come here to fish the offshore islands and nearby isolated beaches and to kayak among the Midriff Islands as far south as Loreto, rather than to see Bahía de Los Angeles. Some have complained that the inshore waters have been fished out, but there is still a yellowtail season from May to October (also the hottest months).

Information

The best source of information on Bahía de Los Angeles and its surroundings is the Museo de la Naturaleza y de la Cultura (see later).

Bahía has a Telnor long-distance office (☎ 6-650-32-06/7); unfortunately, this office does not permit collect calls.

As of 2000, the local Pemex station was closed, but Magna Sin was available at Casa Díaz at the southern edge of town for about US$4 per gallon.

Be warned: Theft, though not epidemic, is increasing. Keep an eye on your belongings, even the large and conspicuous – a small plane recently disappeared from the airfield north of town, and because it was out of reach of radar at Ensenada (to the north) and Loreto (to the south), authorities were unable to track it down.

Museo de la Naturaleza y de la Cultura

The self-supporting museum of nature and culture features well-organized displays of shells, sea turtles, whale skeletons and other local marine life, and exhibits on native cultures (including Cochimí artifacts and rock art displays), mining, and horse gear and *vaquero* (cowboy) culture. Also on the grounds are a desert botanical garden and a good reconstruction of a mining site.

Just uphill from the central plaza, it is open 9 am to noon and 2 to 4 pm daily. Admission is free, but the museum enjoys volunteer labor and depends on donations and sales of books and T-shirts for support. The volunteers, mostly resident gringos, are a good source of information.

Programa Tortuga Marina

The Programa Tortuga Marina is north of town on the coast. Bahía de Los Angeles was once the center of the turtle fishery on the Gulf and, unfortunately, the now illegal practice has not completely disappeared. In a modest facility at the unused Brisa Marina RV Park, the Secretaría de Medio Ambiente, Recursos Naturales y Pesca (Semarnap; Ministry of the Environment, Natural Resources & Fishing) Sea Turtle Program conducts research on sea turtle biology, ecology and conservation. In 1996, the program released a loggerhead turtle named 'Adelita' at Santa Rosalillita on the Pacific side of the peninsula and tracked it by radio transmitter across the ocean to Japan.

The modest program's tanks offer the opportunity to see endangered sea turtle species such as the leatherback, the green and the hawksbill.

Parents should keep close watch on their children – despite its innocuous appearance, the smallish hawksbill will quickly (but not painlessly) amputate a dangling finger.

Mina Las Flores

About 6 miles (10km) south of town on the road to Bahía San Francisquito, all that's left of a once prosperous gold mine are the remains of an adobe house and a sturdy, virtually intact smelter.

Fishing

Casa Díaz (see Places to Stay & Eat, later) and a few other outfitters arrange full-day (6 am to 1 pm) panga excursions for US$100 to US$120.

Those with their own boats can use the launch ramps at Villa Vitta Trailer Park or Guillermo's (see Places to Stay & Eat) for about US$10 per day (use is free if you're staying at either place).

The following list indicates when gamefish species are abundant in the vicinity of Bahía de Los Angeles:

Cabrilla	April to January
Corvina	February to June
Grouper	year round
Halibut	April
Marlin	June to August
Roosterfish	November to April
Sailfish	May to September
Sierra	March
Yellowtail	year round

Sea Kayaking

According to San Diego–based kayaker Ed Gillet, kayaking from Bahía de Los Angeles to the islands around the bay is one of the best and most challenging adventures in the

Sea of Cortez. Northeasterly winds of up to 35 knots can suddenly appear and churn the water into a nasty mess, so expect some exciting paddling.

Isla Coronado, northeast of town, is the most popular local destination for kayakers. To get there, follow the dirt road north out of town for about 5 miles (8km) to Punta La Gringa; in winter there are usually plenty of campers around to watch your vehicle while you paddle. On Isla Coronado, Gillet recommends camping on the western side (near the islet of Mitlán) and fishing on the eastern side. Many kayakers continue north

from Punta La Gringa to Punta Remedios and Isla Angel de la Guarda.

Those exploring offshore islands should take care to avoid disturbing wildlife; careless visitors have scared many birds, most notably pelicans, from their nests, exposing eggs and chicks to predators and the hot sun.

Daggett's Beach Camping (see below), north of town, and a couple of places have rental kayaks for about US$20 for a half day.

Places to Stay & Eat

Bahía de Los Angeles has several motels, RV parks and other campsites north and

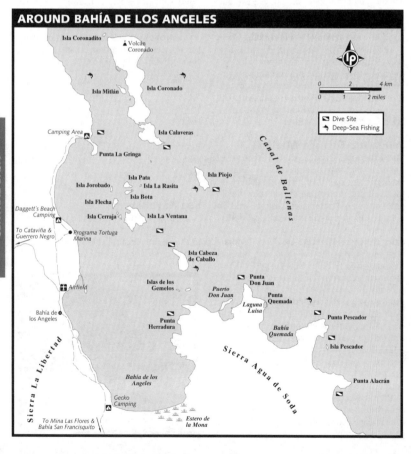

AROUND BAHÍA DE LOS ANGELES

Isla Coronadito

Volcán Coronado

Isla Mitlán

Isla Coronado

Camping Area

Isla Calaveras

Punta La Gringa

Canal de Ballenas

Isla Pata

Isla Piojo

Isla Jorobado

Isla La Rasita

Isla Flecha

Isla Bota

Daggett's Beach Camping

Isla Cerraja

Isla La Ventana

To Cataviña & Guerrero Negro

Programa Tortuga Marina

Isla Cabeza de Caballo

Airfield

Islas de los Gemelos

Puerto Don Juan

Punta Don Juan

Punta Quemada

Bahía de los Angeles

Laguna Luisa

Punta Pescador

Punta Herradura

Bahía Quemada

Isla Pescador

Sierra La Libertad

Sierra Agua de Soda

Punta Alacrán

Bahía de los Angeles

Gecko Camping

Estero de la Mona

To Mina Las Flores & Bahía San Franciscito

0   2   4 km
0   1   2 miles

Dive Site
Deep-Sea Fishing

CENTRAL BAJA

south of town, plus a handful of decent restaurants. Punta La Gringa, a beautiful beach area to the north, has several rugged **campsites** with choice views of offshore islands, but the road is a bit hard to follow, the trash cans are overflowing and toilet facilities are nil.

Daggett's Beach Camping (☎ *6-650-32-06*), just north of the Programa Tortuga Marina, charges US$8 per site. Hot showers are available, and it's much cleaner and tidier than most other area campgrounds. It's also possible to rent kayaks or to arrange fishing tours.

Congenial **Gecko Camping**, in a quiet shoreline location 3½ miles (6km) south of town on the Bahía San Francisquito road, has ramshackle cabins for US$12 to US$16 with flush toilets, bathrooms with hot showers, firewood and regular trash collection. Camping is US$3 per night with access to the same amenities.

In town, **Hotel La Hamacas** (☎ *6-650-32-06*) has clean and spacious doubles for US$30 or US$35 for newer rooms with TV and air-con. Its restaurant is a good choice and a bit cheaper than others in town. Just south of Las Hamacas is **Costa del Sol** (*costadelsolhotel@hotmail.com*), the most upscale of any accommodations options. Large rooms with TV and air-con are US$50.

Hotel Villa Vitta (☎ *760-741-9583 in the US*) offers very clean, comfortable, air-conditioned rooms ranging from US$25 to US$50, depending on the number and size of beds. Its restaurant specializes in moderately priced seafood. Across the road, the shabby, shadeless **Villa Vitta Trailer Park** has suspect toilets and a few beachfront spaces with full hookups for about US$10 per vehicle (hot showers are available at the hotel).

Next door, separated from the beach by an unsightly row of trailers and fishing shanties, **Guillermo's Trailer Park & Restaurant** (☎ *6-650-32-09*) has about 40 spaces for tents and RVs, some with limited shade and a few with full hookups. Tent spaces cost US$4 per night; RV spaces cost US$12 per night. The baths are less than immaculate, but the hot water supply is reli-

able. Its motel annex has singles/doubles with private bath for US$35/45, while meals at the restaurant cost about US$7 to US$10. The food is good; the margaritas are large but watery and expensive – only a good value during the 4 to 5 pm Happy Hour.

Casa Díaz (☎ *6-178-70-07 in Ensenada*) is a family-run trailer park/campground that includes a grocery store, motel and restaurant. The motel, consisting of 14 cozy stone cabins with hot showers, charges about US$20/25. Camping is possible on the motel grounds for about US$5 for two or three people, but Guillermo's is probably a better choice.

Flor del Mar, at the northern approach to town, is a very good seafood restaurant – try the tasty scallops in particular, but note the price difference (about 30%) between the peso and dollar menus.

SANTA ROSALILLITA

Twenty-four miles (39km) south of the Bahía de Los Angeles junction on the Transpeninsular, a road leads 10 miles (16km) west to Santa Rosalillita, an overgrown fish camp on the Pacific coast. The road is graded but unrelentingly washboarded, and resembles nothing so much as an eternal progression of speed bumps. The exit off the Transpeninsular is signed southbound but not northbound. Across Bahía de Sebastián Vizcaíno from Rosalillita, the twin peaks of Isla Cedros are visible in the distance.

For **surfing** enthusiasts, beaches north of Punta Santa Rosalillita, reachable by a difficult 7½-mile (12km) dirt road that requires high clearance, are renowned for exceptional breaks, while Punta Rosarito to the south, known among surfers as 'The Wall,' may be the most consistent break on the entire peninsula.

ROSARITO

Rosarito is a small truck stop 8½ miles (14km) south of the Santa Rosalillita junction and 32 miles (52km) south of the Bahía de Los Angeles junction. For surprisingly good food, try **Restaurant Mauricio**, whose striking onyx counter comes not from the massive quarry at El Mármol (see earlier in the chapter) but from a smaller, local quarry known as El Marmolito. Rosarito (not to be confused with the Playas de Rosarito resort town between Tijuana and Ensenada) offers the most convenient approach to Misión San Borja, one of the most significant and best preserved missions on the peninsula.

MISIÓN SAN BORJA

At Rosarito, a lateral off the Transpeninsular leads 21 miles (34km) east to the extensive ruins of Misión San Borja de Adac, founded here in 1762 by Jesuit Fray Wenceslao Linck because of the area's abundant water supply. The few remaining local families still cultivate grapes, olives and other crops. Of all the Jesuit adobes in Baja California, these are the best preserved.

Dominicans built the now-restored landmark church, made of locally quarried volcanic stone with many outstanding details, well after the Jesuits' expulsion. See the custodian before climbing the spiral staircase to the chorus, and leave a small (or large) donation. Other notable remains include the old mill and wine vats. On October 10, the local saint's day, devotees from throughout the region converge on the tiny ranchería to pray and party.

The well-signed road from Rosarito is rough in spots, but any vehicle with a short wheelbase and the clearance of a small pickup can handle it. The route passes through a spectacular Wild West valley landscape of cirio, cardón, *torote* (elephant tree), *datilillo* (yucca) and cholla beneath broad volcanic mesas. The road forks about 2 miles (3km) before San Borja; a sign indicates that both forks go to the mission, but the left (northern) fork is easier on both car and driver.

An alternative route to San Borja leaves the paved road to Bahía de Los Angeles at Km 44. By reputation, this is a 4WD route, but some locals profess to have taken ordinary passenger vehicles on the road. Along this route are some pre-Columbian **rock paintings**.

PARALELO 28

Marked by a 140-foot (42m) steel monument ostensibly resembling an eagle (but more ac-

curately described by veteran travel writer Joe Cummings as 'the world's largest tuning fork'), the 28th parallel marks the border between the states of Baja California (northern Baja) and Baja California Sur (southern Baja). The time zone changes here: Pacific Time (to the north) is one hour behind Mountain Standard Time (to the south).

The monument also symbolizes the completion of the Transpeninsular. During celebrations of the highway's completion, thousands jammed the amphitheater at its base. For years the facilities were neglected and trashed almost beyond salvation, but the Mexican army has rehabilitated them and installed a new guns-and-drugs checkpoint.

Hotel La Pinta Guerrero Negro (☎ 1-157-30-05), part of the Baja chain of La Pinta hotels, sits precisely on the 28th parallel. It has a restaurant, a bar and 28 comfortable rooms for US$67, but some of its details show wear and tear. *Trailer Park Benito Juárez*, alongside the hotel, has a few palapas and spacious RV sites for US$10 per night.

GUERRERO NEGRO

Guerrero Negro (population 7237), the first settlement south of the 28th parallel, is a company town that owes its existence to the world's largest evaporative saltworks. Most travelers, however, come here to visit famous Laguna Ojo de Liebre (better known in English as Scammon's Lagoon), the mating and birthing site for California gray whales. The Exportadora de Sal (ESSA) dominates the local economy, but the tourist trade is an important supplement, especially during the winter whale-watching season. A more recent economic factor is the Mexican army, which has a new camp at the Paralelo 28 monument north of town.

Named for the *Black Warrior,* a Massachusetts whaler wrecked nearby in the mid-19th century, Guerrero Negro capitalizes on tourism through its annual **Festival Cultural de la Ballena Gris** (Gray Whale Cultural Festival), lasting three weeks in early February. It includes events such as environmental talks, films, bicycle races and a book fair. Other indicators of progress are continuing street improvements, a construction boom and establishment of an FM radio station, but this is still probably the least appealing of any of the whale-watching bases.

Orientation

Guerrero Negro comprises two very distinct sectors: a disorderly strip along Blvd Emiliano Zapata west of the Transpeninsular, and ESSA's orderly company town, with a standard grid pattern that begins shortly after Blvd Zapata curves southwest near the airfield. Most of the town's accommodations and restaurants are in the former area on Blvd Zapata.

Information

Banamex, on Blvd Zapata at the entrance to the ESSA sector, will change US dollars and traveler's checks at reasonable rates (with a minimum of bureaucracy) 8:30 am to 3 pm weekdays. Supermercado La Ballena no longer changes traveler's checks but accepts US dollars in payment for purchases, giving change in pesos.

The town's post office is in the ESSA sector; the postal code is 23940. There are Ladatel phones available on many street corners.

Bring your dirty clothes to Lavamática Express, across the street from Motel Las Ballenas (see Places to Stay, later), open 8 am to 8 pm Monday to Saturday, 10 am to 4 pm Sunday.

The town's Clínica Hospital IMSS (☎ 1-157-04-33) is on the southern side of Blvd Zapata at the point where the road curves southwest.

Guerrero Negro is one of the main gas stops along the Transpeninsular, so the gas station tends to run out of gas on a regular basis. Fill up your tank as soon as you get to town, on the off-chance that there won't be gas when you head back to the station (which usually means an unplanned overnight stay while you wait for the gas truck to arrive).

Campers and RVers can obtain purified drinking water at a reasonable cost at Fresk-Pura on the southern side of Blvd Zapata.

Saltworks

ESSA's saltworks consists of about 70 sq miles (182 sq km) of evaporative ponds, each about 110 sq yards (100 sq meters) in area and about a yard deep, just south of Guerrero Negro. In the intense desert sunlight and high winds, water evaporates quickly, leaving a saline residue that is dredged from the pools, hauled to nearby quays and barged to Isla Cedros for transshipment by freighter. The works produces more than five million tons of salt annually.

Whale-Watching

Guerrero Negro is the northernmost of Baja's whale-watching locales and has the most abundant accommodations of any of them. Tours from Guerrero Negro, however, are usually briefer than tours elsewhere because they require traveling some distance to the whale-watching sites.

Three-hour tours usually start at 8 and 11 am and cost around US$40, including transportation to Scammon's Lagoon and a box lunch. Local operators include Mario's (☎/fax 1-157-01-20) and Malarrimo Ecotours (☎ 1-157-02-50, fax 1-157-01-00), both at their namesake restaurants (see Places to Eat, later). The Web site for Malarrimo is www.malarrimo.com.

Note that whale-watching excursions at Guerrero Negro and more southerly points conform to Mountain Standard Time; southbound visitors who forget to change their watches at the state border will literally miss the bus.

Places to Stay

Accommodations in Guerrero Negro are fairly abundant and reasonably priced, but the winter whale-watching season can put a strain on these resources. For this reason, reservations are advisable from January through March.

Camping is free at most beaches outside town. In town, *Malarrimo Trailer Park (☎ 1-157-01-00, fax 1-157-08-53)* charges from US$5 per site for tent camping, US$12 for RVs. Not all the electrical outlets work, so check before setting up. Hot water is plentiful and the toilets are clean, but one of the showerheads emits a stream thinner than a pencil lead. The largest RVs, especially those with trailers, may have trouble maneuvering into a site.

Well-worn *Dunas Motel* (☎ 1-157-00-55), at Blvd Zapata and División del Norte, has 28 drab but clean rooms with firm beds and hot showers for US$13. The *Motel Brisa Salina* (☎ 1-157-01-15), on the northern side of Blvd Zapata, charges US$17/20 for singles/doubles.

Motel Gamez (☎ 1-157-03-70), on the northern side of Blvd Zapata toward the airfield, has slightly shabby but adequate rooms for US$12 double. Probably the best value in town is nine-room *Motel Las Ballenas* (☎ 1-157-01-16), just north of Hotel El Morro, on Victoria. Clean and tidy, it has hot water and a color TV in every room for US$16/19.

Hotel El Morro (☎ 1-157-04-14), on the northern side of Blvd Zapata, has 35 clean, pleasant rooms for US$22/30 with cable TV and hot showers. The upgraded *Motel San José* (☎ 1-157-14-20), opposite the bus terminal, has rooms with TV and hot showers for US$18/23. *Motel Don Gus* (☎ 1-157-16-11), around the corner from the bus terminal, just off Blvd Zapata, charges US$25/30; it also has a decent restaurant and a bar.

Motel San Ignacio (☎ 1-157-02-70), on the northern side of Blvd Zapata, has clean, spacious rooms with TV for US$25/28. At *Cabañas Don Miguelito* (☎ 157-02-50, fax 157-01-00), part of the Malarrimo restaurant-RV park complex, pleasant rooms cost US$26/31.

Places to Eat

Guerrero Negro's best bargains are the numerous taco stands along Blvd Zapata, which keep erratic hours but maintain high standards. *Supermercado La Ballena* (☎ 1-157-00-55) has reasonably priced takeout food at its cafeteria and a wide selection of groceries and produce for campers who plan to go into the backcountry. Its landmark sign depicts a sperm whale rather than the gray whale that draws tourists to the area.

Highly regarded *Malarrimo* (☎ 1-157-01-00), on the northern side of Blvd Zapata as you enter town, specializes in seafood ranging from fish and shrimp to clams and abalone, in both traditional antojitos and more sophisticated international dishes. While it's not cheap, its portions are abundant and it's still a good value. The margaritas are small but strong.

For good breakfasts, try *Cocina Económica Letty* on the southern side of Blvd Zapata, which also serves very fine antojitos and seafood at prices a fraction of those at Malarrimo. *Mario's* (☎ 1-157-08-08), next door to Hotel El Morro on the northern side of Blvd Zapata, serves excellent, moderately priced seafood.

Getting There & Away

Air Aeropuerto Guerrero Negro is 1¼ miles (2km) north of the state border, just west of the Transpeninsular. Guerrero Negro also has an airfield near the ESSA sector in town.

The AeroMéxico connector airline Aerolitoral (☎ 1-157-17-45) flies daily except Sunday to Hermosillo, with connections to Ciudad Juárez, Ciudad Obregón, Chihuahua, Mexico City, Phoenix, Tucson and Culiacán (the latter is weekdays only). Its offices are on the northern side of Blvd Zapata near the Pemex station, but it leaves from Aeropuerto Guerrero Negro.

You can fly north to Isla Cedros or Ensenada with Aerocedros (☎ 1-157-16-26), which has offices on the northern side of Blvd Zapata in Guerrero Negro. Aerocedros flies Tuesday and Friday at 1:30 pm from Aeropuerto Guerrero Negro to Cedros (US$51), then continues on to Ensenada (US$103).

Bus From Guerrero Negro's bus terminal (☎ 1-157-06-11) on the southern side of Blvd Zapata, Autotransportes de Baja California (ABC) and Autotransportes Aguila offer services throughout the peninsula.

San Quintín – US$20, five hours; 6:30 & 8:30 am, 7:30, 8:30 & 10 pm

Ensenada – US$30, eight hours; 6:30 & 8:30 am, 7:30, 8:30 & 10 pm

Tijuana – US$37, 10 hours; 6:30 & 8:30 am, 7:30, 8:30 & 10 pm

Mexicali – US$49, 12 hours; 2:30 am

Sample southbound fares include the following:

Vizcaíno – US$4, one hour; 1, 5, 6 & 8:30 am, 4:30 & 9 pm

San Ignacio – US$7, three hours; 1, 5, 6 & 8:30 am, 4:30 & 9 pm

Santa Rosalía – US$11, four hours; 1, 5, 6 & 8:30 am, 4:30 & 9 pm

Mulegé – US$16, five hours; 1, 5, 6 & 8:30 am, 4:30 & 9 pm

Loreto – US$21, seven hours; 1, 5, 6 & 8:30 am, 4:30 & 9 pm

Ciudad Constitución – US$29, nine hours; 1, 5, 6 & 8:30 am, 4:30 & 9 pm

La Paz – US$40, 12 hours; 1, 5, 6 & 8:30 am, 4:30 & 9 pm

AROUND GUERRERO NEGRO
Reserva de la Biosfera El Vizcaíno & Laguna Ojo de Liebre

Also known in part as Parque Natural de la Ballena Gris (Gray Whale Natural Park), the 9833-sq-mile (25,566-sq-km) Vizcaíno Biosphere Reserve sprawls from Laguna San Ignacio, Guerrero Negro, Isla Natividad and Isla Cedros across to the Sea of Cortez, taking in part of the Sierra de San Francisco. It is the joint responsibility of Semarnap (☎ 1-157-17-77 in Guerrero Negro) and Ejido Benito Juárez (☎ 1-157-17-33), whose lands the reserve occupies.

Laguna Ojo de Liebre (Scammon's Lagoon) has the greatest number of whales of any of Baja's four main **whale-watching** sites. Local *pangueros* (fishermen with skiffs) take visitors for 1½-hour excursions on its shallow waters for US$25/15 for adults/children. Whale-watching now officially begins December 15 and lasts until April 15, but whales are few at the earliest dates. Late-season trips, those from mid-February on, are likelier to encounter friendly whales.

Five miles (8km) southeast of the Guerrero Negro junction, at Km 208 of the Transpeninsular, a smooth, graded road leads 15 miles (24km) southwest to Laguna Ojo de Liebre. All vehicles must register with the guard at ESSA's checkpoint, which controls the access road. (The road is so smooth because it's almost solid salt; be sure to get your car washed soon after leaving.)

Camping is possible at the lagoon, where savvy visitors choose sites above the sometimes flooded tidal flats; the more remote sites are also closer to the maternity channel, so you can hear the whales up close and personal. The ejido charges US$3 per vehicle for camping or day use. Its ***Restaurant Palapa*** has superb food at very reasonable prices – don't miss the tasty *almejas rancheras* (clams with salsa).

El Arco & Pozo Alemán

About 17 miles (27km) south of Guerrero Negro, a once paved but now graveled 26-mile (42km) lateral leads eastward to El Arco, a 19th-century gold-mining town that now serves as a supply center for surrounding ranchos. The replacement of the road's miserably broken pavement by gravel is a godsend, as it's now possible to drive the route without arranging a chiropractor's appointment in advance. At times, the sandy offshoot of the road that runs alongside provides a smoother ride than the paved road.

El Arco, which retains a smattering of rusting machinery from its mining heyday, is presently undergoing a minor renaissance due to renewed interest in its ores. The area's real highlight is the nearby ghost town of Pozo Alemán, a few miles east on a sometimes rugged dirt road. Its ruins include several residences, the smelter, a blacksmith's shop, a still-functioning windmill and water system and a company store with items still on the counter. Note especially the caves – actually excavations in the steep banks of the arroyo – where the peons resided. A caretaker oversees the ruins and shows visitors around; a small tip is appropriate.

The dirt road continues east to Bahía San Francisquito on the Sea of Cortez. Just west of Bahía San Francisquito, a graded road leads north to Bahía de Los Angeles – the drive takes about three hours – and can be pretty rough at times.

Misión Santa Gertrudis

About 23 miles (37km) east of El Arco via an unpaved road, the isolated Misión Santa

Scammon & the Whales

Laguna Ojo de Liebre takes its English name, Scammon's Lagoon, from Captain Charles Melville Scammon, an American whaler who frequented the area in the 1850s. Born in Maine, Scammon yearned to captain a trading ship but had to settle for command of less lucrative whalers, such as the *Boston* out of San Francisco. In 1857, upon learning from some Mexicans that an estuary near Bahía de Sebastián Vizcaíno was the breeding ground of the gray whale, he headed south.

Each year, gray whales migrate 6000 miles (9700km) from the Bering Sea to the warmer lagoons of Ojo de Liebre, San Ignacio and Bahía Magdalena, where they stay from January to April. The lagoons offer an ideal, protected breeding ground for sexually mature whales (five years or older) to mate, give birth and nurture their offspring. By late March, most have begun the long journey back to the Arctic.

For whalers, the density of whales in constricted, shallow lagoons meant almost literally shooting fish in a barrel, but Scammon's first attempts were disastrous: Whales crushed two of his small whale-boats and seriously injured half the crew. Resorting to 'bomb lances' – bombs fired into a whale from a hand-held gun – instead of harpoons, Scammon and his crew managed to get 740 barrels of oil, filling virtually every container on board, which was later sold in San Francisco as lubricant.

By the end of 1859, Scammon and other whalers had nearly eliminated the gray whale from the lagoons. Whaling did not cease until 1935, and it took many decades for the population to recover. Today, the US and Mexican governments have effective laws, in addition to international agreements, that protect the gray whale and its habitat.

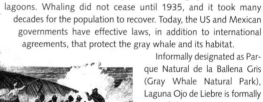

Informally designated as Parque Natural de la Ballena Gris (Gray Whale Natural Park), Laguna Ojo de Liebre is formally part of the massive Reserva de la Biosfera El Vizcaíno, as is Laguna San Ignacio.

Gertrudis La Magna was the focus of the Jesuits' northward missionary efforts. Initially founded as a result of explorations by the famous Jesuit Fernando Consag in 1751, its original adobe church, with a stone foundation, was built under the direction of Fray Sebastián Sisteaga and an extraordinary blind Cochimí Indian named Andrés Comanjí. The German Jesuit Georg Retz took charge of the 600 Cochimí here, digging a well, building *acequias* (irrigation canals) and planting wheat, maize, olives, grapes, dates, pomegranates and figs. The mission also maintained livestock, such as cattle, horses, mules, goats and sheep.

After the Spanish government expelled the Jesuits in 1767, Dominicans took over and finished the small stone church, now undergoing restoration, which bears a ceiling date of 1796. Labor and water shortages forced the mission's abandonment in 1822.

The church museum contains a selection of Guaycura, Cora and Cochimí artifacts, as well as *ofrendas* (offerings) left by pilgrims for Santa Gertrudis – common among the offerings are the lengthy tresses of young women who have visited this popular pilgrimage site. Every November 16, pilgrims jam the village for the **Fiesta de Santa Gertrudis**.

Another landmark is **El Camino Real**, the royal road (really a trail), which still leads 29 leagues (100 miles or 161km) from San Ignacio to San Borja via Santa Gertrudis. Most travelers prefer the improved road from El Arco, passable for any passenger vehicle and even small RVs (though one van with California plates now stands on blocks behind the church). The entire trip from Guerrero Negro takes 2½ to three hours.

BAHÍA SAN FRANCISQUITO

About 52 miles (84km) east of El Arco and 80 miles (129km) south of Bahía de Los Angeles, Bahía San Francisquito contains the remote, rustic fishing resort **Punta San Francisquito** (☎ 619-690-1000 in the US), many of whose guests arrive by private plane. This is one of the most beautiful, isolated beaches in Baja. The road from Bahía de Los Angeles is passable for just about any vehicle, but drive with caution because it has washed away at certain points. The total drive takes about 2½ hours.

Beachfront camping is possible at the resort for just US$5 per site with access to hot showers, and cabañas cost US$15 per person, US$30 with full board. Reservations are essential for cabañas but not for camping. The restaurant is open all year and offers excellent, if pricey, food.

A short distance north of the resort, **Puerto San Francisquito** has equally attractive beachfront camping for US$2.50 per person with a saltwater flush toilet, but there's no fresh water. The resort's mailing address is Apdo Postal 7, San Ignacio, Baja California Sur 23930, México.

ISLA CEDROS

Isla Cedros is a mountainous northward extension of Península Vizcaíno, separated from the mainland by Canal de Kellet, the much smaller Isla Natividad and Canal de Dewey. Reaching altitudes of nearly 4000 feet (1200m) above sea level, this desert island is a rewarding, off-the-beaten-track destination for adventurous travelers.

Early Spanish explorers found surprisingly large numbers of Cochimí Indians on the island, whose intransigence led to their forcible relocation to the mainland mission of San Ignacio by the Jesuits. Manila galleons later used Isla Cedros as a port of refuge on their return across the Pacific. The island supports unusual vegetation, including native tree species and coastal wildlife such as elephant seals and sea lions. Cedros mule deer,

an endangered subspecies, still inhabit the rugged backcountry.

Most of the island's 1465 inhabitants live in the tiny port of Cedros on the sheltered eastern shore, but many also live at ESSA's company town at Punta Morro Redondo at the southern tip of the island, which is the site of the airfield and the transshipment point for salt barged over from Guerrero Negro. The Sociedad Cooperativa de Producción Pesquera, the local fishing cooperative, is the other main employer. Commercial pressure has reduced the offshore abalone, just as earlier hunters vastly depleted the numbers of fur seals and sea otters (otters may have returned to the area). The first abalone divers were Japanese, but the Mexican cooperative took over the business after WWII.

Isla Cedros' commercial abalone season runs from December to June at three different locations: Cabo San Agustín, Cabo Norte and Islas San Benito. Divers work in groups of three and gather up to 100 abalone per day. The lobster season runs from October to April.

The ramshackle village of Cedros faces Bahía de Sebastián Vizcaíno from the slopes beneath towering Cerro Vargas, also called Cerro Cenizo, whose summit (3950 feet or 1185m) is usually hidden by clouds. It's definitely not a stereotypical tourist destination. Cedros has no bank or any other place to change money, and you can't even get a margarita, but there is phone service, an IMSS hospital/clinic and a Capitanía del Puerto (port authority).

Several two-story buildings with porches or balconies facing the bay add a touch of vernacular architectural interest. Electricity is only available 6 am to noon and 5 to 11 pm. Running water is available mornings only, though most houses have storage tanks. Prices are high because nearly everything is shipped in – including salt, despite the mountains of it at Punta Morro Redondo.

In Cedros' tidy hillside church, murals in the curious **Capilla de la Reconciliación** (Chapel of Reconciliation) depict events in Mexican and Baja Californian history, such as the expulsion of the Jesuits, in a comic-book style. According to local residents, the

CENTRAL BAJA

ISLA CEDROS & ISLAS SAN BENITO

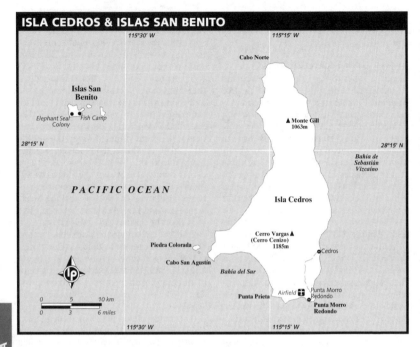

hilltop **Panteón** cemetery harbors the remains of early Japanese divers, but only a single headstone bears a conspicuous Japanese inscription.

Places to Stay & Eat

Accommodations in Cedros are very basic. *Casa de Huésped Aguilar* on the waterfront charges US$10 for rooms with shared bath (no hot water) or US$15 with private bath. To find the unmarked building, walk straight downhill from the church; before entering the grounds of the fishing cooperative, look for the two-story house on your left. If no one is on duty, you'll have to hike up the hill to Manuel Aguilar's house, a brown stucco next to the elementary school and the power plant, to check in.

Cedros has only a few places to eat and, surprisingly enough, prices for abalone are double or triple those on the mainland. *El Marino* charges US$35 to sample this delicacy but also has much more affordable antojitos, fish and shrimp. *La Pacenita* is a bit cheaper, but heavily fried foods are the rule. A friendly taco stand up the main drag from El Marino serves only carne asada.

Getting There & Away

Isla Cedros' airfield is at Punta Morro Redondo, about 5 miles (8km) south of the village. Taxis charge about US$5 per person, but locals will sometimes offer you a ride there. Flights from Guerrero Negro and Ensenada serve Isla Cedros.

Return flights from Isla Cedros to Guerrero Negro (US$51) ostensibly leave at 1 pm (Pacific Time), but travelers should arrive at least an hour ahead of time to avoid being left at the airstrip.

ISLAS SAN BENITO

This tiny archipelago consists of three small islands 30 nautical miles (55km) west of Isla Cedros. The westernmost island, the largest of the three, supports a large winter camp of abalone divers and their families, as well as a substantial breeding colony of northern elephant seals. The seals begin to arrive in December but are most numerous in January and February. Another notable animal is the black storm-petrel, locally known as the *nocturno* because it leaves its nesting burrows only at night. Sea turtles and whales are visible offshore (the islands are just off the gray-whale migration route).

Unless you bring camping equipment and enough food and water to stay overnight, expect to spend no more than an hour on shore. Avoid getting too close to the elephant seals, especially the enormous bulls; not only are they potentially dangerous, but frightened bulls may accidentally crush or injure newborn pups that cannot get out of their way.

Passing yachts often anchor here, and sailors come ashore to see the seals, but budget travelers can catch a lift on the *Tito I*, which carries daily supplies to the abalone divers and returns to Isla Cedros with the day's catch. For a (free) passage on the *Tito I*, visit the Sociedad Cooperativa de Producción Pesquera in the village of Cedros

Northern elephant seal

before it closes to the public at 1 pm. On request, with routine approval by the chief, the secretary will issue a letter to present to the captain that evening for the following day's voyage.

The crew of the *Tito I* are exceptionally friendly and will probably offer breakfast to passengers, but travelers prone to seasickness should refrain from eating too heavily. The four-hour voyage to the San Benitos, against the wind and the northwestern swell, is generally rougher than the voyage back.

PENÍNSULA VIZCAÍNO

One of Baja's most thinly populated areas, Península Vizcaíno is a sparsely vegetated, mountainous extension of the Desierto de Vizcaíno. While you may not need a rugged 4WD vehicle everywhere – roads are generally passable – conditions are terrible in certain areas. Even the best roads are pretty rough, so driving can be very slow.

Both Bahía Tortugas and Bahía Asunción have gas stations, but carry extra fuel in any event.

Vizcaíno

About 40 miles (64km) south of Guerrero Negro, the crossroads town of Vizcaíno is the gateway to the peninsula; good rooms are available at *Motel Kadekaaman* (☎ 1-154-08-12) for US$19/21 singles/doubles. The adjacent RV park charges US$6; improvements are supposedly in order. Across from the Pemex station, *Motel Olivia* (☎ 1-154-07-24) charges US$16/21 for rooms with air-con and TV (with a small selection of channels).

From Vizcaíno's bus terminal (☎ 1-154-07-71), next to Motel Olivia, Aquila buses run north five times daily and south four times daily. Buses also go to Bahía Tortugas (US$10.50; three hours; Monday, Tuesday, Wednesday and Saturday at 5 am) near the western tip of the peninsula, on a partly paved but mostly graded surface negotiable for any vehicle.

Bahía Tortugas

Passing yachts usually anchor at Bahía Tortugas because it's the only port between San

Diego and Cabo San Lucas that has direct refueling facilities, making it a good spot for lifts south despite its remoteness. Hang out on the pier near the tuna cannery. Anglers cruise the offshore kelp beds for bass, mackerel and barracuda, while farther offshore they find bonito and yellowtail. You can hire a guide to take you fishing in a panga for US$50 per day; inquire at the dock.

Bahía Tortugas has a few hotels in town. **Motel Nancy** (☎ 1-158-01-00) on Independencia is a friendly, family-run place, with rooms for US$15/17 singles/doubles. On Altamirano, the **Motel Rendon** (☎ 1-158-02-32) has rooms for US$10.50/13. The decent restaurant next door, **El Moroco**, is run by the same family.

Bahía Asunción

This harbor is reached by a graded road at the southern end of the Sierra Santa María (no public transport) and is a prime site for barracuda, bonito, dorado, yellowfin and yellowtail, but the area is very windy and offshore waters are rough. The lone hotel is part of the **3 Hermanos Restaurant** (☎ 1-154-02-11) and charges US$14/18 singles/doubles. It is also possible to camp free of charge at the beach.

SAN IGNACIO

After the scrub and cacti forests of the Desierto de Vizcaíno, the palm oasis of San Ignacio (population 761) is a soothing sight. In 1728, the Mexican Jesuit Juan Bautista Luyando located Misión San Ignacio de Kadakaamán here, planting dense groves of date palms and citrus in the Arroyo El Carrizal surrounding the town. After the Jesuits' expulsion, Dominican missionaries supervised construction of the lava-block church (finished in 1786) that still dominates the town's laurel-shaded plaza.

San Ignacio has become the jumping-off point for whale-watching excursions to Laguna San Ignacio – probably the best spot for contact with so-called friendly whales – and trips to the spectacular pre-Columbian rock art sites in the Sierra de San Francisco. Surrounding ranchos and fish camps rely on the town for supplies – San Ignacio has

several grocery stores, a handful of restaurants, lodging and modest trailer parks. Its lingering colonial atmosphere contrasts with the bustling development of some other Baja towns.

San Ignacio's Fiesta Patronal (festival in honor of San Ignacio's patron saint) takes place the last week of July.

Orientation & Information

San Ignacio is 88 miles (142km) south of Guerrero Negro. The town proper is about 1 mile (1.6km) south of the Transpeninsular; a paved lateral leads from the highway junction (known as San Lino) past a small lagoon and through groves of date palms into the town. Parking is easy, and the town invites walking.

Most services are found around the plaza, including the post office; the postal code is 23930. International collect calls are quick and easy from Ladatel telephones on the plaza. Cuco Arce (☎ 1-154-02-22 ext 229) is the INAH representative in San Ignacio. The INAH office is part of the museum next to the mission church (see below for hours).

Misión San Ignacio

With lava-block walls nearly 4 feet (1.2m) thick, the former Jesuit Misión San Ignacio de Kadakaamán is one of Baja's most beautiful churches. It has been in continuous use since its founding in 1728. Opposite the plaza, occupying the site of a former Cochimí ranchería and initiated by the famous Jesuit Fernando Consag, the church was completed in 1786 under the direction of Dominican Juan Crisóstomo Gómez. Epidemics reduced the Cochimí population from about 5000 at contact to only 120 by the late 18th century, but the mission lasted until 1840.

Museo San Ignacio

Just south of the mission church, the Instituto Nacional de Antropología y Historia (INAH) has built an impressive new museum that has elaborate displays on the Desierto Central's rock art, including a replica cave-mural site that's the next best thing to descending into Cañón San Pablo (see Sierra de San Francisco, later). From

November to April, it's open 8 am to 6 pm daily; otherwise it closes at 3 pm and all day Sunday (free admission). You must request permission here to visit any rock art site in the area.

Organized Tours

Kuyima (☎/fax 1-154-00-70), a local cooperative on the plaza, arranges whale-watching trips in season as well as visits to rock art sites in the surrounding area. Its mailing address is Apdo Postal 53, San Ignacio, Baja California Sur 23930, México.

It is also possible to hire a guide at Motel La Posada (see later), for about US$31 per person, to take visitors without vehicles to view the easily reached rock art site at Cueva del Ratón, but mule trips can be arranged more cheaply at San Francisco de la Sierra, with approval from INAH in San Ignacio. Motel La Posada also offers whale-watching day trips for US$55. See Sierra de San Francisco and Laguna San Ignacio, later.

Places to Stay & Eat

San Ignacio has several basic RV parks at San Lino on the approach to town. On the eastern side of the lateral into San Ignacio, just north of the Hotel La Pinta San Ignacio, the very basic *Martín Quesada RV Park* charges just US$3 per site. On the western side, free camping is available at *Camping La Muralla*. It is essentially a barren

---

Rock Art of Central Baja

When Jesuit missionaries inquired about the creators and meaning of the giant rock paintings of the Sierra de San Francisco, the Cochimí Indians responded with a bewilderment that was, in all likelihood, utterly feigned. The Cochimí claimed ignorance of both symbols and techniques, but it was not unusual, when missionaries came calling, to deny knowledge of the profound religious beliefs that those missionaries wanted to eradicate.

At sites like Cueva Pintada, Cochimí painters and their predecessors decorated high rock overhangs with vivid red-and-black representations of human figures, bighorn sheep, pumas and deer, as well as more abstract designs. It is speculated that the painters built scaffolds of palm logs to reach the ceilings. Postcontact motifs do include Christian crosses, but these are few and small in contrast to the dazzling pre-Columbian figures surrounding them.

Cueva de las Flechas, across Cañón San Pablo, has similar paintings, but the uncommon feature of arrows through some of the figures here is the subject of serious speculation. One interpretation is that these depict a period of warfare. Similar opinions suggest that they record a raid or a trespass upon tribal territory, or perhaps constitute a warning against such trespass. One researcher, however, has hypothesized that the arrows represent a shaman's metaphor for death in the course of a vision quest. If this is the case, it is no wonder that the Cochimí would claim ignorance of the paintings and their significance in the face of missionaries, unrelentingly hostile to such beliefs.

Such speculation is impossible to prove, since the Cochimí no longer exist. However, the Instituto Nacional de Antropología y Historia (INAH) has undertaken a survey of the Cochimí, the largest systematic archaeological survey of a hunter-gatherer people yet attempted in Mexico, and it has discovered that, in addition to rock art and grinding stones, the Cochimí left evidence of permanent dwellings. In recognition of its cultural importance, the Sierra de San Francisco has been declared a Unesco World Heritage Site. It is part of the Reserva de la Biosfera El Vizcaíno, which includes the major gray-whale calving areas of Laguna San Ignacio and Laguna Ojo de Liebre.

The Sierra de San Francisco remains an INAH-protected archaeological zone, which means that visitors need entry permits to conduct research. Research permits are only issued through the INAH office in Mexico City, not the one in San Ignacio. INAH has also instituted regulations for tourists, in the interest of preserving the paintings. For details, see the Sierra de San Francisco entry in this chapter.

parking lot and lacks shade as well as toilets and showers. Across the road, **Don Chon** has plenty of shade and a nice riverside location but also lacks showers and toilets. Sites cost US$4.

Just south of Hotel La Pinta on the western side of the road, **El Padrino RV Park** (☎/fax 1-154-00-89) has undergone a major cleanup but lacks shade in some areas despite handsome stands of date palms. There are around 100 sites, 15 of which have full hookups; four good showers have a dependable hot water supply. Fees are US$8 per site for camping, US$10 with full hookups. The restaurant here, **Flojos**, serves good, fresh seafood; its lobster is notably cheaper than at Tota's (see below), and the margaritas are strong and well priced. The **Rice & Beans RV Park** (☎ 1-154-02-83), on the road to San Lino, just off the Transpeninsular west of town, has 30 spaces, 24 with full hookup, for US$5 each.

Chalita (☎ 1-154-00-82), a restaurant facing the southern side of the plaza, has a few rooms with private bath for US$8. It serves cheap antojitos in a family atmosphere (literally – it's a living room). **Motel La Posada** (☎ 1-154-03-13) has comfortable but spartan doubles with hot showers for about US$22. It often fills up early and is a bit hard to find – wind around southeast from the Plaza.

Hotel La Pinta San Ignacio (☎/fax 1-154-03-00, 800-336-5454 in the US) is on the main road into town, northwest of the plaza, and sports colonial-style architecture, a tiled courtyard, swimming pool and groves of date palms and citrus. Rooms cost US$65. The restaurant serves fairly pricey Mexican food; their specialty is beef from nearby ranches.

Taquería Los Arcos, just east of the plaza on Hidalgo, rarely keeps to its 5 pm opening time. Serving antojitos next door, **Rene's** occupies a site once held by the popular Tota's. **Tota's** has moved two blocks south but still serves very good, reasonably priced antojitos and seafood dishes 7 am to 10 pm daily.

On the Transpeninsular, west of the San Lino junction, **Quichuley** serves good antojitos at moderate prices.

Getting There & Away

Transpeninsular buses pick up passengers opposite the Pemex station at the San Lino junction. There are at least five northbound buses daily between 6 am and 3 pm and as many southbound between 6 am and 10:30 pm.

AROUND SAN IGNACIO
Sierra de San Francisco

To date, researchers have located about 500 pre-Columbian rock art sites in an area of roughly 4300 sq miles (11,200 sq km) in the Sierra de San Francisco north of San Ignacio. Reached by a graded road from a conspicuously signed junction at Km 118 of the Transpeninsular, 28 miles (45km) north of San Ignacio, the village of San Francisco de la Sierra is the gateway to the area's most spectacular manifestations of Baja's unique cultural heritage.

About 1½ miles (2.5km) west of San Francisco de la Sierra, **Cueva del Ratón** is the most accessible site, featuring typical representations of *monos* (human figures), *borregos* (desert bighorn sheep) and deer, but they are not as well preserved as paintings elsewhere in the area. The site is well worth seeing for day visitors, who must obtain INAH permission at San Ignacio. The INAH staff will also help to arrange for a guide to show you the paintings, which are protected by a chainlink fence and locked gate. Visiting hours are 6 am to 5 pm daily.

The area's most rewarding excursion is a descent into the dramatic Cañón San Pablo to see its famous **Cueva Pintada**, **Cueva de las Flechas** and other magnificent sites. Cueva Pintada, really an extensive rock overhang rather than a cave, is the single most imposing site. Among English-speakers, it is known as Gardner's Cave; the popular American novelist Earle Stanley Gardner wrote several well-known books about his own adventures in the area. Mexicans, however, intensely resent the identification with Gardner and strongly prefer the Spanish term.

Exploring Cañón San Pablo requires a minimum of two days, preferably three. Visitors must obtain permission and contact guides from INAH in San Ignacio (see Orientation & Information under San Ignacio, earlier) as well as agree to a series of INAH guidelines and other restrictions in the interest of preserving the paintings. Visitors may not touch the paintings, smoke at the site or take flash photographs – 400 ASA film easily suffices even in dim light. Campfires and alcoholic beverages are prohibited.

Excursions to Cueva del Ratón can take about three hours in a 4WD car. You must hire a guide, and each guide can take four people. The cost ranges from US$4 for one person to US$8 for four people. Excursions to Cañón San Pablo involve hiring a guide and mule for US$10.50 per day, a mule for each individual in the party for US$8 per day plus additional pack animals, either mules or burros, to carry supplies such as tents and food. Visitors must also provide food for the guide; San Francisco de la Sierra has a small market, but it's better to bring food from Guerrero Negro or San Ignacio.

Backpacking is permitted, but backpackers still must hire a guide and mule. Most visitors will find the steep volcanic terrain much easier to manage on muleback, which leaves more time to explore the canyon and enjoy the scenery. The precipitous muleback descent into the canyon takes about five or six hours, the ascent slightly less; in winter this means almost an entire day devoted to transportation alone. Perhaps the best time to visit is in late March or April, when days are fairly long but temperatures are not yet unpleasantly hot.

San Francisco's residents, descendants of the early vaqueros who settled the penin-

sula along with the missionaries, still maintain a distinctive pastoral culture, herding mostly goats in the surrounding countryside. They also retain a unique vocabulary, with many terms surviving from the 18th century, and produce some remarkable crafts – look at the guides' *polainas* (leather leggings) for riding in the bush, for instance. Such items are generally made to order, but occasionally villagers will have a pair of men's *teguas* (leather shoes) or women's open-toed *huaraches* (sandals) for sale.

At the turnoff to San Francisco de la Sierra, INAH has posted signs that also warn against attempting to visit the rock art sites without its permission. The road from the Transpeninsular is regularly graded, but, because parts of its surface are poorly consolidated at times, there are spots that are difficult for vehicles with poor traction and low clearance (4WD is not necessary, however). It can be very difficult after a rain.

At a signed junction at Km 59 of the Transpeninsular, about 9 miles (15km) east of San Ignacio, a decent road leads 24 miles (39km) north from Ejido Alfredo Bonfil to Rancho Santa Martha, the starting point for excursions to rock art sites at **Cuesta Palmarito**. Following approval from the office in San Ignacio, the local INAH representative will arrange guides and mules for US$10.50 a day.

Punta Abreojos

Reached by a 60-mile (95km) graded road that leaves the Transpeninsular about 16 miles (26km) west of San Ignacio, Punta Abreojos is one of the prime fishing spots on Baja's Pacific coast. Cabaña accommodations are available at ***Campo René (☎ 1-157-00-72, fax 1-157-04-77)***; it's about a 20-minute drive from Punta Abreojos.

Laguna San Ignacio

Along with Laguna Ojo de Liebre and Bahía Magdalena, Laguna San Ignacio is one of the major winter whale-watching sites on Baja's Pacific coast, with probably the highest concentration of 'friendly' whales of any location.

Whale-watching excursions take place from December 15 to April 15, but whales

Primary mode of tranport in the sierra

CENTRAL BAJA

are most abundant in January, February and March. In other seasons, the area is an outstanding site for bird-watching in the stunted mangroves and at offshore **Isla Pelícanos**, where about 150 ospreys and as many as 5000 cormorants nest (landing on the island is prohibited, but pangas may approach it).

This is not Baja's best fishing area, but cabrilla, corvina, grouper, halibut and sierra are found here, and boats can be hired. Keep in mind that fishing is not allowed during whale season. Sea kayaking is allowed – but only in the mangroves, not in the main lagoon.

No Salt, Por Favor

Having survived and recovered from the brutality of commercial whaling, the California gray whale still faces contemporary challenges in Baja California. Recently it was an innocent bystander in a tug-of-war between Mexican government agencies with dramatically different visions of the future of Laguna San Ignacio.

The point of contention was a 203-sq-mile (520-sq-km) saltworks, which Exportadora de Sal (ESSA) wanted to establish at the 184-sq-mile (470-sq-km) lagoon. Those statistics deceptively understate the scale of the project, since ancillary works would have directly affected 819 sq miles (2100 sq km) and indirectly affected up to 5850 sq miles (15,000 sq km) of El Vizcaíno Biosphere Reserve. ESSA, a Guerrero Negro–based and state-owned enterprise with a large holding (49%) by the Japanese multinational Mitsubishi Corporation, proposed a 1-mile (1.6km) canal to pump water continuously from Laguna San Ignacio to a 300-sq-km system of dikes and ponds. A 15-mile (25km) conveyor belt would have shifted the salt to a 1¼-mile (2km) pier near Punta Abreojos, northwest of the lagoon. Projected production was 7 million tons of salt yearly, which would have made ESSA the world's largest salt producer.

Mexico's powerful Secretaría de Comercio y Fomento Industrial (Secofi, Secretariat of Commerce and Industrial Development) backed the project, but the resolute Instituto Nacional de Ecología (INE, National Ecology Institute) vigorously objected because of the potential impact on the gray whale, the endangered peninsular pronghorn antelope and the mangrove wetlands that serve as incubators for fish and shellfish. The impact on the whales, was the biggest, literally and figuratively, and most controversial issue.

Nobody really knows how much disruption the whales can tolerate during courtship and during the birth and raising of their young. ESSA claims that whale numbers have doubled in its three decades of operations at Laguna Ojo de Liebre, but conservationists are skeptical of the company's data. In addition, less than half of the narrower and shallower Laguna San Ignacio is suitable for whales. It might also suffer more from turbulence caused by pumping, which could reduce salinity and temperature in areas frequented by newborn calves. While gray whales have adapted to some human activities at Ojo de Liebre, studies have shown that noises such as oil drilling seriously disturb the big creatures.

The proposed saltworks became an environmental cause célèbre, and Mitsubishi was the target of a vigorous letter-writing and boycott campaign. Organizations such as the US-based Natural Resources Defense Council (NRDC) and the International Fund for Animal Welfare made stopping the project their number-one environmental priority in Mexico.

In March 2000, environmentalists finally won a major victory when President Ernesto Zedillo unexpectedly announced that the Mexican government was canceling the project in order to preserve the entire Vizcaíno Biosphere Reserve. Speaking at a meeting on national environmental policy, President Zedillo said, 'We're dealing with a unique place in the world both for the species that inhabit it and for its natural beauty, which we should preserve.'

At La Laguna and La Fridera fish camps on the southern shore of the lagoon, whale-watching excursions of about three hours cost around US$30 per person. Other guides include Maldo Fischer, at Campo Catarina, or Jorge Peon Rico at La Pista. Camping at each of these places ranges from US$5 to US$10. Free camping is permitted in some areas as well.

Kuyima (☎ /fax 1-154-00-70), a cooperative with offices on the plaza in San Ignacio, operates a whale-watching camp consisting of 20 tent spaces and 10 cabañas. Reservations are required for the cabañas. Rates are about US$150 per night per person, which includes all meals and the whale-watching boat excursion. (Kuyima generally arranges for package trips, including accommodations, guided hikes, bird-watching, nature videos and the whale-watching excursion.) Single-night camping is available in tent spaces and RV sites for US$10 per night.

Camp guests have access to solar shower bags and very clean flush toilets using sea-water; the camp itself is spotless and the English-speaking staff is friendly. Meals may be available for drop-ins – the food is excellent and abundant – but mealtimes are fixed (8 am for breakfast, 1 pm for lunch and 7:30 pm for dinner) and camp guests have priority. Kuyima's cozy solar-powered dining room, out of the prevailing winds, has whale and natural history videos, as well as a library of natural history books.

The road from San Ignacio has deteriorated in recent years; most passenger cars need at least two hours to cover the 40 miles (65km) to La Fridera fish camp (assuming no rain has fallen recently) without wrecking their suspension. The first half of the road from the village is spine-wrenching washboard, but the second half is notably better.

The village of San Juanico, known for good surfing, is about 60 miles south of La Fridera via a graded but potentially hazardous road. The village is more safely reached from La Purísima; for details on the roads to San Juanico, see its section, later in the chapter.

SANTA ROSALÍA

Despite the nearby discovery of copper as early as the 1860s, the erstwhile company town of Santa Rosalía (population 10,190) really dates from the 1880s, when the French-owned Compañía del Boleo (one of the Rothschild family's many worldwide ventures) built it under a 99-year concession from the government of Mexican President Porfirio Díaz. Imported timber from Oregon and British Columbia frames the clapboard houses and French-style colonial homes that still stand along the main streets. The Compañía also assembled a prefabricated, galvanized-iron church designed by Alexandre Gustave Eiffel for the 1889 World Fair in Paris (see the boxed text). The church is still in use, while balconies and porches along the tree-lined streets encourage a spirited street life contrasting with the residential segregation of the mining era.

The French left by 1954, but a palpable legacy remains in the town's atypical architecture, a bakery that sells Baja's best baguettes and building codes decreeing that new construction must conform to the town's unique heritage. Most of the original ore-processing plant is intact; the Trans-peninsular passes beneath its old conveyor belt north of the turnoff into town. Celebrations of Santa Rosalía's Fundación de la Ciudad (Founding of the City) last four days in mid-October.

After the mines closed, the federal government took charge of the facilities in order to preserve jobs, but the Compañía Minera de Santa Rosalía closed in 1985, on the eve of the town's centenary, because of a high incidence of arsenic poisoning among miners and their families. There are rumors of renewed mining.

Public health problems were not the only adverse impact of mining: From the turn of the 20th century, commercial egg collectors raided the gull colonies of the Midriff Islands to supply miners and their families.

Orientation

Santa Rosalía is on the Gulf coast 45 miles (73km) east of San Ignacio and 38 miles

CENTRAL BAJA

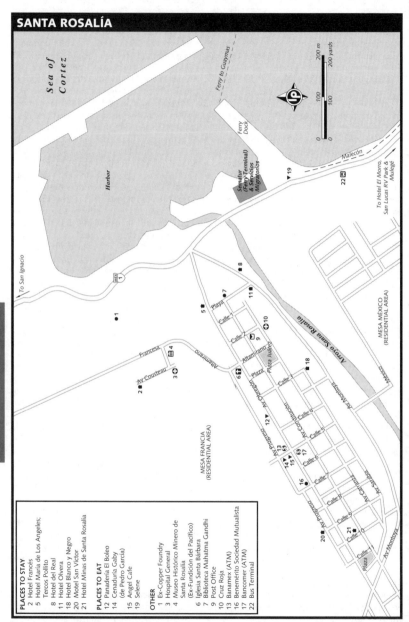

SANTA ROSALÍA

CENTRAL BAJA

PLACES TO STAY
2 Hotel Francés
5 Hotel María de Los Angeles;
   Tercos Pollito
8 Hotel del Real
11 Hotel Olvera
18 Hotel Blanco y Negro
20 Motel San Víctor
21 Hotel Minas de Santa Rosalia

PLACES TO EAT
12 Panadería El Boleo
14 Cenaduría Gaby
   (de Pedro García)
15 Angel Cafe
19 Selene

OTHER
1 Ex-Copper Foundry
3 Hospital General
4 Museo Histórico Minero de
   Santa Rosalia
   (Ex-Fundición del Pacífico)
6 Iglesia Santa Bárbara
7 Biblioteca Mahatma Gandhi
9 Post Office
10 Cruz Roja
13 Banamex (ATM)
16 Benemérito Sociedad Mutualista
17 Bancomer (ATM)
22 Bus Terminal

(61km) north of Mulegé. Most of central Santa Rosalía nestles in its namesake arroyo west of the Transpeninsular, while residential areas occupy plateaus north and south of the canyon. French administrators built their houses on the northern Mesa Francia, now home to municipal authorities, the museum and many historic buildings, whereas Mexican officials occupied the southern Mesa México.

The town's narrow avenidas run northeast-southwest; its short calles run northwest-southeast. One-way traffic is the rule. Large RVs will find it difficult to navigate around town and should park along or near the Transpeninsular.

Plaza Benito Juárez, about four blocks west of the highway, is the focus of the town. The Andador Costero, overlooking the harbor south of downtown, is an attractive *malecón* (waterfront promenade) with good views of offshore Isla Tortuga.

Information

Most tourist-oriented services are on or near Avenida Obregón, but there is no official information office.

The customs office (☎ 1-152-03-13) is in the ferry terminal.

Santa Rosalía has the only banks between Guerrero Negro and Loreto; Mulegé-bound travelers should change US dollars or traveler's checks here. Banamex and Bancomer are on opposite corners of Avenida Obregón and Calle 5; both have ATMs.

The post office is at the corner of Avenida Constitución and Calle 2; the postal code is 23920.

The Hotel del Real, on Avenida Manuel Montoya near the Transpeninsular, has long-distance services, but there are also many Ladatel public phones.

The Hospital General (☎ 1-152-07-89) overlooks the town from a hilltop site on Mesa Francia opposite the historic Fundición del Pacífico (now the town museum). The Cruz Roja (Red Cross; ☎ 1-152-06-40) is on Avenida Carranza near Calle 2.

Historic Sites

Due to its origins as a 19th-century company town, Santa Rosalía's architecture is fasci-natingly atypical for a Mexican town. Its most famous landmark, at the corner of Avenida Obregón and Altamirano, is the **Iglesia Santa Bárbara**. Designed and erected in Paris, disassembled and stored in Brussels, the structure was originally intended for West Africa but finally shipped to Mexico. Here, a director of the Compañía del Boleo stumbled upon it by chance, and in 1895 Alexandre Gustave Eiffel's prefabricated

Eiffel Beyond the Tower

Few know that French engineer Alexandre Gustave Eiffel (1832–1923), so renowned for his tower in Paris, also played a significant role in the New World. New York's Statue of Liberty is his most prominent transatlantic landmark (he was the structural engineer), but his constructions also dot the Latin American landscape from Mexico to Chile. Santa Rosalía's Iglesia Santa Bárbara is only one of many examples.

In 1868, in partnership with the engineer Théophile Seyrig, Eiffel formed G Eiffel et Compagnie, which later became the Compagnie des Etablissements Eiffel. Among their notable creations in South America were the Aduana de Arica (Customs House, 1872; Arica was part of Peru and is now part of Chile), Arica's Iglesia San Marcos, the gasworks of La Paz (Bolivia) and the railroad bridges of Oroya (Peru). Most of these were designed and built in Eiffel's workshops in the Parisian suburb of Levallois-Perret and then shipped abroad for assembly.

What might have been his greatest Latin American monument effectively ended his career. In the late 19th century, Eiffel had argued strongly in favor of building a transoceanic canal across Nicaragua, but a few years later, he obtained the contract to build the locks for Ferdinand de Lesseps' corruption-plagued French canal across Panama. Implicated in irregular contracts, Eiffel was sentenced to two years in prison and fined a substantial amount. Though his conviction was overturned, he never returned to his career as a builder.

church finally reached Santa Rosalía; it was reassembled by 1897 and adorned with attractive stained-glass windows.

On the eastern side of Playa near the Transpeninsular, the **Biblioteca Mahatma Gandhi** was another Compañía del Boleo project. The **Benemérito Sociedad Mutualista** (1916), at the corner of Avenida Obregón and Calle 7, features an interesting clock tower.

Many buildings on Mesa Francia also deserve a visit, most notably the **Fundición del Pacífico**, now a mining museum (see below), and the **Hotel Francés** (US$1 admission) as well as the ruins of the **copper foundry** along the Transpeninsular. Lined with numerous French colonial houses, Avenida Cousteau runs between the Fundición and the hotel; it also displays a wealth of antique mining equipment, including steam locomotives, mine cars and cranes.

Museo Histórico Minero de Santa Rosalía

Once the business offices (Fundición del Pacífico) of the Compañía del Boleo, this museum includes accountants' offices (now filled with scale models of historic buildings like the Benemérito Sociedad Mutualista, the Panadería El Boleo and the Cine Trianon, destroyed by fire some years ago), the purchasing office (filled with maritime memorabilia), the pay office (complete with safe) and the boardroom.

Overlooking the downtown area from Mesa Francia at the southern end of Avenida Cousteau, the museum is open 8 am to 7 pm, closed Sunday. Admission is US$1.25.

Places to Stay

About half a mile (1km) west of the Transpeninsular between Km 181 and Km 182, spacious *San Lucas RV Park* has a good beach and boat launch sites, flush toilets and hot showers. Bird-watching is good in the area. Sites cost US$6 per night.

Travelers have recommended 'very quaint' *Hotel Blanco y Negro* (☎ 1-152-00-80), at the top of a spiral staircase on the 2nd floor of a small building at Avenida Sarabia 1, which has 12 clean, basic rooms at US$13/14 singles/ doubles.

Hotel Olvera (☎ 1-152-02-67), near the corner of Avenida Montoya and Playa, is one of the best deals in town for budget travelers. Spotless wood-paneled rooms, most with carpets and fans, cost US$14/19. Rates rise by about US$2 in summer to compensate for the increased use of air-conditioning.

Hotel del Real (☎ 1-152-00-68), on Avenida Montoya, has small, clean and air-conditioned rooms for US$16/21. Tidy *Motel San Víctor* (☎ 1-152-01-16, Avenida Progreso 36), at the corner of Calle 9, is a pleasant, family-run operation on a shady, quiet street. Its 12 rooms, all with overhead fans and tiled bath, cost US$13/16. *Hotel María de los Angeles* (☎ 1-152-00-75), part of the Tercos Pollito restaurant at the entrance to town, has clean but dark rooms for US$19/21.

Trying awkwardly to capitalize on the town's historic past, the modern but drab *Hotel Minas de Santa Rosalía* (☎ 1-152-10-60), a seemingly half-finished project at the corner of Avenida Constitución and Calle 10, has rooms for US$26.

Hotel Francés (☎ 1-152-20-52, Avenida Cousteau 15), at Mesa Francia, once catered to French idiosyncrasies but now offers an atmospheric bar/restaurant (open 6 am to 11 pm daily), a small swimming pool, wonderful views of the rusting copper foundry and air-conditioned rooms for US$35.

Santa Rosalía's best accommodations are at the cliffside *Hotel El Morro* (☎ 1-152-23-90, fax 1-152-04-14), about 1 mile (1.6km) south of town, just off the Transpeninsular. Along with sea views and a relaxed atmosphere, it offers a swimming pool, restaurant and bar for just US$24/26 a night.

Places to Eat

Taco stands are numerous along Avenida Obregón, but most of them serve nothing but beef. For standard antojitos at good prices, try *Cenaduría Gaby (de Pedro García)*, on Calle 5 just north of Avenida Obregón. *Angel Cafe*, on Obregón at the corner of Calle 5, serves sandwiches and hamburgers in a nice, open patio.

Tercos Pollito (☎ 1-152-00-75), on Avenida Obregón near Playa, in the Hotel María de Los Angeles, specializes in

The US-Mexico (Me Co?) border

RICK GERHARTER

Frontón Palacio on Avenida Revolución (Tijuana)

RICHARD CUMMINS

Woman statue, 56 feet tall (Tijuana)

DAVID PEEVERS

Huichol crafts in the Bazar de México (Tijuana)

DAVID PEEVERS

Floating on Bahía de los Angeles

View from El Mirador (Km 84, La Frontera)

Objets d'art at Coco's Corner (Desierto Central)

chicken but also serves meat and lobster lunches and dinners. South of downtown, the waterfront **Selene** (☎ 1-152-06-85) serves sumptuous seafood dishes at upscale prices.

Started by the French when mining operations were in full swing at the turn of the 20th century, **Panadería El Boleo** (☎ 1-152-03-10) is on Avenida Obregón between Calle 3 and Calle 4. For many travelers, it's an obligatory stop for delicious Mexican and French breads and pastries. Baking begins at 4 am daily, but baguettes usually sell out by 10 am. Occasionally, there's an afternoon batch as well.

The restaurant at Hotel Francés (see Places to Stay), enjoying the same resurgent popularity as the hotel, is well worth a stop, though the service can be slow.

Getting There & Away

Santa Rosalía's small marina offers some possibilities for catching a ride by private yacht north or south along the Gulf coast or across to mainland Mexico.

Bus Autotransportes Aguila and ABC buses between Tijuana and La Paz stop at Santa Rosalía's Terminal de Autobuses (☎ 1-152-01-50), on the western side of the Transpeninsular opposite the malecón. Northbound buses go to Guerrero Negro at 3 pm, to Tijuana and intermediate stops at 4 and 5 am and 5 and 6 pm, and to Mexicali and intermediate stops at midnight. Sample fares are as follows:

San Ignacio – US$7, one hour; 12, 4 & 5 am, 3, 5 & 6 pm

Vizcaíno – US$10.50, two hours; 12, 4 & 5 am, 3, 5 & 6 pm

Guerrero Negro – US$14, four hours; 12, 4 & 5 am, 3, 5 & 6 pm

San Quintín – US$32.50, nine hours; 12, 4 & 5 am, 5 & 6 pm

Colonia Vicente Guerrero – US$33, 11 hours; 12, 4 & 5 am, 5 & 6 pm

Ensenada – US$42, 12 hours; 12, 4 & 5 am, 5 & 6 pm

Tijuana – US$48, 14 hours; 12, 4 & 5 am, 5 & 6 pm

Mexicali – US$59, 16 hours; 12 am

Southbound buses to La Paz and intermediate stops pass at 9, 10 and 11:30 am, and 9:30 pm. Approximate fares are US$4 to Mulegé (one hour); US$10 to Loreto (three hours); US$16 to Ciudad Constitución (five hours) and US$25 to La Paz (eight hours).

Ferry The Sematur ferry terminal (☎ 1-152-00-13/14) is just south of Arroyo Santa Rosalía, right along the Transpeninsular. Ferries sail to the mainland Mexican town of Guaymas (an eight-hour journey without delays) at 9 am Wednesday and Friday; strong winter winds can cause long delays. The return ferries leave from Guaymas at 9 am and arrive in Santa Rosalía at 3:30 pm Tuesday and Thursday.

Ticket windows are open 8 am to 3 pm Monday, Tuesday, Thursday and Saturday, 7 am to 2 pm Wednesday and Friday, closed Sunday. Pregnant women are not allowed on the ferry. Make reservations at least three days in advance and, even if you have reservations, arrive early at the ticket office.

It is not possible to obtain a mainland vehicle permit at Santa Rosalía, so get one at the US border or Ensenada; otherwise you have to go to La Paz. For more information about permits, see Vehicle Permits in the Getting Around chapter.

Approximate one-way fares from Santa Rosalía are as follows: In *Salón* class, US$21; in *Turista*, US$42; in *Cabina*, US$63; in *Especial*, US$84.

Vehicle rates are as follows:

length	price
Up to 5m*	US$205
5.01 to 6.5m	US$266
With trailer up to 9m	US$368
9.01 to 17m	US$694
Motor home	US$429
Motorcycle	US$47
*1m = 3 feet 3 inches	

ISLA SAN MARCOS

At 6 am every Friday, a free boat carries residents of the magnesium mining settlement on this offshore island to their weekly

CENTRAL BAJA

shopping spree in Santa Rosalía. Travelers interested in hiking the island are welcome to hop aboard the return voyage at 10:30 am (ask at the harbor for the exact docking site), but you will have to wait a week or contract a launch to return to the mainland. It's also possible to hire a boat in the tiny fish camp of San Bruno, about midway between Santa Rosalía and Mulegé, and visit an offshore sea lion colony.

Sierra de la Giganta

The Sierra de la Giganta parallels the Gulf, dividing the region into an eastern semitropical zone and a western region of arid lowlands and high plateaus.

MULEGÉ

South of Santa Rosalía, the Transpeninsular tracks the base of the eastern scarp of the northern edge of the Sierra de la Giganta, passing the peninsula of Punta Chivato before winding through the Sierra Azteca and dropping into the subtropical oasis of Mulegé (population 3169). Beaches to the south along Bahía Concepción attract more conventional vacationers than do areas to the north, but the Mulegé area is especially popular with divers.

Mulegé straddles the verdant Arroyo Santa Rosalía (also known as Río Mulegé) about 2 miles (3km) inland from the Sea of Cortez. Scrawny mangroves extend along the lower reaches of the river's estuary, frequented by large numbers of birds, while date palms line its banks farther inland. Avoid swimming at the badly polluted mouth of the estuary.

Information

Mulegé has no formal tourist office. The bulk of visitor services are on the northern side of the river, on or near Jardín Corona, the town plaza. If you're planning on spending quite a bit of time around here, you might consider buying Kerry Otterstrom's self-published guidebook, *Mulegé,* available around town or from the writer himself, who works at the popular bar/restaurant El

Candil. From December to April, the biweekly English-language paper, the *Mulegé Post,* is another useful source of information, including data like tide tables.

Visitors needing to change traveler's checks or obtain cash advances on credit cards should do so in Santa Rosalía or Loreto, the closest towns with banks, before arriving in Mulegé. Many Mulegé merchants will change US dollars or accept them as payment.

Mulegé's post office is on Avenida General Martínez, almost across from the Pemex station; the postal code is 23900.

Long-distance telephone and fax services are available at the Mini Super Padilla grocery on Zaragoza at Avenida General Martínez (fax 1-153-01-90), and there are plenty of Ladatel phones around town.

Efficient Lavamática Claudia (☎ 1-153-00-57), at the corner of Zaragoza and Moctezuma, is open 8 am to 7 pm daily except Sunday. A full load costs about US$3, washed, dried and folded. The laundromat is also a community meeting place with a useful bulletin board, worth checking for rides and the like.

For medical needs, Mulegé's Centro de Salud is on Madero (☎ 1-153-02-98) opposite the Canett Casa de Huéspedes.

Drivers of large RVs (or anything bigger than a van conversion) should not even consider entering downtown Mulegé's narrow, irregular and sometimes steep streets. Besides risking scrapes and dents to your vehicle, you're likely to cause serious and potentially hazardous congestion. Visitors who park downtown should pay special attention to red zones – parking in one can tie up traffic for hours.

Aqua 2000, on Avenida General Martínez east of Zaragoza, sells purified water and ice at reasonable prices.

Misión Santa Rosalía

Across the Transpeninsular and near the southern bank of the river, restored Misión Santa Rosalía de Mulegé stands atop a hill above the town. Founded in 1705 and completed in 1766, the mission functioned until 1828, when the declining Indian population

SIERRA DE LA GIGANTA & LLANO DE MAGDALENA

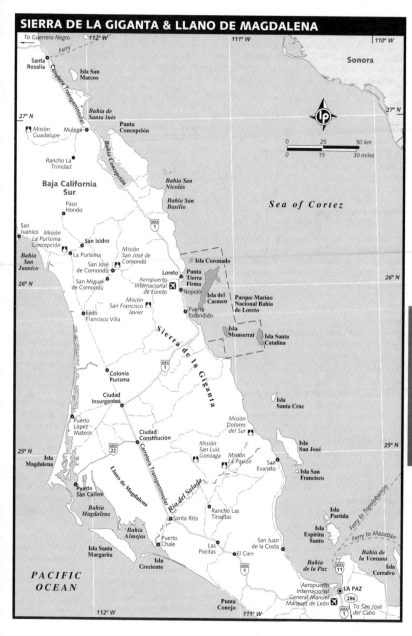

To Guerrero Negro
112° W
111° W
110° W

Ferry

Sonora

Santa
Rosalía

Isla San
Marcos

Bahía de
Santa Inés

Punta
Concepción

27° N   27° N

Misión
Guadalupe   Mulegé

Rancho La
Trinidad

Baja California
Sur

Bahía San
Nicolás

Paso
Hondo

Bahía San
Basilio

Sea of Cortez

MEX 1

San
Juanico   Misión
La Purísima
Concepción

San Isidro

Misión
San José de
Comondú

Bahía
San
Juanico

La Purísima

San José
de Comondú

Isla Coronado

San Miguel
de Comondú

Aeropuerto
Internacional
de Loreto

Loreto

Punta
Tierra
Firma

26° N   26° N

Nopoló

Misión
San Francisco
Javier

Ejido
Francisco Villa

Isla del
Carmen

Parque Marino
Nacional Bahía
de Loreto

Puerto
Escondido

Isla
Monserrat

Isla Santa
Catalina

Colonia
Purisma

MEX 1

Ciudad
Insurgentes

Isla
Santa Cruz

Misión
Dolores
del Sur

Puerto
López
Mateos

Ciudad
Constitución

MEX 22

Isla
San José

25° N   25° N

Misión
San Luis
Gonzaga

Misión
La Pasión

San
Evaristo

Isla
Magdalena

Isla San
Francisco

Puerto
San Carlos

Bahía
Magdalena

Rancho Las
Tinajitas

Isla
Partida

Bahía
Almejas

Santa Rita

Puerto
Chale

Las
Pocitas

San Juan
de la Costa

Isla
Espíritu
Santo

Isla Santa
Margarita

Isla
Creciente

El Cien

MEX 1

Bahía
de la Paz

Bahía de
la Ventana

PACIFIC
OCEAN

Aeropuerto
Internacional
General Manuel
Márquez de León

MEX 286

LA PAZ

MEX 11

Isla
Cerralvo

Punta
Conejo

To San José
del Cabo

112° W
111° W

Ferry to Topolobampo

Ferry to Mazatlán

CENTRAL BAJA

led to its abandonment. Remodeled several times, the church is less architecturally distinguished than its counterparts at San Ignacio and San Borja – it is imposing but utilitarian, with fewer enticing details. The exterior is still faithful to the original, but the succeeding centuries have greatly altered the interior.

Behind the church, a short footpath climbs a volcanic outcrop to an overlook with soothing views of the palm-lined Arroyo Santa Rosalía and its surroundings. This is one of the visual highlights of the area, well worth a detour even for travelers not intending to stay in town.

Museo Mulegé

Federal inmates from Mulegé's 'prison without doors,' a strikingly whitewashed neocolonial building on Cananea, overlooking the town, traditionally enjoyed a great deal of liberty. Except for the most serious felons, who were confined in its inner compound, prisoners at the Prisión Federal Territorial usually left at 6 am for jobs in town, returning at 6 pm; in some cases. They could even attend town dances and a number of them married locally.

Now the town museum, the building was to undergo a major restoration after decades of neglect, but there's been little progress since the peso crisis of 1994. Its interesting but eclectic artifacts – archaeological and religious materials, cotton gins, antique diving equipment and firearms – are more coherently organized than in the past, but pigeons perch in and soil nearly every room in the building. The museum is open 9 am to 1 pm weekdays (free admission).

Activities

Mulegé's best **diving** spots are around the Santa Inés Islands (north of town) and just north of Punta Concepción. There is excellent beach diving and snorkeling at Punta Prieta, near the lighthouse at the mouth of Arroyo Santa Rosalía.

Cortez Explorers (formerly Mulegé Divers, ☎/fax 1-153-05-00), at Moctezuma 75A, owned by a Swiss couple, offers diving instruction and excursions, snorkel equip-

ment rental and bike rental. It's open 10 am to 1 pm and 4 to 7 pm, closed Sunday. A four-hour scuba course costs US$70, including all equipment and a guided underwater dive tour. Diving excursions (including a boat, a dive-master guide, two tanks and a weight belt) cost US$50; there is a minimum charge of US$100 (two-person minimum). Snorkeling trips cost US$25 to US$30 per person, with a US$70 minimum (two-person minimum).

Rental equipment is also available on a daily basis, including buoyancy compensators (US$8 each), weight belts (US$3), tanks with air (US$7), regulators with pressure gauge and depth gauge (US$8), wet suit jackets (US$5) and masks and fins (US$5). Check out its Web site at www.cortez-explorer.com for more information.

For **mountain biking**, Cortez Explorers offers bike rentals for US$15 the first day, US$10 the following days.

Mulegé is a popular **fishing** destination as well. Game-fish species available all year in the area include bonito, cabrilla, corvina, crevallo, grouper, pargo, sierra and skipjack. Seasonal species include dorado (May to November), needlefish (June to November), roosterfish (April to October), sailfish (July to October), striped marlin (June to October) and the especially popular yellowtail (November to May). Wahoo make rare appearances.

Bahía Concepción, south of Mulegé, is the main destination for **sea kayaking**. El Candil (see Places to Eat, later) rents kayaks for US$29 per day.

Places to Stay

Mulegé lacks upscale accommodations; visitors seeking luxury will have to lower their sights, but the general quality of lodging is good.

Camping Eastbound Madero and Romero Rubio merge into a single dirt road leading to *beach camping* areas near the lighthouse, 2 miles (3km) northeast of town. This is also a popular party spot for local youth, so there's no guarantee of any sleep, at least on weekends.

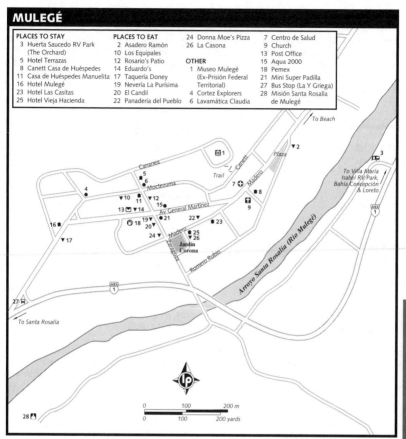

MULEGÉ

PLACES TO STAY
3 Huerta Saucedo RV Park
   (The Orchard)
7 Hotel Terrazas
8 Canett Casa de Huéspedes
11 Casa de Huéspedes Manuelita
16 Hotel Mulegé
23 Hotel Las Casitas
25 Hotel Vieja Hacienda

PLACES TO EAT
2 Asadero Ramón
10 Los Equipales
12 Rosario's Patio
14 Eduardo's
17 Taquería Doney
19 Nevería La Purísima
20 El Candil
22 Panadería del Pueblo

24 Donna Moe's Pizza
26 La Casona

OTHER
1 Museo Mulegé
   (Ex-Prisión Federal
   Territorial)
4 Cortez Explorers
6 Lavamática Claudia

7 Centro de Salud
9 Church
13 Post Office
15 Aqua 2000
18 Pemex
21 Mini Super Padilla
27 Bus Stop (La Y Griega)
28 Misión Santa Rosalía
   de Mulegé

Abounding with palms, mangoes and citrus, friendly **Huerta Saucedo RV Park** (popularly known as 'The Orchard'; ☎ 1-153-03-00) is half a mile (1km) east of town on the river side of the Transpeninsular. RVs driving from central Mulegé should take the highway or the road that passes beneath the Transpeninsular bridge; only small vehicles should take the road on the river's south bank. Spaces with full hookups cost US$16; those without are US$5 for two people, plus US$1.50 for each additional person. Hot (sometimes lukewarm) showers, decent toilets and a boat ramp are available. Canoe

rentals are US$3.50 per hour; paddleboats are US$4 per hour. The park also offers frequent Mexican buffets and other special meals at bargain prices.

Just beyond Huerta Saucedo, **Villa María Isabel RV Park** (☎ /fax 1-153-02-46) charges US$6 per person for sites without hookups, US$15 with full hookups, but the real reason to stop here is the fabulous bread and cinnamon rolls at its first-rate bakery – well worth a stop.

Guesthouses Cheapest of Mulegé's several guesthouses is the plain, eight-room **Canett**

Casa de Huéspedes (☎ *1-153-02-72*) on Madero. It's not a bad place, but late sleepers should know that the church bells across the street chime loudly every quarter-hour from 6 am; singles/doubles with private bath cost just US$10.50/13.

Casa de Huéspedes Manuelita (☎ *1-153-01-75*), kitty-corner from Lavamática Claudia on Moctezuma, offers rooms for US$13.

Hotels & Motels Friendly and modern *Hotel Mulegé* (☎ *1-153-00-90*), near the Y-intersection at the entrance to town, has singles/doubles for US$24/29.

Sharing a courtyard with its namesake restaurant, *Hotel Las Casitas* (☎ *1-153-00-19*, *fax 1-153-01-90*), on Madero near the junction with Avenida General Martínez, was once home to poet Alán Gorosave. All rooms have hot showers, air-con and plenty of shade trees in front. Rooms cost US$20/24. *Hotel Terrazas* (☎ *1-153-00-09*), on Zaragoza just north of Lavamática Claudia, has 20 fine rooms with views for US$31.

Suffering from frequent management changes, *Hotel Vieja Hacienda* (☎ *1-153-00-21, Madero 3*), at the northeastern corner of the plaza, seems to be an ongoing construction project. Rooms with twin beds, fridge, air-con and hot showers cost US$31. There's a small pool, a bar and a shady patio.

Places to Eat

Nevería La Purísima, on Zaragoza next to El Candil, serves homemade Mexican-style ice cream. For homemade bread and pastries, try the *Panadería del Pueblo*, on Madero across the street from Las Casitas.

At the western end of Mulegé just before the Transpeninsular, *Taquería Doney* serves up some of the region's best tacos. *Donna Moe's Pizza*, at the northwestern corner of the plaza, draws steady crowds as well.

At the intersection of Romero Rubio and Madero, *Asadero Ramón* (formerly Taquería Dany's) offers a variety of fillings, from carne asada to carnitas to chicken to fish. Prices are more than reasonable. *La Almeja*, on the beach near the road to the lighthouse, serves low-priced beer, fish tacos and other seafood.

Local expatriates suggest *Eduardo's* (☎ *1-153-02-58*), across from the Pemex station on Avenida General Martínez, which has transcended its fast-food origins to offer varied cuisine, including Friday ribs and a Sunday Chinese special. *El Candil*, on Zaragoza near the plaza, has filling meat and seafood dishes at moderate prices. Its bar is a popular gringo meeting place, with international sports on satellite TV, but later in the evening it draws a more Mexican crowd.

Try *Las Casitas* (☎ *1-153-00-19*) on Madero at the Hotel Las Casitas, one of Mulegé's more upscale places, for typical antojitos (with daily specials) and a few seafood dishes, plus unusual drinks like mango daiquiris. A good breakfast value is the generous combination fruit plate. Popular *La Casona* (☎ *1-153-02-08, Madero 3*) is a large, open restaurant with food ranging from antojitos to steak sandwiches. *Rosario's Patio*, on Zaragoza between Moctezuma and General Martinez, serves similar fare.

Specializing in Sonoran beef, *Los Equipales* (☎ *1-153-03-30*), on Moctezuma just west of Zaragoza, serves outstanding meals that, if dearer than most in town, are worth the money.

Getting There & Away

Mulegé has no formal bus terminal, but buses running from Tijuana to La Paz stop daily at the Y-junction (known locally as 'La Y Griega') on the Transpeninsular at the western edge of town. Buy tickets at the store up the hill from the stop.

Santa Rosalía – US$4, one hour; 4 & 7 pm

Loreto – US$6, two hours; 10:30 & 11 am, 2, 8:30 & 10 pm

Ciudad Constitución – US$13, four hours; 10:30 & 11 am, 2, 8:30 & 10 pm

La Paz – US$22, seven hours; 10:30 & 11 am, 2, 8:30 & 10 pm

Ensenada – US$42, 13 hours; 4:30 & 10:30 pm

Tijuana – US$48, 15 hours; 4:30 & 10:30 pm

AROUND MULEGÉ
Cañón La Trinidad

In Cañón La Trinidad, 18 miles (29km) southwest of Mulegé via a bumpy dirt road (passable for most vehicles with high clearance), visitors can go on a hike-and-swim excursion to view several pre-Columbian rock art sites in impressive volcanic overhangs. Another route involves hiking only, but it's longer and less interesting than passing through the canyon's deep pools, especially when the weather's hot. The drive to the canyon from Mulegé involves taking several unmarked junctions from the westbound (San Estanislao) road and can be difficult for a first-timer.

The rock paintings themselves are multicolored Cochimí depictions of human figures and wildlife, including fish and sea turtles. Those at the lower site, visited prior to the swim up the canyon, are more vivid and better preserved, thanks to their more sheltered location. All visitors must check in with the INAH caretakers at Rancho La Trinidad, who lead hikes up the canyon for a very modest fee.

Longtime Mulegé resident Kerry Otterstrom, a bartender at El Candil (see Places to Eat under Mulegé, earlier), leads day trips to Cochimí rock art sites at Cañón La Trinidad for US$25 per person and overnight trips for US$50. The day hikes include a hot

AROUND MULEGÉ

To Santa Rosalía
Isla San Marcos
La Mina
Piedra Lobos
San Bruno
MEX 1

Boca de Magdalena

Carretera Transpeninsular

Punta Chivato
Punta Santa Inés
Isla Alto
Isla Razo
Isla Santa Inés
Bahía de Santa Inés
Playa Santa Inés

Sea of Cortez

0   5   10 km
0   3   6 miles

Dive Site

CENTRAL BAJA

Punta Prieta
Lighthouse
Punta Santo Domingo
Mulegé
MEX 1

Punta Concepción
Punta Pilares
Punta María
Punta La Trinidad

To Misión Guadalupe

Posada Concepción
EcoMundo
Playa Santispac
Playa Escondida
Playa El Burro
Playa El Coyote
Isla Coyote
Isla Guapa
Playa Buenaventura
El Requesón
Playa La Perla
Playa Armenta

Cerro Colorado
▲ 490m

Punta Santa Rosa
Punta Colorada
Bahía San Lino
Punta Santa Teresa

Sierra Los Gavilanes

Rancho La Trinidad

Cañón La Trinidad

Sierra Coyote

Bahía Concepción
Punta La Pasajera

Isla San Ildefonso

Bahía San Nicolás

San Sebastián

Punta Pulpito

MEX 1
To San Isidro, La Purísima & Loreto

meal (all-you-can-eat bean burritos with fresh vegetables) and cold beer or soda at Rancho La Trinidad at the end of the hike. Day trips leave from El Candil at 9 am (make reservations there in advance). The trip entails an 18-mile drive into the canyon, followed by a 3½ mile (5.5km) hike. Otterstrom provides dry bags for carrying camera equipment through the canyon as well as wet suits for winter trips, when the air temperature is generally pleasant but the water in the shady canyon can be chilly.

Another bilingual guide is Salvador Castro (☎ 1-153-02-32).

Misión Guadalupe

The dirt road leading from Mulegé to the Rancho La Trinidad junction continues onward to San Estanislao. There, a marked branch leads to the ruins of remote Misión Nuestra Señora de Guadalupe de Huasinapi (established 1720), of which only foundations remain.

BAHÍA CONCEPCIÓN

Along Bahía Concepción, south of Mulegé, are more than 50 miles (80km) of beaches; the most accessible (and most crowded) run along the western edge of the bay, but few people travel the dirt road to Punta Concepción at the peninsula's northern tip. Camping is possible on almost every beach in the area, but most of the best sites charge for the privilege.

EcoMundo

Established in 1989, the EcoMundo kayaking and natural history center is an extension of Roy Mahoff and Becky Aparicio's longrunning Baja Tropicales company. Baja Tropicales continues to offer local kayak trips from its facilities, south of Mulegé at Km 111 of the Transpeninsular, between Posada Concepción and Playa Escondido. In addition to accommodations (see Places to Stay & Eat, below), the EcoMundo project includes an educational center (a natural history museum is planned for the future). It also has a recycling site.

Baja Tropicales' guided kayak day trips on Bahía Concepción cost US$49 per person, including meals and beverages, for a minimum of four people. Experienced kayakers may rent kayaks for US$25 per day. Snorkeling gear can be rented for US$5. For more information, inquire at Hotel Las Casitas in Mulegé or contact Baja Tropicales (☎/fax 1-153-04-09, ecomundo@aol.com), Apdo Postal 60, Mulegé, Baja California Sur 23900, México.

Places to Stay & Eat

EcoMundo (see above) has accommodations, including bungalows (with hammocks or cots and lights) for US$12 and tent sites for US$6. Hot showers and outhouses are available, and the restaurant offers breakfast and lunch.

At *Playa Santispac*, 13 miles (21km) south of Mulegé, 35 campsites with palapas at water's edge are available for US$6 apiece. Amenities are limited, but there are cold showers; bring drinking water. *Ana's* has served meals, freshly baked bread and desserts for more than a decade here, and also sells groceries. Large RVs can't use the narrow beachside road south of the main area, which leads to less crowded spots.

Playa El Burro is just south of EcoMundo. Consisting of a large stretch of beach, this is a very pleasant place to camp; sites are US$6. Outhouses and showers are available, and flush toilets are being built. *Bertha's Restaurant* on the beach offers some of the best breakfasts in the area.

RV Park El Coyote, 18 miles (29km) south of Mulegé, is a fine area for beach camping, although it's close to the highway and often unpleasantly crowded. Rates are about US$6 per vehicle.

South, at Km 94.5 of the Transpeninsular, the area's best accommodations are at *Resort Hotel San Buenaventura* (☎/fax 1-153-04-08). It's an attractive stone building with singles/doubles, each with its own shaded patio, starting at US$50/62. It is also possible to camp on the beach for US$10 or to rent a cabaña (with two cots, lights and a fan) for US$20. There's a boat launch at the beach, and kayaks are available for rent. Also on site is *George's Olé Sports Bar & Grill*.

El Requesón, 28 miles (45km) south of Mulegé, once made a *Condé Nast Traveler* list of Mexico's top 10 beaches, but its scanty services keep it suitable for short-term camping only. One attractive feature is the *tombolo* (sandspit beach) that connects it to offshore Isla El Requesón except during very high tides. Despite its proximity to the highway, it's relatively quiet; camping here is free.

A short distance south of El Requesón is *La Perla*, where camping sites are US$5. It's a small beach but doesn't tend to get as crowded as some of the other beaches in the area. Free camping is possible at *Playa Armenta*, just south of La Perla. It has a short but sandy beach, and although it's more exposed to the highway than El Requesón, it's less crowded.

SAN ISIDRO & LA PURÍSIMA

South of Bahía Concepción, the paved Transpeninsular continues to Loreto, but at Km 60 a graded alternative route crosses the Sierra de la Giganta to the twin villages of San Isidro and La Purísima, both also accessible by a very good paved highway from Ciudad Insurgentes (see San José de Comondú, later). Travelers who prefer not to retrace their steps may wish to take the graded road either north- or southbound. Drivers with high-clearance vehicles will find it more enjoyable, whereas those with RVs or trailers will find it difficult; 4WD is unnecessary, however.

This area was the site of **Misión La Purísima Concepción**, founded in 1717 by Jesuit Nicolás Tamaral, but only foundations remain. The major landmark is the steep-sided volcanic plug of **El Pilón**, a challenge for technical climbers, which lies between the two villages. From La Purísima, a graded road goes northwest to San Juanico, one of the Pacific coast's prime surf spots, and to Laguna San Ignacio, a major whale-watching area. See their entries, later in this chapter.

Neither San Isidro nor La Purísima has a Pemex station, but private gasoline sellers offer both Nova and Magna Sin at about a 25% markup – look for hand-painted signs.

San Isidro's very simple *Motel Nelva*, behind the church and conveniently adjacent to the bus terminal, charges US$6 per person; the shared baths have hot water. San Isidro has a basic lonchería and a taco stand, while La Purísima has a taco stand and the ordinary *Restaurant Claudia*, with basic antojitos and a few seafood dishes.

San Isidro and La Purísima offer bus service to La Paz (US$7, five hours; daily at 6:30 am and 3 pm) with Autotransportes Aguila, which picks up most of its passengers in Ciudad Constitución. Buses leave from San Isidro and pass through La Purísima.

Paso Hondo, 19 miles (31km) north of San Isidro by a dirt road (inquire at the bus terminal about its condition), features Cochimí rock art sites.

SAN JOSÉ DE COMONDÚ

South of San Isidro, a bumpy, rocky, undulating road (which is never really difficult, at least for high-clearance vehicles) crosses a volcanic upland before dropping steeply into San José de Comondú, site of the Jesuit **Misión San José de Comondú**. The temple dates from the 1750s, although the mission proper began in 1707.

San José de Comondú, midway between the Pacific Ocean and the Sea of Cortez, was a promising site for a mission because of its perennial spring, where several groups of Indians lived. The Jesuit Franz Inama, an Austrian, oversaw the construction of the church, abandoned in 1827 and demolished in part at the turn of the century. Harry Crosby's *Antigua California*, working from probably the most elaborate records available for any Jesuit mission in Baja, recreates daily life at San José de Comondú in considerable detail.

Only part of the mission temple remains intact, but there are extensive walls surrounding it. Restoration is lagging, but the building contains good examples of traditional religious art, though the canvases are deteriorating badly. Note the historic photos, dated 1901, when a major *recova* (colonnade) and two short *campanarios* (bell towers) still existed. Ask for the key to the temple at the bright-green house 30 yards to the east.

West of San José de Comondú is its almost equally picturesque twin, **San Miguel de Comondú**. Most inhabitants of the area are fair-skinned descendants of early Spanish pioneers, in contrast to later mestizo arrivals from mainland Mexico.

For vehicles without high clearance, access to San José de Comondú is easier by a graded lateral from Ejido Francisco Villa that leaves the paved highway about 40 miles (64km) north of Ciudad Insurgentes. One tricky stream ford may present problems for vehicles with low clearance.

Driving north from San José de Comondú to San Isidro, the steep climb over loose rock may cause some problems. At the crest of the hill, take the left fork to San Isidro.

SAN JUANICO
About 30 miles (48km) northwest of La Purísima and 60 miles (97km) south of Laguna San Ignacio, the village of San Juanico is well known among surfers for nearby **Punta Pequeña** at the northern end of Bahía San Juanico. Its right-point breaks, some believe, provide the highest-quality surf on the peninsula in a southern swell. The best months for surfing are September and October. Other area activities include windsurfing, sea kayaking, diving and sportfishing for corvina, halibut and especially roosterfish.

Scorpion Bay (☎ 1-138-28-50), a well-run campground operated by an American in cooperation with the local ejido, offers sites for US$4 per person per day. The palapa restaurant serves excellent food.

San Juanico is most easily accessed by a good graded dirt road heading north from La Purísima. Unfortunately, the road south to San Juanico from Laguna San Ignacio, despite depiction as a graded surface on the AAA map, is potentially hazardous, even for high-clearance vehicles.

The road from Laguna San Ignacio veers off from the graded road approximately 8 miles south of Laguna San Ignacio. This is the Baja 1000 road – and passable by most trucks – as long as drivers know how to

drive dirt roads. The road passes through a number of sand dunes and seems to be in the middle of nowhere, which means it's very easy to get lost and you'll be isolated if you happen to break down. If you're lucky, the drive will take about four hours.

LORETO
In 1697, the Jesuit priest and explorer Juan María Salvatierra established the Misión Nuestra Señora de Loreto on the Gulf coast as the first permanent Spanish settlement in the Californias. In concentrating local Indians at mission settlements instead of dispersed rancherías and converting them to Catholicism, the Jesuits directly extended the influence and control of the Spanish crown in one of the empire's most remote areas.

It was a convenient staging point for missionary expansion even after the official expulsion of the Jesuits in 1767 – in 1769, Franciscan Padre Junípero Serra trekked northward to found the now-famous chain of missions in mainland California. Also the first capital of the Californias, Loreto (population 9200) served that role until its near destruction by a hurricane in 1829.

Loreto's spectacularly restored mission underscores its role in the history of the Californias. The town remains a modest fishing port with cobblestone streets, though some of its historic past has now fallen beneath developers' onslaughts.

A positive development, due largely to activism by the grassroots environmental organization Grupo Ecologista Antares, is the Mexican congress' creation of Parque Marino Nacional Bahía de Loreto. Comprising 799 sq miles (2077 sq km) of shoreline and offshore islands, Baja's second offshore national park protects the areas north, south and east of town from pollution and uncontrolled fishing. The park's boundaries also overlap with the Reserva de la Biosfera Islas del Golfo, which includes all of the Sea of Cortez islands.

Loreto is an ideal base for all types of outdoor activities, and a number of outfitters cover the range from kayaking and diving along the reefs around Isla del Carmen, to horseback riding and hiking in the Sierra de la Giganta.

Loreto's main fiestas are early September's Día de Nuestra Señora de Loreto and mid-October's Fundación de la Ciudad, which celebrates the city's founding in 1699.

Orientation

Between the Transpeninsular and the shores of the Gulf of California, Loreto is 210 miles (338km) north of La Paz and 84 miles (135km) south of Mulegé. It has a slightly irregular street plan, but the colonial mission church on Salvatierra is a major landmark; most hotels and services are within easy walking distance of it.

The Plaza Cívica, as the *zócalo* (central plaza) is known, is just north of Salvatierra between Madero and Davis. Salvatierra itself is a de facto pedestrian mall (vehicle access is limited and inconvenient), lined with topiary laurels, between Independencia and the beach. The beach's attractive malecón is ideal for evening strolls along the Gulf.

Information

Tourist Offices Loreto's Departamento de Turismo Municipal (☎ 1-135-04-11, fax 1-135-07-40), in the Palacio de Gobierno on the western side of the Plaza Cívica at Madero and Salvatierra, is open 8 am to 3 pm weekdays. The staff doesn't speak much English but does have a good selection of brochures and fliers.

The Marine Park Office (☎ 1-135-04-77), next to the marina, is a good source of information for all water activities in the Gulf (including kayaking, fishing and camping on the islands). Because Loreto's shoreline and offshore islands are protected, by registering with the Marine Park you will ensure that you know all the guidelines for traveling in the park. In addition, the staff provides information about such things as fish populations, dive locales and campsite occupancy. The office is open 9 am to 3 pm Monday to Saturday.

Immigration Loreto's Oficina de Migración y Aduana (☎ 1-135-12-54) is at the airport, south of town. Its in-town office is in the Casa de la Cultura (☎ 1-135-12-66) on Paseo Tamaral.

Money Bancomer, at the corner of Salvatierra and Madero, changes US dollars and traveler's checks from 8:30 to 11:30 am with a minimum of bureaucracy; there's an ATM there as well. It sometimes runs short on cash, so it's better to get there early. The next closest full-service banks are in Santa Rosalía and Ciudad Constitución. The majority of stores in Loreto do not accept US dollars, although some may accept traveler's checks.

Post & Communications Loreto's post office is on Deportiva just north of Salvatierra; the postal code is 23880. There are Ladatel phones throughout town. Servifax, Salvatierra 75 opposite the laundry, is the best phone office but closes as early as 7 pm. There's an Internet cafe on Madero between Café Olé and Las Parras Tours. It's open 9 am to 1 pm and 4 to 7 pm weekdays, to 2:30 pm Saturday, and charges US$3 for every half hour.

Travel Agencies Viajes Pedrín (☎ 1-135-02-04, fax 1-135-07-88) is on the southern side of Avenida Miguel Hidalgo next to Hotel Plaza Loreto.

Laundry Lavandería El Remojón is located on Salvatierra between Independencia and Ayuntamiento.

Medical & Emergency Services Loreto's Centro de Salud (☎ 1-135-00-39), Salvatierra 68, is near the corner of Allende. The Cruz Roja (Red Cross; ☎ 1-135-11-11) is also on Salvatierra, just west of Allende. At press time, Loreto did not have a decompression chamber to treat diving accidents.

Misión Nuestra Señora de Loreto

Above the entrance to this mission, downtown on Salvatierra, the inscription 'Cabeza y Madre de las Misiones de Baja y Alta California' (Head and Mother of the Missions of Upper and Lower California) describes its role in the history of the Californias aptly. Featuring a floor plan in the shape of a Greek cross, it suffered serious damage when the ceiling and bell tower collapsed during the 1829 hurricane; it has been restored only over the last 25 years.

It's polite to take off your hat when you enter the mission. During mass, you should sit down and resist the urge to shoot photos.

Museo de las Misiones

Alongside the mission church, INAH's museum recounts the European settlement of Baja California in a generally chronological manner. It pays attention to the peninsula's indigenous population, honoring the accomplishments of the Jesuits and their successors without ignoring or denying the native demographic collapse caused by the missions. It also displays a fine selection of the implements of daily life, such as horsegear and household tools, from the early days of European settlement.

Other noteworthy features include an early mission bell, a room of religious art, antique weapons like swords and a cannon, a horse-powered *noria* (mill) in the interior courtyard and a very large kettle. Of par-

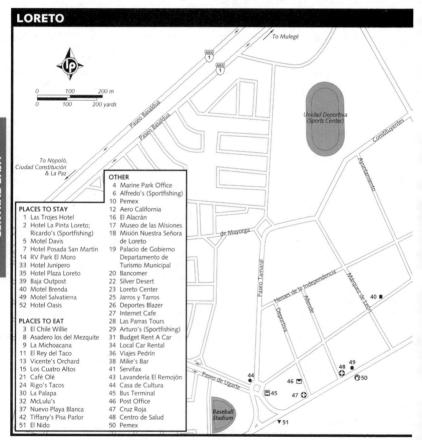

LORETO

To Mulegé

0   100   200 m
0   100   200 yards

To Nopoló,
Ciudad Constitución
& La Paz

Paseo Basaldúa

Unidad Deportiva
(Sports Center)

de Mayorga

Paseo Tamaral

Héroes de la Independencia

Deportiva

Allende

Márquez de León

Constituyentes

Ayuntamiento

Paseo de Ugarte

Baseball
Stadium

PLACES TO STAY
1   Las Trojes Hotel
2   Hotel La Pinta Loreto;
    Ricardo's (Sportfishing)
5   Motel Davis
7   Hotel Posada San Martín
14 RV Park El Moro
33 Hotel Junípero
35 Hotel Plaza Loreto
39 Baja Outpost
40 Motel Brenda
49 Motel Salvatierra
52 Hotel Oasis

PLACES TO EAT
3   El Chile Willie
8   Asadero los del Mezquite
9   La Michoacana
11 El Rey del Taco
13 Vicente's Orchard
15 Los Cuatro Altos
21 Café Olé
24 Rigo's Tacos
30 La Palapa
32 McLulu's
37 Nuevo Playa Blanca
42 Tiffany's Pisa Parlor
51 El Nido

OTHER
4   Marine Park Office
6   Alfredo's (Sportfishing)
10 Pemex
12 Aero California
16 El Alacrán
17 Museo de las Misiones
18 Misión Nuestra Señora
    de Loreto
19 Palacio de Gobierno
    Departamento de
    Turismo Municipal
20 Bancomer
22 Silver Desert
23 Loreto Center
25 Jarros y Tarros
26 Deportes Blazer
27 Internet Cafe
28 Las Parras Tours
29 Arturo's (Sportfishing)
31 Budget Rent A Car
34 Local Car Rental
36 Viajes Pedrín
38 Mike's Bar
41 Servifax
43 Lavandería El Remojón
44 Casa de Cultura
45 Bus Terminal
46 Post Office
47 Cruz Roja
48 Centro de Salud
50 Pemex

ticular note is a 15th-century French astronomical globe. The museum bookstore sells a variety of Spanish-language books about the archaeology, anthropology and history of Mexico and Baja California.

The Museo de las Misiones (☎ 1-135-04-41) is open 9 am to 1 pm and 1:45 to 6 pm, closed Tuesday. Admission is US$1.25.

Activities

Many guides are available for all-day **fishing** trips, but fishing near Loreto is poorer than it once was. The creation of the offshore national park is beginning to have a positive impact on the fish population (in part because professional shrimpers are no longer allowed in the park area).

Bonito, cabrilla, corvina, crevalle, grouper, pargo, sierra and skipjack are all-year game species. Dorado swarm offshore from April to October, but striped marlin, needlefish, roosterfish and sailfish also inhabit these waters. From November to May, yellowtail are the main attraction.

Some outfitters that arrange all-day fishing trips include Alfredo's Sportfishing (☎ 1-135-01-32, fax 1-135-05-90), on Calle de la Playa (Blvd López Mateos) between

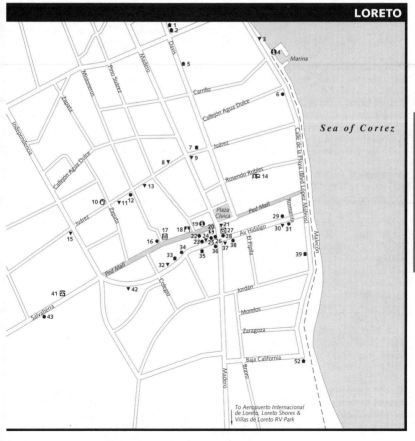

LORETO

Juárez and Callejón Agua Dulce; Arturo's (☎ 1-135-07-66, 1-135-01-26), on Avenida Hidalgo near the intersection with Romanita (an inconspicuous block-long street near the waterfront); and Ricardo's (☎ 1-135-00-25) at Hotel La Pinta Loreto (see Places to Stay). For about US$100, you can hire a local guide to take you out for a day trip; inquire at the marina.

Reefs around Isla del Carmen, Isla Coronado and other sites are superb for water sports. From April to November, the water temperature averages 75° to 85°F (24° to 29°C), and visibility is about 60 to 80 feet (18 to 24m). From December to March, the water temperature averages 60° to 70°F (15° to 21°C); visibility is about 30 to 50 feet (9 to 15m).

Diving and **snorkeling** excursions can be arranged at Baja Outpost or the Loreto Center (see below). Two-tank diving excursions cost about US$75 per person. Deportes Blazer (☎ 1-135-09-11), on Avenida Hidalgo east of Madero, rents and sells scuba gear.

Las Parras Tours (see below) rents opentop kayaks, ranging from US$5 for one hour to US$25 for eight hours. It also arranges four-hour guided tours for US$25.

Organized Tours

Baja Outpost (☎ 1-135-11-34), a well-run outfitter on the waterfront between Jordán and Hidalgo, offers diving, snorkeling, whale-watching and kayaking expeditions.

Las Parras Tours (☎ 1-135-10-10, fax 1-135-09-00), on Madero just north of Avenida Hidalgo, also offers hiking, cycling, horseback riding and sea kayaking tours. Its prices are a little higher than other operators', but it also makes a special effort to involve local people in its business, hiring them as drivers, for example.

The Loreto Center (☎ 1-135-07-98), on Hidalgo and Pino Suárez, offers diving, hiking, fishing and whale-watching expeditions (plus a childcare center).

Places to Stay

Budget Only half a block from the beach and a few blocks from the mission, *RV Park El Moro* (☎ 1-135-05-42, *Rosendo Robles 8*)

has about 13 sites with full hookups for US$8 for cars to US$10 for RVs. Tent spaces cost US$4. It's very friendly and tidy, with clean baths and hot showers, but has limited shade. There are also eight rooms available, with air-con and TV, for US$30/40 singles/doubles.

Spacious *Loreto Shores* (☎ 1-135-06-29, fax 1-135-07-11), on the beach across the Río Loreto, has full hookups, clean bathrooms, hot showers and a laundry room but very little shade. Office hours are 8 am to 6 pm (although it is possible to get through by phone at all hours). Rates are US$5 for camping without hookups, US$14 with hookups; nonguests can use the showers for US$3. The mailing address is Apdo Postal 219, Loreto, Baja California Sur 23880, México.

Nearby *Villas de Loreto* (☎/fax 1-135-05-86) is one of the best options for camping. It has full-hookup sites for US$15 and 10 double rooms for US$70, including breakfast. This is a nonsmoking resort. There are kayaks available to rent, and use of their bikes is free for guests. The mailing address is Apdo Postal 132, Loreto, Baja California Sur, 23880; its Web site is at www.villasdeloreto.com.

Very basic *Hotel Posada San Martín* (☎ 1-135-07-92), at the corner of Juárez and Davis, has rooms for US$26/31, but it's often full. Cheaper and even more basic, *Motel Davis*, on Davis between Constituyentes and Carrillo, lacks hot showers but is otherwise passable, with rooms for US$10.

The *Motel Salvatierra* (☎ 1-135-00-21, *Salvatierra 123*), between Allende and Márquez de León, has clean but small rooms with air-con and hot showers for US$19/21. The best choice is this category is probably *Motel Brenda* (☎ 1-135-07-07), on Juárez between Márquez de León and Ayuntamiento, where clean and comfortable rooms with air-con, TV and hot water cost US$21/23.

Mid-Range Loreto generally lacks midrange accommodations, but *Hotel Junípero* (☎ 1-135-01-22), on Avenida Hidalgo near the mission plaza, has become popular in part for its reasonable prices (US$30/35) and balconies overlooking the avenue or the mission.

Attractive *Hotel Plaza Loreto* (☎ *1-135-02-80, fax 135-08-55, Avenida Hidalgo 2)*, across from the mission, has rooms for US$45/55. Set just off the beach, *Las Trojes Hotel* (☎ *1-135-02-77)*, on Davis just north of Hotel La Pinta, has eight pleasant rooms for US$45.

Baja Outpost (☎ *1-135-11-34, 888-649-5951 in the US)*, on the waterfront between Jordán and Hidalgo, offers beautiful rooms for US$56.

Top End On the beachfront at the corner of Calle de la Playa (Blvd López Mateos) and Baja California, the 35-room *Hotel Oasis* (☎ *1-135-01-12, fax 1-135-07-95)* offers subtropical gardens and rooms with private bath, hot water, air-con and all meals for about US$60/70 (October to March), US$88/125 (April to September).

Hotel La Pinta Loreto (☎ *1-135-00-25, fax 1-135-00-26, 800-336-5454 in the US)*, on Davis about 1 mile (1.6km) north of the plaza, has a swimming pool (not always filled), a restaurant and bar and easy beach access. Its 48 air-conditioned rooms have TVs, showers and private balconies facing the Gulf, but some guests have complained that the lack of heating makes winter nights chilly. Rooms range from US$75 to US$85.

Places to Eat

La Michoacana, on Madero near the corner of Juárez, has decent ice cream but much better paletas and aguas. For fresh fruit, go to *Vicente's Orchard* on Juárez. Taking up an entire block (directly behind the mission), it's a garden where you can pick and cut your own fruit, vegetables or flowers.

There are several taco stands definitely worth stopping at in Loreto. *Rigo's Tacos*, on Hidalgo at Madero, specializes in carne asada, as does *Asadero los del Mesquite*, on Juárez at Madero. *El Rey del Taco*, on Juárez at Zapata, was the first fish taco stand in Loreto, and *McLulu's*, on Hidalgo, has become popular in recent years.

Café Olé (☎ *1-135-04-96, Madero 14)*, just south of the Plaza Cívica, serves good, inexpensive breakfasts (with especially tasty hotcakes) and antojitos. American-owned *Tiffany's Pisa Parlor* (☎ *1-135-00-04)*, at the corner of Avenida Hidalgo and Independencia, appeals to an exclusively gringo clientele, and the prices reflect it, but quality is also high, and it's tobacco-free.

El Nido (☎ *1-135-00-27, Salvatierra 154)*, across from the bus terminal, is the local branch of the Baja steakhouse chain. *Los Cuatro Altos*, at the corner of Juárez and Independencia, is a respectable upstairs bar and grill.

El Chile Willie (☎ *1-135-06-77)* is becoming something of a Loreto institution. Set on the water at López Mateos just past the marina, the restaurant's menu ranges from eggs benedict to chile relleno with lobster. It's a little bit pricey but is a fun place to dine.

Nuevo Playa Blanca (☎ *1-135-11-26)*, on Avenida Hidalgo at the corner of Madero, serves decent seafood dishes; the lobster dishes cost about US$16. *La Palapa*, a very good seafood restaurant on Avenida Hidalgo just half a block from the beach, is a direct descendant of the popular but now defunct Caesar's.

Entertainment

Mike's Bar (☎ *1-135-11-260)*, next to the Nuevo Playa Blanca on Hidalgo, offers music nightly after 10 pm. On Hidalgo and Madero, *Jarros y Tarros* ('Mugs and Jugs') is a good place for playing pool.

Shopping

For the best selection of specifically Baja handicrafts, browse the selection at Las Parras Tours (see Organized Tours, earlier). For items from throughout Mexico, try El Alacrán (☎ 1-135-00-29), at the corner of Salvatierra and Misioneros.

The Silver Desert (☎ 1-135-06-84), at Salvatierra 36, next to the bank, offers silver jewelry, local handicrafts and clothing. Prices are reasonable, and the owners are very helpful and friendly.

CENTRAL BAJA

Getting There & Away

Aeropuerto Internacional de Loreto (☎ 1-135-04-54) is reached by a lateral off the Transpeninsular, just across the Río Loreto. Aero California (☎ 1-135-05-00, 1-135-05-55 at the airport, fax 1-135-05-66), with an office on Juárez between Misioneros and Zapata, flies once daily to and from Los Angeles.

Aerolitoral, represented by Viajes Pedrín (see Travel Agencies, earlier), flies daily to and from La Paz. Connections to many mainland Mexican cities can be made in La Paz (see the Cape Region chapter).

Loreto's bus terminal (☎ 1-135-07-67) is near the traffic circle where Salvatierra, Paseo de Ugarte and Paseo Tamaral converge. The following are some of the main schedules and fares:

Santa Rosalía – US$9.50, three hours; 2 & 5 pm

La Paz – US$16, five hours; 8, 10 & 12 am, 1, 2 & 11 pm

Guerrero Negro – US$22.50, five hours; 11 pm

Tijuana – US$57, 18 hours; 12:30 am & 3 pm

Mexicali – US$68, 19 hours; 9 pm

Getting Around

Taxi rides to or from the airport cost about US$7.

Loreto's two car rental agencies are Budget Rent A Car (☎ 1-135-10-90), on Hidalgo just before López Mateos, and Local Car Rental (☎ 1-135-00-48, fax 1-135-00-13), at Hidalgo 2.

Las Parras Tours (see Organized Tours, earlier) rents mountain bikes for US$5 per hour, US$15 per half-day and US$25 per full day (eight hours). Mountain-bike tours are also available.

AROUND LORETO
Isla Coronado

About 3 miles (5km) northeast of Loreto, opposite Punta Tierra Firma, Isla Coronado is one of the Gulf's most accessible islands and the northernmost island in the Parque Marino Nacional Bahía de Loreto. The turquoise waters along its sparkling sandy beach, facing the mainland, are ideal for snorkeling. There are also many seabirds,

mostly pelicans, and the rocky eastern shore has a small sea lion colony.

Many kayakers make the trip to Coronado. Camping is possible, and several palapas are available for shade. Las Parras Tours in Loreto (see earlier) can also arrange a panga circumnavigation and beach stop.

Nopoló

In the 1980s, Fonatur, the federal tourist development agency also responsible for mainland Mexican debacles like Cancún and Ixtapa, plopped this incongruous resort complex onto an erstwhile goat ranch 4 miles (6.5km) south of Loreto. Despite construction of an international airport and an elaborate street plan off a single palm-lined avenue, it remains a cluster of largely vacant and weedy lots except for its single upscale hotel, lighted tennis courts, sprawling 18-hole golf course and a handful of private houses. Nopoló also has its own clinic and fire department.

The Campo de Golf Loreto (☎ 1-133-05-54) features a cart bridge that many isolated rural communities might start a revolution to get. Greens fees are US$40, while cart rentals cost US$35 and club rentals US$20.

The *Eden Resort* (☎ 1-133-07-00, fax 1-133-03-77) is an adults-only facility featuring two swimming pools (sometimes heated), tennis courts (sometimes with nets) with a stadium for competitive matches, a nightclub, a bar, two restaurants and a nude beach.

The resort's daily rates range from about US$200 to US$300 per night for two people; nonguests can use the hotel facilities for US$35 per day. The Web site is at www.eden-resorts.com.

Puerto Escondido

An ostensibly Mediterranean-style marina in a scenic natural port 16 miles (26km) south of Loreto, Puerto Escondido was the site of yet another ambitious Fonatur scheme. A joint venture with a French investment company, it was intended as a resort complex with five-star hotels, luxurious private homes, condominiums, stores, a fitness center and moorings for 300 yachts.

The paved but potholed access road off the Transpeninsular beyond Tripui Resort RV Park aptly symbolizes the ragged results.

Tripui Resort RV Park *(☎ 1-133-08-18, fax 1-133-08-28),* a short distance east of the Transpeninsular, is an RV park/campground/fortress in a noisy location remote from the bay. Full hookups, a swimming pool, lighted tennis courts, a laundry room, restaurant and grocery store are available. Rates are US$16 per vehicle and US$5 for a tent. RV-club members should ask for discounts. Tripui's mailing address is Apdo Postal 100, Loreto, Baja California Sur 23880, México.

Misión San Francisco Javier

Built from blocks of volcanic stone in the Sierra de la Giganta west of Loreto, San Francisco Javier de Viggé-Biaundó is one of the Californias' best-preserved mission churches, in perhaps the most spectacular setting of any of them. Founded in 1699 at nearby Rancho Viejo by the famous Jesuit Francisco María Piccolo, the Californias' second mission moved to its present site in 1720 but was not completed until 1758.

The church itself is in very good condition, with original walls, floors and venerable religious artworks, but visitors may no longer climb the spiral staircase to the chorus. Irrigation canals of Jesuit vintage, the first on the peninsula, still water the local fields. Every December 3, hundreds of pilgrims celebrate the saint's fiesta here.

Just over a mile (1.6km) south of Loreto is the junction for the spectacular 22-mile (35km) mountain road to the village of San Javier, which takes about 1½ hours, not counting photo stops. The dirt surface is graded only to Rancho Viejo but is passable for most passenger cars despite a few bumpy spots and arroyo crossings. Rancho Las Parras, in a verdant canyon halfway to San Javier, grows figs, dates, olives and citrus, but livestock have contaminated most of the water along the route – do not drink without treating it. A spring just before Km 20 westbound should be potable, and there are a couple of potential swimming holes.

With an early start, this would be a good day trip on a mountain bike, but parts of the road are steep enough that even the strongest cyclist will probably have to walk for short stretches. The village's only tourist facility is ***Restaurant Palapa San Javier***, where the owner serves simple meals, cold beer and sodas under a shady palapa alongside his house. Ask about camping; there may even be rustic accommodations available.

The road leading southwest from San Javier, passing a series of remote ranchos before reaching the intersection with the paved Ciudad Insurgentes–San Isidro highway just north of Colonia Purísima, is much improved and passable for any vehicle with good clearance. While this interesting road is slower than the paved Transpeninsular, it allows drivers to avoid the unpleasant Judiciales checkpoint south of Nopoló.

Llano de Magdalena

Beyond Puerto Escondido, the Transpeninsular twists and climbs through the Sierra de la Giganta before turning westward into the Llano de Magdalena (Magdalena Plain), a major agricultural zone that offers visitors activities including whale-watching, fishing, surfing and windsurfing.

A bronze monument to pioneer agriculturalists graces the road north from the highway junction at Ciudad Insurgentes, an increasingly prosperous town with restaurants, groceries and a Pemex station, but still no accommodations. If you're planning to continue west to Puerto López Mateos or north to San José de Comondú, stock up on supplies here.

One of the key whale-breeding sites on the coast, popularly known as 'Mag Bay' among English-speakers, Bahía Magdalena has had a colorful history despite (or perhaps because of) its thinly populated coastline. In colonial times, Sebastián Vizcaíno anchored nearby, but, finding no surface water, soon departed. Some years later, missionary Clemente Guillén found no suitable harbor, and, though the Jesuits built a lowland chapel under the jurisdiction of Misión San Luis Gonzaga, they never really colonized the area.

Both before and after Mexican independence, the area attracted smugglers; foreign whalers worked the area from 1836 to 1846, assisted by laborers from San José de Comondú. During the Mexican-American War, the US Navy promised local residents US citizenship in return for their support. These residents were forced to leave after the signing of the Treaty of Guadalupe Hidalgo and the failure of secret negotiations that would have kept Baja California under US control in exchange for a cash indemnity.

There were several other failed attempts to take over the Baja Peninsula, but accelerating agricultural development in the latter half of the 20th century finally consolidated Mexican control of the area. Today, the region, particularly around Ciudad Constitución, is booming. Its main lure for travelers – whale-watching – brings visitors from around the globe to its small but very appealing port towns. Bahía Magdalena is also one of the largest remaining wetlands on the Pacific coast of North America.

PUERTO LÓPEZ MATEOS

Protected by the barrier island of Isla Magdalena, Puerto Adolfo López Mateos (population 2400), 20 miles (32km) west of Ciudad Insurgentes by a good paved road, is one of Baja's best **whale-watching** sites. The bay is narrow, so you don't have to travel as far by boat to see the whales. Boca de Soledad, only a short distance north of the port, boasts the highest density of whales anywhere along the peninsula. The annual Festival del Ballenato, celebrating the birth of gray-whale calves, takes place in early February.

The cooperative Unión de Lancheros (☎ 1-131-51-78) and the Sociedad Cooperativa Aquendi (☎ 1-131-51-15) run whale-watching pangas from the new pier near their headquarters near the lighthouse; other authorized pangueros include Sergio Tapia García (☎ 1-131-51-19) and Modesto Camacho Beltrán (☎ 1-131-51-23). Trips cost US$50 per hour for up to six persons. Because people begin to arrive the night before for early-morning departures and camp at nearby Playa Soledad, it's easy to form groups to share expenses. Pangueros stay out as long as their clients wish.

Free camping, with pit toilets only (bring water), is possible at **Playa Soledad**. López Mateos' only other accommodations are at the small and simple but new and tidy **Posada Ballena López**, within easy walking distance of the whale-watching pier, for US$10/15 single/double.

Besides a few so-so taco stands, López Mateos has several decent restaurants. The **Restaurant California** (☎ 1-131-52-08) serves good, moderately priced seafood, as does **Cabaña Brisa**. At the entrance to town, **La Ballena Gris** offers decent seafood.

Autotransportes Aguila provides daily buses from Ciudad Constitución (US$3.50); return service to Constitución leaves at 6:30 am and 2:30 pm. The bus stop is next to the Restaurant California.

CIUDAD CONSTITUCIÓN

Having grown dramatically with the Llano de Magdalena's rapid expansion of commercial agriculture, Ciudad Constitución (population 35,000) bears all the marks of a 'progressive' city: clean, broad paved streets (at least in the center), several banks and even high culture – state and national cultural organizations visit the local Teatro de la Ciudad (City Theater) on their tours.

At the northern entrance to town, at the turnoff to Puerto San Carlos, is a monument to General Agustín Olachea Avilés, a Todos Santos native who participated in the famous Cananea copper strike in Sonora. Olachea Avilés joined the revolutionary forces in 1913, became a general in 1920 at the age of 28 and put down a Yaqui Indian rebellion in Sonora in 1926. Later, as governor of Baja California's Territorio Sur, he promoted agricultural development in Ciudad Constitución.

Fresh water for cultivation was a serious problem before the exploitation of huge aquifers beneath the plain. Israeli technicians have since advised farmers on water conservation and crop substitution to take advantage of newly drilled wells. Water-efficient crops like garbanzos (chickpeas) and citrus are superseding thirsty, pesticide-dependent cotton.

Because Constitución is primarily an agricultural service center, most travelers find little of interest here, but the city is very convenient to the major whale-watching centers of Puerto San Carlos and Puerto López Mateos, which have only limited accommodations. It is also the *cabecera* (administrative center) of the *municipio* of Comondú.

Orientation

This city is 134 miles (216km) northwest of La Paz, 89 miles (143km) southwest of Loreto and 36 miles (58km) east of Puerto San Carlos on Bahía Magdalena. The north-south Transpeninsular is the main street, known as Blvd General Agustín Olachea Avilés and more commonly as Blvd Olachea, but the city has matured beyond the strip-development phase (unlike such northern Baja towns as San Quintín). Still, most important services are within a block or two of Blvd Olachea, where passing delivery trucks have clipped,

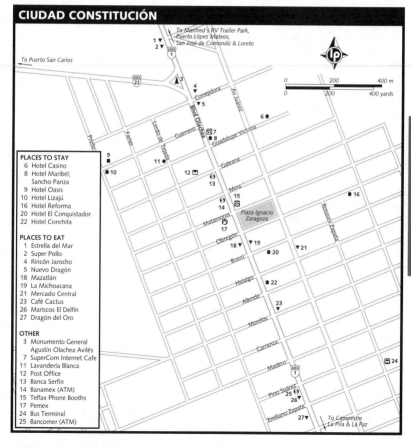

CIUDAD CONSTITUCIÓN

To Manfred's RV Trailer Park,
Puerto López Mateos,
San José de Comondú & Loreto

To Puerto San Carlos

PLACES TO STAY
6 Hotel Casino
8 Hotel Maribel;
    Sancho Panza
9 Hotel Oasis
10 Hotel Lizajú
16 Hotel Reforma
20 Hotel El Conquistador
22 Hotel Conchita

PLACES TO EAT
1 Estrella del Mar
2 Super Pollo
4 Rincón Jarocho
5 Nuevo Dragón
18 Mazatlán
19 La Michoacana
21 Mercado Central
23 Café Cactus
26 Mariscos El Delfín
27 Dragón del Oro

OTHER
3 Monumento General
    Agustín Olachea Avilés
7 SuperCom Internet Cafe
11 Lavandería Blanca
12 Post Office
13 Banca Serfin
14 Banamex (ATM)
15 Telfax Phone Booths
17 Pemex
24 Bus Terminal
25 Bancomer (ATM)

To Campestre
La Pila & La Paz

CENTRAL BAJA

bent and twisted the city's once shiny Banamex street signs; traffic seems to cross Olachea at every corner. The other major street is the parallel Avenida Juárez, one block east.

Information

Constitución has no cambios, but three banks on Blvd Olachea change US dollars or traveler's checks: Banca Serfin at the corner of Galeana, Banamex at the south-western corner of Mina and Bancomer on Pino Suárez just west of Blvd Olachea. All have ATMs.

The post office is at 236 Galeana just west of Blvd Olachea; the postal code is 23600. Besides Telmex and Ladatel public phones, try the private Telfax phone booths on the eastern side of Blvd Olachea between Matamoros and Mina.

SuperCom Internet Café is located on Olachea between Guadalupe Victoria and Guerrero; access is US$2 every half hour.

For laundry services, Lavandería Blanca (☎ 1-132-07-69) is at the corner of Avenida Lerdo de Tejada and Guadalupe Victoria.

Places to Stay

Camping The RV park *Campestre La Pila (☎ 1-132-05-62, fax 1-132-02-29)* is at the end of a dirt road south of town that leads west for about half a mile (1km); turn right off Olachea at the large factory. There are hot showers, electrical outlets, toilets and a swimming pool. On weekends, the park proper is a popular picnic ground – a pleasant, grassy area surrounded by a farm (with accompanying animal sounds) and a few shade trees. At harvest times, freshly picked vegetables are available from the farm. The rate for two people is about US$9; US$5 for each extra person.

At the northern end of town near the junction with the highway to Puerto López Mateos, Austrian-run *Manfred's RV Trailer Park (☎ 1-132-11-03)* has spacious sites for US$14/16 for one/two people. The rate for cyclists and motorcyclists is US$8 per site; for car campers it's US$13 per site. Thanks to an elaborate drip-irrigation system, the park is increasingly shady; it also has hot

showers, a swimming pool, an Austrian restaurant and a spacious apartment with private bath available for US$28 per night.

Hotels Some budget choices include *Hotel Reforma (☎ 1-132-09-88, Obregón 125)*, with rooms for US$8/10 singles/doubles, and *Hotel Lizajú (Guerrero 521)*, with doubles for US$10.

Hotel Casino (☎ 1-132-14-15), on Guadalupe Victoria about one block east of Hotel Maribel, has very spartan rooms for about US$20; the go-cart track across the street can wreak havoc on your afternoon siesta, and the improbable transvestite bar next door could also be a distraction. The much better *Hotel Conchita (☎/fax 1-132-02-66, Blvd Olachea 180)* charges US$13/18. *Hotel Oasis (☎ /fax 1-132-44-58, Guerrero 284)* is a very good choice for US$20 per double.

Hotel Maribel (☎ 1-132-01-55, Guadalupe Victoria 156), near Blvd Olachea, has comfortable rooms – each with telephone and TV – for about US$28/32 upstairs, US$19/23 downstairs. The attached restaurant offers basic Mexican dishes.

Hotel El Conquistador (☎ 1-132-27-45, Bravo 161) is a three-star place charging US$24/30 downstairs, US$31/38 upstairs. It's a bit dark and formal, but its restaurant has decent meals.

Places to Eat

For Constitución's cheapest eats, try the many taquerías on Blvd Olachea (which have finally caught up with the fish taco craze) or the *Mercado Central*, on Avenida Juárez between Hidalgo and Bravo. *La Michoacana*, on Blvd Olachea half a block south of Plaza Ignacio Zaragoza, has dependably good ice cream, paletas and aguas. Hotel Maribel's *Sancho Panza* is worth a try for Mexican food.

Super Pollo (☎ 1-132-28-88), just north of the Olachea monument, specializes in grilled chicken, Sinaloa style. Next door, *Estrella del Mar (☎ 1-132-09-55)* is a good seafood restaurant, as is *Rincón Jarocho (☎ 1-132-25-25)* on the eastern side of Blvd Olachea just south of the monument.

Other seafood choices include **Mariscos El Delfín**, at Blvd Olachea and Emiliano Zapata, and **Mazatlán**, on Blvd Olachea between Bravo and Obregón. **Café Cactus** (☎ 1-138-35-01), on Olachea at the corner of Morelos, offers coffee, sandwiches and good desserts.

Constitución has two Chinese restaurants, both on Blvd Olachea: **Nuevo Dragón** (☎ 1-132-29-22), at the corner of Correjidora, and **Dragón del Oro** (☎ 1-132-53-43), just south of Emiliano Zapata.

Getting There & Away
North-south ABC and Autotransportes Aguila buses on the Transpeninsular stop at Constitución's terminal (☎ 1-132-03-76) at the corner of Avenida Rosaura Zapata and Pino Suárez, two blocks east of Blvd Olachea.

The following are buses bound for destinations north and south of Constitución:

Puerto San Carlos – US$3, one hour; 10:45 am, 5:30 & 7 pm

Puerto López Mateos – US$3, one hour; 12:30 pm

Loreto – US$7, two hours; 11:30 am, 2, 4 & 8:30 pm

San Isidro – US$7, three hours; 9:45 am & 6 pm

La Paz – US$9, 2½ hours; 10 times daily 6:30 am to 6 pm

Santa Rosalía – US$16, five hours; 11:30 am & 2:30 pm

Los Cabos – US$17, five hours; 3 pm

Guerrero Negro – US$29, nine hours; 11:30 pm

Tijuana – US$64, 19 hours; 10:30 pm

Mexicali – US$75, 19 hours; 6:30 pm

PUERTO SAN CARLOS
Increasingly popular for some of southern Baja's best whale-watching, Puerto San Carlos (population 3600) is a dusty and windy but friendly deep-water port on Bahía Magdalena, about 36 miles (58km) west of Ciudad Constitución (watch for livestock, including cattle and even pigs, on the paved highway). Puerto San Carlos ships cotton and alfalfa from the fields of the Llano de Magdalena, and a minor building boom has given it the best accommodations of any of

Baja's whale-watching destinations. Nearby beaches on Bahía Magdalena are fine for camping, clamming and sportfishing.

In the late 19th century, a US Navy coaling station in the area became a major political controversy in mainland Mexico. A recent Japanese concession of 5000 acres (2000 hectares) for a tourist development south of Puerto San Carlos is on hold; the offshore Isla Magdalena, a barrier island, is under control of the Mexican navy and off-limits to this enterprise.

All Puerto San Carlos' streets are named for Mexican port cities. Gasoline, including Magna Sin and diesel, is available at the Pemex station. Puerto San Carlos lacks a tourist office but has a post office (postal code 23740), long-distance telephone service and an IMSS clinic.

The new Museo Ballena Sudcaliforniana (Southern Baja Whale Museum) is very rudimentary, displaying only a single gray-whale skeleton and a few rusting artifacts from 19th-century whaling days, but mid-February's Festival de la Ballena Gris (Gray Whale Festival) is becoming a big-time event.

Whale-Watching
From mid-January through March, local pangueros take up to six passengers to view friendly whales in Bahía Magdalena for US$50 per hour. Some people come for the day from Loreto or La Paz (both about 2½ hours away by car) or even fly in from Cabo San Lucas, but early morning is the best time to see whales.

Among the local operators are Ulysturs (☎ 1-136-00-17, fax 1-136-00-86) and Mar y Arena (☎ 1-136-02-32, fax 1-136-00-76), at the corner of Blvd Puerto La Paz and Puerto Loreto. Most hotels in town can arrange for tours as well.

Places to Stay & Eat
Free camping is possible on the fairly clean public beach north of town, but the aging palapas are falling into disrepair and there are no toilets. South of town, people camp among the mangroves near the whale-watching launch sites; it's messier, but there's

a good selection of bird life, perhaps suggesting that aesthetics are more important to humans than to wildlife.

RV Park Nancy (☎ *1-136-01-95*) has nine small, shadeless spots for US$5. Hotel accommodations are more abundant than in the past, but whale-watching season still puts a strain on local capacity, and reservations are a good idea. Friendly, family-oriented *Motel Las Brisas* (☎ *1-136-01-52*), on Puerto Madero, has basic but clean singles/doubles from US$14/16. The *Hotel Palmar* (☎ *1-136-00-35*), on Puerto Morelos, charges US$20/25. The attractive *Hotel Alcatraz* (☎ *1-136-00-17, fax 1-136-00-86*) has rooms with TV for US$50/70. Its shady *Restaurant Bar El Patio* is by far the best in town.

A comparable hotel is the *Hotel Brennan* (☎ *1-136-02-88, fax 1-136-00-19, 510-428-5464 in the US*), whose well-appointed rooms cost US$40/50. Owned by the same family, *Molly's Suites* (☎ *1-136-01-31*), on Puerto La Paz, offers pleasant rooms for US$50/60.

Mariscos Los Arco, on Puerto La Paz, just east of Puerto Mexico, has excellent shrimp tacos and seafood soup.

Getting There & Away

Based in a small house on Puerto Morelos, Autotransportes Aguila offers buses to Ciudad Constitución (US$4) and La Paz (US$13) at 7:30 am and 1:45 pm daily. This is the only public transportation.

MISIÓN SAN LUIS GONZAGA

Founded back in 1737 by German Jesuit Lambert Hostell, the date-palm oasis of Misión San Luis Gonzaga, southeast of Ciudad Constitución, closed with the Jesuits' departure in 1768, after an original Indian population of 2000 had fallen to only 300. The Alsatian Jesuit Johann Jakob Baegert left a detailed record of the mission's last two decades.

San Luis' well-preserved church, dating from the 1750s but lacking the embellishments of the San Borja and San Francisco Javier churches, is not one of the mission system's gems, but its twin bell towers are unusual. Besides the church, there are ruins of more recent vintage with elaborate neo-

classical columns. The village's only facilities are a school and a Conasupo (small store).

At Km 195, about 9 miles (14km) south of Ciudad Constitución on the Transpeninsular, a graded lateral good enough even for low riders or mammoth RVs, leads 25 miles (40km) east to the edge of the Sierra de la Giganta and San Luis Gonzaga. Keep watching for the sign reading 'Presa Iguajil.'

Just across the arroyo from the mission, a road suitable for high-clearance, short-wheelbase vehicles only (4WD is not essential) leads 16 miles (26km) south past Ranchos Iraquí, La Palmilla (Conasupo and cold drinks), El Caporal and Pozo de Irití to Rancho Las Tinajitas. There, it meets another lateral from Santa Rita that climbs eastward into the sierra to the extensive but poorly preserved ruins of Misión La Pasión (see next). This route is more difficult but much more interesting than the corresponding segment of the Transpeninsular.

MISIÓN LA PASIÓN

From Km 128 on the Transpeninsular, a graded dirt road climbs east to Rancho Las Tinajitas and Rancho Los Ciruelos, beyond which the ungraded surface to the Jesuit Misión La Pasión becomes difficult for vehicles without high clearance. The ruins themselves are just west of Santa María Toris, a friendly rancho beyond which a 4WD route continues toward **Misión Dolores del Sur**, but stops just short of those ruins – they're an hour's hike or five minutes away by panga from the end of the route. Santa María Toris itself has a Conasupo market and an *internado* (boarding school) but has no other facilities. There are cave paintings in the canyon below Toris, among its numerous volcanic plugs and mesas, but these are difficult to locate without a guide.

Only foundations remain of Misión La Pasión, which lasted from 1737 until the Jesuits' expulsion in 1767, when its Indians were transferred to Todos Santos. Those foundations are very extensive, however; barely a decade ago, according to local residents, the last standing wall fell. Note that the usually reliable AAA map places the ruins on the wrong (northern) side of the road and has several other inaccuracies.

At the junction 3 miles (5km) west of Toris, the right fork leads south to Rancho Las Animas, beyond which a dangerously exciting road, sloping and riddled with gullies (4WD only, with great caution), leads to Rancho Soledad and the Gulf coast fish camp of San Evaristo, where another, less difficult road leads south to La Paz. (See the Cape Region chapter for more details.) The road from Las Animas to Soledad offers truly awesome panoramas of the Sierra de la Giganta, but don't take your eyes off the road unless you stop the car.

PUERTO CHALE

About 36 miles (58km) south of Ciudad Constitución, a 15-mile (24km) graded dirt road leads west from the village of Santa Rita on the Transpeninsular to Puerto Chale, a tiny Pacific coast fish camp popular with windsurfers.

EL CIEN & AROUND

So called because it lies exactly 100km northwest of La Paz on the Transpeninsular, El Cien has a Pemex station and a decent restaurant; it is 35 miles (56km) south of Santa Rita.

Twelve miles (19km) farther south, at Km 80 just beyond the microwave station 'El Coyote,' is a junction with a 12-mile (19km) unmarked, dirt road to **Punta Conejo** (some smaller RVs have successfully navigated this route but not without cosmetic damage).

Countless tiny crabs scurry over Punta Conejo's firm, sandy beach to the safety of their burrows, wary of the gulls overhead; the bicycle-tire-like tracks disappear under a rock overhang, where hermit crabs hide from their pursuers. The area attracts many surfers to its right break, mostly in southerly swells, but it's far from crowded; surf fishing is also popular.

At the southeastern end of the beach, a jutting headland consists of a marine conglomerate composed almost entirely of fossils. Follow the informal trail at the base of the cliff to some smaller, more secluded beaches, but be prepared to scramble over the rocks. Remember that Mexican law prohibits fossil hunting; in any event, all these fossils are fairly recent.

There are oyster beds 5 miles (8km) south of Punta Conejo, but drifting sand makes the road difficult beyond that point even for 4WD vehicles. Surfers headed south to **Punta Márquez** might find it easier to approach via the graded road from the Transpeninsular to Ejido Conquista, between Kms 55 and 54.

Cape Region

Comprising the modern southern city of La Paz and areas to its south along the Transpeninsular and México 19, the Cape Region also includes the popular resorts of Los Cabos (San José del Cabo and Cabo San Lucas). This is the costliest and most tourist-oriented part of the peninsula, but it still offers unconventional opportunities for determined travelers.

Highlights

- Scuba diving, sea kayaking or strolling the malecón in La Paz
- Windsurfing at La Ventana or Los Barriles
- Watching the sun set over Land's End, margarita in hand, from a Corridor resort
- Exploring the Sierra de la Laguna, an ecological wonderland
- Hauling in a fish dinner on the East Cape or Cabo San Lucas
- Swimming with tropical fish and manta rays in Cabo Pulmo, the only coral reef on North America's west coast
- Surfing at Playa Los Cerritos, south of Todos Santos

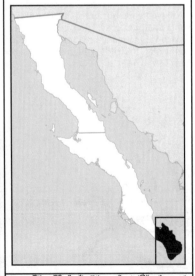

LA PAZ

Kaleidoscopic sunsets over the bay, a palm-studded *malecón* (waterfront promenade), neocolonial architecture and nearby Península Pichilingue's sandy beaches are the main attractions of La Paz (population 182,418), the capital of Baja California Sur. Although undercut by NAFTA tariff reductions, La Paz remains a notable port and has become a resort city as well.

Most activities in the area are beach-oriented, but authorities acknowledge that Bahía de La Paz proper is badly polluted. Areas beyond the Pemex shore facilities and ferry terminal, toward Playa Tecolote at the tip of Península Pichilingue, are cleaner, pleasanter and safer.

Thanks to its university, several good museums and an important theater and cultural center, La Paz is also a locus for cultural activities. Pichilingue, on the peninsula north of town, is the port for ferries between La Paz and the mainland Mexican ports of Topolobampo and Mazatlán.

History

In 1535 on Península Pichilingue, Hernán Cortés established Baja's first European settlement. But despite the discovery of pearls in the Gulf of California, it was soon abandoned due to Indian hostility and food and water shortages.

By the late 16th century, England and Holland were disputing Spain's maritime hegemony and buccaneers were raiding Spanish ships throughout the world; the treasure-laden galleons that sailed from Manila to Acapulco were especially popular targets. After the turn of the century, in response to incursions by Northern Europeans, Viceroy Gaspar de Zuñiga y Acevedo of

CAPE REGION

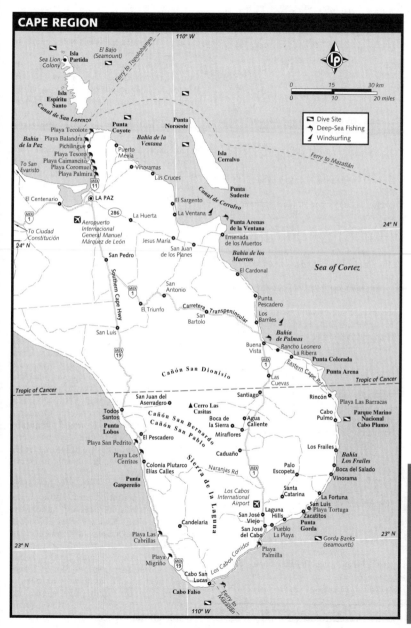

CAPE REGION

The Dutch in the Pacific

New World piracy was largely the province of the English, but other Northern European countries eagerly joined in the battle against Spanish wealth and hegemony in the Americas. The French and especially the Dutch were most active in the Caribbean and on the coast of Brazil, but the Dutch had Pacific ambitions as well.

Since the late-16th-century voyage of Sir Francis Drake, British buccaneers had frequented the Pacific coasts of North and South America, despite the distances between their homes and their convenient, well-watered island bases in the Caribbean. Thomas Cavendish's capture of the *Santa Ana* off Cabo San Lucas in 1587 attracted privateers' interest to New Spain (Mexico) and Baja California; British pirates lay in wait for treasure-laden galleons returning from Manila and sometimes took other major prizes.

The Netherlands, having rebelled against Spanish domination in 1566, was eager to make its mark on the seas. The Dutch became rivals of the Spaniards in the Caribbean and the Portuguese in Brazil, and they soon rounded the Horn to the Pacific. Though they lurked at Cabo San Lucas in hopes of emulating Cavendish's windfall, their earliest voyages had limited success. Profit was not the only motive that spurred the Dutch; they were fanatical Protestants who resented the reactionary Catholicism the Spaniards had imposed on them in Europe.

In 1615, the surprisingly genteel occupation of Acapulco by the Dutch privateer Joris van Speilbergen induced the Spaniards to build the famous port's landmark castle, the Fuerte de San Diego. For decades, though, the menace of Dutch privateers forced the Spaniards to send patrols from the mainland to the Cape Region. Península Pichilingue, north of La Paz, even takes its name from the Dutch privateers whom the Spaniards called 'Flexelingas,' after their home port of Vlissingen just north of the modern Belgian border.

New Spain granted Sebastián Vizcaíno a license to exploit the pearl fisheries of the Cape Region and establish settlements to discourage privateers.

Though Vizcaíno renamed Bahía de la Santa Cruz as Bahía de La Paz (Bay of Peace), he abandoned the idea of a settlement there because of the shortage of supplies and the area's limited agricultural potential. In 1720, the Jesuits established a mission, but epidemics and Indian uprisings led to its abandonment 29 years later. La Paz was briefly occupied by US Marines during the Mexican-American War, then attacked by William Walker during his preposterously incompetent attempt to annex Baja California to the USA.

Mining at nearby El Triunfo, along with pearling and fishing in the Gulf, contributed to the city's postindependence growth. Its political status advanced with the grant of statehood to Baja California Sur in 1974.

Orientation

As the Transpeninsular approaches the city, it runs parallel to Bahía de La Paz and becomes Calzada (Calle) Abasolo. To continue to Cabo San Lucas without visiting downtown La Paz, turn right (south) on 5 de Febrero and follow the signs to 'Carretera al Sur' (the southbound Transpeninsular) and 'Cabo San Lucas.'

Four blocks east of 5 de Febrero, Abasolo becomes Paseo Alvaro Obregón, running along the malecón and eventually to Península Pichilingue. On weekend nights, Paseo Obregón is a mile-long traffic jam, while the malecón attracts hordes of teenyboppers.

Most of La Paz has a regular grid pattern that makes orientation easy, although the city center's crooked streets and alleys change their names almost every block. In this area, locals occasionally use different street names as well – the official name of block-long Lerdo de Tejada, for instance, is usually ignored in favor of Santos Degollado, the name of its longer extension. Note also that the numbering system along Paseo Obregón is so irregular that it seems completely improvised.

On Avenida Independencia, four blocks from the Muelle Turístico (tourist pier) on the malecón, Plaza Constitución is the traditional heart of the city. Both Plaza Constitución, known officially as Jardín Velasco, and the Muelle Turístico have attractive bandshells. Many tourist activities take place on the Muelle Turístico on weekends.

Information

Tourist Offices The Coordinación Estatal de Turismo, allied with the Secretaría de Turismo del Estado (Secture), has an office (☎ 1-122-59-39) on the waterfront at the corner of Paseo Obregón and 16 de Septiembre. The well-organized, English-speaking staff distributes a variety of leaflets and keeps a current list of hotel rates. It's open 8 am to 10 pm weekdays, noon to 10 pm weekends.

There's a second office, located in the Fidepaz building at Km 5 of the Transpeninsular, southwest of downtown (☎ 1-124-01-00, fax 1-124-07-22, turismo@gbcs .gob.mx). It's open 8 am to 8 pm weekdays.

Immigration Servicios Migratorios (☎ 1-125-34-93, fax 1-122-04-29), in the Edificio Milhe at Paseo Obregón 2140 between Allende and Juárez, is open 9 am to 6 pm weekdays. On weekends, immigration officials staff the ferry terminal at Pichilingue and the airport (☎ 1-124-63-49), but tourist card extensions are available only at the Paseo Obregón office.

Money Most banks and *cambios* (currency exchange houses) are on or around 16 de Septiembre, and all have ATMs.

Bancomer and Citibank are at the intersection of 16 de Septiembre and Esquerro. Banco Santander and Banamex (the latter is probably the most efficient bank in town) are across the street from each other at the junction of Agustín Arreola and Esquerro. Banco Internacional (Bital) is at the corner of 5 de Mayo and Madero.

Shopping centers like the Centro Comercial Californiano, across from the Palacio de Gobierno, and the Centro Comercial Colima, near the corner of Abasolo and Colima, will change a traveler's check if the holder makes a purchase worth at least 10% of the check's face value. There are also ATMs here.

Post & Communications The post and telegraph office is at the corner of Constitución and Revolución, one block east of Jardín Velasco (Plaza Constitución). The downtown postal code is 23000.

Ladatel phones are abundant, so it's easy to make long-distance calls with magnetic phone cards, with credit cards or by reversing charges (remember to avoid the predatory blue phones). At private phone booths on Paseo Obregón and elsewhere, verify charges before calling, as rates can vary up to 50% between offices.

There are numerous Internet cafes throughout the city. The usual rate is US$2 every 30 minutes. Katun Café (☎ 1-127-10-07) on 16 de Septiembre, at the corner of Paseo Obregón, is open 9 am to 10 pm Monday to Saturday. Café Internet (☎ 1-125-93-80), at Madero and Constitución, is open 8 am to 8 pm Monday to Saturday. There's also an Internet cafe on Paseo Obregón near the corner of Muelle.

Travel Agencies Turismo Express (☎/fax 1-125-63-10) is alongside the tourist office on the Muelle Turístico. It has recently expanded its offices to include an Internet cafe and also rents kayaks and bikes. Viajes Coromuel (☎ 1-122-80-06, fax 1-125-43-13) is at the corner of Paseo Obregón and Rosales. Viajes Palmira (☎/fax 1-122-40-30), on the malecón across from Hotel Los Arcos, also offers all the usual travel services.

Viajes Lybsa (☎ 1-122-60-01, fax 1-122-84-11), at the corner of Obregón and Lerdo de Tejada, is a full-service travel agency. Viajes Baja (☎ 1-122-36-60, 1-122-41-30) is at Obregón 2110 at Allende.

Bookstores Librería Contempo (☎ 1-122-78-75), Agustín Arreola 25-A, near Paseo Obregón, keeps a selection of US newspapers and magazines and usually carries the most recent issue of the English-language Mexico City *News*. Libros Libros Books

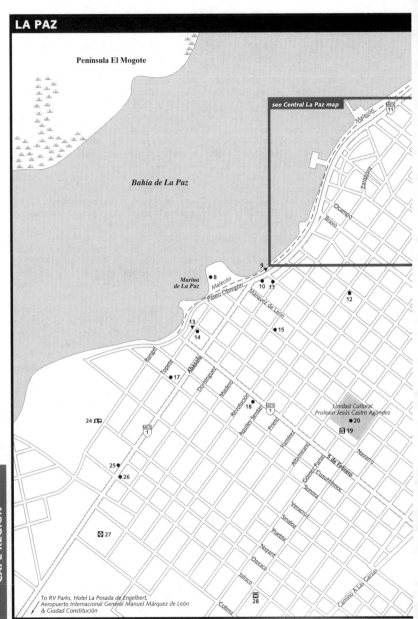

LA PAZ

Península El Mogote

Bahía de La Paz

Marina
de La Paz

Malecón

Paseo Obregón

● 8

● 9

● 10 ● 11

Márquez de León

♠ 12

▲ 13
● 14

● 15

Rangel

Topete

Abasolo

Domínguez

● 17

Madero

Revolución

● 18

Aquiles Serdán

MEX 1

Prieto

Ramírez

Altamirano

Gómez Farías

Cuauhtémoc

5 de Febrero

Navarro

Unidad Cultural
Profesor Jesús Castro Agúndez
● 20
🏛 19

24 🕮

MEX 1

25 ●
● 26

Sonora

Veracruz

Sinaloa

Puebla

Nayarit

Oaxaca

Jalisco

🏕 27

Camino A Las Garzas

📷 28

Collima

see Central La Paz map

Malecón

MEX 11

Zaragoza

Ocampo

Bravo

To RV Parks, Hotel La Posada de Engelbert,
Aeropuerto Internacional General Manuel Márquez de León
& Ciudad Constitución

CAPE REGION

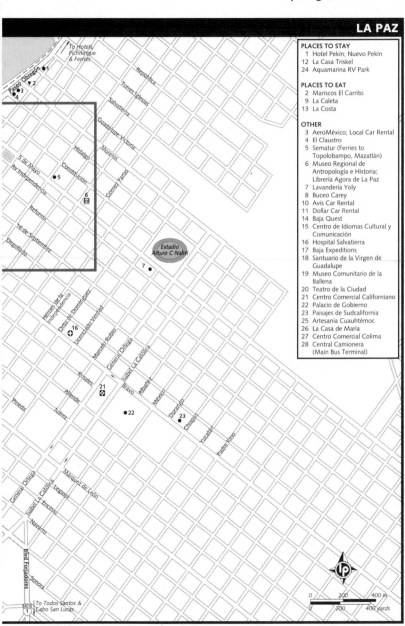

LA PAZ

PLACES TO STAY
1 Hotel Pekín; Nuevo Pekín
12 La Casa Triskel
24 Aquamarina RV Park

PLACES TO EAT
2 Mariscos El Carrito
9 La Caleta
13 La Costa

OTHER
3 AeroMéxico; Local Car Rental
4 El Claustro
5 Sematur (Ferries to Topolobampo, Mazatlán)
6 Museo Regional de Antropología e Historia; Librería Agora de La Paz
7 Lavandería Yoly
8 Buceo Carey
10 Avis Car Rental
11 Dollar Car Rental
14 Baja Quest
15 Centro de Idiomas Cultural y Comunicación
16 Hospital Salvatierra
17 Baja Expeditions
18 Santuario de la Virgen de Guadalupe
19 Museo Comunitario de la Ballena
20 Teatro de la Ciudad
21 Centro Comercial Californiano
22 Palacio de Gobierno
23 Paisajes de Sudcalifornia
25 Artesanía Cuauhtémoc
26 La Casa de María
27 Centro Comercial Colima
28 Central Camionera (Main Bus Terminal)

CAPE REGION

Books (☎ 1-122-14-10), Constitución 195, at the corner of Madero, offers a small selection of books in English.

The Museo Regional de Antropología e Historia (see below) has a good selection of Spanish-language books on Baja California and mainland Mexico.

Next door, Librería Agora de La Paz (☎ 1-122-62-04) is even better, offering many of the same items for more reasonable prices.

Laundry La Paz Lava is centrally located at Ocampo and Mutualismo. Lavandería Yoly is on 5 de Mayo between Licenciado Verdad and Marcelo Rubio, opposite the baseball park.

Medical & Emergency Services La Paz's Hospital Salvatierra (☎ 1-122-14-96, 1-122-15-96) is on Bravo between Licenciado Verdad and Ortiz de Domínguez. Another option is the Cruz Roja (Red Cross; ☎ 1-122-11-11 or 1-122-12-22).

Museo Regional de Antropología e Historia

Set behind an attractive cactus garden at the corner of 5 de Mayo and Altamirano, this first-rate anthropological and historical museum (☎ 1-122-01-62), run by the Instituto Nacional de Antropología y Historia (INAH), chronicles the peninsula's past from prehistory to the Revolution of 1910 and its aftermath.

Exhibits cover pre-Columbian rock art, native peoples, the mission era, various mining booms, the arrival of independence, the Mexican-American War and William Walker's invasion (don't miss the replica of Walker's flag and the bonds used to finance his adventures).

A small gallery contains rotating exhibits by local artists and photographers or seasonal displays on topics like November's Day of the Dead, Mexico's most famous informal holiday. The museum also contains a bookstore with a good selection on both Baja California and Mexico in general.

The museum is open 9 am to 6 pm weekdays, to 1 pm Saturday (free admission).

Catedral de Nuestra Señora de La Paz

Nothing remains of La Paz's first cathedral, built in 1720 under the direction of Jesuit missionaries Jaime Bravo and Juan de Ugarte near the site of present-day Jardín Velasco. The present structure dates from 1861 but mimics the style of California mission architecture.

Biblioteca de la Historia de las Californias

La Paz's former Government House, now a history library, contains a small but valuable collection of books and newspapers in both Spanish and English about the Californias. It also displays thematically appropriate artwork ranging from ghastly (a kitschy representation of Calafia, the mythical Amazon whose name presumably survives in the word 'California') to mediocre (privateer Thomas Cavendish's crew boarding the Manila galleon *Santa Ana)* to respectable (a replica mural of Desierto Central rock art). The library, on the northwestern side of Jardín Velasco, is open 8 am to 8 pm weekdays.

Teatro de la Ciudad

At the entrance to La Paz's city theater, the Rotonda de los Hombres Ilustres (Rotunda of Distinguished Men) is a sculptural tribute to figures who fought against filibuster William Walker's invasion of La Paz in 1853 and the French mainland intervention of 1861. The theater proper offers performances by musical and theatrical groups such as Guadalajara's Ballet Folklórico, as well as occasional film series.

A sprawling concrete edifice, the theater (☎ 1-125-00-04) is the most conspicuous element of the Unidad Cultural Profesor Jesús Castro Agúndez (☎ 1-125-19-17), a cultural center that takes up most of the area bounded by Altamirano, Navarro, Héroes de la Independencia and Legaspi. Other units within the center include the Galería Maestro José Carlos Olachea, exhibiting works by contemporary Mexican artists; the Archivo Histórico Pablo L Martínez, a research archive named in honor of a famous Baja California historian; and the Biblioteca Central Filemón C Piñeda, a general library.

A new feature on the periphery of the grounds on Navarro close to the corner of Altamirano is the **Museo Comunitario de la Ballena** (Community Whale Museum), open 10 am to 1 pm daily.

Santuario de la Virgen de Guadalupe

Paying homage to Mexico's greatest religious icon, the Santuario, on 5 de Febrero between Revolución and Aquiles Serdán, is La Paz's biggest religious monument, built partly in a mission style with various modernistic touches.

Diving & Snorkeling

The main diving and snorkeling destinations in Bahía de La Paz (beware of contaminated water) and the Gulf are **Isla de las Focas**, an island just north of Península Pichilingue's Punta Coyote that is renowned for its beaches and sea lion colony; **Los Islotes**, a group of islets just north of Isla Partida with various shipwrecks, underwater caves, reefs and sea lion colonies; and **Isla Cerralvo**, east of Península Pichilingue. Snorkeling trips to Isla de las Focas cost about US$45, whereas two-tank scuba trips to Los Islotes run around US$85. Prices usually include food and drinks, but try to clarify what's included before booking a trip.

Probably La Paz's best-established dive shop is Baja Diving & Service (☎ 1-122-18-26, fax 1-122-86-44), Paseo Obregón 1665, Local 2. Baja Expeditions (☎ 1-125-38-28, fax 1-125-38-29, 800-843-6967 in the US), 585 Sonora at the corner of Abasolo, gets recommendations for its dive packages. Its Web site is at www.bajaex.com. You can arrange trips through the San Diego office at 2625 Garnet Ave, San Diego, CA 92109.

Sea Scuba (☎ 1-123-52-33), at 460 Paseo Obregón, Suite 208, at the corner of Ocampo, arranges dive trips and rents equipment, as does Buceo Carey (☎ 1-123-23-33), located in the La Paz Marina. Scuba Baja Joe (☎ 1-122-40-06, fax 1-122-40-00) is around the corner on Ocampo; its mailing address is Apdo Postal 361, La Paz, Baja California Sur

23000, México. Rates are US$85 per day (9 am to 4 pm) for trips to sites in the immediate La Paz area, US$95 for trips to El Bajo (a seamount near Isla Partida) and Isla Cerralvo. Deportiva La Paz (☎ 1-122-73-33), on Paseo Obregón at the corner of the Calle La Paz (pedestrian walk), sells diving equipment but doesn't offer rentals.

Baja Quest (☎ 1-123-53-20, fax 1-123-53-21), Navarro 55, between Abasolo and Topete, is a newcomer that specializes in diving but also offers sea kayaking and whale-watching trips. Its snorkeling trips cost US$60 per person, whereas two-tank dives cost US$100 and three-tank dives US$125. The Cortez Club (☎ 1-121-61-20, fax 1-121-61-23, 800-999-2242 in the US and Canada) at La Concha Beach Resort (see Places to Stay) specializes in diving but also rents kayaks, windsurfing equipment, Hobie cats and the like. The US postal address is 7860 Mission Centre Court, Suite 202, San Diego, CA 92108-1331. Check out its Web site at www.cortezclub.com. The Hotel Marina (☎ 1-121-62-54, fax 1-121-61-77) also has a water-sports center that offers snorkeling and diving (see Places to Stay). A two-tank dive costs US$162.

Fishing

Game-fish species available all year in the vicinity of La Paz include bonito, corvina, crevalle, grouper, needlefish, pargo, rock bass, sierra and skipjack. Seasonal species include black and blue marlin (both July to October), dorado (April to December), roosterfish (May to January), sailfish (June to October), snook (December to June, but rare), striped marlin (May to October), yellowfin tuna (July to November, sporadically) and yellowtail (December to May).

The Hotel Los Arcos lobby (see Places to Stay) contains an information desk for the Dorado Vélez Fleet (☎ 1-122-27-44 ext 608, fax 1-125-43-13), which offers trips on boats ranging from 22 to 30 feet and provides all equipment, licenses and transportation. Its mailing address is Apdo Postal 402, La Paz, Baja California Sur, México. Most of La Paz's other major hotels and travel agencies can also arrange trips.

CENTRAL LA PAZ

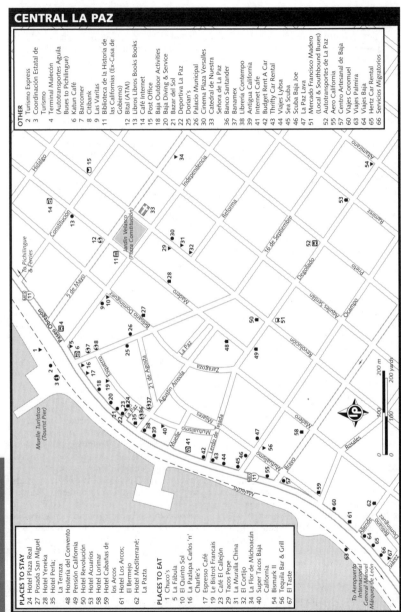

CAPE REGION

PLACES TO STAY
24 Hotel Plaza Real
27 Posada San Miguel
28 Hotel Yeneka
35 Hotel Perla;
    La Terraza
48 Hostería del Convento
49 Pensión California
50 Hotel Revolución
53 Hotel Acuarios
58 Hotel Lorimar
59 Hotel Cabañas de
    los Arcos
61 Hotel Los Arcos;
    El Bermejo
62 Hotel Mediterrané;
    La Pazta

PLACES TO EAT
1   Chuco's
5   La Fábula
10 El Quinto Sol
16 La Pazlapa Carlos 'n'
    Charlie's
17 Espresso Café
19 Le Bistrot Francais
23 Café El Callejón
29 Tacos Pepe
31 La Muralla China
32 El Cortijo
34 La Flor de Michoacán
40 Super Tacos Baja
    California
54 Bismark II
56 Tequila Bar & Grill
67 El Taste

OTHER
2   Turismo Express
3   Coordinación Estatal de
    Turismo
4   Terminal Malecón
    (Autotransportes Aguila
    Buses to Pichilingue)
6   Katun Café
7   Bancomer
8   Citibank
9   Las Varitas
11 Biblioteca de la Historia de
    las Californias (Ex-Casa de
    Gobierno)
12 Bital (ATM)
13 Libros Libros Books Books
14 Bazar del Sol
15 Café Internet
18 Post Office
20 Baja Outdoor Activities
21 Deportiva La Paz
22 Dorian's
25 Palacio Municipal
30 Cinema Plaza Versalles
33 Catedral de Nuestra
    Señora de La Paz
36 Banco Santander
37 Banamex
38 Librería Contempo
39 Antigua California
41 Internet Cafe
42 Budget Rent A Car
43 Thrifty Car Rental
44 Viajes Lybsa
45 Sea Scuba
46 Scuba Baja Joe
47 La Paz Lava
51 Mercado Francisco Madero
    (Local & Southbound Buses)
52 Autotransportes de La Paz
55 Aero California
57 Centro Artesanal de Baja
60 Viajes Coromuel
63 Viajes Palmira
64 Viajes Baja
65 Hertz Car Rental
66 Servicios Migratorios

Mulegé, straddling the verdant Arroyo Santa Rosalía in central Baja

WAYNE BERNHARDSON

Natural arch at Land's End (Cabo San Lucas)

LEE FOSTER

Gray whale sighting

WAYNE BERNHARDSON

Waves at Playa Los Cerritos (Western Cape)

WAYNE BERNHARDSON

LEE FOSTER

Popular El Squid Roe club (Cabo San Lucas)

JOHN NEUBAUER

Sipping away in Margaritavilla (Cabo San Lucas)

JOHN NEUBAUER

Inside El Squid Roe (Cabo San Lucas)

DAVID PEEVERS

Colorful Pancho's restaurant (Cabo San Lucas)

LEE FOSTER

Touristy beach resorts take over the southern coastline of Baja.

Jonathan Roldan's Sportfishing Services (☎ 626-333-3355 in the US) at the Cortez Club (see Diving & Snorkeling, earlier) offers four-night packages, including two days of *panga* (skiff) fishing, at La Concha Beach Resort for US$339 per person, double occupancy.

Sea Kayaking & Whale-Watching

Baja Outdoor Activities (☎/fax 1-125-56-36), an Anglo-Mexican company on Paseo Obregón a few doors west of La Pazlapa Carlos 'n' Charlie's, offers kayak trips ranging from half a day (US$30) to a full day (US$80) on and around Isla Espíritu Santo, as well as overnight excursions. Rental kayaks cost US$25 to US$45 per day, with weekly rentals at a slight discount. Try its Web site at www.kayactivities.com. Its mailing address is Apdo Postal 792, La Paz, Baja California Sur 23000, México.

Baja Quest and the Cortez Club (see Diving & Snorkeling, earlier) also rent kayaks.

Many hotels can arrange whale-watching tours. The Hotel Marina (see Places to Stay) offers day trips that cost about US$100 per person.

Language Courses

Centro de Idiomas, Cultura y Comunicación (☎ 1-125-75-54), Calle Madero 2460, offers introductory, intermediate and advanced Spanish lessons and a total-immersion program. Se Habla…La Paz is a new language school. See Language Courses in the Facts for the Visitor chapter for details.

Special Events

Carnaval is in February or March. These pre-Lenten celebrations are probably the peninsula's best and among the country's best. Fundación de la Ciudad is from May 1 to 7, when *Paceños* (people of La Paz) celebrate the founding of La Paz in 1535. Events include a dramatization of Hernán Cortés' landing, sports events like a half-marathon and a commercial exhibition.

Día de la Marina (Navy Day) is June 1, and Festival de las Artes (Arts Festival) is held in late November.

Places to Stay

Budget At Km 4 on the Transpeninsular, just before town in a partly shaded area distant from the beach, the well-organized *El Cardón Trailer Park* (☎ 1-124-00-78, fax 1-124-02-61) has 90 spaces, each with full hookups, electric light and a small *palapa* (palm-leaf shelter). Facilities include a laundry room, a swimming pool, hot showers, clean toilets, a small paperback book exchange, a travel agency and an Internet cafe. Car spaces cost US$10, while RV spaces cost US$12. The postal address is Apdo Postal 104, La Paz, Baja California Sur, México.

Just west of El Cardón, shady, secure and well-kept *RV Park Casa Blanca* (☎ 1-124-00-09, fax 1-125-11-42) has a pool, a restaurant and sites with full hookups for US$15 per night.

La Paz Trailer Park (☎ 1-122-87-87, fax 1-122-99-38, Brecha California 120) is a deluxe facility about 1 mile (1.6km) south of downtown. Facilities include very clean bathrooms and showers, a fine restaurant, a Jacuzzi, a swimming pool and a book exchange. Rates are about US$17 for a vehicle site, US$12 for a tent site.

Closest to town is the bayside fortress of *Aquamarina RV Park* (☎ 1-122-37-61, fax 1-125-62-28), at the foot of Nayarit. The place is highly regarded, but its heavy-duty security gives it an intimidating feeling. Sites cost about US$18.

Longtime budget favorite *Pensión California* (☎ 1-122-28-96, Degollado 209) features a patio surrounded by tropical foliage; its walls are lined with quirky artwork. Each basic room has a ceiling fan, fluorescent light, adjustable blinds and a shower for US$10.50/14 single/double. Under the same management, basic *Hostería del Convento* (☎ 1-122-35-08, Madero 85) is dark and dilapidated, with less-than-spotless toilets. Rooms cost US$9/14.

Built around a central patio, the 14-room *Posada San Miguel* (☎ 1-122-88-88, Belisario Domínguez 1510) is a pleasant, pseudo-colonial place whose dark but clean rooms each have a private bath, but the hot water can be erratic. Rates are US$10.50/13.

Motel-style *Hotel Yeneka* (☎ *1-125-46-88, Madero 1520*) has 20 rooms and a quasicafe with eclectic automotive decor including hub caps and countless bumpers with mud-splattered license plates. Clean rooms with firm beds (mattresses set over concrete) cost US$19/22.

Hotel Revolución, formerly the María Cristina I (☎ *1-125-80-22, Revolución 85*), near Degollado, has rooms with air-con and pool for US$17/21. Rooms at *Hotel Pekín* (☎ *1-125-53-35, Paseo Obregón 875*), near Guadalupe Victoria, cost US$23/26.

For an excellent value, try *Hotel Lorimar* (☎ *1-125-38-22, fax 1-125-63-87, Bravo 110*), near Madero, with an attractive courtyard. Bright rooms with air-con and tiled shower with hot water cost either US$19/24 or US$30/34 for new rooms; there is good laundry service here. It is also possible to arrange for shuttle service out to Tecolote Beach for US$8.

La Casa Triskel (☎ *1-123-05-01, 305 Allende*) is a bed and breakfast that offers rooms for US$14. Some of the rooms are shared, hostel style.

Mid-Range At the corner of Calle La Paz and Esquerro, *Hotel Plaza Real* (☎ *1-122-93-33, fax 1-122-44-24*) charges US$39 for doubles. The rooms are very basic, but it's a central location.

Recommended *Hotel Acuarios* (☎ *1-122-92-66, fax 1-125-57-13, Ramírez 1665*), at Degollado, has a restaurant and a swimming pool. Rates are US$42/45 for rooms with air-con, full carpeting, TV and telephone.

One of the nicest places to stay (if you don't mind being a bit out of town) is the *Club El Moro* (☎ *1-122-40-84, fax 1-125-28-28*), where a standard double is US$40. The suites are a particularly good deal, offering spacious rooms with kitchenettes and living rooms for US$50 to US$70. It's located on the road to Pichilingue; the mailing address is Apdo Postal 357, La Paz, Baja California Sur, México. The more central *Hotel Mediterrané* (☎ *1-125-11-95, Allende 36-B*) has rooms ranging from US$55 to US$80. An Italian restaurant, La Pazta, is located in the hotel (see Places to Eat).

Historic *Hotel Perla* (☎ *1-122-07-77, fax 1-125-53-63, Paseo Obregón 1570*), has a swimming pool, a restaurant, a bar and a nightclub. Some rooms offer bay views, while others overlook the pool; all have air-con, TV and private bath. Rates run around US$72 for a double.

Top End Rates at bayside *Hotel Marina* (☎ *1-121-62-54, fax 1-121-61-77, 800-826-1138 in the US*), at Km 2.5 on the Pichilingue road, start at US$95 a double. Suites start at US$150.

On Avenida Reforma, the Spanish-style *Hotel La Posada de Engelbert* (☎ *1-122-40-11, fax 1-122-06-63*), owned by crooner Engelbert Humperdinck, has 25 bungalow-type rooms with brick fireplace; facilities include a private beach, a swimming pool, tennis courts, a restaurant and a bar. Rates are US$75/95.

The *Araiza Inn Palmira* (☎ *1-121-62-00, fax 1-121-62-27*), about 1½ miles (2.5km) north of downtown on the Pichilingue road, is a modern hotel appealing to vacationing families and small conventions, with a swimming pool, tennis courts, a restaurant and a nightclub. Its rooms start at US$95.

Set among lush tropical gardens on Mutualismo near Paseo Obregón, highly regarded *Hotel Cabañas de los Arcos* (☎ *1-122-27-44, fax 1-125-43-13*) offers cabaña-style rooms with fireplace, tiled floor, thatched roof, TV, air-con and minibar. Rates are about US$75 for a cabaña, US$60 for a double. Its US representative is Baja Hotels (☎ *949-450-9000, 800-347-2252, fax 949-540-9010*), 6 Jenner St, Suite 120, Irvine, CA 92618.

Its larger but rather less appealing sister, *Hotel Los Arcos* (*Paseo Obregón 498*) near Rosales, has two swimming pools, a sauna, a restaurant and a coffee shop. All rooms have air-con, telephone, color TV and showers. Rooms range from US$75 for a double to US$80 for a room with a bay view.

At Km 5 on the road to Pichilingue, the 107-room *La Concha Beach Resort* (☎ *1-121-61-61, in the US* ☎ *800-999-2252, fax 619-294-7366*) is a beachfront hotel with palm trees, a swimming pool (with poolside bar), a fine Mexican restaurant and a watersports center (though the water is very shallow). It charges around US$95 for comfortable, air-conditioned rooms, all with balconies overlooking the bay.

Places to Eat

Two blocks southeast of Jardín Velasco, on 5 de Mayo between Prieto and Aquiles Serdán, *La Flor de Michoacán* sells delicious aguas, paletas, licuados, ice cream and sandwiches. Frequented more by Mexicans than gringos, the *Espresso Café (Paseo Obregón 10),* near 16 de Septiembre, is a popular coffee bar that also offers drinks and light meals.

Super Tacos Baja California, a stall at the corner of Agustín Arreola and Mutualismo, thrives on both local and tourist trade. It's a bit dearer than most taco stands, but the quality of its fish, shrimp, clam and scallop tacos, plus outstanding condiments, more than justifies the extra peso – what other taquería offers sweet-and-sour shrimp tacos? It's open 8 am to 6 pm.

Mariscos El Carrito, at the corner of Paseo Obregón and Morelos, is a palm-shaded seafood stand with tables for taco lovers weary of standing while eating. *Tacos Pepe*, on Revolución between Reforma and Avenida Independencia, has outstanding carnitas.

El Quinto Sol (☎ 1-122-16-92) is a very popular vegetarian landmark and health-food market at the corner of Avenida Independencia and Belisario Domínguez. Besides its bean specialties, it offers large breakfast servings of yogurt (plain, with fruit or with granola or muesli). Licuados, fresh-baked breads and pastries are other specialties.

Another good restaurant that offers vegetarian options is *Le Bistrot Francais* (☎ 1-125-60-80, 10 Calle Esquerro). The courtyard tables provide a particularly pleasant atmosphere.

Chuco's, on the malecón at 16 de Septiembre, is the best place to eat dinner and watch the sun go down. The margaritas are especially good. *La Media Luna* (☎ 1-122-19-19, Paseo Obregón 755), between Iglesias and Salvatierra, offers a menu ranging from seafood to steak. Its three-storied

palapa offers views of the bay. *La Costa* (☎ 1-122-88-08), at Topete and Navarro, serves the best lobster in La Paz.

One of downtown's best values, *Café El Callejón*, on the Calle La Paz ped mall, has cheap and very good antojitos; try the chicken mole. *El Cortijo* (☎ 1-122-25-32, Revolución 1460) is a popular Mexican place that's been around since 1960.

Bismark II (☎ 1-122-48-54), at the corner of Degollado and Altamirano, is popular with locals for generous helpings of excellent, reasonably priced seafood. *La Caleta* (☎ 1-123-02-87), right on the malecón at the corner of Pineda, is very popular for its reasonably priced meals and drinks; there's live music tending toward jazz and ballads.

For pizza, try *La Fábula* (☎ 1-122-41-01), across the malecón from the tourist office, open noon to 11 pm daily. *La Pazta* (☎ 1-125-11-95, Allende 36-B), just south of the malecón in the Hotel Mediterrané, has good Italian specials at reasonable prices. Also serving Italian food, upscale *El Bermejo*, at the corner of Paseo Obregón and Rosales, is part of Hotel Los Arcos.

El Taste (☎ 1-122-81-21), on Paseo Obregón at Juárez, is a good place to go for antojitos and margaritas. Serving a predominantly Mexican crowd, *La Pazlapa Carlos 'n' Charlie's* (☎ 1-122-92-90), on Paseo Obregón near 16 de Septiembre, is part of the extensive chain more noted for drinking than for dining. Down the block at the corner of Paseo Obregón and Calle La Paz, Hotel Perla's *La Terraza* restaurant has good food and an attractive, open terrace.

Tequila Bar & Grill (☎ 1-122-52-17), at the corner of Mutualismo and Ocampo, is another good spot to stop for antojitos. They serve excellent margaritas as well.

Restaurant/Bar El Moro (☎ 1-122-70-10), near the Araiza Inn Palmira on the Pichilingue road, features Sonoran beef, salad, pasta and a few Cantonese dishes. *Nuevo Pekín* (☎ 1-125-09-95, Paseo Obregón 875), near Guadalupe Victoria in the Hotel Pekín, is a so-so Chinese restaurant very popular with locals. *La Muralla China* (☎ 1-122-06-06, Revolución 1440) is comparable.

Entertainment

Most of La Paz's nightlife is concentrated on and around Paseo Obregón, but it never gets as raucous as Cabo San Lucas. Note that La Paz's uneven sidewalks, many with steps of varying sizes, are virtual minefields for tipsy pedestrians.

Longtime favorite nightclub *Las Varitas* (☎ 1-125-20-25, *Avenida Independencia 111*), near Belisario Domínguez, regularly offers live music and dancing; there's a US$2 cover charge.

The current hot nightspot is *El Claustro* (☎ 1-122-45-44), located on Paseo Obregon at Hidalgo. It's a combination restaurant and nightclub.

Cinema Plaza Versalles (☎ 1-122-95-55), on Revolución near the corner of Avenida Independencia, offers first-run international films on four screens. Admission costs about US$4.

Shopping

Peter Gerhard, in his classic *Lower California Guidebook* of the 1960s, tells of a tourist who bought a black pearl in La Paz only to learn that it was an exquisitely burnished ball bearing! Few visitors are so gullible, but local stores have plenty of junk alongside the good stuff.

Centro Artesanal de Baja (☎ 1-125-88-02), at Abasolo and Bravo, sells jewelry, handicrafts and clothes. Bazar del Sol (☎ 1-122-36-26), Paseo Obregón 1165, near Calle La Paz, is loaded with kitsch. Antigua California, on Paseo Obregón between Agustín Arreola and Muelle, features a wide selection of crafts from throughout the country.

A bit west of downtown, La Casa de María (☎ 1-122-56-06), on Abasolo between Jalisco and Oaxaca, is a good choice for handicrafts and especially furniture. Artesanía Cuauhtémoc (☎ 1-122-45-75), across the street at Abasolo 3315, is a weavers' cooperative. Paisajes de Sudcalifornia (☎ 1-123-37-00), Bravo 1890, specializes in southern Baja art and crafts.

Dorian's, on 16 de Septiembre between Esquerro and 21 de Agosto, is one of the city's major department stores.

On weekends during the Christmas season, countless baubles change hands at the Mercado Navideño, which turns downtown Madero and Avenida Independencia (at right angles to each other) into pedestrian malls.

Getting There & Away

Air Aeropuerto Internacional General Manuel Márquez de León (☎ 1-122-14-66/7), more commonly known as La Paz International Airport, is just 6½ miles (10km) southwest of downtown, at the end of a short lateral off the Transpeninsular.

AeroMéxico (☎ 1-122-00-91), at Paseo Obregón between Hidalgo and Morelos, flies daily between La Paz and Los Angeles, Tucson, Tijuana, Culiacán, Durango, Guadalajara, Guaymas, Mazatlán and Mexico City. Its subsidiary Aerolitoral, at the same address, flies daily to and from Loreto.

Aero California (☎ 1-125-10-23, 800-237-6225 in the US) has offices at the airport and at Paseo Obregón 550 near the corner of Bravo. Hours are 8 am to 8 pm daily. It operates two daily flights between La Paz and Los Angeles, daily flights to Tucson via Hermosillo and one daily nonstop to Tijuana. It also offers many flights to mainland Mexican destinations, including Los Mochis (for the Barranca del Cobre train), Mazatlán and Mexico City. Most flights have onward national and international connections.

Bus Autotransportes de Baja California (ABC; ☎ 1-122-30-63), Autotransportes Aguila (☎ 1-122-42-70) and Autotransportes de La Paz (☎ 1-122-21-57) operate intercity buses.

ABC and Aguila use the Central Camionera (main bus terminal) at the corner of Jalisco and Héroes de la Independencia, whereas Autotransportes de La Paz has its own terminal at the corner of Degollado and Prieto. Aguila also has a separate terminal on the malecón at Independencia.

The following are northbound ABC/Aguila routes:

Ciudad Constitución – US$9, 2½ hours; five times daily 7 am to 9:30 pm

Puerto San Carlos – US$12, four hours; daily at 8 am & 2:30 pm

Puerto López Mateos – US$12, four hours; daily at 10 am & 4:30 pm

Loreto – US$16, five hours; five times daily 9 am to 10 pm

La Purísima-San Isidro – US$16, five hours; daily at 7 am & 3:30 pm

Mulegé – US$22, seven hours; three times daily 9 am to 10 pm

Santa Rosalía – US$25, eight hours; four times daily 9 am to 10 pm

San Ignacio – US$31.50, nine hours; four times daily 10 am to 10 pm

Guerrero Negro – US$40, 12 hours; four times daily 10 am to 10 pm

San Quintín – US$57, 17 hours; three times daily 10 am to 10 pm

Ensenada – US$67, 20 hours; daily at 10 am, 8 & 10 pm

Tijuana – US$73, 22 to 24 hours; daily at 10 am, 8 & 10 pm

Mexicali – US$84, 24 hours; daily at 4 pm

Southbound ABC/Aguila buses depart several times daily for El Triunfo (US$2, one hour), San Antonio (US$3, 70 minutes), Buena Vista (US$5, 1½ hours), Miraflores (US$7, 2½ hours) and San José del Cabo via the Transpeninsular (US$10, three hours).

Aguila buses take the Southern Cape Highway (México 19) from La Paz to Cabo San Lucas (US$9) and to Todos Santos (US$5) at least five times daily between 7 am and 7 pm.

Autotransportes de La Paz operates buses from the station at the corner of Degollado and Prieto to Todos Santos (US$3.50, 1½ hours) and Cabo San Lucas (US$8, 2½ hours) eight times daily between 6:45 am and 7:45 pm.

Ferry The major terminal for Sematur ferries to the mainland towns of Topolobampo and Mazatlán is in Pichilingue, about 14 miles (22km) north of central La Paz. Sematur (☎ 1-125-23-4612) maintains La Paz offices at the corner of Prieto and 5 de Mayo.

Before they will ship your vehicle, ferry officials require you to show a vehicle permit. For details on how to obtain one, see the Vehicle Permits section in the Getting Around chapter.

To leave your vehicle in La Paz while returning to the USA or crossing to mainland Mexico, theoretically you will need authorization from Mexican Customs, who may require that you leave the vehicle in a *recinto fiscal* (official impound lot).

Ferry tickets must be confirmed by 2 pm on the day before departure. At 3 pm, seats that have not been confirmed are sold on a first-come, first-served basis, which sometimes results in shoving matches to see who gets to the head of the line.

Weather permitting (high winds often delay winter sailings), the Topolobampo ferry (10 hours) leaves at 10 pm daily and arrives in Topolobampo at 8 am. The Tuesday sailing does not permit women or boys under age 18 because it carries *carga negra* (hazardous materials). The return ferry from Topolobampo departs at 10 pm daily.

The ferry to Mazatlán (17 hours) departs at 3 pm daily, arriving at 8 am the following morning. The return ferry leaves Mazatlán at 3 pm, arriving at 8 am in La Paz.

Approximate one-way fares from La Paz are as follows:

class	to Topolobampo	to Mazatlán
Salón	US$19	US$26
Turista	US$38	US$53
Cabina	US$57	US$79
Especial	US$79	US$105

Vehicle rates are as follows:

length	to Topolobampo	to Mazatlán
Up to 5m*	US$163	US$265
5.01 to 6.5m	US$210	US$345
With trailer up to 9m	US$290	US$477
9.01 to 17m	US$547	US$895
Motor home	US$339	US$451
Motorcycle	US$39	US$54

*1m = 3 feet 3 inches

Private Yacht Between November and March, according to one Lonely Planet correspondent, La Paz is a good place to catch a lift on a private yacht to mainland Mexico:

The Marina de La Paz, which houses the Dock Restaurant, the Penthouse Racing Club and the Club Cruceros, are the best places to hang out. Club Cruceros has a bulletin board where you can get information about people looking for help crewing their yachts. It's a pretty good source of information. There is a VHF radio at Club Cruceros, and plenty of people to show you how to use it. Their Web site is www.clubcruceros.org.

The most frequent trip is La Paz to Puerto Vallarta with stops at Bahía de los Muertos, Los Frailes (great coral snorkeling), then Isla Isabél and Puerto Vallarta. Allow about one week, with two to three nights at sea.

Getting Around

The government-regulated Transporte Terrestre (☎ 1-125-32-74, 1-125-62-29) minivan service charges US$10 per person to or from the airport, while private taxis cost about US$15.

Autotransportes Aguila buses leave downtown for Península Pichilingue and the ferry terminal from the Terminal Malecón (☎ 1-122-78-98) at the corner of Paseo Obregón and Avenida Independencia hourly between 7 am and 6 pm. The fare is about US$16.

Most local buses leave from the front of the Mercado Francisco Madero at the corner of Degollado and Revolución.

Car rental rates start around US$45 per day, including 300km of travel; taxes and insurance are extra. International rental agencies include the following:

Avis (☎ 1-122-26-51, 1-124-63-12 at the airport) Paseo Obregón 820 near Márquez de León

Budget (☎ 1-123-36-22, 1-124-64-33 at the airport, fax 1-122-51-40) Paseo Obregón between Muelle and Tejada

Dollar (☎ 1-122-60-60, fax 1-122-60-40) Paseo Obregón at Pineda

Hertz (☎ 1-122-53-00, 1-124-63-30 at the airport, fax 1-122-09-19) Paseo Obregón between Juárez and Allende

Local (☎ 1-122-51-40, fax 1-123-36-22) Paseo Obregón 582 between Morelos and Hidalgo

Thrifty (☎ 1-125-96-96, 1-124-63-65 at the airport) Paseo Obregón at the corner of Lerdo de Tejada (☎ 1-122-65-44) La Concha Beach Resort, Km 5 on the Pichilingue road

AROUND LA PAZ
Beaches

There are several small but pleasant beaches north and west of La Paz. To the west are the bayside **Playa El Comitán** and **Playa Las Hamacas**, but no public transportation serves them. El Comitán has deteriorated in recent years and swimming is no longer advisable there.

On Península Pichilingue to the north, the beaches nearest to La Paz are **Playa Palmira**, **Playa Coromuel** and **Playa Caimancito**. Playa Palmira has the *Araiza Inn Palmira*, a marina and a few condominium complexes with restaurant and bar, while the latter two have restaurants and bars, toilets and shady palapas. Playa Coromuel also has a big Plexiglas waterslide, and its seafood restaurant is good. **Playa Tesoro**, the next beach north, also has a restaurant and shade.

Camping is possible at **Playa Pichilingue**, 110 yards (100m) north of the ferry terminal; it has a restaurant and bar, toilets and shade. The road north of Pichilingue is paved to the exceptional beaches of **Playa Balandra** (whose sheltered location is not good for camping because of mosquitoes in its mangroves) and **Playa Tecolote** (where, across the Canal de San Lorenzo, Isla Espíritu Santo looks like a chunk of southern Utah's canyon country floating on the sea). **Playa Coyote**, on the Gulf side of the peninsula, is more isolated.

Surprisingly uncrowded even in ideal winter weather, Tecolote's wide, sandy beach lacks potable water and other amenities. It does have the nearby steak-and-seafood **Restaurant El Tecolote**, where the fish is excellent but the drinks are watery. Club de Playa El Tecolote (☎/fax 1-122-88-85), on the beach and in La Paz on Belisario Domínguez between Avenida Independencia and 5 de Mayo, offers tours from La Paz, arranges kayak trips to Espíritu Santo and rents water-sports equipment.

Most hotels can arrange shuttles to the beaches for about US$8. Aquila buses also leave from the Malecón terminal to Tecolote at noon and 2 pm, with return buses leaving the beach at 5:30 pm. The trip costs US$2 each way.

Local expatriates warn that stealthy and skillful thieves break into campers' cars at Tecolote and other isolated beaches – even while the campers are sleeping.

El Centenario to San Evaristo

West of La Paz, just beyond the village of El Centenario, a paved but potholed bumpy spur off the Transpeninsular leads north along the western shore of Bahía de La Paz to **San Juan de la Costa**, a phosphate-mining port with a passable restaurant and a detachment of Mexican marines. It's a nice drive out to San Juan de La Costa, right along the cliffs of the bay. The road continues to its northern terminus at San Evaristo, a small fish camp opposite Isla San José, on a sparkling inlet of the Gulf of California.

North of San Juan, the graded coastal road skirts the eastern scarp of the Sierra de la Giganta. The layered sediments of this multicolored mountain range resemble a cutaway of Arizona's Grand Canyon, most impressive in the morning sun, which accentuates the mountains' vivid colors. The road is badly washboarded in spots but passable even for low-clearance vehicles until a difficult climb at Punta El Mechudo, around Km 54.

The **Cuesta El Mechudo** consists of four crests. The last is relatively easy, but the preceding three are abrupt climbs on narrow roadways with many loose rocks – meeting another vehicle en route could be disastrous. Driving along this road is an adventure; the steep, winding climb along the cliffs allows for some hair-raising moments. A 4WD vehicle is preferable but not essential; high clearance and close attention to the roadway are imperative. According to residents at San Evaristo, a Volkswagen Beetle once made the trip, but no one can confirm that it returned successfully to La Paz. Because of the hairpin turns, it would be very difficult to maneuver this road in a large vehicle. One fisherman claims to drive the route at night so he needn't look down.

In April and May, San Evaristo swarms with boaters and campers, who enjoy bountiful fishing for snapper and cochinito. Most of the beaches along the San Juan-San Evaristo route are rocky or gravelly, but determined campers will find a few pleasant, sandy and isolated spots.

Just south of San Evaristo, an occasionally graded dirt road leads to the date-palm oasis of El Bosque and to Rancho Soledad, where a slightly dangerous 4WD road (with awesome panoramas of the Sierra de la Giganta's volcanic plateau) continues north to Rancho Las Animas, the ruins of Misión La Pasión and well-preserved Misión San Luis Gonzaga. (See the Desierto Central to Llano de Magdalena chapter for more details; sites in this section appear on the Sierra de la Giganta & Llano de Magdalena map in that chapter.)

Two-wheel-drive vehicles with good clearance can probably make it to El Bosque and Rancho Soledad, where a more passable road leads southwest to intersect the Transpeninsular at Las Pocitas, at Km 110. This is the easiest route into San Evaristo, even though it is not the most scenic. The San Evaristo-Soledad road is easier west-to-east (downhill) than east-to-west (uphill).

La Ventana & Ensenada de los Muertos

Southeast of La Paz (about a 45-minute drive), just before the village of San Juan de los Planes, a paved spur off highway BCS-286 turns north toward La Ventana, on its namesake bay opposite Isla Cerralvo. This is one of the best sites for windsurfing in Baja.

La Ventana Campground is a large campground with basic services; sites cost US$3. The campground gets very crowded during the prime windsurfing months (November to February). There are also a couple of unnamed *RV parks* in town, where sites cost US$6. The pleasant *Baja Joe's* (☎ 1-126-23-22 in La Paz) offers rooms on the water ranging from US$25 to US$85. Bikes and kayaks are available to guests, and windsurfing rentals are US$40 per day (lessons are also available). There are a few restaurants in town and a market as well.

About 32 miles (51km) southeast of La Paz, BCS-286 turns northeast just beyond San Juan de los Planes, where the paved road surface ends, and continues to Ensenada de los Muertos, on its own namesake bay, with plenty of places to camp. The bay is a popular fishing area; it's one of the main destinations for fishing packages organized in La Paz.

Just before the turnoff to Ensenada de los Muertos, there's a dirt road that takes you to Punta Arenas de la Ventana. The upscale *Las Arenas Resort* (☎ 1-122-31-46; in the US ☎ 619-460-4319, fax 619-460-4918) is a beautiful hotel located right on the water. Spacious rooms cost US$100/160 single/double with all meals included. Most people come to Las Arenas for the fishing; packages range from US$150 for a day trip to up to US$460 for four days out.

From a junction just southeast of San Juan de los Planes, an unpaved lateral climbs the Cuesta de los Muertos (Crest of the Dead) and continues south to Los Barriles. Though unsuitable for RVs of any sort, this route is an interesting alternative for visitors with high-clearance vehicles. For more details, see North of Los Barriles, later in this chapter.

Eastern Cape

Still among the less developed coastal areas in the Cape Region, the East Cape is where you're most likely to catch a glimpse of the Old Baja magic. It was wealthy American fishermen and adventurers who first 'discovered' the area – which stretches from Bahía Las Palmas, about 75 miles (120km) south of La Paz, all the way to San José del Cabo – in the 1940s and '50s. Hollywood celebrities such as John Wayne, Bing Crosby and Errol Flynn flew here in their private aircraft, making perilous landings on improvised airstrips. Deep-sea fishing and white-winged-dove hunting were favorite pastimes of this testosterone-driven crowd. The original fly-in resort, the Rancho Buena Vista, where many of them stayed, is still in operation today.

Fishing in these rich waters continues to be the East Cape's main draw. But other outdoor enthusiasts will find plenty to do as well. Remote beaches and clear waters are great for swimming and lounging. There's world-class windsurfing at Los Barriles. Diving off Cabo Pulmo, the only coral reef on the west coast of North America, may yield encounters with huge manta rays and schools of tropical fish.

For the most part, the infrastructure of the East Cape is still relatively basic; most roads are unpaved and there are many places without phone connections. In recent years, however, small-scale development has begun to encroach upon the area's pristine beauty, especially south of Los Barriles. Real estate prices have surged as North Americans have snapped up beachfront lots for their vacation homes, and 'towns' like Buena Vista and Los Barriles, until a few years ago little more than dusty outposts, are growing at a steady clip.

The Transpensinsular brushes the coast at Los Barriles from where a rough dirt road leads north to Punta Pescadero and El Cardonal. At Las Cuevas, near Km 93, a paved road leads to the coastal village of La Ribera. After about 6 miles (10km) on this road, another paved road veers off to the right. This is the Eastern Cape Road to Cabo Pulmo, Los Frailes and beyond, culminating at San José del Cabo after about 60 miles (100km).

Just before reaching Cabo Pulmo, after about 17 miles (27km), pavement abruptly gives way to a tooth-clattering dirt road. Most 2WD vehicles can usually get through, but it may become impassable after any sort of rain. Always check conditions locally before heading out. Under favorable conditions, smaller RVs should be able to make it at least to Los Frailes.

About 12 miles (19km) south of Los Frailes, at Vinorama, another dirt road called Palo Escopeta Road heads west and joins back with the Transpeninsular just south of Los Cabos International Airport. This road is usually in a fair state.

Aguila buses from La Paz to Los Cabos travel along the highway, stopping for pickups and dropoffs along the way (there are no bus terminals). Check the La Paz and San José del Cabo sections for details.

LOS BARRILES

Fast-growing Los Barriles (population 600), Baja's windsurfing capital, has a post office, police station, Ladatel phones, a Cruz Roja station, two supermarkets and several restaurants. Baja Money Exchange, in Plaza del Pueblo, changes cash and traveler's checks (closed Sunday). Faxes may be sent from Tío's Tienda. A modern self-service laundry is across from Mañanas restaurant (closed Sunday).

Windsurfing

Brisk 'El Norte' winds averaging 20 to 25 knots descend the 6000-foot (1800m) *cordillera* (mountain range) toward the mid-morning launch site at Playa Norte, about 2 miles (3km) north of Los Barriles. The wind picks up around 11 am at more southerly locations. The wind direction and curving shoreline, running south and then east into the Gulf, make it possible to sail 20 miles (32km) out to sea without losing sight of the shore.

San Francisco Bay Area–based Vela Windsurf Resorts (☎ 831-461-0820, 800-223-5443, fax 831-461-0821, info@velawindsurf.com) operates its Baja Highwind Center out of Los Barriles' Hotel Playa del Sol from mid-November to the first week in March. These world-class instructors teach seminars using state-of-the-art equipment

(boards by F2 and HiFly and sails by Neil Pryde).

Packages include accommodations at either the Playa del Sol or Hotel Palmas de Cortez (see Places to Stay, later), all meals, unlimited use of equipment, daily seminars, plus activities like mountain biking, snorkeling and kayaking. Weeklong trips start around US$887 per person, double occupancy. Reservations are essential as space is limited to 32 sailors and the resort is usually completely booked from December 1 to January 31. Note that seminars are best suited for intermediate to advanced sailors.

Also see Windsurfing under Buena Vista, later.

Mountain Biking

The people of Vela Windsurf Resorts have built a 30-mile trail network around Los Barriles. Trails are generally paved in thorns, making 'slime tubes' (self-sealing puncture tubes) essential. You'll also need fairly wide tires to ride safely on sandy trails.

A good long-distance trip is the triangular circuit up the Transpeninsular to San Antonio, continuing north through the arroyo to San Juan de los Planes and back down the coast to Los Barriles (72 miles, 115km).

Also see the Sierra de la Laguna section, later, for the popular Naranjas Road ride.

Places to Stay

Convivial *Martín Verdugo's Beach Resort* (☎/fax 1-141-00-54) can accommodate 61 RVs with full hookups for US$13 and an additional 15 tents at US$11 each. Facilities include hot showers, laundry rooms and the cleanest bathrooms we saw on the Cape. It also offers large and nicely decorated beachfront motel rooms, ranging from US$46 to US$56. Fishing boats rent for US$130 for a 22-foot panga to US$190 for a 23-foot super-panga and US$290 for a 28-foot supercruiser.

Juanito's Garden RV Park (☎ /fax 1-141-00-24, hotellosbarriles@cabonet.net.mx) charges US$12 for sites with full hookups, though most are taken up by permanent

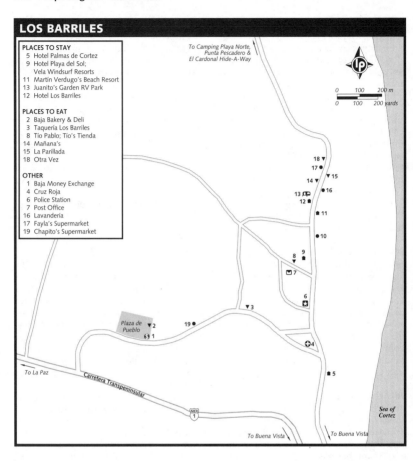

LOS BARRILES

PLACES TO STAY
5 Hotel Palmas de Cortez
9 Hotel Playa del Sol;
   Vela Windsurf Resorts
11 Martín Verdugo's Beach Resort
13 Juanito's Garden RV Park
12 Hotel Los Barriles

PLACES TO EAT
2 Baja Bakery & Deli
3 Taquería Los Barriles
8 Tío Pablo; Tío's Tienda
14 Mañana's
15 La Parillada
18 Otra Vez

OTHER
1 Baja Money Exchange
4 Cruz Roja
6 Police Station
7 Post Office
16 Lavandería
17 Fayla's Supermarket
19 Chapito's Supermarket

To Camping Playa Norte,
Punta Pescadero &
El Cardonal Hide-A-Way

Plaza de
Pueblo

To La Paz

Carretera Transpeninsular

To Buena Vista   To Buena Vista

Sea of
Cortez

residents. There is no tent camping. Hacienda-style **Hotel Los Barriles**, part of Juanito's, has 20 large rooms with Mexican furnishings and handpainted tiles built around a freeform pool for US$45/55 single/double.

At the time of research, a new campground, **Camping Playa Norte**, was being built on the beach about a mile or so north of Los Barriles proper. Once completed, it will offer hookups, flush toilets and other facilities. Rates, which may rise as infrastructure improves, are US$7 for tents and US$10 for RVs. **Hotel Playa del Sol** (☎/fax 1-141-02-12) has 26 clean, recently remodeled rooms for US$65/100 with full board. A traditional favorite among fisherfolk, the larger **Hotel Palmas de Cortez** (☎ 1-141-00-50) is an older facility with 31 rooms, 15 suites and 10 condominiums, all of them with ocean views. Nice touches include an aviary with parrots and the cabaña suites with private hammocks. Rates, including all meals, are US$75/120, US$150 for suites and US$220 (without meals) for the condos. The US contact for these last two hotels is ☎ 818-591-9463, 800-368-4334, fax 818-591-1077.

CAPE REGION

Places to Eat

A good place to start the day with gourmet coffee and fresh bakery items is the squeaky-clean **Baja Bakery & Deli** (☎ 1-141-03-81) in Plaza del Pueblo. It also serves hot breakfasts and sandwiches for around US$5 and is open 6:30 am to 2 pm daily. There are two markets in town, Fayla's and Chapito's.

Locals swear by the makeshift **Taquería Los Barriles** (also known as 'Blue Tarp Taquería'), whose owner Sylvia puts up an especially mouthwatering display of condiments to complement your fish, shrimp or meat tacos. It's open 8 am to 3 pm, closed Tuesday.

On weekends, big appetites flock to **La Parillada**, a little shack serving succulent charbroiled chicken for US$3.50/7 per half/whole, along with French fries, salsa and tortillas. It's open 5 to 10 pm Friday to Sunday.

Another place known for its gut-busting portions is the ever-popular **Tío Pablo** (☎ 1-141-03-30). Most people come for the pizza and burgers, but it's famous for the 28oz (840g) 'beltbuster steak.' There's also an all-you-can-eat salad bar. Tío's Tienda next door is a general-goods store.

Mañana's (☎ 1-141-03-44) has an American vibe and offers wood-fired pizza in two sizes (from US$6), salads and Mexican standards. The industrial-size nachos are great, but the salsa is soupy. The more extensive and gourmet-oriented dinner menu is only slightly more expensive.

The indoor **Otra Vez** (☎ 1-141-02-49) has an ambitious menu featuring Thai, Mexican and American dishes, mostly under US$10. Low-fat and vegetarian choices are available too.

NORTH OF LOS BARRILES

North of Los Barriles, a mostly graded but rough and potentially dangerous road, not suitable for large RVs, hugs the coast to Punta Pescadero and El Cardonal, and even crosses the very difficult Cuesta de los Muertos en route to San Juan de los Planes and La Paz. Conditions get worse the farther north you go, with narrow, steep and curvy sections quite common. While most beaches north of Los Barriles are rocky or gravelly, some are suitable for free camping. Check locally about road conditions before heading out.

After about 8 miles (13km), you'll reach remote **Hotel Punta Pescadero** (☎ 1-141-01-01, fax 1-141-00-69, 800-426-2252 in the US). A consummate getaway, the resort hugs a narrow but long ribbon of sandy beach. Each of the 21 newly remodeled rooms has an oceanview terrace, lounge area, fridge, satellite TV and coffee-maker. Rooms cost US$140. Meals cost US$8/10/15 for breakfast/lunch/dinner. Sportfishing trips cost US$150 on a panga, US$220 on a super-panga and US$250 to US$300 on a cruiser. Scuba rentals, surf-fishing equipment and horses are also available.

It takes determination to continue for 6 miles (10km) to reach the Canadian-run **El Cardonal Hide-A-Way** (☎/fax 1-141-00-40, in the US and Canada ☎ 514-467-4700, fax 514-467-4668, elcardonaleddy@hotmail.com), but you'll be rewarded with a spectacular, remote setting and the sense that you've really made it off the beaten path. Beachfront suites feature two double beds and full kitchenettes and cost US$39 per day, US$259 per week. Tents and small campers are charged US$7, while RVs pay US$10 for full hookups. Children stay free, and the restaurant is open all day. Activities include diving and snorkeling, horseback riding, kayaking and fishing, all fee-based. You can also play volleyball, badminton and horseshoes. Rock-art excursions to Rancho Boca del Alamo can be arranged.

BUENA VISTA

What windsurfing is to Los Barriles, sport-fishing is to tiny Buena Vista (population 200). This small village about 1 mile (1.6km) south grew up around the East Cape's first fly-in fishing resort, the Rancho Buena Vista, once frequented by Hollywood hotshots. There are a few other hotels now but little infrastructure otherwise.

Hikers will be rewarded with fine bay views from the top of Flat Top Mountain, reached via an easy 30- to 45-minute trail. Ask for directions at Rancho Leonero (see Places to Stay & Eat, later); they're the people who built the trail. Less ambitious folk can walk, drive or bike up to the Flag Monument for equally impressive views. Look for the turnoff around Km 105.5 off the Transpeninsular.

Mountain bikers can take the Pemex Ridge Trail from behind the Pemex station at Km 109, which runs through a cactus forest and offers great bay views.

Fishing

The following list indicates the prime seasons for the various fish species on the East Cape. Many of the hotels and resorts listed under Places to Stay have their own fishing fleet, open to guests and nonguests.

Blue marlin	June to November
Cabrilla	March to May
Dorado	March to November
Roosterfish	April to June
Sailfish	June to November
Sierra	December to March
Striped marlin	March to June
Yellowfin	May to November
Yellowtail	February to May
Wahoo	June to November

Windsurfing

A slightly cheaper alternative to the Los Barriles options is Baja Adventures (☎ 1-141-02-71). One-week packages with B&B lodging at Casa Miramar in Buena Vista start at US$575/695/1390 bunk/single/double. Prices include unlimited use of windsurfing equipment, mountain bikes, snorkeling gear, sea kayaks and Hobie Cats. Nonsailors pay US$375/575/950. Baja Adventures also offers kiteboarding packages, a new sport that's been compared to kite-powered waterskiing.

Diving & Snorkeling

Vista Sea Sport (☎/fax 1-141-00-31) offers dive tours to Cabo Pulmo (US$100), Los Frailes (US$100), Punta Pescadero (US$75), Isla Cerralvo (US$120) and the Gordo Banks (US$140), and snorkeling tours (US$25 to US$50) in the Los Barriles area. Baja Adventures (☎ 1-141-02-71) at Casa Miramar runs similar excursions and also

rents sea kayaks, Hobie Cats and windsurfing equipment.

Places to Stay & Eat

About half a mile (800m) south of Hotel Buena Vista Beach Resort (see below) is the rustic *La Capilla Trailer Park (no phone)*. The dirt road to Rancho Leonero (turnoff at Km 103.5; see below) also provides access. Sites, which cost US$10, hug the beach and have full hookups. Bathrooms are rather grimy, but hot showers are usually available. Vacancies are rare in winter, when the place fills with 'snowbirds.'

The East Cape's most original digs are at *Casas Ramada (☎/fax 1-141-00-38)*, a quartet of Afghani-style huts overlooking the beach that rent for US$20. Made from local materials, these round huts come complete with refrigerator, small gas stove, fans and private outdoor hot tub. Showers and toilets were inside the rooms at the time of our visit, but the owner was planning on building attached cubicles. The office is in the house with the painted portraits at the southern edge of town. The owner is also an agent for vacation homes renting from US$175 to US$750 per week.

Mexican-owned *Hotel Calafia (☎ 1-141-00-28)*, at Km 107 on the Transpeninsular, has seven small, simple but clean rooms for US$23/28 single/double and a restaurant as well.

Casa Miramar (☎/fax 1-141-02-71, 800-533-8452 in the US, mrbill@windriders.com) is a six-room B&B catering mostly to sports enthusiasts. Rates are US$45/77; a bed in a three-person bunkroom is US$25, and the four-person suite goes for US$125. Rates include a full breakfast. It's right off the Transpeninsular at the end of a little dirt road opposite the Pemex station at Km 109.

Historic *Rancho Buena Vista Hotel (☎ 1-141-01-77, fax 1-141-00-55, in the US ☎ 805-928-1719, 800-258-8200, fax 805-925-2990)* remains the sentimental favorite of anglers and their families, although the Hollywood glamour has decidedly worn off. Facilities include a swimming pool, a bar, a restaurant, tennis courts and a fleet of 15 fishing cruisers (US$240 to US$335). Comfortable rooms cost US$80/140/180 single/double/triple with full board. The entrance is opposite the Flag Monument at around Km 105.5.

Hotel Buena Vista Beach Resort (☎ 1-141-00-33, fax 1-141-01-33, in the US ☎ 619-429-8079, 800-752-3555, fax 619-429-7924, info@hotelbuenavista.com) is just half a mile (800m) south and has a pretty garden setting, a hot mineral spa and swim-up pool bar. Its extensive menu of activities ranges from kayaking, horseback riding and birdwatching to tours to Indian rock paintings and mineral hot springs. The resort's sportfishing fleet includes a 23-foot superpanga (US$220), a 28-foot deluxe cruiser (US$330) and a 29-foot luxury cruiser (US$385). Room rates are US$60/120 or US$85/135 with full board. For slightly better rooms add US$15 per person.

For a special treat, ensconce yourself at *Rancho Leonero (☎ 1-145-36-36, fax 1-141-02-16, in the US ☎ 714-692-6965, 800-646-2252, fax 714-692-6976, rancholeonero@worldnet.att.net),* an isolated resort on a spectacular beachfront location reached by taking a turnoff at Km 103.5. Manly fisherfolk mix with gregarious families, and stories of marlins that got away (or not) fly fast and furious at the bar each night. Their famed dining room, overlooking the sea, often serves up the day's catch sushi-style, in delicious ceviche or grilled over a wood fire. Leonero's fishing fleet consists of well-maintained cruisers, superpangas and pangas costing US$300/220/160, respectively. Nonanglers can relax poolside or in the soft sand, glide over the ocean in a sea kayak, tone biceps in the outdoor gym or go diving or horseback riding. There's even a rock reef right off the beach for great snorkeling. Remnants of an Indian midden and marine fossil beds are steps away along the beach.

Spotless, spacious rooms have thatched roofs, stone walls, tiled floors and some of the best showers on the East Cape. Standard rooms with full board start at US$110/140; deluxe rooms and bungalows are US$140/170. Even larger oceanview bungalows are US$170/200. Off-season

rates are US$25 less. Its Web site is at www.rancholeonero.com.

There are a few taco stands around the Pemex station, but outside the resorts the only restaurants are *La Gaviota* and *Calafia*, both serving standard Mexican seafood and antojitos.

LA RIBERA & AROUND

From Rancho Leonero, the dirt road continues south to tiny La Ribera, also accessible via a paved lateral from Las Cuevas, about 8 miles (13km) south of Buena Vista on the Transpeninsular. La Ribera is the last point for supplies southbound on the Eastern Cape Road, so stock up here if you're headed to Cabo Pulmo or beyond.

There are no hotels, but the *Correcaminos Trailer Park (☎ 1-145-99-00, fax 1-145-39-01),* close to the beach, has 25 mostly shady sites in a mango orchard with hookups for US$12; tent spaces are US$8.

About 4 miles (6km) farther south is *Hotel Punta Colorada (☎ 1-141-00-50, fax 1-141-00-46, in the US ☎ 818-222-5066, 800-368-4334, fax 818-591-1077),* another anglers' favorite. Singles/doubles/triples/quadruples cost US$60/100/150/180 with full board; day rates for fishing trips range from US$195 to US$300.

CABO PULMO

The Eastern Cape Road leads to what many consider the most spectacular site on the East Cape, the secluded Cabo Pulmo (population 100). It is home to the only coral reef on the west coast of North America, estimated to be 25,000 years old. On the cusp of tropical and temperate waters, it harbors 220 species of colorful tropical fish and a dozen species of petrified coral. The reef and 127 sq miles (70 sq km) of ocean surrounding it constitute the **Parque Marino Nacional Cabo Pulmo**, a legally protected area founded in 1995. The marine park is bounded by Playa Las Barracas in the north and Bahía Los Frailes in the south.

The coral reef consists of seven fingers jutting into the sea right from the shoreline. The reef system is very fragile and especially susceptible to pollution. Planned on-shore resort and housing developments pose the biggest threats, as does petrochemical pollution from two-stroke outboard motors. The University of La Paz is developing an Integrated Area Management Plan (IAMP) to determine the level of impact with which the park can cope.

Fishing is not permitted in the park but is possible in areas outside the boundaries. Diving, snorkeling and sea kayaking are extraordinary. Green turtles nest at Playa Las Barracas, about 15 minutes north of Cabo Pulmo, in August and September. Nondivers can take snorkeling and sightseeing tours with Pepe (see below), including trips to the Sierra de la Laguna. Rock climbers will find challenging seaview routes on the nearby granite (there is also some basalt and other volcanic rock). For hikers, the Vista Trail is a two-hour loop around Pulmo Mountain.

The village of Cabo Pulmo has a few hotel facilities, restaurants and dive centers but no other infrastructure. It's entirely solar-powered and the park director has the only phone line.

Diving & Snorkeling

Optimal conditions for underwater explorations are found in June and July when glassy waters allow for visibility up to 100 feet. It's lower in May, August and September, but the greater amount of plankton attracts more and different marine life, including many pelagics and manta rays. From December to March, heavy winds often make diving impossible.

There are 14 dive sites in the national park of which **El Bajo** has the highest concentration of fish, including the gigantic and rare whale shark and ore fish. **El Cantil** is the largest reef and has good coral, plus bat rays, hammerhead sharks and manta rays. **El Vencedor**, a tuna boat sunk in 1981, is a good place to spot baby eels and sea cucumbers; it was even featured in a Jacques Cousteau video. **Rock Island/El Islote** has the best sea fans, plus frog fish, sea horses and big groupers. **Los Frailes** to the south is a submarine canyon whose walls are home to manta rays and turtles. Water depths range from 25 to 100 feet.

There's also a sea lion colony in Bahía Los Frailes.

There's snorkeling right off the beach, but the best place is at **Playa La Sirenita** (Mermaid Beach), about a 10-minute boat ride away.

Affable and English-speaking José Luis Murietta, better known as Pepe, is the park director and also runs a full service dive shop, Pepe's Dive Center (☎/fax 1-141-00-01, pepesdive99@mail.com). Guided dives cost US$45 for one tank, US$65 for two; night dives cost US$55. His resort courses, which get you down to about 40 feet, cost US$75; four-day full PADI certification runs US$350; referral courses are US$180. Pepe also leads three-hour snorkeling excursions for US$35 per person, gear included.

The dive center at the Cabo Pulmo Beach Resort (see Places to Stay & Eat) has similar prices.

Places to Stay & Eat

Beachfront tent and RV sites cost a nominal US$2 for garbage removal. Showers are available at Pepe's for US$1 and tents may be rented for US$10 per night.

Pepe's wife, Libby, rents several villas, some with kitchens, from US$55 to US$75 for two people; additional persons pay US$10 and kids under 12 stay free. A comfortable camper with an outside shower costs US$40. You should check at the dive shop or restaurant for availability; call or fax ☎ 1-141-00-01 or send an email to pepesdive99@mail.com.

More formal accommodations are available at US-owned **Cabo Pulmo Beach Resort** (☎ 1-141-02-44, in the US ☎/fax 208-788-8823, 888-997-8566), where small bungalows cost US$60. Larger rooms cost US$85. *Casitas* (cottages) sleeping up to four people cost US$120, and the beachhouse for up to six people rents for US$165. All have kitchen or kitchenette. Monthly rentals are available. The resort also operates a PADI dive center and offers sea kayaking, climbing, hiking and snorkeling.

El Caballero has a large menu with straightforward Mexican fare. At the relatively basic *Tito's*, you can dine on a patio deck made from a local shipwreck. For gourmet quality and possibly the best food – and wine – anywhere on the Cape, go to American-run *Nancy's*, where you'll have a memorable outdoor dining experience. The fish burger, homemade bread and tasty margaritas get two thumbs up.

BAHÍA LOS FRAILES & AROUND

About 5 miles (8km) south of Cabo Pulmo, Bahía Los Frailes is a beautiful crescent-shaped bay with free beach camping on its northern end. *Hotel Bahía Los Frailes* (☎ 1-141-01-22, 800-934-0295 in the US) is a quiet luxury hideaway with lovely rooms right on the beach. Rates, including full board, are US$200 for a distinctive room with two queen-size beds and US$250 for a one-bedroom suite. The two-bedroom cabaña that sleeps four guests goes for US$450. Fishing pangas and sea kayaks are available for rent.

Past Los Frailes, the road becomes increasingly rough but still passable for vehicles with good clearance and a short wheelbase. After about 8 miles (13km), the road reaches Rancho Boca del Tule and, after another 3½ miles (5.5km), Rancho Boca La Vinorama, where some extravagant housing development has already occurred.

A short distance south, a graded dirt road heads west to the village of Palo Escopeta,

hitting the Transpeninsular just north of the Los Cabos International Airport after about 22 miles (35km). This is a smoother and faster ride compared to the rest of the coastal road, which, past this point, is practically impassable for anything larger than a pickup truck. Plans are underway to completely pave this road, in large part to accommodate the new part-time residents in their vacation homes.

For additional information on this road, see the Around San José del Cabo entry later in this chapter.

Central Cape

The Central Cape begins about 15 miles (24km) south of La Paz, roughly where México 19 (the Southern Cape Highway) splits off from the Transpeninsular. The latter continues through several villages, which had their heyday during the 19th-century mining era. These days, most of them are agricultural centers that export much of their crop (including cherry tomatoes, basil and peppers) to the US. Framed by the two highways is the scenic Sierra de la Laguna, an ecological wonderland that deserves explicit national park status.

EL TRIUNFO & SAN ANTONIO

El Triunfo (population 350), on the Transpeninsular, is the first town beyond the junction of the two highways, followed by San Antonio (population 600), about 5 miles (8km) to the east. Both towns were part of a large cattle ranch under the Jesuits in the early 18th century, but the population quickly swelled after gold and silver strikes in 1748. At its peak, San Antonio counted a population of more than 10,000 and was the largest settlement in the Cape Region, mostly home to mestizo miners and Yaqui laborers from the state of Sonora.

When Loreto was obliterated by a hurricane in 1829, San Antonio briefly became the capital of the Californias; a year later, the capital was moved to La Paz. The boom revived after the discovery of even higher quality ore at El Triunfo in 1862, but the mines ran dry in the late 19th century, and by 1925 both settlements were virtual ghost towns.

These days, small-scale mining has resumed in El Triunfo, and San Antonio is a modest farming community in a picturesque canyon. Both are worth a brief stop. Places worth a look in El Triunfo include the old smelter, the Casa Municipal and the small, pretty church. Local artisans sell colorful handwoven baskets, and there's a small restaurant for refreshments. Cobbled streets and restored buildings give San Antonio a more prosperous appearance. Stop here if only to peak at the interesting church.

Opposite San Antonio's Pemex station, a graded 14-mile (22km) road follows Arroyo San Antonio to a junction with BCS-286, the paved highway between San Juan de los Planes and La Paz. This is a particularly good mountain-bike route, winding gradually downhill through the arroyo.

Just about 8 miles (14km) east of San Antonio, at Km 141, is the **Rancho Verde RV Park** (☎ 1-146-91-03, in the US ☎ 406-889-3030, 888-516-9462, ranchoverde@mexonline .com), nicely located on a 3000-acre ranch in a lush valley. Rates are US$11 for full-hookup RV sites and US$7 for tents. An informative natural trail explains the dense vegetation.

SANTIAGO

Tranquil Santiago (population 2500), a charming village about 6 miles (10km) south of Las Cuevas and 1 mile (1.6km) west of the Transpeninsular, was the site of one of the bloodiest episodes in Baja's history. Pericú Indians revolted and murdered the Jesuit Lorenzo Carranco and several other Spaniards here before being subdued by Spanish soldiers and European epidemics. No trace remains of the mission, which closed in 1795, but a lovely little church has been built near the original site.

Although landlocked, Santiago has grown considerably since tourism came to the area. Many locals are employed in construction, fishing and general services. Santiago is also an important supplier of palm fronds used in thatched roof construction.

Prosperity and pride led the residents to establish Baja's only zoo in 1983. The tidy **Zoológico Santiago** contains a variety of animals, including a Bengal tiger, a black bear, emus and ostriches, deer, monkeys, native reptiles (mostly rattlesnakes), peccaries and a collection of colorful macaws. Only some of the cages are labeled. There are swing sets, and many families enjoy a Sunday barbecue here. Admission is free, but donations are welcome – and encouraged.

Modest but friendly **Hotel Palomar** (☎ 1-132-21-65 ext 128, fax 1-132-21-90), downhill from the plaza, has singles/doubles with hot shower for US$30/60; you can set up tents on the fruit-tree covered grounds for US$5. The restaurant, which gets customers from as far away as San José del Cabo, is noted for its fine seafood, priced mostly under US$10. The English-speaking owner, Sergio Gómez, is a good source of information on the Sierra de la Laguna.

There's also a small **taquería** on the plaza, next to the Pemex station.

AROUND SANTIAGO

Just past the zoo, a dirt road reaches the village of **Agua Caliente** after about 5 miles (8km). Another 2½ miles (4km) farther west by another dirt road is **El Chorro**, where natural hot spring water is being piped into a concrete reservoir. The amount of water, its cleanliness and temperature vary widely every year, depending on rainfall and other conditions. The best time to visit is in October and November, right after the fall rains. There are other hot springs in San Jorge and Santa Rita, both at the end of a dirt road north of Agua Caliente. Ask in Santiago about road conditions and for detailed directions.

Sol de Mayo

If hot springs don't do it for you, how about a cool swimming hole fed by a 30-foot waterfall? Getting there requires a bit of scouting, but it's worth the effort. From Santiago, turn right onto a dirt road just before reaching the plaza. At the store, take the road to San Dionisio (signed), then keep left at the junction (you should see the palm-studded valley below). After three-quarters of a mile (1.2km), turn right just before the air field, then continue for 1½ miles (2.5km) until the road forks. Take the right fork (a sandy, narrow dirt road). It dead ends after about 3¾ miles (6 km), with the trail starting right past the gate. You'll see the waterfall after a minute or two, but getting down to it requires a challenging scramble that should only be attempted by the physically fit. The last 20 feet are real ankle-busters, so use absolute caution. You'll certainly have earned your dip in the pool.

Tropic of Cancer
Precisely at latitude 23.5°N, just south of Santiago, a concrete sphere on the Transpeninsular marks the tropic of Cancer, which also passes through Hawaii, Taiwan, central India, Saudi Arabia and the Sahara Desert. Locals have built an elaborate shrine to the Virgin of Guadalupe – and a bar right next to it.

SIERRA DE LA LAGUNA
South of where the Transpeninsular and México 19 intersect, the precipitous heart of the Cape Region begins. This is one of the

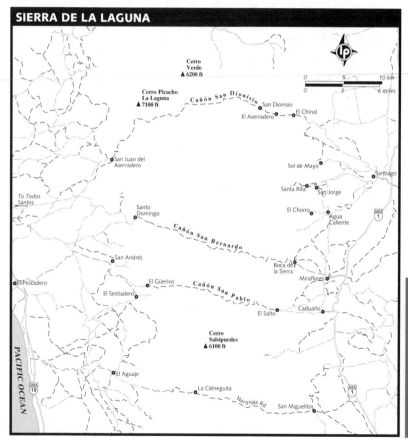

SIERRA DE LA LAGUNA

most rugged and inaccessible areas of the entire peninsula, with top elevations of around 7000 feet (2100m). It is traversed – east to west – by a succession of steep canyons, the larger of which double as backpacking routes. The Sierra receives more water than any other area in southern Baja, which accounts for its extraordinary lushness.

The area's complete wilderness and isolation make for adventurous backpacking. The terrain is difficult and unpredictable and should only be attempted by experienced hikers. Trails are not marked and are often hard to find. Water sources are not dependable, and weather conditions can change suddenly. Be prepared for anything.

Several foothill villages provide access to these unique mountains of the interior, which are also accessible from Todos Santos on their Pacific slope. Hikers should plan on spending several days crossing the Sierra; the best time is from November to February after the fall rains have filled the canyons with fresh water. However, days are short at this time of year, and the mercury can drop below freezing at night in January and February.

Those not wanting to go it alone should consider hiring a local guide. Ask around in Santiago or check with Señor Gómez of the Hotel Palomar. English-speaking Marco Hernandez of San José–based Nomadas (☎ 1-142-43-88) is also available for guided tours (also see Organized Tours under San José del Cabo, later).

The best guidebook for hiking in the Sierra de la Laguna is Walt Peterson's *The Baja Adventure Book* (see the Facts for the Visitor chapter for more information).

Cañón San Dionisio
The northernmost of the east-west routes is the most popular, perhaps because of its unique ecology – cacti, palms, oaks, aspens and pines grow virtually side by side. A route highlight is La Laguna, a flat meadow at 5600 feet (1700m) that was once a lake.

Most people start the crossing from the Todos Santos side, where a steep trail climbs into the mountains from near San Juan del Aserradero (La Burrera), about 15 miles

(24km) northeast of Todos Santos. From the trailhead, it's about 7 miles (11km) to La Laguna. From here it's another 8 miles (13km) to the eastern trailhead at the town of San Dionisio. The entire crossing can be negotiated in about five to six days. Going the other way, San Dionisio can be reached from Santiago (12 miles, 19km) via a dirt road passable for any passenger vehicle driven with caution. You can also try to hitch a ride or hire a taxi (about US$30).

Cañón San Bernardo
The central route across the Sierra is considered a bit easier and is also popular with day hikers. The trailhead is near the village of Boca de la Sierra, at the end of a dirt road about 4 miles (6km) west of Miraflores. Miraflores itself, accessible by paved road from the Transpeninsular at Km 71, is a dusty town of little interest.

The trail soon ascends into a wonderland of native vegetation and wildlife, including hairy tarantulas and other spiders, peculiar insects that look like walking twigs, and colorful tree frogs. It also passes a series of attractive granite pools, some suitable for swimming. After about 14 miles (22.5km) the trail comes out at Santo Domingo from where it's connected to México 19 by a series of signed dirt roads. The entire trip across takes about five days.

Cañón San Pablo
The southernmost route traverses the Sierra via Cañón San Pablo and picks up at the town of El Salto, about 5 miles (8km) west of Caduaño, terminating at El Güerivo after about 10½ miles (17km). From here dirt roads lead northwest to San Andrés and El Pescadero back to México 19. The turn-off to Caduaño is at about Km 68 on the Transpeninsular. Budget about five days to cross the sierra on this route.

Naranjas Road
Near Km 55 on the Transpeninsular, a narrow dirt road shoots west toward the mountains, spilling into México 19 after about 34 bone-shattering miles (55km). Only sturdy vehicles, preferably 4WD, should

attempt this road, which is characterized by steep grades, sudden and sharp turns and potholes the size of small craters. Also a popular day trip for mountain bikers, the ride is moderately difficult with a fair amount of elevation gain. The road is usually closed for months after the fall rains. Always check locally about conditions before setting out.

Los Cabos

The southern tip of Baja California is the most developed and heavily visited on the peninsula. The *municipio* (county) of Los Cabos has three quite distinct personalities. Its capital, San José del Cabo, is a tranquil Mexican coastal town, well-kept and with nice architecture, shopping and dining. The international airport serving the entire area is a few miles north of here.

West of town, the Los Cabos Corridor is an 18-mile (29km) stretch of the Trans-peninsular paralleling the coast and connecting San José with Cabo San Lucas. Along here are fancy resorts and golf courses perfect for the well-healed with a penchant for tranquility. It is also the area experiencing the heaviest development.

Finally, there is Cabo San Lucas, a roaring resort town with a youthful vibe, full menu of activities and a spectacular natural setting.

History

Baja's southern tip has been, in succession, a sleepy haven for Pericú Indians, a sheltered hideaway for pirates and a string of sedate fishing communities. The Pericú inhabited the foothills of the Sierra de la Laguna to the north, never settling around the Cape proper because fresh water was scarce there. The majority of them died soon after the arrival of Europeans and their deadly diseases.

When Europeans first saw the peninsula in the 16th century, water shortages made the southern Cape an unappealing place for permanent settlement, but its secluded anchorages offered privateers an ideal base for raiding Spain's Manila galleons.

By the early 17th century, the Spanish had lost enough gold and silver to prompt the es-tablishment of a small *presidio* (military outpost) at Cabo San Lucas. Around 1730, the Jesuits established Misión San José del Cabo, which became a more permanent settlement. The presidio deterred the pirates and, eventually, both encampments became villages whose inhabitants relied on fishing and fish-canning for their livelihood. During the Mexican-American War, US troops occupied the area, as did the eccentric William Walker's forces a few years later.

After WWII, US private pilots brought tales of the area's big game fish and magnificent beaches to listeners north of the border. As more North Americans arrived, upscale hotels and restaurants sprouted and the federal government built an international airport near San José del Cabo. Cruise ships soon included Cabo San Lucas on their itineraries, and a ferry service (since discontinued) began to operate to and from the mainland city of Puerto Vallarta. In recent years, hordes of North American tourists and retirees have frequented the area, downtown Cabo San Lucas lost its village ambiance and a string of multi-story luxury resort hotels, not to mention several golf courses, has disfigured the coastline between Cabo San Lucas and San José del Cabo.

SAN JOSÉ DEL CABO

San José del Cabo (population 50,000) has a pedestrian-friendly historic center characterized by century-old Spanish colonial-style brick and adobe structures and anchored by a shady plaza and imposing church. As the capital of the municipio of Los Cabos, the town is well-maintained, clean and sedate. A quiet, laid-back atmosphere prevails. About 1 mile (1.6km) south of here is the more modern part of San José, especially along the beachfront's *zona hotelera*. There are a few resorts, but overall, San José is uncluttered and preserves plenty of wide open spaces. March 19 marks the Fiesta de San José, a celebration of the town's patron saint; festivities last four or five days.

Orientation

San José del Cabo is 20 miles (32km) east of Cabo San Lucas and 112 miles (179km) south

SAN JOSÉ DEL CABO

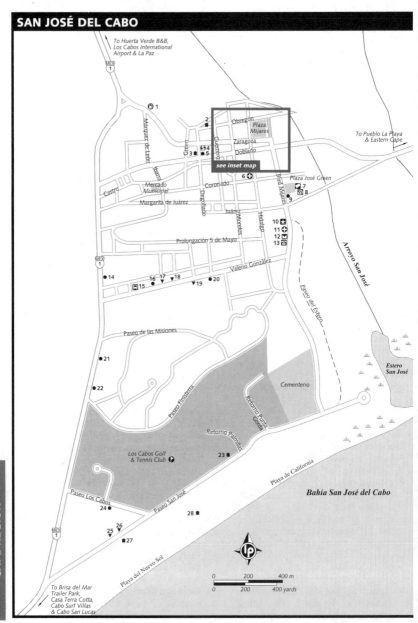

To Huerta Verde B&B,
Los Cabos International
Airport & La Paz

MEX 1

1

2

Obregón

Plaza Mijares

Zaragoza

Doblado

To Pueblo La Playa
& Eastern Cape

3 4
5

Guerrero

see inset map

6

Bulevar Mijares

Plaza José Green
7
8
9

Mercado
Municipal

Castro

Márquez de León

Ibarra

Degollado

Coronado

Margarita de Juárez

Juárez

Morelos

Hidalgo

10
11
12
13

Prolongación 5 de Mayo

Valerio González

MEX 1

14

15 16 17 18
19 20

Arroyo San José

Paseo del Estero

Paseo de las Misiones

21

22

Estero
San José

Paseo Finisterra

Retorno Punta Gorda

Cementerio

Retorno Palmillas

Los Cabos Golf
& Tennis Club

23

Paseo Los Cabos

24

Paseo San José

28

Playa de California

Bahía San José del Cabo

MEX 1

25 26

27

Playa del Nuevo Sol

To Brisa del Mar
Trailer Park,
Casa Terra Cotta,
Cabo Surf Villas
& Cabo San Lucas

0   200   400 m
0   200   400 yards

CAPE REGION

of La Paz. The historic downtown is linked to the zona hotelera by manicured Blvd José Antonio Mijares. San José's commercial center orbits Plaza Mijares, the northern terminus of Blvd Mijares.

About 1½ miles (2.5km) east of downtown is Pueblo La Playa, a tranquil fishing village that is also the starting point of the unpaved Eastern Cape Road (see Around San José del Cabo, later this chapter).

Information

San José's tourist office (☎ 1-142-04-46 or 1-142-29-60 ext 150) on Plaza Mijares is usually open 8 am to 3 pm weekdays and 10 am to 1 pm Saturday. It has accommodating – and usually English-speaking – staff as well as pamphlets on area activities, hotels and restaurants.

The cambio at Los Cabos International Airport offers poor rates. In town, several cambios keep long hours, but banks pay better rates. Bancomer and Banca Serfin in downtown cash traveler's checks and have ATMs. Telecomm, next to the post office, can arrange international money transfers.

The post office is on Mijares north of González; the postal code is 23400. For fax service and Internet access, try CaboCafe.com (☎ 1-142-52-50) in Plaza José Green, where 10/30/60 minutes of surfing cost US$2/4/7.

Libros Libros Books Books (☎ 1-142-44-33) offers a decent selection of American magazines and English-language novels as well as a few guidebooks and maps. It's on Mijares, north of Coronado.

Viajes Damiana (☎ 1-142-07-52 or 1-142-37-52), at Zaragoza and Morelos, is a widely respected full-service travel agency.

Lavandería Vera and Lavamática San José are both on Valerio González, east of the bus terminal, and open 8 am to 8 pm (closed Sunday).

The general IMSS hospital (☎ 1-142-01-80 for emergencies, otherwise ☎ 1-142-00-76) is at Hidalgo and Coronado. The Cruz Roja (Red Cross; ☎ 1-142-03-16) is on Mijares just north of the post office. The police station (☎ 1-142-03-61) is almost next door.

Iglesia San José

This imposing replica of the original mission church lords over Plaza Mijares. Note the mosaic above the front portal depicting a 1734 local Indian uprising.

Estero San José

San José's most delightfully peaceful spot is the estuary adjacent to the Hotel Inter-Continental in the zona hotelera. In colonial times, between raids on Spanish galleons, pirates took refuge in what is now a protected wildlife area replenished by a subterranean spring. It's a birdwatcher's delight, with frigate birds, sparrow hawks, white herons, red tailed hack and other species making their home here. From the corner of Juárez, a palm-lined pedestrian trail parallels Mijares all the way to the zona hotelera. This is a delightful alternative to the boulevard, but it may not always be passable because of high water levels, especially after rains.

Beaches

White sandy beaches are a major attraction for visitors. Playa del Nuevo Sol and its eastward extension, Playa de California, at the southern end of Blvd Mijares, are both good for swimming. La Playita in Pueblo La Playa has excellent surf fishing.

Fishing

Fishing is not as big a pastime in San José as it is in Cabo San Lucas and on the East Cape, but several operators do offer excursions. For a fish calendar, see Fishing under Cabo San Lucas, later in this chapter.

Victor's Sportfishing (☎ 1-142-10-92 or 1-142-22-55), at the Hotel Posada Real (see Places to Stay), organizes six-hour super-panga trips from Playa Palmilla for US$185 (maximum three people) and eight-hour cabin-cruiser trips from US$325 (maximum four) to US$395 (maximum six).

Panga trips cost about the same with Gordo Banks Pangas (☎/fax 1-142-11-47, 619-447-4098 in the US, gordobanks@cabonet .com.mx), based at La Playita, the beach in Pueblo La Playa. La Playa Sport Fishing is another operator. If your Spanish is up to it,

you might try negotiating a deal with one of the independent panga owners hanging around the beach, who are usually a few dollars cheaper.

Surfing

In town, Killer Hook Surf Shop (☎ 1-142-24-30), on Guerrero just south of Doblado, is a good source of surfing information and gear. The closest surfing beach, and the best in the Los Cabos area, is Zipper's Beach, at Km 28.5 on the Transpeninsular. Experienced surfers claim that summer reef and point breaks match the finest in Hawaii. Costa Azul Surf Shop (☎ 1-147-00-71), on the north side of the highway, has rental equipment (surfboards, snorkels and body boards) and also does repairs. Stop here for the latest surf report and to pick up their free surf break location map.

A concession at Brisa del Mar Trailer Park (see Places to Stay under Los Cabos Corridor, later) also rents surfboards.

Golf, Tennis & Bicycling

The nine-hole, par-35 course at Los Cabos Golf & Tennis Club (☎ 1-142-09-05) charges a very reasonable US$30, making it by far the cheapest course in Los Cabos. Tennis courts rent for US$15 per hour during the day, double that per hour at night.

Brisa del Mar Trailer Park (see Los Cabos Corridor) rents mountain bikes for US$20 per day.

Organized Tours

Nomadas de Baja California is an ecologically minded adventure tour company that offers a wide range of explorations along the coast, the Los Cabos hinterlands and the Sierra de la Laguna. Options include trips to waterfalls and hot springs (US$65), a sunrise hike (US$40) and biking through the desert (US$65). The popular Cabo Pulmo excursion can be tailored to kayakers, snorkelers or divers (or any combination; US$85 to US$140).

Nomadas' bilingual owner, Marco Hernandez, can also customize guided hiking treks to the Sierra de la Laguna for individuals or groups. The office (☎/fax 1-142-43-88,

1-147-05-17 mobile phone, nomadas@1cabonet.com.mx) is located on Doblado at Degollado.

Places to Stay

Budget accommodations are decent but scarce and demand is high. If possible, make reservations in the peak winter months. Prices below reflect peak season rates and are usually about 25% to 40% lower the rest of the year.

Budget Free beach camping is possible at Pueblo La Playa. Also here is Swedish-run *El Delfín Blanco* (☎ 1-142-12-12, fax 1-142-11-99, eldelfin@bcsl.telemex.net.mx) in a garden filled with palm and banana trees, where amenities include a barbecue area and outdoor kitchen. Tent sites cost US$10, or US$15 if you don't have your own tent. It also has neatly decorated, thatch-roof cabañas with shared bath for US$30/36/43 for one/two/three people. Larger casitas with private bath cost US$45/52/59 for two/three/four people.

Though urgently in need of plaster and paint, the friendly *San José Inn* (☎ 1-142-24-64), on Obregón between Degollado and Guerrero, has spacious singles/doubles with private bath, ceiling fans and hot water (usually) for US$12 to US$18. It's fairly quiet and the owner assures us that a renovation is forthcoming. Keep us posted.

Backpackers from around the world congregate at convivial *Posada Señor Mañana* (☎/fax 1-142-04-62, Obregón 1), just north of Plaza Mijares, despite rooms that are basic at best and could easily be called grimy. The staff is friendly, though, and there's a small pool and communal kitchen. Rates range from US$30 to US$40, depending on room size and location. Ask to see several before registering.

Hotel Diana (☎ 1-142-04-90, Zaragoza 30) has air-conditioned rooms with satellite TV for US$20 to US$24.

Another good bet is family-run *Hotel Colli* (☎ 1-142-00-52), on Hidalgo near Zaragoza. Rooms, which are smallish and a little worn but very clean, cost US$30 to US$35.

Mid-Range A few pesos extra buy more comfortable and stylish digs.

Right in town on Mijares, north of Coronado, is the *Tropicana Inn* (☎ 1-142-09-07, fax 1-142-15-90, 510-939-2725 in the US, correo@tropicana.cabo.com), with a tropical garden around its swimming pool. Each of the 40 doubles has satellite TV and costs US$86, taxes included. Suites cost US$106.

Also central, friendly *Posada Terranova* (☎ 1-142-05-34, fax 1-142-09-02, terranova@1cabonet.com.mx), on Degollado between Doblado and Zaragoza, has bright, clean and cheerful rooms with air-con for US$55 (also see Places to Eat).

Time seems to move a bit slower at the flower-festooned *El Encanto Inn* (☎ 1-142-03-88, fax 1-142-46-20, Morelos 133). The sun-yellow, colonial-style hotel in a quiet location has 19 rooms and suites, all with phone and TV, for US$59 to US$79.

The beachfront *Hotel La Palmita* (☎ 1-142-04-34), on Paseo San José overlooking the golf course, is a handsome, modern inn with nicely decorated rooms for US$55. There's a deli and small store right outside.

At Pueblo La Playa, *La Playita Resort* (☎/fax 1-142-41-66, in the US ☎ 626-962-2805, 888-242-4166), almost in the sand, has large, comfortable rooms costing US$60 and three penthouses for US$130, including continental breakfast. They're flexible with the rates if business is slow or if you're planning a multiday stay.

Top End After a US$2 million make-over, the *Best Western Hotel Posada Real* (☎ 1-142-01-55, fax 1-142-04-60, 800-528-1234 in the US) sparkles once again. Oceanview rooms are in a three-floor structure wrapped around a beautiful cactus garden. Rooms cost US$115.

Hotel Fiesta Inn (☎ 1-142-07-93, fax 1-142-04-80), on the beach to the west, is now an all-inclusive resort (meaning all meals, drinks and most activities are included in the price) with per-person rates from US$90 to US$120. It's popular but a bit low on charm.

Across town to the north, the same cannot be said about *Casa Natalia* (☎ 1-142-51-00, fax 1-142-51-10, 310-793-0025 in the US, *casa.natalia@1cabonet.com.mx, Blvd Mijares 4)*, on the northeastern corner of Plaza Mijares, a tasteful, homey retreat run by a European couple. Each of the 18 rooms gets its character from different art objects, and all come with private patio (where breakfast is served) and sunken shower/tub. Special touches include embroidered robes and a hammock. Rates are US$220 for rooms and US$325 for a spa suite. Its popular restaurant serves gourmet-quality fare.

Out toward the airport is ***Huerta Verde*** *(☎ /fax 1-148-05-11, 303-431-5162 in the US, lovemexico@aol.com)*, an enchanting B&B tucked into a terraced hillside. There are seven suites, some with kitchenettes, costing US$115 to US$140. It's all set in a lush garden (the name translates as 'Green Orchard'), home to many bird species. It's a bit remote, so phone ahead for availability and directions.

Places to Eat

The main restaurant scene is concentrated around Plaza Mijares and its side streets, and the overall quality is very high. Look for more casual eateries along Valerio González and Doblado.

Around the Plaza A trio of fine restaurants orbits Plaza Mijares. On the east side, popular ***Damiana*** *(☎ 1-142-04-99)* is inside a restored 18th-century house with wood-beam ceilings and traditional decorations. At night, the courtyard, canopied with bougainvillea, is especially romantic. If you pick and choose carefully, you can make a meal for about US$20, although it's easy to spend twice as much. It's open for lunch and dinner; reservations are recommended.

At nearby ***Floriska*** *(☎ 1-142-46-00, Mijares 16-1)*, French-born chef Michel Mustiere gets creative with fish, seafood and meat. Concoctions like fish fillet with almond damiana sauce are typical and best enjoyed on the candlelit patio embellished with hand-painted murals. It's open for lunch and dinner.

La Cenaduría *(☎ 1-148-22-83, Zaragoza 10)* serves up honest-to-goodness food at some of the best prices in town. The vast

menu ranges from antojitos like tamales and ceviche tostadas (US$1.50 each) to more substantial seafood and grilled dishes (US$6 to US$13). Check out the rooftop terrace with a view of the plaza and church. Its open for breakfast, lunch and dinner.

South of the Plaza The following places fall along Blvd Mijares. On Mijares at Doblado, Almacenes Goncanseco is a good-size supermarket. Almost next door, ***Helados Bing*** has tasty ice cream, paletas, milkshakes and other refreshing concoctions.

Lively ***Tropicana Bar & Grill*** *(☎ 1-142-09-07)* has a large, open sports bar and a sidewalk cafe. No-nonsense Mexican-American main courses, like baby-back ribs and a lobster-steak combination, characterize the mid- to top-priced menu.

Across the street, ***Iguana Bar*** *(☎ 1-142-02-66)* is the stomping ground of gregarious expats chowing down on moderately priced Mexican and American staples. After dark, it morphs into a throbbing nightclub.

A few steps west of Mijares, on Doblado, is the classy ***Tequila*** *(☎ 1-142-11-55)* whose main drawing card is the 90 varieties of its namesake. The menu is Mediterranean with Mexican and Asian touches (mains from US$12); dining takes place beneath ancient fruit trees on the breezy patio. It's open for dinner only.

West of the Plaza On Morelos between Obregón and Zaragoza, ***La Michoacana*** serves excellent aguas and licuados. For a sugar fix, nothing beats ***Pan del Triunfo*** on Morelos at Obregón. All its lip-smacking breads, cookies, pastries and donuts are made right on the premises. Its open daily to 9 pm, Sunday to 8 pm.

At the French-country-style ***La Provence*** *(☎ 1-142-33-73)*, in a heritage building at Obregón and Morelos, you can dine under the stars amid flowers, birds and fountains. Main courses start at US$14. It's open for dinner only.

Nearby, in the El Encanto Inn behind a heavy wooden door, is the traditional ***Alfonso's*** *(☎ 1-142-03-88, Morelos 133)*, where plates groan beneath continental favorites like lamb chop, beef filet and grilled lobster. Main courses range from US$8.50 to US$22.50, but the best bargain is the three-course set lunch for just US$6.50. It's closed Sunday.

Fandango (☎ 1-142-22-26, Obregón 19) does Pacific Rim cuisine in a casual setting accented by brightly pigmented murals. Main courses average US$13. Its open for breakfast, lunch and dinner (closed Sunday).

Andalé (☎ 1-142-41-14), on Morelos north of Zaragoza, does inspired pasta dishes from US$5 to US$10 and meat and fish main courses clocking in at US$7 to US$12. Artsy decor and a secluded upstairs patio add to the relaxed ambience.

Across the street, *Jazmín's* (☎ 1-142-17-60) serves Mexican, seafood and vegetarian meals in a peaceful setting with excellent, unobtrusive service and, incongruously, a paperback book exchange. *Xochimilco* (☎ 1-142-54-32), on Zaragoza between Morelos and Guerrero, charms with sophisticated decor and a small but distinctive midpriced menu of specialities from around Mexico.

Elsewhere in Town Across from the Hotel Fiesta Inn, *El Sinaloense* is a casual seafood restaurant with an outdoor terrace. Next door is *Tropicana Pizza*, where pies come in three sizes and cost from US$4 to US$14.

Next to the bus station on Valerio González is *La Picazón*, a super-friendly, outdoor eatery with possibly the town's best margaritas, US$1 tacos and excellent fish burgers. The affiliated *Pica Grill* next door specializes in carne-asada-based meals. Farther east, *Cesar* has a reputation for making the best Caesar's salad in town.

At the *Mercado Municipal*, on Ibarra between Coronado and Castro, numerous loncherías offer simple, inexpensive and good meals (open from 7:30 am to late afternoon).

Entertainment

San José is definitely not the place for after-dark partying. Tropicana Bar and Iguana Bar are two establishments with Happy Hours popular with gringos (see Places to Eat). The latter draws a slightly younger clientele, as does the rooftop bar *Piso 2*, on Zaragoza between Guerrero and Morelos, which has pool tables on the ground floor.

Cactus Jacks, Mijares near Juárez, does karaoke Wednesday through Saturday nights and also hosts the occasional live band. It too has pool tables (free) and a large-screen TV showing sporting events.

Shopping

Souvenir shops cluster near the plaza and on northern Blvd Mijares, but San José excels at shops selling high-quality interior design items and crafts. Selections include ceramics, woven rugs, lamps, glassware, vases, small furniture and wall decorations. Among stores worth a visit are Arte Diseño Decoración (☎ 1-142-27-77) on Zaragoza at Hidalgo; Antigua Los Cabos (☎ 1-142-18-10), a few doors west; Casa Paulina (☎ 1-142-55-55), also on Zaragoza between Guerrero and Morelos; and Galerias de Arte Fino (☎ 1-142-19-50) at Mijares 33-A. La Mina (☎ 1-142-37-47) next door has stylish silver jewelry.

On the eastern side of Plaza Mijares, Copal (☎ 1-142-30-70) has a good assortment of crafts, including interesting Christmas decorations. The Huichol Collection, on Mijares at Zaragoza, sells rainbow-colored, beaded animal sculptures made by the mainland Mexican Huichol tribe.

Getting There & Away

Air Serving both San José del Cabo and Cabo San Lucas, Los Cabos International Airport (☎ 1-142-03-41, 1-142-21-11) is 6½ miles (10km) north of town. Mexicana (☎ 1-142-15-30, 1-142-06-06 at the airport) has an office at Plaza Los Cabos between the beachfront Paseo San José and Paseo Los Cabos; most of the other airlines have their offices at the airport itself.

Alaska Airlines (☎ 1-142-10-15, fax 1-142-10-16) has direct flights daily to San Diego, at least three times daily to Los Angeles, daily to San Francisco and up to five times daily to Seattle. Its sister airline Horizon Air also goes to Phoenix, but only seasonally (usually from October to March).

Continental Airlines (☎ 1-142-38-40) flies daily between Houston and Los Cabos, while America West (☎ 1-142-28-80) serves

Phoenix twice daily. American Airlines (☎ 1-142-27-35) has one direct flight daily to and from Dallas/Fort Worth year round. From November to April, it also operates one nonstop flight from Chicago.

AeroMéxico (☎ 1-142-03-41) flies daily to San Diego and also serves many mainland Mexican destinations, with international connections via Mexico City. Aero California (☎ 1-142-09-43, fax 1-142-09-42) has one daily flight to Los Angeles.

Mexicana flies twice daily to Los Angeles and daily to Mexico City, both nonstop and via other mainland Mexican cities; it also flies to Denver on Thursday and Sunday. Aerolitoral, in the same offices as Mexicana, flies to Los Mochis.

Bus The main bus terminal (☎ 1-142-11-00) is on Valerio González just east of the Transpeninsular. Autotransportes Aguila goes to La Paz at least 14 times daily between 6 am and 7:30 pm; seven buses travel straight north *(via corta)*; the other seven go via Cabo San Lucas and Todos Santos *(via larga)*. Fares are the same (US$10), but the via larga route takes about half an hour longer.

The fare to Todos Santos is US$6, to Cabo San Lucas US$1.50. Local buses to Cabo cost the same and operate more frequently. There are also buses to Loreto (US$25, nine hours) at 9:45 am and to Tijuana (US$80, 24 to 26 hours) at 4 pm daily.

Getting Around

San José is small enough to be pedestrian-friendly; even from the zona hotelera the walk into town takes only about half an hour. Outside town, buses, taxis or bicycles may be necessary.

Taxis from the airport to downtown San José or the zona hotelera cost about US$5 per person or US$12 to US$15 for the entire taxi. Top-end hotels often arrange transportation for their guests. Local buses from the terminal on Valerio González to the airport junction on the Transpeninsular cost less than US$1, but taking one means a 20- to 30-minute walk to/from the air terminal.

All major car rental agencies have offices at the airport; some also have branches downtown. The car rental scene on the Southern Cape is more competitive than elsewhere on the peninsula, and some good deals with unlimited mileage are available. Agencies include the following:

Advantage (☎ 1-146-00-04)
Alamo (☎ 1-146-06-26)
Avis (☎ 1-142-11-80 at the airport)
Dollar (☎ 1-142-01-00)
Hertz (☎ 1-146-50-88 at the airport)
National (☎ 1-142-24-24, 1-146-50-20 at the airport)
Thrifty (☎ 1-142-23-80)

AROUND SAN JOSÉ DEL CABO

Pueblo La Playa marks the southern terminus of the Eastern Cape Road, a gritty dirt road leading east-northeast toward Los Frailes, Cabo Pulmo and La Ribera. Badly gullied, it is suitable only for narrow vehicles with short wheelbases and may be completely impassable after rain.

Despite the area's remoteness, development has arrived. About 5 miles (8km) east of San José are the beachfront villas of **Laguna Hills**, just before **Punta Gorda** and popular – and increasingly populated – **Santa Cruz de los Zacatitos**, the site of the original construction assault on this part of the East Cape. Most of the homes here are largely self-sufficient, producing their own solar energy and obtaining water through desalination. About 6 miles (10km) offshore are the famous **Gorda Banks**, two seamounts that are prime fishing grounds for marlin and other big game fish; they are also popular with divers.

Back on land, a few miles farther east is **Playa Tortuga**, named for the turtles who nest here, and then **San Luis**, the new vacation home hotspot. Another 8 miles (13km) farther is the turnoff to the Palo Escopeta Road back to the Transpensinular. The East Cape Road continues north to Los Frailes and Cabo Pulmo. See the Eastern Cape section earlier in this chapter for details.

LOS CABOS CORRIDOR

The 18-mile (29km) stretch of the Transpeninsular between San José del Cabo and Cabo San Lucas is commonly referred to as

LOS CABOS CORRIDOR

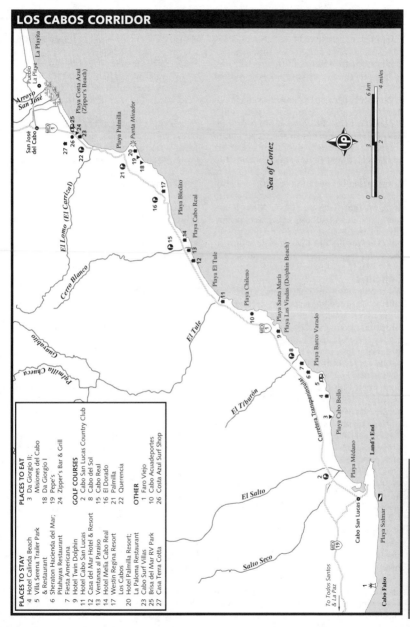

Sea of Cortez

La Playita

Pueblo La Playa

Arroyo San José

Playa Costa Azul (Zipper's Beach)

San José del Cabo

Playa Palmilla

Punta Mirador

El Lomo (El Carrizal)

Cerro Blanco

Playa Bledito

Playa Cabo Real

Guadélbio

Palmilla Chueca

Playa El Tule

Playa Chileno

El Tule

Playa Santa María

Playa Las Viudas (Dolphin Beach)

El Tiburón

Playa Barco Varado

Carretera Transpeninsular

Playa Cabo Bello

El Salto

Playa Médano

Land's End

Cabo San Lucas

Salto Seco

Playa Solmar

To Todos Santos & La Paz

Cabo Falso

PLACES TO STAY
4 Hotel Calinda Beach
5 Villa Serena Trailer Park & Restaurant
6 Sheraton Hacienda del Mar; Pitahayas Restaurant
7 Fiesta Americana
9 Hotel Twin Dolphin
11 Hotel Cabo San Lucas
12 Casa del Mar Hotel & Resort
13 Ventanas al Paraíso
14 Hotel Meliá Cabo Real
17 Westin Regina Resort Los Cabos
20 Hotel Palmilla Resort; La Paloma Restaurant
23 Cabo Surf Villas
25 Brisa del Mar RV Park
27 Casa Terra Cotta

PLACES TO EAT
3 Da Giorgio II; Misiones del Cabo
18 Da Giorgio I
19 Pepe's
24 Zipper's Bar & Grill

GOLF COURSES
2 Cabo San Lucas Country Club
8 Cabo del Sol
15 Cabo Real
16 El Dorado
21 Palmilla
22 Querencia

OTHER
1 Faro Viejo
10 Cabo Acuadeportes
26 Costa Azul Surf Shop

CAPE REGION

'The Corridor.' This state-of-the-art, divided four-lane highway parallels the most beautiful stretch of coast in the Los Cabos area. It's a visual feast of secluded coves, jutting points, generous sandy beaches, teeming tidal pools, rolling desertscape and drop-dead gorgeous ocean views.

Naturally, it's also the arena for the area's most aggressive developers, who have snapped up the choice beachfront properties to build sprawling resorts and condo complexes. Practically all of them are of the sophisticated and posh variety, intended to appeal to upscale (read: filthy rich) travelers. Interspersed between the hotels are world-class golf courses – seven at last count – with more in the planning stages. Most locals seem to welcome all this expansion, primarily for its job- and income-creating potential. Meanwhile, old-time travelers lament the area's loss of charm and natural beauty.

Beaches

All along the Transpeninsular, you'll see blue beach access signs sporting pictographs of the types of activities available (snorkeling, fishing, diving, surfing, etc) at the particular beach. Parking is along the highway or in parking lots. If you're using the bus, ask the driver to drop you off at your beach of choice. By law, all Mexican beaches are open to the public, but access from the highway is becoming increasingly restricted because of developments.

The Corridor beach closest to San José is **Playa Costa Azul** at Km 28, also known as Zipper's Beach, which is quite popular with surfers. Access is through Zipper's restaurant. Surfers also hang out at the much smaller adjacent **Playa Acapulquito**, accessible at Km 28 just before the lookout. Also see Surfing under San José del Cabo, earlier.

Next up is **Playa Palmilla** at Km 27, a long crescent of fine sand popular with swimmers and water-sports enthusiasts. Facilities include a dive shop, equipment concession and restaurant.

The Hotel Melía Cabo Real at Km 19.5 sits on a lovely cove known as **Playa Cabo Real**, which is protected by a breakwater, making it safe for swimming and water

sports. The hotel also provides access to **Playa La Concha**, a beach club (admission is charged). East of here is **Playa Bledito**, sought out by beachcombers.

One of the largest open stretches of beach is at **Playa El Tule** at Km 15, reached through the arroyo at Puente Los Tules. Surfers come here, as do the occasional beach campers. There are zero facilities.

Next up is **Playa Chileno** at Km 14, which offers good swimming and snorkeling and fresh-water showers. Cabo Acuadeportes (☎ 1-143-01-17) rents kayaks, snorkeling and dive equipment (also see Diving & Snorkeling, below). The beach is easily accessible from the road and just a short walk from a large parking lot. On weekends it fills up with local families.

Perhaps the nicest Corridor beach is **Playa Santa María**, a sheltered cove teeming with underwater creatures. Numerous snorkeling excursions from San José and Cabo San Lucas come here, so waters may occasionally get crowded. Snorkeling gear and beach chairs are available for rent, but there's no infrastructure otherwise. It's reached via a sandy road near Km 12 and there's a guarded parking lot (free).

Access to **Playa Las Viudas**, also known as Dolphin Beach, is via a sandy road next to the Hotel Twin Dolphin turnoff at Km 12. Depending on road conditions, it may be advisable to walk the quarter-mile (400m) to the beach, which is secluded and good for swimming.

Playa Barco Varado now fronts the mega-sized Cabo del Sol development and is better for diving and snorkeling than for swimming. Access is through the Cabo del Sol entrance at Km 10. The closest surf beach to Cabo San Lucas is **Playa Cabo Bello**, right below the Da Giorgio restaurant and reached via the Misones del Cabo turnoff at Km 5.

Diving & Snorkeling

The best snorkeling along the Los Cabos Corridor is at Playa Santa María. From Playa Chileno, Cabo Acuadeportes runs two-hour snorkeling trips for US$25 – though you can do much the same on your own by going right to the cove. Its dive excursions cost US$38/66 for one/two tanks and take you to various dive sites.

Golf

The popularity of golf has skyrocketed in recent years, so it was only a matter of time before a developer would have visions of the pristine Los Cabos coastline covered with velvety green blankets. This man was Don Koll from Orange County, California, owner of the Hotel Palmilla (see Places to Stay, below). So when he, in 1990, asked golfing guru Jack Nicklaus to design three nine-hole courses near the hotel, Los Cabos took the first step toward becoming a premier golfing destination.

In the 1990s, four more courses were thrust upon the desert terrain, all of them with 18 holes. These include two more by Nicklaus: the El Dorado near the Westin Regina resort (☎ 1-144-54-40; US$198 in winter, US$138 in summer) and the Cabo del Sol (☎ 1-145-82-00; US$209/138). The Cabo Real course came courtesy of Robert Trent Jones Jr (☎ 1-144-00-40; US$176/116), while the Cabo San Lucas Country Club (☎ 1-143-46-53; US$143/100) boasts a Roy Dye signature course. Nicklaus' 18 holes at Palmilla (☎ 1-144-52-50) cost US$198/127. All prices include greens fees, cart, tax, bottled water and use of driving range.

By the time you're reading this two more courses should have opened, one by Tom Weiskopf at Cabo del Sol, and the Corridor's first private course, Querencia, near Palmilla. There seems to be no end in sight.

By all accounts, each of these coastal courses is a golfer's dream – and an environmentalist's nightmare – although local regulations at least require all golf courses to be irrigated with gray water.

Places to Stay

About 2 miles (3km) southwest of San José, at Km 28.5 on the Transpeninsular, **Brisa del Mar Trailer Park** (☎ 1-142-39-99, mortimer@brisadelmar.com) has tent sites for US$10 and US$12 and RV spaces (with full hookups) from US$18.50 to US$30. There are hot showers, toilets, a restaurant/bar and a guest laundry. Also beachfront but more expensive are its small cabañas, which rent for US$50 to US$60.

At Km 7.5, **Villa Serena Trailer Park** (☎/fax 1-143-05-09, 044-114-1-96-96 cell phone, ☎ 800-932-5599 in the US) has 56 sunny sites with full hookups for US$15 and a great blufftop restaurant (see Places to Eat, later).

Clinging to a hillside near Zipper's Beach at Km 28.5 on the Transpeninsular, **Casa Terra Cotta** (☎/fax 1-148-05-37, info@terracotta-mex.com) is a snug B&B set in a tropical garden. Each of the four casitas has a private patio with hammock and view of the Sea of Cortez. Rates are US$113 to US$142, plus US$8 for optional kitchen use.

Nearby at Km 28 is **Cabo Surf Villas** (☎/fax 1-140-51-63, 800-896-8196 in the US), right on Playa Acapulquito. Rooms are decorated with Mexican furniture and have ocean-facing patios. A planned expansion in 2000 is supposed to add 28 rooms to the current eight. Rates are US$125 to US$250.

All the resorts on the Corridor are in the five-star luxury category with amenities and prices to match. Breathtaking bay views, gorgeous landscaping and top-rated service are de rigeur, as are facilities like swimming pool(s) with swim-up bar, lighted tennis courts, multiple restaurants and bars, a fitness center and room service.

Rooms are usually oceanview and have a private terrace, minibar, TV, air-con, direct phone, in-room safe and other amenities. Rarely do they cost less than US$200 per night. Some hotels enforce minimum stays (especially around holidays and on weekends).

All resorts can arrange for a wide range of activities from sportfishing to horseback riding to diving. Size, location and architecture are the main elements that set properties apart. Even if you have no intention of staying here, you may enjoy dropping in for a drink, meal and sweeping ocean views.

Rates below are for peak periods and do not include 10% IVA, 2% lodging tax and – in most places – compulsory service charge (usually 15%). Listed from east to west, the resorts are as follows:

Hotel Palmilla Resort

At Km 27.5 on Playa Palmilla; ☎ 1-144-50-00, fax 1-144-51-00, in the US ☎ 714-935-2000, 800-637-2226, fax 714-935-2030. Built in 1956 by Rod Rodríguez, son of a former Mexican president, this is the Corridor's original Hollywood hideaway, including a golf course. Rates are US$395 to US$595; three-night minimum on weekends.

Westin Regina Resort Los Cabos

At Km 22.5; ☎ 1-142-90-00, fax 1-142-90-10, 800-625-5144 in the US, relos@westin.com. Mega-resort with daring, modern architecture and landscaping designed to complement the desert colors and surroundings. Rates are US$285 to US$630.

Hotel Melía Cabo Real

At Km 19.5 on Playa Bledito; ☎ 1-144-00-00, fax 1-144-01-01, 800-336-3542 in the US, caboreal@1cabonet.com.mx. Easily recognized by its glass and marble pyramid lobby, this 302-room resort sits on a lovely, breakwater-protected cove next to the Cabo Real golf course. Rates are US$250 to US$700.

Ventanas al Paraiso

At Km 19.5; ☎ 1-144-03-00, fax 1-144-03-01, in the US ☎ 310-824-7781 or 888-525-0483, lvap@1cabonet.com.mx. In a class by itself, the exclusive Ventanas oozes Zen-like serenity and charms with deceptively simple landscaping and architecture. A luxurious spa and golf course are adjacent. Rates are US$525 to US$625. Minimum stay of four or seven days required in January, February and around most holidays.

Casa del Mar Hotel & Resort

At Km 19.5; ☎ 1-144-00-30, fax 1-144-00-34, 800-221-8808 in the US, casamar@cabonet.net.mx. Comparatively intimate (24 rooms and 36 suites), the Casa del Mar, like the Melía, is part of the Cabo Real development that also includes the Ventanas, a condo complex and a golf course. Rates are US$325 to US$375.

Hotel Cabo San Lucas

At Km 14 on Playa Chileno; ☎ 1-144-00-14, fax 1-144-00-15, in the US ☎ 323-655-2323, 800-733-2226, cabotravel@earthlink.net. Set on a bluff amid 2500 acres (1000 hectares) of luxuriant tropical gardens, this is another of the Corridor's old-timers, dating to 1962. Rates are US$195 to US$545.

Hotel Twin Dolphin

At Km 12 on Playa Las Viudas; ☎ 1-145-81-90, fax 1-145-81-96, in the US ☎ 213-386-3940, 800-421-8925, fax 213-380-1302. Also an original Corridor resort, the Twin Dolphin is built on a more intimate scale (50 rooms and suites). Assets include a jogging trail and free shuttle to Cabo San Lucas. Rates are US$285 to US$485 (suites); add an optional US$55/78 per person for half-board/full board.

Fiesta Americana

At Km 10.3; ☎ 1-145-62-00, fax 1-415-62-01, reserv@fiestaamericana.com.mx. Neighboring the Hacienda, the colorful Fiesta Americana is part of a Mexican chain. The peak rate is US$389.

Sheraton Hacienda del Mar

At Km 10; ☎ 1-145-80-00, fax 1-145-80-08, 888-672-7137 in the US and Canada, information@haciendadelmar.com.mx. Part of the Cabo del Sol development, which also encompasses a golf course, the new all-suites Hacienda del Mar is distinguished by its dramatic, riverlike pool and original colonial artworks. Rates are US$300 to US$1700.

Hotel Calinda Beach

At Km 6.5, ☎ 1-145-80-44, fax 1-145-80-57, 800-424-6423 in the US and Canada. The closest resort to Cabo San Lucas, the cliffside Calinda Beach has some of the best views of Land's End. It also has the best Corridor rates: US$176 to US$198.

Places to Eat

Eating along the Corridor takes place mostly at the resort hotels. Special mention goes to *La Paloma* (☎ 1-144-50-00) at the Hotel Palmilla, which serves nouveau Mexican built around organically grown produce and seafood. The Sunday brunch is legendary.

The Sheraton Hacienda del Mar is home to **Pitahayas** (☎ 1-145-80-10), which specializes in Pacific Rim cuisine, including vegetarian selections. Dining takes place beneath a giant palapa. It's open for dinner only.

Notable eateries outside the resorts include the casual **Zipper's Bar & Grill** at Km 28, which caters to surfers and specializes in mesquite-grilled beef; there's usually live music on Friday night.

Almost alongside Hotel Palmilla is the popular **Pepe's** (☎ 1-144-50-40), serving Mexican seafood. **Da Giorgio** (☎ 1-142-19-88), west of the Palmilla at Km 25.5, offers various Italian-style seafood dishes, pizza and pasta at mid- to top-range prices. There's a second branch (☎ 1-145-81-60) at the Misiones del Cabo development at Km 5.5. Its dramatic, terraced clifftop setting makes it one of the best Corridor places to watch the sun set over Land's End.

Cheaper and also with a good view is **Villa Serena** (☎ 1-145-82-44), at Km 7.5, which has US$10 lobster specials daily and paella feasts on Sunday (also US$10). The trailer park is listed in Places to Stay, above.

CABO SAN LUCAS

To many people, arriving at the southern tip of Baja California after traversing seemingly endless, nearly deserted stretches of the peninsula, Cabo San Lucas (population 55,000) comes as a culture shock. Its sprawling hotels, streets filled with zooming cars and people, bustling bars and restaurants, a string of malls and other trappings of 'civilization' are more reminiscent of a beach town in Florida, California or Hawaii than Mexico. And that's exactly how the half-million tourists a year – most of them American and Canadian – like it.

But Cabo is no Cancún. Despite persistent development, it still preserves some small-town character – at least so far. Away from the beaches and the four-lane main drag, you're more likely to bump into Enrique and María from Cabo than Bob and Wilma from Dubuque. Small mercados, flower shops, taquerías and other eateries line the narrow, mostly unpaved streets. There are only three traffic lights in the entire town. And there's also little of the poverty so often encountered in other parts of the country: Cabo's population enjoys one of the highest standards of living.

Much of Cabo's reputation as a party town is well deserved. But if conga lines, karaoke and silly party games don't do it for you, you'll also find plenty of quieter, more sophisticated – though not necessarily more expensive – places, including some on the beaches.

To many visitors, Cabo's natural treasures are the main attraction. The arches of Land's End are a landmark. There's great swimming, boating and water sports. Superb snorkeling and diving are just a five-minute boat ride away from the harbor. And to fisherfolk, the mystique of 'Marlin Alley' is legendary.

But in recent years, Cabo's natural beauty has come under threat from potentially irresponsible development. New construction on Playa Médano was not in the mold of the venerable Hacienda Beach Resort, whose low-rise structures are practically concealed by a forest of mature palms. Rather, the new resorts are humongous hunkered-down blocks that jut from the desert landscape as weirdly as the tall kid in your third grade picture. To the west, Pedregal is a closed-gate hillside community of exclusive villas with stunning ocean views reserved only for very wealthy residents. On Blvd Marina, time-share hawkers (see the boxed text 'I'd Love a Cabo Time-Share, But…') are as irksome as a cloud of mosquitoes at your lakeside picnic.

But despite all this, Cabo is fun. There's an energy and buzz in the streets that's not found anywhere else on the peninsula. There's a lot of enjoyable things to do – on and off the water. And there's always the local population, friendly and quick with a smile, to make you feel welcome.

Orientation

At the southernmost tip of the Baja Peninsula, Cabo San Lucas is 1059 miles (1694km) from Tijuana and 137 miles (219km) from La Paz. After splitting south of La Paz, the paved Transpeninsular and the Southern

CAPE REGION

CABO SAN LUCAS

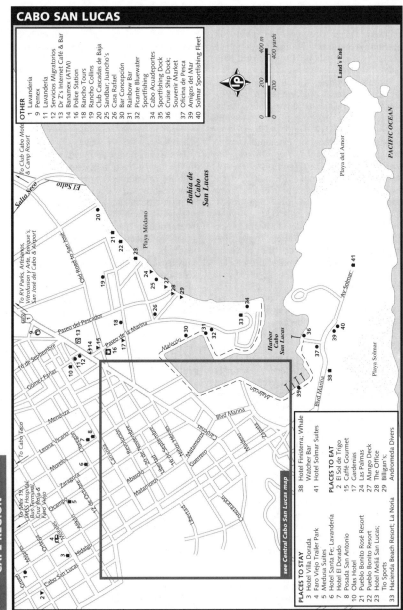

OTHER
1   Lavandería
9   Pemex
11 Lavandería
12 Servicios Migratorios
13 Dr Z's Internet Café & Bar
14 Banamex (ATM)
16 Police Station
18 Rancho Tours
19 Rancho Collins
20 Club Cascadas de Baja
25 Sandbar; Juancho's
26 Casa Rafael
30 Bar Concepción
31 Rainbow Bar
32 Picante Bluewater
    Sportfishing
34 Cabo Acuadeportes
35 Sportfishing Dock
36 Cruise Ship Dock;
    Souvenir Market
37 Oficina de Pesca
39 Amigos del Mar
40 Solmar Sportfishing Fleet

PLACES TO STAY
3   Hotel Villa Dorada
4   Faro Viejo Trailer Park
5   Medusa Suites
6   Hotel Santa Fe; Lavandería
7   Hotel El Dorado
8   Posada San Antonio
10 Olas Hotel
21 Pueblo Bonito Rosé Resort
22 Pueblo Bonito Resort
23 Hotel Meliá San Lucas;
    Tio Sports
33 Hacienda Beach Resort; La Noria

38 Hotel Finisterra; Whale
    Watcher Bar
41 Hotel Solmar Suites

PLACES TO EAT
2   El Sol de Trigo
15 Caffé Gourmet
17 Gardenias
24 Las Palmas
27 Mango Deck
28 The Office
29 Billigan's;
    Andromeda Divers

see Central Cabo San Lucas map

Cape Highway (México 19) rejoin at Cabo San Lucas, making a fine driving or bicycle circuit. The Transpeninsular is also called 'Carretera a San José del Cabo,' whereas México 19 is referred to as 'Carretera a Todos Santos.' A bypass road skirting Cabo's northeastern edge connects the two.

The town's main drag, Blvd Lázaro Cárdenas, is essentially a continuation of the Transpeninsular. Past the intersection with Zaragoza, it peters out into a minor shopping street while most of the action continues along Blvd Marina, culminating at Land's End. Tourist-oriented shops, restaurants, bars, a post office, police and other infrastructure are all along this road. The commercial area just north of here has a more local flair.

Cabo does not use street numbers, so addresses always specify the nearest cross streets.

Information
Tourist Offices Cabo San Lucas does not have an official tourist office, but there are several free publications with more or less useful information available around town (see the boxed text 'What's Up in Cabo').

Signs saying 'Tourist Information' are usually time-share booths. If you can ignore the aggressive come-ons, ask for free maps and other information and then just walk away. If you're in the US or Canada, you can get free vacation planners from the Los Cabos Tourism Board by calling ☎ 800-847-4822 (800-VISITCABO).

Immigration Servicios Migratorios (☎ 1-143-01-35), at Cárdenas and Gómez Farías, is open 9 am to 2 pm weekdays.

Money US dollars are widely accepted at stores, restaurants and hotels, but the exchange rate may not be favorable. Banks with 24-hour ATMs and exchange services (usually until 1 pm only) include Banca Serfin in Plaza Arámburo; Banamex at Cárdenas and Paseo de la Marina; and Banco Santander at Cárdenas and Avenida Cabo San Lucas.

Cambios, like those by Baja Money Exchange (several branches around town), have

longer hours but poorer exchange rates, plus commission fees. American Express (☎ 1-143-57-66), which cashes its own traveler's checks for free, has an office on Morelos, just south of Cárdenas (closed Sunday).

American Express and Telecomm/Western Union by the post office can arrange instant international cash transfers.

Post & Communications The post office, on the eastern side of Cárdenas near 16 de Septiembre, is open 9 am to 4 pm weekdays and to noon Saturday. The postal code is 23410. There are plenty of Ladatel phones around town. Faxes may be sent from the

What's Up in Cabo?

The following local publications – wholly or partly in English – contain plenty of useful information to help you navigate around town. Look for them in restaurants, bars, hotel lobbies and shops. Almost all are free.

Baja Sun – Los Cabos – monthly all-English edition catering mostly to residents but still featuring the occasional useful article.

Destino: Los Cabos – quarterly, partly bilingual paper without much advertising and with good articles about lesser-known area attractions as well as hotel and restaurant profiles (not widely available).

Gringo Gazette – English-language biweekly publication with an offbeat but surprisingly informative editorial approach, despite the preponderance of real estate–related articles. Geared toward both the visitor and resident.

Los Cabos Magazine – published twice yearly, this is the most useful and informative of the bunch, packed with hotel and restaurant reviews, details about beaches, golfing and other activities, plus several good maps. It has a sticker price of US$4.95 but may also be available for free.

Los Cabos News – mostly Spanish biweekly, with some articles in English, covering general and tourism-related news in the Los Cabos area.

Telecomm office (see earlier), from Mail Boxes Etc on Morelos just south of Cárdenas, and from most Internet cafes.

Internet cafes are popping up all over Cabo. Dr Z's Internet Café & Bar (☎ 1-143-53-90), on Cárdenas across from the Pemex station, has about a dozen terminals and charges around US$4/6/7.50 for 15/30/60 minutes. It's open 9 am to 6 pm (closed Sunday). Other places to try are Francisco's Café (☎ 1-143-23-66), next to Margaritavilla, and Café Cabo Mail, next to Banca Serfin on Zaragoza. Libros Libros Books Books (see Bookstores) is cheapest (US$5/hour) but has only two terminals.

Internet Resources Nearly all the Cabo-related Web sites are advertising-driven and provide little valuable information. Exceptions are the site maintained by the Los Cabos Tourism Board at www.visitcabo.com and the online version of the magazine *Los Cabos Guide* at www.loscabosguide.com (searchable).

Travel Agencies Well-established Los Delfines (☎ 1-143-13-96 or 1-143-30-96, fax 1-143-13-97), on Morelos at 16 de Septiembre, has an English-speaking staff and publishes current flight schedules in the *Los Cabos News*. American Express (see Money, earlier) is also a full-service agency.

Bookstores Come to Libros Libros Books Books (☎ 1-143-31-73), at Blvd Marina 20, for a good selection of English-language novels and magazines, or even to surf the Internet.

Laundry Self-service lavanderías are sprinkled throughout town. Locations include near the Olas Hotel on Revolución and Gómez Farías, on Mendoza between Revolución and 16 de Septiembre, in the Hotel Santa Fe on Zaragoza at Obregón, and on Matamoros just north of Mijares.

Medical & Emergency Services Cabo's general IMSS hospital (☎ 1-143-15-94 for emergencies, otherwise ☎ 1-143-15-89) is just north of the Pemex station on México 19. The Cruz Roja (☎ 1-143-33-00) is at

Km 121 on the same road. A decent pharmacy, Farmacia Arámburo, is on Cárdenas near Ocampo.

The central police station (☎ 1-143-39-77) is next to McDonald's at Cárdenas and Paseo de la Marina.

Dangers & Annoyances A major annoyance is the gauntlet of time-share salespeople lined up along Blvd Marina like buzzards on a fence. They will try to entice you with free meals, drinks or rounds of golf if you attend a 'short' tour and presentation, which usually ends up taking up half of your vacation day. Because nearly their entire income comes from sales commissions, they will put serious pressure on you to take advantage of the 'unique opportunity' offered by buying into their properties. The best advice is, of course, to ignore them, but this may be hard to do. For tongue-in-cheek suggestions of how to handle these people, see the boxed text 'I'd Love a Cabo Time-Share, But....'

Completely harmless but a major nuisance are the many beach vendors, usually poor Indian migrants from mainland Mexico, who are especially prevalent along Playa Médano but who also work more remote Corridor beaches like Playa Chileno and Playa Santa María. A simple 'no gracias' will usually send them on their way, but it gets to you after the 30th time. By the way, if you are inclined to buy something, you'll probably pay less than in stores.

Beaches

Cabo San Lucas has three main beaches. The most popular is **Playa Médano** (Dune Beach), which runs northeast for about 2 miles (3km) from the Hacienda Beach Hotel. Calm waters make it ideal for swimming, although you'll need to watch out for jet skis. Bars and restaurants abound, as do ambulant souvenir vendors. If you want greater peace and quiet, head to the stretch past the Club Cascadas development.

Playa Médano is action central for all water sports. Cabo Acuadeportes (☎ 1-143-01-17), by the Hacienda Beach Resort, has the largest stable of toys. Kayaks rent for

I'd Love a Cabo Time-Share, But...

Cabo's most sinister bottom feeders are not offshore sharks but real-estate agents and time-share sellers. No visitor can completely avoid these predators, who may be either gringos or Mexicans, but the following phrases may discourage them:

No hablo inglés ni español.	I don't speak English or Spanish.
¿Habla Ud albanés/swahili/tibetano?	Do you speak Albanian/Swahili/Tibetan?
Lo siento, pero el doctor dice que me quedan solo dos meses de vida.	I'm sorry, but the doctor says I have only two months to live.
Lo siento, pero acabo de declarar bancarrota.	I'm sorry, but I've just declared bankruptcy.
Lo siento, pero la DEA confiscó todos mis bienes.	I'm sorry, but the DEA confiscated all my assets.
¿El contrato permite mi víbora cascabel?	Does the contract allow my pet rattlesnake?
Mi abogado dice que no puedo hacer inversiones hasta no cumplir mi libertad condicional.	My lawyer says no more investments until my parole is over.
Si Ud piensa que soy tan estúpido para comprar un tiempo compartido, me gustaría venderle un puente que tengo en Brooklyn.	If you think I'm dumb enough to buy a time-share, I have a bridge in Brooklyn I'd like to sell you.

US$10/15 single/double per hour. Windsurfing equipment costs US$20 and wave runners cost US$40/70 per half-hour/hour. Parasailing flights, offered here and by Juancho's next to the Las Palmas restaurant, cost US$30. Tio Sports (☎ 1-143-33-99), at the Hotel Melía San Lucas, has similar equipment but slightly higher prices.

Flanked by towering rocks, quiet **Playa del Amor** (Lover's Beach) – with access to both the Pacific and the bay waters – is Cabo's most scenic beach. Swimming near the arches should be avoided, but snorkeling on the bay side is excellent. Access is by water taxi (US$5 roundtrip) from Playa Médano or the Plaza Las Glorias docks. Alternatively, arrange a drop-off (and pick-up) with a glass bottom boat (US$8; see below). The only other access is via a class 3 scramble over the rocks from Hotel Solmar (not recommended).

Playa Solmar, on the Pacific side, has a reputation for unpredictable, dangerous breakers that drown several unsuspecting tourists every year. Locals jokingly call it 'Divorce Beach.' It's quieter, though, and well suited for sunbathing.

For beaches between Cabo San Lucas and San José del Cabo, see Los Cabos Corridor, earlier in this chapter.

Cruises

Dos Mares (☎ 1-143-10-57) operates 45-minute bay tours aboard its glass bottom boats for US$8. Departures are hourly from the Plaza Las Glorias docks and from Playa Médano. Drop-offs and pick-ups at Lover's Beach can be arranged at no extra charge.

Sunset Cruises Capping off a day at the beach with a sunset cruise is a popular pastime among Cabo vacationers. Trips last two to three hours, and prices usually include drinks and snacks. Boats depart from the Plaza Las Glorias docks.

The 42-foot catamarans *Pez Gato I* and *Pez Gato II* (☎ 1-143-37-97) are segregated into 'booze cruises' and 'romantic cruises,' each costing US$30/15 adults/children. The *Jungle Cruise* (☎ 1-148-76-74), another wild party boat, and the much tamer *Encore* (☎ 1-143-20-15), a 60-foot ocean-racing yacht, also charge US$30. *Sun Rider* (☎ 1-143-22-52) and *Vancouver Star* (☎ 1-143-21-88) do drinks,

CAPE REGION

dinner and dancing for US$40/20. *Kaleido-scope* (☎ 1-148-73-18) is a 100-foot catamaran with adults-only cruises for US$37.

For something a little different, take a 'pirate cruise' aboard the *Sunderland* (☎ 1-143-27-14), a beautiful 19th-century four-masted tallship that lets you glide into the sunset without noisy engine sounds. The crew is dressed in pirates' garb, and the captain himself will shower you with tales of Cabo's sordid corsair past. The cost is US$37, free for kids under 12 (one per adult).

Most operators also run snorkeling cruises to Playa Santa María (see the Los Cabos Corridor section, earlier) in the mornings.

Whale-Watching During the peak of the gray whale migration, from January to March, you can easily spot whales right from the shore. Many of the operators listed under Sunset Cruises also run whale-watching trips during those months (around US$40).

Fishing

Cabo's claim as 'Marlin Capital of the World' may be hyperbole, but there's no doubt that the Cape Region is one of the world's best places for game fishing. Fishing is best during hurricane season (July to early October), when rougher seas bring out the marine life.

Competition among sportfishing charters is fierce, but quality varies. Always ask what's included in a boat charter. Most rates for eight-hour outings include fishing licenses and permits, tackle, crew and ice. Sometimes they also include beer and soda, cleaning and freezing, and tax. Live bait is usually available at the docks for US$2 each. Things to bring on your own include a hat, sunscreen, sunglasses and anti-seasickness medication.

Prices depend on the size and type of boat and range from US$260 for a 26-foot cruiser (for up to three passengers) to US$350 for a 29-footer (four people) to US$650 for a 42-footer (eight people).

The most professional place in town to stock up on rods, reels, line, leaders, lures, etc, is Minerva's Baja Tackle (☎ 1-143-12-82,

PLACES TO STAY
8 Cabo Inn
20 Chile Pepper Inn
21 Las Margaritas Inn
32 Hotel Mélida
35 Bungalows Breakfast Inn
36 Hotel María Elena
37 Hotel Los Milagros
45 Hotel Mar de Cortez
60 Siesta Suites Hotel
61 Hotel Dos Mares

PLACES TO EAT
1 La Michoacana
2 Los Paisas
7 Almacenes Castro
9 Mariscos Mocambo
13 El Pollo de Oro
14 Mercado Morelos
15 Rico Suave
16 El Pescador
17 La Palapa
25 La Trattoria
26 Aramburo Supermarket
33 Antojitos Doña Lolita
39 Pane, Pizza e Vino
42 Margaritavilla
49 Sanlíz Supermarket
50 O Mole Mio
56 Mi Casa
57 Pastelería Suiza
67 Sancho Panza

OTHER
3 Lavandería
4 Budget Rent A Car
5 Telecomm/Western Union
6 Post Office
10 Dollar Car Rental
11 Los Delfines
12 Buses to San José
18 Pazzo's Cabo
19 Thrifty Car Rental
22 Café Cabo Mail
23 El Squid Roe
24 Hard Rock Café
27 Banca Serfin (ATM)
28 Kokomo
29 Cortes
30 Dos Lunas
31 American Express; Mail Boxes Etc
34 Farmacia Arámburo
38 Galerías Zen-Mar
40 Budget Rent A Car
41 Libros Libros Books Books
43 Nowhere Bar
44 Francisco's Café
46 Faces of Mexico
47 Cabo Wabo Cantina
48 Minerva's Baja Tackle
51 Dollar Car Rental
52 Avis Car Rental
53 The Giggling Marlin
54 National Car Rental
55 Banco Santander (ATM)
58 Aero California
59 US Consulate
62 Payless Car Rental
63 Baja Money Exchange
64 TangaTanga
65 Pancho's
66 National Car Rental
68 Dos Mares
69 Land's End Divers; Neptune Divers
70 Baja Dive International
71 Pisces Sportfishing Fleet
72 *Pez Gato* Boats

CAPE REGION

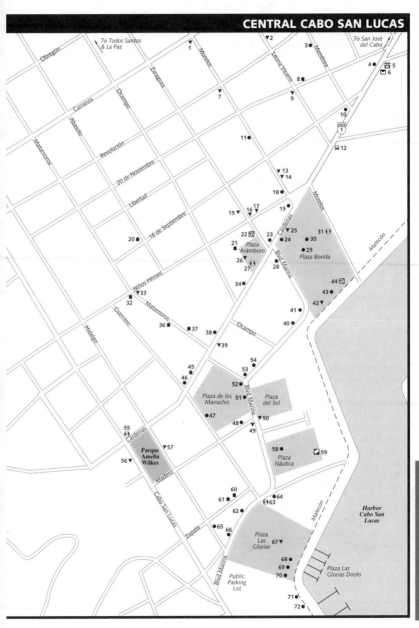

CENTRAL CABO SAN LUCAS

fax 1-143-04-40, minerv@allaboutcabo.com) at Blvd Marina and Madero. Serious fisherfolk swear by the store's quality and selection and give high marks to the friendliness and know-how of the staff. Minerva is a real Cabo character who also operates her own fishing fleet.

Some other reputable operators include Pisces Sportfishing Fleet (☎ 1-143-12-88, fax 1-143-05-88, pisces@piscessportfishing.com) by the Plaza Las Glorias docks; Solmar Sportfishing Fleet (☎ 1-143-35-35, fax 1-143-04-10,

Catch & Release

More than 40,000 marlin are caught annually off Los Cabos alone, but most of them are returned to the ocean to fight another day. Although each boat is legally allowed to kill one billfish (marlin, swordfish, sailfish) per daily outing, most fisherfolk follow the advice of the Sportfishing Association of Los Cabos and opt to catch and release. Billfish releases are reported to the Billfish Foundation, which will send the proud angler a Release Certificate. Fish need not be killed in order to be taxidermied. Experts can make replica mounts from photographs taken of the fish.

Unless done correctly, fish can be so seriously injured in the release process that they die anyway after being returned to the sea. Avoid treble or stainless-steel hooks; instead use long-shank, unplated iron hooks that can be more easily removed. Dragging a fish overboard and holding it in an upright position can lead to internal damage. Try to remove the hook with the fish still in the water. If possible, avoid touching the animal, as this can damage the skin, subjecting it to bacterial infections. If a fish's gills are damaged, or it is already bleeding, it will likely succumb to its injuries.

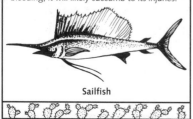

Sailfish

in the US ☎ 310-459-9861, 800-344-3349, caboresort@aol.com) at the Hotel Solmar; and Picante Bluewater Sportfishing (☎ 1-143-24-74, fax 1-143-59-69, in the US ☎ 714-572-6693, fax 714-572-6695, picante@cabotel.com.mx) in the marina near Bar Concepción (see Entertainment, later).

Another possibility is a fishing trip aboard a *panga* (skiff). Rates start around US$30 per hour, with a six-hour minimum for three people.

Charters usually include fishing licenses, but if not you can obtain one from the Oficina de Pesca right by the cruise ship docks (US$9 per day, US$18 per week). The office is open 8:30 am to 3 pm weekdays.

The following list indicates the prime months for the various fish species, but most species actually inhabit Cabo's waters year round. For more 'fishy' information, see the relevant section in the Activities chapter.

Blue Marlin	July to October
Dorado	July to November
Roosterfish	July to December
Sailfish	August to October
Shark	January to May
Striped Marlin	November to June
Tuna	June to October
Wahoo	August and September

Diving & Snorkeling

Underwater explorations in Cabo may yield encounters with manta rays, sea lions, turtles, hammerhead sharks, marlin and an entire aquarium's worth of colorful tropical fish. Best of all, some of the finest diving sites are just a five-minute boat ride away from the marina.

Roca Pelicano (Pelican Rock, 25 to 80 feet) is perfect for beginners and has lots of tropical and schooling fish, while nearby **Land's End** (50 to 60 feet) gives intermediate to advanced divers a chance to frolic with sea lions. Even more experienced types won't want to miss the **Sand Falls** (30 to 100 feet), steep sand banks that plunge into a submarine canyon just 30 yards offshore. (Jacques Cousteau made a documentary on this spectacular place.) Another challenge is **Neptune's Finger** (80 to 100 feet), an amazing canyon wall dive.

Snorkelers can hit the water right off Playa del Amor (on the bay side only).

Dive shops cluster near the Plaza Las Glorias docks and on Playa Médano. Two-hour snorkeling tours cost about US$25 (gear included); one-tank dives cost US$35 to US$45; two-tank dives cost around US$60; one-tank night dives go for US$50. Introductory (resort) courses cost around US$90, and full PADI certification is about US$400.

Rates usually include tanks and weights. Regulators, buoyancy compensator jackets and full wetsuits rent for about US$10 each; airfills and weight belt cost US$5 each. Mask, fins and snorkel average US$10.

Most operators also organize tours to sites farther afield, including all-day trips to Cabo Pulmo (see the Eastern Cape section, earlier) or Gorda Banks (see Around San José del Cabo, earlier) for US$125 and three-hour snorkeling excursions to Playa Santa María (see the Los Cabos Corridor section, earlier) for US$40 to US$50. Most companies mentioned under Cruises, earlier, also run snorkeling trips in the mornings.

Reputable dive outfitters include the following:

Amigos del Mar (☎ 1-143-05-05, 1-143-08-07), near the cruise ship dock at the southern end of Blvd Marina

Andromeda Divers (☎ 1-143-27-65), Playa Médano at Billigan's

Baja Dive International (☎ 1-143-38-30), Plaza Las Glorias

Cabo Acuadeportes (☎ 1-143-01-17), Playa Médano at Hacienda Beach Resort

Land's End Divers (☎ 1-143-22-00), Plaza Las Glorias

Neptune Divers (☎ 1-143-71-11), Plaza Las Glorias

Tio Sports (☎ 1-143-33-99), Playa Médano at Hotel Melía San Lucas

Horseback Riding & Bicycling

Rancho Collins (☎ 1-143-36-52), based just off the driveway to the Hotel Melía San Lucas (see Places to Stay, below), offers one-to 1½-hour beach rides for US$20 to US$25 and longer sunset tours to the Faro Viejo (see Around Cabo San Lucas, later) for

US$45. Red Rose Riding Stables (☎ 1-143-48-26), at Km 4 on the Transpeninsular, has similar rates.

Tio Sports (☎ 1-143-33-99 or 1-143-29-86) rents mountain bikes for US$5 per hour, US$20 per day. Guided tours cost US$30 per person.

Special Events

Cabo San Lucas has several popular annual events, including many fishing tournaments. The most prestigious is the Bisbee's Black & Blue Marlin Jackpot Tournament, held in late October. A week before is the Gold Cup Sportfishing Tournament and in late November the Los Cabos Billfish Tournament. The Festival San Lucas, which celebrates the town's patron saint, kicks off on October 18 or 19.

Places to Stay

Cabo San Lucas has plenty of accommodations in all price categories. Luxury resorts have claimed the beachfront, but plenty of comfortable and more affordable hotels are just a short walk away in downtown. Campgrounds and RV parks are just east of town.

Prices fluctuate significantly by season. Rates quoted below apply to peak season (usually November to May), so expect to pay 25% to 50% less at other times. Unless noted, prices do not include a lodging tax of 12%. Almost all of the big resorts, B&Bs and boutique hotels also charge a compulsory service charge of 10% to 15% in lieu of tipping. Note that many smaller, family-run establishments don't accept credit cards.

Budget Cabo's only in-town campground, *Faro Viejo Trailer Park (☎/fax 1-143-42-11),* on Morales between Matamoros and Abasolo, appeared closed during our repeated visits but may well have reopened since. Keep us posted.

All other campgrounds are east of town on the Transpeninsular. Closest and most congenial, with dependable services, is the Dutch-operated *Club Cabo Motel & Camp Resort (☎/fax 1-143-33-48, clubcabo@ cabonet.net.mx),* about 1 mile (1.6km) east of Club Cascadas de Baja. Full hookups cost

US$16; tent campers pay US$7.50 per person. They also rent thatched-roof cabañas with more than a modicum of style for US$45 to US$80. The grounds, which lie adjacent to a migratory bird refuge, are quiet, well maintained and feature a large swimming pool, Jacuzzi and barbecue area. It's a bit hidden but well signposted once you turn toward the beach at the intersection of the Transpeninsular and the Cabo bypass road (look for Club Cascadas).

About 2 miles (3km) east on the Transpeninsular, **Vagabundos del Mar Trailer Park** (☎ 1-143-02-90, fax 1-143-05-11, in the US ☎ 800-474-2252 or 707-374-5511, xe2htd@ prodigy.net.mx) has 95 sites that are usually occupied by longterm residents but may have occasional openings for US$16; facilities include full hookups, a swimming pool, drinking water and an ice machine. Next to Vagabundos, the **San Vicente Trailer Park** (☎ 1-143-07-12, fax 1-143-25-70, sanvicente@ cabonet.net.mx) has 34 shady, thatched-roofed sites for US$10 but also tends to be booked solid.

Your chances may be better at **Los Arcos Trailer Park** (☎ 1-143-16-86), about 1 mile farther east at Km 5.5 on the north side. It has 85 spaces with full hookups and hot showers for US$12/15 per tent/RV. Its restaurant serves Mexican fare and seafood.

Offering rock-bottom rates, if not much in the way of character, is **Hotel Villa Dorada** (no phone), a long walk away from downtown at Calle de la Juventud and Hidalgo. Large rooms with TV and fan cost US$18. The 'reception' is in the attached 24-hour mini-market. For information, call its sister property, the **Hotel Dos Mares** (☎ /fax 1-143-03-30 or 1-143-47-27), on Zapata between Hidalgo and Guerrero. Rooms at the Dos Mares itself could use sprucing up, and with rates ranging from US$28 to US$45 (tax included), they are somewhat overpriced.

A much better choice is the **Hotel El Dorado** (☎ 1-143-28-10, fax 1-143-67-37), on Morelos between Carranza and Obregón, whose 36 large, clean rooms wrap, motel-like, around a central parking area. All have TV and cost US$25 (with ceiling fan) or US$30 (with air-con).

Almost next door, **Posada San Antonio** (☎ /fax 1-143-73-53 or 1-143-27-09) has dark, no-frills rooms for US$20/25 single/double. An extra US$5 buys a 3rd-floor room with better furniture and fridge.

A step up is the hospitable and quiet **Olas Hotel** (☎/fax 1-143-17-80) on Revolución near Gómez Farías. A small supermarket and coin laundry are across the street, and there's a cafe on the premises. Rooms, with TV, fans (some with air-con) and patio are a good value at US$34/38.

A pleasant newcomer on the Cabo budget circuit is **Hotel Mélida** (☎ 1-143-65-64, fax 1-143-73-95), at Matamoros and Niños Héroes. The dozen or so rooms at this family-run property all have air-con and TV and range from US$30 to US$50, depending on size.

Mid-Range Those who can afford a little more have plenty to choose from.

Cabo Inn (☎ /fax 1-143-08-19, caboinn@ cabotel.com.mx), in a quiet spot on 20 de Noviembre between Mendoza and Leona Vicario, offers comfort and character. Its courtyard bursts with jungley foliage, and there's a barbecue grill to cook your day's catch. Renovated rooms have air-con (some also have kitchenettes) and cost US$53. The rooftop 'Love Palace' comes with private patio for sleeping under the stars (US$75).

Hotel Los Milagros (☎/fax 1-143-45-66, 800-524-5104 in the US, fish@1cabonet .com.mx, Matamoros 116) is an oasis of good taste, style and charm. Rooms feature scalloped brick ceilings and Mexican manor-style furniture. All have air-con but no phones or TV to emphasize the retreat atmosphere; some have kitchenettes. Rates are a great value at US$65.

Cabo's most secluded hideaway is the nonsmoking **Bungalows Breakfast Inn** (☎ 1-143-05-85, fax 1-143-50-35, bungalow@ cabonet.net.mx), off Calle Libertad (follow the signs from Constitución). A palm-fringed pool gives way to 16 light-flooded studios and two-bedroom bungalows with Mexican furnishings, fridges, air-con, TV and VCR (in-house video library). The gourmet breakfasts garner rave reviews. Rates range from US$85 to US$105.

Spicing up this price category is the American-run *Chile Pepper Inn* (☎ /fax 1-143-47-80 or 1-143-05-10, chilepepper@ cabonet.net.mx), at 16 de Septiembre and Abasolo. Assets include hand-crafted furnishings, original artwork, direct phones (free local calls) and TV with CNN and HBO. Regular rates are US$66, though discounts for long-term stays are available.

The colonial-style *Hotel Mar de Cortez* (☎ 1-143-00-32, fax 1-143-02-32, in the US ☎ 831-663-5803, 800-347-8821, fax 831-663-1904, info@mardecortez.com), at Cárdenas and Guerrero, is an old Cabo standby. Rooms range from US$37/41 single/double in the older wing to US$10 more for larger ones in the newer wing. Suites sleeping up to four are available too. There's also a swimming pool and an outdoor bar/restaurant.

Hotel María Elena (☎ 1-143-32-96), on Matamoros half a block north of Cardeñas, is a small family-run affair whose dozen rooms with TV, air-con, fridge or kitchenette cost US$43.

Those bent toward self-catering might opt for one of Cabo's suite hotels. Best of the bunch is the sparkling *Siesta Suites Hotel* (☎ /fax 1-143-27-73, 602-331-1354 in the US, siesta@cabonet.net.mx), on Zapata between Hidalgo and Guerrero. Contemporary rooms with full kitchen cost US$50. There's a barbecue area and free coffee in the morning.

Las Margaritas Inn (☎ 1-143-67-70, fax 1-143-04-50), at Plaza Arámburo, has 16 one- and two-bedroom apartments for US$45 to US$75. It's right in the heart of the nightlife strip, so earplugs may come in handy unless you're part of the party crowd.

Medusa Suites (☎ 1-143-34-92, fax 1-143-08-80), at Ocampo and Alikán, is a cute Spanish-style cottage with nine compact suites around a pool and bar area. Each comes with fridge, TV, telephone and kitchenette and a price tag of US$56. Discounts are available for longer stays.

A step up in comfort is the nearby *Hotel Santa Fe* (☎ 1-143-44-01, fax 1-143-25-52, 800-366-2291 in the US, santafe@go2mexico.com), at Zaragoza and Obregón. All 46 spacious studios cost US$80 and have satellite TV,

kitchenette, air-con and a sofa bed. A small market, cafe and coin laundry are adjacent to the hotel.

Top End Cabo's luxury resorts line the beachfronts of both the Pacific side (Playa Solmar) and the bay side (Playa Médano). Facilities at each are similar and include swimming pools, Jacuzzis, tennis courts, restaurants and bars.

The grande dame of Playa Médano is the glorious *Hacienda Beach Resort* (☎ 1-143-01-22, fax 1-143-06-66, 800-733-2226 in the US, hhbrcabo@cabonet.net.mx), a five-star Mission-style hotel with fountains and tropical gardens so lush that the complex blends in perfectly with its natural surroundings. One of the original Cabo hotels, it oozes old-time charm and tradition in its public areas.

Rooms are comfortable and all have ocean views; some are right next to the sand. Beachfront souvenir vendors and time-share hawkers are kept off the premises. Cabo Acuadeportes operates a water-sports center on the beach in front of the hotel. The bar (killer margaritas) and restaurant (see Places to Eat) are popular locals' hangouts. Rates range from US$130 for garden-patio rooms to US$375 for townhouses. Its Web site is at www.haciendacabo.com.

Hotel Melía San Lucas (☎ 1-143-44-44, fax 1-143-04-20, 800-336-3542 in the US, mslven@cabotel.com.mx) is a popular saffron-colored behemoth with a nicely landscaped pool area and palapa-roof swim-up bar. Spacious, nicely decorated rooms have air-con, minibar, safe and TV, and most also have oceanview terraces. Rates start at US$245 and crest at US$495.

Next up is the *Pueblo Bonito Resort* (☎ 1-143-29-00, fax 1-143-19-95, 800-990-8250 in the US), whose mega-proportions are mitigated by Moorish-style blue-tiled domes. The opulent lobby is another eye-catcher. Rooms with all the perks range from US$200 to US$340.

The adjacent sister property, the all-suite *Pueblo Bonito Rosé Resort* (☎ 1-143-55-00, fax 1-143-55-23, 800-990-8250 in the US), is even bigger and boasts a state-of-the-art spa. Rates are from US$260 to US$450. People under 18 stay free at either.

On Playa Solmar, just off Blvd Marina, *Hotel Finisterra* (☎ *1-143-33-33, fax 1-143-05-90, 800-347-2252 in the US, finister@cabonet.net.mx*) commands an impressive clifftop location. Rooms, some with fireplace, have either ocean or marina views and start at US$175.

Farther east is *Hotel Solmar Suites* (☎ *1-143-35-35, fax 1-143-04-10, in the US ☎ 800-344-3349, 310-459-9861*), a secluded beachfront resort with oceanview studios, suites and condos costing US$165 to US$325. The resort is famous for its sportfishing fleet (see Fishing, earlier).

Places to Eat

Cabo's culinary scene features everything from American fast-food chains to gourmet restaurants. Prices are high for Baja, but, generally, so is the quality. Most places are casual and feature outdoor seating. Smoking is permitted in all restaurants.

The two largest and most centrally located supermarkets are Arámburo (☎ 1-143-14-50), in Plaza Arámburo, and Sanlíz, at Blvd Marina and Madero. Both are open until 11 pm and are popular with gringos, which unfortunately sends prices soaring. Almacenes Castro (☎ 1-143-05-66), on Morelos at Revolución, and Mercado Morelos, on the same street just north of Niños Héroes, are cheaper.

Mexican Friendly *Gardenias*, on Paseo de la Marina, just south of Cárdenas, has consistently excellent tacos (fish, barbecue beef, marinated pork, shrimp; US$1 each), served with your own set of seven condiments. If you're hungry, you could order the three-course *comida corrida*. It's open for lunch only.

Antojitos Doña Lolita, at Niños Héroes and Matamoros, serves delicious homestyle Mexican fare from an outdoor kitchen of wood-burning stoves and black iron pots. The daily changing menu usually features four main dishes and a soup. It's open for lunch and dinner.

Calle Leona Vicario has been dubbed 'Taco Alley' for good reason. Places to try include *Los Paisas*, north of Revolución, which is renowned for its beef tacos and stuffed potatoes, and *Cabo Taco*, farther north at 5 de Febrero, which specializes in marlin, dorado and manta ray tacos. For great chicken, head to *El Pollo de Oro*, on Morelos between Niños Héroes and 16 de Septiembre; a quarter bird plus rice, beans and tortilla costs just US$3.

Wrought-iron furniture, Mayan fertility figures, colorful lanterns – the decor at *O Mole Mio* (☎ 1-143-75-55), in the Plaza del Sol mall, is as creative as the food. Even standards like enchiladas are presented with a whole new twist. Main courses average US$15, and the margaritas are good. It's open for lunch and dinner daily.

Energetic *Margaritavilla* (☎ 1-143-00-10), at Blvd Marina in Plaza Bonita, is (in)famous for its gargantuan margaritas, roaming mariachis and great appetizers. More demanding palates should try *Mi Casa* (☎ 1-143-19-33), in a flower-festooned patio on Avenida Cabo San Lucas, across from Parque Amelia Wilkes. Dishes from around Mexico are served with warm tortillas made freshly on the premises. Main dishes start at US$13.

Playa Médano is home to a string of casual eateries where you eat with your toes dug into the sand. All serve the usual antojitos, seafood and Mexican combos at midrange prices and are open all day.

Billigan's (☎ 1-143-04-02) has daily Happy Hour from 2 to 7 pm. *The Office* (☎ 1-143-34-64) is known for its raucous Mexican fiestas held several times weekly, while *Mango Deck* (☎ 1-143-09-01) is a quieter affair. Cheery *Las Palmas* (☎ 1-143-04-47), which specializes in seafood (they will prepare your catch of the day), also has large salads and respectable sushi.

For a special treat, visit *La Noria* (☎ 1-143-06-63), in the Hacienda Beach Resort, where dining takes place on the waterfront terrace or the high-ceilinged *comedor*. The place gets top marks from the locals for its gourmet takes on traditional dishes, superb service and reasonable prices. La Noria is open all day.

Seafood At Leona Vicario and 20 de Noviembre, *Mariscos Mocambo* (☎ 1-143-21-22) is touristy but renown for its large portions of fresh fish and shellfish. Main courses start at US$8.50, but most hover around US$12. It's open for lunch and dinner daily.

The menu at modest and friendly *El Pescador*, at Zaragoza and Niños Héroes, is an oceanic treasure trove: Shrimp, fish, oysters, snails, crab, octopus – you name it, it's served here. Two doors east, *La Palapa* (☎ 1-143-08-08) draws big crowds with budget breakfasts and good-value seafood dinners. Its free tuna-dip appetizer is a treat.

Outside town, *Enriques* (☎ 1-143-25-18), at Km 4 on the Transpeninsular, is one of the area's best bargains. Lobster combinations (lobster tail plus choice of shrimp or steak) cost just US$10, including soup or salad.

Vegetarian Although there's only one dedicated meatless restaurant, vegetarians should have no trouble getting their fill in Cabo. The family-run *El Sol de Trigo* (☎ 1-143-29-12), Avenida Cabo San Lucas between Mijares and Green, has a three-course lunch that changes daily but is consistently delicious (US$5, including a nonalcoholic drink). Alas, it's only open weekdays for lunch.

Other At Cárdenas and Paseo de la Marina, *Caffé Gourmet* does nice cakes, lattes, cappuccinos and other java fixes in an almost Viennese coffeehouse setting, though it's pricey. *Pastelería Suiza*, on Hidalgo opposite Parque Amelia Wilkes, sells yummy bread, bagels, pastries and pies.

La Michoacana, at Morelos and Carranza, serves the usual superb aguas and paletas. *Rico Suave* (☎ 1-143-05-50), on Zaragoza just north of Niños Héroes, features outstanding juices but also does tortas, sandwiches and salads for around US$3.

In conversations about who makes the best pizza in town, *Pane, Pizza e Vino* (☎ 1-143-30-90), on Cárdenas at Matamoros, is mentioned frequently. Open for dinner nightly, its Neapolitan chef cranks out pie after pie costing from US$8 to US$11 and – usually – large enough to feed two. *La Trattoria* (☎ 1-143-00-68) is an upscale, classic Italian restaurant on Cárdenas next to the Hard Rock Café.

Those with fatter wallets should treat themselves to dinner at *Sancho Panza* (☎ 1-143-32-12), in Plaza Las Glorias, which is as much a visual as a culinary treat. The chef cleverly fuses Mediterranean and Latin tastes, and there's a great wine bar as well.

Entertainment

Cabo San Lucas is a proud party town, and drinking establishments definitely dominate downtown. Alcohol consumption is encouraged all day long, from the welcome margarita at your hotel to free-drink coupons in the newspapers to all-day Happy Hours.

Bars Bar hopping is the quintessential Cabo activity; places downtown are mostly of the loud and raucous variety. *TangaTanga* is an open-air sidewalk bar on Blvd Marina advertising 'rhythm & booze.' The *Nowhere Bar* (☎ 1-143-44-93), on the waterfront next to Margaritavilla, is another dedicated watering hole with a small dance floor.

Also in the marina are *Bar Concepción* (☎ 1-143-49-63) and the *Rainbow Bar*, Cabo's lone gay and lesbian haunt, though it generally draws a mixed crowd. *Pancho's* (☎ 1-143-09-73), a brightly pigmented outdoor eatery at Hidalgo and Zapata, competes with the Museo de Tequila in Rosarito (see the La Frontera chapter) for having the largest selection of tequila. Panchos has about 400 varieties.

A great place to escape the madness is the low-key *Sandbar* on Playa Médano, next to the Hotel Meliá San Lucas. Here you can sip your drink snuggled into a comfy beach chair while toasting your tootsies beside a crackling bonfire right in the sand.

Jazz fiends might enjoy the nightly concerts at the classy wine bar at Sancho Panza (see Places to Eat, earlier), whereas *Casa Rafael* (☎ 1-143-07-39), a boutique hotel and restaurant on Paseo de la Marina, is a romantic spot for a drink and live piano music. The best bars for watching the sun plop into the Pacific are at the Playa Solmar hotels, especially the Hotel Finisterra's *Whale Watcher Bar*.

Clubs & Live Music Cabo nightlife concentrates along Blvd Marina, which, flooded with neon, is beginning to resemble a miniature Las Vegas. This is where legendary watering holes like *The Giggling Marlin* (☎ 1-143-11-82) and *El Squid Roe* (☎ 1-143-06-55) pull in throngs of gregarious gringos in search of a good time.

The party scene here is sort of fraternity party meets street carnival, with lots of audience participation, risqué floor shows and lost inhibitions. It's silly and frivolous, but everyone seems to be enjoying themselves. *Kokomo* (☎ 1-143-52-52), near El Squid Roe across from Plaza Bonita, is in much the same vein. The *Hard Rock Café* (☎ 1-143-37-79), a perennial favorite, also has a dance floor and pop bands, but overall it's a much tamer scene.

For live music, head on over to *Cabo Wabo Cantina* (☎ 1-143-11-88), on Guerrero between Madero and Cárdenas. This cavernous club is owned by ex–Van Halen bass player Sammy Hagar, who occasionally takes to the stage himself.

Pazzo's Cabo (☎ 1-143-43-13), on Morelos just north of Cárdenas, is primarily a restaurant whose cantina offers a varied musical menu, from live blues to salsa and reggae.

Shopping

Downtown Cabo is littered with souvenir shops hawking more or less the same cheesy trinkets, usually at inflated prices. Competi-

tion seems to be so fierce that zealous (or desperate) shop owners wait outside, cajoling you in to take a look.

Plaza Bonita has the most upscale shops, including Dos Lunas (☎ 1-143-19-69), which has reasonably priced resort wear made from natural fibers as well as some nice jewelry. Cortes (☎ 1-143-17-70) is worth a look for its high-quality Mexican-made furnishings and crafts.

Faces of Mexico, on Cárdenas at Guerrero, has a good selection of artisanal goods. Galerías Zen-Mar (☎ 1-143-06-61), on the same street near Ocampo, offers traditional Indian crafts, Zapotec weavings, bracelets and spectacular masks.

For the best selection in hand-painted ceramics and pottery, head to Artesanos (☎ 1-143-38-50), a large warehouse at Km 4.1 on the Transpeninsular, which has decent prices. For margarita glasses, vases and other handblown-glass items, check out Vitrofusion y Arte (☎ 1-143-02-55 or 1-143-01-20). It's on the Cabo bypass, about a third of a mile (0.5km) past the intersection with the Transpeninsular (look for a small sign). Most days you can watch the glass blowers at work in the factory behind the store.

Getting There & Away

For information on air travel to and from the Los Cabos International Airport, see Getting There & Away in the San José del Cabo section, earlier in this chapter. Aero California (☎ 1-143-37-00) has an office in Plaza Náutica, off Blvd Marina.

Bus Long-distance buses operated by Autotransportes Aguila (☎ 1-143-78-80) leave from the main terminal at the junction of México 19 and the Cabo bypass (across from the Pemex station). From here, it's a 20- to 30-minute walk south to downtown, which is also served by local bus (see Getting Around, later).

Todos Santos – US$4.50, 1½ hours; 12 times daily
La Paz – US$8, 2½ hours via Todos Santos and
   3½ hours via San José del Cabo; 16 times daily
Loreto – US$23, 8 to 10 hours; daily at 10:30 am
Tijuana – US$77, 24 hours; daily at 4:40 pm

Car Most major international car rental agencies have multiple branches in downtown, mostly along Cárdenas and Blvd Marina. Some also have desks inside the major hotels.

Prices vary a little between companies (Dollar is the most expensive), but renting an economy car shouldn't set you back more than US$50 a day, insurance included (and *do* get that insurance). Mexico-made VW bugs (new cars but the old models) are usually about US$12 cheaper. You might get better rates by prebooking in your home country. Agencies include the following:

Avis (☎ 1-143-46-07)
Dollar (☎ 1-143-41-66 or 1-143-12-50)
Hertz (☎ 1-142-03-75 or 1-142-41-32)
National (☎ 1-143-18-18)
Payless (☎ 1-143-52-22)
Thrifty (☎ 1-143-16-66)

Getting Around

Bus A fleet of modern orange/blue or green/yellow buses shuttle between Cabo San Lucas and San José del Cabo along the Corridor at approximately half-hour intervals from early morning to about 8 pm.

In Cabo, the main bus stop is on the south side of Cárdenas at Leona Vicario. Upon request, the driver will stop at any of the hotels or beaches along the Corridor. The flat fare is US$1.50. Aguila buses departing from the main bus terminal on México 19 also stop in San José del Cabo on their way to La Paz.

Car & Motorcycle For details about renting a car, see Getting There & Away, earlier. Rancho Tours (☎ 1-143-54-64) rents single and double scooters, though these are hardly a bargain at US$10/30/50 per hour/half-day/day. Call ahead or contact them through your hotel activity desk.

As Cabo San Lucas is growing, finding parking is becoming a problem. Street parking is scarce in the downtown, as are paid lots. However, there is free public parking in the dirt lot at the southern end of Blvd Marina, past Plaza Las Glorias (free, for now anyway). Some of the finer restaurants are now beginning to offer valet parking.

Taxis & Shuttles Taxis are plentiful but lack meters and are not cheap; fares for destinations within downtown should not exceed US$5. New to Cabo are pedi-cabs, which charge US$1.50 per person per ride. They are based on the south side of Blvd LázaroCárdenas at Morelos, or you can flag them down.

To or from the airport, a regular taxi costs around US$45 to US$60 for up to four people, whereas *collectivo* taxis (nine-passenger minivans) charge about US$12 per person.

There's also an airport shuttle service leaving from outside the Plaza Las Glorias Hotel six times daily (US$12 per person). Most hotels offer shuttle service at about the same rate.

AROUND CABO SAN LUCAS

About 3 miles (5km) northwest of town is Cabo San Lucas' historic lighthouse, **Faro Viejo**, perched high above Cabo Falso (False Cape), so named because it was once erroneously thought to be the southernmost point on the Baja Peninsula.

Surrounded by a spectacular dunescape, the lighthouse was in operation from 1895 to 1961, when it was replaced by a candy-striped cousin on a hillside above. The latter is worth a visit for extraordinary 360-degree views of the ocean, city and sierras. Most likely, it will be just you and the wind – unless, of course, a herd of 'dune warriors' on ATVs happens to be tearing through the countryside below (usually in the late afternoon). We recommend that you consciously avoid ATV tours, which tear up the delicate dune ecology.

If you're traveling by car or mountain bike, follow México 19 for about 2½ miles (starting from the Pemex station), and then turn left about half a mile (800m) past the Km 120 sign onto a dirt road just in front of the Coca-Cola distributorship. Turn right when you get to a T-junction, then left at Smokey's Bar and straight on up to the lighthouse.

CAPE REGION

Western Cape

The Western Cape, from Todos Santos south along the Southern Cape Highway (México 19), has so far been spared the development of Cabo San Lucas, but subdivision signs continue to sprout along its sandy Pacific beaches. The near absence of potable water may yet save the area.

TODOS SANTOS

In recent years, the placid historical village of Todos Santos (population 3800) has seen a major influx of North American expatriates, including artists for whom Santa Fe and Taos have grown too large and impersonal. In 1985, the completion of the paved Southern Cape Highway (México 19) through Todos Santos created a straighter and quicker western alternative to Cabo San Lucas than the serpentine Transpeninsular, improving access to beaches south of town. Nevertheless, Todos Santos proper remains a charming destination.

History

Founded in 1724 as a Jesuit *visita* (outstation) dependent on La Paz, Misión Santa Rosa de Todos Los Santos became a full-fledged mission a decade later, but a two-year Pericú rebellion nearly destroyed it. When the La Paz mission was abandoned in 1749, it became Misión Nuestra Señora del Pilar de Todos Santos. Epidemics killed Indians relocated from San Luis Gonzaga and La Pasión, and Todos Santos then limped along until its abandonment in 1840.

In the late 19th century, the former colonial village became a prosperous cane-milling town with four red-brick *trapiches* (mills) producing the dark sugar known as *panocha*. The first mill was shipped from San Francisco to Cabo San Lucas and then overland to Todos Santos. The depleted aquifers eliminated most of the thirsty sugar industry, though mills still operate in nearby Pescadero and San Jacinto. Some farmers have instituted multicropping methods to grow fruits and vegetables with less reliance on chemical fertilizers.

Despite its small size, Todos Santos has produced many notable historical figures for the peninsula and Mexico at large. Among them are General Manuel Márquez de León (who fought against the French intervention of 1861 and later, less heroically, led a Sinaloa rebellion against Porfirio Díaz when he felt insufficiently rewarded for his support of Díaz), Colonel Clodomiro Cota Márquez (also active against the French intervention), General Agustín Olachea Avilés and General Melitón Albañez (notable participants in the Mexican Revolution), and Dionisia Villarino Espinoza (a heroine of the Revolution).

Orientation

Like many Mexican towns, Todos Santos has a fairly regular grid plan, but local residents rely more on landmarks than street names for directions (though street names do exist).

Information

Amid a cluster of stores at the corner of Juárez and Avenida Hidalgo, the English-language bookstore El Tecolote Libros functions as Todos Santos' de facto tourist office. Available here is a very detailed (some might say cluttered) town map and a sketched map of nearby beach areas. It also sells Lee Moore's thorough *Todos Santos Book,* with up-to-date local information on everything from the best restaurants and art galleries to how to contact a local *curandero* (Mexican folk healer). It maintains an outstanding selection of books and magazines specializing in Baja California; it also carries a selection of Lonely Planet guides. A two-for-one paperback book exchange is available.

BanCrecer, at the corner of Juárez and Obregón, changes foreign currencies.

The post office is on Heróico Colegio Militar, between Avenida Hidalgo and Márquez de León. The postal code is 23300.

The Message Center (☎ 1-145-00-03, fax 1-145-02-88), adjacent to El Tecolote Libros, at the corner of Juárez and Avenida Hidalgo, provides phone, fax and message services. It is open from 8 am to 5 pm week-

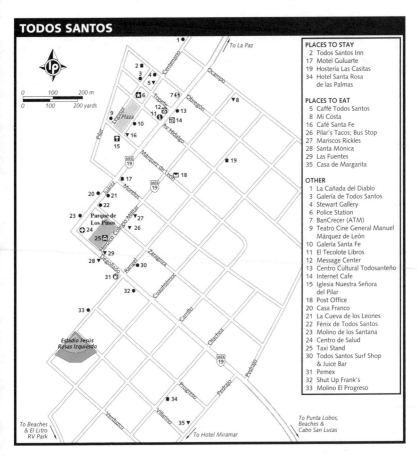

TODOS SANTOS

PLACES TO STAY
2 Todos Santos Inn
17 Motel Guluarte
19 Hostería Las Casitas
34 Hotel Santa Rosa
   de las Palmas

PLACES TO EAT
5 Caffé Todos Santos
8 Mi Costa
16 Café Santa Fe
26 Pilar's Tacos; Bus Stop
27 Mariscos Rickles
28 Santa Mónica
29 Las Fuentes
35 Casa de Margarita

OTHER
1 La Cañada del Diablo
3 Galería de Todos Santos
4 Stewart Gallery
6 Police Station
7 BanCrecer (ATM)
9 Teatro Cine General Manuel
   Márquez de León
10 Galería Santa Fe
11 El Tecolote Libros
12 Message Center
13 Centro Cultural Todosanteño
14 Internet Cafe
15 Iglesia Nuestra Señora
   del Pilar
18 Post Office
20 Casa Franco
21 La Cueva de los Leones
22 Fénix de Todos Santos
23 Molino de los Santana
24 Centro de Salud
25 Taxi Stand
30 Todos Santos Surf Shop
   & Juice Bar
31 Pemex
32 Shut Up Frank's
33 Molino El Progreso

days, to 2 pm on Saturday. The Message Center also offers Internet connection for US$2 per 30 minutes. There's another Internet cafe just across the street that charges about US$3/5 for 30/60 minutes. It's open 9 am to 5 pm Monday to Saturday.

For medical or emergency services, Todos Santos' Centro de Salud (☎ 1-145-00-95) is at the corner of Juárez and Degollado.

Things to See & Do

The restored **Teatro Cine General Manuel Márquez de León** (☎ 1-145-01-22), on the northern side of the plaza, no longer shows films, but occasional live concerts and other performances still take place.

Murals at the **Centro Cultural Todosanteño**, Todos Santos' former schoolhouse (Escuela General Melitón Albañez) and current cultural center, on Juárez near Topete, date from 1933; their nationalist and revolutionary motifs depict missionaries and Indians, the Spanish conquistadores, Emiliano Zapata, cooperativism, rural laborers, industry, athletics ('vigor in mind and muscle') and 'emancipation of the rural spirit.'

Scattered around Todos Santos are the remains of former **mills**, including Molino

El Progreso, on Rangel at Progreso, and Molino de los Santana, on Juárez opposite the clinic. Molino Cerro Verde and Molino Jesús Amador are on the northern outskirts of town.

Only about 1 mile (1.6km) from Todos Santos, through the fields behind Hotel California (see Places to Stay, below), lie pleasant but rarely visited **beaches**. These spots are also accessible via the dirt road that leads west from the Pemex station (follow Rangel to reach the road); passing the ballpark, it becomes steep, rutted and gullied. The shoreline lagoons are good spots for bird-watching, and camping is possible, but bring water (local expatriates report that Todos Santos' tap water is drinkable). Visitors not wishing to hike the roundabout route to the beaches west of Todos Santos can hire a taxi at Parque de Los Pinos, diagonally across from the bus stop.

More accessible but more populous beaches are south of town and 6½ miles (10km) northwest of town. See Around Todos Santos, later in this chapter, for details.

For **surfing** information, contact Pat Baum at the Todos Santos Surf Shop & Juice Bar (fax 145-02-88, teampaty@baja.net.mx) on Rangel, just east of Degollado. Board rentals cost US$10 a day; lessons cost US$15 an hour.

Special Events

Todos Santos' annual Festival de Artes (art festival) lasts two days in late January. Local artists, such as Charles Stewart, can be visited in their homes/studios, where their works are for sale.

In late February, Todos Santos holds a tour of local historic homes.

Places to Stay

El Litro RV Park (☎ 1-146-57-13), in the area southwest of the baseball park, offers spacious camping sites for US$5 and RV sites with hookups for US$10.50. The toilets are spotless and there are three bathrooms, two with showers.

In recent years, Todos Santos' accommodations have improved in quality and in-

creased in quantity, but they are still limited in all categories. *Hotel Miramar* (☎ 1-145-03-41), at the corner of Verduzco and Pedrajo southwest of the town center, has only limited ocean views from the 2nd-floor balconies, but it's clean and reasonably priced at US$8/11 single/double.

Motel Guluarte (☎ 1-145-00-06), at the corner of Juárez and Morelos, has a swimming pool; if no one is on duty at the desk, check the market next door. Rooms cost about US$16/27. *Hostería Las Casitas* (☎ 1-145-02-55) is a Canadian-run B&B on Rangel between Obregón and Avenida Hidalgo. Its rolled palapa roof edges, rarely seen nowadays, add authentic detail to the remodeled, five-room building. Prices run from about US$45 for a double with a shared bath, to US$65 for a double with a private bath. Breakfast is included. Las Casitas' mailing address is Apdo Postal 73, Todos Santos, Baja California Sur 23300, México.

Set among pleasant gardens on Olachea between Villarino and Progreso, the pleasant *Hotel Santa Rosa de las Palmas* (☎ 1-145-03-94) has eight rooms, each with a living room and kitchenette, for US$35. It lacks air-con but has fans and a swimming pool.

The most genteel accommodations are at the US-owned *Todos Santos Inn* (☎ /fax 1-145-00-40, Legaspi 33), a B&B in a restored 19th-century building. Rates range from US$85 to US$120 a double, depending on the room.

Places to Eat

For fine food at bargain prices, try any or all of the taco stands along Heróico Colegio Militar between Márquez de León and Degollado; each has its own specialty, be it fish, chicken, shrimp or beef.

Family-run *Casa de Margarita* (☎ 1-145-01-84), on Pedrajo between Progreso and Villarino, has attracted a devoted following for fine, reasonably priced antojitos and seafood. It also offers a Sunday champagne brunch.

Caffeine junkies can down their cappuccinos at *Caffé Todos Santos* (☎ 1-145-03-00,

Centenario 33), between Topete and Obregón. It offers savory pastries and visually enticing fruit salads, and the deli-style sandwiches are also outstanding.

Mi Costa, on Militar and Ocampo, specializes in seafood, as does *Mariscos Rickles,* on Heróico Colegio Militar between Zaragoza and Morelos.

Las Fuentes (☎ 1-145-02-57), at the corner of Degollado and Heróico Colegio Militar, serves excellent antojitos (the chicken with mole sauce is exceptional) and seafood specialties in a shady patio among colorful bougainvillea and three refreshing fountains. Prices are moderate.

Well-regarded *Santa Mónica* (☎ 1-145-02-04), Todos Santos' oldest restaurant, is just across the street.

In a class all by itself, *Café Santa Fe* (☎ 1-145-03-40) entices patrons from as far away as La Paz and Cabo San Lucas to its plaza location at the corner of Centenario and Márquez de León. The grub here is Italian and prices are high, but service is excellent and it's well worth a splurge; reservations are a good idea during holiday periods.

Entertainment

Proud of its tranquillity, Todos Santos is no party town, but *La Cueva de los Leones,* on Juárez between Morelos and Zaragoza, features live norteña and banda music on weekends.

Most visitors will find walking around town entertaining enough, but the cheap, powerful margaritas at *La Cañada del Diablo,* a low-key palapa bar at the eastern end of Centenario, may leave you incapable of doing so. Snacks are available but not full meals.

Shut Up Frank's – colloquially known as 'Callate Pancho' – is a sports bar and grill that keeps erratic hours; it's on Degollado between Rangel and Cuauhtémoc.

For live action, enthusiastic amateur baseball teams from Todos Santos and nearby communities play several nights weekly (plus daytime games on weekends) at Estadio Jesús Rosas Izquierdo, at the corner of Rangel and Villarino.

Shopping

As an artists' colony, Todos Santos has numerous stores and galleries open to the public, displaying samples of local crafts and artwork. Try Casa Franco, on Juárez between Morelos and Zaragoza, or Fénix de Todos Santos, on Juárez at the corner of Zaragoza, for jewelry, artwork and clothes.

Galería de Todos Santos, at the corner of Topete and Legaspi, features imaginative artwork by Mexican and North American artists, with regular openings. Galería Santa Fe, alongside its namesake restaurant on the southern side of the plaza, is well worth a visit, as is the Stewart Gallery on Obregón between Legaspi and Centenario.

Getting There & Away

Todos Santos has no official bus terminal, but buses between La Paz and Cabo San Lucas stop at Pilar's Tacos at the corner of Heróico Colegio Militar and Zaragoza. At least eight buses daily go to La Paz (US$5) between 7 am and 8 pm and to Cabo San Lucas (US$5) between 7 am and 9 pm.

AROUND TODOS SANTOS

At the **Punta Lobos** beach, about 1½ miles (2.5km) south of Todos Santos, *pangueros* (skiff operators) sell their catch in the late afternoon, offering a cheaper, better selection than local markets.

Farther south on Mexico 19, across from a botanical garden, a 2½-mile (4km) dirt road leads to **Playa San Pedrito,** a sandy crescent beach with surfable breaks.

Spacious *San Pedrito RV Park* (☎ 1-145-01-47) charges US$3 per person for camping without hookups, US$15 for RV sites with all hookups and US$45 double for modest cabañas. Amenities include a restaurant and a swimming pool and laundry. The gates are closed from 10 pm to 7 am.

In a northern swell, the crescent beach at **Playa Los Cerritos** has a good right break but has become more crowded in recent years. There is also good fishing from the rocky headland to the north. The Todos Santos Surf Shop has set up a hut at the beach, where you can rent equipment or sign up for lessons. It also rents camping equipment.

At Km 65, *Los Cerritos RV Park* operates on a shoestring budget, but the toilets flush and the cold showers work (water is expensive because it's trucked in – consider a 'sea shower' to conserve this precious commodity). There is some shade but no electricity. Ejido Pescadero keeps the area weed-free, charging US$4 to park outside the fence, US$5 to park inside. There have been reports of thefts, so secure your possessions at night.

South of Playa Los Cerritos, livestock are common along the Southern Cape Highway (México 19); drive with care. At an unmarked turnoff at about Km 83, **Playa Las Cabrillas** features a long but steep sandy beach unsuitable for surfing. However, there are many good rustic campsites just off the highway.

At Km 97, a dirt road (actually more like a sand trail – suitable only for 4WD) leads half a mile (1km) west among mangroves to **Playa Migriño** and Estero Migriño, a good bird-watching site that also has a right break in the winter months. Cow patties and insects are both abundant, so watch your step and bring bug repellent.

Spanish for Travelers

Speaking a few words of Spanish goes a long way toward establishing rapport with locals and will enhance the experience of your trip. Mexicans normally will be flattered by such attempts, so do not feel self-conscious about vocabulary or pronunciation. Many words are similar to English, so if you're stuck, try Hispanicizing an English word – it is unlikely that you'll make a truly embarrassing error. Do not, however, admit to being *embarazada* unless you are in fact pregnant!

When asking information, avoid leading questions that may invite incorrect responses. Instead of asking, 'Is this the road to San Borja?' (a question that begs a positive answer, whether or not it is the correct road), ask 'Which road goes to San Borja?' (a form that gives the respondent an option). Though it's unlikely that a respondent would purposely lead you astray, a willingness to please can have the same results.

Phrasebooks & Dictionaries

Lonely Planet's *Latin American Spanish phrasebook* is a worthwhile addition to your luggage. Another useful book is the *University of Chicago Spanish-English, English-Spanish Dictionary,* whose small size, light weight and thorough entries make it very convenient for foreign travel.

Pronunciation

Most of the sounds in Spanish have equivalents in English, and written Spanish is mostly phonetic.

Stress, often indicated by visible accents, is very important, since it can change the meaning of words. In general, words ending in vowels or the letters 'n' or 's' have stress on the next-to-last syllable, whereas those with other endings have stress on the last syllable. Thus *vaca* (cow) and *caballos* (horses) both have accents on their next-to-last syllables.

Visible accents, which can occur anywhere in a word, dictate stress over these general rules. Thus *zócalo* (plaza or town square), *América* and *porción* (portion) have stress

on different syllables. When words are written in capital letters, the written accent is often omitted but is still pronounced.

Useful Phrases

Below are English phrases with useful Mexican Spanish equivalents, most of which will be understood in other Spanish-speaking countries. Words relating to food and restaurants are covered in the Menu Guide following this chapter.

At the Border

tourist card	*tarjeta de turista*
visa	*visado*
passport	*pasaporte*
identification	*identificación*
birth certificate	*certificado de nacimiento*
driver's license	*licencia de manejar*
car title	*título de propiedad*
car registration	*registración*
customs	*aduana*
immigration	*migración*
border (frontier)	*la frontera*

Civilities

Like other Latin Americans, Mexicans are very conscious of civilities in their public behavior. Never, for example, approach a stranger for information without extending a greeting like *'Buenos días'* or *'Buenas tardes.'*

Sir/Mr	*Señor*
Madam/Mrs	*Señora*
Miss	*Señorita*
yes	*sí*
no	*no*
please	*por favor*
Thank you.	*Gracias.*
You're welcome.	*De nada.*
Excuse me.	*Perdóneme.*
Hello.	*Hola.*
Goodbye.	*Adiós.*
Good morning.	*Buenos días.*
Good afternoon.	*Buenas tardes.*
Good evening.	*Buenas noches.*
Good night.	*Buenas noches.*

I understand.	*Entiendo.*
I don't understand.	*No entiendo.*
Please repeat that.	*Repítelo, por favor.*
I don't speak much Spanish.	*Hablo poco castellano* or *español.*

Questions

Where?	*¿Dónde?*
Where is … ?	*¿Dónde está … ?*
Where are … ?	*¿Dónde están … ?*
When?	*¿Cuando?*
How?	*¿Cómo?*
How much?	*¿Cuanto?*
How many?	*¿Cuantos?*
I want …	*Quiero …*
I do not want …	*No quiero …*
I would like …	*Me gustaría …*
Give me …	*Déme …*
What do you want?	*¿Que quiere usted?*
Do you have … ?	*¿Tiene usted … ?*
Is/are there … ?	*¿Hay … ?*
How much does it cost?	*¿Cuánto cuesta?*

Some Useful Words

and	*y*
to/at	*a*
for	*por, para*
of/from	*de, desde*
in	*en*
with	*con*
without	*sin*
before	*antes*
after	*después*
soon	*pronto*
already	*ya*
now	*ahora*
right away	*ahorita*
here	*aquí*
there	*allí*
bad	*malo*
better	*mejor*
best	*el mejor*
more	*más*
less	*menos*

Family & Friends

I	*yo*
you (familiar)	*tú*
you (formal)	*usted*
you (plural)	*ustedes*
he/him	*él*
she/her	*ella*
we/us	*nosotros*
they/them (masculine and mixed groups)	*ellos*
they/them (feminine)	*ellas*
my wife	*mi esposa*
my husband	*mi esposo*
my sister	*mi hermana*
my brother	*mi hermano*

I am …	*Soy …*
a student	estudiante
American	americano(a)
a US citizen	estadounidense
Australian	australiano(a)
British	británico(a)
Canadian	canadiense
French	francés (francesa)
German	alemán (alemana)

Transportation

car	*auto*
airplane	*avión*
train	*tren*
bus	*autobus*
ship	*barco, buque*
taxi	*taxi*
truck	*camión*
pickup	*camioneta*
motorcycle	*motocicleta, moto*
bicycle	*bicicleta*
airport	*aeropuerto*
train station	*estación del ferrocarril*
bus station	*estación del autobús*
one-way/roundtrip	*ida/ida y vuelta*
luggage storage	*guardería, equipaje*

first/last/next
  primero/último/próximo
1st/2nd class
  primera/segunda clase
I would like a ticket to …
  Quiero un boleto a …
What's the fare to … ?
  ¿Cuánto cuesta hasta … ?
When does the next plane/train/bus leave for … ?
  ¿Cuándo sale el próximo avión/tren/autobus para … ?

Around Town

tourist information	oficina de turismo
bathing resort	balneario
street	calle
boulevard	bulevar
avenue	avenida
road	camino
highway	carretera
corner (of)	esquina (de)
block	cuadra
to the left	a la izquierda
to the right	a la derecha
on the left side	al lado izquierdo
on the right side	al lado derecho
straight ahead	adelante
north	norte
south	sur
east	este
west	oeste

Post & Communications

post office	correo
letter	carta
parcel	paquete
postcard	postal
airmail	correo aéreo
registered mail	certificado
stamps	estampillas, timbres
telephone office	caseta de teléfono
telephone booth	cabina de teléfono
local call	llamada local
long distance	larga distancia
person to person	persona a persona
collect call	por cobrar
busy	ocupado

At the Hotel

guesthouse	casa de huéspedes
room	cuarto, habitación
single room	cuarto solo, cuarto sencillo
double room	cuarto para dos, cuarto doble
double bed	cama de matrimonio
with twin beds	con camas gemelas
with private bath	con baño
shower	ducha
hot water	agua caliente
air-conditioning	aire acondicionado
blanket	frasada
towel	toalla

soap	jabón
toilet paper	papel higiénico
toothpaste	pasta dentífrica
dental floss	hilo dental
locked safe	caja fuerte
the bill	la cuenta
too expensive	demasiado caro
cheaper	mas económico
May I see it?	¿Puedo verla?
I don't like it.	No me gusta.

What is the price?
  Cuál es el precio?
Does that include taxes?
  ¿Están incluídos los impuestos?
Does that include service?
  ¿Está incluído el servicio?

Money

money	dinero
bank	banco
traveler's checks	cheques de viajero

currency exchange house
  casa de cambio
I want to change money.
  Quiero cambiar dinero.
What is the exchange rate?
  ¿Que es el tipo de cambio?
Is there a commission?
  ¿Hay comisión?

Driving

gasoline	gasolina
unleaded	sin plomo
leaded	con plomo
tire	llanta
spare tire	llanta de repuesto
puncture	agujero
flat tire	llanta desinflada

Fill the tank, please.
  Llene el tanque, por favor.
How much is gasoline per liter?
  ¿Cuánto cuesta el litro de gasolina?
My car has broken down.
  Se me ha descompuesto el carro.
I need a tow truck.
  Necesito un remolque.
Is there a garage near here?
  ¿Hay garage cerca?

Time

Telling time is fairly straightforward. For example, eight o'clock is *las ocho*, while 8:30 is *las ocho y treinta* (literally, 'eight and thirty') or *las ocho y media* (eight and a half). However, 7:45 is *las ocho menos quince* (literally, 'eight minus fifteen') or *las ocho menos cuarto* (eight minus one-quarter).

Times are modified by morning *(de la mañana)* or afternoon *(de la tarde)* instead of 'am' or 'pm.' It is also common to use the 24-hour clock, especially with transportation schedules. Midnight is *medianoche*, and noon is *mediodía*.

While Mexicans are flexible about time with respect to social occasions like meals and parties, schedules for public events (like bullfights and movies) and transportation (like airplanes and buses) should be taken very literally.

Days of the Week

Monday	*lunes*
Tuesday	*martes*
Wednesday	*miércoles*
Thursday	*jueves*
Friday	*viernes*
Saturday	*sábado*
Sunday	*domingo*

Toilets

The most common word for 'toilet' is *baño*, but *servicios sanitarios* (services) is a frequent alternative. Men's toilets will usually bear a descriptive term like *hombres, caballeros* or *varones*. Women's restrooms will be marked *señoras* or *damas*.

Geographical Terms

The expressions below are among the most common in this book and in Spanish-language maps and guides:

bay	*bahía*
bridge	*puente*
cape	*cabo*
farm	*rancho*
hill	*cerro*
island	*isla*
lake	*lago, laguna*
marsh	*estero*
mountain	*cerro*
mountain range	*sierra, cordillera*
national park	*parque nacional*
pass	*paso*
point	*punta*
river	*río*
waterfall	*cascada, catarata, salto*

Numbers

0	*cero*
1	*un, uno* (m), *una* (f)
2	*dos*
3	*tres*
4	*cuatro*
5	*cinco*
6	*seis*
7	*siete*
8	*ocho*
9	*nueve*
10	*diez*
11	*once*
12	*doce*
13	*trece*
14	*catorce*
15	*quince*
16	*dieciséis*
17	*diecisiete*
18	*dieciocho*
19	*diecinueve*
20	*veinte*
21	*veintiuno*
22	*veintidós*
30	*treinta*
31	*treinta y uno*
32	*treinta y dos*
40	*cuarenta*
50	*cincuenta*
60	*sesenta*
70	*setenta*
80	*ochenta*
90	*noventa*
100	*cien*
101	*ciento uno*
143	*ciento cuarenta y tres*
200	*doscientos*
500	*quinientos*
700	*setecientos*
900	*novecientos*
1000	*mil*
2000	*dos mil*

Menu Guide

Antojitos

Antojitos (little whims) are traditional Mexican snacks or small meals. They can be eaten at any time, on their own or as part of a larger meal. There are many, many varieties, but here are some of the more common ones:

burrito – any combination of beans, cheese, meat, chicken and seafood, seasoned with salsa or chilies and wrapped in a flour tortilla
chilaquiles – fried tortilla chips with scrambled eggs or sauce, often with grated cheese on top
chile relleno – poblano chilies stuffed with cheese, meat or other foods, dipped in egg whites, fried and baked in salsa
enchilada – ingredients similar to those in tacos and burritos, wrapped in a flour tortilla, dipped in sauce and then baked or fried
enfrijolada – soft tortilla in a frijole sauce with cheese and onion on top
entomatada – soft tortilla in a tomato sauce with cheese and onion on top
gordita – fried maize dough filled with refried beans, topped with cream, cheese and lettuce
guacamole – mashed avocados mixed with onion, chili, lemon, tomato and other ingredients
machaca – cured, dried and shredded beef or pork mixed with eggs, onions, cilantro and chilies
quesadilla – flour tortilla topped or filled with cheese and occasionally other ingredients, then heated
sope – thick patty of corn dough lightly grilled then served with green or red salsa and frijoles, onion and cheese
taco – ingredients similar to the burrito, wrapped in a soft or crisp corn tortilla
tamale – steamed corn dough stuffed with meat, beans or chilies and wrapped in corn husks
torta – Mexican-style sandwich in a roll
tostada – flat, crisp tortilla topped with meat or cheese, tomatoes, beans and lettuce

Sopa (Soup)

birria – a spicy-hot soup (almost a stew) of meat, onions, peppers and cilantro, served with tortillas
caldo – broth *(caldo tlalpeño* is a hearty chicken, vegetable and chili variety)
gazpacho – chilled vegetable soup spiced with hot chilies
menudo – tripe soup made with the spiced entrails of various four-legged beasts
pozole – rich, spicy stew of hominy (large maize kernels) with meat and vegetables
sopa de arroz – not a soup at all, but just a plate of rice, commonly served with lunch
sopa de pollo – chicken soup in broth

Huevos (Eggs)

huevos cocidos – hard-boiled eggs (specify the number of minutes if you're in doubt)
huevos estrellados – fried eggs
huevos fritos (con jamón/tocino) – fried eggs (with ham/bacon)
huevos mexicanos – eggs scrambled with tomatoes, chilies and onions (representing the red, green and white of the Mexican flag)
huevos motuleños – tortilla topped with slices of ham, fried eggs, cheese, peas and tomato sauce
huevos pasados por agua – lightly boiled eggs (too lightly for many visitors' tastes)
huevos poches – poached eggs
huevos rancheros – fried eggs on tortillas, covered in salsa

Pescado & Mariscos (Fish & Seafood)

atún – tuna
cabrilla – sea bass
ceviche – raw seafood marinated in lime and mixed with onion, chili, garlic and tomato
filete de pescado – fish fillet
huachinango or *pargo* – red snapper
jurel – yellowtail
lenguado – flounder or sole
pescado al mojo de ajo – fish fried in butter and garlic
pez espada – swordfish

sierra – mackerel
tiburón – shark
trucha de mar – sea trout
mariscos – shellfish
abulón – abalone
almejas – clams
callos – scallops
camarones – shrimp
camarones gigantes – prawns
cangrejo – large crab
jaiva – small crab
langosta – lobster
ostiones – oysters

Carnes & Aves (Meat & Fowl)

asado – roast
barbacoa – barbecued over hot coals (eg, *barbacoa de carne* is barbecued beef)
biftec – thin beef filet
cabra – goat
carne – meat
carne al carbón – charcoal-grilled meat
carne asada – grilled beef
chicharrones – deep-fried pork rinds
chorizo – pork sausage
chuletas de cerdo – pork chops
cochinita – suckling pig
conejo – rabbit
cordero – lamb
cordoniz – quail
costillas de puerco – pork ribs or chops
hígado – liver
jamón – ham
milanesa – breaded beefsteak
patas de puerco – pig's feet
pato – duck
pavo or *guajolote* – turkey
pollo – chicken
pollo asado – grilled chicken
pollo con arroz – chicken with rice
pollo frito – fried chicken
puerco – pork
tocino – bacon or salt pork

Frutas (Fruit)

coco – coconut
dátil – date
fresa – strawberry; often used to refer to any berry
guayaba – guava
higo – fig

limón – lime or lemon
mango – mango
melón – melon
naranja – orange
papaya – papaya
piña – pineapple
plátano or *banana* – banana
tomate – tomato
toronja – grapefruit
uva – grape

Verduras (Vegetables)

aceituna – olive
aguacate – avocado
calabaza – squash or pumpkin
cebolla – onion
champiñon – mushroom
chícharo – pea
ejote – green bean
elote – corn on the cob
jícama – root crop, resembling potato or apple, eaten with a touch of lime, chili and salt
lechuga – lettuce
papa – potato
papitas fritas – potato chips
zanahoria – carrot

Dulces (Desserts)

flan – custard
helado – ice cream
nieve – flavored ice; Mexican equivalent of US 'snow cone' and UK 'slush puppy'
paleta – flavored ice on a stick; equivalent to US popsicle, Australian icy-pole and UK ice-lolly
pan dulce – sweet roll
pastel – cake
postre – dessert

Other Foods

azúcar – sugar
sal – salt
pimienta negra – black pepper
leche – milk
mantequilla – butter
crema – cream
queso – cheese
bolillo – French-style bread rolls
mole – sauce made from unsweetened chocolate, chili and many spices, often served over chicken or turkey

salsa – sauce made from chili, onion, tomato, lemon or lime juice and spices

At the Table
tenedor – fork
cuchara – spoon
cuchillo – knife

plato – plate
taza – cup
vaso or *copa* – glass
menú – menu
cuenta – bill
propina – tip, usually 10% to 15% of the bill
servilleta – napkin or serviette

Glossary

For general information on the Spanish language, see the Spanish for Travelers chapter. For a list of food and drink terms, see the Menu Guide.

acequia – irrigation canal, often stone-lined, in Baja California missions

agave – century plant

agua purificada – purified water

alto – stop; also means 'high'

antojitos – Mexican snacks (enchiladas, burritos, gorditas, etc)

Apdo – abbreviation of *Apartado* (Box); in addresses, stands for 'Post Office Box'

asentamientos irregulares – shantytowns of Tijuana, Mexicali and other border towns

asistencia – in colonial times, a way station between missions

avenida – avenue

bajacaliforniano – resident of Baja California

ballena – whale; also a colloquial term for a liter-size bottle of Pacífico beer

banda – style of dance music

béisbol – baseball

biznaga – barrel cactus

bolillo – typical Mexican bread

borrego – bighorn sheep, a rarely seen species in the sierras of Baja California that is frequently represented in the pre-Columbian rock art of the peninsula

bracero – literally, 'farmhand'; used to describe work program established by the US and Mexican governments during WWII that allowed Mexicans to work north of the border to alleviate wartime labor shortages in the US

cabaña – cabin

cabecera – the administrative seat of a *municipio* (see later)

cabina – phone booth

caguama – any species of sea turtle, but most commonly the Pacific green turtle; also a colloquial term for a liter-size bottle of Tecate beer

calle – street

campanario – bell tower

Canaco – Cámara Nacional de Comercio (National Chamber of Commerce)

cardón – either of two species of *Pachycereus* cactus, a common genus in Baja

carga negra – hazardous cargo

cambio or casa de cambio – currency exchange house

casa de huéspedes – guesthouse, a relatively inexpensive but uncommon form of accommodations in Baja

cascabel – rattlesnake

casita – cottage

charreada – rodeo, frequently held during fiestas and other special occasions; particularly popular in northern Mexico

charro – Mexican cowboy or horseman; mariachi bands often dress in gaudy charro clothing

chilango – native or resident of Mexico City; depending on context, the term can be very pejorative

cholismo – rebellious youth movement, akin to punk, that has had some influence on the visual arts in Baja California

choza – hut

chubasco – in the Cape Region of southern Baja, a violent storm approaching hurricane force, associated with summer low-pressure areas in the tropical Pacific

científicos – a group of largely Eurocentric advisers who controlled the direction of Mexico's economy under dictator Porfirio Díaz

cirio – a 'boojum' tree, a slow-growing species resembling an inverted carrot, common only within a limited range of the Sierra La Asamblea in north-central Baja

CITES – Convention on International Trade in Endangered Species of Wild Fauna and Flora, which regulates trade in such species

colonia – neighborhood in Tijuana or other large city; literally, 'colony'

corrida de toros – bullfight

corrido – folk ballad of the US-Mexico border region; corridos often have strong but subtle political content

Cotuco – Comité de Turismo y Convenciones (Committee on Tourism & Conventions)
coyote – smuggler who charges up to US$2000 to spirit illegal immigrants across the US-Mexican border
Cruz Roja – Red Cross
curandero – folk healer

datilillo – yucca
delegación – administrative subdivision of a municipio (see later)

ejidatario – a member of an *ejido*
ejido – cooperative enterprise, usually of peasant agriculturalists, created under the land reform program of President Lázaro Cárdenas (1934–40); ejidos also participate in economic activities such as mining, ranching and tourism
encomienda – system of forced labor and tribute, which the Spanish crown instituted in mainland New Spain and other densely populated parts of its empire

fianza – bond posted against the return of a motor vehicle to the USA
fideicomiso – 30-year bank trust that has fostered the construction and acquisition of real estate by non-Mexicans in Baja California
Fonatur – Mexican federal government tourist agency
fraccionamiento – synonym for colonia (see above)
fronterizo – an inhabitant of the US-Mexico border region
frontón – venue for jai alai (see below)

glorieta – city traffic circle; most numerous in Mexicali and Tijuana
gotas – water purification drops
gringo – term describing any light-skinned person, but most often a resident of the USA; often but not always pejorative
güero – 'blond,' a term often used to describe any fair-skinned person in Mexico

hacienda – local treasury department
hielo – ice
hipódromo – horseracing track
huerivo – aspen tree

INAH – Instituto Nacional de Antropología y Historia (National Institute of Anthropology & History), which administers museums and archeological monuments such as the cave paintings in the Desierto Central
indígena – indigenous person
internado – rural boarding school
IVA – *impuesto de valor agregado,* or value-added tax

jai alai – game of Basque origin resembling squash
Judiciales – Mexican state and federal police

Ladatel – *Larga Distancia Automática,* or Automatic Long Distance phones
La Frontera – the area where Dominican priests built their missions in colonial times (from 1774); it extends from immediately south of present-day San Diego (mainland California) as far as El Rosario, at about the 30th parallel
librería – bookstore
licorería – liquor store; also called *vinos y licores*
llantera – tire repair shop, common even in Baja's most out-of-the-way places
lonchería – casual eatery, often a counter in markets, serving breakfast and lunch only

machismo – an exaggerated masculinity intended to impress other men more than women; usually innocuous if unpleasant
Magonistas – followers of the exiled Mexican intellectual Ricardo Flores Magón, who attempted to establish a regional power base in the towns of northern Baja California during the Mexican Revolution
maguey – any of several species of a common Mexico fiber plant *(Agave* spp), also used for producing alcoholic drinks like tequila, mescal and pulque
malecón – waterfront promenade
maquiladora – industrial plant in Tijuana, Mexicali or another border town that takes advantage of cheap Mexican labor to assemble US components for re-exportation to the north
matador – bullfighter

mestizo – person of mixed Indian and European heritage

moneda nacional – national money, meaning the Mexican peso as distinguished from the US dollar (both use the symbol '$'); often abbreviated as 'm/n'

mono – human figure, as represented in the pre-Columbian rock art of the Desierto Central

mordida – bribe; literally, 'the bite'

municipio – administrative subdivision of Mexican states, roughly akin to a US county; Baja California (Norte) consists of five, Baja California Sur of four municipios

NAFTA – North American Free Trade Agreement, a pact between the USA, Canada and Mexico that reduces or eliminates customs duties and other trade barriers

nao – in colonial times, a Spanish galleon on the Acapulco-Manila trade route; such galleons frequently took shelter in Baja ports on their return voyages

neophyte – a new convert (in this case of the Indians by the missionaries)

nopal – any cactus of the genus *Opuntia* that produces edible fruit *(tuna)*, which was common in the diet of pre-Columbian Baja and is still widely consumed today

noria – water- or animal-driven mill

ofrenda – offering to a saint in exchange for a wish or wishes granted

ola – wave

palafito – walled *palapa*

palapa – palm-leaf shelter

PAN – Partido de Acción Nacional, a free-market-oriented populist party that is strong in Baja California (Norte); its acronym, more than coincidentally, reproduces the Spanish word for 'bread'

panga – fiberglass skiff used for fishing or whale-watching

panguero – one who owns or pilots a skiff; in practice, the word is synonymous with 'fisherman'

parque nacional – national park

pastillas para purificar agua – water purification tablets

peatonal – pedestrian walk

peligro – danger

Pemex – Petróleos Mexicanos, the Mexican government oil monopoly

piñata – papier-mâché animal full of candy, broken open by children at celebrations like Christmas and birthdays

pitahaya dulce – organ pipe cactus, a key element of the traditional diet of Baja's native peoples

plaza de toros – bullring

pollero – synonymous with 'coyote'; a smuggler of undocumented immigrants *(pollos,* or 'chickens') into the USA

Porfiriato – de facto dictatorship of Porfirio Díaz, who held Mexico's presidency from 1876 until the Revolution of 1910; under his rule, much of Baja California was granted to foreign companies for ambitious colonization projects, most of which soon failed

posada – at Christmas, a parade of costumed children reenacting the journey of Mary and Joseph to Bethlehem

presidio – during colonial times, a military outpost

PRI – Partido Revolucionario Institucional, the official party of government in Mexico from 1929 until 2000

propina – tip, at a restaurant or elsewhere

pueblo – town

ranchería – subsistence unit of hunter-gatherers in the contact period with Europeans, or, later, units associated with missions; implies a group of people rather than a place

rancho – tiny rural settlement, ranging from about 20 to 50 people

rebozo – shawl

recinto fiscal – official vehicle-impound lot

recova – colonnade (architectural term)

registro – local records office

reglamento de tránsito – the Mexican drivers' manual

Secture – Secretaría de Turismo del Estado (State Tourism Office)

SEDUE – Secretaría de Desarrollo Urbano y Ecología, a Mexican government agency that regulates foreign hunting activity in Baja California and elsewhere in Mexico

Semarnap – Secretaría de Medio Ambiente, Recursos Naturales y Pesca, the Mexican government's primary conservation agency

Servicio Postal Mexicano – the Mexican national postal service

Servicios Migratorios – Immigration Office

SIDA – AIDS (Acquired Immune Deficiency Syndrome)

s/n (sin número) – street address without a specific number

todo terreno – mountain bike

tombolo – sandspit beach

tope – speed bump

torote – elephant tree

tortillería – tortilla factory or shop

tortuga carey – hawksbill turtle

tortuga laúd – leatherback turtle

trapiche – sugar mill

turista – tourist; also a colloquial name for diarrhea contracted by tourists

ultramarino – small grocery store

Unesco – United Nations Educational, Scientific and Cultural Organization

vado – ford, as of a river; can also refer to a dip in a road

vaquero – Mexican cowboy

veda – seasonal or permanent prohibition against hunting or fishing of a given species

villa deportiva juvenil – youth hostel

visita – during colonial times, a mission's outstation

yodo – iodine, sold in pharmacies for water purification

zócalo – central plaza, a term more common in mainland Mexico than in Baja California

zona de tolerancia – in border cities like Tijuana and Mexicali, an area in which prostitution and related activities are concentrated

zona hotelera – hotel zone

Acknowledgments

THANKS

Many thanks to the travelers who used the last edition and wrote to us with helpful hints, useful advice and anecdotes. Your names follow:

Eduardo Ayacardi, Eduardo Aycardi, Roger Baker, Cathyo Bianc, Scott Bishopp, Steve Bowers, Helen Burton, Celia Condit, David Croome, Bill Denny, Martin Dillig, Patrick Diveu, Martin & Michaela Dohnalkova, Klaus Dunder, Frank Fox, Astrid Frey, Rick Gerharter, Meghan Gibbons, Judy Gibson, Jim Isaacs, P Kalberer, Adam Kent, Rachele Lamontagne, Andrew J Lampkin, Lee Lau, Harvey Lozano, Glenn MacCrimmon, Liene Maeckelburgh, Alessandro Marcolin, Sheri Marcus, Chris & Jeff McFarland, George Merchant, Jonathan Miles, Michael Monterey, James Nelson, Nancy Nixon, Steve Novosel, Dennis Oman, Jorgos-Rita Palimetakis, Wendy Postier, Harald Praschinger, Sage Rich, Mauro Ruffino, Andy & Bea Sidler, Heidi Smith, Peter Steiner, R Tokgoz, Tom Tyler, Steven Verdekel, Paola Vozza, Jeff Walter, Sally Walton, Myra Winfield, Nancy Wright

LONELY PLANET

You already know that Lonely Planet produces more than this one guidebook, but you might not be aware of the other products we have on this region. Here is a selection of titles which you may want to check out as well:

Diving & Snorkeling Baja California
ISBN 0 86442 572 4
US$16.95 • UK£10.99 • 130FF

World Food Mexico
ISBN 1 86450 023 9
US$11.95 • UK£6.99 • 95FF

Mexico
ISBN 1 86450 089 1
US$24.99 • UK£14.99 • 179FF

Latin American Spanish phrasebook
ISBN 0 86442 558 9
US$6.95 • UK£4.50 • 50FF

Available wherever books are sold.

LONELY PLANET

Guides by Region

Lonely Planet is known worldwide for publishing practical, reliable and no-nonsense information in our guides and on our Web site. The Lonely Planet list covers just about every accessible part of the world. Currently there are 16 series: Travel guides, Shoestring guides, Condensed guides, Watching Wildlife guides, Pisces Diving & Snorkeling guides, City Maps, Road Atlases, Out to Eat, World Food, Journeys travel literature and Pictorials.

AFRICA Africa on a shoestring • Cairo • Cape Town • Cape Town City Map • East Africa • Egypt • Egyptian Arabic phrasebook • Ethiopia, Eritrea & Djibouti • Ethiopian (Amharic) phrasebook • The Gambia & Senegal • Healthy Travel Africa • Kenya • Malawi • Morocco • Moroccan Arabic phrasebook • Mozambique • Read This First: Africa • South Africa, Lesotho & Swaziland • Southern Africa • Southern Africa Road Atlas • Swahili phrasebook • Tanzania, Zanzibar & Pemba • Trekking in East Africa • Tunisia • Watching Wildlife East Africa • Watching Wildlife Southern Africa • West Africa • World Food Morocco • Zimbabwe, Botswana & Namibia
Travel Literature: Mali Blues: Traveling to an African Beat • The Rainbird: A Central African Journey • Songs to an African Sunset: A Zimbabwean Story

AUSTRALIA & THE PACIFIC Auckland • Australia • Australian phrasebook • Australia Road Atlas • Bushwalking in Australia • Cycling Australia • Fiji • Fijian phrasebook • Healthy Travel Australia, NZ and the Pacific • Islands of Australia's Great Barrier Reef • Melbourne • Melbourne City Map • Micronesia • New Caledonia • New South Wales & the ACT • New Zealand • Northern Territory • Outback Australia • Out to Eat – Melbourne • Out to Eat – Sydney • Papua New Guinea • Pidgin phrasebook • Queensland • Rarotonga & the Cook Islands • Samoa • Solomon Islands • South Australia • South Pacific • South Pacific phrasebook • Sydney • Sydney City Map • Sydney Condensed • Tahiti & French Polynesia • Tasmania • Tonga • Tramping in New Zealand • Vanuatu • Victoria • Watching Wildlife Australia • Western Australia
Travel Literature: Islands in the Clouds: Travel in the Highlands of New Guinea • Kiwi Tracks: A New Zealand Journey • Sean & David's Long Drive

CENTRAL AMERICA & THE CARIBBEAN Bahamas, Turks & Caicos • Baja California • Bermuda • Central America on a shoestring • Costa Rica • Costa Rica Spanish phrasebook • Cuba • Dominican Republic & Haiti • Eastern Caribbean • Guatemala • Belize, Guatemala & Yucatán: La Ruta Maya • Healthy Travel Central & South America • Jamaica • Mexico • Mexico City • Panama • Puerto Rico • Read This First: Central & South America • World Food Mexico • Yucatán
Travel Literature: Green Dreams: Travels in Central America

EUROPE Amsterdam • Amsterdam City Map • Amsterdam Condensed • Andalucía • Austria • Baltic States phrasebook • Barcelona • Barcelona City Map • Berlin • Berlin City Map• Britain • British phrasebook • Brussels, Bruges & Antwerp • Budapest • Budapest City Map • Canary Islands • Central Europe • Central Europe phrasebook • Corfu & the Ionians • Corsica • Crete • Crete Condensed • Croatia • Cycling Britain • Cycling France • Cyprus • Czech & Slovak Republics • Denmark • Dublin • Dublin City Map • Eastern Europe • Eastern Europe phrasebook • Edinburgh • Estonia, Latvia & Lithuania • Europe on a shoestring • Finland • Florence • France • Frankfurt Condensed • French phrasebook • Georgia, Armenia & Azerbaijan • Germany • German phrasebook • Greece • Greek Islands • Greek phrasebook • Hungary • Iceland, Greenland & the Faroe Islands • Ireland • Istanbul • Italian phrasebook • Italy • Krakow • Lisbon • The Loire • London • London City Map • London Condensed • Madrid • Malta • Mediterranean Europe • Mediterranean Europe phrasebook • Moscow • Munich • Norway • Out to Eat – London • Paris • Paris City Map • Paris Condensed • Poland • Portugal • Portuguese phrasebook • Prague • Prague City Map • Provence & the Côte d'Azur • Read This First: Europe • Romania & Moldova • Rome • Russia, Ukraine & Belarus • Russian phrasebook • Scandinavian & Baltic Europe • Scandinavian Europe phrasebook • Scotland • Sicily • Slovenia • South-West France • Spain • Spanish phrasebook • St Petersburg • St Petersburg City Map • Sweden • Switzerland • Trekking in Spain • Tuscany • Ukrainian phrasebook • Venice • Vienna • Walking in Britain • Walking in France • Walking in Ireland • Walking in Italy • Walking in Spain • Walking in Switzerland • Western Europe • Western Europe phrasebook • World Food France • World Food Ireland • World Food Italy • World Food Spain
Travel Literature: Love and War in the Apennines • The Olive Grove: Travels in Greece • On the Shores of the Mediterranean • Round Ireland in Low Gear • A Small Place in Italy

INDIAN SUBCONTINENT Bangladesh • Bengali phrasebook • Bhutan • Delhi • Goa • Healthy Travel Asia & India • Hindi/Urdu phrasebook • India • Indian Himalaya • Karakoram Highway • Kerala • Mumbai (Bombay) •

LONELY PLANET

Mail Order

Lonely Planet products are distributed worldwide. They are also available by mail order from Lonely Planet, so if you have difficulty finding a title please write to us. North and South American residents should write to 150 Linden St, Oakland, CA 94607, USA; European and African residents should write to 10a Spring Place, London NW5 38H, UK; and residents of other countries to Locked Bag 1, Footscray, Victoria 3011, Australia.

Nepal • Nepali phrasebook • Pakistan • Rajasthan • Read This First: Asia & India • South India • Sri Lanka • Sri Lanka phrasebook • Tibet • Trekking in the Indian Himalaya • Trekking in the Karakoram & Hindukush • Trekking in the Nepal Himalaya
Travel Literature: The Age of Kali: Indian Travels and Encounters • Hello Goodnight: A Life of Goa • In Rajasthan • A Season in Heaven: True Tales from the Road to Kathmandu • Shopping for Buddhas • A Short Walk in the Hindu Kush • Slowly Down the Ganges

ISLANDS OF THE INDIAN OCEAN Madagascar & Comoros • Maldives • Mauritius, Réunion & Seychelles

MIDDLE EAST & CENTRAL ASIA Bahrain, Kuwait & Qatar • Central Asia • Central Asia phrasebook • Dubai • Hebrew phrasebook • Iran • Israel & the Palestinian Territories • Istanbul • Istanbul City Map • Istanbul to Cairo on a shoestring • Jerusalem • Jerusalem City Map • Jordan • Lebanon • Middle East • Oman & the United Arab Emirates • Syria • Turkey • Turkish phrasebook • World Food Turkey • Yemen
Travel Literature: Black on Black: Iran Revisited • The Gates of Damascus • Kingdom of the Film Stars: Journey into Jordan

NORTH AMERICA Alaska • Boston • Boston City Map • California & Nevada • California Condensed • Canada • Chicago • Chicago City Map • Louisiana & the Deep South • Florida • Hawaii • Hiking in Alaska • Hiking in the USA • Las Vegas • Los Angeles • Miami • Miami City Map • New England • New Orleans • New York City • New York City City Map • New York City Condensed • New York, New Jersey & Pennsylvania • Oahu • Pacific Northwest • Puerto Rico • Rocky Mountains • San Francisco • San Francisco City Map • Seattle • Southwest • Texas • USA • USA phrasebook • Vancouver • Virginia & the Capital Region • Washington, DC • Washington, DC City Map • World Food Deep South, USA
Travel Literature: Caught Inside: A Surfer's Year on the California Coast • Drive Thru America

NORTH-EAST ASIA Beijing • Cantonese phrasebook • China • Hiking in Japan • Hong Kong • Hong Kong City Map • Hong Kong Condensed • Hong Kong, Macau & Guangzhou • Japan • Japanese phrasebook • Korea • Korean phrasebook • Kyoto • Mandarin phrasebook • Mongolia • Mongolian phrasebook • Seoul • South-West China • Taiwan • Tokyo
Travel Literature: In Xanadu: A Quest • Lost Japan

SOUTH AMERICA Argentina, Uruguay & Paraguay • Bolivia • Brazil • Brazilian phrasebook • Buenos Aires • Chile & Easter Island • Colombia • Ecuador & the Galapagos Islands • Healthy Travel Central & South America • Latin American Spanish phrasebook • Peru • Quechua phrasebook • Read This First: Central & South America • Rio de Janeiro • Rio de Janeiro City Map • Santiago de Chile • South America on a shoestring • Trekking in the Patagonian Andes • Venezuela
Travel Literature: Full Circle: A South American Journey

SOUTH-EAST ASIA Bali & Lombok • Bangkok • Bangkok City Map • Burmese phrasebook • Cambodia • Hanoi • Healthy Travel Asia & India • Hill Tribes phrasebook • Ho Chi Minh City • Indonesia • Indonesian phrasebook • Indonesia's Eastern Islands • Jakarta • Java • Lao phrasebook • Laos • Malay phrasebook • Malaysia, Singapore & Brunei • Myanmar (Burma) • Philippines • Pilipino (Tagalog) phrasebook • Read This First: Asia & India • Singapore • Singapore City Map • South-East Asia on a shoestring • South-East Asia phrasebook • Thailand • Thailand's Islands & Beaches • Thailand, Vietnam, Laos & Cambodia Road Atlas • Thai phrasebook • Vietnam • Vietnamese phrasebook • World Food Thailand • World Food Vietnam

ALSO AVAILABLE: Antarctica • The Arctic • The Blue Man: Tales of Travel, Love and Coffee • Brief Encounters: Stories of Love, Sex & Travel • Chasing Rickshaws • The Last Grain Race • Lonely Planet Unpacked • Not the Only Planet: Science Fiction Travel Stories • On the Edge: Extreme Travel • Sacred India • Travel with Children • Travel Photography: A Guide to Taking Better Pictures

Index

Bold indicates maps.

Bold indicates maps.

Bold indicates maps.

Boxed Text

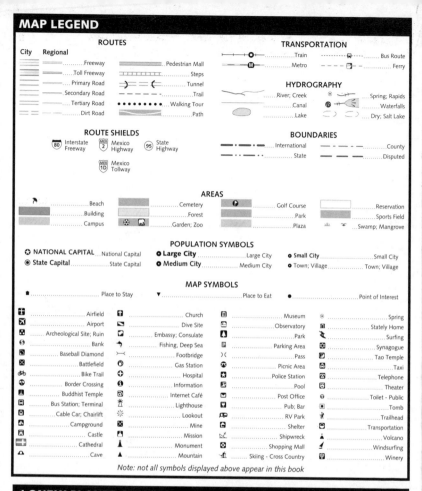

MAP LEGEND

ROUTES

City **Regional**

Freeway
Toll Freeway
Primary Road
Secondary Road
Tertiary Road
Dirt Road

Pedestrian Mall
Steps
Tunnel
Trail
Walking Tour
Path

TRANSPORTATION

Train
Metro
Bus Route
Ferry

HYDROGRAPHY

River; Creek
Canal
Lake
Spring; Rapids
Waterfalls
Dry; Salt Lake

ROUTE SHIELDS

(80) Interstate Freeway
(2) Mexico Highway
(95) State Highway
(1D) Mexico Tollway

BOUNDARIES

International
State
County
Disputed

AREAS

Beach
Building
Campus
Cemetery
Forest
Garden; Zoo
Golf Course
Park
Plaza
Reservation
Sports Field
Swamp; Mangrove

POPULATION SYMBOLS

NATIONAL CAPITAL ... National Capital
State Capital ... State Capital
Large City ... Large City
Medium City ... Medium City
Small City ... Small City
Town; Village ... Town; Village

MAP SYMBOLS

Place to Stay
Place to Eat
Point of Interest

Airfield
Airport
Archeological Site; Ruin
Bank
Baseball Diamond
Battlefield
Bike Trail
Border Crossing
Buddhist Temple
Bus Station; Terminal
Cable Car; Chairlift
Campground
Castle
Cathedral
Cave

Church
Dive Site
Embassy; Consulate
Fishing, Deep Sea
Footbridge
Gas Station
Hospital
Information
Internet Café
Lighthouse
Lookout
Mine
Mission
Monument
Mountain

Museum
Observatory
Park
Parking Area
Pass
Picnic Area
Police Station
Pool
Post Office
Pub; Bar
RV Park
Shelter
Shipwreck
Shopping Mall
Skiing - Cross Country

Spring
Stately Home
Surfing
Synagogue
Tao Temple
Taxi
Telephone
Theater
Toilet - Public
Tomb
Trailhead
Transportation
Volcano
Windsurfing
Winery

Note: not all symbols displayed above appear in this book

LONELY PLANET OFFICES

Australia
Locked Bag 1, Footscray, Victoria 3011
☎ 03 9689 4666 fax 03 9689 6833
email talk2us@lonelyplanet.com.au

USA
150 Linden Street, Oakland, California 94607
☎ 510 893 8555, TOLL FREE 800 275 8555
fax 510 893 8572
email info@lonelyplanet.com

UK
10a Spring Place, London NW5 3BH
☎ 020 7428 4800 fax 020 7428 4828
email go@lonelyplanet.co.uk

France
1 rue du Dahomey, 75011 Paris
☎ 01 55 25 33 00 fax 01 55 25 33 01
email bip@lonelyplanet.fr
www.lonelyplanet.fr

World Wide Web: www.lonelyplanet.com *or* AOL keyword: lp
Lonely Planet Images: lpi@lonelyplanet.com.au